THE ORIGINS OF EVIL IN HINDU MYTHOLOGY

THE ORIGINS OF EVIL IN HINDU MYTHOLOGY

WENDY DONIGER O'FLAHERTY

UNIVERSITY OF CALIFORNIA PRESS
Berkeley · Los Angeles · London

for DANIEL H. H. INGALLS

and in memory of ROBIN ZAEHNER

University of California Press
Berkeley and Los Angeles, California
University of California Press, Ltd.
London, England

First Paperback Printing 1980
ISBN 0-520-04098-8
Library of Congress Catalog Card Number: 75-40664
Printed in the United States of America

3 4 5 6 7 8 9

The paper used in this publication meets the minimum requirements of American National Standard for Information Sciences—Permanence of Paper for Printed Library Materials, ANSI Z39.48–1984. ♾

Preface to the Paperback Edition

When the first edition of this book was in press, and I was fighting a losing battle against the temptation to keep adding to it, Philip Lilienthal in final desperation wrenched the typescript from my obsessive fist and consoled me with the promise that there would always be a second edition. Thus the ink of the first edition was not yet dry when I had amassed a steadily growing file of "Evil Errata and Addenda," and now is the moment to open it.

The major correction I would make is in the discussion of karma (pp. 14–20). In the course of writing and editing a book on this subject (*Karma and Rebirth in Classical Indian Traditions*, University of California, 1980), I have come to have more respect for the internal consistency and usefulness of the karma theory as a theodicy. These concepts are too complex to outline here, and the reader is referred to that work.

Other changes are of a more positive nature: I have found material that substantiates and clarifies certain of the ideas in this book. I now know, for example, that when Śaṅkara is quoting Vyāsa (pp. 91–92), he is citing *Mahābhārata* 14.19.54; that in another South Indian variant of the myth of the Triple City (p. 187), the demons are released from their bondage and become the guardians of Śiva's door;[1] that another non-Hindu version of the incarnation of Viṣṇu as the Buddha (p. 204) appears in the *Ain-i-Akbari*; and that, like the *Mahābhārata* (pp. 258–259), the *Matsya Purāṇa* states that demons killed in the battle between gods and demons were reborn on earth, where they torment all human beings.[2] A strange variant of the story of Dvārakā (p. 269) appears in the *Ghata Jātaka* (454): the sons of Kṛṣṇa are evil, and the only survivor of the flood is a black woman named Kṛṣṇā. In another telling of this story, the sage is asked why, if Kṛṣṇa just wanted to relieve the earth's burden, he killed good people and left bad ones alive; the answer is that there have to be some wicked people left because it is the Kali Age.[3] Another aspect of this logic is reflected in the statement that when the heavens and worlds became full of men in the Kali Age, and Yama complained that hell was unused, Viṣṇu produced Kalkin and killed

1. *Tiruvācakam* 14.4 and 15.9. 2. *Matsya* 47.26–27. 3. *Devībhāgavata* 6.11.

all but a few survivors;[4] this myth combines the theme of the overcrowded heaven with the contrasting motifs of the overburdened earth and the empty hell.

A notable instance of the hate-love motif (p. 309) is the myth of Rāvaṇa, who wants to fight Rāma in order that he may be killed and released.[5] In the discussion of the transfer of Indra's Brahminicide (pp. 153–160), Dumézil's analysis of the parallel transfer of Indra's virtues is illuminating: Indra's first sin (the beheading of Triśiras) causes him to lose his spiritual power, which becomes incarnate in Yudhiṣṭhira; his second sin (Namuci) causes him to lose his physical force and his manhood, which become incarnate in Bhīma and Arjuna; his third sin (the seduction of Ahalyā) causes his beauty to enter the Aśvins.[6]

These changes are in the nature of bandaids applied here and there to patch the more obvious weaknesses. Short of a major operation (for were I to write this book today, I would go about it in an entirely different way) I am content to let it stand. I am grateful to the University of California Press for giving it a new avatar that will make it more accessible to my students and other potential theodicists.

Chicago, January, 1980.

4. *Bhaviṣya* 3. 4. 24–25. 5. Tulsī Dās, p. 310. 6. Dumézil (1970), *passim*.

Contents

Acknowledgments

This book was begun at Harvard with Daniel H. H. Ingalls and completed at Oxford with R. C. Zaehner; and many other friends have read or listened to parts of it over the years. I would particularly like to thank Professor Thomas Burrow, Dr. John Marr, Dr. Richard F. Gombrich, and Professor Thomas R. Trautmann for their painstaking reading of any early draft, and Dr. Rodney Needham, Mr. Alex Gunasekara, Mrs. Audrey Hayley, and Professors Brenda Beck, A. M. Piatigorsky and J. C. Heesterman for their inspiring comments on parts of the second draft. I cannot express my gratitude to David Shulman, not only for finding and translating all the Tamil myths that I have used, but for providing many perceptive insights into these and the Sanskrit myths as well. To the learned and energetic staff of the Indian Institute Library in Oxford, and in particular to Mrs. de Goris and Mr. Alderman, I offer my heart felt thanks. Parts of the book were originally published in the journals *History of Religions* and *Art and Archaeology Research Papers*; chapter XI was read at a meeting of the Royal Asiatic Society and chapter V at a conference at the School of Oriental and African Studies, and I am grateful to members present at those meetings for their spirited reactions.

Finally, I should like to thank all of my students and colleagues in England, where I was so happily occupied during the past decade. Many of the ideas in this book were inspired by talks with them, corrected by their criticisms, and augmented by materials from their various fields of expertise. I can never forget how much I owe to Professors Kenneth A. Ballhatchet and Christoph von Fürer-Haimendorf, my good genii, who steered the course of my teaching and publishing through the deceptively still waters of English academia. I shall miss them all very much.

Oxford, 22 March, 1975

Shall there be evil in a city, and the Lord hath not done it?
Amos 3:6

I

INTRODUCTION: THE PROBLEM OF EVIL

1. The Nature of Theodicy

Theodicy, the term used to designate the problem of evil and its attempted resolution, is derived from the Greek *theos*, god, and *dikē*, justice; it was put into general currency by Leibniz,[1] who used it to signify the defense of the justice of God in face of the fact of evil.

A clear formulation of the implications of theodicy is offered by John Hick: "If God is perfectly good, He must want to abolish all evil; if He is unlimitedly powerful, He must be able to abolish all evil; but evil exists; therefore either God is not perfectly good or He is not unlimitedly powerful."[2] In a similar definition, C. S. Lewis emphasizes the absence of happiness rather than the presence of evil: "If God were good, He would wish to make His creatures perfectly happy, and if God were almighty He would be able to do what He wished. But the creatures are not happy. Therefore God lacks either goodness, or power, or both."[3]

It might appear that theodicy is a problem only in religions which presuppose a single, benevolent, omnipotent god. If this were so, the problem of evil might be solved if one were to accept any of three alternatives to benevolent monotheism: "Either there is no spirit behind the universe, or else a spirit indifferent to good and evil, or else an evil spirit."[4] Gananath Obeyesekere has suggested that no fundamental logical contradiction need arise "either in polytheism, where good and bad deities have their respective sphere of influence, or in Zoroastrian-

[1] Gottfried Wilhelm von Leibniz, *Essai de Théodicée* (Amsterdam, 1710).

[2] Hick, p. 5. [3] Lewis, p. 14. [4] *Ibid.*, p. 3.

ism, where [there are two forces], the one benevolent but not powerful, the other powerful but not benevolent," or in the Indian doctrine of karma, which dispenses with deity altogether.[5] Logically, a theodicy is necessary in any religion where any god is regarded as invariably benevolent and omnipotent, though typically it arises in monotheistic religions.[6] But Max Weber extends the use of the term *theodicy* to the existential need to explain suffering and evil,[7] and Talcott Parsons explains how, in Weber's view, such a theodicy arises from experiences such as premature death:

> Weber attempted to show that problems of this nature, concerning the discrepancy between normal human interest and expectations in any situation and society and what actually happens, are inherent in the nature of human existence. They pose problems of the order which on the most generalized line have come to be known as the problem of evil, of the meaning of suffering, and the like. . . . It is differentiation with respect to the treatment of precisely such problems which constitute the primary modes of variation between the great systems of religious thought.[8]

In this view, not only is theodicy not confined to monotheism, but it is the touchstone of all religions, an existential rather than a theological problem. Obeyesekere takes exception to Weber's definition but offers another, which also extends theodicy to nonmonotheistic religions: "When a religion fails logically to explain human suffering or fortune in terms of its system of beliefs, we can say that a theodicy exists."[9] Here, theodicy is regarded as a logical rather than a psychological problem; ideas that fail to explain suffering or that pose logically untenable contradictions incite theodicy. However, as we shall see, neither theology, nor logic, nor psychology can be entirely excluded from the battlefield of theodicy. Obeyesekere admits that "strictly speaking there can be no resolution of a theodicy. I use the term 'resolution' to describe the attempt to resolve the cognitive (logical) impasse posed by any theodicy."[10] When logic fails, and theology fails, irrational resolutions are offered by other modes of religious thought–notably mythology–and these, proving psychologically satisfactory, are acceptable to the members of that faith, however inadequate they may appear to professional philosophers.

Arthur Ludwig Herman, in an extensive study of Western and Indian theodicy, sets forth three criteria for a satisfactory solution: common sense, consistency, and completeness.[11] Any "solution" which denies the perfection, omniscience, or benevolence of God, or the existence of evil, "cannot be a *bona fide* but only a spurious solution".[12] Hindu myths do in fact deny any or all of these hypotheses from time to time and so cannot be said to supply a logical solution. Herman groups the classical "solutions" into five major categories, with

[5] Obeyesekere, p. 9. [6] *Ibid.*, p. 8. [7] *Ibid.*, p. 11. [8] Parsons (1949), pp. 62–63.
[9] Obeyesekere, pp. 11–12. [10] *Ibid.*, p. 39. [11] Herman, p. 195. [12] *Ibid.*, pp. 139–140.

twenty-one subdivisions: the aesthetic (the whole is good because, or even though, the parts are not); the idea of discipline (suffering builds character); free will (evil is man's fault); illusion (evil is merely an illusion); and limitation (God's choice at the time of creation was limited).[13] Within these five categories he subsumes the arguments of contrast, recompense, and imbalance (good outweighs evil); teleology; justice and rebirth; privation (evil is merely the absence of good); and the concepts of prevention (our evils are necessary to prevent greater evils), the impersonal wicked substance (evil matter), the personal wicked substance (Satan), metaphysical evil (the imperfection of creation itself), and, finally, the argument of mystery—the presence of evil cannot be rationally justified. All of these appear in some form in Hindu mythology. All have some flaw.

It is useful to note the different problems arising from three kinds of evil: superhuman, (gods, powers, and fallen angels), human, and subhuman (including animals and plants).[14] More important is the division into another triad: moral evil (sin); suffering (teleological evil, sometimes further divided into ordinary and extraordinary suffering), and natural evil (death, disease).[15] One may further speak of the three theological hypotheses of the problem of evil: the ethical thesis (God is good), the omnipotent thesis, and the omniscient thesis;[16] any one of these may be combined with the hypothesis of the existence of evil without contradiction, but problems arise when this hypothesis is combined with any two or more hypothetical properties of God.[17]. Herman feels that the most satisfactory theodicy is offered by the Hindu Vedāntists, who account adequately for all three types of evil (superhuman, human, and subhuman),[18] absolving God from all blame by the hypothesis of *līlā*, the playful spirit in which God becomes involved in creation: "Who after all can blame a child for acts done in joy and playful exuberance?"[19] The answer to this is simply "The Hindus, that's who," for the Vedāntic argument did not put an end to Indian attempts to solve the problem.

2. The Problem of Evil in India

Herman argues that although all the theses necessary to generate the theological problem of evil can be found in Indian philosophical and religious literature, with many interesting variations, and although all three theological theses have been both accepted and questioned, defended and attacked,[20] nevertheless the Indians are "strangely silent" about the problem of evil, a problem that plagued Western but not Indian philosophy:[21] "Classical and medieval Indian philosophy

[13] *Ibid.*, p. 200. [14] *Ibid.*, p. 143. [15] *Ibid.*, p. 162. [16] *Ibid.*, p. 145. [17] *Ibid.*, p. 183.
[18] *Ibid.*, p. 519. [19] *Ibid.*, p. 510. [20] *Ibid.*, pp. 8, 411, 417, 439–440. [21] *Ibid.*, pp. 1 and ii.

has not shown any great concern for the problem of evil in any of its theological forms. . . . When a problem of evil appears, consequently, it appears as a practical problem about evil, i.e. one states that all is suffering, *saṃsāra* [the cycle of rebirth] is itself evil. . . . When the problem of evil itself is discussed in the older texts it is almost as an aside, or it appears secondarily in the context of Who made the world?"[22] This "strange silence" he attributes largely to the satisfactory nature of the solution provided by the doctrine of rebirth. Similarly, John Bowker maintains that, in the Indian view, "the problem of Job cannot arise, because it may always be the case that occurrences of suffering are a consequence of activities, not simply in this existence, but in previous ones as well."[23] We shall see, however, that the doctrine of rebirth was not regarded as totally satisfactory by all Hindus, nor, indeed, was it accepted at all by many. The "secondary" occurrences of the problem of suffering—the problem of Job—in texts about the origin of the world form an enormous body of literature, on which the present work is based.

The belief that Indians did not recognize the problem of evil is widespread. "For Hindu thought there is no Problem of Evil," writes Alan Watts,[24] and a Hindu scholar concurs: "Hinduism is not puzzled by the Problem of Evil."[25] Similarly, it is often said that there is no concept of evil at all in India. Mircea Eliade remarked that not only was there no conflict between good and evil in India, but there was in fact a confusion between them. He suggested a reason for this confusion: "Many demons are reputed to have won their demonic prowess by good actions performed in previous existences. In other words: *good* can serve to make *evil*. . . . All these examples are only particular and popular illustrations of the fundamental Indian doctrine, that good and evil have no meaning or function except in a world of appearances."[26] Sir Charles Eliot regarded this tendency to confuse good and evil as an innate characteristic of pantheism, which "finds it hard to distinguish and condemn evil."[27] Statements of this kind are generally based on Vedāntic Hinduism and Buddhism, which are concerned more with ignorance than with sin, valuing virtue only as an adjunct to knowledge, by means of which the philosophic saint rises above both good and evil; and many varieties of Indian religion regard suffering rather than sin as the fault in the world.[28] These beliefs do not, however, apply to most of Purāṇic Hinduism.

Another source of the statement that Indians do not have a Problem of Evil is the belief that evil is unreal in Indian thought. "Wrong . . . in India is *māyā* [illusion], *asat* [nonexistent], by definition not real. . . . The problem of evil is a false one, [and] the brahmin gives it the treatment false problems deserve."[29] The

[22] *Ibid.*, p. 415 and p. 2. [23] Bowker, p. 215. [24] Watts (1957), p. 35.
[25] Buch, p. 9. [26] Eliade (1938), pp. 202ff., and (1965), p. 96. [27] Eliot, I, ci.
[28] *Ibid.*, I, lxxii and lxxix. [29] Smith, p. 10.

counterargument is simply that, though many Vedāntists did maintain that evil was logically unreal, suffering was always subjectively accepted as real.[30] From the "other" Indian point of view—the same affective strain that rejects the implications of karma[31]—"evil, suffering, waste, terror, and fear are real enough. . . . Therefore there is a sense in which evil is real, and a sense in which karma and rebirth are real as well. The dogma of unreality is betrayed by the activity and concern of the faithful."[32]

Philosophers and theologians may set up their logical criteria, but a logical answer to an emotional question is difficult both to construct and to accept. The usual example of extraordinary evil given in Indian texts is the death of a young child. If one says to the parents of this child, "You are not real, nor is your son; therefore you cannot really be suffering," one is not likely to be of much comfort. Nor will the pain be dulled by such remarks as "God can't help it" or "God doesn't know about it." It is only the ethical hypothesis that is *emotionally* dispensable: God is not good, or God does not wish man to be without evil (two very different arguments). And this is the line most actively developed by Hindu mythological theodicy.

That this theodicy does in fact exist was recognized by Max Weber, who, though giving the doctrine of karma pride of place among the world's theodicies, remarked: "All Hindu religion was influenced by [the problem of theodicy] . . . ; even a meaningful world order that is impersonal and supertheistic must face the problem of the world's imperfections."[33] A very early example of an explicit statement of the problem of evil—the justice of God—occurs in a Buddhist text that satirizes the Hindus' failure to come to terms with the problem:

The world is so confused and out of joint, why does Brahmā not set it straight? If he is master of the whole world, Brahmā, lord of the many beings born, why in the whole world did he ordain misfortune? Why did he not make the whole world happy? . . . Why did he make the world with deception [māyā], *lies, and excess, with injustice* [adhamma]*? . . . The lord of beings is unjust. There is such a thing as* dhamma,[34] *but he ordained* adhamma.[35]

The problem of evil is still an important part of contemporary Hinduism on the village level, where "the cult presumes the existence of a dominant deity (Vishnu, Siva or Brahma) who, though not all-powerful or all-kind in the monotheistic sense, has enough power and compassion to assist humans in their quest for salvation, and to grant the this-worldly aspirations of his devotees."[36] Throughout the mythology that spans the period from the Buddhist text to the

[30] Herman, pp. 436–438. [31] See below, chap. II, sec. 1. [32] Herman, p. 439.

[33] Weber (1963), p. 139. [34] See below, chap. V, sec. 1, for a working definition of this important term (Sanskrit *dharma*). [35] *Bhūridatta Jātaka*, number 543, verses 153c–156. [36] Obeyesekere, p. 23.

present, theodicy is present not only implicitly, in the stories, but in specific questions posed by the sages to whom the myths are told: Why is there death? How could God do such an evil thing? How did evil originate?

Scholars have also been wrongly led to deny the presence of theodicy in Indian religion by the fact that many myths are about minor deities of an extravagantly anthropomorphic nature, ludicrous clowns who commit countless peccadilloes of the type notorious in the affairs of Zeus and Loki. This has tended to obscure the fact that there is also an extensive mythology of a much more serious nature in which *the* god commits evil actions of cosmic significance. Thus C. G. Jung remarked,

> Of course one must not tax an archaic god with the requirements of modern ethics. For the people of early antiquity things were rather different. In their gods there was absolutely everything: they teemed with virtues and vices. Hence they could be punished, put in chains, deceived, stirred up against one another, without losing face, or at least not for long. The man of that epoch was so inured to divine inconsistencies that he was not duly perturbed when they happened.[37]

This is a fair description of Indra in the Purāṇic period, and of Śiva in some Vaiṣṇava myths, but it is not valid when applied to Indra in the Vedic period or Śiva in the Śaiva myths; these gods do indeed have "absolutely everything," but the worshipper *is* perturbed by the implications of this, as the myths clearly reveal. Myths of theodicy are perennial in India; they do not seem to arise, or to proliferate, at any particular time, under stress of social, political, or economic upheaval. The answers may change, but the problem itself endures.

3. The Indian Concept of Evil

The Oxford English Dictionary defines evil (adj.) as "the antithesis of GOOD. Now little used . . . "; the noun is "that which is the reverse of good, physically or morally," and the second cited example is "The greatest of all mysteries–the origin of evil (Tait & Stewart)." The Sanskrit term *pāpa*–widely used, unlike its English equivalent–may be applied adjectively or nominally and denotes both physical and moral nongoodness. But Christian theology has always emphasized the distinction between moral evil ("evil that we human beings originate: cruel, unjust, vicious and perverse thoughts and deeds") and natural evil ("the evil that originates independently of human actions: in disease bacilli, earthquakes, storm, droughts, tornadoes, etc.").[38] This has led to a false distinction between "primitive" religions that are largely concerned with dispelling natural evils, and "higher" religions concerned with sin.[39] In Indian religions, these two forms of evil are logically distinguished but regarded as aspects of a single phenomenon, for which a single explanation must be sought.

[37] Jung (1954), p. 13. [38] Hick, p. 18. [39] See below, chap. VI, sec. 7.

Pāpa (henceforth to be translated as evil) in the Ṛg Veda often has a moral sense: people are evil-minded; adultery is evil; incest is evil.[40] People can "do" (*karoti*) evil, and this we might translate as "commit a sin." But even sin may occur without the will of the sinner in Indian thought, so that a sense of personal repentance is rare, and one may pray for deliverance from sins committed by others in the same way as for those committed by oneself.[41] Thus the Ṛg Vedic poet prays, "O gods, deliver us today from committed and noncommitted sin [*enas*]";[42] both of these are evil. Similarly the Artharva Veda distinguishes between natural and moral evil, but regards them as inextricably intertwined: "Sleep, exhaustion, misery—these divinities called evils—and old age, baldness, and greyness entered the body. Then theft, bad deeds, falsehood, truth, sacrifice, fame and power entered the body."[43] This blurring of natural and moral evil is further encouraged by the Indian tendency to regard sin as a mistake of the intellect rather than the result of a flaw of character. "Since the intellectual has no intentional error, he can only go wrong on imperfect information or misunderstanding, which is not really his fault. Wrongness is not sin, though it may be unfortunate."[44] If evil is not man's fault, karma cannot "solve" the problem of evil.[45] There are some striking exceptional examples of a true sense of sin and repentance in Hinduism, such as some Ṛg Vedic hymns to Varuṇa,[46] some poems of Tamil Śaivism, and a Sanskrit verse still recited by many sophisticated Hindus today: "Evil am I, evil are my deeds. . . ."[47] But these are outweighed a thousandfold by instances of sin regarded as the fault of nature. Evil is not primarily what we do; it is what we do not wish to have done to us. That evil which we do commit is the result of delusion (*moha*) or deception (*māyā*)—and it is God who creates these delusions and deceptions. Thus once again we are forced to deny the ethical hypothesis: God is not good.

4. The Confrontation of Evil in Hindu Mythology

There would appear to be two good reasons why one should *not* write a book about the problem of evil in Hindu mythology: Indologists have long maintained that there is no problem of evil in Indian thought, and philosophers regard the problem as one best confined to the discipline of philosophy (or theology) rather than mythology. But one should never take too seriously the attitudes either of Indologists or of philosophers, and I think these two objections cancel one another out: scholars have overlooked the problem of evil in Indian thought because they have sought it in philosophy rather than in mythology.

[40] *RV* 4.5 and 10.10. [41] Rodhe, pp. 146–147. [42] *RV* 10.63.8.; cf. *RV* 5.85.8.

[43] *AV* 11.8.19–20. [44] Smith, p. 10. [45] See below, chap. II, sec. 5. [46] *RV* 5.85.

[47] "Pāpo 'ham, pāpakarmo 'ham." Personal communication from Dr. Tapan Raychaudhuri, of Oxford.

The theodicy that is developed in Hindu mythology demonstrates a more popular, general, and spontaneous attitude toward evil than may be found in the complex arguments of the Hindu theologians. Moreover, the myths are on the whole far more provocative and original than the textual discussions, for reasons which Heinrich Zimmer has pointed out:

Theologians very rarely produce first rate poetry or art. Their outlook on life's ambiguous and ambivalent features is narrowed by their dogmatism. They lack (this is a result of their training) that cynicism and that perilous innocence, candid and childlike, which are basic requirements for anyone dealing with myths. They lack (and this is their virtue, their duty) that touch of "amorality" which must form at least part of one's intellectual and intuitive pattern, if one is not to fall prey to predetermined bias and be cut off from certain vital, highly ironical, and disturbing insights.[48]

Since the main body of Hindu mythology—the medieval Purāṇas—was compiled by Brahmins with a considerable knowledge of theology, some of these texts degenerate into little more than the narrow-minded diatribes that Zimmer had in mind. Other texts, however, rise to the true level of myth, and these provide a more "candid and childlike" response to the problem of evil.

The theologians have a reply to Zimmer, in defense of their hallowed territory:

In general, religious myths are not adapted to the solving of problems. Their function is to illumine by means of unforgettable imagery the religious significance of some present or remembered fact or experience. But the experience which myth thus emphasizes and illumines is itself the locus of mystery. . . . When this pictorial presentation of the problem has mistakenly been treated as a solution to it, the "solution" has suffered from profound incoherences and contradictions.[49]

But this pictorial presentation of the problem is in itself a great achievement when the problem is, as we have seen theodicy to be, inherently contradictory;[50] the theologian wants answers, but the myth is content to ask, like Gertrude Stein, "What is the question?" Moreover, the very forcefulness, or even crudeness, of the myth may be its greatest strength; William James, describing the deep melancholy and terror of the suffering sick soul, suggested that "the deliverance must come in as strong a form as the complaint, if it is to take effect; and that seems a reason why the coarser religions, revivalistic, orgiastic, with blood and miracles and supernatural operations, may possibly never be displaced."[51] The philosophical pessimism and melancholy of the Upaniṣads, when confronted with the orgiastic and evil gods of primitive Tantrism, resulted in the integrated theodicy of Purāṇic Hinduism.

Another antimythological argument often maintains that stories about gods and demons are irrelevant to the study of the *human* problem of suffering. This is

[48] Zimmer, p. 179n. [49] Hick, p. 285. [50] O'Flaherty (1973), pp. 36–38; Lévi-Strauss (1967), pp. 29–30; Leach (1970), p. 57. [51] James, p. 168.

sheer nonsense. Myths are not written by gods and demons, nor for them; they are by, for, and about men. Gods and demons serve as metaphors for human situations; the problems of the virtuous demon and the wicked god are the problems of ambitious low-caste men and sinful kings. Sir James George Frazer once remarked that no country has ever been so "prolific of human gods" as India;[52] the demons are even more human, and are explicitly said to represent human impulses.[53] The specific, factual, human nature of myth has been well defended by Jung: "Myth is not fiction: it consists of facts that are continually repeated and can be observed over and over again. It is something that happens to man, and men have mythical fates just as much as the Greek heroes do."[54]

The myths of evil appear to be about origins, but implicit in them is a concern for the way things *are*. The pseudo-historical framework is merely a manner of speaking, a metaphor for theoretical ideas about the relation of good to evil, gods to men, the individual to society. The myth elucidates the nature of evil by means of an invented story of its origin. The techniques of philosophy are necessary but not sufficient; they are presupposed, and often rejected, by the myths. Philosophy supplies the vocabulary with which the problems can be stated; myth begins from the premises of philosophy but is then driven by a commonsense logic which discards the more elaborate solutions of the Vedāntins and seeks a more direct answer, an answer illuminated by the "coarse" ritual imagery which philosophy scorns. Myth is a two-way mirror in which ritual and philosophy may regard one another. It is the moment when people normally caught up in everyday banalities are suddenly (perhaps because of some personal upheaval) confronted with problems that they have hitherto left to the bickerings of the philosophers; and it is the moment when philosophers, too, come to terms with the darker, flesh-and-blood aspects of their abstract inquiries.

5. Notes on Method

In a study of Śaiva mythology, I discussed various methods of analysis and ended up using a somewhat modified structuralist technique because it seemed appropriate to that particular problem.[55] The problem of evil does not easily lend itself to a structuralist approach, perhaps because so many of its jagged facets prove stubbornly irreducible, perhaps because it is almost always viewed in conceptual rather than symbolic terms (though symbolism is appropriate to certain aspects of it[56]). I have therefore used any tool that would do the job—a bit of philology, a measure of theology, lashings of comparative religion, a soupçon of anthropology, even a dash of psychoanalysis—rather like a monkey piling up complex

[52] Frazer, I, 402. [53] See below, chap. IV, sec. 4, and chap. XI, secs. 6–8. [54] Jung (1954), p. 75.
[55] O'Flaherty (1973), pp. 11–21. [56] See below, chap. XI, sec. 2.

scientific gadgets into a miscellaneous heap in order to pluck the banana from the top of the cage. I trust that, though I may have misused the specialist's equipment, I have neither damaged it nor disgraced it. My only excuse for this undisciplined trespass is that it seems to work, to render accessible at least some of the answers I have sought.

In addition to the classical Sanskrit texts pertaining to this subject, I have occasionally drawn upon myths recorded by anthropologists conversant with the religions of Indian tribal communities. Although this material diverges from that of the Purāṇas in many significant respects, it is nevertheless possible to regard the two traditions as adjacent, if not actually contiguous; undoubtedly, there has been considerable borrowing in both directions. Verrier Elwin, who has produced many valuable studies of tribal mythology, has noted this continuity between his materials and those of the "Sanskrit" tradition: "My collection . . . will also provide material for the study of the diffusion of legends and will indicate how far the influence of the all-pervading Hindu tradition has proceeded. . . . The book may, in fact, be regarded as a sort of Aboriginal Purāṇa."[57] These tribal myths were all recorded during the last two centuries and are therefore liable to show traces of the influence of Christian missionaries, but such influences are usually immediately apparent, and the general agreement between tribal and Purāṇic mythology is striking.

In an early draft of this book, I included a number of parallels from Greek and Judeo-Christian mythology, which I subsequently decided to omit. Theologians and scholars of comparative mythology do not need me to point out the native varieties growing in their own backyards, and for the Indologists it is perhaps better merely to indicate that many of the "Hindu" concepts do appear outside of India (as the biblical citations at the head of each chapter are designed to demonstrate) than to provide a sketch of the non-Indian myths out of their context. Some ideas, such as the Fall or the loss of the Golden Age, are so immediately evocative of their Western associations that it would be awkwardly pedantic to avoid mentioning them; but these passing references are not meant to substitute for a detailed comparative study. Indeed, it is my fond wish that the present work may provide raw material for a single facet—the Hindu facet—of just such a cross-cultural analysis, perhaps used in conjunction with such studies of the Western approach to the problem of evil as the works of John Bowker, John Hick, C. G. Jung, C. S. Lewis, and Paul Ricoeur.

Even after omitting the comparative material, I found that the Hindu texts alone provided an *embarras de richesse*. The Sanskrit Purāṇas are garrulous and digressive, and in order to include as wide a selection of myths as possible I have summarized rather than translated, omitting large bodies of material superfluous

[57] Elwin (1949), pp. x and xi.

to the present study, such as hymns of praise, ritual instructions, detailed descriptions of people and places, and lengthy philosophical discourses. This extraneous material is not only unwieldy but would have tended to obscure the patterns that emerge from the more selective treatment. I have also omitted certain portions of the text that seem hopelessly corrupt, and in some instances where the meaning seems quite clear in spite of the garbled text, I have given the best sense I could make of it; where obscurities remain, I have included the ambiguous Sanskrit text. I have not (knowingly) added anything that is not in the text, but I may omit in one version certain details that also occur in another. For the sake of convenience, I have set long translations from the Sanskrit in italics but these do not indicate word-for-word translations, as is the usual convention, nor have I employed ellipsis points to indicate omissions, as these would have occurred so frequently as to render the text unreadable. Long quotations from secondary sources are printed in reduced type.

In attempting to trace the mythology of evil from the period of the Vedas to the present day, I encountered a number of significant variations and contradictions, and it is difficult to generalize and set forth "the" Indian attitude to certain pivotal problems. Where the attitude has changed in the course of time, I have tried to trace it from the earliest known sources; where sectarian biases reverse the original conclusions, I have so indicated. Historians of religion may regret that I have not followed the historical development of the entire mythology of evil but have instead treated the separate philosophical strands. There are two reasons for this. In the first place, it is notoriously difficult to date Indian religious texts, though it is reasonable to postulate several broad areas of Indian mythology: Ṛg Veda (c. 1200 B.C.), Brāhmaṇas and Atharva Veda (c. 900 B.C.), Upaniṣads (c. 700 B.C.), *Mahābhārata* (c. 300 B.C.–A.D. 300), *Rāmāyaṇa* (c. 200 B.C.–A.D. 200), early Purāṇas (*Brahmāṇḍa, Mārkaṇḍeya, Matsya, Vāyu*, and *Viṣṇu*, c. 300 B.C.–A.D. 500), middle Purāṇas (*Kūrma, Liṅga, Vāmana, Varāha, Agni, Bhāgavata, Brahmavaivarta, Saura, Skanda,* and *Devī,* c. A.D. 500–1000), later Purāṇas (all others, c. A.D. 1000–1500), modern Hindu texts. Wherever possible, within the discussion of a particular question, I have treated what appear to be the earlier texts first and indicated the emergence of later concepts. In particular, I have found it useful to distinguish three broad periods (or recurrent textual traditions): Vedic, Epic-Purāṇic (orthodox or post-Vedic), and devotional (bhakti).

There is a more basic argument against treating the entire corpus of myths through a history of the texts: There are several recognizably different conceptual attitudes to evil, and I found it more illuminating to trace each one of these separately than to divide the material into historical eras and summarize all the different philosophical concepts of evil that emerge in each era. The final objection to the historical method arises from the fact that there *is* no clear-cut development in Hindu mythology. Archaic concepts emerge again in late texts, often in direct conjunction with contradictory later concepts. This is due in part to the Indian habit of retaining everything old and simply adding new ideas like Victorian wings built on to Georgian houses, but it may also indicate a basic refusal to discard *any* possible approach to the problem of evil. Certain broad historical trends may be discerned, nevertheless, and I have indicated these where it seems most appropriate.

I must confess at the start to a violently Procrustean selection of my materials. If the devil may quote scripture, surely a scholar may follow suit by citing only those parts of scripture which give the devil his due and depict god in an unfavorable light. I find myself here firmly on the side of the demons, who in previous Indological studies have lacked an advocate. There are of course many Indian texts that depict the gods as good and the demons as evil—*ça va sans dire*—and a book based on these texts would be neither challenging to write nor interesting to read (a consideration which has not prevented a number of scholars from writing that book over and over again). The present study assumes that the reader will assume that the Hindus assume their gods to be good, their demons evil; proceeding from this chain of half-truths, I have set out to rectify the imbalance by setting forth the less obvious corollary—that the gods are not good, nor the demons evil, in any consistent or significant sense of these important words.

I must also admit another lacuna in this work. One of Stephen Potter's best ploys was the one in which the Lifesman, finding himself involved in a conversation on a subject of which he was totally ignorant, while Opponent was an acknowledged expert, would simply remark from time to time, "Not in the South."[58] I fear that any Lifesman could go far with that phrase, were he forced to discuss this book. South Indian Tamil texts are a world unto themselves, encompassing theological tracts and local myths that treat the problem of evil in a manner directly at variance with the attitudes prevailing in the texts on which my work is based, Sanskrit texts predominantly from the North Indian tradition. I have included a few Tamil myths when they were so apt that I could not resist them; but one could write another long book on the Hindu mythology of evil, using only the Tamil texts that I have *not* consulted. I am deeply indebted to David Shulman for discovering and translating the Tamil myths that I have cited; until he writes that other book let the reader be warned: not in the South.

6. The Questions and the Answers

The questions that I have tried to answer are basically threefold: What solutions did the Hindus offer to the problem of evil? How did these arise and develop

[58] Potter, pp. 26–28.

historically? How, if at all, can these various solutions be subsumed under a unified world view? Myths view problems in terms of characters, and there are four possible candidates for the role of villain in this drama: man, fate, devils, and gods. The first of these appears as a tentative solution in many Hindu texts (chapter II), but the myths of the Fall ultimately blame fate, rather than man, a logically consistent hypothesis, which is nevertheless ultimately rejected in its turn: it is not emotionally satisfying, and it bypasses the essential components of theodicy. Most Hindus preferred to believe that God was above fate, that he programmed evil into his creation willingly or unwillingly (chapter III). Moreover, the failure of Manichean dualism (chapter IV), and the belief that many demons were good rather than evil (chapter V), passed the buck back to the gods again. The benevolent motives of the god who recognized the necessity of evil (chapter III) were now replaced by the malevolent needs of demonic gods who thrust their own evil indiscriminately upon good and evil demons and men (chapters VI through IX). But in bhakti mythology, though God is still responsible for evil, he is benevolent once more (chapter X), and it is then left to the individual man to resolve, within himself, the problem of his own evil (chapter XI). These various approaches to the problem (chapter XII), most of which might have been eliminated or at least modified by other religions in order to strike a single theological note, are all retained in Hinduism in a rich chord of unresolved harmony.

And when the woman saw that the tree was good for food, and that it was pleasant to the eyes, and a tree to be desired to make one wise, she took of the fruit thereof, and did eat, and gave also unto her husband with her; and he did eat.
Genesis 3:6

II
TIME, FATE, AND THE FALL OF MAN

1. The "Solution" of Karma

It has been argued that "the most complete formal solution of the problem of theodicy is the special achievement of the Indian doctrine of *karma*, the so-called belief in the transmigration of souls."[1] This doctrine, simply stated, "solves" the problem by blaming evil on itself: one's present experience is the direct result of the action (karma), good and bad, accumulated in past lives and affixed to the transmigrating soul. Karma is a thing that can be transferred to one person from another, whittled away by good deeds performed in the present life, but never entirely destroyed; it is the outward visible sign of past invisible deeds. The evil that we experience is thus justified by evils of the past and will be balanced by rewards in future births; it is not God's fault, nor man's fault, nor a devil's fault; it is part of the eternal cycle, and ultimately all is justified and balanced.

The flaws in this solution are immediately apparent. The hypothesis of karma violates the hypothesis of omnipotence[2] and thus bypasses rather than resolves theodicy. If God is under the sway of karma, he is not omnipotent; if, as some theologians insist, God controls karma, then once again the blame is cast at his feet: "While the problem of extraordinary or gratuitous evil can be explained by a reference to previous Karma, this cannot, the plain man might feel, justify that evil."[3]

Even if the doctrine can be made rationally sound, it is never emotionally satisfying. This is apparent in village Buddhism in Ceylon (where some Hindu influence may have occurred) as well as in Hinduism:

[1] Weber (1963), p. 145. [2] Herman, p. 417. [3] *Ibid.*, p. 511.

> In the context of day-to-day behaviour the *karma* theory of causation presents logical problems which arise from ordinary human social and personal "needs." . . . It is impossible for the deities to help human beings to alter their *karma* because the deities themselves are *karma*-bound. Yet, despite the theory, the human need for such a supernatural intercession is manifest.[4]

In Buddhism, this results in "a behavioural position which involves a paradox of the theodicy type whereby gods endowed with power to alter the state of human grace are allowed to exist alongside a belief in karma which cannot be so altered."[5] In Hinduism, particularly in monotheistic devotional cults, karma becomes relatively unimportant and can be overcome by devotion.[6] This paradoxical symbiosis of cognitive religion (here represented by the philosophy of karma) and affective religion (devotion to the gods) has been noted in the Buddhism of Ceylon,[7] northeast Thailand, and Burma.[8] Ursula Sharma has observed a similar process in village Hinduism, where she distinguishes three levels of theodicy: cognitive (the problem of injustice), psychological (the need for comfort), and theological (the classical problem of monotheism); karma answers the first and obviates the need for the third, but it does not satisfy the second.[9] This psychological level is so acute that, although the villagers accept the doctrine of karma, they supplement it so that the afflicted person is protected from "feelings of anxiety about past deeds."[10] (This anxiety may have been alleviated in the classical texts by de-emphasizing sin in general: "The absence of sin introduces an irrationality to life; for karma must be just, yet what appalling creatures we must have been if we are only getting our just deserts all the time. It does not bear believing."[11]) Moral guilt does not constitute a special problem in village Hinduism, as it would if karma were strictly interpreted; people do not believe that there is nothing they can do to avoid or remove karma. Hindus often behave as if they did not believe in karma, and some definitely claim that they do not accept karma or believe in a supreme deity.[12] There is a clear gulf between philosophy and cult here, as Devendranath Tagore recognized when he criticized the Upaniṣads: "I became disappointed. . . . These Upanishads could not meet all our needs. Could not fill our hearts."[13] It is the particular talent of mythology to bridge the gap between the affective and cognitive aspects of religion—to fill the heart.

This pattern of differentiation has been observed in another Hindu village as well: the theory of karma generates anxiety and guilt about one's probable (but unknown) past sins, as well as feelings of helplessness, but "the beliefs concerning ways whereby fate can be subverted seem to function to allay such feelings—to give the individual mother some feeling of control over her social environ-

[4] Obeyesekere, pp. 20 and 22. [5] *Ibid.*, p. 23. [6] *Ibid.*, p. 24. [7] Gombrich (1971), *passim*.
[8] Tambiah, *passim*; Ling, *passim*. [9] Sharma, p. 350. [10] *Ibid.*, p. 357. [11] Smith, p. 10.
[12] Sharma, p. 350. [13] Tagore, p. 161.

ment."[14] Ghosts and evil spirits, as well as semi-gods who have achieved powers from asceticism, are "agents working outside fate"; devotion to God can overcome karma.[15] This simple faith has an elaborate, classical foundation in the philosophy of Rāmānuja, who maintained that God could "even override the power of *karma* to draw repentant sinners to him."[16] Thus the doctrine of karma is deeply undermined by other important strains of Indian religion in which the individual is able to swim against the current of time and fate.

Karma as a philosophy merely formalizes an intuition that has depressed most of the pessimists among us at one time or another—the feeling that we cannot escape our past, we cannot start fresh, that, as F. Scott Fitzgerald wrote, "we beat on, boats against the current, borne back ceaselessly into the past." Placing the initial wave of this current in a previous birth, or in a birth at some other point on a circle, simply transfers the blame from the realm of known events to the realm of unknown ones; in this way, the emotional intuition of the force of the past becomes logically airtight. The idea of the Golden Age is also based on a widespread (though by no means universal) intuition—a feeling that the skies were bluer, apples sweeter, when we were young. The myth reintroduces these underlying natural emotions into a philosophical framework which was invented precisely in order to form a rigid superstructure to protect that intuition in the first place.

How did Indians come to accept these alternative, conflicting views of theodicy? Obeyesekere, arguing against Weber's "existential" level of theodicy, attacks this question:

> In what sense could we say that a theodicy existed previous to the development of *karma*? Certainly not in the classical European sense of theodicy, which is explicitly related to the attributes of a monotheistic deity. . . . In a culture which possesses a theory of suffering like that of *karma* the problem of explaining unjust suffering simply cannot arise.[17]

But there are problems of the theodicy type in many texts of the Vedas and Brāhmaṇas, though karma does not appear until the later period of the Upaniṣads.[18] The concept of the sinful deity, which explains the origin of evil as a result of the malevolence of gods toward men, definitely predates the doctrine of karma and continues to prevail despite karma.[19] The wish to escape death (the basis of the antagonism between gods and men) and the fear of premature death (one of the classical sources of theodicy) are also well attested in Vedic texts. In karma-influenced texts this fear of death is changed into the wish to escape from life, but this line is seldom developed in the mythology, which reverts to Vedic assumptions, allows mortals to challenge death, and describes the resulting wrath of the gods—and our resulting suffering. Thus the patterns of theodicy were established before the doctrine of karma and continued to develop alongside it.

[14] Kolenda, p. 78. [15] *Ibid.*, pp. 76–77, and 79. [16] Basham, p. 332.

[17] Obeyesekere, pp. 10–11. [18] Keith, pp. 570 ff. [19] See below, chap. VI, secs. 3–4.

Karma is often used as a makeshift excuse to account for the temporary weakness of a god: Bali is able to usurp Indra's throne because of the evil karma that Indra had amassed in destroying the foetus in the womb of Diti,[20] and Vajrāṅga is able to steal Indra's treasures as a result of the same act. As the poet remarks, "The immortals have become unhappy because of their own karma; Indra has reaped the fruit of his evil act."[21] The gods may also escape punishment for their sins by blaming this same karma: when Indra had raped Utathya's pregnant wife and hidden in shame, Bṛhaspati consoled Indra by saying, "Don't worry. All this universe is in the sway of karma," and Indra bathed at a shrine and became purified and powerful again.[22] So too Gautama excused Indra for having seduced Ahalyā (Gautama's wife) and said that it was the fault neither of Ahalyā nor of Indra, but a result of karma.[23] The gods simply cannot lose, for another argument, that they are *not* ruled by karma as men are, is also cited in justification of their immoralities: "What the gods do bears no fruit, good or bad, as it does for men."[24] This statement, that the gods are above the laws of karma, appears as frequently as its converse.

2. The Problem of the Beginning of Time

One difficulty that arises directly out of the inadequacy of the karma solution is the problem of origins. Karma "solves" the problem of the origin of evil by saying that there *is* no origin—there is no beginning to time, simply an eternal cycle where future and past melt into one another. But this ignores rather than solves the problem; as Alan Watts inquired, "Why and how does the reincarnating individual first go wrong?"[25] One medieval Indian philosopher clearly stated the paradox: "Though, originally, all beings were associated with particular kinds of *karma*, . . . the original responsibility of association with *karma* belongs to God."[26] This, too, is no solution, for "at the time of original association the individuals were associated with various kinds of *karma* and were thus placed in a state of inequality."[27] The quandary leads logically in the Indian tradition to the myth of the Fall, calling upon an assumption that destroys the effectiveness of rebirth as a solution.

The myth of the Fall, or the loss of the Golden Age, entails three presuppositions: there was a beginning of human action, a first wicked act, and a previous period in which God had created everything in perfection.[28] But how can this be used to qualify the cycle of rebirth, which has no beginning? Herman states the problem nicely:

If the Vedas mention, as they do in their various cosmogenic moods (e.g. RV X.190; 129),

[20] *Vāmana* 49–50. [21] *Śiva* 2.3.14.18–24. [22] *Skanda* 2.7.23.8–40.
[23] *MBh.* 12.258.42. [24] *Matsya* 4.6. [25] Watts (1964), p. 39.
[26] Śrīpati Paṇḍita, cited in Dasgupta, V, 185. [27] Dasgupta, V, 185. [28] Herman, pp. 469–470.

origins of the Universe, then are these rather straightforward metaphysical myths to be subjected to Procrustean therapy just to save a nasty puzzle? . . . If the mythology of creation does indeed say that there was a beginning in some sense of that word, in non-being, or Puruṣa, or in an act of Indra or Brahmā, and if you are inclined to take your *śruti* [Vedic canon] seriously, then isn't it the better part of philosophic valor to admit to beginnings and face the philosophic music?[29]

The Indian answer to this paradox is simple, and brilliant: the Fall itself is cyclical; it happens again and again, over and over, within the cycle of rebirth. This is the Indian myth of the four Ages of man.

The myth of the four Ages is difficult to date. It is foreshadowed in the Brāhmaṇas in its broadest sense—the concept that the universe proceeds through time cycles of definite duration[30]—but its striking similarities to myths of Iran and Greece may indicate that the three myths represent parallel syntheses of diverse elements from all three cultures and from Mesopotamia, exchanged between the eighth and the third centuries B.C.[31] The four Ages decrease in goodness and virtue. This idea, that man lives in an age of degeneration, may have evolved simultaneously in Hindu thought with the whole cyclical theory of time-reckoning;[32] or the progression may have been more episodic: first a cyclic vision of time, then the myth of four Ages, then moral deterioration, and finally periodic destruction in fire and flood.[33] Even if the dharma element accrued to the myth last, it is included in the earliest recorded Indian variants of the myth, c. 200 B.C.,[34] and it may be obliquely challenged in an Aśokan edict of the fourth century B.C.[35] Certainly the theory of degenerative time is known to the *Mahābhārata*,[36] and it is fully developed in all of the earliest Purāṇas.

However piecemeal its origins, the synthetic theory is totally consistent. The inevitability of the decline, in spite of the original apparent balance of good and evil, or even the original prevalence of good, is based on the Hindu view of the relative activity and inactivity of evil and good: good is quiescent; evil is chaotic and life-creating.[37] "The growth of evil as the *yugas* [Ages] succeed each other is due to an expanding realization or actualization of the inherent polarity in man and the universe. . . . The Purāṇas tend to use a static conception of good and a dynamic conception of evil."[38] The world begins over and over again; each time, it is created out of water, and the Golden Age takes place. This Age degenerates until finally the fourth Age is reached, the present Kali Age, which is destroyed by fire and flood; all is once again water, out of which the world is created anew.

This myth not only provides the ideal framework for Indian cosmic mythology but itself reveals a number of profound symbolic insights:

[29] *Ibid.*, pp. 514–515. [30] *Śata.* 13.6.2.9–10. [31] Church (1973*a*), *passim.*

[32] Kane, III, chap. 34. [33] Church (1971) and (1974), *passim.* [34] Kane, III, xvii.

[35] Aśoka's fourth rock edict. [36] *MBh.* 3.188.9–13, etc.

[37] O'Flaherty (1973), pp. 310–313, and (1975), 11–14. [38] Huntington (1964), p. 38.

The [day of creation and night of destruction]motif can be understood either as (1) a root metaphor, or as (2) a central idea. The metaphorical pattern can be expressed as follows: (1) as full moon is to new moon, . . . spring is to winter; (2) good is to evil, *dharma* is to *adharma*; . . . The central idea can also be expressed simply: just as nothing lives forever, nothing ever dies. In the Yuga Story it is time itself that maintains the balance of opposites, the vehicle that unites both the dissolution and regeneration of all things.[39]

3. Free Will and the Fall

Though the myth of the Ages accounts for the ultimate balance of good and evil, it does not solve the problem of origins; it merely points out that the origin happens over and over again. In India man is not usually held responsible for the origin of evil, but this cannot be attributed to the absence of a belief in free will.[40] Though karma somewhat qualifies free will, it does not negate it. Indeed, as Christoph von Fürer-Haimendorf has pointed out, in an important sense karma is based on the assumption of free will: "The theory of *karma* presupposes man's moral responsibility for each of his actions and hence the freedom of moral choice."[41] Karma is clearly distinguished from fate (*daiva*); the latter is used often to explain otherwise inexplicable occurrences which even karma is regarded as inadequate to justify.

Karma is the hand one is dealt; one can play it badly or well. (Of course, the ability to play is also part of one's karma, and this leads to metaphysical intricacies). This is not the place, nor am I the scholar, for a lengthy exposition of the Indian doctrine of free will. Suffice it to say that Indian ideas on this subject differ radically from Western ones; in particular, we must face the disquieting ability of Indians to believe several seemingly contradictory tenets at once. Thus we find, in varying proportions, the concepts of free will, fate, and God's grace emerging from different texts at different periods. Moreover, there is significant evidence of a difference of opinion on this subject within individual texts: When the wicked Kaṃsa learns that he is "fated" to be killed by a child of his cousin, he boasts, "This is a matter that concerns mere mortals, and so it can be accomplished by us though we are mortal. It is known that people like me can overcome fate and turn it to advantage by the right combination of spells, and herbal medicines, and constant effort."[42] Unfortunately for Kaṃsa, his fate does not turn out to be surmountable (for the child fated to kill him is Kṛṣṇa, no "mere mortal"), and when Kaṃsa's scheme backfires he changes his tune, saying that it was not he but fate that arranged events, that he could *not* overcome fate by mere human effort. Yet the means that Kaṃsa set such store by must have been accepted by many people in ancient India.

[39] Church (1971), p. 177. [40] von Fürer-Haimendorf (1974), p. 549. Cf. Strauss, *passim*.

[41] *Hari.* 48.39. [42] *Hari.* 47.1–15.

An early text combines the will of the godhead with karma in a way that seems to leave no room for free will: "He causes him whom he wishes to lead up from these worlds to perform good action; and him whom he wishes to lead downward to perform bad action."[43] A medieval philosopher discussed the paradox of predetermination, man's will, and God's grace implicit in the above text:

> God only helps a person when he wishes to act in a particular way; or to desist from a particular way of action. So a man is ultimately responsible for his own volition; which he can follow by the will of God in the practical field of the world.[44]

And a later commentator on this second text further muddied the already muddy waters but left more scope for free will:

> It is . . . meaningless to say that it is He, the Lord, that makes one commit sins or perform good deeds merely as He wishes to lower a person or to elevate him. For . . . God does not on his own will make one do bad or good deeds, but the persons themselves perform good or bad actions according to their own inclinations as acquired in past creations.[45]

Here one's inclinations are determined by the past—but one is nevertheless responsible for them.

The belief that God intended man to live in a state of perfection, but that man, by the exercise of his free will, destroyed this perfection and thus either brought about the evils of the world or caused God to destroy him, arises very seldom in Sanskrit texts. There the blame is usually cast either upon God (who through his own shortcomings causes man to be born with the imperfections that are inevitably to result in his downfall) or (rarely) upon demons who spoil the world for mankind and cause the gods to destroy it: men are good until evil gods corrupt them. The belief that man himself is the author of his woes is, however, entirely consonant with the early mythology of the degeneration of civilization and the evil nature of man, and it reemerges in certain myths of heresy in which men corrupt one another.

4. The Indian Myth of the Fall

There are a few, atypical Indian texts that blame man for the Fall; prominent among them is the corpus of myths that account for low caste status as a result of past sins. This concept appears in myths that attribute the status of demons to a fall from caste and in others that describe the loss of the Golden Age as a process of moral and social disintegration.[46] There are also numerous local traditions of this sort which rationalize the status of specific castes. Manu regarded the Greeks and other foreign "barbarians" as Śūdras (servants) who had sunk from their

[43] *Kau. Up.* 3.9. [44] Śrīkaṇṭha on *Brahmasūtra* 2.3.41, cited in Dasgupta, V, 89.

[45] Appaya Dīkṣita on *Śrīkaṇṭha*, II, 47–48, cited in Dasgupta, V, 87. [46] See below, chap. IV, sec. 3.

former status as Kṣatriyas (warriors, nobles) when they disregarded Brahmins.[47] The sect of Kāpālikas are thought to have been Brahmins in former times.[48] According to Jain theory, all castes once professed Jainism, but certain groups fell into false ways and became Brahmins who formulated a cult sanctioning the slaughter of animals[49]—a myth that reverses the usual assumptions of the Hindu myth and describes a fall *into* Brahmin-hood rather than *from* it.

Many castes consider themselves fallen Brahmins and justify their change of occupation (when they move up the scale) by stating that they are merely resuming their former status. Ambedkar revived the traditional myth when he argued that the Untouchables, and many Śūdras, were Buddhists who had suffered from the hatred of Brahmins when the Hindu renaissance occurred.[50] Local Hindus accepted the claim made by certain Untouchables that their ancestors had been kings who had fallen to their present status through some sin; one variation of this myth states that, when fighting the Muslims, the Kṣatriya ancestors of certain Untouchables pretended to be Untouchables and were cursed to remain in that state as punishment for their cowardice.[51] Yet even this belief, based on the philosophy of karma and an admission of one's own past guilt, is denied by many low castes, who do not attribute their status to sinful past lives of members of their castes but rather say that they were somehow tricked out of their former high rank,[52] just as the demons were tricked out of theirs.

The Ṛg Veda contains an unusual verse which states that "brotherless women, deceiving their husbands, evil, lying, . . . have made this deep place."[53] The commentator, Sāyaṇa, takes this "deep place" to be hell, but his reading is not supported by any other Ṛg Vedic text. Later Vedic texts, however, do occasionally revive this point of view. One myth that appears in the Brāhmaṇas seems to imply that man committed a moral error, which forced the gods to destroy him:

Prajāpati created beings, but they were gripped by poverty and anxiety, and so Varuṇa seized them. They treated him with disdain and left him. Prajāpati then became Varuṇa and seized them.[54]

Even here, the original impulse stems not from man but from some external force that inflicts poverty and anxiety upon him; it is this "evil"—one can hardly call it a sin—which drives man to reject Varuṇa, a sin for which he is punished. The meaning of this rather obscure myth emerges more clearly upon comparison with another Brāhmaṇa:

When they were created, all the creatures ate the barley corn belonging to Varuṇa, and

[47] Manu 10.43–44. [48] Gonda (1963), p. 210; and see below, chap. X, sec. 2.
[49] Prasad, p. 225. [50] Ambedkar, p. 78. [51] Pocock (1955), final par.; (1964), p. 303; and personal communication from Pocock. [52] Kolenda, p. 75; and see below, chap. IV, sec. 3.
[53] *RV* 4.5.5. [54] *Tait. Br.* 1.6.4.1; cf. *Mait. Sam.* 1.10.19 and *Kāṭh. Sam.* 36.5.

because of that Varuṇa seized them. They became swollen [with dropsy, the punishment sent by Varuṇa, god of the waters] but Prajāpati healed them and freed them from Varuṇa's snare, and his creatures were born free of disease or fault. Prajāpati created an abundance [of food] and freed the creatures.[55]

The original sin is here directly related to hunger, and the cure is simple: Prajāpati creates an abundance of food. The conflict between the two gods is apparent. Prajāpati creates man and protects him, while Varuṇa punishes him. Yet neither acts as the devil, and the blame is laid upon man—though man is restored in a manner acceptable to Vedic mythology, in contrast with the later Purāṇic myths where hunger begins an irreversible process of decay.

It is in the tribal mythology of India, however, that one often encounters myths corresponding to the Western idea that God is forced to destroy man because of man's wickedness, and this may be due to Christian missionary activity among the tribes, whose traditions were recorded only after such activity had been taking place for some time. Many of these myths are used to explain the origin of death, which may be regarded in simple terms as a manifestation of the separation of man from god (i.e., mortal from immortal):

When God first made the world, He [created man and woman from ashes and] then called the man by name, saying, "Manoo [Manu, the first man]," and the man replied, "Hoo" instead of "Ha Jee" (Yes, Life) respectfully, as he should have done. For this reason was everlasting life denied him.[56]

A similar myth is told among the Kuruk of Middle India:

[Mahapurub made a boy and a girl.] When they grew up they quarrelled. Mahapurub called them and said, "You are disturbing me with your quarrels." He picked them up and killed them.[57]

The Jhoria believe that there was no death until men and gods began to fight against each other; then Mahaprabhu created the waters of death and immortality and tricked men into accepting the former.[58] Although the pattern of this myth is that of the Vedic myths of the wars between gods and demons (who fight against one another for the drink of immortality, which the gods obtain by tricking the demons), the antagonism between men and gods rather than demons and gods is more characteristic of Purāṇic mythology.[59]

5. The Natural Origin of Evil

In contrast with these scattered instances of evil originating from man's sin, most Indian myths of the loss of the Golden Age do not blame man at all: he is

[55] *Śata.* 2.5.2.1–3 and 5.2.4.1–2. [56] Dracott, p. 5. And see below, chap. IV, sec. 8, and chap. VIII. sec. 8. Cf. Haimendorf (1974), pp. 541–543 and 548. [57] Elwin (1949), p. 42.

[58] *Ibid.*, p. 510. [59] See below, chap. IV, secs. 1 and 5.

the victim, not the cause. This generally prevalent view first appears in the *Mahābhārata*:

Formerly Prajāpati brought forth pure creatures, who were truthful and virtuous. These creatures joined the gods in the sky whenever they wished, and they lived and died by their own wish. In another time, those who dwelt on earth were overcome by desire and anger, and they were abandoned by the gods. Then by their foul deeds these evil ones were trapped in the chain of rebirth, and they became atheists.[60]

The reference to "another time" may signify the appearance of the Kali Age or may simply describe the eventual appearance of the evil inherent in desire and anger and the subsequent loss of purity and immortality. For the original people are not mortals at all, but pure creatures who do not eat or die. They become physically corruptible (i.e., subject to carnal decay and rebirth) when they are morally corrupted; the two characteristics are inextricably linked, for in Hindu mythology embodied humans are corrupt, in both senses of the word. Although this myth shares important assumptions with the myth of Eden, its emphasis is on the development of the evil chain of rebirth implicit in the myth of the four declining Ages.

This myth of a lost Golden Age appears in Buddhist texts as well as Hindu and is widely distributed outside India as well. Charles Drekmeier has suggested a reason for its widespread appeal:

The Buddhist doctrine shares much with certain theories of psychoanalysis. Freud never postulated an idyllic natural state like the golden age that haunts Buddhist cosmogony. Before men united in civil societies they were governed by the rule of the strong. But there is a golden age in the life of man. The quest (explicit in Buddhism, innate in man according to the psychoanalyst) is for this golden age before the organism had distinguished itself from its surroundings.[61]

This analysis implies that the Golden Age is characterized by a lack of differentiation, an implication supported by those Indian texts which point out that there was no need for class separations in the Golden Age:

In the Golden Age, people were happy and equal. There was no distinction between high and low, no law of separate classes. Then, after some time, people became greedy, and the wishing-trees disappeared, and passions arose.[62]

But it is also clear that both the psychoanalytic view and the Indian view of this golden time are more complex than Rousseau's theory that when man is at one with nature and free of civilization he is "good." The "rule of the strong" applies even without society; this appears in Hindu mythology as the "rule of the fishes,"

60 *MBh.* 3.181.11–20.

61 Drekmeier, p. 105. Cf. Robert Frost's "Nothing Gold Can Stay" and Masson (1974*a*), p. 456; but cf. Haimendorf (1974), p. 555.

62 *Skanda* 1.20.40.173–185.

whereby the big fish eats the smaller fish, a metaphor for the dreaded state of anarchy.

Moreover, in the majority of Purāṇic myths, the Golden Age is only temporary, a passing phase, rather than the basic or natural state of man. Inevitable decay characterizes another myth of the origin of evil:

In former times there was no king, nor was there any rod of chastisement; of their own accord, and by means of dharma, all creatures protected one another. But then they wearied of this, and delusion entered them. Religion and dharma were destroyed, greed and desire overcame people, and the gods became afraid, saying, "Now that dharma is destroyed, we will become equal with the mortals, for their dwelling will rise and ours will fall when they cease to perform the rituals." (Then, for the benefit of the gods, Brahmā established government and Viṣṇu created kings—Vena and Pṛthu.)[63]

As in the usual Vedic view, the gods wish men to be virtuous so that they will continue to offer sacrifice to the gods; but a hint of the later, opposing, Purāṇic view appears in the statement that the gods fear not only their own decline but the rise of men, a situation which in later mythology leads the gods to bring about the moral corruption of mankind rather than to reestablish dharma among mortals on earth.[64] Sheer boredom seems to suffice to sow the seed from which corruption must develop, for it is dharma that bores them, dharma of which they "wearied." Stemming from these same assumptions, several lawbooks use the premise of the destruction of man's original dharma to justify coercive authority, the chastising rod of the king.[65]

The Purāṇas relate the story of man corrupted by nothing but time (*kāla*):

In the beginning, people lived in perfect happiness, without class distinctions or property; all their needs were supplied by magic wishing-trees. Then because of the great power of time and the changes it wrought upon them, they were overcome by passion and greed. It was from the influence of time, and no other cause, that their perfection vanished. Because of their greed, the wishing-trees disappeared; the people suffered from heat and cold, built houses, and wore clothes.[66]

Unlike the myths justifying the establishment of kingship, this text seems to imply that civilization—property and clothing—is a source of further greed and sin, not a cure for them. This much the Hindu philosopher shares with Rousseau, but his basic attitude lies closer to Hobbes: with the passage of time, man's inherent evil must come to the fore. The Hindu myth views the necessity of clothing as a sign of the loss of simple physical innocence: people are no longer immune to the weather. Greed, however, is regarded as a sin, and it is this sin that destroys the magic fruit of paradise.

[63] *MBh.* 12.59.13–30; and see below, chap. XI, sec. 1.

[64] See below, chap. IX, sec. 1, and chap. IV, sec. 8. [65] *Nārada Smṛti* 1.1–2. [66] *Vāyu* 1.8.77–88.

The belief that time is morally destructive is the basis of the myth of the four Ages:

In the Golden Age, dharma was complete. There was no sorrow or delusion or old age or misery, no injury or quarrels or hate or famine. Men lived a long life. . . . In the Dvāpara [the third] Age, dharma was only half left, and injury, hatred, falsehood, delusion, evil, disease, old age, and greed arose. Castes became mixed.[67]

A Buddhist text offers what may well be a satire on this facile view of the corruption of man:

At first, all sages were virtuous ascetics, but then came a reversal, and they began to covet one another's wealth, wives, and horses, and to slaughter cows. Indra, the gods, demons, and Rākṣasas cried out against this adharma; and thus the three original diseases (desire, hunger, and old age) developed into ninety-eight.[68]

Though the gods' disapproval of the adharma on earth links this myth with the Vedic concept of the need for sacrifice and virtue, the manner in which the myth offers the expansion of three evils into ninety-eight as an "explanation" of the loss of virtue may be a travesty of Brāhmaṇical number mysticism. The text does not indicate whether the plague of evils arises directly from the loss of the sages' virtue or from the subsequent indignation of the gods—and, significantly, of the demons—but the perversion occurs in the first place simply in the course of time.

The power of time reasserts itself in spite of the moral efforts of the corrupted mortals:

When the Tretā [the second] Age began to wane, after a long time, and because of the change in creatures, greed and passion arose; and because of this change in them, caused by time, all the wishing-trees were destroyed. People thought about this, and as they meditated truly, the trees reappeared. . . . But in course of time greed again returned to them, and they tore up the trees. Then the dual sensations arose, and they were oppressed by cold rain and hot sun, thirst and hunger. Again their perfections appeared, and rain fell, and again the trees appeared. But again passion and greed arose in them, because of the inevitable fate ordained for the Tretā Age.[69]

At first the trees vanish of their own accord when men become greedy; then the greedy men themselves tear up the trees. But the original impulse is caused by time, an impulse that reasserts itself over and over again despite the strenuous moral efforts of men.

This degenerative process seems to imply a belief in original sin, or at least in an original tendency to sin. The Brāhmaṇas do not assert the inheritance of original sin, for one early text states, "As little guilt as there is in a child just born,

[67] *Bṛhaddharma* 3.12.1–24. [68] *Sutta Nipāta, Brāhmana-dhammika Sutta*, pp. 51–55.

[69] *Liṅga* 1.39.23–56.

so little guilt is there in him who performs the Varuṇapraghāsa sacrifice,"[70] implying that a newborn child is more or less guilt free; but this view was certainly not shared by later Hindus; Manu states that the elaborate birth ceremony is necessary to remove the impurity which the newborn child inherits from the womb and the seed.[71] In the Hindu view, human beings caught up in the process of time are inherently, naturally inclined to fall prey to evil. The pure creatures of the original Golden Age are not a part of time at all; for them, karma doesn't exist; they are beyond good and evil. Their "fall" consists of passing from eternity into time; once caught up in the flow of time, they are no longer immune to evil. The creatures of the Golden Age, though they may dwell upon earth, are not the first members of the human race; almost by definition, as soon as they become "human" the Golden Age must immediately disappear. The Hindu concept of the Golden Age thus lacks any vision of pristine human innocence or the corresponding belief in a separate agency of evil. To the Hindu, the original state of perfection is doomed to quick extinction from within, and there is no need for a serpent or a devil to initiate the process.

Max Weber interpreted this Hindu relativity of paradise and sin in sociological terms:

> The conception of an "original sin" was quite impossible in this world order, for no "absolute sin" could exist. There could only be a ritual offense against the particular dharma of the caste. In this world of eternal rank orders there was no place for a blissful original state of man and no blissful final kingdom. Thus there was no "natural" order of men and things in contrast to positive social order.[72]

Though it is true that ritual offenses usually occupy in Hindu myth the place Weber allots to "sin," there is a contrast throughout the mythology between the positive social order and the "natural" social order which becomes so quickly corrupt. Moreover, although the individual could offend against his caste law, the caste as a whole could violate a more universal law—the law of dharma—as is evident from the myths of Brahmins who "fall" to become Untouchables or demons.

The fleeting and insubstantial nature of the original paradise, and the pessimistic view of the nature of man, characterize the Hindu myths. In these myths, men—and even demons—are originally good, but evil passions inevitably appear soon after creation, and *this* is the natural (albeit not original) state of man. The inability to explain the loss of the Golden Age prevails even in tribal mythology. The Todas believe that once, long ago, gods and men inhabited the hills together. "The Todas can now give no definite account of their beliefs about the transition from this state of things to that which now exists."[73]

[70] *Mait. Sam.* 1.10.10 and *Kāṭh. Sam.* 36.5; cf. Heesterman (1971), p. 13.

[71] *Manu* 2.27. Cf. also *Tāṇḍya* 18.1.24, *Śata.* 2.5.2.22, 4.4.5.23, *Kau. Br.* 5.3.

[72] Weber (1958), p. 144. [73] Rivers, p. 183.

6. Women and the Origin of Evil

The connection between procreation and evil, the implication that sexual creation is the epitome of sin, recurs constantly in the Hindu mythology of evil; women are not only the abstract cause of a number of evils and sins in the world, they are also used as the specific instrument of the gods to corrupt individual sages and demons. This is the natural consequence of the general misogyny of the Indian ascetic tradition and the Upaniṣadic doctrine of the chain of rebirth: reproduction traps men in the painful cycle of existence. Orthodox Hinduism, too, was prone to misogyny in its caste laws restricting the freedom of women.

As this tendency developed, abstract goddesses were cited with increasing frequency as the cause of evil on earth. Death, originally a male god, began to appear as a goddess; the stallion, the symbol of Aryan supremacy in the Vedic period, was now replaced by the dangerous mare, in whom the doomsday fire lurked, ready to destroy the universe.[74] In the Epic myths of the origin of evil, the goddesses of disease and destruction initiate the downfall of mankind; the vague "natural tendencies" of corruption are replaced by anthropomorphic (perhaps one should say gynecomorphic) goddesses of doom.

According to the *Mahābhārata*, men originally lived without fear of death and did not know of sexual intercourse; in the Tretā Age people were born by imagination, but in the Dvāpara there arose copulation, and in the Kali Age, pairing; then there was death.[75] The distinction between copulation and pairing is obscure, but the latter may refer to twins, the brother and sister who are the (incestuous and therefore immoral) primeval couple in Vedic mythology (Yama and Yamī) and who appear in Jain and Hindu creation myths:

When Brahmā first performed creation, he meditated upon truth, and from his mouth he created pairs (of human beings) who were made of truth; from his breast he created pairs made of passion; from his thighs those made of passion and ignorance; from his feet, those made of ignorance. All of these pairs loved one another and began to mate. But although they had intercourse, women did not menstruate and so they did not bear offspring. At the end of their life-span they brought forth a pair (of children to reproduce themselves). They were free of strife and hatred and jealousy. They lived without houses, and they were without desire, remaining happy and righteous. All were equal and remained young for four thousand years, without any affliction. As time went by, people began to be destroyed, and gradually their perfections vanished. When they were all destroyed, liquids fell from the sky, and from this liquid wishing-trees arose, which formed houses and food. Then, in time, without any cause, lustful passion arose, and because of their passion women began to menstruate, and they conceived again and again. Then, after an interval of time, greed came over them, and they fenced in the trees, and because of this misdeed the trees perished. People became hungry. They built cities.[76]

[74] O'Flaherty (1971*a*), *passim*. [75] *MBh.* 12.200.34–40. [76] *Mārk.* 46.1–35; *Kūrma* 1.28.15–40.

Although degenerative forces of time reappear constantly in this myth, which even states that lustful passion arose "without any cause," the motif of sexual passion is also clearly essential. In keeping with Hindu beliefs that fertility and eroticism are not necessarily connected and that it is necessary to control sexual passion even while procreating,[77] mankind encounters its greatest difficulties not when sexual reproduction appears, but only when passion appears. It is clear, however, that reproduction also entails an element of evil, for the first troubles begin, not when people merely reproduce, but when they begin to increase—that is, to produce more than a pair of children. This increase is symbolized by the menstrual flow, which reappears throughout Hindu mythology in association with sin and pollution. Before menstruation, intercourse did not cause the trees to disappear—because, in this myth, there *are* no trees, nor any need for them, before the original fall takes place.

The significance of the increase in population is linked with Indian ideas of food and death and their connection with sexual reproduction. As in the *Mahābhārata*, death arises only when sexual increase appears; clearly, this is a result of the Hindu fear of overpopulation, which is manifest at a surprisingly early period, at a time when, because of high infant mortality, it may not have been a realistic worry on a major scale. Transition from rural to urban life at this time may have produced pockets of actual overpopulation and contributed to a more general mentality of overcrowding and a resurgence of the Vedic lust for *Lebensraum.* Bluntly expressed, the logic implicit in the Indian fear of overpopulation is simply that if too many people are born, some must die; if death is feared, birth must be feared. The connection with food is equally obvious: not only are hunger and desire two basic appetities, but they are closely associated in Indian mythology, and they are interconnected through the theme of overpopulation: when too many people are produced, food becomes scarce—the trees vanish. This may be the significance of the strange liquid that falls from the sky when the perfection of mankind is destroyed. The liquid that is associated with man's ensnarement in the cycle of rebirth may be traced back to the Upaniṣads: men, upon cremation, are transformed eventually into clouds; they rain down, grow as plants, are eaten and emitted as semen.[78] One translator of this myth either misunderstands this verse or has a different text, for he seems to associate it with the myth of the Fall from heaven: "Men [in place of "liquids"] fell down from the sky."[79] The translator, or his text, may have been influenced by the Buddhist myth in which beings from the brahma-world fall to earth when their merit is exhausted,[80] beings further reminiscent of the pure creatures of the *Mahābhārata*

[77] O'Flaherty (1973), pp. 255–292. I am indebted to Professor Anne Draffkorn Kilmer for her insights into problems of ancient myths of overpopulation. [78] *Ch. Up.* 5.10.6.

[79] Pargiter (1904), 49.27 (p. 239). [80] *Visuddhimagga* 13.44; see below, chap. VIII, sec. 7.

myth, for they are self-luminous until they begin to eat (i.e., to have bodies) and to crave, whereupon their light leaves them. The magic liquid becomes necessary when people cease to live on their virtue alone; if man is prey to passion, he must have food.

The literal fall of men from heaven (as well as the fall of liquids) recurs in William Buck's interpretation of the *Mahābhārata* myth of the Fall:

> At the beginning of Time men lived in the clear air and moved at will without any effort. Then the Earth was honey, sweet and delicious, and, few by few, men dipped down from the sky to taste her. Then they took more than a taste, though they needed no food to live, and as they ate they became too heavy to fly and their wings dropped off from them, while Earth grew crusted and dry and made her seeds, and the rains began to fall.[81]

The fall of rain is simultaneous with the fall of man—it is the beginning of dangerous fertility, the jungle-like growth of plants and creatures heralding the end of Eden. In another text, the Golden Age is characterized by the absence of lust, rain, and time: "No one desired another man's wife; everyone was born and died in equal proportions; the clouds did not rain, and there was no development of time."[82] Yet even this age cannot last forever.

7. Hunger and Sin

The symbol of paradise is the self-creating source of food, the magic tree. In India, the magic trees are *meant* to be eaten. When the trees disappear, sin appears, for hunger is born. This is merely another way of saying that evil is natural to human being; the original pure creatures had no lust or hunger—but they were not human beings. Once *we* appear upon the scene, hungry and lustful, the Golden Age is doomed. This assumption is challenged in other myths of this corpus: men remain virtuous until the source of food begins to diminish, and only then do they become evil. This is perhaps the closest that the ancient Indians ever came to the concept of a virtuous natural state of man, who violates the moral law only when threatened by an external force.

Yet the very nature of that external force was given moral overtones in some texts. This is evident from a medieval Jain myth that begins, like the Buddhist and early Hindu creation stories, with the postulation of limitless food coming from the wishing-trees:

But with the passing of time in that place, the power of the wishing-trees became weak, like that of ascetics who have violated their vows. As if by some evil fate, the trees had been changed, replaced by others. As the consequence of such a time, passions such as anger appeared in people, who informed their king of the sins that had arisen. He ordained food for them to eat, and a fire arose from the branches of trees rubbing together, and people

[81] Buck, p. 318. [82] *Skanda Purāṇa, Sahyādri Khaṇḍa* 2.45–51.

began to cook their food. When they were frightened of the fire and asked the king what it was, he replied, "This fire arises because of the fault of a time that is both harsh and smooth. It does not exist in a period that is altogether harsh nor in one that is altogether smooth." Then he began to institute social order and laws of conduct and punishment.[83]

As is usual in such myths, time is made to bear the major portion of the guilt, and the workings of an evil fate (*durdaiva*) are also suggested, for time and fate are closely linked. But nature herself seems to have moral qualities, which inevitably decline. The trees waste away, not because of the sins of mankind but because of the loss of power of the trees themselves, a power that is likened to a loss of chastity–the sin usually associated with the people who lose the trees. When moral law further decays, the king provides food, first raw and then cooked; civilization enters at this point, and the king's explanation of the birth of fire is significant: fire is symptomatic of the ambiguous time–a mixture of good and bad–that characterizes the Hindu universe[84] (though the Jain text states that we now live in a completely harsh era, the fifth of six). This text thus makes explicit what is implicit in all the myths of this cycle: that man and nature inevitably interact in such a way as to corrupt one another; that man's sin causes food to decrease, and hunger causes man to violate the moral law. Once more we are caught in a circle of evil.

The connection between hunger and evil is an ancient one. In Vedic texts, hunger and drought do not merely *cause* evil (i.e., moral evil, sin); they themselves *are* evil, and are listed in Vedic texts describing evil–natural evil. In the Brāhmaṇas, hunger is demonic; the demons create hunger as a weapon against the gods, but it rebounds against them.[85] Elsewhere, hunger is a demonic part of human beings; the demonic half of the serpent Vṛtra becomes the stomachs of men.[86] The Ṛg Veda says: "The gods did not give us hunger as an instrument of slaughter; for various deaths overcome one who has eaten."[87] But creators' intentions often miscarry, and by the time of the Brāhmaṇas a more realistic and cynical attitude toward hunger and thirst prevailed: "Whenever there is drought, then the stronger seizes upon the weaker, for the waters are dharma."[88] When Brahmā began to create in his passionate form, he produced hunger whence was born anger and the starving Rākṣasas; and when Śiva created the Rudras they threatened to eat him.[89] In many creation myths of this type, the first evil creatures that the creator produces are hungry, and they trouble the universe until they are assigned suitable food. Thus it is said that Prajāpati feared that Agni would eat him, since there was no other food, and he satisfied Agni by offering

[83] *Triṣaṣṭiśalākāpuruṣacaritra* I (*Ādīśvaracaritra*) 2.148–163; 2.893–894; 2.941–944.

[84] Lévi-Strauss (1970), pp. 136–195; and see below, chap. III, sec. 1. [85] *Tait. Br.* 1.6.7.2.

[86] *Śata.* 1.6.3; see below, chap. V, sec. 4, and chap. VI, sec. 4. [87] *RV* 10.117.1; cf. *Bṛhadāraṇyaka Up.* 1.2. [88] *Śata.* 11.1.6.24. [89] *Viṣṇu* 1.5.41–43; *Bṛhaddharma* 3.12.26–41.

him a wife, Svāhā (the oblation), the food of fire.[90] It is significant that the original threat posed by hunger is ultimately removed by the satisfaction of the closely related sexual drive; Svāhā is both Agni's food and his wife.

This link endures in a much later Purāṇic myth:

The demon Ruru attacked the gods, who sought refuge with the Goddess. She created goddesses who killed Ruru and his army, but then they asked for food. The Goddess summoned Rudra Paśupati, who offered them the food that pregnant women have defiled, and newborn children, and women who cry all the time. They refused this disgusting food, and at last Rudra said, "I will give you the two balls resembling fruits below my navel. Eat those testicles and be satisfied." The goddesses were delighted and praised him.[91]

Both forms of the food offered to the goddesses are sexual in nature; the first is closely associated with the pollution of procreation and with procreative women in particular and emotional women in general; the second is more crudely sexual. Another, earlier version of this same myth omits the second food, for the goddesses immediately accept the original offer of food defiled by pregnant women and others;[92] this part of the myth also follows the pattern of those stories in which an evil force is distributed among sinful mortals.[93]

A tribal myth preserves the basic link between the dangers of hunger and sexual desire: "[A man saw a beautiful maiden] and he wanted to devour her, for he had no penis and he could only find pleasure in swallowing. [Mahadeo came there and made sexual organs for the man and the woman.] The world was saved."[94] As is often the case, the tribal myth recognizes the same basic problems that are treated in the Hindu texts but is content to settle for a solution of the immediate quandary without considering the implications of the enduring philosophical conflict.

In human terms, hunger is the epitome of *āpad-dharma*, the extremity in which normal social conventions cease to function:

Once there was a twelve-year drought, when Indra sent no rain. All dharma was destroyed and people ate one another. The great sage Viśvāmitra came to a place inhabited by outcastes who ate dogs; seeing a dead dog, he tried to steal it, reasoning that theft was permissible in time of extremity. An outcaste tried to stop him from committing the sin of eating a dog, but in vain. Viśvāmitra ate the rump of the dog and burned away his sin by performing asceticism, and eventually Indra sent rain.[95]

The initial premise of a twelve-year drought is a frequent motif in later myths of heresy, as is the complete reversal of moral roles—the sage being instructed by the outcaste.

[90] *Śata.* 9.1.1.1; 2.2.4.1. [91] *Padma* 5.26.91–125; cf. *Liṅga* 1.106.1–27; *Matsya* 252.5–19; 179.7–187.
[92] *Varāha* 96.1–144. [93] See below, chap. VI, secs. 3 and 6. [94] Elwin (1949), p. 261.
[95] *MBh.* 12.139.13–92; see below, chap. X, sec. 4.

In fact, the satisfaction of hunger, rather than hunger itself, is often considered the cause of the evil: "When the starving creatures devoured one another, Adharma was born. His wife was Nirṛti [destruction], who had three terrible, evil sons: Fear, Terror, and Death."[96] Improper eating (the basic caste tabu) is the source of sin. A Pāñcarātra myth dating from the fifth century A.D.[97] seems to connect the eating of the fruit of the knowledge of good and evil with the Fall from Eden,[98] but there is a significant difference: "Here the ground idea seems to be not that any devil has spoilt the world but that ignorance is necessary for the world process, for otherwise mankind would be one with God and there would be no world."[99] The myth itself is brief and obscure:

Knowledge became a cow, with a portion of herself, that is, she became a cloud. Then the milk called "the year" flowed from her and became food. But all the Manus, who had been omniscient, ate that milk of knowledge and lost their knowledge. Thereupon the Text was promulgated by the Manus.[100]

The Text is the Pāñcarātra canon of the author of this myth. An immediate reversal of the Judeo-Christian theme is apparent: the first beings lose their omniscience by eating of the fruit of knowledge. This apparent paradox results from the Indian emphasis on ignorance (darkness, delusion), loss of knowledge, in place of sin–loss of virtue resulting from acquisition of knowledge. This "knowledge" in the present myth, however, may be orthodox scriptural knowledge as contrasted with the intuitive knowledge that is supposedly contained in the Text. The myth has been interpreted as signifying that "souls have naturally unlimited knowledge," which "for some reason becomes limited and obscure, so that religion is necessary to show the soul the right way."[101] But these absolute statements must be qualified. Souls once had unlimited knowledge for a brief time, but the casual manner in which this knowledge was destroyed indicates the necessity of religious law (just as it justifies regnal law)–particularly of the Text which is appropriate to the lowly condition of fallen man.

8. The Chain of Evil and the Evil of Civilization

In some of these myths, the corrupting influence–sexual passion or hunger–simply arises in the course of time; other myths, however, sought an explanation for this inevitable corruption and found it in the doctrine that "former sins" caused the loss of the Golden Age, the doctrine of karma: evil is a chain that has no beginning or end.

An interesting Buddhist example of this chain of reasoning may be considered here, but it must be taken with a grain of salt. The Buddhist doctrine of the origin

[96] *MBh.* 1.60.52–53. [97] Schrader, p. 97. [98] *Ibid.*, p. 78.

[99] Eliot, I, lxxx, n. 1. [100] *Ahirbudhnyasaṃhitā* 7.59b–63a. [101] Eliot, I, lxxx.

of evil, which lies outside the scope of this work, is a central and widely discussed point of Buddhist belief; the second noble truth enunciated by the Buddha states that misery arises from craving, and a basic tenet of the Buddhist canon is the theory known as the chain of dependent origination. These ideas obviously bear a close resemblance to the Hindu theories of evil, but they arise in a different context; the Buddhists tended to face the problem of evil in terms of psychological factors within man rather than cosmological factors acting through or upon gods, and most cosmogonic myths in Buddhism are probably intended as satires on Hindu myths. Nevertheless, these texts often reproduce in faithful detail the main points of the Hindu myths, for, whether or not they accepted them, early Buddhists were well aware of the common pre-Buddhist corpus of Indian legends upon which both they and the later Hindus drew.

The "chain of evil" is a very Buddhist idea, since the Pali canon explained the origin of evil in terms of causal links in the chain of misery. Thus a Buddhist myth of the origin of evil uses both Hindu and Buddhist elements to explain the Fall by postulating earlier evil:

The original creatures were made of mind, eating only joy; they lived in the air, without sexual distinctions. Then the earth became fragrant and sweet as honey. At first no one touched it, but then a certain being, born greedy [the commentator remarks, "Greedy from a former birth"], said, "What can this be?" and tasted it, and craving overcame him. The others followed his example and tasted the earth greedily. Their bodies became solid. Some people became beautiful, others ugly. The beautiful despised the ugly. Therefore the sweet food disappeared. Then women were differentiated from men, and passion arose. People began to couple, and when others saw them doing so they threw dust and ashes and cow dung at them and shouted, "Perish, you foul one. How could one person treat another like that?" Then men built huts to conceal their sexual intercourse. . . . Then someone of a greedy disposition appropriated another field that had not been given to him. . . . From such beginnings arose theft, censure, false speech, and punishment.[102]

Physical beauty here causes differentiation between the previously "pure" spiritual creatures. A related Buddhist text also uses this criterion but blames the ugly, not the beautiful, for the final link in the chain of immorality: "Those who were ugly envied the beautiful and committed adultery with their wives. . . . Thus sexual wrong-doing arose."[103]

Sexual appetites and hunger initiate the degenerative process, as they do in many Hindu myths (sometimes in that order, sometimes reversed). The earth is made of honey, as are the wishing-trees in the Hindu versions, and the Buddhist myth goes on to explain the origin of caste in what appears to be a satire on the

[102] *Dīgha Nikāya, Aggañña Suttanta* xxvii.10 ff., vol. III, p. 84 ff; *Sumaṅgalavilāsinī* of Buddhaghosa, III, 865; Visuddhimagga 13.49.

[103] *Dīgha Nikāya, Cakkavatti Sīhanāda Suttanta*, III, pp. 69–70.

Mahābhārata description of this process.[104] But certain assumptions are shared by the Buddhists and Hindus. Punishment is in itself regarded as an evil institution (grouped with theft and lying) rather than a satisfactory answer to the problem of the evil nature of man, which results from various wicked dispositions from former births. Property, the direct result of passion or greed, introduces all the evils of civilization. Other Hindu texts similarly imply that the need for houses (civilization) arises directly from the increased sensitivity to pain, heat, and cold, which afflicts mortals when human nature is no longer perfect (i.e., indifferent);[105] when the wishing-trees perish, men are forced to build cities.[106]

This concept of civilization as one of the links in the downfall of man is inherent in the idea of the Golden Age as a state of nature. The cumulative effects of the evils of civilization are noted in a Buddhist description of a much later stage of society, in which one of the Universal Emperors fails to rule properly:

He did not give to the poor, and so poverty became widespread. Soon a certain man took what had not been given to him, and this was called theft. They caught him and accused him before the king, who gave him wealth. People heard of this and thought they would do the same in order to receive wealth from the king. To put a stop to this, the king began to execute thieves. Thus arose poverty, theft, murder, and falsehood.[107]

Once need (nature) has caused men to sin, the cycle has begun and cannot be arrested, even by the correction of need (civilization). The king's belated generosity only inspires further wrongdoing, and coercive authority (though regarded as tantamount to yet another evil—murder) must take effect. Since need is originally responsible for man's fall, since hunger is man's eternal condition, temporary satisfaction merely masks the flaw.

Interesting evidence of the antiquity of this myth (and hence of the even greater antiquity of the Brāhmaṇic myth on which it is based) appears in the report which Strabo attributes to Onesicritus, who entered India with Alexander in 327 B.C. and heard this tale from a naked "sophist":

In olden times the earth was full of barley and wheat; fountains flowed with water, milk, honey, wine and olive oil. But man's gluttony and luxury led him into boundless arrogance [hubris], *and Zeus, hating this state of things, destroyed everything. When self-control and the other virtues reappeared, blessings were again abundant, but the state of man is again increasing in arrogance and the destruction of all existence is imminent.*[108]

The basic elements of the Indian myth are faithfully reproduced here, in spite of the apparent Hellenization evident in the olive oil and Zeus. Food is at first

[104] Cf. *MBh.* 12.181.10–13; and see below, chap. IV, sec. 3. [105] *Viṣṇu* 1.6.17–20; cf. *Vāyu* 1.8.77–88.
[106] *Kūrma* 1.28.15–40; *Mārk.* 46.1–35. [107] *Dīgha Nikāya, Cakkavatti Sīhanāda Sutta,* III, 65–70.
[108] Strabo, bk. 15, chap. 1, par. 64.

limitless; greed appears naturally; the gods hate man and destroy his welfare; virtues reappear; but man is near his ultimate destruction (i.e., the end of the Kali Age). This degeneration, preordained in spite of all episodes of virtue, is inherent in all the Indian versions of the myth. When the magic trees disappear, creatures are reborn as Brahmins, Kṣatriyas, Vaiśyas, and Śūdras according to their respective deeds in previous births.[109] Not time alone, nor hunger alone, but both of these, coupled with the individual predilection to sin, destroy the Golden Age.

For the true force of the myth is not that it happened "once in the past," in a split second, but that "it is the fall in every individual life, and in each day of each individual life."[110] Pierre Teilhard de Chardin has seen in the myth of the Fall the "inevitable chance of evil . . . which accompanies the existence of all participated being . . . a universal and unbreakable law of reversion or perversion—the price that has to be paid for progress."[111] The Golden Age of release from this "inevitable chance of evil" (the evil of time itself) must be sought, in spite of this antiprogressive view of history, neither in the past nor in the present, but in the future: "Man has never lived in a pre- or unfallen state, in however remote an epoch. . . . We must speak instead in hope of a radically better state which will be."[112] This teleological viewpoint is an important part of the Indian myth, too, for by combining the theory of degenerating ages with the cyclic force of the chain of rebirth, Hindus are led ineluctably to the conclusion that the end of the Golden Age leads, inevitably, through the present Kali Age to the next Golden Age.

9. The End of the Kali Age

The Kali Age ends in a great conflagration and flood.[113] The flood motif occurs in the very oldest layers of Indian mythology, where it accounts for Viṣṇu's avatar as the fish or boar;[114] at first it is not a punishment for man's wickedness but merely an inevitable natural occurrence, corresponding to the great flood that takes place at the end of every era. However, since the end of the era is the end of the Kali Age, in which wickedness thrives so that Viṣṇu must become incarnate as Kalkin to destroy sinful mankind, it is easy to see how these motifs came to be combined in Indian mythology. Thus the flood is called a "washing away", a term also applied to a purifying ritual ablution.[115]

The Santal Parganas have a myth that combines the myth of the Golden Age with the myth of the flood. Though the initial sexual act takes place between a brother and sister, as often occurs in tribal mythology (though rarely in Sanskrit texts),[116] it is prompted not by the devil, nor by a serpent, but by the benevolent

[109] *Vāyu* 1.8.154–159. [110] Lewis, p. 63. [111] Teilhard de Chardin (1971), pp. 40–41.
[112] Hick, p. 270 and p. 180. [113] *Matsya* 2.1–19. [114] Suryakanta Shastri, *passim.*
[115] *Mbh.* 3.185.27. [116] Cf. *RV* 10.10.1–14, and O'Flaherty (1973), pp. 112–114.

bonga (spirit) himself, Maran Buru, who gives them the magic food (rice beer) which causes them to lose their innocence and repressions. When the boy and girl became ashamed and said, "What a bad thing we did," Maran Buru laughed and said, "No harm is done," and went away. But the descendants of this pair "became more and more"—a sign of impending disaster—and at last the unexplained corruption took place:

Men grew wicked and became like buffaloes. When he saw this, Thakur [the creator] became very angry and decided to destroy mankind if they did not return to him. He searched for them and said, "Return to my ways." But they did not heed him. Then Thakur called Pilcu Haram and Pilcu Budhi and said, "Your children are not heeding my words so I shall kill them. Go into a cave on the mountain and you will be saved." The pair heard Thakur's words and went to the mountain cave. As soon as they had entered, Thakur rained down fire for seven days and seven nights without stopping. He killed every human being and animal; and only the two in the cave at Harata were saved.[117]

The sexual nature of the "wickedness" is in harmony with Hindu, Christian, and tribal concepts (behaving "like buffaloes" denoting promiscuity: Santals say, "He is like a buffalo in rut"[118]), as is the punishment consisting of both fire and water—a rain of fire—the survival of the pair, and the motif of seven days' fury. One suspects actual Christian influence here, as one of the earliest records of the myth was made by an old Santal dictating to a missionary, though the Santals as a whole are not Christian.[119]

Other tribal myths reflect these same nontribal traditions, Hindu and Christian. According to the Kamar, "Bhagavan made the world virtuous, yet after a time it sank into sin," and he sent a flood to destroy it.[120] The Kols also attribute the flood to man's wickedness, which "so provoked the deity that he determined to punish them"; they believe that Sirma Thakoor destroyed the earth with water or fire "because people became incestuous and unmindful of God."[121] The Bhils believe that the earth simply sinks naturally into the flood waters,[122] as it does in Hindu mythology.

A motif closely related to that of the flood sent to destroy sinners does appear in Sanskrit texts, however, and that is the myth of the earth sinking into the cosmic waters because of an excessive weight placed upon her, a burden which God removes by destroying those who are causing the earth to sink.[123] When the burden is caused by the weight of mankind in general, death is introduced to remove the excess; this then corresponds to the myths in which the flood occurs naturally at the end of the era, devoid of any moral stigma. Since overpopulation is linked to sexual procreation, however, it may be said that even here man's "wickedness" causes God to destroy him. A still closer parallel occurs in the myths in which the excess burden of evil demons causes the earth to sink until God destroys the demons. Here, however, the myth differs from the tribal

[117] Archer, pp. 262–264. [118] Personal communication from William Archer. [119] *Ibid.* [120] Elwin (1953), p. 5. [121] Elwin (1949), p. 20, and p. 24. [122] *Ibid.*, p. 20. [123] See below, chap. IX, sec. 3.

corpus in that it absolves mankind of any part of the sin that causes God to destroy the race; nor in fact is mankind destroyed. Quite the contrary: by killing the demons, God raises the earth and *prevents* the flood. In short, Sanskrit tradition offers no true parallel to the Western idea that man's wickedness forces God to punish him with a cosmic flood.

But a flood (and a fire) does mark the end of the Kali Age, when wickedness prevails. All moral bounds are blurred; people become heretics and abandon the rules of separate classes;[124] Śūdras instead of Brahmins preach the Vedas, and the earth is crowded with heretics.[125] The Kali Age is almost always marked by overpopulation, the inevitable accompaniment of evil times as well as the recurrent Indian problem of the present (Kali) Age. The final "Fall" is thus merely an exaggeration of the problem of the original loss of the Golden Age.

Two interesting arguments develop from the premise of the natural wickedness of man in the Kali Age. One is the doctrine of the *kalivarjya*, the belief that certain actions, such as widow remarriage, though previously acceptable, are only to be considered immoral in the present Kali Age, when men are not strong enough to indulge in them without ill effect. This doctrine is implicit in an Epic myth:

In the past, women were free to indulge their desires, and this was dharma. This ancient dharma is still practised by birds and animals. But then one day Śvetaketu saw his mother being abducted by a Brahmin in the presence of his father. The boy was angry, but his father explained that it was considered proper. Then Śvetaketu established the moral boundaries.[126]

Animals still follow the earlier, freer morality; it is only the shortcomings of mankind (implicit both in the lust of the Brahmin and in the incestuous jealousy of Śvetaketu) which makes a strict moral code necessary. By this rather circular reasoning, a more strict level of morality must be sought in the Kali Age, since man himself is less moral.

The doctrine of the *kalivarjya* is not an example of moral relativism, though this can be found elsewhere in Indian thought. "The idea that Good and Evil are relative terms, that the moral value of an act is susceptible to be appreciated differentialy from epoch to epoch, is an idea of the modern world which could not have come into our authors' heads."[127] The same has been remarked about the Buddhist concept of the vanishing of the good law: the law itself does not change, for it is a law of nature; only our ability to follow it declines.[128] Dharma is unchanging truth; man's capacity to obey the moral law changes in different ages.

[124] *Viṣṇu* 6.1.37; *Brahma* 230.13; *Vāyu* 1.58.59; *Brahmāṇḍa* 2.31.59–66; *Matsya* 144.40; *Kūrma* 1.29.16–25. [125] *Bṛhannāradīya* 38.54; *Viṣṇu* 1.6.45. [126] *MBh.* 1.113.3 ff.

[127] Lingat (1962), p. 12; (1973), p. 188. [128] Lamotte, I, 212.

David Pocock regarded the theory of the *kalivarjya* as an indication that the Kali Age "is not homogeneous with the other *yugas*, it is opposed to them, and the radical difference is that it is the age of time which is actually lived."[129] The Kali Age is the period in which man's true nature is at last revealed; moral laws are valid *now* only if they take into account this low moral condition, this chasm between the idea and the reality. Another inversion of values appears in the statement that the Kali Age is best in the sense that by a small effort now one will win the merit that would require great asceticism in the Golden Age;[130] the commentator interprets this as an allusion to the worship of Kṛṣṇa. Here the "easiest" path is equated with the best, but it is also the Tantric path suited only for the "worst" of men; whatever its moral value, good or bad, it is the only path that applies to the present state of man. That this argument is double-edged is apparent from the common statement that among the evils of the Kali Age is the fact that even Śūdras are allowed to practise asceticism;[131] this orthodox view regards the fact that even the lowest of men are allowed to participate in religion as evidence of the disruption of the proper social order—which is precisely the *virtue* of the Kali Age from the Tantric point of view (a view which is itself an inversion of the doctrine of the *kalivarjya*).

Another argument exalts the Kali Age because it is the last stage before the return to the Golden Age. At the end of the Kali Age, Viṣṇu will come as Kalkin to uproot the barbarians and heretics and usher in the Golden Age again.[132] The Kalkin avatar is first described in the *Mahābhārata*:[133] In the Kali Age, the earth will be overrun with heretics and barbarians; then, at the end of the Age, in order to cause mankind to increase again, Kalkin, a part of Viṣṇu,[134] will be born, and he will destroy all the barbarians and establish dharma and the Golden Age.

The Purāṇas add that Kalkin will ride on a swift horse given by the gods,[135] that he will live for twenty-five years and give up his life at the confluence of the Ganges and the Yamunā, at Prayāga,[136] or that he will subdue the barbarians and establish himself between the Ganges and the Yamunā.[137] His resemblance to the "rider on the white horse," whose cloak is soaked in blood and who is sent to put the pagans to the sword,[138] is striking; and there is almost certainly a historical connection between the two images.[139] Moreover, the concept of a Golden Age following the deluge appears together with the image of the horseman in the Book of Revelation, where, after the rider on a white horse has appeared, an angel binds the Devil, Satan, for a thousand years in a bottomless pit; later Satan is

[129] Pocock (1964), p. 312. [130] *Viṣṇu* 6.1.60; cf. 6.2.34–36. [131] *Rām.* 7.74.27.

[132] *Bhāgavata* 2.7.36–39. See below, chap. VII, sec. 6. [133] *MBh.* 3.188.14–93, 3.189.1–13.

[134] Cf. Gonda (1954), p. 149. [135] *Bhāgavata* 12.2.19.

[136] *Vāyu* 2.36.103–155; *Brahmāṇḍa* 2.3.73.104, 115–117, 125; 2.3.74.206.

[137] *Hari.*, 4 inserted after 31.148. [138] Revelation 19:11–15.

[139] See below, chap. VII, sec. 6.

cast into hell forever and the world is created again, this time without death or sorrow.[140]

The *Kalki Purāṇa*, a late work, describes the interaction of Kali and Kalki (*sic*):

At the end of the Age, Brahmā created from his back an evil one known as Adharma. From him Kali was descended, foul-smelling and lustful, with gaping mouth and lolling tongue. He begat Fear and a daughter named Death; thus were born the many descendants of Kali, revilers of dharma. Men then became lustful, hypocritical, and evil, intent upon penis and stomach, adulterers, drunkards, evil-doers. Ascetics took to houses, and householders were devoid of discrimination. The earth yielded few crops. Men abandoned the study of the Vedas and sacrifices, and they ceased to offer oblations. The gods were all without sustenance, and they sought refuge with Brahmā.

Then Viṣṇu was born as Kalki. He amassed a great army to chastise the Buddha; he fought the Buddhists, who were led by the Jina, and he killed the Jina and defeated the Buddhists and the barbarians who assisted them. The wives of the Buddhists and barbarians had also taken up arms, but Kalki taught them bhakti-yoga, karma-yoga and jñāna-yoga [the three paths of the Bhagavad Gītā]. *Kalki then continued his march and met Dharma, who had been driven out by Kali. Kalki defeated Kali and his allies, but Kali escaped to another age.*[141]

Several elements from the oldest corpus of myths of evil are retained here: the Kali Age brings a dearth of food (the initial condition for degeneration) and the gods are weakened by the decline in religious practices among mortals. The next chronological level is manifest in the typical Purāṇic description of the Kali Age: the caste lines and stages of life are destroyed, Buddhists and Jains (undifferentiated) are rampant, and barbarians hold sway. Kali is personified as a demon: the lolling tongue and gaping mouth are typical demonic features, as is his foul smell. In place of the usual Purāṇic motif of the god corrupting the women of the demon's city in order to weaken them and the demon,[142] the god here enlightens the women in order to win them to his side; this is in keeping with the Vedic assumption, in this text, that the gods are weakened by man's failure to offer sacrifice. Unlike most battles between gods and demons, however, this apparent victory is immediately undercut, for Kali escapes to reappear in "another age"–in our age, or the next Kali Age.

In this escape of Kali, as in the implication that the Kali Age is best because it is the gateway to the renewed Golden Age, the Indian view of the cyclic nature of evil is apparent. In some descriptions of the Kali Age, when civilization is completely destroyed men are said to dwell in the woods living on roots and fruits and wearing rough bark garments.[143] This return to nature, though hardly equivalent to Rousseau's idea of the noble savage, is strongly reminiscent of the

[140] Revelation 19–21. [141] *Kalki* 1.1.14–39; 2.6–7; 3.6–7.

[142] See below, chap. VII, secs. 1–4. [143] *Vāyu* 2.37.389–407.

Indian ideal of the holy man in the wilderness; by being reduced to his lowest state, man begins to regain his virtues. The state of nature is thus both the condition of innocent perfection (that of the sages) and the condition in which the animal appetites of man assert themselves (the state of the fallen men of the Kali Age). Some Western observers have found this resemblance odd: "It is rather strange that the condition of men, in what appeared to the writer of this Purana as the most miserable he could imagine, where their dress was bark and their food consisted of roots and fruits, was in the earliest ages regarded as the most desirable. It was thus the old Rishis lived, who are held in the greatest esteem."[144] But in the Indian view, there is nothing strange in this; the Kali Age is the turning point, where evil is transformed back into the good from which it evolved in the Golden Age. Often, individuals prone to evil may be cursed, homeopathically, to become so evil that they must eventually reform; one extreme leads to the other.[145] Similarly, mankind in general may be delivered from the sins of the Kali Age only by being corrupted so completely that true enlightenment is the only possible consequence.

This is evident from several myths of the Kali Age. We have seen how the beginnings of disintegration in the Tretā Age produced meditation and repentance; this process is repeated in the third age, the Dvāpara: when drought, death, and disease harass people, sorrow will arise in them; from sorrow, depression and complete indifference to worldly objects; and from this, deep thought about liberation from suffering, and a realization of defects; and from this realization, knowledge.[146] This chain of development bears a striking resemblance to the Buddhist four noble truths (suffering arising from craving and, through the correct mental discipline, being relieved through the absence of craving). The text describes the process as it recurs in the Kali Age in even more Buddhist terms:

In the Kali Age, men will be afflicted by old age, disease, and hunger, and from sorrow there will arise depression, indifference, deep thought, enlightenment, and virtuous behavior. Then the Age will change, deluding their minds like a dream, by the force of fate, and when the Golden Age begins, those left over from the Kali Age will be the progenitors of the Golden Age. All four classes will survive as a seed, together with those born in the Golden Age, and the seven sages will teach them all dharma. Thus there is eternal continuity from Age to Age.[147]

The belief that the end of the Kali Age is a period of transfiguration as well as destruction occurs in several texts.

The people of the Kali Age will take refuge in the chasms between mountains, and they will eat honey, vegetables, roots, fruits, leaves, and flowers. They will have too many children, and they will be forced to endure cold, wind, sun, and rain. No one's age-span will reach twenty-three years. . . . Then Kalkin will destroy men of evil acts and thoughts,

[144] Wilkins, p. 247. [145] See below, chap. X, sec. 7. [146] *Liṅga* 1.39.66–70. [147] *Ibid.* 1.40.72–83.

and he will reestablish everything in its own dharma. Immediately at the conclusion of the exhausted Kali Age, the minds of the people will become pure as flawless crystal, and they will be as if awakened at the conclusion of a night. These men, the residue of mankind, will be transformed, and they will be the seeds of creatures and will give birth to offspring, conceived at that very time, who will follow the ways of the Golden Age.[148]

Viṣṇu destroys the evil of the Kali Age to ensure a residue and to prevent a break, a discontinuity between the evil men of the Kali Age (totally destroyed) and the good men of the Golden Age (created ex nihilo). Kalkin thus merely acts in anticipation of the inevitable Golden Age, catalyzing the natural transformation from evil to good, which takes place at the end of the Kali Age, just as a natural transformation from good to evil takes place at the end of the Golden Age. For, as the commentator on the myth remarks, the offspring of the Kali Age will follow the ways of the Golden Age "because of the very nature of time itself."[149] In Hindu cosmogony, as in nature, there are no saltations.

The cyclic nature of time is emphasized in several Buddhist myths:

There will come a time when moral conduct will disappear, immoral conduct will flourish, and even the word "moral" will no longer exist among humans. Then for Seven Days of the Sword, men will look on each other as wild beasts and kill each other. But a few will think: "We do not want anyone to kill us, and we do not want to kill anyone. Let us hide and live on the fruits of the forest." Thus they will survive. And after the Seven Days of the Sword they will come out and embrace one another and say, "My friend, how good it is to see you still alive. We have lost so many of our kinsfolk because we took to evil ways; now we must do good and stop taking life." Then they will increase in age and beauty, and they will practise virtues. India will be as crowded then as Purgatory, with people like reeds in a jungle.[150]

A few men seem to escape the corrupting influence of time by withdrawing into the ambiguous state of nature, and they do succeed in initiating a new Golden Age without the intervention of a wrathful god, whether against the flow or simply after the end of the age of evil. But India then becomes as crowded as hell, an ominous simile albeit ostensibly meant as an indication of prosperity; for the next cycle has already begun, with overcrowding on earth.

Another Buddhist text gives an explicit reason for this cycle:[151]

After a hundred thousand years, the cycle is to be renewed, and so the gods who inhabit the heaven of sensual pleasure wander about, weeping and saying, "After a hundred thousand years, the cycle is to be renewed, and this world will be destroyed. . . . Therefore

[148] *Viṣṇu* 4.24.25–29. [149] Commentary on *Viṣṇu* 4.24.29.

[150] *Dīgha Nikāya, Cakkavatti Sīhanāda Suttanta* III, 71–75. [151] *Visuddhimagga, Abhiññānaddeso, Pubbenivāsānussatiñāṇakathā*, 13.34.

cultivate love, sympathy, pity, and equanimity; serve your mothers and fathers, and honor your elders."

The philosophy underlying this passage is clearly akin to that cited in other Buddhist and Hindu discussions about death: only when destruction is imminent will mankind reform.[152] Yet both Hindu and Buddhist texts more commonly state that this reformation takes place only *after* the final cataclysm. Kalkin destroys the wicked cities of the Hindu plain, and in the Buddhist view the nature of the final destruction corresponds directly to the nature of the prevalent sin that causes it. When passion preponderates, the world perishes by fire; when hatred preponderates, it perishes by water (some say the opposite, passion causing fire and hatred causing the flood); when delusion preponderates, it perishes by wind.[153] The Hindu texts, leaving nothing to chance, usually state that it is destroyed by fire, water, *and* wind.

Thus the cycles move up as well as down; after the Kali Age comes the Golden Age again, and against the framework of the degenerating cycles of cosmic time the Indians set the progressive cycles of individual time–rebirth. Although an evil action can cause one to be reborn in a lower form, the Indian ideal was for gradual improvement from birth to birth until final release from the cycle was achieved; thus the individual could not only rise in the cycle but escape from it altogether; the personal moral code could supersede the cosmic. As David Pocock has said of the *kalivarjya* theory, "Parallel to this and at another level we may consider the great theory of successive births which is a counterpart of the caste hierarchy";[154] into the hierarchical warp is woven the thread of the individual's life.

Optimistic reformers might thus think it possible to hasten or even reverse the inevitable turning point of the cycle of evil, and indeed Manu states that the king, by his good or bad behavior, produces the character of the Kali or Golden Age, not the reverse.[155] Similarly, the *Arthaśāstra* suggests that the king, by maintaining the code of the Vedas, may cause the world to progress and not to perish.[156] The *Mahābhārata,* too, says that the king's action makes the time–the best time being the Golden Age, the time of dharma.[157] The individual sage may also escape from the Kali Age by trying to conform to the precepts of the eternal law. In doing this he is not turning backwards through time, or reverting to the past, but simply adapting himself to the true order of things, or reinstating that order.[158]

If it is possible for a king or a sage to resist the flow of the Kali Age, why cannot God resist it altogether? The simple answer is that God *is* the Kali Age.

[152] See below, chap. VIII, sec. 4. [153] *Visuddhimagga, Abbiññānaddeso, Pubbenivāsānussatiñāṇakathā,* 13.64. Cf. Robert Frost, "Fire and Ice." [154] Pocock (1964), p. 312. [155] *Manu* 9.301–302. [156] *Artha.* 1.3.14–17. [157] *MBh.* 12.70.6–8. [158] Lingat (1962), p. 14; (1973), p. 186.

Śiva, the great destroyer, is often identified with the Kali Age[159] and is said to be the god of the Kali Age.[160] God's reason for bringing about this evil time and the final destruction of mankind may be explained in benevolent terms (the world is so wicked that release is impossible for anyone, and so it may therefore "be good of God to stop all that wickedness"[161]) or in terms of necessity ("The Lord has no choice. The cosmic process is automatic . . . destruction must occur whatever God's feelings in the matter"[162]). But this brings us back to the limitation of omnipotence: "If the Lord is responsible for the end, and the end contains evil, then it would seem *prima facie* that the Lord is responsible for evil."[163] Despite this snag, the "necessity" view is held by many orthodox Hindus,[164] while others claim that God cannot help destroying mankind.[165]. But many devotional texts maintain that God is in fact above karma, that, as a deus ex machina, he may interrupt the process of karma, and does so from time to time:

> The progression of the cycle from freshness to decay, from dawn to sad evening is inexorable. The gods themselves are no less subject to it. Nevertheless we find the element of intervention even here. We have the belief growing in strength from the Middle Ages onwards that Vishnu plays with the cycles of time. His avatars come increasingly to be considered as interventions on the behalf of society or some virtuous individual. He is believed to break through the progressive decay, arrest its course, and even reverse it. This is a remarkable contradiction and one of which our texts seem to be aware, for we find some attempt at reconciliation. The final avatar of Vishnu, Kalki, is to intervene in that he punishes the wrongs of that time but, because his intervention coincides with the last moments of the Kaliyuga, the righteousness which he restores is in fact the inauguration of a new Kṛta [Golden] age.[166]

Thus the idea that evil automatically develops into good is given a devotional overlay with the statement that Viṣṇu intervenes in order to make it do precisely that. For the universal process and the individual are parallel: "Just as *bhakti* is opposed to, cuts through, the inevitable succession of rebirths, so Vishnu cuts through the inevitable succession of the yugas."[167] God does not, therefore, actually oppose fate; he superimposes his benevolent intentions on a fate already made to appear ultimately benevolent. In this way, karma is once more overruled by myth; God is *felt* to be responsible both for original evil and for final good, to use karma for his own ends. Just as the pure creatures of the Golden Age are not yet ensnared in the coils of time at all, so too the creatures of the Kali Age may be extricated from these coils, from the entire mundane level on which time functions. It is God's privilege to "play" with time in this way, for, as Viṣṇu points out in the *Bhagavad Gītā,* he *is* time.[168]

The new bhakti attitude to the inevitability of fate may be seen not only in

159 *MBh.* 13.17.150. 160 *Kūrma* 1.28.18. 161 Herman, p. 496.

162 *Ibid.* See below, chap. III, sec. 2. 163 Herman, p. 498. 164 See below, chap. VI, sec. 1.

165 See below, chap. IX, sec. 4. 166 Pocock (1964), p. 313.

167 *Ibid.*, p. 314. And see below, chap. IV, sec. 5, for bhakti. 168 *Gītā* 11.32.

the increased powers of the gods—the belief that Viṣṇu may counteract the force of time—but in the higher moral nature of the gods—the belief that the gods want us to be good, rather than evil.[169] Nevertheless, this is not a universal, broadly accepted change; traditional Hinduism reasserts itself and warns against the dangers inherent in any challenge to cosmic decay:

The demon Bali, ruling in the Kali Age, protected the universe with great virtue. When Kali saw this he sought refuge with Brahmā, for his own nature was being obstructed. Brahmā said, "Bali has destroyed the nature of the whole universe, not just your nature." Then Kali went to a forest, and the Golden Age took place: asceticism, noninjury, truth, and sacrifice pervaded the world. Indra complained that his kingdom had been taken, but Brahmā explained that Indra was merely reaping the fruits of his evil deed in having destroyed the embryo in the womb of Diti. To atone for this sin, Indra performed asceticism for a year and bathed in a holy river. Then Viṣṇu conquered Bali and made him rule in hell.[170]

In seeking the original, past cause of present sins, this text arives at a compromise. Indra's encounter with Diti is somewhat justified (for he fears that Diti's unborn child will usurp his throne,[171] even as Bali has just done) and easily expiated; but underlying the doctrine of individual karma—Indra's karma—is the deeper necessity of the karma of the universe, for evil to come when it is ripe. By his virtue, Bali does not merely threaten the gods in heaven (a problem that is solved by making the virtuous demon rule in hell, where the demons belong) but he threatens the nature of the Kali Age, the nature of the whole universe, which must be evil at this moment. In a late text, a virtuous king named Kṣemaka performs a sacrifice of barbarians that threatens to destroy Kali until Viṣṇu himself offers to preserve the "multiform age" by creating the ancestor of a new race of barbarians (the inverse of the usual act of Kalkin); this ancestor is none other than Adam (Ādama), whose wife, Eve (Havyavatī), Kali tricks into eating "the fruit of evil", Kali himself taking the form of a serpent.[172]

These orthodox assumptions are overruled in a South Indian text that regards the Kali Age as anti-Vedic and therefore to be avoided:

The gods complained to Śiva about the evils of the Kali Age, when Brahmins perform improper rites and dharma is hidden in the forest. Śiva sent them to a shrine where Kali, disease, and Yama [the god of death] had no power.[173]

Here, as in so many Tamil texts, the Vedic and devotional beliefs that men should be good combine to overrule the orthodox assumption that the evils of the Kali Age fill a necessary role. Orthodoxy is similarly challenged in another Tamil myth about Kali incarnate:

169 See below, chap. IV, sec. 5. 170 *Vāmana* 49.1–14, 50.1–26. 171 *Rām.* 1.46–47.

172 *Bhaviṣya* 3.1.4.1–46. 173 *Katirkāmapurāṇavacanam* 15 (pp. 45–46; *Takṣinakailāsam* 11).

A sage, wishing to escape the adharma of the Kali Age, went to a Śaiva shrine. Kali pursued him, saying, "Stop! You are in my power," but Śiva prevented Kali from touching the sage. Kali begged to be allowed to dwell near the shrine, to expiate his sins.[174]

Here Kali is not destroyed, nor indeed does he cease to function in general; like Yama in another Tamil text,[175] he is allowed to continue his necessary evil work but is constantly forgiven–and he cannot touch the devotee. The process continues but the individual is freed; this belief (which may be traced back to the Upaniṣadic concept of the enlightened man's release from the cycle of rebirth) is the compromise achieved by late devotional mythology.

The Kali Age must take place, and the Golden Age after it, and God may *appear* to intervene, to motivate the inevitable changes wrought by time. Nature corrupts mankind and the gods of Hinduism are themselves in the power of these natural forces; they are therefore the instruments of time or karma in bringing about the moral corruption of mankind. It is inevitable that the universe should be destroyed at the end of the Kali Age, and before God destroys us he must first weaken us with sin–thereby justifying his act of destruction and transforming it into an act of benevolence, for it makes possible the rebirth of the Golden Age.

[174] *Tiruvāñciyakṣettirapurāṇam* 39; *Kāñcippurāṇam* 13; *Tiruvārūrppurāṇam* 109.1-75.

[175] See below, chap. VIII, secs. 5-6.

Then said his wife unto him, Dost thou still retain thine integrity? curse God, and die. But he said unto her, Thou speakest as one of the foolish women speaketh. What? shall we receive good at the hand of God, and shall we not receive evil?
Job 2:9–10

III

THE NECESSITY OF EVIL

From the myths of the Fall it would appear that man is not responsible for evil; nor is karma made to bear the brunt of the blame, since the gods are in some views capable of overcoming karma. These conclusions lead to several myth cycles in which God creates evil as a positive element of the universe, acting either as a direct agent of fate or himself determining that there should be evil; either willingly or unwillingly, God creates the necessary good and evil in the universe. In the Indian view, there is no significant distinction between these two variants. Since dharma is both what *is* and what *ought* to be, it does not matter whether God approves of the dictates of fate or not; the universe *is* good and evil, and so God creates it thus. Nevertheless, we may distinguish between texts in which God is *forced* to create evil because the universe (predetermined before he arrives on the scene) must have it, and those in which he himself *decides* to create an ambivalent universe.

1. God Willingly Creates Evil

One eighteenth-century Indologist compared the implications of the Western view that God creates evil against his will with the "Indian" view that he creates it willingly; he remarked that the problem of the origin of moral evil had led some (Western) authors to

very strange conclusions. . . . "That God was necessitated to admit moral evil in created beings, from the nature of the materials he had to work with; that God would have made all things perfect, but . . . to produce good exclusive of evil, is one of those impossibilities, which even infinite power cannot accomplish. . . ." How much more rational and sublime the text of Brahmah, which supposes the Deity's voluntary creation, or permission of evil, for the exaltation of a race of beings, whose goodness as free agents could not have existed without being endued with the contrasted, or opposite powers of doing evil.[1]

Both of the ideas contrasted here (that God creates evil of necessity, and that he creates it willingly) may, together, be in turn contrasted with the belief that God is not responsible for the origin of evil at all, a concept that occurs far less often in Hinduism. The first of the original pair is more prevalent than the second, but Hindus frequently and facilely combine it with the second: because God recognizes that evil is necessary, he willingly creates it. The contrast here stated in moral terms—that goodness within an individual becomes valuable only when it is pitted against evil—is recognized by the Hindus in cosmological terms: that the good in the universe is valuable only because it exists together with evil.

In justifying the wickedness of kings, Arjuna argues, "I do not see any creature in this world that lives without injuring others; animals live upon animals, the stronger on the weaker. . . . No act is entirely devoid of evil."[2] This doctrine is further developed and more specifically related to the gods in a Tantric hymn describing Śiva's cosmic dance: "By the stamping of your feet you imperilled the safety of the earth and scattered the stars of the heavens. But you dance in order to save the world. Power is perverse."[3] The commentator explains that Śiva behaves in the manner of a king protecting his subjects, an allusion to the view that, if a village is troubled by robbers or demons, the king's army will protect it, but the village will then have to tolerate the evils resulting from the presence of the army itself (rape, pilfering, etc.). Sin is necessary for the balance of earthly society; it is necessary for there to be Untouchables in order for there to be Brahmins; purity depends on impurity. Goddesses of disease and filth are worshipped throughout India; the Hindus recognize the necessity of coming to terms with evil. Goodness cannot, by definition, exist without evil, any more than (to adopt the Zen analogy) there can exist the sound of one hand clapping.

Not only is evil inevitable, it is desirable. When a sage asks why Bṛhaspati, the guru of the gods, told a lie, the reply is simple: "All creatures, even gods, are subject to passions. Otherwise the universe, composed as it is of good and evil, could not continue to develop."[4] First it is a fact that the gods are subject to evil; then it is said that this is a good thing, a dynamic factor. This attitude underlies several important creation myths. The creator purposely incorporates evil into his world: "In order to distinguish actions, the creator separated dharma and adharma and made the pairs of opposites such as happiness and unhappiness. And whatever he assigned to each at the first creation, truth or falsehood, that quality clung spontaneously to it."[5] The creator is explicitly said to be pleased with the

[1] Holwell, p. 70. [2] *MBh.* 12.15.20 and .50. [3] *Mahimnastotra* 16.

[4] *Devībhāgavata* 4.13.1–35. [5] *Manu* 1.26, 1.29.

mixed nature of the creation and with the plenitude thus ensured: "Whatever karma they had achieved in a former creation, they received this karma as they were created again and again, harmful or benign, gentle or cruel, full of dharma or adharma, truthful or false. And when they are created again, they will have these qualities; and this pleased him. The lord Creator himself diversified the variety and differentiation of all the objects of the senses, properties, and forms."[6] Yet in spite of this statement of the creator's intentions, the author finds it necessary to draw upon the doctrine of karma as well, a doctrine which contradicts the hypothesis of the creator's will. The creator emits his creatures, good and evil, from his own body; yet they bring with them even before that act some overriding force, for part of them and part of him is evil: "Brahmā's power is the will to create and he is impelled by the powers of the things to be created," concludes the text.

The evil which is an essential part of God even results in the evil which denies that god:

That portion of Viṣṇu which is one with Death caused created beings to fall, creating a small seed of adharma from which darkness and desire were born, and passion was brought about. Those in whose minds the seed of evil had been placed in the first creation, and in whom it increased, denied Vedic sacrifices and reviled the gods and the followers of the Vedas. They were of evil souls and evil behavior.[7]

Just as a seed of goodness must survive the Kali Age to be born in the Golden Age, so in the Golden Age the first seed of evil must be present.

Other texts also attribute to God the explicit wish to make the universe ambivalent by means of heresy as well as evil fortune (Alakṣmī):

Viṣṇu made the universe twofold for the sake of delusion. He made the Brahmins, Vedas, and the goddess Śrī [prosperity], and this was the best portion. Then he made Alakṣmī and the lowest men, outside the Vedas, and he made adharma. Alakṣmī, the Eldest [Jyeṣṭhā], must dwell far from where men follow the path of the Vedas and worship Viṣṇu and Śiva. But she may enter wherever husband and wife quarrel, wherever there are heretics, atheists, and hypocrites, Buddhists or Jains.[8]

This myth accounts for the presence of wicked people on earth by making them fodder for the goddess Jyeṣṭhā in the usual manner,[9] but it also accounts for the heresies of Buddhism and Jainism; or, to be more precise, the myth implies that heretics exist as part of the "other" portion of the universe created by Viṣṇu, for he created the Vedas and therefore had to create people beyond the pale of the Vedas. In a similar manner, Hinduism describes the origin of a "left-hand"

[6] *Viṣṇu* 1.5.59–65; *Mārk.* 45.39–45; O'Flaherty (1975), p. 46.

[7] *Viṣṇu* 1.6.14–15, 29–31. [8] *Liṅga* 2.6.1–57.

[9] See below, chap. IV, sec. 4.

heresy: "Prajāpati, in order to conceal (the true) teaching, created [a sect] which deluded even the sages, let alone ordinary men."[10] No motivation is given for Prajāpati's act, but the corpus of myths of heresy can supply any one of a number of possibilities, perhaps the most basic of which is the simple belief that evil and heresy are as necessary as good and orthodoxy. Just as it is necessary for certain men to perform unclean tasks,[11] so too is it necessary for the gods to provide evil to fill a place in the universe. The belief that the gods wish men to be heretics is basic to the mythology; it is said that pleasure in the company of heretics and in their arguments arises in those fools who have fallen into the ocean of Viṣṇu's power of delusion.[12] Only fools will fall in, but the ocean of delusion is the work of God.

This view of evil, though not completely dominant in Hindu texts, has been accepted by many Western scholars as "the Indian view of evil" and has led to many mistaken generalizations. Thus Alan Watts remarks, "For Hindu thought there is no Problem of Evil. The conventional, relative world is necessarily a world of opposites. Light is inconceivable apart from darkness, order is meaningless without disorder, and likewise, up without down, sound without silence, pleasure without pain."[13] This is indeed an accurate representation of one set of Hindu texts, but it can hardly be said to solve the problem of evil for all Indians. It solves the classical theodicy by limiting the potency of God (as karma does) or by implying that God freely chooses evil (a denial of the ethical thesis).

In Hinduism, evil must be rightly ordered and kept in its place, away from the gods, distributed among men or demons or both. Only in this way would there be a true balance, a true plentitude; were evil to weaken the gods or to disappear altogether—were all men to become virtuous, or all demons godly—there would be no universe at all, for there would be no "contrasting pairs." In this view, God is powerful and good; he chooses to place evil and suffering in the universe, not because he is forced to do so by karma, nor because he is so evil that he enjoys seeing others suffer, but because if he wishes to create a universe at all, it is by definition necessary for that universe to contain evil as well as good.

This view is sometimes contradicted in Indian texts which state that God is either powerless or malevolent.[14] The hypothesis of necessity is perhaps the most satisfactory "solution" from both a philosophical and an emotional standpoint; yet it could not have been totally satisfactory, for Indian thinkers continued to generate other approaches to the problem of evil. Preeminent among these is the belief that God, against his will, is forced to create evil, under the influence of time or karma, or through some fault of his own, that he does not consider evil "a good thing" but cannot avoid it.

[10] *Vaikhānasasmārtasūtra* 8.11. [11] See below, chap. V, sec. 1.

[12] *Viṣṇudharma Purāṇa*, chap. 3, fol. 11b, cited in Hazra (1958), p. 146.

[13] Watts (1957), p. 35; see above, chap. I, sec. 2. [14] See below, chap. VI, sec. 4, and chap. IV, sec. 8.

2. God Creates Evil Against His Will

Many Indians rejected both the hypothesis of omnipotence and that of benevolence. The gods do not wish for evil in the first place, but given its existence, they would rather have it survive among mankind than among themselves; and men would rather have it here than among the gods.[15] The reason for the persistence of this view is well expressed in a conversation between E. M. Forster and the Maharajah of Dewas Senior:

When I asked him why we had any of us ever been severed from God, he explained it by God becoming unconscious that we were parts of him, owing to his energy at some time being concentrated elsewhere. . . . If you believe that the universe was God's *conscious* creation you are faced with the fact that he has consciously created suffering and sin, and this the Indian refuses to believe. "We were either put here intentionally or unintentionally," said the Rajah, "and it raises fewer difficulties if we suppose it was unintentionally."[16]

It is hardly correct to state that "the Indian refuses to believe" that God consciously created evil—indeed, it is the prevalent Indian view—but the Rajah's philosophy is also supported by hallowed texts:

Prajāpati created the golden egg of the universe. He created the gods, and there was daylight. Then, by his downward breathing, he created the demons, and they were darkness for him. He knew that he had created evil for himself; he struck the demons with evil and they were overcome. Therefore, the legend which tells of the battle between gods and demons is not true, for they were overcome because Prajāpati struck them with evil.[17]

Here we encounter a logical inversion that haunts these myths: because the demons were evil, Prajāpati made them evil, a corollary to the theory of the chain of evil. The gods are accidentally responsible for the creation of evil demons; then, to overcome these demons, they corrupt them further. This ancient text already explicitly rejects another "orthodox" view—the view of total moral contrast between gods and demons as depicted in the myth of their battle.

An early Upaniṣad attributes a basic evil, hunger and thirst, to an apparently inadvertent act of the primeval Self:

In the beginning, the Self created a Man made of fire, wind, the sun, the quarters of heaven, plants, the moon, death, and water. As soon as these divine powers had been created, they fell headlong into the great sea. The Self placed hunger and thirst in the Man. The divine powers said to the Self, "Give us a place to live and food to eat." He led the Man up to them and they entered into their respective abodes—fire as speech in the mouth, wind as breath in the nostrils, the sun as sight in the eyes, the quarters of heaven as hearing in the ears, plants as hairs in the skin, the moon as emotion in the heart, death as

[15] See below, chap. VI, sec. 6. [16] Forster, p. 25.

[17] *Śata.* 11.1.6.1–11; cf. below, chap. VIII, sec. 2.

the out-breath in the navel, waters as semen in the penis. Then hunger and thirst said to the Self, "Give us, also, a place to live," and he gave them a share in the divine powers.[18]

The creatures of the original creator are flawed, so that they suffer an immediate and literal fall, from which he rescues them only by placing them (flawed as they are) in Man; he also places hunger and thirst, the seed of further flaws, in Man. In an attempt to justify this act of the creator, the commentator points out that the sea is the sea of ignorance, desire, disease, death, and so forth, and that it is in order to stir them from it that he acts as he does. Moreover, he continues, since the original Man had hunger, thirst, and other faults, so the divine powers made from him had them—pushing the original cause farther back without explaining it. In fact, the pattern of this myth was so evidently malevolent that the central role was assigned not to the creator but to the demons in other texts of this same period.[19] Demons like Vṛtra enter man and become hunger within him; demons enter man and create his flawed senses; demons are hungry and are given evil men as their abode and food. Even in the text cited above, our headlong fall into the ocean of misery, as well as the hunger that tortures us (and corrupts us) within it, must be blamed on God, who does not seem to design these events but seems rather to fall prey to them against his will, to be led from one mistake to another in escalating delusion.

The first Vedāntic treatise on a monist Upaniṣad states that God was deluded by his own power of delusion,[20] and an allegorical play describes at great length how Delusion overcame God.[21] In most of the creation myths, delusion appears and continues to generate evil forces:

When Brahmā was thinking about creation, at the beginning of the era, there appeared a creation preceded by ignorance and made of darkness; from it was born fivefold ignorance, consisting of darkness, delusion, great delusion, gloom, and blind-darkness. Seeing that this creation was imperfect, Brahmā began to create again. . . . His fourth creation produced creatures in whom darkness and passion predominated, afflicted by misery; these were mankind.[22]

The qualities of passion and darkness (*rajas* and *tamas*) appear in the course of creation as the natural complement to the third basic quality—*sattva*, light and truth. These three components of matter are known as the "strands" because they are inextricably intertwined like the strands of a rope, and they continue to influence subsequent creation. As usual, it is mankind who bears the burden of God's inadequacy.

Demons, too, are created unintentionally by Brahmā:

[18] *Ait. Up.* 2.1–6; Śaṅkara on *Ait. Up.* 2.1. [19] See below, chap. IV, sec. 4.

[20] *Kārikā* of Gauḍapada, 2.19. [21] *Prabodhacandrodaya*, Act I.

[22] *Viṣṇu* 1.5.1–18; cf. *Liṅga* 1.70.138–302.

After creating the gods, demons, ancestors, and mankind, Brahmā became afflicted with thirst and hunger, and he took another body composed of passion and darkness. In that darkness he created deformed creatures thin with hunger, and they began to eat his body, for they were the Rākṣasas and Yakṣas. When Brahmā saw them he was displeased, and his hair fell out and became serpents. And when he saw the serpents he was angry, and the creatures born of his anger were the fierce, flesh-eating Piśācas. Thus Brahmā created cruel creatures and gentle creatures, dharma and adharma, truth and falsehood.[23]

Hunger and thirst are the germinal evil-producing force for Brahmā as they are for mankind on earth. The chain reaction then takes over, and his displeasure and anger lead to further unsatisfactory creations, with which Brahmā is explicitly said to be dissatisfied. Though he seems to be attempting to create a world devoid of all evil, the text demonstrates that his creation is, as always, composed of equal measures of good and evil.

The passage cited above appears in texts that go on to insist that God *chose* to create abstract evil.[24] In the vain attempt to account for radical evil, these texts also provide a third approach to the problem, on the genealogical model. After enumerating the dynasties of the good sages and their wives, and the sons of Dharma, the author suddenly begins to discuss Adharma. Injury was his wife, in whom he begot a son, Falsehood (Anṛta), and daughter, Destruction (Nirṛti), who married each other and begot fear, hell, deceit, and torture; from these were born death and pain; from death was born disease, old age, sorrow, greed, and anger. None of these have any wives or children; all have drawn up their seed in chastity.[25]

The origin of Adharma—the crux of the myth—is awkwardly glossed over in this text; but the commentator supplies the missing link:[26] "Having told of the lineage of Dharma, in order to tell of its counterpart, he tells this verse. Dharma and Adharma are the two sons of Brahmā, for it is said, 'From his right breast Dharma was born; Adharma was born from his back.' "[27] The parentage of Adharma remains obscure in the text itself, though his offspring are all too familiar.

In spite of the fact that the original text specifies that the sons of Death and Destruction remained chaste, in contrast with the daughters of Dakṣa, who are procreative and benevolent, one variant goes on to insert a long passage describing the offspring of Death and another wife, Alakṣmī. These fourteen children live in the organs of the senses and in the mind, causing men to fall prey to passion, anger, and other emotions and thus to become destroyed through adharma.[28] Evidently these creatures absolve man of the responsibility for his evil

[23] *Mārk.* 45.18–40; *Viṣṇu* 1.5.59–65; O'Flaherty (1975), p. 44. [24] See above, n. 6.

[25] *Mārk.* 47.29–32; *Viṣṇu* 1.7.29–32. [26] Commentary on *Viṣṇu* 1.7.29.

[27] See below, chap. VI, sec. 1. [28] *Mārk.* 47.33–37; cf. below, chap. IV, sec. 4.

actions, a responsibility that must ultimately devolve upon Brahmā himself, the author of our woes.

One of these fourteen sons is then described in a longer passage, which makes even more explicit the helpless ambivalence of Brahmā in opposition to his evil offspring. Duḥsaha (the Intolerable) was ravaged with hunger, for Brahmā had created him to eat all beings; yet Brahmā begged him *not* to devour the universe, and to throw off the passion and ignorance in which he had been created. Duḥsaha then asked for food, and Brahmā granted him as food all that is unclean and people who disobey the moral law;[29] Duḥsaha's offspring, too, harm only the sinful, not the righteous.[30] In this way, the author of the text attempts to ethicize the darker side of creation; though Brahmā unintentionally creates evil, ultimately it serves to keep the universe good.

Unfortunately, this afterthought cannot justify the radical evils of death, disease, and misfortune, which strike down all mankind, sinful and virtuous. A Tamil text attributes our own meager life-span not to the jealousy of the gods (as most Sanskrit texts do[31]) but to the primeval human flaw, lust, in the creator himself:

Brahmā created the worlds, including a beautiful woman whom he desired. Shamelessly he made love to her, forgetting about creation; creatures then became short-lived.[32]

Brahmā's notorious proclivity to incest injures his creatures[33] until he becomes a devotee of Śiva, who restores his creative powers–though Śiva himself neglects the process of creation when he is overpowered by lust.[34]

The vain attempt of the gods to prevent evil from overcoming their creation is described at some length in a much later text, which explicitly rejects the chain-reaction theory used to explain the origin of evil in many earlier Purāṇas. When the sage simply states, "In the Dvāpara Age, dharma was only half left, and injury, hatred, envy, quarrels, and cruelty arose, and then came falsehood, anger, evil, disease, old age, and greed,"[35] the listener interrupts to ask, "*How* did the dharmas of injury, hatred, and so forth arise, and how did dharma disappear?" The sage then replies:

Formerly, the eleven Rudras were born of Brahmā's anger; they were terrible and destructive, ruining the universe. Brahmā saw that they were unsuitable for that time, and so he instructed Dakṣa to restrain them, for Dakṣa was capable of doing this. But when Dakṣa reached them he developed an evil disposition from contact with them. Then Śiva himself arrived and suppressed them. Because of this, they became anger, injury, old age, and so forth. They stood there, terrified of Śiva's strength, but then in the Dvāpara

[29] *Mārk*. 47.38–97. [30] *Mārk*. 48.1–123. [31] See below, chap. IV, sec. 8, and chap. VIII, sec. 3.

[32] *Tiruvāṉaikkāval māhātmiyam* 26 (pp. 184–187). [33] O'Flaherty (1975), pp. 25–35.

[34] *Śiva* 2.2.22.68, 2.4.1.24; *Matsya* 158.29; *Skanda* 6.245.50–51, 6.246.1; O'Flaherty (1973) pp. 300–302. [35] See above, chap. II, sec. 5.

Age they overran him. When Śiva saw them he was frightened and tried to protect himself with his trident. Then they were terrified and begged him to give them a position, saying, "If you do not find a place for us, we will eat you." Hearing this, Śiva said, "Go to Brahmā. He will give you a livelihood, for he is the creator." They left Śiva and went to Brahmā, saying, "We are injury and your other sons. Since we were frightened of Śiva, we remained hidden, as we had no opportunity to act. But now that dharma is dwindling we have found our opportunity, and we want a position and a livelihood." Brahmā said, "I have a son named Desire, who will help you. When Desire is born in someone's body, anger arises, and from anger comes delusion, and thence come greed, doubt, old age, disease, and death. And I have another son, Adharma, and when he terrifies Dharma you heroes will do your work." Then they took refuge in the work of assisting Desire and Adharma.[36]

The series of attempts to contain the evil which Brahmā had accidentally created merely transforms it from one level to another. At first, the Rudras are simply destructive demons; when Dakṣa tries to control them, they pollute him; when Śiva tries to suppress them, they turn into the personifications of all evils; when he threatens them with his trident, they seem to subside, but in truth they merely remain waiting for a chance to reemerge. Eventually, when Śiva has shifted the responsibility to Brahmā and he in turn has sent them to Desire, the evils find their usual lodging place—within the human body. Thus Śiva and Brahmā fall back on what amounts to the traditional solution: when the hungry forces of evil threaten to eat them, they offer in place of themselves human beings for food, and they attempt to mitigate this selfish and cowardly act by stipulating that only evil beings (in this instance, those who have fallen prey to desire, the usual mortal flaw) will provide demon-fodder. The belief that evil must emerge sooner or later, in one form or another, is here combined with the theory of degenerating eras. Although Śiva appears to suppress the forces of evil, they merely remain in hiding until they find their "opportunity," the chink in the armor of time—the Dvāpara Age when dharma is fated to decay anyway.

Śiva commits another error because of his conflict with Desire, which results in the same postponement of evil:

When Rudra destroyed Kāma (Desire), Kāma's wife Rati wept and her friends commiserated. Spring (Madhu), the best friend of Kāma, wished for revenge, hoping to cheer Rati up by creating an obstacle to the worship of Śiva. Assisted by Delusion, Deceit, Anger, Greed, and Logic, the servants of Kali, Spring asked Brahmā to promise that they might oppose the worship of Śiva. "Not now, but in the future," Brahmā replied. And so in the Kali Age, Spring became born as the evil heretic Madhu, son of a widow and a Brahmin, spreading his evil doctrine over India and reviling Śiva.[37]

[36] *Bṛhaddharma* 3.12.1–50. [37] *Saura* 40.10–74. See below, chap. VII, sec. 7.

The heresy of Śiva-hatred (here blamed on a Vaiṣṇava philosopher) stems from Śiva's own emotional outburst, his rash destruction of Kāma.

In a multiform of the creation myth, the goddess Jyeṣṭhā, goddess of misfortune, appears from the ocean when it is churned by the gods, who instruct her to dwell wherever there are quarrels or false speech and to eat people who lie and who fail to wash their feet.[38] The existence of the evil goddess on earth is the fault of the gods, who produce her—as they produce the Kālakūṭa poison, which immediately precedes her and threatens to destroy the universe—when their greedy determination to obtain the elixir of immortality causes them to churn the ocean too fast. But, like the demons and mortals whom Prajāpati corrupts, she may only prey upon those who are already evil—though, as usual, the text fails to explain how these deserving victims became evil in the first place.

In one Purāṇa, heresy arises through the mistaken ideas of the sectarian gods Viṣṇu and Brahmā, who have replaced Prajāpati as creators. This late text specifies heresy rather than the older concept of general evil:

Brahmā and Viṣṇu were arguing, each shouting that he was supreme. In anger, Brahmā cursed Viṣṇu: "You will be deluded and your devotees will have the appearance of Brahmins, but they will be against the Vedas and the true path to Release."[39]

The ultimate expression of this belief that the gods are responsible for all the troubles of mankind appears in the mythology of the Hill Saora, who state that the gods *are* the troubles of mankind:

In the days before gods and the Dead troubled men, there were no priests. But in time the gods were born for every caste and they began to trouble them and men fell ill.[40]

This idea recurs among the Koya tribe, who view with remarkable cynicism the gods' need for sacrificial food:

There were no gods, no priests, no sorcerers at first. Man increased in number and prosperity. The gods were living with Deur and he found it a great burden. Deur thought, "I'll send these gods to men and they'll have to see about feeding them." [He lowered the gods to earth and told them to force men to feed them by inflicting fever, blindness, and so forth upon mankind, who would have to seek help from the gods.][41]

The belief that the gods create evil for man in order that man should depend on the gods—and the priests—recurs in the Sanskrit texts.[42] The gods find evil necessary for their very existence; they allow the demons to thrive in order that they themselves may thrive as gods, to force men to worship them.[43] The gods' desire for a balance of good and evil may be selfish in origin but it is also philosophically justifiable. Zimmer points out that Viṣṇu becomes incarnate to

[38] *Padma* 6.260.22–23. [39] *Parāśara Purāṇa*, chap. 3, cited in *Tantrādhikāranirṇaya*, 34.

[40] Elwin (1953), p. 503. [41] *Ibid.*, p. 591.

[42] See above, chap. II, sec. 7. [43] See below, chap. IV, secs. 6–8.

prevent demons from destroying mankind, but not to annihilate the demons, for he wishes to keep the forces of good and evil in equilibrium. Kṛṣṇa scotches the serpent Kāliya but does not kill him:

> There could be no elimination, once and for all, of this presence which to man seemed wholly negative. Krishna effected only a kind of boundary settlement, a balanced judgment as between demons and men. For the good of the human kingdom, Kāliya was assigned to a remoter sphere, but he was allowed to remain unchanged both in nature and power. Had he been transformed, redeemed, or altogether eliminated, productive and destructive energies would have been disrupted.[44]

Thus there are both benevolent and malevolent reasons for the gods to create and tolerate evil. The myths of necessity emphasize the former, or resort to the rejection of the hypothesis of omnipotence; but the lack of benevolence—the antagonism between god and man—underlies the major corpus of Indian mythology, the less philosophical and abstract corpus, to which we must now turn.

[44] Zimmer, p. 87.

And there was war in heaven: . . . And the great dragon was cast out, that old serpent, called the Devil, and Satan, which deceiveth the whole world: he was cast out into the earth, and his angels were cast out with him.
Revelation 12:7 and 9

IV

GODS, DEMONS, AND MEN

When fate and man have been ruled out as comprehensive sources of evil, the theologian finds himself, *volens nolens*, in the realm of mythology. Moreover, this same process of elimination reveals that there is a true problem of theodicy in India, that the responsibility for evil must be placed on personal gods—or personal demons.

The view that demons, rather than gods, are responsible for the origin of evil is found in its purest form in Manicheanism, a religion originating in Persia in the third century A.D., composed of Gnostic Christian, Mazdean, and pagan elements, and representing Satan as co-eternal with God. The term "Manichean," as a descriptive adjective, is therefore often applied to any religion which holds similar views of ethical and cosmic dualism, though technically, as a proper name, it should denote only the religion of the followers of Mani. For want of any better term, I have used "Manichean" throughout the present work to denote such trends in Indian religion, whether or not they show evidence of actual Persian influence or arise after the third century A.D.

In India, the solution offered by Manichean dualism—that the devil is responsible for evil, and that God is therefore not responsible—is seldom invoked, because the ambiguous nature of the demons (called Asuras, Daityas, or Dānavas) in Hinduism makes them totally unsuitable to bear the blame for the origin of evil.

1. The Consanguinity of Gods and Demons

In the Ṛg Veda, gods and demons are opposed, but the nature of this opposition is far from clear. As W. Norman Brown remarked, "The cause of the epic quarrel between the Ādityas and Dānavas . . . is never stated, but we may reasonably assume that it lay in the antithesis between their natures."[1] This rather begs the question, however, for the "nature" of the demons is a matter of considerable dispute; a typically ambiguous example is Tvaṣṭṛ,[2] about whom Brown admits that his "part in the war seems uncertain." According to Jan Gonda, the central myth from the time of the Vedas on is the myth of the conflict of the gods (representing the powers of good) against the powers of evil (Indra vs. Vṛtra, Rāma vs. Rāvaṇa, Buddha vs. Māra), the conflict between good and "the evil power of destruction, starvation, and death."[3] But the demons do not always represent these misfortunes, which are often attributed to the gods; nor by any means do the gods always represent unmitigated "good"; nor, finally, are destruction, starvation, and death always regarded as "evil." The one invariable characteristic of the gods is that they are the enemies of the demons, and the one invariable characteristic of the demons is that they are opposed to the gods. For this reason, when the later myths begin to apply new moral codes to the characters of individual gods and demons in myths, a number of inconsistencies arise, for the two groups, as groups, are not fundamentally *morally* opposed.

Since these uncertainties are inherent in the myths, it is not surprising that they have found their way into the assessments of scholars. In order to understand the myths, it is necessary to distinguish between presuppositions and conditions. It is a presupposition of the myths that gods and demons are different; it is a condition of the myths that they are in fact alike—as is immediately apparent from any myth about the battle. By nature, gods and demons are alike; by function, however, they are as different as day and night. In fact, one reason for their perpetual conflict is the simple fact that they only become distinct—and therefore real to the Hindus hearing the myths—when they are engaged in battle.

Each myth begins with the Vedic presupposition that the gods and demons are locked in equal combat, or indeed that the demons are winning, and each myth ends with the demons retreating to hell with their tails between their legs; yet, at the opening of the next chapter, the demons have somehow emerged again from hell to pose a new, seemingly unanswerable challenge. Overnight, the gods have lost the ground won in the previous myth (which now must be regarded, in retrospect, as a mere episode) and are back at square one; like Penelope, the ancient Indian weaver of tales nightly unravels the work of the day. This is due in part to the ritual nature of myth: we must fight and win the same fight every day. In an early text, the gods ask their creator, Prajāpati, "Is there not some means by which we might defeat the demons once and for all and never have to fight them again?"[4] Prajāpati teaches them the ritual that accomplishes this end; but of

[1] Brown (1942), p. 91. [2] See below, chap. V, sec. 3.

[3] Gonda (1954), p. 162. [4] *Śata.* 1.2.4.8.

course one must go on performing the ritual forever, and the battle is merely another form of agonistic ritual. The stubborn persistence of the paradox of the strife between consanguine and identical gods and demons is ensured by the deep-rooted nature of the two contradictory assumptions: that the gods must always win, and that strife must never be totally annihilated. So the game goes on forever, because you cannot tell the players without a scorecard.

Ananda K. Coomaraswamy pointed out this phenomenon years ago: "Although distinct and opposite in operation, [gods and demons] are in essence consubstantial, their distinction being a matter not of essence but of orientation, revolution, or transformation. . . . The Titan is potentially an Angel, the Angel still by nature a Titan."[5] Mircea Eliade further developed Coomaraswamy's hypothesis and interpreted it in terms of two levels of religious potential:

> The Vedic mythology and religion present us with a situation which is at first sight paradoxical. On the one hand there is a distinction, opposition and conflict between the Devas and the Asuras, the gods and the "demons," the powers of Light and Darkness. . . . But on the other hand, numerous myths bring out the consubstantiality or brotherhood of the Devas and Asuras. One has the impression that Vedic doctrine is at pains to establish a double perspective: although, as an immediate reality, and as the world appears to our eyes, the Devas and the gods [*sic*] are irreconcilably different by nature and condemned to fight one another, at the beginning of time, on the other hand, that is to say before the Creation or before the world took its present form, they were consubstantial. . . . In man's immediate experience, in his concrete, historical existence, the Devas and Asuras are opposed, and he must pursue virtue and combat evil. *What is true of eternity is not necessarily true in time.*[6]

Thus Eliade places the "consubstantial" aspect of gods and demons in the Golden Age before time began, and sees their "apparent" conflict as the only reality relevant to the present age–the Kali Age, when man must "combat evil" as the gods do. This is an attractive interpretation but one which is undermined by numerous Indian texts in which the "consubstantiality" of gods and demons (the wickedness of gods, the virtue of demons, the brotherhood in actual lineage as well as in behavior) is depicted as continuing through the present time, while the conflict between gods and demons is said to occur *as soon as they are created*–leaving no interim Golden Age for them to be at peace. Eliade's basic distinction between the two levels–the apparent conflict masking the true consubstantiality–remains valid in *all* periods of Hindu mythological time. In terms of chronological development within a single myth, the texts frequently begin with apparent equality, if not identity, between gods and demons (deadlocked in struggle), and end with inequality: the gods win. Viewed in Eliade's terms, the "true" identity is obscured in the course of the myth by the "apparent" (but functionally more valid) opposition.

[5] Coomaraswamy (1935), pp. 373–374. [6] Eliade (1965), pp. 88–89 and 94.

In assessing the myth of the Buddha avatar of Viṣṇu, Charles Coleman found the behavior of Viṣṇu "more demoniacal than divine, and more in accordance with the character of a minister of evil, than of the preserving deity of the universe."[7] The function of gods as devils is an important motif to which we shall often have occasion to return; for the moment, let us concentrate on the manner in which the two powers exchange roles. Hindu gods and demons are the very embodiment of the palindrome "Dog as a devil deified lived as a god."

According to the Brāhmaṇas, Prajāpati at first created gods and demons alike and did not distinguish between them.[8] Early texts always stress the similarity between the two groups, though an attempt is sometimes made to distinguish between their functions: "The gods took refuge in day, the demons in night; they were of equal strength, and one could not distinguish between them. The gods were afraid of night, darkness, death."[9] The demons are associated with qualities which the gods (and we, their worshippers) fear, but Hindus did not regard these qualities as morally evil. Even in the Purāṇas, where the battle lines are more clearly drawn, the gods admit to Brahmā their inability to discern the true nature of things: "Even though we and the demons are both born of portions of you, nevertheless we see the universe as divided, a distinction caused by ignorance. The demons are virtuous."[10] In order to *make* a distinction corresponding to the gods' deluded view, Viṣṇu becomes the Buddha (a demonic act, as Coleman remarks) to corrupt the demons. That the gods and demons are brothers is often remarked, usually to the discredit of the gods; Arjuna asks rhetorically, "Do the gods prosper without killing their kinsmen, the demons? The gods won their places in heaven by fighting. Such are the ways of the gods and the eternal dictates of the Vedas."[11] Elsewhere it is said, "Brothers kill brothers for the sake of a kingdom. Even the gods, knowing dharma well, killed the demons."[12]

The moral ambiguity of the demons may be seen even in the etymological confusion inherent in their name (Asura); in Iranian mythology, Ahura designates the great god, Ahura Mazda (other gods being called Bogas), while in Sanskrit, Asura comes to mean a demon. In the early Ṛg Veda, Asura still designates a god; only in the later books does it come to mean a demon. The myths with which the present work is concerned, however, all derive from the later period, in which Asura is linguistically no longer ambiguous, though it still retains its moral ambiguities. By a false etymology which takes the initial *A* of Asura as privative, the word *Sura* (i.e., "not A-sura") is coined for "god." This term, *Sura*, finally comes to be explained by a myth which states that the gods (Suras) drank wine (*surā*), while the others, who had refused the wine, became

[7] Coleman, p. 185; see below, chap. VII, sec. 4.

[8] *Tait. Br.* 1.4.11. Cf. *Mait. Sam.* 4.2.1; *Śata.* 1.2.4.8, 1.5.3.2, 1.7.2.22.

[9] *Ait. Br.* 4.5.

[10] *Viṣṇu* 3.17.19–43.

[11] *MBh.* 12.8.28. Cf. *Bṛhadāraṇyaka Up.* 1.3.1.

[12] *Skanda* 5.2.66.18. Cf. *Rām.* 7.2.6–17, *MBh.* 13.12.26.

Asuras.[13] This episode occurs in the myth of the churning of the ocean, and the wine is a multiform of the Soma which the gods obtain at that time by defeating the demons; the Soma is the elixir of immortality, the possession of which distinguishes the gods from the demons. Before the elixir appeared, gods and demons were alike and at peace; afterwards, as only one side could have the Soma (the unexplained assumption of the myth), the battle rages forever. One Tamil myth apparently challenges this assumption. When the Soma first appears, gods and demons agree to share it in peace at a site of harmony among enemies; but the demons suspect that the gods will trick them, and the gods fear that the proud, strong demons will harm them; and so Śiva declares that anyone infected with pride will lose the strength gained by drinking the Soma.[14] Even when the Vedic conflict is ethicized so that the opposition god/demon is replaced by the opposition good/evil (enlightened/proud), the primeval conflict reasserts itself, and the gods attempt to destroy all the demons, whether or not they are infected with pride.

This is one of the archetypal myths of the struggle between gods and demons, and a recent analysis of it by J. Bruce Long highlights several basic factors. Using as his *point de'appui* Lévi-Strauss's distinction between myths (which begin with a state of asymmetry between polar oppositions and end with an equilibrium or a state of symmetry) and games (which begin with structural symmetry between the opponents and end with asymmetry or inequality), Long demonstrates that the myth fits the model of the game better than that of the myth; the artificial or functional symmetry with which the myth begins (a temporary truce between gods and demons) leads to the ultimate (albeit also temporary) victory of the gods, which demonstrates "the *real*, as contrasted to the attested or theoretical, superiority of the divine forces" (this theoretical superiority being originally given to the older brothers, the demons).[15] The churning of the ocean, an allotrope of the pressing of the Soma in the Soma sacrifice, is a ritualistic myth, which is based on an agonistic model, like a game; what J. C. Heesterman has demonstrated for the Vedic model[16] is still true of this Epic myth and of the myth of the battle between gods and demons; whether it is true of *all* Hindu myths (some of which lack a ritualistic basis) remains to be seen.

The demons are often called Daityas and Dānavas, terms derived from the names of the mothers of two great families of demons, Diti and Danu; the fact that the demons are identified by matronymics rather than patronymics is of great significance in the mythology. An etymological confusion the inverse of that which hedges *Asura* is found in the ordinary word for god in Sanskrit, *deva*, which comes to mean "devil" in Persian and in the Avesta, which particularly

[13] *Rām.* 1.44.21–23.

[14] *Tirukkaṭṭavūr* 2–4 (pp. 18–37).

[15] Long (1975), *passim*. [16] See below, n. 31.

characterizes Indra as an evil spirit.[17] These linguistic labyrinths compound an already formidable moral haze.

The demons are physically indistinguishable from the gods—or indeed from anyone else, as gods and demons share the power of illusion (*māyā*), which allows them to assume any form at will. In the Buddhist *Jātakas*, the fact that the demon (Yakka) casts no shadow marks him as a nonhuman creature; but this is a sign of a god as well.[18] As E. W. Hopkins says of the demons, "Opposition to light and goodness, love of and use of *māyā*, illusion or deception, a roaring voice, ability to assume any shape, or to disappear, are their general characteristics; in which they differ from Rākṣasas [a lower form of demon, flesh-eating and hideous] not at all and except for the first element not from the gods."[19] The gods are said to use "demon tricks" in their immoral enterprises[20] and are often expressly said to behave like demons. In Buddhism, the gods are always righteous (*dhammika*) and the demons unrighteous; but demons do not have any true significance in Buddhist cosmology, perhaps because they are all subsumed under Māra.[21]

The fact that gods and demons do not differ is the very basis of their strife; it is only through battle that they can be made distinct, and the distinction consists in no more and no less than that quality which distinguishes winners from losers. The strife is intensified by the sibling rivalry of the brothers:

> Strife rooted in nature never disappears. Thus there is enduring strife between mungoose and snake . . . water and fire—gods and devils—dogs and cats—herbivorous creatures and those armed with claws—rival wives—lions and elephants—hunter and deer—crow and owl—scholar and numskull—wife and harlot—saint and sinner. In these cases, nobody belonging to anybody has been killed by anybody, yet they fight to the death.[22]

In this list, distinctions of nature (water and fire) are mixed with functional differences (wife and harlot, saint and sinner); gods and devils would fall into the latter group. In any case, the strife between them is eternal—because it does not have any specific cause and so cannot have a specific solution.

Patañjali lists gods and demons in the category of "enmity" but *not* under "eternal opposition" (such as that of crows and owls, dogs and jackals, Brahmin and non-Hindu ascetics); Indian grammatical tradition maintains that this implies that the enmity of gods and demons is *not* eternal, that they might someday be reconciled. But this view of the grammarians is not shared by the authors of the myths; and the *Mahābhārata* states that gods and demons, being brothers, are locked in an enmity that is innate and therefore constant and perpetual.[23]

[17] Burrow, p. 5. [18] *Jātaka*, V, no. 513; *MBh*. 3.57.23.

[19] Hopkins (1915), p. 48. [20] *Daśakumāracarita*, chap. II, p. 85.

[21] Ling, p. 23; see below, chap. VIII, sec. 1. [22] *Pañcatantra*, prose at 2.1.25–26 (Ryder, p. 223).

[23] Patañjali on Pāṇini 2.4.9 and 4.3.125; cf. *MBh*. 5.98.18.

2. The Ambiguous Virtue of Demons

A superficial difference between gods and demons might be sought in the presence of benevolence in gods, malevolence in demons, but "in Indian religions, it is not suitable to call a god demon as soon as he is malignant."[24] As Max Weber has commented,

> The only qualitative differentiation that is made between these anthropomorphic gods and demons is that between powers useful to man and those harmful to man. Naturally, the powers useful to him are usually considered the good and high gods, who are to be worshipped, while the powers harmful to him are usually the lower demons, frequently endowed with incredible guile or limitless spite, who are not to be worshipped but magically exorcised. Yet the differentiation did not always take place along this particular line. . . . Powers of clearly diabolical character, such as Rudra, the Hindu god of pestilence, are not always weaker than the good gods, but may actually be endowed with a tremendous power potential.[25]

Although the demonic nature of Rudra is more complex than Weber's passage seems to imply,[26] the statement that power rather than benevolence characterizes the Hindu gods is entirely justified. Zoroastrianism distinguishes between two forces, one benevolent but not powerful, the other powerful but not benevolent;[27] this scheme may be applied to Hinduism, but with the stipulation that the first group (benevolent but not powerful) refers to the virtuous demons, while the second group (powerful but not benevolent) refers to the wicked gods.[28]

The principle factor that distinguishes gods from men is immortality; therefore, when men become immortal, blurring the necessary functional distinction, they must be destroyed.[29] The crucial distinction between gods and demons is power; therefore when demons become powerful (often through virtue, though sometimes through trickery or brute strength), they must be destroyed. In later devotional texts, when the groups violating classification cannot be destroyed, they are reclassified—made into gods. Thus the conflict between gods and demons in Hinduism does not represent a conflict between good and evil, not because good and evil do not conflict in the Hindu view (though many texts would support this view) but because these moral categories simply do not apply to the two superhuman factions.

Nor can it be said that the gods and demons represent a conflict between life and death. These two forces may also be said to be unconflicting in some Hindu texts (since, in the philosophy of rebirth, life-and-death together are seen to contrast with release from the cycle of rebirth); but in most Hindu texts, even when life is clearly desired and death feared, death is not the key to the struggle between gods and demons. For although they fight for the elixir of immortality,

[24] Rodhe, p. 58. [25] Weber (1963), pp. 33–34. [26] See below, chap. X, secs. 1–2.

[27] Obeyesekere, p. 9. [28] See below, chaps. V and VI. [29] See below, chap. VIII, sec. 3.

and the gods are said to win it ultimately, gods and demons are equally mortal and equally murderous to mankind. Finally, though the gods and demons are sometimes identified with light and darkness, these are merely symbolic expressions of contrast rather than true oppositions.

The opposition between the gods and demons is purely structural; they are alike in all ways except that, by definition, they are opposed. The two groups are functionally but not essentially opposed, in conflict over the acquisition of power–the same power, but utilized differently in each case. Our allegiance to the gods is based not on moral factors but on agonistic ones: the gods always win, and so we are always on their side. (This is particularly true when "we" are the Brahmin authors of the texts; when the factor of asceticism is introduced, the alignment of gods and men is more complicated.[30]) Heesterman has demonstrated that the Vedic sacrifice itself is an agonistic ritual between two sacrificing partners, the parties of life and death, who are symbolized by gods and demons; in the course of this ritual, the two parties *change places*–and this is the pattern of the battle between gods and demons, which requires that the two opponents be basically alike, and hence opposed.[31]

This opposition is so basic and so necessary to the myths that the gratified structuralist coming upon them might almost suppose that the ancient Indians had read Lévi-Strauss and constructed the category of demons precisely in order to provide a structural counterpart to the gods, this being their total raison d'être in Hinduism. As logical entities, the gods and demons are what a linguistic philosopher might regard as "yea-nay" or "boo-hoorah" terms: there are no qualitative differences, but merely differences relative to the position of the speaker (or myth-maker). We say "Boo!" to the demons and "Hoorah!" to the gods, and this is the difference between them.

It has been said that the demons, like the gods, perform sacrifices but "in the wrong manner, . . . with the wrong result, according to the Devas [gods]."[32] Naturally, the gods accuse the demons of behaving wrongly, since the demons are their enemies; even when the demons are patently virtuous, they are "other" and must be slain, since by definition the gods must always win. Time and time again it is said that, since certain demons follow the precepts of the Vedas, they cannot be slain;[33] yet it is always assumed that they *must* be slain. This stubborn and apparently illogical attitude is in part responsible for the quandary of the virtuous demon: it is the particular duty of demons to be evil, but it is evil to disregard one's own duty.[34] Thus, whatever they do, the demons lose; the gods (and Brahmins) have loaded the dice against them.

Though the demons were at first barely differentiated from the gods, they came

[30] See below, secs. 5 and 7. [31] Heesterman (1964), pp. 1-31; (1975), pp. 8-9.

[32] Dange, p. 87. [33] Cf. *Viṣṇu* 3.17.39. [34] See below, chap. V, sec. 1.

gradually to be regarded as morally neutral enemies and, finally, to be described as hideous and immoral. Most of the myths of evil fall within the middle period. Gods and demons are "separate but equal," rather like two separate castes; each has his own job to do—the gods to encourage sacrifice, the demons to destroy it—but there is no immorality in the demons; they are merely doing their job, a destructive one, just as the sweepers perform their unclean tasks. Although this apparently tolerant attitude would seem to have more in common with orthodox Hinduism than with the less caste-oriented texts of the earlier and later periods, this is not in fact the case. The amoral view of the demons is prevalent largely in the earliest mythological texts, the Brāhmaṇas, and in the latest texts, in which the doctrine of caste duty is superseded by the idea of individual salvation;[35] here the demons merely play their role and are inevitably defeated (in the Brāhmaṇas) or released altogether (in the devotional texts). But the large body of Purāṇic material composed between these two periods regards the demons as "evil" in spite of the fact that these texts emphasize the necessity of following one's preordained path in life. For these orthodox scriptures often display the same intolerance toward the demons as they do toward human heretics: to be other is to be bad.

3. The Fall of the Demons

In this way, the originally nonqualitative opposition between gods and demons comes to assume a moral dimension in some texts. But since even these texts agree that the demons and gods were originally created equal, it is necessary to explain how they became unequal—unequal in power (in all texts) and sometimes unequal in moral quality as well. This problem remains real to contemporary Hindus who blame evil spirits for creating evil; as a young Sweeper remarked, "*Bhuut-preets* [evil spirits, ghosts] wander around. Their own salvation has not been settled by God. I don't know why they cause trouble; maybe because they are crazy."[36] This last refuge—the statement that evil is the work of a madman—is occasionally applied to God, as well as to demons; thus Śiva is often said to be a madman.[37] It is not an explanation but an admission of the inability of reason to account for evil at all.

One definition of the term for a demon (*Asura*) draws upon the myth of the Fall: the demon is called "one who was formerly a god" (*pūrva-deva*).[38] In the late Ṛg Veda, though the demons come to represent the powers of darkness and the gods the powers of light, they do not dwell apart. It is only by the time of the Brāhmaṇas that the demons are said to inhabit a place of darkness below the

[35] See below, chap. V, sec. 13. [36] Kolenda, p. 77. [37] Dasgupta, p. 151; O'Flaherty (1973), p. 215; *Skanda* 7.2.9.24; *Bhāgavata* 4.2.11–16. [38] *Amarakośa* 1.1.7.

earth; indeed, it is only at this period that the universe becomes "ethicized" to any degree, and the Atharva Veda is the first text to know of hell at all.[39] Thus, between the Ṛg Veda and the Purāṇas, the demons may be said to have fallen from heaven to hell.

The gods are usually the ones who make the demons into demons, because of the divine disinclination to share heaven:

Gods and demons, both born from Prajāpati, were vying against one another; the demons won the world and began to divide it. "Who shall we become if we do not have a share in it?" thought the gods, and they went there and tricked the demons into giving them the sacrifice, which is the whole earth.[40]

Although the demons in this text are said to be jealous and grudging, they do give the gods something—and the gods take it all, leaving the demons with nothing.

The belief is often expressed that the demons were not only the equals of the gods but their superiors—the older brothers,[41] the original gods from whom the gods stole the throne of heaven. (William Buck expresses this well when he refers to the Asuras as the "dark, olden gods" and the Devas as "the mortal gods of heaven."[42]) The original superiority of the demons is explicit in the *Kāṭhaka Saṃhitā*:

The gods and demons performed the sacrifice; whatever the gods did, the demons did. The demons were greater, and better; the gods were younger and more evil, like younger brothers. Then the gods saw the first part of the Soma libation and grabbed it, and with it they became first.[43]

The gods overcome their superiors by a ritual sleight of hand, as usual; the *Kāṭhaka* cites in explanation of this ritual battle an episode in the mythical battle in which the bitch Saramā helps the gods to grab the cows from the older demons and thus to become first, that is, preeminent.

One Vedic hymn may imply that the demons were made to revere their brothers, the gods.[44] The hymn refers to the manner in which "the gods placed faith in the mighty demons" (perhaps implying that the gods obtained the demons as their sacrificial patrons) and asks that they now place faith in sacrificers—hopefully, in sacrificers as generous as demons.[45] Sāyaṇa's commentary expands on this: "The gods, Indra and the others, placed faith in the demons whose might was threatening them; thinking, 'These must be killed,' they paid great attention to them." Sāyaṇa thus finds in the Vedic stanza the inference that the demons threatened the gods and that the gods, in turn, placed faith in them in order to

[39] Gombrich (1975), p. 116. [40] *Śata* 1.2.5.1–10; O'Flaherty (1975), pp. 177–178; see below, chap. VII, sec. 1. [41] *Śata* 14.4.1.1; *Bṛhadāraṇyaka Up.* 1.3.1. [42] Buck, p. 9.
[43] *Kāṭh. Sam.* 27.9, citing *RV* 3.31.6; cf. *MBh.* 12.34.13. [44] Geldner, III, 383. [45] *RV* 10.151.3.

kill them. Karl Geldner sees here a reference to the "belief in the recognition of their own power which the rising younger generation of gods placed in the older generation of Asuras." As the losers in the competitive sacrificial ritual, the demons would be left behind with impurities shed by the gods—who would ascend to heaven, like the sacrificial priest. In later mythology, the demons are often ruined by being converted to belief in the gods, though in earlier texts the gods usually destroy the demons' faith in the sacrifice in order to overcome them; on some occasions, the gods place faith in men for this purpose, but not in demons.[46]

In some texts, the fall of the demons results not from the machinations of the gods but from a flaw in their own demonic nature. Though the fall of the demons is not described in the Ṛg Veda, it is recorded in ancient Iranian mythology, which may imply a pre-Vedic origin of the myth: "Infatuation (or delusion) came upon them as they took counsel together, so that they chose the worst thoughts (or the most evil mind)."[47] The manner in which "infatuation" causes the demons to be thrust out of the divine pantheon and regarded as devils is described in several different Hindu texts. Gods and demons were created alike, but the demons placed their oblations in their own mouths, while the gods offered theirs to one another, and so the sacrifice became the property of the gods.[48] Both gods and demons sent representatives to Prajāpati to learn about the Self; the gods understood the doctrine better and thus gained all their desires.[49] Another text describes this conflict in terms of the transfer of merit, like the transfer of karma:

The gods and demons both spoke truth, and they both spoke untruth. They were alike. The gods relinquished untruth, and the demons relinquished truth. The truth which was within the demons beheld this and went over to the gods, and the untruth of the gods went to the demons.[50]

Although in each case the change in status results from a moral error, intellectual failure, or ritual mistake on the part of the demons, the chain is self-reinforcing, and the demons are further corrupted by their own incipient evil. This is expressed in terms of the transfer of good karma from the demons to the gods, and the bad karma in the opposite direction. That the gods are only too pleased to help the process along, to keep the demons demonic, is evident from the *Gītā*, where Kṛṣṇa admits that he hurls cruel, hateful men into demonic wombs in birth after birth, so that they never reach him but go the lowest way (to hell).[51]

[46] *Tāṇḍya* 17.1.1; cf. Heesterman (1962), p. 33.

[47] *Gāthas, Yasna* xxx, 5–6; xxxv.3; cited in Moulton, p. 307, and Zaehner (1961), p. 42.

[48] *Śata.* 5.1.1.1; 11.2.1.1–2; Meyer (1937), II, 251.

[49] *Ch. Up.* 8.7–12; see below, n. 76 and chap. V, sec. 10.

[50] *Śata.* 9.5.1.12–15; see below, chap. VI, sec. 2.

[51] *Gītā* 16.19–20.

In Epic mythology, the goddess of prosperity (Śrī) is transferred, like good karma, from demons to gods:

Śrī dwelt among the demons in former times because they followed the dharma of truth; but when she realized that they had been perverted, she preferred to dwell among the gods. For at first the demons were firm in their own dharma and delighted in the road to heaven; they honored their gurus and worshipped the gods. But then, with the passage of time and the change in their quality, their dharma was destroyed and they were in the grip of desire and anger. They became sinners and atheists, evil and immoral. Then Śrī left them.[52]

Here the demons are destroyed by the same forces that corrupt mankind: the passage of time and the appearance of desire and anger.

Another Epic passage interprets the demons' downfall in terms of the older, Brāhmaṇa concept of the demons' natural disinclination to behave well:

Formerly the gods delighted in dharma and the demons abandoned dharma. Then pride entered those who dwelt in adharma, and from pride came anger. Lakṣmī [the goddess of good fortune] entered the gods, and Alakṣmī entered the demons. Then the spirit of Kali entered the demons, and they were destroyed.[53]

The cumulative effects of evil culminate in the arrival of the Kali Age, but the demons are responsible for initiating this process.

These myths generally account for the differentiation between gods and demons but do not usually involve mankind. The demons who lose the right to rule in heaven are driven down beneath the earth and are thus not necessarily any closer to mortals on earth than are the gods in heaven. In one myth, however, the fall of the demons is viewed in human terms:

Brahmā created Brahmins out of his own energy, and he gave them truth and dharma and purity conducive to heaven. He made men, demons, Rākṣasas, Piśācas, and others, but they became full of lust, anger, and so forth, and they abandoned their svadharma *and became other classes. Thus they became ignorant through greed, and those who do not understand the Godhead are of many sorts—Piśācas, Rākṣasas, and all the barbarian castes.*[54]

Two important assumptions seem inherent in this text. At first Brahmā created only Brahmins, in each species—Brahmin men, Brahmin demons, and so forth; these, through their own fault, and in the familiar manner, lost their Brahmin status and became Kṣatriyas, Vaiśyas, and Śūdras, as well as barbarians. In this context, men and demons fall together. But then it is said that those who fell in this way became Piśācas, Rākṣasas, and barbarians, which seems to imply that these demonic species did not exist at all before the Fall, that there was originally

[52] *MBh.* 12.221.26–78. [53] *MBh.* 3.92.6–10. [54] *MBh.* 12.181.1–20. Cf. *MBh.* 12.34.13–18.

no such thing as a Brahmin Rākṣasa. This latter concept seems to have influenced the Abbé Dubois' interpretation of the myth: "Brahmin giants (the most mischievous of the race)" were Brahmins who had been turned into giants (i.e., Rākṣasas) as a punishment for former crimes: "Occasionally they adopted a hermit's life, without thereby changing their character, or becoming better disposed."[55] Either of these two contradictory original assumptions leads to the conclusion that present-day demons were once better than they are now, and fell in status through their own fault.

Certain Western commentators, perhaps influenced by ideas from Christian theology, have interpreted the fall of the demons from heaven in terms of a subsequent Fall of man. This attitude appears in the terminology they apply to demons; the demons in the Pāli canon are said to be fallen beings, "devas in opposition or in revolt or disgrace,"[56] and some eighteenth-century Hindus encountered by the Danish missionaries were said to have believed that human souls are "heavenly spirits, which for their sins are driven out of heaven."[57] Another eighteenth-century observer recorded at greater length a myth of this type, from "Brahmāh's Shastah":

> [The initial creation was a state of joy and harmony] which would have continued to the end of time, had not envy and jealousy taken possession of Moisasoor [Mahiṣāsura, the buffalo demon] and other leaders of the angelic bands.... They spread their evil imaginations among the angelic host, deceived them, and drew a large portion of them from their allegiance. The eternal One then commanded Sieb [Śiva] to go armed with his omnipotence, to drive them from Mahah Surgo [heaven], and plunge them into the Onderah [hell], there doomed to suffer unceasing sorrows.... Part of the angelic bands rebelled and were expelled from the heavenly regions; the leaders of the rebellion, . . . in process of time, regained their influence, and confirmed most of the delinquents in their disobedience.[58]

The assumption that paradise "would have continued to the end of time" conflicts with the general Hindu view of original creation, which is more closely represented by the statement that the demon rebels regained their influence "in process of time." The statement that Śiva was to drive the demons from heaven corresponds with a more typical pattern of Hindu myths, in which the demons are the victims and the gods the initiators of corruption,[59] a contradiction of the initial premise of this text.

One tribal myth of the origin of evil shows the obvious influence of Christian mythology (particularly in the attitude toward the devil), but retains certain Indian ideas as well:

> [In the olden times, God gave people everything they needed. There was no shame of

[55] Dubois, p. 516. [56] Ling, p. 22. [57] Orme, I, 179. I am indebted to Dr. Peter Marshall of King's College, University of London, for the transcript of the Orme manuscript.

[58] Holwell, pp. 71 and 57. [59] See below, chap. VII, secs. 1–4.

nakedness, and people lived for a thousand years. Then one man's heart became bold, and he thought that he did not need God. He tried to kill God, but God stripped off his wings and threw him down into hell and called him a devil. God allowed the devil to come up to earth only on the day of the dark moon.

There were two beautiful people living on earth. When the devil saw how happy they were, while he suffered in hell, he resolved to destroy God's intention, thinking, "If I do not cause this to cease, shall I be a devil?" God had told the people on earth not to eat certain griddle cakes, but the devil took the form of a snake and told the woman that if she ate the griddle cakes she would fly like a god. She ate them and felt shame. The snake, overjoyed, returned home. The woman made the man eat the cakes, and then they both covered themselves with leaves.][60]

The myth of Eden has been only slightly modified, and the ideas shared by Indian and Christian mythology (the role of sex in the loss of paradise, the danger of eating tabu food) appear in the Western form. But the devil's concern about the fulfilment of his own role (" . . . shall I be a devil?") is a particularly Indian feature, on which the whole myth revolves.

4. Evil Created by Demons

Hindu mythology hardly ever blames the demons for the corruption of mankind, though isolated texts with this implication do appear from time to time. These ideas may have been further encouraged in India by Zoroastrian cults, which were brought to India by invaders from Iran and Central Asia by about A.D. 200 and which certainly affected other aspects of Hinduism (such as cults of the sun). Zoroastrianism itself was originally a monotheistic religion, which later solved the theodicy by splitting the attributes of the single deity into two independent causal agents controlling the universe;[61] the evil powers after the Fall "rush headlong into Fury that they might thereby extinguish the existence of mortal men," and a man's actions were thought to contribute not only to the struggle between good and evil but to the determination of his own ultimate fate. Manicheanism, founded by Mani in the third century A.D., affirmed "an ultimate dualism of good and evil, light and darkness."[62] Yet in spite of the possible influence of Manicheanism in India (Iran and India being historically and geographically closely linked), it seems superfluous to postulate such an influence, since moral dualism was never strong in India, and what dualism there was seems to have been as prevalent before A.D. 200 as after it.

One possibly Manichean myth appears in the *Mahābhārata*:

Prajāpati created all creatures, including Rākṣasas, in eternal dharma, in which the gods dwelt. But then the lords of demons transgressed the command of the Grandfather and caused a decrease in dharma, because they were full of anger and greed. Then all of

[60] Emeneau, pp. 174–191. [61] Zaehner (1961), pp. 42–43. *Yasna* 35.3. [62] Hick, p. 44.

them—Prahlāda, Virocana, and the others—strove against the gods, making this the pretext: "We are all of equal birth [jāti], *the gods and we."*[63]

Probably only the demons' virtue is destroyed in this way, though they may have been responsible for a more general corruption as well. Yet the ostensible cause for their action belies any truly dualistic basis of the conflict. The demons claim (rightly) that they and the gods are of equal birth; apparently they have been unjustly deprived of their birthright. In the course of the resulting battle, however, the demons (often inadvertently) create various forms of evil, which continue to afflict mankind: "Gods and demons were contending, and the gods were made powerful by chanting the Vedic hymn; the demons combined it with evil"[64] (though it is also said that the gods kept the demons out of heaven and avoided death by mixing the hymns with evil).[65] This Manichean attitude to the Vedas continues in modern Hinduism, for Dayānand Sarasvatī, the founder of the Ārya Samāj and champion of the "Return to the Vedas" movement, maintained that "whatever was written about the eating of flesh—that part of the Veda was composed by demons."[66]

By the time of the late Upaniṣads, demonic evil (*āsura pāpman*) was regarded as the main obstacle to the enlightenment of the gods. The gods wished to know the Self; demonic evil grasped them; they wished to swallow that demonic evil, and by religious exertions they succeeded in overcoming this obstacle.[67] But even in the classical Upaniṣads there are at least two striking examples of demonic evil viewed in a Zoroastrian manner, demonic evil directed against the gods but ricochetting into the essence of mankind:

When the gods and demons, both descendants of Prajāpati, strove against one another, the gods took up the loud chant [*of the Sāma Veda*], *thinking, "With this we shall overcome them." They worshipped the loud chant as the breath from the nose; the demons afflicted it with evil, and so with it one smells both the sweet-smelling and the ill-smelling, for it is afflicted with evil. When the gods went on to worship the loud chant as speech, the eye, the ear, and the mind, the demons struck these faculties with evil, making them capable of sensing and expressing evil as well as good; but when the gods worshipped the chant as the breath in the mouth, and the demons attempted to strike this too, the demons fell to pieces like a lump of clay striking a solid stone, and so the breath from the mouth is free from evil, smelling neither good smells nor bad smells; when this breath departs, the mouth gapes open in death.*[68]

From this text it is apparent that the demons have brought about the moral ambiguity of all our senses, having defiled them as they defiled the Vedic verses and as the demon Vṛtra defiles the essences of smell, taste, sight, touch, and

63 *MBh.* 12.160.16–29. 64 *Jai. Up. Br.* 1.18.1–11. 65 *Jai. Up. Br.* 1.16.1–12.

66 Dayānand Sarasvatī, 12th *Samullāsa* of his *Satyārthaprakāś*, cited in Alsdorf, p. 37.

67 *Nṛsiṃhatāpanīya Up.* 2.6.2. 68 *Ch. Up.* 1.2.1–7.

hearing.[69] Life alone remains pure goodness, free from demonic influence. A similar Upaniṣadic text begins with the same struggle between the gods and their older brothers, the demons, fighting to obtain these worlds:

The gods had the loud chant sung by speech, the breath (in the nose), the eye, the ear, and the mind; each time, the demons pierced it with evil, so that one speaks evil as well as good, sees evil as well as good, and so forth. Finally, the breath in the mouth sang the chant, and the demons, wishing to pierce him with evil, were destroyed. The gods increased while the demons became inferior; the divinity who is the essence of the limbs removed evil, that is death, from these deities. Freed from death, speech became fire, smell became wind, the eye became the sun, the ear became the quarters of heaven, the mind became the moon.[70]

Here again, the demons succeed in making the senses morally ambivalent, but now—in contrast with the first text, where the departing breath dooms the body and all its senses to death—the breath of life makes the senses univalent from the standpoint of *power*, the true essence of divinity: the senses become immortal and are actually translated to heaven. Indeed, in an almost identical episode it is explicitly said that the gods did *not* contend against the demons, that the gods introduced evil into each of the senses except breath in order to overcome death and evil and to enter heaven.[71] That these divine faculties play out their scene originally on a human stage—a stage which the demons pollute in the course of the action—is clear from the assumed locus of the senses and is made explicit by Śaṅkara's gloss on the first text: "The gods, called Devas because they shine forth (*dīv*), are the action of the senses highlighted by the textbooks: the demons are opposed to the gods and are called Asuras because they delight (*ra*) in life (*asu*), that is in the activities of the life's breath and in all sensations; these latter, demonic actions of the senses have darkness (*tamas*) as their nature."[72] The opposition of light and darkness is implicit in the name of the gods, though the demonic etymology is perhaps forced; but the essence of Śaṅkara's definition is that gods and demons are opposed (*viparītās*) and that their battle takes place within the human senses. These strikingly Manichean texts and commentary present a basic assumption that is upheld in the majority of myths, where man's evil, resulting directly from the misuse of the senses (through lust and anger), is a casualty of the cosmic battle—a battle often equated with the sacrifice performed by men. But the corollary—that the demons create that evil—is contradicted by these myths, which generally blame the belligerent gods. In some Purāṇic texts, as we have seen, these ideas combine in the statement that the evil impulses of man are caused by the demonic descendants of Alakṣmī and Death—themselves ultimately descended from Brahmā himself.[73]

[69] See below, chap. VI, sec. 3. [70] *Bṛhadāraṇyaka Up.* 1.3.1–17; cf. *Śata.* 14.4.1.1–8.

[71] *Jai. Up. Br.* 2.10.1–22; see below, chap. VIII, sec. 2.

[72] Śaṅkara on *Ch. Up.* 1.2.1. [73] See above, chap. III, sec. 2. (*Mārk.* 47.33–37).

In order to remove religious power from the gods, the demons may try to destroy it altogether. "Śiva created all of this," states one late text, "but the demons, Yakṣas, Rākṣasas and Piśācas have made an obstacle to it."[74] The demons' willing participation in their own corruption and the subsequent corruption of others is already implicit in the Upaniṣads:

The gods and demons came to Brahmā and asked him to tell them the Self. He thought to himself, "These demons desire a different Self [from the true Self]." Therefore a very different doctrine was taught to them, a doctrine which fools here believe in, praising what is false.[75]

The "fools here" are mortals on earth, apparently; if so, this myth makes demons responsible for an important heresy, though Brahmā invents it and presses it upon them. This possibility is enhanced by another Upaniṣadic myth:

Prajāpati said that the one who understands the Self obtains all worlds and all desires. Both the gods and the demons heard this, and the gods sent Indra from among them, while the demons sent Virocana. Without speaking to each other, the two of them approached Prajāpati and lived as disciples with him for thirty-two years. . . . Prajāpati taught them that the Self that they saw reflected in a mirror or a pan of water was the true Self. The two of them went forth, satisfied, and Prajāpati thought, "They have not comprehended the Self. Whoever has such a doctrine, whether they be gods or demons, shall perish." Virocana came to the demons and taught them, "Whoever makes himself happy here on earth obtains both worlds, this world and the world beyond." Therefore even now here on earth they say of one who does not give [money to Brahmins], who does not believe, and who does not sacrifice, "He is like a demon," for this is the doctrine of the demons. But Indra was dissatisfied with what he had learned, and he went back to Prajāpati for a hundred and one years and learned the doctrine of the Self, and since the gods had this doctrine they obtained all worlds and all desires.[76]

The doctrine that the demons learn seems to be a kind of Materialism. Although Prajāpati is the one who teaches them (and the myth might thus be included in the more common group of those in which the gods delude the demons, rather than with those in which the demons are the deluders), it is nevertheless evident that the demons and gods are exposed to the same temptation, and that some flaw in the demons causes them to accept the false doctrine, while the gods go on to seek the truth. Moreover, whatever the source of their own corruption, the demons are definitely responsible for the creation of heresy among men on earth, the Materialism that is known as the doctrine of the demons. The demonic doctrine which the *Bhagavad Gītā* calls atheistic ("They say the universe is

[74] *Skanda Purāṇa*, Sahyādri Khaṇḍa 16.77.

[75] *Mait. Up.* 7.10. [76] *Ch. Up.* 8.7–12.

without a lord"), lascivious, deluded, and harmful to others is identified by Śaṅkara as Materialism.[77]

Some orthodox Hindus have maintained that Materialism was called the demon philosophy[78] because "degenerates attracted each other."[79] The *Vāyu Purāṇa* contains an episode that specifically describes the demons' intention to create a heresy: "During the battle between gods and demons, the conquered demons changed all men into heretics; this was not part of the creation by Prajāpati."[80] These were the Jains, Buddhists, and the naked ones who do not practise dharma, the barbarian Niṣādas, atheists, and other evil-doers.[81] A later text describes at length a similar perversion:

In ancient times, the mortals, being pious through the due performance of their duties, could go to heaven at the mere wish, and the gods also grew stronger by getting their due share in the sacrifices. Consequently, the Daiteyas and Asuras could not prevail upon the gods. In course of time two Daiteyas, Śaṇḍa and Marka by name, intended to annihilate the gods and performed a dangerous *kṛtyā* (a magic rite or witch meant for destructive purposes), from which came out a dreadful figure called Mahāmoha ["Great delusion"], who had a very dark body resembling a mass of darkness and was extremely fierce, haughty, deceitful and lazy. . . . This Mahāmoha, who was *adharma* in person and was polluted by pride and other vices, took his position among the people and deluded them in various ways. By his misleading instructions he turned them worthless through infatuation and made them discard their conscience as well as their respective duties enjoined upon them by their castes. . . . Thus they led themselves as well as others to hell.[82]

This text preserves an assumption more representative of the mythology of the Brāhmaṇas than that of the Purāṇas, which rarely attribute a heresy to the demons; this is the assumption that, as the gods are strengthened by the sacrifices of devout men, it is to the advantage of the demons to interfere with human morality. That the demons interfere with the sacrifice is a belief shared by Brāhmaṇas and Purāṇas alike; it is the main business of demons. But that they should do so by corrupting men, though this would seem an obvious expedient, is a corollary which one encounters surprisingly rarely. Moreover, the text fails to make clear how this corruption has the effect intended by the demons; though they are successful in their attempts to mislead mankind, they themselves are also doomed to hell.

A myth which equates heretics with demons is used to justify the killing of a heretic by a Brahmin:

A Materialist who was a Rākṣasa disguised as a Brahmin beggar approached Yudhiṣṭhira and chastised him for having murdered his kinsmen. The Brahmins then told Yudhiṣṭhira, "This is a Rākṣasa named Materialist, who has assumed the form of a wandering beggar." They struck him down and burnt him up, and when Yudhiṣṭhira

[77] *Gītā* 16.7–18; Śaṅkara on 16.8. [78] Chattopadhyaya, pp. 14ff.

[79] *Ibid.*, p. 17, Shastri, D. R., *passim*. [80] *Vāyu* 78.29–30. [81] *Vāyu* (Bombay) 2.16.29–35.

[82] *Viṣṇudharma Purāṇa*, chap. 25, cited in Hazra (1958), p. 128. See below, chap. V, sec. 8.

expressed concern they said, "Formerly, in the Golden Age, there was a Rākṣasa named Materialist, who performed great asceticism, so that Brahmā granted him safety from all creatures. Then the evil one heated the gods [with his ascetic power], and the gods asked Brahmā to slay him. Brahmā said, "He will be killed soon, for he will be the friend of Duryodhana [the enemy of Yudhiṣṭhira], and out of love for Duryodhana the Rākṣasa will dishonor Brahmins, who will kill him."[83]

As usual, the demon is associated with the Materialist heresy, though here it amounts to little more than the nonviolent misgivings expressed elsewhere by Yudhiṣṭhira himself and voiced by Arjuna in the *Gītā*. This heresy fails to bring about the corruption of mankind; quite the contrary: the demon's love for an evil mortal destroys the demon. This myth is patterned on the common motif of the virtuous or powerful ascetic who must be made to utter a heresy in order to justify his destruction. Nevertheless, it does support the argument that at least some heretics were regarded as demons.

A later manifestation of the dualistic philosophy of evil appears in a Sanskrit play in which the heresies themselves, personified, are said to attempt to corrupt the orthodox virtues in order to preserve their own race:

Hypocrisy entered and said, "Great Delusion has commanded me thus: 'Discrimination and his ministers have sent Tranquility, Self-control, and the others to various holy shrines in order to encourage Enlightenment. The destruction of our race is imminent, and you must take pains to prevent it. Go to the city of Benares, the holy place where beatitude is obtained, and interrupt the religious performances of those who are engaged in asceticism.' "[84]

The forces of evil act here in opposition to the forces of good, and mankind is caught in the cross fire.

The belief that the gods wish men to be good but that demons make them evil occurs from time to time in Sanskrit texts:

A Rākṣasa carried off the wife of a Brahmin, but he did not eat her. A king questioned him about this and received the following reply: "We are not man-eaters; that is another kind of demon. We eat the fruit of a good deed. When we eat the patience of men, then they become angry; when we have eaten their evil nature, they become virtuous."[85]

The demon in this story is responsible for the disruption of the chain of karma in both directions. He destroys the power that causes men to pay for their past actions and thus changes evil men to good, as well as the reverse.

A more subtle accusation of demon heresy may be present in a Brāhmaṇa text which states that the demon Kapila, son of Prahlāda, introduced the system of the four stages of life (student, householder, forest-dweller, ascetic) when the

[83] *MBh.* 12.39.22–49. [84] *Prabodhacandrodaya*, act II, prose before verse 1.

[85] *Mārk.* 67.17–18.

demons were competing with the gods.[86] This act would have weakened the gods, since they could not received offerings from forest-dwellers or ascetics.[87] Thus the system would drain off participants in the householder stage and deprive the gods of the fruits of the sacrifice. It would also deprive the Brahmins of their sacrificial fees—one reason for the antiascetic bias of the Brahmin authors of the texts.

There is one late, strikingly Manichean Hindu myth that may in fact derive directly from Persian influence; it concerns the mythological hagiography of Śaṅkara, as "revised" by his enemies:

In the Kali Age, knowledge of the Vedas at first reigned supreme. But then the demons conspired to spread false doctrines. The demon Śakuni, urged by the son of a Materialist, pointed out that other heresies such as those of the Materialists, Jains, and Pāśupatas, had all failed. Therefore the demon Maṇimat, who alone had sufficient skill, became incarnate as a Brahmin ascetic in order to destroy the Vedānta while pretending to explain it. He was born as Śaṅkara.[88]

Maṇimat (who appears in the Epic) might owe his name to the Manicheans, a term given by Indians to the many Persians living there at the time this text was composed. It is possible that the author of the text, who was said to speak the language of the foreigners, was acquainted with Manicheanism.

The Indian tribal tradition contains several manifestations of the belief that demons rather than gods are responsible for the corruption of man. As in the myths of the Fall, some of these show apparent Christian influence:

[God created man, who lived happily without pain. God made a tree as a covenant; men could climb up and down the tree to heaven, but must not cut it down. A monster from the bottom of the ocean was jealous of the happiness of men. He tricked men into cutting down the tree, lest it grow to hide the light of the sun, moon, and stars. When they cut it down, the sun and moon hid; there was darkness, and sin and pain arose.][89]

The image of the tree is equally familiar to Hindu and Christian mythology, and the generosity with which God allows man to climb up to heaven is equally foreign to both. The tree that brings darkness when cut down is reminiscent of the "limb" of Śiva that causes darkness when it is cut down in the Pine Forest,[90] and the monster from the bottom of the ocean may be a form of the destructive submarine mare.[91] The Reverend Heras read several Christian motifs into this myth, for he regarded the monster as a "stranger who was a demon in disguise," who "tempted man with the strange food," so that "the entire human race had

[86] *Baudhāyana Dharmasūtra* 2.6.11.28, citing "a Brāhmaṇa." [87] Lingat (1973), p. 50.

[88] *Maṇimañjarī*, chap. 5, vv. 1–29; Grierson, p. 236; see below, chap. VII, sec. 7.

[89] Narayan, pp. 454–462. [90] See below, chap. X, sec. 5, and O'Flaherty (1973), pp. 172–209.

[91] O'Flaherty (1973), pp. 289–292, and (1971*b*).

become subject to the power of the demon,"[92] but none of this is implicit in the extant text of the myth.

Another Indian tribe believed that while God slept the devil performed certain destructive actions and brought death into the world.[93] The devil is responsible for death in a myth from middle India:

[Mahadeo wanted to teach the Gonds certain magic] but Naita Dhobnin thought, "If these twelve brothers become adepts at this art, . . . [and] if they eat Mahadeo's body, . . . no one in the world will die." [She tricked Mahadeo so that he became ill, and she told the Gonds to cook and eat him. But then, saying, "What a great sin is this!", she tricked the Gonds into throwing the flesh into the river. She took the form of a crocodile and swallowed the flesh, and so she became a great witch.][94]

Once again the corruption of man is associated with a woman and with a food tabu, but here no blame rests on mankind or the gods. A similar witch appears in the popular tradition as Jātahāriṇī, "a certain goddess who plays tricks with mankind. If a son when grown up acts differently from what his parents did, people say that he has been changed in the womb"; it is she who is held responsible for transforming a Brahmin's son, raised in the strictest orthodoxy, into "a high Buddhist, or in other words an utter atheist."[95]

The Sanskrit tradition, however, does not usually regard demons in this way. One Rākṣasa maintains that it is mankind who make demons evil, rather than the reverse:

"We are hungry and eternally devoid of dharma," said the Rākṣasa. "We do not do all the evil that we do because of our own desire; it is because of your evil karma, and your disfavor toward us. Our faction increases because of the Brahmins who behave like Rākṣasas and the evil actions of the other three classes. Those who dishonor Brahmins become Rākṣasas, and our ranks are swelled by the sexual sins of evil women."[96]

In one text of this myth, the sages to whom the Rākṣasa makes this complaint take pity on him and designate various sorts of unclean food for him; then, for their salvation, the sages produce the Sarasvatī river for the Rākṣasas to bathe in, and the Rākṣasas are released from their sins and go to heaven.[97] Thus the force of karma may be transferred in either direction; the demons cannot be made to bear the entire blame, for often they are simply produced by evil mortals or reborn from mortals who were evil in a former life and cursed to become demons.[98] (One late text reverses this assumption and states that those who were formerly Rākṣasas became Brahmin heretics in the Kali Age.)[99] The more usual belief, that evil men become or nourish Rākṣasas, leads to the corollary that demons are given as their food various groups of sinners and are allowed to dwell in the houses of

[92] Heras, p. 237. [93] Lewin pp. 225–226. [94] Elwin (1949), p. 451.
[95] Burton, p. 162. Cf. *Mārk.* 48.103–104. [96] *Vāmana S.* 19.31–35.
[97] *MBh.* 9.42.14–26. [98] Dubois, p. 516. [99] *Devībhāgavata* 6.11.42.

evil men.[100] This is implicit in the statement that when the demons have eaten the evil nature of men, the men become virtuous; from this point of view, the demons ultimately destroy evil rather than produce it. As Obeyesekere remarks, "Only the sinner can come to harm [from demons]. This amounts to an ethicization of the actions of demons."[101] This ethicization may even be read back into the previous lives of the demons; as Eliade remarks, "The goddess Hariti is said to have obtained the right to eat children as a consequence of merits gained in a previous existence."[102] Here the demons eat food that is "innocent," and yet their actions are justified by their own previous innocence, their own good karma, which functions as the equivalent of the bad karma of their victims.

These scattered myths about demons who cause evil and heresy to arise on earth form no coherent pattern. Most of them are isolated reversals of more common patterns in which the demons are *not* responsible for the creation of evil. In fact, the majority of these myths seem to be more concerned with an attempt to explain how the demons themselves came to be evil (usually through the agency of gods or men) rather than how, if at all, they cause others to be evil.

5. The Three Stages of Alignment of Gods, Demons, and Men

Thus the Manichean solution, in Indian texts, is not a solution. The rejection of the possibility that the devil could be made responsible for evil resulted in a polarization of the two remaining forces–God and man. God was made to replace the devil as the source of evil, and man became God's enemy not because of man's sinfulness but because of man's godliness and because of the weakness–the ungodliness–of God. This failure of Manicheanism makes God malevolently responsible for evil; God is the devil. The evolution of this concept can best be understood in the context of the evolution of Indian religion under the influence of the three major trends: sacrifice, asceticism, and devotion (bhakti).

In addition to all the usual problems of arbitrary periodization, the division of Indian religion into three distinct periods is complicated by the continuity of the Indian tradition; by the absence of data regarding nonreligious events (economic, social, political) which might have inspired sudden changes; by the tendency of attitudes to persist from one period, in addition to new ideas which one might have expected to replace them; and by the frequent occurrence of intentional archaism–the resurrection of old ideas in order to lend an air of tradition to a late text. In designating these three periods as Vedic, post-Vedic (or orthodox), and devotional (bhakti), one is referring not to three discrete strata of

[100] *Mārk.* 47.42–61. [101] Obeyesekere, p. 34.

[102] Eliade (1938), pp. 201ff.; (1965), p. 96. See above, chap. I, sec. 2.

texts but rather to three attitudes, each one a reaction to the one preceding it and thus "later" in an ideological sense, though not necessarily in a chronological sense. The Vedic period includes the Ṛg Veda and many Brāhmaṇas and Upaniṣads, but the Vedic attitude also persists in many parts of the *Mahābhārata,* the *Rāmāyaṇa*, and the Purāṇas. The post-Vedic stage includes some late Brāhmaṇas and Upaniṣads, though it is mainly composed of Epic and Purāṇic texts; as this is the prevalent, "orthodox" Hindu attitude, this group also draws upon the Dharmaśāstras. The bhakti myths appear in many of these same texts (though not in the Dharmaśāstras) and in some Tantras as well.

In the first, the Vedic period, gods and demons are clearly opposed to one another, and gods unite with men against the demons. In Vedic times, when gods were thought to live on sacrificial offerings provided by devout men, the gods wished men to be virtuous, for then they would continue to offer sacrifices;[103] the demons interfered with the sacrifice in order to weaken the gods; occasionally this action may have incidentally corrupted mankind. Though men served merely as pawns in the cosmic battle, it was in their interest to serve the gods, for the demons would try to kill men (in order to divert the sacrifice from the gods) —unless men were protected by gods sated by sacrificial offerings. The origin of evil is not directly discussed in the Ṛg Veda, which merely establishes the fundamental relationship between gods and men; nor do the Brāhmaṇas come to grips with the problem, though they formulate the basic terms in which subsequent texts viewed the matter; the Brāhmaṇas are content with an immediate solution on the ritual level, the mythic belief that anything that was dealt with successfully "then," at the time of primeval creation, is satisfactorily redisposed of whenever that ritual is reenacted. In this period, sacrifice is power.

This straightforward alignment of forces—men and gods vs. demons—changed radically in the second period, the post-Vedic, when sacrificial power came largely to be replaced by ascetic and meditative power. Myths of this period began to be drafted from the standpoint of men, as Brahmins came to regard themselves as more important to cosmic order than the gods themselves. The Brahmin authors of these texts felt that men and demons might threaten the gods with ascetic virtue; jealous gods treated good men as their enemies, while ascetic demons were more dangerous to the gods than were "demonic" demons. These were the first myths to attempt to explain the problems and evils of men, and they did so simply by applying to men the role that had originally been taken by demons. Thus there is a basic antagonism between gods and men in post-Vedic mythology arising at first not from a theological hypothesis but rather from an inherited pattern of myth: the gods corrupt and destroy men because they treat men as they treated demons.

[103] See above, chap. II, sec. 5.

In spite of the great importance of asceticism in Hindu philosophy and cult, Hindu mythology is generally antiascetic.[104] The ascetic is regarded as virtuous, good, and holy, and he may achieve his goal within a myth, but he causes trouble, often provoking the gods to overcome him by placing some form of evil in him. When the Brahmins recast the Vedic myths in the second period, men had acquired new sources of religious power. This power appeared in two distinct spheres of Indian religious thought. Within the ritual tradition, the Brahmins maintained that they alone, by performing the sacrifice, could ensure the achievement of the ends for which the sacrifice was being performed, without the participation of the gods at all. A very different kind of emphasis on human, individual religiosity appeared at roughly the same period in the Upaniṣadic texts, which maintained that, without participation in ritual, a man could achieve a kind of immortality equal or indeed superior to that of the gods, through his own individual efforts. The attitude of the Brahmins reworking the myths was very different with regard to these two groups (orthodox priests and individual ascetics), and it must be remembered that priests were the authors of almost all the texts in which the myths appear.

The role of the human priest was one of mediation between gods and men. In the mythology of the first stage, priests were thought to mediate between the two opposed powers, gods and demons. When, in the second stage, mankind began to be regarded as a force important enough to participate more actively in the myths, there were only two roles from which they could choose their part in the rigid, inherited pattern of the cosmic drama: divine heroes or demonic villains. At the time of this recasting, the position of the priests was already assured; they called themselves "gods on earth" or "human gods,"[105] and they were willing to extend the benefits of their lofty contacts to their ritual patrons. But it was in the interest of the Brahmins to convince these patrons that the gods regarded powerful human beings of the nonritual sphere as demons and treated them accordingly. Thus the pattern that had been established in Vedic myths of gods and demons were now applied to gods and men: excessive power or virtue in an opponent was to be destroyed. And so, at this second stage, the priests came to mediate between the gods and their twofold challengers—men and demons—who (without the intervention of the priests) would be destroyed or corrupted by the gods. Thus the Brahmin authors of the texts regarded human beings who remained within the ritual contexts—Brahmins and their patrons—as gods; but those mortals who aspired to religious power outside the ritual sphere inherited the role of demons in the cosmic masque.

Gods were competing against men and demons for a limited quantity of what both sides desired—power, immortality, heaven. In the context of this antagon-

[104] O'Flaherty (1973), pp. 40–82. [105] *Manu* 9.317, 319; *Śata.* 2.2.2.6.

ism, the problem of evil as it exists in the West is irrelevant; it is not surprising that an omniscient and omnipotent god will inflict suffering and delusion on men, if men are his enemies. This assumption persists until and indeed well into the bhakti period; it underlies the majority of classical Hindu texts and may be called the "orthodox" Hindu view, the view against which bhakti and Tantrism later rebelled.

These ethical developments are reflected in changes in the cosmologies of the first two periods. In the Vedic period, heaven and earth were the two great worlds, joined (or, from the Hindu point of view, separated) by the intervening ether. All the essential activity of the cosmos was transacted between gods in heaven and men on earth; demons were outside the system altogether, though they threatened both worlds from the outside. But in the Purāṇic period, the two great worlds were heaven and hell, joined (or, again, separated) by earth; Sumeru ("good Meru"), the world-mountain at the center of the earth, the umbilical link between gods and men, was now given a demonic counterpart, a mirror-image in the underworld–Kumeru ("bad Meru"). The world-mountain, which had provided access upwards, now extends down as well–and the gods oppose human and demonic ascetics who, by interiorizing these pillars within the spinal column, would mount to heaven. Evil has been assimilated into the system, and cosmology has become ethically dualized.

A secondary result of the reaction against asceticism in the orthodox period was the emphasis on the code of *svadharma*, one's own role in the social order. The ascetic and Upaniṣadic ideal implied an absolute view of evil and a way in which it could be overcome. An individual could break away from the evil of his own caste, or his own time, and swim against the current of the universe to find his own release. Hindus and Buddhists agreed that evil was implicit in human life, but the orthodox Hindu view then stated as the corollary to this theory the belief that certain individuals were doomed to remain at least temporarily in the toils of that evil. Each member of society has his own *svadharma*, and of necessity some of these must be evil roles (the slaughterer of animals, the presser of seeds), the benefits of whose labors are enjoyed by castes too pure to indulge in them themselves. As these tasks are necessary, they are not considered conducive to damnation. On the contrary, it is only by abandoning one's own impure *svadharma* in aspiration to a higher way of life that, in the classical Hindu system, the individual is damned. These texts of the second period see the conflict between good and evil in a particular, temporal framework: dharma is what is good or right for the particular occasion, what one should do given the social and familiar position occupied and in the face of the particular obstacles of the moment (hence the need for *āpad-dharma*, the dharma of emergencies). Though this code changed from time to time, the myths betray little doubt as to what was dharma and what was adharma; yet there was no absolute good or evil recognized as the enduring standard.

The ascetic violated this relativistic order by attempting to create a new, non-sacrificial, antisocial form of power. Asceticism introduces ambiguities into the post-Vedic alignment of loyalties: while Vedic gods want men to be good (sacrificial), post-Vedic gods do not want men to be good (ascetic). The sacrifice helps the gods, creating mutual dependence; asceticism hurts the gods, producing a challenge from men which breaches the basic Vedic relationship of human dependence on the gods or demonic inferiority to the gods. Asceticism negates the distinction between the categories of gods, demons, and men, producing a problem which can be resolved in either of two ways: one can negate the negation (destroy the ascetic power of the man or demon) or negate the categories (make the ascetic man or demon into a god). The first solution is usually adopted by post-Vedic mythology; the second occurs in the devotional mythology of the third period, the bhakti period.

Bhakti resolves the conflict between gods and good men or demons by reintroducing the Vedic concept of dependence on the gods; thus devoted (*bhakta*) men and devoted demons are protected by the gods, who encourage virtue in men–and (unlike the Vedic corpus) in demons too. In the Vedic age, gods and men are complementary, while demons are antagonistic to both; in the post-Vedic age, men and demons are complementary, in that often they are both antagonistic to the gods; and in the bhakti age, men and good demons are complementary to each other and to the gods, who oppose only evil demons and evil men. Against the élitist, Establishment view, the bhakti texts set the alternative which the priests had previously obscured, that the gods might be willing to make good men or demons into gods. This view eliminates the need for any priests at all, for men and gods are now joined in a mutual dependence, which is direct and personal, unlike the Vedic dependence, which relied on priestly mediation. Thus bhakti mythology displays an increasingly cynical attitude to the now logically superfluous but nevertheless persistent figure of the priest of the demons or the gods.[106]

The manner in which bhakti myths can resolve the conflicts between Vedic and post-Vedic assumptions is evident from a Tamil text:

The gods complained to Śiva that sinners without merit were worshipping at a certain shrine and reaching Śiva. "What is the use of the preeminence you have given us?" they asked. "No one worships us, we receive no sacrificial portions or horse sacrifice, and hell is deserted." Śiva said, "You yourselves reached your present status by performing asceticism at a shrine. Would it be right to stop others from worshipping there? And you should worship there, too, and obtain release."[107]

[106] See below, chap. V, secs. 4, 12, and 15.

[107] *Viruttācalapurāṇam* 6.1–24.

The gods are troubled both by receiving no sacrifice (i.e., mortals are not virtuous enough in the Vedic sense) and by losing their preeminence of ascetic power (i.e., mortals are too virtuous in the post-Vedic sense). The gods are being bypassed just as priests are bypassed in bhakti cults, their preeminence threatened just as the priestly hierarchy was disregarded. The solution is that gods and mortals will be united by bhakti and that the jealousy as well as the sacrificial requirements of the gods will become superfluous when the gods obtain release (just as demons are often rendered innocuous by being "helped" to seek release[108]).

The texts of the bhakti period reflect the humanizing effects of later Buddhism and of the sectarian movements, expressing the view that the gods participate willingly in the evils of the human condition because of their love for mankind. This aspect of the bhakti cult coincided superficially with one attitude of the orthodox texts: God committed sins and taught them to mankind, not (as in the earlier view) because of his own inevitable weakness or malevolence, but in order to save mankind.[109] The motive has changed, but the effect is the same.

The three stages somewhat approximate the three paths described in the *Bhagavad Gītā*: the sacrificial stage (karma-yoga), when sacrifice is power; the second stage (jñāna-yoga), when asceticism or knowledge is power; and the third stage (bhakti-yoga), when devotion is power. The alignments of the three groups of forces (gods, demons, and men) remain remarkably rigid in each stage, regardless of the apparent "virtue" or "sin," the dharma or adharma, of any of the individuals involved in the myths. Indeed, attitudes appropriate to earlier alignments often persist in later myths where the moral qualities of the characters make these attitudes totally illogical. The individual is judged by the group to which he belongs; though he may free himself from that group by asceticism or devotion, ultimately the judgment of *svadharma* prevails in most texts (one reason for calling this the "orthodox" view); it is certainly the majority view, the conceptual framework in which the bulk of Hindu mythology is set. In order to understand the role of demons under this prevalent attitude, it is best to examine first the original attitude from which it diverged and then to compare representative texts from the second period.

6. The First Stage: Vedic Sacrifice (Gods and Men vs. Demons)

W. Norman Brown describes the demons as creatures who oppose creation, "patrons of inertia and destruction" who live in darkness under the earth, where there is no cosmic order:

> Regrettably, deities and human beings cannot pursue their duties without interference; the demons living in the Asat [the area of nonexistence and nongoodness, outside cosmic

[108] See below, chap. V, sec. 12. [109] See below, chap. X, sec. 7.

order] are ever active to prevent them. . . . The gods seem not to be vulnerable to the demons' attack, perhaps because of copious draughts of Soma. . . . To foil the demons, gods and human beings unite their efforts, the gods by use of their might, which is greater than that of the demons, especially when they are well fortified with Soma, men by providing plentiful offerings in the sacrifice . . . and by giving them Soma, which arouses the gods' fighting fury to slay the demons, who fortunately are mortal. . . . The warfare between the gods and the demons is never-ending, for the demons breed prolifically; each morning there is a new brood.[110]

In later Vedic times, the demons were divided into two groups: the Asuras, the enemies of the gods, and the flesh-eating Rākṣasas, lower powers, the enemies of men.[111] But Rākṣasas and Asuras join forces in most battles, blurring again the attempted distinction; gods, men, and ancestors fight together against Asuras, Rākṣasas, and Piśācas.[112] Since Asuras, not Rākṣasas, are almost always the initiators of cosmic problems, these problems must be regarded as primarily an affair of the gods, in which men are embroiled. These distinctions are not of great significance in the Vedic period, but they are implicit in and essential to the post-Vedic myths.

Gods and demons may be consanguine in the Vedic period, but they are often sharply distinguished—to the discredit of the demons (a qualification that does not always pertain in the post-Vedic period). Often the demons are the direct opponents of men:

Manu [the ancestor of all mankind] had a bull whose roar killed Asuras and Rākṣasas. The Asuras said, "Alas! This bull inflicts evil on us. How can we destroy him?" The two priests of the demons tricked Manu into sacrificing the bull, but the voice then entered Manu's wife; again they tricked him into sacrificing her, and the voice entered the sacrificial vessels, where it always resides, killing Asuras.[113]

Sometimes the gods intervene to help men pitted against demons:

The gods and demons, both born of Prajāpati, once fought for supremacy. The demons then defiled, partly by magic, partly with poison, the plants on which men and beasts live, hoping thus to overcome the gods. Because of this, men and beasts began to starve, and when the gods heard of this they rid the plants of poison by means of a sacrifice.[114]

Here, however, it is clearly in the gods' own interest to help men, who were only attacked by demons in the first place in order that the true enemies of the demons—the gods—would be harmed, not (as in the Manu myth) because of any basic enmity between demons and men.

[110] Brown (1942), p. 88; (1941), pp. 76–80 (re *RV* 7.104); (1972), p. 62.

[111] Keith (1925), I, 239. [112] *Tait. Sam.* 2.4.1.

[113] *Śata.* 1.1.4.14–17, and see below, chap. V, sec. 8. [114] *Śata.* 2.4.3.2–3.

Self-interest motivates the gods in other instances when they assist men or banish evil from men. The usual method of the gods is to create a sort of *capo regime* to keep unruly mortal men in line:[115]

The gods and men failed to subdue the people by kindnesses, and so the gods disappeared. Then Prajāpati said to them, "Who will protect creatures now that you have vanished? People, unprotected, will be afflicted with adharma, and they will cease to make the offerings which are our livelihood." Then the gods made a king to protect dharma.[116]

The gods' concern for the virtue of men is even more selfish in another Brāhmaṇa text:

Those mortals who made offerings in former times touched the altar while they were sacrificing. They became more evil. Those who washed their hands became righteous. Then men said, "Those who sacrifice become more evil, and those who do not sacrifice become righteous." No sacrificial food then came to the gods from this world. The gods therefore said to Bṛhaspati, the son of Aṅgiras, "Men no longer believe; teach them the sacrifice," and he did.[117]

A mere ritual accident accounts for the fact that men become evil in the first place, though a better reason for the origin of sin is implicit in the remark that men, observing the apparent injustice in the lack of reward for religious exertion, lose faith. But this is not an important point in the myth, which does not have to explain the origin of evil, since evil as a permanent force is denied: the gods teach men the sacrifice and everyone lives happily ever after. This fortunate state of affairs is typical of the Brāhmaṇas.

In the formula recited at the end of the Vedic ritual, the priest says, "The god has accepted the offering, he has become strengthened, he has won greater might," and the sacrificer replies, "May I prosper in accordance with the prosperity of the god."[118] This interdependence persists in later traditional Hinduism as expressed in the *Gītā* (which preserves sacrifice as one of the three paths): "With this [sacrifice] cause the gods to grow, and they will nourish you."[119] Śaṅkara says that this indicates that Indra and the other gods will give such things as rain: "Nourishing one another, you will obtain the supreme good."

Occasionally, however, the element of freely bestowed offerings takes on a more sinister hue, when it appears that men are made to sacrifice under duress, as victims of a kind of protection racket; this is apparent from a myth which emphasizes the role of Agni (fire) as a mediator between gods and men—the divine counterpart of the voracious priest:

[115] See above, chap. II, sec. 8. [116] Viśvarūpa commentary on *Yājñavalkyasmṛti* 1.350. Ghoshal (p. 20) thinks that this is "probably from a lost Brāhmaṇa." [117] *Śata*. 1.2.5.24–25.

[118] Keith (1925), p. 259. [119] *Gītā* 3.11.

Now when Prajāpati created living beings, he created Agni, who tried to burn everything here. Everyone tried to get away from him, and Agni went to man [puruṣa] *and said, "Let me enter you. If you reproduce me and keep me in this world* [*i.e., if you kindle fires*] *then I will reproduce and keep you in that world* [*i.e., give you life after cremation*]*." Man replied, "So be it," and when he dies and they place him on the fire, then he is reproduced from out of the fire. And he* (*Agni*) *who was his son before, now becomes his father.*[120]

At first, Agni behaves like a demon, threatening to eat everyone and to usurp another body.[121] Man then saves himself—and the gods—from Agni by an act of appeasement: Agni is allowed to dwell within men (as the digestive fire) as well as in the sacrificial fire; sacrifice controls Agni by feeding him, even as demonic gods may be controlled by being constantly bribed with sacrificial food. The element of mutual interdependence is here clearly tinged with a hint of threat in addition to the usual bribery.

Although the Ṛg Veda seems to freely allow the sacrificer to mount to heaven after death,[122] this doctrine sits uneasily when preserved in a later text that apparently accepts the Vedic premise but views it in a more sophisticated light: "In ancient times the mortals, being pious through the due performance of their duties, could go to heaven at the mere wish, and the gods also grew stronger by getting their due share in the sacrifices. Consequently, the Daiteyas and Asuras could not prevail upon the gods."[123] Although the gods seem to allow mortals to ascend to heaven, this situation does not ultimately prevail in this text; the mortals are corrupted—not by the gods but, in a rare Manichean episode, by the demons who wish to drain the sacrificial power of the gods.[124] This is a curious imposition of the values of Vedic mythology on a situation and plot more typical of second-stage, post-Vedic mythology.

The use of demons to corrupt inconveniently virtuous mortals is a device that frequently forms a bridge between myths of the first and second stages. The gods want mortals to sacrifice, but even excessive sacrificial virtue becomes a danger in the second period.[125] When it is demons who "have" the sacrifice—usually having stolen it from the gods—there is no question of conflicting ethics: the sacrifice must be taken from them.[126] Yet one text of this group falls back on the assumptions of the Vedic period in stating that, when demons fail to sacrifice, the gods are weakened:

The demon Raktāsura conquered the gods and ruled the triple world. One day he said to the demons, "Sacrifice to me and honor me. I will kill anyone who defends the gods. Abandon all contributions to Brahmins and enjoy the wives of the gods as much as you

[120] *Śata.* 2.3.3.1–5. cf. 2.2.4.1–8. [121] See below, chap. V, sec. 6. [122] *RV* 9.113.7–11.
[123] *Viṣṇudharma Purāṇa*, chap. 25, cited in Hazra (1958), p. 128. [124] Cf. *Jai. Up. Br.* 1.18.1–11.
[125] See below, chap. XI, sec. 3. [126] See below, chap. V., sec. 2.

please." Thus the ritual of sacrifice was destroyed, the world was without dharma, and Indra's strength was therefore reduced. The demons, knowing this, attacked Indra and conquered him. Bṛhaspati sought the help of the Goddess, who killed the demons, and the gods rejoiced.[127]

In this myth, Bṛhaspati acts, as he often does in the Brāhmaṇas, to restore sacrificial power to the gods, though here he takes the sacrifice away from the demons, instead of giving it to mortals as he does in the earlier texts.

Another uneasy balance between the benevolent gods of stage one and the malevolent gods of stage two appears in the Vedic justification for the existence of evil demons to oppose gods and men alike. W. Norman Brown has commented on the fact that the demons produce a new brood every morning to ensure that the fight will continue despite their mortality; in analyzing the Indra cycle, he suggests another reason for the resilience of the demons—the tacit compliance of the gods:

> [When Indra killed Vṛtra, everyone rejoiced.] The one flaw was that evil was not extinguished. . . . Not all the wicked were destroyed. There remained demons (Rākṣasas), who lurked in that fell place below the earth by day, but at night emerged to ensnare men, especially those who by sinning have put bonds on themselves and cannot escape. . . . Good was triumphant, therefore, but not unrivalled.
>
> It was just as well, from the gods' point of view. If they had completely annihilated evil, man would not have had any incentive to serve them, and then they would have perished for lack of the daily sacrifices. Especially would Indra, this demiurge, have lost his Soma.[128]

Apparently the gods here create—or tolerate—human evil of their own accord, not merely *faute de mieux*, just as, in tribal mythology, they create diseases so that men will have to sacrifice to them in order to be rid of diseases.[129] The myth makes it clear that some demons remain to threaten men, but this is immediately qualified by the statement that it is only sinners who are in danger—sinners who have put "bonds" on themselves (though it is the gods who usually bind men with sin[130]). This is a very good reason for men to avoid sin and to serve the gods: for the goblins will get them if they don't watch out. Thus sin is placed by the gods not *in* men but *against* men, in the form of demons; this is a typical act of divine jealousy, appropriate to post-Vedic mythology but set firmly in the context of Vedic sacrificial interdependence. The gods still want men to be good, to offer sacrifice, but in order for this to be so there must be evil elsewhere in the universe, evil against which one must sacrifice. This is why the victory of the gods is never complete—not because they are unable to conquer the demons, but because they do not wish to do so. For without demons, there would be no reason for the gods to exist at all; without Untouchables, there could be no Brahmins.

[127] *Saura* 49.7–143.

[128] Brown (1942), p. 98. [129] See above, chap. III, sec. 2.

[130] See below, chap. VI, sec. 8.

7. The Second Stage: Post-Vedic Antiascetic Orthodoxy (Gods vs. Demons and Men)

Thus even in the first stage there are implications of antipathy between gods and men, and these become explicit in the second stage. Sacrifice was a two-edged sword: though it did strengthen the gods, it sometimes also strengthened the enemies of the gods (sacrificiant demons or mortals). The confusion which this could induce even in the minds of the gods themselves is apparent from a Purāṇic myth in which a king attempts to perform a hundred horse sacrifices to Indra, an act which should strengthen Indra. But Indra prides himself on being the god of a hundred horse sacrifices (Śatakratu); originally this must have indicated a god *to whom* a hundred sacrifices were to be performed, but when the gods were recast as sacrificers as well as recipients of the sacrifice, the name was reinterpreted to mean "one who has performed a hundred sacrifices." Therefore Indra (who, in the good old days, would have welcomed precisely the homage to which his name entitled him) became jealous of the king and stole the stallion in order to prevent the sacrifice from taking place.[131] Similarly, Indra performs horse sacrifices, and Soma sacrifices, in order to expiate the sin of having killed a Brahmin demon, an act which, in Vedic times, was not a sin but a much applauded feat, and one which Indra grew powerful enough to perform by receiving the offerings of the sacrifice. Indra is sometimes said to have won his throne by asceticism, but he is so frequently threatened by other ascetics that the common phrase "fruits of asceticism" could be glossed: "becoming Indra, and so forth."[132]

Asceticism, unlike sacrifice, could only strengthen the enemies of the gods and do no good to the gods, although the gods themselves could produce ascetic power (even as they could perform sacrifices). Whereas in the first period men were encouraged to imitate the gods, men were brought into conflict with the gods by emulating them in the second period.[133] This is a complex issue in Hinduism, because religious activity could take so many different forms, some to be imitated, some not to be imitated. R. C. Zaehner noted this danger of asceticism: "The whole ascetic tradition, whether it be Buddhist, Platonist, Manichean, Christian, or Islamic, springs from that most polluted of all sources, the Satanic sin of pride, the desire to be 'like gods.' We are not gods, we are social, irrational animals, designed to become rational, social animals."[134]

From this it might appear that in Hinduism the cause of evil is considered to be man's offense against the gods as he tries to become godlike through the power of asceticism or by eating the fruit of the tree of omniscience. But this is not the case. Pride is a sin in many Hindu texts—demons in particular learn to their peril that

[131] See below, chap. XI, sec. 3, and chap. VI, sec. 5. [132] Mallinātha on *Kumārasambhava* 1.57.

[133] See below, chap. X, sec. 3, but cf. *Śata.* 1.2.2.9; 1.7.2.9; 3.1.2.4–5; 3.2.2.16.

[134] Zaehner (1974), p. 235.

pride cometh before a Fall—but the mere possession of ascetic power, in all humility, was enough to pose a dangerous threat. Moreover, trying to be like a god was not necessarily regarded as a manifestation of pride. Divinity was cheap in ancient India (priests were said to be human gods, and kings had a kind of divinity as well), but the priests who wrote the texts in which the myths appear presented their own point of view: a priest might legitimately emulate the gods, but an ascetic should not. An ambitious priest was like a god; an ambitious ascetic was like a demon.

Just as Hindu gods and demons often behaved alike, so, in the second-stage myths, men and demons often share roles. When you separate the devil from God and banish the devil—that is, when Manicheanism appears and is rejected—man becomes the source of evil and is opposed to God.[135] The Hindu texts maintain that there are only two forces in the world, truth and falsehood, and no third force;[136] but these powers are associated with different factions at different times. At first it is said that Prajāpati created the gods out of truth and the demons out of falsehood;[137] but another text makes it clear that these are not inherent qualities, but ones that were achieved after original creation took place;[138] and it is also said that, while the gods are truth, men are falsehood.[139]

8. The Jealousy of the Gods

The opposition between men and gods arises, therefore, not from any sin committed by mankind, but rather from a structural opposition between men and gods, resembling (and often replacing) the opposition between demons and gods. The gods are in competition with men in the post-Vedic period, just as they are in competition with demons in the Vedic period. Even in the Vedic period, the enemies of the gods (Panis, Dasyus or Dāsas) are regarded sometimes as human, sometimes as demonic; as Keith remarks, "Their name denotes 'Niggard,' especially with regard to the sacrificial gifts, and thus, no doubt, an epithet of human meanness has been transferred to demoniac foes."[140] The Brahmin authors of these texts were equally prone to transfer the evils wrought by demons to the accounts of the human sinners par excellence—the niggardly sacrificers. In the *Mahābhārata*, too, demons and evil men are joined in battle against the gods, though, in typical Hindu fashion, men are still mere pawns in the cosmic battle, this time on the side of evil:

In the ancient battle between gods and demons, the gods were the younger brothers, the demons the older. They fought a bloody battle for Śrī, and the gods conquered the demons and attained heaven. Nevertheless, certain Brahmins, learned in the Vedas, obtained the earth, became deluded by pride, and assisted the demons. They became known as "dogs" or

[135] Jung (1954), p. 37. [136] *Śata.* 1.1.1.4; 1.1.2.17; 3.3.2.2; 3.9.4.1.
[137] *Mait. Sam.* 1.9.3. [138] *Śata.* 9.5.1.12–27; see above, chap. IV, sec. 3.
[139] *Śata.* 1.1.2.17; *Air. Br.* 1.6; *Śata.* 1.1.1.4–5. [140] Keith (1917), p. 166.

"jackals," and the gods killed eighty-eight thousand of them, for those evil ones who oppose dharma are to be slain as the gods slew the venomous demons.[141]

The Hindu gods at first appear to be jealous in their ambivalent relationship with men. They are jealous of other gods in that they require men to sacrifice to them (though not necessarily to sacrifice only to them; they are generally tolerant in this respect[142]); and they are also jealous of men, jealous enough to fight to keep for themselves, and to keep away from men, those qualities which distinguish them–in particular, the quality of immortality and the right to reside in heaven,[143] for death and heaven distinguish man from god.

The line between Hindu gods and men is not inalienably fixed. The elusive quality of immortality may be purchased or stolen like any other treasure:

The qualitative superiority of anthropomorphically conceived gods and demons over man himself is at first only relative.... They are neither omniscient nor omnipotent, ... nor necessarily eternal.... However, they often have the ability to secure their glamorous existence by means of magical food and drink which they have reserved for themselves, much as human lives may be prolonged by the magical potions of the medical man.[144]

Read "priest" for "medical man" and the reason for the persistence of this kind of mythology in Hinduism is obvious. Throughout the Vedas, the gods jealously refuse to share the Soma with the demons; in the *Mahābhārata,* when men begin to threaten them, the gods refuse to share the Soma with men.[145]

From time to time, mortals become immortals and the hierarchy is upset. This creates in Indian mythology the circumstance that mortals come up to heaven and trouble the gods, in contrast, for example, with the Greek, where the gods usually interfere in the affairs of men on earth. For, just as the gods oppose the demons because gods and demons are alike, so they compete with men because they fear that men, too, may be no different from gods. The exception to this general rule is the avatar (primarily associated with Viṣṇu, though Śiva also has avatars, usually called *svarūpas*, "forms of himself," and often appears in disguise as a mortal). But the avatar is temporary and "playful" (undertaken in a spirit of play, *līlā*, or illusion, *māyā*); moreover, avatars usually occur in response to a challenge from a mortal or demon who has usurped divine powers and reversed the avatar process. This transfiguration of a mortal (known as *āropa*) is regarded as a danger in pre-bhakti texts, which pit the gods against virtuous demons and men, but it comes to be regarded as a desirable process in later bhakti texts, which assume that God loves men and wishes to help them find salvation. In these latter texts, men are encouraged to become immortal and to go to heaven; but this is certainly not the prevalent attitude of pre-bhakti texts, nor is it the prevailing Indian attitude in general.

141 *MBh.* 12.34.13–18. 142 See below, chap. VII, sec. 7. 143 See below, chaps. VIII and IX.
144 Weber (1963), p. 33. 145 O'Flaherty (1975), pp. 56–60; *MBh.* 14.45.12–35.

The concept that the gods are sometimes jealous of mortals occurs in Indian tribal mythology. The Agaria believe that the loss of the Golden Age and the fall of the Agaria kingdom were due to the jealousy and subsequent treachery of Bhagvan, the Lord.[146] The Marias consider the gods to be both jealous and petty-minded:

A Kol story from Bondi shows the Supreme Chando so exasperated at the sight of the parents of mankind enjoying sexual intercourse that he killed them out of jealousy. A Kuruk tale describes how Mahapurub destroyed his own children for making too much noise.[147]

In classical mythology of the earliest period, even in the Brāhmaṇas, the gods' own sense of insecurity leads them to corrupt mankind. This may be implicit in the statement that the gods were displeased with man and visited upon him the evils of sleep, sloth, anger, hunger, and the love of dice and women.[148] A specific reason for the gods' displeasure toward men who aspire too high is given in another Brāhmaṇa text:

Prajāpati created creatures who did not yield him supremacy. Therefore he took away the essence [rasa] *of these creatures and of the quarters of the sky, and he made a garland and put it on. Then the creatures yielded him supremacy.*[149]

It is not evident how the creatures challenged him, but he responds like a demon, stealing their essence; and the challenge becomes clear by the time of the Upaniṣads:

"*I am* brahman [*the godhead*]"*–whoever among gods, sages, or men became enlightened to this, he became it all; even the gods had no power to prevent him becoming thus, for he became their self. But whoever worships another divinity is like a sacrificial animal for the gods, and each person is of use to the gods just as many animals would be of use to a man. Therefore it is not pleasing to those (gods) that men should know this.*[150]

This lack of differentiation (that men will become the "self" of the gods) is superimposed on the basic Vedic theory that men who sacrifice (instead of seeking what this text considers the better religion–Upaniṣadic enlightenment) are like sacrificial animals, of which the more the merrier–for the gods.[151] Śaṅkara remarks on this text that the gods exercise their mastery against men–but only against the man who does not have knowledge. Apparently Śaṅkara thereby infers that the gods would not oppose the truly enlightened man; yet the text does not say this. Quite the opposite attitude emerges from the very text that Śaṅkara cites in this same context: "As Vyāsa says, 'By rituals one reaches the

[146] Elwin (1942), pp. 92 and 87. [147] Elwin (1943), p. 181.

[148] *Jai. Br.* 1.97. See below, chap. IX, sec. 1. [149] *Tāṇḍya* 16.4.1.

[150] *Bṛhadāraṇyaka* 1.4.10. [151] See below, chap. VI, sec. 8.

world of the gods; and the gods do not wish that there should be upward mobility for mortals.' Therefore they make obstacles to their knowledge."

The Brāhmaṇas present many examples of the beginning of the second stage of religion–that the gods fear or simply dislike men. The gods secrete themselves from men[152] or withdraw from them in pique:

When gods and men lived together in the world, men kept asking the gods for all that they lacked, saying, "We don't have this. Let us have it." The gods began to hate all these demands, and they vanished.[153]

The gods want to keep heaven as a private club for themselves, and this is tantamount to keeping men on earth or in hell. One Brāhmaṇa text states that the need for a distinction first caused the gods to seek immortality: "At first, the gods were like men. They wished to dispel need, evil, and death, and to reach the place of the gods. And they did."[154] Evil and death leave the gods–and enter mankind.

This view of the relationship between man and god is defined by Paul Ricoeur in a chapter entitled "The Wicked God and the 'Tragic' Vision of Existence,"[155] a motif which he finds exemplified in ancient Greek mythology. In this archaic view, "the sacred reveals itself as superhuman destruction of man . . . the Sacred is perceived, in the archaic stage of the religious consciousness, as that which does not permit a man to stand, that which makes him die."[156] This view is based, as we have seen to be the case in India as well, on "the non-distinction between the divine and the diabolical."[157] Archaic though it may be, yet this view survives and persists, and Ricoeur well understands the reasons for this persistence in the West, reasons that apply to India as well:

The tragic is always personal, but it makes manifest a sort of cosmic sadness which reflects the hostile transcendence to which the hero is a prey. . . . That is why the tragic vision always remains possible, resisting any logical, moral, or esthetic reconciliation. . . . The theme of the wrath of God, the ultimate motive of the tragic consciousness, is invincible to the arguments of the philosopher as well as of the theologian. For there is no rational vindication of the innocence of God.[158]

Once again, theodicy proves immune to logic, and the brutal reality of the tragic vision cannot be argued away. Ricoeur rejects with even shorter shrift the possibility of countering the tragic vision with a theology based on emotion rather than logic: "That the theology of love cannot become a systematic theology appears evident. Its powerlessness to integrate justice conceptually is nothing compared to its powerlessness to account for the position of evil in the

[152] *Śata.* 3.1.1.8. [153] *Ibid.* 2.3.4.4. [154] *Tait. Sam.* 7.4.2.
[155] Ricoeur, pp. 211–241. [156] *Ibid.*, p. 33 and p. 43. [157] *Ibid.*, p. 214.
[158] *Ibid.*, pp. 323 and 326.

world."[159] Logically, this is indeed evident; yet in India, at least, a theology of love (bhakti) was often felt to provide a specific counterargument to the tragic vision.

In most Hindu myths, evil is the fault of the gods, a result of the gods' malevolence against virtuous demons and virtuous men. But the third stage, the bhakti stage, when God is benevolent and reconciled with man, begins to transfigure the myths in this cycle; often the devotee is allowed to win his reward, even when this reward involves immortality or the usurpation of the privileges of the gods. In early myths, demons are purposely left unredeemed, demonic, to maintain a force of evil and distinguish them from gods;[160] but in bhakti myths, even demons may be saved. In addition to this transformation of the myths based on an assumption of malevolence, the bhakti spirit generates an entire cycle of its own, in which even the apparently unrelenting malevolent acts of God–acts which do not allow the mortal or demon to be "saved" by a final act of grace–are nevertheless regarded as being of ultimate benefit to mankind and as deriving from God's love of man.[161]

[159] *Ibid.*, p. 326n. [160] See above, sec. 2.

[161] See below, chap. X, sec. 7.

Thou believest that there is one God; thou doest well: the devils also believe, and tremble.
James 2:19

V

THE PARADOX OF THE GOOD DEMON: The Clash Between Relative and Absolute Ethics

1. Svadharma and Eternal Dharma

Dharma is the fact that there are rules that must be obeyed; it is the principle of order, regardless of what that order actually is. The concept of dharma is thus to some extent normative, but it is also descriptive; for dharma includes within its many semantic ranges the idea of one's nature (*bhāva* or *svabhāva*). The behavior of a demon priest is said to be based on his demonic nature—which is sometimes the same as his demonic dharma but sometimes opposed to his priestly dharma. Nature forms one set of natural laws such as the law of gravity; as nature is the way people are, it may be contrasted with dharma in the normative sense, what people should be. Yet, to the extent that "the dharma of the world" is descriptive, dharma subsumes nature.

That *dharma* is both a normative and a descriptive term is essential to an understanding of Hindu mythology. *Dharma* implies that "should" and "is" are one—that one should do what one's nature inclines one to do. The nature of an individual is the source of his own dharma and that of the group to which he belongs;[1] it is the nature of snakes to bite, of demons to deceive, of gods to give,

[1] Strauss, p. 242.

of sages to control their senses[2], and so it is their dharma to do so. This means that people who have "evil" dharmas should follow them; it is the dharma of thieves to steal. In this way, Hinduism sidesteps many of the problems of Western theodicy, in which one strives against one's evil nature, or wicked man strives against a good god; for in India, nature, man, and god all consist of a mixture of good and evil. The only wrong, the only "evil," is to strive against nature–in some cases, to strive against evil; the demon may abandon his demon nature, but this causes serious problems in all but bhakti texts. Thus the moral code (dharma) in India is nature, whereas in the west it usually consists of a conflict with nature. The dharma of a demon is both his characteristic as a type and his duty as an individual; they may be separated, for he may refuse his duty or even deny his nature, but Hindus regard this conflict as an unnatural one, one which must be resolved one way or the other.

The Hindus recognize two different levels of dharma: relative (*svadharma*, one's own particular dharma) and absolute (called *sāmānya*, "equal," the same for everyone, or *sādhāraṇa*, "common, general"). *Svadharma* is as complex as the caste system; absolute or eternal (*sanātana*) dharma is rather like the ten commandments–easily memorized, not so easily followed. The term *dharma* is usually taken in the relative sense, to designate the specific duty of a class (*varṇa*) or a stage of life (*āśrama*), hence it is often called *varṇāśrama dharma*.[3] Some authorities distinguish five kinds of dharma: the dharma of class, of stage of life, of class and stage of life together, the dharma dependent on a particular cause (such as expiation), and the dharma inherent in the possession of certain qualities.[4] Others add a sixth type of dharma: absolute dharma, the dharma for everyone, even outcastes; this includes the duty to speak the truth and refrain from injuring living beings.[5] The *Arthaśāstra* states that all men must cultivate noninjury, truth, purity, good will, mercy, and patience.[6] Later texts somewhat modify this list: the ten-limbed dharma for all classes is noninjury, truth, purity, not stealing, charity, forbearance, self-restraint, tranquility, generosity, and asceticism.[7]

Scholars and authors of the lawbooks generally state that there is no conflict between the two forms of dharma: "The Purāṇas have made a successful attempt at reconciling *sādhāraṇa dharma* with *svadharma*."[8] Absolute dharma demands that all of us behave properly in certain general ways, in addition to the particular requirements of our social class and stage of life. It soon becomes apparent, however, that the two forms of morality cannot always be resolved; indeed, even within the so-called "absolute" category there are irreconcilable contradictions.

There is an element of relativity even in absolute dharma. Manu prescribes one

[2] *MBh*. 14.26.9–10. [3] *Manu* 1.2; *Yājñavalkya* 1.1.0 Kane, I, 4. [4] Medhātithi on *Manu* 1.2.
[5] Mitākṣara on *Yājñavalkya* 1.1. Cf. also *Yājñavalkya* 1.122; *Manu* 10.63; *Matsya* 52.8–10.
[6] *Arthaśāstra* 1.3.13. [7] *Vāmana* 14.1. [8] Venkateswaran, p. 287.

set of duties for all men in the Golden Age (of which the most important is asceticism), one in the Tretā Age (in which knowledge is most important), one for the Dvāpara (sacrifice), and one for the Kali Age (charity). Since, in addition, Prajāpati is said to have assigned separate duties for the four classes, the first list must correspond to "common" dharma.[9] Thus the degenerative nature of time makes even "eternal" dharma relative, at least in the sense that our ability to conform to the immutable ideal changes, and so our modified actual goals change too.

Absolute dharma applies primarily to attitudes of mind, while svadharma applies to specific behavioral roles; to this extent, their ranges of application might be kept separate and unconflicting. But absolute dharma also includes certain precepts that imply action, and these conflict not only with many instances of svadharma but even with each other. These active precepts are noninjury and asceticism. Noninjury conflicts with many types of svadharma; in addition, it conflicts with another aspect of eternal dharma, the precept of asceticism, for asceticism is often interpreted to include sacrifice (which involves animal slaughter).[10] As V. Raghavan drily remarks, "Outside of the Veda-enjoined sacrifices, the principle of *ahimsā* [noninjury] should be observed in all matters."[11] This is a major "exception"; noninjury as an ideal first appears in the late Vedic period and continues to conflict with the injunction to sacrifice until the bhakti period, when at last it is possible to replace animal sacrifice with the sacrifice of fruit or flowers, and at last eternal dharma becomes internally consistent. The triumph of bhakti is in one sense the triumph of absolute ethics; although in orthodox myths svadharma usually prevails over eternal dharma, and bhakti myths often simply overrule both forms of dharma, nevertheless bhakti itself is a form of absolute and universal morality, a new form of eternal dharma.

The conflict between relative and absolute dharma is more persistent in the case of noninjury. The duty to kill is an ancient Hindu duty derived from the ancient code of the Vedic warriors (the Kṣatriya class); the duty *not* to kill enters Hinduism at the time of the rise of Buddhism and Vedānta. The conflict between them appears often in the *Mahābhārata*, notably in the dilemma of Yudhiṣṭhira (who is often called a crypto-Buddhist by his more hawklike companions), in the sin of Indra (who slaughters the Brahmin demon),[12] and in the famous conversation between Arjuna and Kṛṣṇa recorded in the *Bhagavad Gītā.* Theological texts such as the *Gītā* offer sophisticated and not altogether satisfactory answers to the problem, but the most dramatic examples of the conflict appear in Hindu myths.

The contradiction first became acute in the post-Vedic age, when svadharma became rigidly codified in the lawbooks and absolute dharma became defined in a

9 *Manu* 1.86–87. 10 Venkateswaran, p. 288: *ijyā* and *devapūjā.* Cf. *Brahmāṇḍa* 1.2.30.1–48.

11 Raghavan, p. 356. But cf. Alsdorf, *passim.* 12 Cf. Dumézil (1969 and 1970), and Zaehner (1970).

nonsacrificial context. The Hindus attempted to resolve, or at least to combine, these two codes in opposition to a third category, which differed from both of them more than they differed from each other; this third ideology is the code of asceticism. The conflict between ascetic and nonascetic Hinduism remains a paradox even to contempoary Hindu villagers, who experience a tension between caste dharma (blood sacrifice) and virtuous behavior (noninjury) on one level, and a tension between society and religion on another; they prefer a sinful man who provides for his children to a sinless ascetic.[13] Svadharma and absolute dharma developed together within society in the tradition of the Ṛg Veda and the Upaniṣads; in spite of their occasional conflicts, they are both forms of social law, in contrast with the religion of release (*mokṣa*), the negation of social law. Yet asceticism is often included as a form of eternal dharma, and *mokṣa*, release, is the fourth of the orthodox goals.[14] But asceticism is morally neutral; it may be used for good or evil purposes, and so its dharma varies accordingly. Moreover, the code that asceticism challenged—sacrifice—is also morally neutral; there are good sacrifices and bad sacrifices, depending on the intention of the sacrificer. For both of these religious activities are forms of power, and power is amoral.

These concepts tend to blur the distinction between thought and action in Indian religion. It has been suggested that orthopraxy, rather than orthodoxy, is typical of mainstream Hinduism, where much stress is placed on proper behavior, although people are permitted to believe in any or none of a bewildering range of doctrines. In the later sectarian movements, however, as in Buddhism and Jainism, doctrine is all-important, and people of widely varying behavior are allowed to join the order as long as they share the common doctrinal assumptions.[15] Thus mainstream Hinduism emphasizes svadharma, while bhakti cults emphasize their own brand of absolute dharma. The conflict between thought and action appears in the myths in the form of conflicts within characters torn between contradictory ethical claims: Viśvarūpa speaks for the gods but thinks for the demons.[16] In some texts, this means that the gods benefit from Viśvarūpa's actions (i.e., that what he actually does is most important, as in the orthodox, or rather orthoprax, view), but usually Viśvarūpa's duplicity is taken as an indication that the demons benefit, for, as the text explicitly notes, the person whom one *secretly* honors is the one who truly benefits; and this is the sectarian, apparently nonorthoprax view. The doctrine of the demonic Śukra[17] is the same as that of the divine Bṛhaspati, but Śukra's action is directed toward benefiting the demons, and hence he is regarded as demonic by the orthopraxic view. Intention in general is usually secondary to the action of the myth; the meaning is carried by the action rather than by the explanation of the action, which may

[13] Beals, pp. 49–50. [14] O'Flaherty (1973), pp. 76–82.

[15] Staal (1959), pp. 215–218, and (1975), pp. 65 and 173n.

[16] See below, chap. V, sec. 4. [17] See below, chap. V, sec. 9.

frequently be a later accretion. But the intention of demons often seems to be the definitive point: apparently they do good works (sacrifice or asceticism) with evil intention and so are a danger to the world. This is not in fact the way the Hindus regarded the situation. To them the demons are dangerous by definition, regardless of their intentions, as are the pious ascetics who threaten to upset the balance of good and evil.

The contradictions in the formal moral system are particularly sharp in the case of demons, whose class and stage of life may be clear (there are Brahmin demons, ascetic demons, householder demons, demon kings) but who are said to have a basic, characteristic demonic dharma of their own. Although the myth of the Brahmiṇs who become Rākṣasas may be read to imply that Brahmins and Rākṣasas are mutually exclusive classes, there are numerous instances in which this is not so: there are many Brahmin Rākṣasas.[18] Similarly, the gods are divided into four classes: there are Brahmin gods (Agni, Bṛhaspati), Kṣatriya gods (Indra, Soma, Yama, Rudra, Varuṇa), Vaiśyas (the Maruts, Rudras, Vasus, and Viśvedevas), and Śūdras (Pūṣan); it is also said that the gods are Brahmins and the demons are Śūdras.[19] The Brahmin demon and ascetic demon are paradoxical (because of the elements of sacrificial generosity and nonviolence implicit in the Brahmin class and ascetic stage of life) while the householder demon and demon king are not paradoxical. Further confusion is encountered because of the uncertainty in the force of the adjective *demonic* (*āsura*): is it descriptive or prescriptive? The adjective is applied to several types of marriage, of which three are demonic: marriage by purchase (*āsura*), marriage by capture (*rākṣasa*), and marriage by trickery (*paiśāca*).[20] Similarly, one of the three types of conquest is demonic—conquest in which rape and pillage take place.[21] In these contexts, the adjective *demonic* is almost certainly descriptive rather than prescriptive; but the duty of demons to do the things thought to be typical of them—killing men and opposing the gods—is often taken in a prescriptive sense. In early myths, svadharma usually prevails when any conflict arises, and demons are expected to behave demonically; but in many of the later bhakti texts, "good" demons are allowed to abandon their svadharma as demons.

The priests of the demons form a transitional bridge between gods and demons. Not knowing the actual parentage (god or demon) of some of the most important priests accentuates the ambiguity; there are priests who are demons, priests who merely sacrifice for demonic demons, and priests who sacrifice for "good" demons. The priest's role is ambivalent, but there is no question of his primary loyalty. His priestly aspect predominates; his membership in the union takes precedence over his ties to his boyhood gang of gods or demons. In Vedic

[18] See above, chap. IV, sec. 3. [19] *Bṛhaddevatā* 2.63; *Śata*. 9.1.1.15; 14.4.2.23–26; *Tait. Br.* 1.2.6.7; *Bṛhadāraṇyaka Up*. 1.4.11 lists gods who are Kṣatriyas. [20] *Arthaśāstra* 5.2.2. [21] *Ibid*., 12.1.3.

times, the demon priests follow their svadharma as priests rather than demons and thus avoid any conflict with absolute dharma. They perform the sacrifice, and it does not matter whether they sacrifice for gods or for demons—who, in Vedic texts, pursue the same goal (sacrificial power). Thus the priest helps either side to complete a sacrifice, and the treachery of the demon priest who defects to the gods serves a purpose in the battle between gods and demons but does not affect the character of the priest himself. At the second stage, when it becomes necessary for good demons to be corrupted by evil gods, the treacherous priest of the gods mediates by corrupting the virtuous demons. Finally, in the bhakti myths, the demon priest acts either as priest (advising the demon devotee to worship the god) or demon (advising the demon devotee to try to destroy the god).

The dilemma of the demon priest shows that the division of dharma into relative and absolute morality was possible only in theory. The problem raised by the conflict between svadharma and eternal dharma was inherent in the very condition of existence, for it is a conflict between the real and the ideal.

2. The Vedas of the Demons

The divided loyalties of "good" demons may serve as metaphors for tensions between Hindus of different backgrounds, particularly for people who marry into families whose ethics differ from that of their parents, where first one faction and then the other claims them. This function supplies part of the answer to an objection that might be raised regarding the myths to which I have applied this ethical problem: Is eternal dharma, involving sacrifice to the gods, intended to apply to demons at all?

It could be argued that, in the Ṛg Veda, *ṛta* (the Vedic antecedent of dharma) applies only to human beings and deities in the region of *sat*, reality and order; below the earth lies *asat*, the dwelling place of demons—all of whom "abhor the Ṛtá."[22] This may be an accurate generalization about Vedic mythology, though demons are only vaguely and faintly delimited there, and dharma is equally unspecific. By the time of the Epic, however, demons do aspire to follow the precepts of eternal dharma; this troubled at least one scholar, who remarked, "When it is said that [the demons] 'worshipped the gods,' credulity is strained."[23] The belief that demons offer sacrifice never seemed to strain the credulity of Hindus, however, and elaborate rationalizations were constructed for such anomalies as the sacrifice offered by the demon Bali:

It might be argued, "It is inconceivable that Bali, the enemy of the gods, would offer sacrifice, since there could be no gods to be gratified by a sacrifice, because of his hatred of

[22] Brown (1972), p. 61. [23] *MBh*. 12.221.27–28; see above, chap. IV, sec. 3; Hopkins (1915), p. 48.

Indra and the others." But this is not so, for there are two kinds of gods, those who are gods by birth and those who have more recently become gods by means of karma, such as Indra. The gods by birth receive sacrifice but cannot offer sacrifice; the karma gods, like Indra, perform sacrifice and pose obstacles (to sacrificers like Bali).[24]

This neat division solves the problem of the sacrificiant demon and the antisacrificiant god, grouping them together as ambitious parvenus in contrast with the higher gods to the manner born. But one cannot assume that all the authors of Purāṇic myths knew (or accepted) such a hair-splitting solution to the paradox.

In the Purāṇas absolute dharma definitely comes to include the demons, who are by that time thoroughly assimilated into the ethicized universe. Similarly, on the human level, the dharma of barbarians (Mlecchas) outside the Hindu fold includes Vedic rites and noninjury,[25] and there is a complex dharma for robbers.[26] In the Brāhmaṇas, the demons perform sacrifice and even fight the gods for this privilege; later they perform asceticism; and finally they are capable of bhakti. Thus they are always capable of "good" dharma as well as of dharma in the broader sense—nature or conduct of any quality.

The belief that the demons perform sacrifice in order to become strong, like the gods, is implicit in the mythology of the Brāhmaṇas; that the demons are sacrificing to their enemies, the gods, is an implication which does not usually seem to trouble the Brahmin authors of these texts. But in order to perform the sacrifice (to which they are not entitled, or of which they have been unjustly deprived by the gods) they must steal it, and this is precisely what the Brahmin priest is at such pains to prevent. In Purāṇic times it was often said that the demons worshipped the gods and performed sacrifice, a state of affairs that for various (often conflicting) reasons is intolerable. Virtue as a substance (transferable karma or prosperity incarnate in the goddess Śrī) is stolen by the demons and stolen back from them by the gods; and when this virtue is the virtue of performing sacrifice, it is usually said that the demons "stole the Vedas," an act which not only makes them pious and powerful but simultaneously deprives the gods of these sources of victory. The gods' act of stealing back the Vedas from the demons is thus the antecedent of the later, more sophisticated concept of perverting the demons, making them into heretics.

The myth of the stealing of the Vedas is associated primarily with Viṣṇu. At first it is said that the demons Madhu and Kaiṭabha stole the Vedas, and Viṣṇu rescued them by assuming the form of the Horse-headed One (Hayagrīva).[27] This is a particularly apt form for this task, for the sacrifice (of a stallion) is horse-headed, and horse-headed figures (such as Dadhyañc) are often associated

[24] Comm. on *Rām.* 1.29.6 (Bombay ed.), cited in Muir, IV, 131–132. [25] *MBh.* 12.65.14–22.
[26] *Cilappatikāram* XII. [27] *MBh.* 12.335.21–65; *Viṣṇu* 5.17.11; *Bhāgavata* 5.18.1–6.

with the many myths of finding the lost sacrifice.[28] Then the more sophisticated idea of corruption is grafted onto this simple myth, and Viṣṇu assumes his delusory form of Great Illusion (Mahāmāyā), the form he assumes when he corrupts the demons and makes them Buddhists; in this form, he deludes Madhu and Kaiṭabha.[29] The horse-headed figure lost in this version reappears in a third variant of the myth, but on the other side: a horse-headed demon (Hayagrīva) steals the Vedas, and Viṣṇu becomes a fish to steal them back again.[30] This myth links Viṣṇu with two other cycles of "rescue": the story of Prajāpati, who becomes a fish in order to rescue Manu, the Seven Sages, and the Vedas from the cosmic flood; and the myth of Viṣṇu's becoming a boar to rescue the earth from the flood.[31]

Tamil sources offer further developments of the myth of the stolen Vedas; though these are late texts, they still maintain the assumption of Vedic mythology—that the gods themselves must perform sacrifices:

Brahmā created gods and demons; without any reason, the two groups began to fight. The gods used Vedic incantations as weapons; seeing this, the demons resolved to steal the Vedas. Madhu and Kaiṭabha, aided by Māyā, cast a spell on the gods, took the Vedas, chopped them into pieces, and hid them at the bottom of the ocean. Without the Vedas the gods were unable to perform rites and Brahmā was incapable of creation. Śiva's female power (śakti) *helped Viṣṇu recover the Vedas.*[32]

Here the demons use the power of illusion to steal the Vedas, as Viṣṇu used it against the demons in the Sanskrit text; illusion is a force that changes sides frequently, just as the Horse-head appears sometimes as a god, sometimes as a demon. Another Tamil text attributes the theft of the Vedas to the demon Somaka, who is conquered by Viṣṇu in his fish avatar.[33] And a final South Indian text weaves together all of these threads:

[A demon named Somaka stole the Vedas and took them to his golden city in the middle of the sea. The world was] stripped of all learning; and the gods complained to Śiva of the prevailing ignorance among mankind. Śiva told them that he would not kill the Asura, who was his devotee, and asked Bṛhaspati to assume the form of a Buddhist monk and instruct the Buddhist faith to the Asura. [Viṣṇu killed the demon and recovered the Vedas from the midst of the sea. Then] Viṣṇu got rid of the sin of killing the Asura by worshipping the *liṅga* at Veda pura.[34]

The gods complain now not of a loss of sacrificial power but of the general ignorance in the world, for by stealing the Vedas away from *men*, the demons have not only diverted the sacrifice for their own purposes, as usual, but have

28 See O'Flaherty (1971*b*), *passim*, and (1975), 56–91. 29 *Mārk*. 81.49–77. 30 *Bhāgavata* 8.24.7–57; *Agni* 2.1–17. 31 O'Flaherty (1975), pp. 179–196; see below, chap. IX, sec. 3.

32 *Tiruvoṟṟiyūr purāṇam*, 5. 33 *Kāñcippurāṇam* 55.3–9. 34 *Vedapuristhalapurāṇam*, summarized by T. Mahalingam, Mackenzie mss., Madras, 1972, pp. 255–256.

annihilated sacrifice altogether, as in the Tamil myth where they chop all the Vedas into bits. The reaction of the gods, however, serves not to remedy this state of ignorance but rather to exacerbate it, for they corrupt the demons in the usual Purāṇic manner. They send Bṛhaspati to make the demons nonsacrificers, even as they send him to make men sacrificers in similar situations (a more effective expedient, one would think); the corruption of demons becomes the normal expedient employed by Bṛhaspati in the later stratum of the mythology.[35] Finally, Viṣṇu must expiate the sin of killing the demons (as well as that of encouraging heresy[36]) by *liṅga* worship, that is, by bhakti to Śiva, in whose favor this entire myth has been recast.

From these, and many other examples,[37] it is evident that demons do often make a claim on the dharma of sacrifice, the eternal dharma, though this claim is often challenged by the gods, for their own reasons. But in any case, it is far more significant for the purposes of the present study that the virtuous demon is taken *by the myth* to represent an anomaly that tests the entire classificatory system, and as such his problem is the problem of society as a whole.

3. Indra against Tvaṣṭṛ

The myths of the treacherous "good" demon begin with the mysterious figure of Tvaṣṭṛ, whose complex relationship to Indra, king of the gods, is originally one of psychological significance based on kinship, later overshadowed by partisan opposition. Some Ṛg Vedic hymns seem to imply that Tvaṣṭṛ is Indra's father and that Indra kills Tvaṣṭṛ.[38] More certain is the fact that Tvaṣṭṛ is the father of Indra's enemy, Vṛtra, whose mother is the demoness Danu.[39] Among Danu's many demon sons (the Dānavas) is Puloman,[40] the father of Paulomī Śacī, the wife of Indra (and, according to one text,[41] the wife of Tvaṣṭṛ and mother of Vṛtra). Indra marries Puloman's daughter and then kills him,[42] just as he kills Tvaṣṭṛ in order to obtain the Soma that Tvaṣṭṛ has hidden from him. In one tradition, Indra is Tvaṣṭṛ's grandson: When Indra fled from Vṛtra, he entered into some cows, who were Tvaṣṭṛ's daughters, and they brought Indra forth.[43] The parallels with later Śiva mythology are close. Indra kills his father, Tvaṣṭṛ, when Tvaṣṭṛ excludes him from drinking Soma because Indra has killed Tvaṣṭṛ's son, just as Śiva kills his father-in-law, Dakṣa, when Dakṣa excludes him from the Soma sacrifice because Śiva has killed Dakṣa's father, Brahmā.[44] In both instances, the gods must perform elaborate expiations for having committed Brahminicide.

In one Brāhmaṇa, Indra clearly attempts to kill Tvaṣṭṛ:

[35] See above, chap. IV, secs. 5–6, and below, chap. VII, secs. 1–2. [36] See below, chap. VII, secs. 3–4.
[37] See above, chap. IV, secs. 1–2. [38] *RV* 4.18 and 8.77. Cf. Brown (1950 and 1942).
[39] *RV* 1.32.9. [40] *MBh*. 1.65.21. [41] *Skanda* 6.296.16. [42] *Hari*., app. 1, no. 5, 1.116.
[43] *Jai. Br*. 3.19; *Tāṇḍya* 12.5.19–21. [44] O'Flaherty (1973), pp. 84–89; see below, chap. X, sec. 1.

Tvaṣṭṛ excluded Indra. Indra thought, "If he excludes me now from this sacrifice, I will always be excluded. I will slay him." With his thunderbolt in his hand, Indra pursued Tvaṣṭṛ. Tvaṣṭṛ took refuge with the wives, and Indra did not follow him there. Then Indra drank Soma, and Tvaṣṭṛ came afterwards and asked, "Is anything left?" They gave him the remnant, which he threw into the fire, and Vṛtra was born.[45]

Tvaṣṭṛ also seeks refuge with "the wives" (probably the wives of the gods, though perhaps Tvaṣṭṛ's own) when not only Indra but all of the gods attack him, for no stated reason: "The gods desired to slay Tvaṣṭṛ; he took refuge with the wives, who did not surrender him."[46] A possible reason for the conflict is offered by one Ṛg Vedic episode in which the Ṛbhus—mortals who are brought to the heaven of the gods—are said to have been artisans, like the divine Tvaṣṭṛ, and to have made four cups from the cup fashioned by Tvaṣṭṛ (the cup that enabled the gods to bring their wives to heaven[47]). When Tvaṣṭṛ saw this he hid himself among the wives and wished to kill the Ṛbhus for desecrating the drinking vessel of the gods.[48] It has been suggested that Tvaṣṭṛ tried to kill the Ṛbhus but "was thwarted by his daughter, who seems to have become their common wife."[49] This statement may result from a confusion of the myth of the Ṛbhus with the myth of Indra (who is saved by Tvaṣṭṛ's daughters); in any case, treacherous women provide the link between the gods and the demons, women who are related by blood to the demons and by choice to the enemies of the demons. This pattern of transferred allegiance persists in the myths of Devayānī, Satī, and so forth. The blood ties of the woman may be ambivalent in themselves; the Atharva Veda invokes a goddess who is a "daughter of the demons, sister of the gods."[50] Tvaṣṭṛ may have been the leader of those gods who "hated the Ṛbhus because of their human smell,"[51] while Indra is often said to have been the particular friend of the Ṛbhus. "We have therefore the cause of a conflict between, on the one side, the *devas* who hated the Ṛbhus . . . , all led by Tvaṣṭṛ (also moved by personal jealousy), and, on the other side, the *devas* who invited the Ṛbhus to their company, at whose head was Indra."[52] The first group of gods, according to this view, became the "fallen angels," or demons, while the second remained the gods in heaven.

The primary conflict between Tvaṣṭṛ and Indra is a conflict between two gods, father and son. (Tvaṣṭṛ's antipathy to his sons recurs in other myths: Tvaṣṭṛ's daughter married Vivasvat, the sun, and Tvaṣṭṛ "trimmed" the glory of his son-in-law by placing him on his lathe.[53]) Tvaṣṭṛ's conflict with Indra is greatly exacerbated by the presence of two other sons, whom Tvaṣṭṛ supports and Indra opposes—Viśvarūpa and Vṛtra, the demon priests. Thus the main field of battle in

45 *Jai. Br.*, 2.155. 46 *Tait. Sam.* 6.5.8.4. 47 *RV* 4.33.5–6; *Tait. Sam.* 6.5.8.1–2. 48 *RV* 1.161.4–5.
49 Brown (1972), p. 59. 50 *AV* 6.100.3. 51 *Ait. Br.* 3.30 (13.6). 52 Heras, p. 214.
53 *RV* 10.17.1–2; *Bṛhaddevatā* 6.162–3; 7.1–6; see below, chap. XI, sec. 4; *Mārk.* 103–105.

this corpus is transferred from the Oedipal conflict to the more familiar sibling rivalry of gods and demons.

4. Indra Against Viśvarūpa and Vṛtra, the Demon Priests

The key to this rivalry is the treacherous domestic priest (*purohita*) who leaves the demons to aid the gods. One possible Ṛg Vedic instance of this figure may be seen in the reference to the sun as the demonic (*asurya*) domestic priest of the gods.[54] The "demon" in this case is almost certainly the early Vedic figure not yet opposed to the gods, yet Sāyaṇa takes the term in its later, oppositional sense, and hence finds it necessary to reverse its meaning, glossing it as "killer of demons." In most late Vedic texts, however, the demonic priest is truly demonic, yet truly a priest of the gods. The most important of these figures are Viśvarūpa and Vṛtra.

Vṛtra is the son of Tvaṣṭṛ who figures most prominently in the Ṛg Veda as the enemy of Indra; he is a serpent with one head.[55] Tvaṣṭṛ's other son, Viśvarūpa ("assuming all forms"), is a three-headed monster who appears only briefly in the Ṛg Veda[56] but plays an important part in later mythology, where he is always said to have been created before Vṛtra; indeed, Indra's murder of Viśvarūpa is usually cited as the cause of Tvaṣṭṛ's creation of Vṛtra.

In the Brāhmaṇas, Viśvarūpa is a domestic priest and a hypocrite:

Viśvarūpa the son of Tvaṣṭṛ was the priest of the gods, but he was the son of a sister of the demons. His three heads ate Soma, wine, and food. Openly he promised the share to the gods, secretly to the demons. Indra feared that Viśvarūpa was diverting the sovereignty of Indra, and he cut off his heads.[57]

Often the gods use a "secret" sacrifice to defeat the demons:

The gods and demons were contending, and the demons were more numerous and stronger than the gods. Prajāpati thought, "If I perform the sacrifice openly, the demons will destroy it." So he performed it secretly, and the gods prospered while the demons perished.[58]

Viśvarūpa's attempt to bring off this ruse, however, ultimately fails; though Indra often fears that Viśvarūpa will become Indra,[59] he manages to kill the contender and then is led to commit a second murder (of Vṛtra). Indra must then perform expiation for the sin of Brahminicide, for it is emphasized that Tvaṣṭṛ's son, though a demon and therefore by definition one who must be killed, is a Brahmin who must not be killed. Caught between two conflicting ethics—his svadharma to kill demons, and the eternal dharma not to kill anyone, particularly a Brahmin—Indra must do the deed and pay the price.

[54] *RV* 8.101.12. [55] *RV* 1.52.10. [56] *RV* 1.32.7 and 10.8.8–9.

[57] *Tait. Sam.* 2.5.1. [58] *Tāṇḍya* 18.1.1–5. [59] *Mait. Sam.* 2.4.1; *Kāṭh. Sam.* 12.10.

The necessity of Viśvarūpa's murder is justified in a number of ways:

The son of Tvaṣṭṛ was so powerful that he could perform the sacrifice alone [without using three priests, as was usual], for he sang, praised, and recited with his three heads. Openly he promised a share to the gods, secretly to the demons; for one promises secretly to the one whom one prefers. Indra was frightened because Tvaṣṭṛ's son was the son of a demon woman and because he was so powerful. Indra said, "He is demoniacal, this son of a demon woman, and he speaks secretly for the demons. I must kill him." He cut off Viśvarūpa's heads with the thunderbolt.[60]

The "demoniacal" nature of Viśvarūpa—his birth (svadharma) rather than his function (eternal dharma of sacrifice)—is the primary cause of Indra's fear; then Indra adds that the demon is mighty and treacherous, further reasons for killing him.

A slightly later text states both causes of the conflict (demon birth and treacherous behavior) but introduces ambiguities regarding the true motives and divided loyalties of the demon: "The three-headed Viśvarūpa became the priest of the gods, for he wished to please them, since he was the son of a sister of the demons." An alternative reading, however, states that he became the priest of the gods "because he wished to destroy them."[61] The first reading emphasizes his outward purpose, the second his secret purpose. Other texts of this period say nothing about Viśvarūpa's demon birth or priestly function, but merely state that he was Tvaṣṭṛ's son, that Indra hated him and beheaded him, and that Indra was forced to perform expiation for killing a Brahmin.[62] Tvaṣṭṛ's hatred of Indra is emphasized in a brief variant of the myth in the fifth book of the *Mahābhārata*, which also indicates the usual reason for Indra's hatred of the demon (who wants to ursurp Indra's place) and the usual attempt to avoid Brahminicide (by destroying the demon's virtue):

Tvaṣṭṛ, in his hatred of Indra, created a three-headed son, Viśvarūpa, who desired to take Indra's place. With his three heads he read the Vedas, drank wine, and looked as if he would swallow the universe. When Indra saw his great ascetic powers, his courage, his truth, and his infinite energy, he worried lest Viśvarūpa should become Indra, and he thought, "How may he become addicted to sensual pleasures, so that he does not swallow the triple world?" Though he sent celestial nymphs to seduce Viśvarūpa, this ruse failed, and Indra killed him.[63]

The twelfth book of the *Mahābhārata* preserves and reworks the older version of the enmity based on Viśvarūpa's demon birth (his demon mother) and consequently almost entirely excluding Tvaṣṭṛ (the nondemonic father):

Viśvarūpa, the son of Tvaṣṭṛ and of a sister of the demons, was the priest of the gods;

[60] *Jai. Br.* 2.153–155. [61] *Bṛhaddevatā* 6.149. [62] *Śata.* 1.6.3.2, 5.5.4.3. [63] *MBh.* 5.9.3–25.

secretly he offered the share to the demons. Then the demons offered a boon to their sister, the mother of Viśvarūpa, saying "Sister! Your son and Tvaṣṭṛ's, the three-headed Viśvarūpa, priest of the gods, has been giving the share openly to the gods but secretly to us. Therefore the gods are growing stronger while we are waning away. You should prevent this, so that we may have the share." Then Viśvarūpa's mother went to him in Indra's garden and said, "My son, why do you help the side of the enemy to increase while you destroy your mother's side? You should not do this." Viśvarūpa, thinking that one could not disregard his mother's command, went to the demon king Hiraṇyakaśipu and became his priest. Then Vasiṣṭha (who had been the priest of Hiraṇyakaśipu until then) cursed the demon king: "Since you chose another priest, your sacrifice will not be completed, and you will be killed." When Viśvarūpa performed asceticism in order to bring prosperity to his mother's faction, Indra wished to break his vow; he sent many lovely celestial nymphs who disturbed Viśvarūpa's mind and attracted him. When the demon asked them to stay with him, they said, "We prefer Indra," and Viśvarūpa replied, "Today the gods will no longer have an Indra." Then he grew great and with one mouth he drank up all the Soma that had been offered in sacrifices in all the worlds. When Indra saw him he became worried and asked Brahmā for help. Indra then slew Viśvarūpa, from whose body Vṛtra was born; and then he slew Vṛtra.[64]

In this version, Tvaṣṭṛ's role is reduced to nothing. The other demons urge Viśvarūpa's mother, not his father, to stir his demonic nature up, and Tvaṣṭṛ does not even create Vṛtra or deprive Indra of Soma; Viśvarūpa himself accomplishes these ends by "fathering" Vṛtra from his own body and by drinking all the Soma with his third head (a motif taken from the older corpus but only here expanded to reveal its full implication, the theft of sacrifice). The initial treachery of Viśvarūpa is not regarded as benefiting the demons here, and so he is made more treacherous still, first by the demons and then by Indra, who tempts him with celestial nymphs (successfully now, in contrast with their failure in the other Epic variant) and kills him. Viśvarūpa's devotion to his mother is clearly symbolic of his return to the svadharma of demons (his maternal heritage) from the eternal dharma of a priest serving the gods. This demonic attachment to the mother is further emphasized by the *Bhāgavata Purāṇa*, which also depicts Viśvarūpa's quarrel with the gods in a more subtle light:

Indra insulted Bṛhaspati, who vanished. Then Indra said, "Alas! Today I have behaved like a demon, though I am lord of the gods." The demons took refuge in their own guru, Śukra, and attacked the gods, who fled to Brahmā; Brahmā advised them to worship Viśvarūpa, a Brahmin ascetic. The gods approached Viśvarūpa and said, "You should grant the desire of your ancestors [literally "fathers"]. The highest dharma of sons is to serve fathers. We choose you as our guru and teacher, so that we may quickly conquer our

[64] *MBh*. 12.329.17–30.

enemies." Viśvarūpa agreed to be their domestic priest, though he remarked that he would not perform the rituals, which pleased only stupid, evil-minded men, and which he himself despised. When he had become their priest he took the prosperity of the enemies of the gods (which was protected by a magic spell of Śukra) and gave it to Indra by means of a magic spell of Viṣṇu. Protected by this, Indra conquered all the demons in battle. Now, Viśvarūpa spoke aloud for his paternal kin, the gods, but secretly he gave the share to the demons, because he was overpowered by affection for his mother. When Indra discovered Viśvarūpa's contempt for the gods and his transgression of dharma, he was frightened.[65]

Though the gods continually appeal to his father's lineage, Viśvarūpa despises them–indeed, he despises all Vedic ritual, since he is an ascetic–and he finally allows his love for his mother to lead him to transgress dharma–the dharma of the gods and Vedic sacrifice, eternal dharma. In spite of this text's apparent endorsement of Vedic values, the true power which Viśvarūpa takes from the demons and gives to the gods is not the power of sacrifice, nor even that of his own asceticism, but the magic spell which Śukra had won from Śiva and which Viśvarūpa now wins through the opposing magic spell of Viṣṇu–that is, the magic of sectarian bhakti.[66] The conflict between nature and function here takes place not within Viśvarūpa but within Indra, who, in despising a Brahmin, assumes a demonic nature, or rather acts as if he had one, just as the real demon acts like a god. Viśvarūpa actually becomes a god in later Hindu mythology, where he appears as an important iconographic form of Viṣṇu.[67]

Indra's role in inciting Viśvarūpa to treachery is further expanded in one of the few texts that seem to question why a demon should be the priest of the gods in the first place. This is a Tamil text, which draws upon the *Mahābhārata* but reverses the role of the nymphs, who here act against Indra rather than for him:

Once, Indra was lustfully watching the celestial nymphs dancing and singing. Plunged into an ocean of joy, he did not bow to Bṛhaspati, the guru of the gods, who had come there. When Bṛhaspati saw that Indra was deluded by the nymphs, he went away, and Indra's prosperity diminished. Indra realized that this misfortune had come about because he had committed a sin in failing to bow to his guru when he saw him; he searched for Bṛhaspati in vain, and then he went to Brahmā, who told him, "Until you see your guru, take as your guru Viśvarūpa, the three-headed son of Tvaṣṭṛ. Though he is a demon, from the family of descendants of Danu, he is exalted in wisdom and in deeds." Indra consented to this, not knowing the scheme or the evil intention of the intriguing Brahmā, and he took Viśvarūpa as his guru. Viśvarūpa said, "Let the gods prosper," but then he changed his mind, and he thought, "Let the demons prosper." Indra found out and cut off his heads, which became birds, and he let the female demons consume his blood and flesh.[68]

[65] *Bhāgavata* 6.7.2–40; 6.8.1–42; 6.9.1–4. [66] *Matsya* 47.81.

[67] Maxwell, *passim*. [68] *Tiruviḷaiyāṭaṟpurāṇam* 1.1–11.

The text first emphasizes that Viśvarūpa was "exalted," and then casts doubts on this statement by implying that Brahmā is scheming against Indra by advising him to seek Viśvarūpa's help. Viśvarūpa does prove to be treacherous, changing his mind, behaving finally according to his demon birth rather than his "good" character. The conflict between the divine king Indra and his priest Bṛhaspati is reiterated in the friction between the demon king Hiraṇyakaśipu and his priest Vasiṣṭha, a friction which underlies the encounter between the demons and their priest Śukra.[69]

The trouble between Indra and his priest recurs in the *Brahmavaivarta Purāṇa*:

Indra disregarded Bṛhaspati one day; because of a curse of nature, he did not bow to his guru. Bṛhaspati became angry and cursed Indra to be ruined. Indra went to his mother, Tārakā, who told him to wait until his guru returned. . . . Indra raped Ahalyā and was cursed by her husband, the sage Gautama, to lose all his prosperity. . . . And then, one day, because of his guru's anger, Indra was overcome by Brahminicide. For when Indra was abandoned by his guru he was swallowed by his fate; oppressed by the demons, Indra sought refuge with Brahmā, who told him to make Viśvarūpa his priest. And as Indra's wits had been destroyed by fate, he placed his trust in him. But when he realized the true nature of the son of the daughter of a demon, Indra quickly beheaded him. Then Tvaṣṭṛ created Vṛtra.[70]

Ecclesiastical forces truly conspire against Indra here. His own nature causes him to insult a Brahmin; then another Brahmin (Brahmā himself) gives him bad advice, which makes him trust a third Brahmin (Viśvarūpa) after a fourth Brahmin (Gautama) has cursed him. As if this were not enough, fate deprives Indra of what little wit he has, and his own mother (who appears here in place of the demon's mother) gives him scant solace.

A closely related Sanskrit text introduces yet another Brahmin guru, Śukra, the guru of the demons, who has until now played only a minor role:

Indra lost his kingdom because he disregarded his guru, ignoring him because of his fascination with the dancing nymphs. Therefore the gods churned the ocean to obtain prosperity incarnate, and in the resulting battle between gods and demons, Śukra practised asceticism to obtain victory for the demons. The demons had been weakened by transgressing against their guru,[71] *but had become strong again by propitiating Śukra. They routed the gods. Now, Indra was ruling without a guru, but he was advised by Viśvarūpa, the son of Tvaṣṭṛ, a Brahmin who served Indra as his domestic priest. The three-headed Viśvarūpa performed a sacrifice for gods, demons, and men; the Brahmin cried aloud for the gods, silently for the demons, and with the medial stroke for men. One day, Indra insulted his guru, and when Viśvarūpa noticed this he decided to perform a*

[69] *Vāyu* 2.35–36; *Brahmāṇḍa* 3.72–73. [70] *Brahmavaivarta* 4.47.11–45.

[71] A reference to the episode of Śukra and Bṛhaspati; see below, sec. 12.

miracle for the success of the demons. Indra thought, "He is our priest, but he wishes to give the fruits of the sacrifice to others." He took his thunderbolt and beheaded him.[72]

The "insult to the guru" is repeated several times in this passage; the first incident results in the loss of the entire kingdom and of prosperity, a loss that is rectified not by seeking a substitute guru but by obtaining prosperity incarnate, by churning the ocean. The demons then insult their guru and suffer for it. When Indra insults Bṛhaspati again, however, the substitute guru (who has come upon the scene inconspicuously) takes advantage of this lapse to perform a destructive sacrifice, with the usual results. At this point, however (when Indra is suffering from Brahminicide), Indrāṇī, the wife of Indra, curses Bṛhaspati in return.[73] This passage does not explain why Indra chose a demon to be his priest; indeed, no subsequent texts find it necessary to explain this circumstance, but several try to explain why the demon suddenly began to act like the demon he was; and this present text uses the Bṛhaspati episode to explain precisely that. The ambivalence of the demon is here cleverly assimilated to the motif of the three heads, which now do not merely eat three substances or perform three ritual functions but serve three masters.

The problem of the demon Brahmin is more explicitly developed in another episode dealing not with Viśvarūpa but with Vṛtra:

Vṛtra, the son of Tvaṣṭṛ, was born in the daughter of the demon Puloman. Abandoning his demon nature, he was devoted to Brahmins. He worshipped Brahmā, who offered him a boon, and Vṛtra chose to become a Brahmin. While he performed asceticism, the gods killed the demons and destroyed their dynasty. The demons, with Vṛtra's mother, approached Vṛtra; they asked him to kill the gods, and she asked him to marry and settle down with a family. He agreed, saying, "This is the highest dharma, for a son to obey his mother." Vṛtra was consecrated as king of the demons, and he set out to destroy Indra. As the demons were conquering the gods, Bṛhaspati advised Indra to make a false treaty to trick Vṛtra; Indra said, "Go yourself and make this pact." Bṛhaspati approached Vṛtra, who bowed and welcomed Bṛhaspati, for Vṛtra was always devoted to Brahmins. Bṛhaspati said, "Make a pact with Indra—you take the earth, and let him rule heaven." Vṛtra agreed to this, but Indra killed him anyway and was afflicted by the sin of Brahminicide.[74]

Vṛtra here shares both Indra's father (Tvaṣṭṛ) and Paulomī (Indra's wife and Vṛtra's mother): Vṛtra is thus Indra's half brother and also Indra's stepson. He is both god and demon; moreover, he is both Brahmin and king. Though Vṛtra tries to abandon his demon nature and demon dharma, he cannot abandon the dharma of his birth, which is embodied in his duty to obey his mother and his duty to beget demons. His attachment to eternal dharma (generosity, devotion to Brahmins) is then his undoing, for he is caught between his conflicting loyalties.

[72] *Bhāgavata* 6.7.1–40. *Skanda* 1.1.9–15. [73] *Skanda* 1.1.16.6–7. [74] *Skanda* 6.269.16–60.

The ambivalent virtue of Vṛtra is exaggerated in a Tamil text:

When Indra sinned by destroying a great shrine,[75] *Vṛtra conquered Indra's throne and ruled the worlds, but he was still dissatisfied and wished to destroy Indra; to do this, he began to worship Śiva for a thousand years. When Indra learnt of this, he killed Vṛtra; then the sin of Brahminicide drove Indra to a cave in the middle of the sea. Indra complained, "Why should I suffer from Brahminicide? I have killed many demons and never suffered any ill effects before." But Brahmā said, "Vṛtra was not like other demons. He knew the Vedas, performed asceticism, and sacrificed; and you killed him unfairly, from ambush; that is why you suffer from Brahminicide." Finally Indra restored the shrine, bathed in it, became whole again, and returned to heaven.*[76]

Vṛtra has great virtue, but it is not his virtue alone that frightens Indra; in spite of sacrificing (to the gods, one must assume), he reverts to type by trying to kill Indra even after taking Indra's throne (just as Indra kills Vṛtra even when Vṛtra cedes heaven to Indra). The conflict between the demands of Vedic religion and the Purāṇic threat can be resolved only by devotion–bathing in the shrine.

The statement that the demon chose to be a Brahmin appears in another myth, which uses this fact explicitly to account for Indra's Brahminicide, as the Tamil text does. A demon (Rākṣasa) was not by his birth a Brahmin, yet when Indra killed him the sin of Brahminicide came upon Indra, since the demon had been born when his demon mother had been given a boon by a sage.[77] Many texts describe the virtues of Vṛtra at some length; in one episode of the *Mahābhārata*, Vṛtra discourses on dharma for many chapters and finally attains salvation: "When the great demon, the great yogi, had been killed, he went to the highest place of Viṣṇu; for it was because of his devotion to Viṣṇu that he had formerly pervaded the universe, and therefore when he was slain in battle he reached the place of Viṣṇu."[78] Thus Viṣṇu enables Vṛtra to conquer Indra as well as to achieve salvation. Indra addresses Vṛtra as a devotee who has abandoned his demon nature and found the Godhead, though he remarks in the same text, "This is a great miracle that you, with passion as your nature, have become devoted to Viṣṇu."[79] The text explains this "miracle" by the device of reincarnation:

Once the demigod (Vidyādhara) Citraketu mocked Śiva for embracing his wife in public. Pārvatī became furious and cursed Citraketu to be born as an evil demon, so that he could no longer offend the great in heaven. He propitiated her, pointing out that he was a devotee of Viṣṇu, and she mitigated her curse. He was born as Vṛtra, son of Tvaṣṭṛ, but he remained a devotee of Viṣṇu.[80]

Another text elaborates upon this episode. After Pārvatī's curse, the demigod

[75] See below, chap. VI, sec. 3. [76] *Tiruvārūrppurāṇam* 13.1–53. [77] *Skanda* 3.1.11.7–70.
[78] *MBh.* 12.273, and 12.274.55–58. [79] *Bhāgavata* 6.12.20–21. [80] *Bhāgavata* 6.17.1ff.

(Gandharva) Citraratha fell from heaven and became the demon Vṛtra; he could not be slain in battle, but one night Vṛtra fell asleep and forgot to worship Śiva, and so Indra was able to kill him.[81] Here Vṛtra is a devotee of Śiva rather than of Viṣṇu; but in spite of the bhakti overlay, the Vedic opposition must take place, and a lapse of virtue makes the demon demonic once more.

5. Indra Against the Treacherous Nephews of Tvaṣṭṛ

The ambivalences of the descendants of Tvaṣṭṛ sometimes lead to confusion in the minds of the redactors of the texts. Two almost identical texts differ only on the most essential points, in narrating the tale of Tvaṣṭṛ's nephews. According to both of these texts, Śukra married the mind-born daughter of the Soma-drinking ancestors; in one text she is called Aṅgī ("the body"), and in the other she is Gau ("the cow").[82] She bore him four sons: Tvaṣṭṛ, Śaṇḍa, and Marka, and Varūtrin (or Varatrin). These sons shone like suns and caused many problems: Tvaṣṭṛ, Śaṇḍa, and Marka are familiar in their own right;[83] Varūtrin is merely the father of troublesome children, grandsons of Śukra and nephews of Tvaṣṭṛ:

Varūtrin's sons sacrificed to the gods, but they instructed Manu in order to destroy sacrificial dharma. When Indra saw that dharma would thus be discarded, he said to Manu, "Using them (as sacrificial offerings), I will cause you to obtain your desire as a sacrificer." When they heard this, they left that place, and when they had disappeared, Indra took their wife, Cetanā ("mindfulness"), released her, and followed her. When Indra saw the evil ascetics who were bent on destroying Indra, he killed them and gave their heads to the jackals to eat. Then he went to sleep on the southern altar of Śiva.[84]

There are several puzzling elements in this text. If the demons are sacrificing to the gods, as is stated, it is not clear how they are trying to destroy sacrificial dharma. Indra then uses their wife (whose name indicates virtue, as does their own designation as "sacrificers to the gods") to track the "evil ones" (who are at last explicitly said to be determined to destroy Indra) and kills them, apparently by beheading them. (Indra "releases" their wife from bonds meaningless in this text but central to others.) The jackals who enter the scene are known from the Vṛtra myth (when Indra kills Vṛtra, Vṛtra's memory leaves him in the form of a jackal) and from early Brāhmaṇa references to Indra's sin in having "given the heads of the ascetics to the jackals."[85] Only at the end of the passage are the sons of Varūtrin called ascetics, a direct contradiction of their earlier designation as sacrificers (and a contradiction which Vṛtra shares); and when Indra goes to sleep on the inauspicious southern altar, one can only describe it as an incongruous act of bravado.

[81] *Skanda* 1.1.17.92–197. [82] *Vāyu* 2.4.75–84; *Brahmāṇḍa* 2.3.1.76–85; *MBh.* 1.59.35–6.

[83] See below, sec. 8. [84] *Vāyu* 2.4.75–84. [85] *MBh.* 12.272–273; O'Flaherty (1975), p. 87.

Many of these obscurities vanish upon examination of the second text, which is probably earlier and certainly more consistent. The sons of Varatrin were sacrificers to the *demons*; they caused Manu to sacrifice on their behalf, to destroy the sacrificial dharma of the gods; when the demons fled, Indra used *Manu's* wife (called Acetanā, "mindlessness") to track them; then he laughed and *burnt them* on the southern half of the altar, and gave their heads to the jackals.[86] This plot is quite straightforward. The demons, aided by Manu, were sacrificing to the demons and against the gods; Indra made true his threat to use them as sacrificial offerings, upon the southern, demonic altar. Manu's involvement is clearer and more complete: his wife (who has an appropriately inauspicious name) replaces the demons' wife as the woman seduced by Indra and led to betray her husband.[87]

The role of Manu's wife and the intentions of the demons in this myth are further clarified by a group of older variants in the Brāhmaṇas:

Manu had a bull with a demon-killing voice that crushed Asuras and Rākṣasas. The Asuras said, "How can we destroy this bull who inflicts evil on us?" Now Kilāta and Ākuli were the two Brahmins of the Asuras. They said, "Let us see how much faith in the gods this Manu has." They offered to sacrifice for him with the bull, and he agreed. They killed the bull, but its voice entered Manu's wife and continued to crush Asuras and Rākṣasas. Again they persuaded Manu to let them sacrifice for him with his wife, but the voice entered the sacrificial vessels and they could not expel it.[88]

The demons "test" Manu's faith in the gods in order to ruin him and win their own strength back. Sylvain Lévi has commented on the peculiar neutrality of Manu, the symbol of all mankind: "Preoccupied only with the effects of the sacrifice, Manu shows the same indifference to gods and demons, regarding them both merely as agents for the all-powerful sacrifice. With impartial and imperturbable *sang-froid*, he gives the divine and demonic sacrificers his utensils, bull, even his wife."[89] This aspect of Manu's character would make him the symbol of priesthood rather than of mankind as a whole.

The expanded version of the Brāhmaṇa myth comes closer in essence (and in the names of the demons) to the Purāṇic episode that links them with Tvaṣṭṛ. It seems at first to begin where the other Brāhmaṇa text had finished; the demon-killing voice is within the sacrificial vessels:

Manu had sacrificial vessels which destroyed all demons who heard them resound. There were two Brahmins among the demons, Tṛṣṭa and Varutri; they said, "Manu, you have faith in the gods; give us the vessels." He gave them to them, and they destroyed them in fire, but a bull licked the flames and the voice entered him. Tṛṣṭa and Varutri asked Manu to let them sacrifice the bull for him; he agreed; the voice entered Manu's wife;

[86] *Brahmāṇḍa* 2.3.1.76–85. [87] See below, chap. VII, sec. 3.

[88] *Śata.* 1.1.4.14–17; see above, chap. IV, sec. 6. [89] Lévi, p. 118.

preparing to sacrifice her, having asked Manu, they led her around the fire. But Indra saw that the two demons were depriving Manu of his wife, and so Indra took the form of a Brahmin and approached Manu; when Manu asked who he was, Indra replied, "I am a Brahmin. What need is there to ask a Brahmin who his father and mother are? The sacred sciences are his parents." He then told Manu that he would sacrifice, using the two (demon) Brahmins as offerings, and Manu agreed, but when they saw Indra approaching, they fled. Then Indra told Manu to free his wife, and Manu set her free.[90]

Here Indra is clearly on Manu's side (or rather on Manu's wife's side); this may be contradicted by another text of this period, which states that Indra caused Manu to sacrifice his wife—but then adds that "he" (Indra or Manu) let her go.[91] This text also states that the offering was intended for Tvaṣṭṛ—the final link with the garbled Purāṇic texts. Manu and his wife are pawns in a complex struggle involving Indra on one side and an alternating group of demons on the other: Tvaṣṭṛ (sometimes as Tṛṣṭa), Varūtrin, Kilāta, and Ākuli. Manu sides with whichever team seems to offer the best prospects, and Indra alternately aids or impedes Manu, depending on Manu's allegiance at the particular moment. (Unlike the demons, Indra denies his parents and is thus free to change sides at will.) Manu's ambivalence in the Brāhmaṇas remains in the Purāṇas, where it introduces a new ambivalence in the demons themselves.

The myth itself is of importance in this corpus, but even more significant is the manner in which it remained part of the Purāṇic cycle even when most of the basic premises were apparently reversed. The ambivalence of Tvaṣṭṛ's family makes the myth "valid" whether the demons sacrifice to the gods or to the demons. At first they are overtly demonic, then hypocritical, but in either case they must be destroyed in order to preserve the sacrificial dharma—and to save Indra's skin.

6. Indra Against Agni and Soma

The treachery of the demons sometimes rebounds to their disadvantage, for in one cycle of myths as old as the myth of Viśvarūpa's treachery (though not as old as the myth of Indra's slaughter of Viśvarūpa) the demon priests turn against the demons to help the gods. This presupposes a simpler, and probably later, alignment of forces than that of the Vṛtra myths; the gods and demons are no longer so incestuously related that one could expect the reader to accept the premise that a demon would serve as the priest of the gods; here, the demons have a demon priest and the gods have a divine priest. Yet although this is the initial premise, the myth often reintegrates the Vedic belief in the interchangeability of demonic and divine priests, for the priest of the demons changes sides and serves

[90] *Mait. Saṃ.* 4.8.1; cf. 4.1.6; *Kāṭh. Saṃ.* 2.30.1; *Tait. Br.* 3.2.5.9. [91] *Tait. Saṃ.* 6.6.6.1.

the gods after all, albeit only temporarily; the imposter is unmasked and punished.

The treachery of Agni and Soma may be traced back to the Vṛtra cycle in the Ṛg Veda. In one hymn, Indra invites Agni to come to him; Agni replies, "Leaving the nongod secretly and by hidden ways, as a god I go to immortality. Deserting him, I go from my natural friends to a strange household." Varuṇa then follows Agni from the demon father, going from the portion that is without sacrifice to that which has the sacrifice; and Soma also chooses Indra and deserts the father. Indra remarks, "These demons will be without magic resources if you bestow your love on me. Separating the false from the true, come rule my kingdom. Let us kill Vṛtra." Then they all forsake Vṛtra with loathing.[92] The demon father is Vṛtra, who is deserted by the demonic Agni and Soma when they are bribed by Indra with the traditional reward, a portion of the sacrifice.[93] Several of the motifs of this obscure hymn recur in the mythology of treacherous demons: the demons who are false, the gods true; the demon who finds immortality among the gods; the stealing of the demons' superior magic.

The link between Agni, Soma, and Vṛtra appears in one story of Vṛtra's birth. When Indra tried to kill Tvaṣṭṛ, Tvaṣṭṛ created Vṛtra by casting into the fire the remnant of the Soma that Indra had drunk. "Therefore," states the text, "they say that Agni and Soma are demons."[94] Here, Agni and Soma are the parents of Vṛtra; in the Ṛg Veda, on the other hand, Agni and Soma refer to Vṛtra as their father. This inversion of parentage appears elsewhere in Hindu mythology, notably in the relationship of Viṣṇu to Brahmā and of Brahmā to Śiva.[95]

The treachery of Agni and Soma emerges clearly from another episode, in which it would appear that Agni and Soma are not demonic by nature at all; they are gods who have entered into Vṛtra, and who are called back again by Indra. Thus their treachery is directed here first against Indra and only later against Vṛtra (the starting point of the episode in the Ṛg Veda):

Tvaṣṭṛ cast the remnant of the Soma into the fire, and it became Vṛtra, endowed with Agni and Soma, and with all science, glory, nourishment, and prosperity. Indra pursued Vṛtra and addressed Agni and Soma, saying, "You belong to me and I belong to you. That one is nothing to you; so why do you support that barbarian and oppose me? Come over to me." They asked what reward he would give them, and he promised them a particular share. They went over to him, and after them went forth all the gods, all the sciences, glory, nourishment, and prosperity; thus Indra became what Indra is now. Then Indra cut Vṛtra in two. Since all the gods were abiding in Indra, they say that Indra is all the deities, chief of all the deities.[96]

Agni and Soma are followed by all the powers into Vṛtra, and then the powers

[92] *RV* 10.124.1–8. [93] Brown (1919), pp. 100–103.

[94] *Jai. Br.* 2.153–155. [95] O'Flaherty (1973), p. 111. [96] *Śata.* 1.6.3.8, 13–15, 17, 22.

and the gods follow them back into Indra. It is not clear what would be the answer to Indra's question: Why, indeed, if Agni and Soma belong to Indra, do they support Vṛtra? Their role in Vṛtra's birth, obscure here but clearer in the earlier text, may provide one answer, since they are bribed not by the demons but by the gods; their blood ties are demonic. But more significant is the fact that together they symbolize the neutral sacrifice, for which the gods and demons compete in sibling rivalry.

This ambiguous treachery recurs in Brāhmaṇa literature: "Indra took up his thunderbolt to slay Vṛtra. Agni and Soma said, 'Do not hurl it; we are within.' 'Come to me,' he said. They asked for a share and he granted this, and he created cold and fever heat.[97] Agni and Soma left Vṛtra, and Indra killed him."[98] The demonic nature of the forces that desert Vṛtra is established by yet another variant, in which, when Indra raises his thunderbolt three times to kill Vṛtra, Vṛtra himself cries out each time, "Do not strike me; there is power within me; I will give it to you." When he has given Indra his powers, Indra is able to kill him.[99] Elsewhere, Vṛtra gives up to Indra the Yajur, Sāman, and Ṛg Vedas, which had been within Vṛtra.[100] Thus the divine elements within Vṛtra—the gods or Vedas who dwell within him—desert him and are ultimately his undoing, as was his "devotion to Brahmins" in the Purāṇic myth.

The role of Agni as traitor may also be viewed in the context of the many Ṛg Veda myths in which Agni treacherously flees from the gods and must be bribed to come back.[101] In the *Mahābhārata*, this theme is embroidered with another betrayal: Agni betrays a sage's wife to the demons (Rākṣasas) and is cursed for this, whereupon he flees from the sacrifice until the gods seek him out and bring him back.[102] Soma's role in the Ṛg Veda myth of Vṛtra may similarly be derived from the Ṛg Veda "seeking of Soma" corpus, though Soma is usually unwillingly abducted by the demons, instead of collaborating as Agni does.

7. Kaca, the Son of Bṛhaspati, Against the Daughter of Śukra

The swallowing of the Soma is a frequent motif in the Vṛtra cycle. In the *Mahābhārata,* Kaca, the son of Bṛhaspati, is sent to steal the secret of immortality from the demons; instead of swallowing it, he is himself swallowed by Śukra. But Śukra is persuaded to revive Kaca at the importunity of Devayānī, the daughter of Śukra, whom Kaca has led up the garden path and whom he abandons as soon as he has learnt the secret of revival and taken it back to the

[97] Cf. *MBh.* 12.272. [98] *Tait. Sam.* 2.5.2.2–5.

[99] *Tāṇḍya* 20.15.6; *Tait. Sam.* 6.5.1. [100] *Śata.* 5.5.5.2–5.

[101] *RV* 10.51.1–9; *Śata.* 1.2.3; *Bṛhaddevatā* 7.61–4; *Tait. Sam.* 2.6.6.1–5; *MBh.* 13.84. Cf. O'Flaherty (1975), 98–104, and see below, chap. VI, sec. 2. [102] *MBh.* 1.5–6.

gods.[103] Thus the daughter of the demons' guru, who rescues the son of the gods' guru, joins the long gallery of demon women who defect to the gods. These women seem to form two distinct categories: the mother of the ambivalent demon causes him to revert to his primary, demonic allegiance, his blood loyalty; but the wife or daughter of the demon is an erotic rather than a maternal female,[104] and she betrays the demon. This distinction between the loyal mother and the treacherous enchantress, so typical of Hindu mythology, is somewhat complicated here by the fact that the loyal woman is loyal to the "wrong" side, while the treacherous woman defects to the "right" side. (It would thus appear that, although deceit and treachery are regarded as demonic traits among male humans–and gods–the pattern is reversed in women: loyalty is demonic, treachery divine). This pattern further reinforces the evidence that Hindus placed far greater importance on blood ties than on marriage ties when the two came into conflict; nature prevails over society.

8. Indra Against Śaṇḍa and Marka, the sons of Śukra

Śukra's sons prove even more treacherous than their sister, for the gods bribe and corrupt them in an important series of myths. Śukra is the father of the arch-troublemaker, Tvaṣṭṛ, and of Varūtrin, whose sons are tricked by Indra. The remaining sons of this quartet, Śaṇḍa and Marka, are, like Viśvarūpa and Vṛtra, priests, and hence more direct sources of power than are Tvaṣṭṛ and Varūtrin. At first there is only one son: "Śaṇḍa, the priest of the demons, was the son of Śukra. Since the gods drink Soma in the house of Śukra, Śukra is a divinity."[105] Other texts give Śaṇḍa a brother, Marka:

Bṛhaspati was the priest of the gods; Śaṇḍa and Marka were the priests of the demons. The gods and demons strove together in battle, but the gods could not win. The gods invited Śaṇḍa and Marka, who replied, "Let us choose a boon; let cups (of Soma) be drawn for us also." For them they drew these cups for Śukra and Manthin; then the gods became the gods and prospered, and the demons became demons and were defeated. Having driven the two of them away, the gods offered themselves to Indra. Śukra is the sun, and Manthin is the moon. . . . The two eyes of Prajāpati were Śukra and Manthin. Śaṇḍa and Marka were the priests of the demons. The gods could not kill the demons, who possessed religious truth; the gods offered Śaṇḍa and Marka a share, and they accepted and came to the gods.[106]

Other texts emphasize the priests' power to bestow victory:

Indra knew that both the gods and the demons possessed religious truth. The gods invited Śaṇḍa and Marka, who chose to drink Soma among the gods. Indra gave them Śukra

[103] *MBh.* 1.71–72; O'Flaherty (1975), 281–289. [104] See below, chap. XI, secs. 3–4.

[105] *Vāj. Sam.* 7.12.13. [106] *Tait. Sam* 6.4.10.1; *Mait. Sam.* 4.6.3.

and Manthin as shares. Then the kingdom (of the demons), having no priest, was overcome by the gods. . . . Śukra is the eater, and Manthin is the food. There are two demons named Śaṇḍa and Marka. When the gods drove away the demons, they could not drive away these two; but whatever (sacrificial) work the gods performed, those two disturbed and then quickly fled. The gods said, "Let us draw two cups (of Soma) for them; they will come down to us and we shall seize them and drive them away." They did, and that is why the cups are drawn for Śaṇḍa and Marka but offered to deities.[107]

From these texts it is evident that Śaṇḍa is merely a multiform of Śukra, with Marka added to form a parallel to Manthin, the celestial alter ego of Śukra. The two demon priests succeed in their treachery against the gods at first—they destroy the sacrifice and cannot be driven away—but in the end they are driven away and cheated in their turn by the gods, so that they do not enjoy the Soma for which they betrayed their faction. It is particularly significant that, at this early stage, the demons hold the religious truth that the gods must steal in order to conquer; sometimes the gods have this power, too, but while both factions are equal there can be no victory. Later, the demons alone have the magic formula of revival, which is the key to victory.[108]

In the Purāṇic version of this legend, the treachery that must disturb the balance of powers is initiated not by the gods but, as in the Viśvarūpa cycle, by the demons:

In the battle between the gods and demons, Śukra assured the demons, "These two disciples of mine will bring you all that is created by Bṛhaspati for the gods." Then Prahlāda and the demons rejoiced and departed. As the demons were conquering the gods, the gods took counsel and said, "Let us invite these two to a sacrifice, and then we will conquer the demons." The gods promised to become devotees of Śaṇḍa and Marka, who thereupon helped the gods to conquer the demons.[109]

Here it would appear that Śaṇḍa and Marka, though serving the demons, are somehow managing to steal the sacrificial merit produced for the gods by Bṛhaspati, just as Viśvarūpa siphons off the fruits of the gods' sacrifices. Therefore the gods must bribe them, and in this text it seems that Śaṇḍa and Marka are allowed to keep, at least temporarily, the reward for their defection.

A late Purāṇic text attributes to Śaṇḍa and Marka an act of treachery not against the demons but rather on behalf of the demons and against gods and mortals; mortals were virtuously performing sacrifices, strengthening the gods, and so the demons could not win; therefore Śaṇḍa and Marka created heresy, delusion, and adharma, corrupting mankind.[110] In fact, the effect of this elaborate ruse is precisely the same as that described in the earlier episode: Śaṇḍa and Marka

[107] *Kāṭh. Saṃ.* 27.8; *Śata.* 4.2.1-5. [108] *MBh.* 1.71.7-8. [109] *Matsya* 47.224-234.

[110] *Viṣṇudharma Purāṇa* 25; see above, chap. IV, sec. 4.

prevent the gods from receiving the fruit of the sacrifice. Here they possess not religious truth but religious falsehood; yet in this they imitate Viṣṇu, who takes the form of delusion to corrupt the demons.[111]

9. Indra Against Śukra

Śukra himself sometimes assumes the role of the treacherous priest of the demons. The gods drink Soma in the house of Śukra when Śaṇḍa is priest of the demons.[112] One Brāhmaṇa states that when Śukra was priest of the demons, the gods won him over with wishing-cows called Auśanasas[113] ("The cows of Uśanas," as Kāvya Uśanas is another name of Śukra). Another text expands upon this:

The gods and demons fought, but there was no decisive victory. Bṛhaspati was priest of the gods, Śukra of the demons. Whatever rite the gods performed forward, the demons did it backward, so that it had no effect. A three-headed Gandharva knew which of them would have the decisive victory. He lived in the waters. Indra knew that the three-headed Gandharva knew which of them would have the victory, and so he spoke to flatter the wife (of the Gandharva) and asked her to ask her husband whether gods or demons would win. She asked the Gandharva, who said, "Bṛhaspati and Śukra are two Brahmins with the same knowledge. If either of them goes to the other side, that side will win." When Indra heard this he turned into a green parrot, went to Śukra among the demons, and summoned him with the wishing-cows of Virocana, son of Prahlāda. Then these two (Indra and Śukra) ran forth with the cows, and the demons pursued them. The two erected a pillar to heaven; the demons could not go beyond this. These two came to the gods with the wishing-cows. . . . Śukra among the gods desired the immortal world of the Gandharva. He alone among the gods obtained the immortal world of the Gandharva.[114]

The aggression in this episode begins with the gods: Indra compounds his usual felony by stealing from the demons the cows with which he bribes their own priest. He uses a woman (the Gandharva's wife, a celestial nymph) to help him steal the demons' cows as well as their guru, even as a woman often helps him steal Soma from the demons or the Gandharvas (and Manu's wife holds the balance of power between gods and demons).[115] For these thefts, Indra takes the form of a bird, the form he usually assumes in order to steal Soma or secrets from the demons or from the Gandharvas.[116] The three-headed Gandharva is reminiscent of Viśvarūpa, another mediating figure; yet the Gandharva—who represents the all-seeing and treacherous sun—is unknowingly treacherous to the demons, while Viśvarūpa is knowingly treacherous to the gods.

The ambivalence of the Gandharvas is evident from another myth:

[111] See below, chap. VII, sec. 4. [112] *Vāj. Sam.* 7.12. [113] *Tāṇḍya* 7.5.20.

[114] *Jai. Br.* 1.125–127. [115] *Air. Br.* 1.27; *Tait. Sam.* 6.1.6.5; *Mait. Sam.* 3.7.3. [116] *Tait. Sam.* 2.1.9.1.

Gods, ancestors, and men were on one side; demons (Asuras, Rākṣasas, and Piśācas) were on the other; and the Kali-Gandharvas were in the middle, helping neither side. The gods and their forces overcame the demons and divided the three worlds among gods, ancestors, and men. Then the Kali-Gandharvas asked for a share, but the gods refused, saying that the Gandharvas had been neutral. "But," said the Gandharvas, "in our minds *we were on your side." The gods gave them the land of the Kalindas where the Gandharvas practise asceticism.*[117]

The Gandharvas are explicitly said to behave neutrally; yet, like Viśvarūpa, they secretly take sides—or so they claim. They here form a mediating group between gods and demons, for the usual tripartite structure (gods, demons, men) is disrupted: gods and men are on one side (with the ancestors brought in to occupy the world of hell), while the demons are divided into three subgroups.

Another version of the myth of Indra and the Gandharva's wife adds several illuminating details:

Bṛhaspati and Śukra both had religious truth, so neither gods nor demons were victorious. The Gandharva Sūryavarcas, who lived on a golden boat in the ocean, knew which would win. Indra was on joking terms with the Gandharva's wife, and at Indra's behest she asked her husband which side would win; to overhear them, Indra became first a golden ray of sunlight and then (when the Gandharva whispered) a green parrot. The Gandharva said, "Whichever side has Śukra will win." Indra went to Śukra and invited him, offering him Indra's daughter Jayantī and four wishing-cows. Śukra went from the demons to the gods, and the gods won.[118]

Here Śukra is tempted not only with cows but, as in the later myth of his treachery,[119] with Jayantī, daughter of Indra, who supplements both the Gandharva's wife and the cows, just as Tvaṣṭṛ's "cow" daughters aid Indra and Śukra's wife is called "the cow." The myth continues, and Śukra begins to behave like the archetypal treacherous priest, Viśvarūpa:

Śukra, living as the guru (of the gods), received much wealth from the demons, drinking it in like poison. He said, "I am your guru," and received much wealth from the demons. "Do not sacrifice," they said. Bṛhaspati the son of Aṅgiras performed a great sacrifice and vomited forth gold. Seeing this, Śukra said, "Ah, I will steal this for the demons." Indra, learning of this, made a mountain, and the descendants of Śukra Uśanas, called the Auśanasas, went to the mountains in Kurukṣetra.[120]

This brief text links the motif of the treachery of the demon priest (Śukra) in favor of the gods to the treachery of the demon priest (originally Viśvarūpa, here Śukra again) against the gods. Bṛhaspati vomits forth the wealth that Viśvarūpa usually swallows up, and Śukra attempts to swallow (or steal) it, just as he

[117] *Jai. Br.* 1.154–155. [118] *Baudhāyana Śrauta Sūtra* 18.46.

[119] *Vāyu* 2.35–36; *Matsya* 47. [120] *Baudhāyana Śrauta Sūtra* 18.47.

swallows the demons' bribes—bribes that consist of the same "great wealth" which the gods had used to bribe him in the first place. Śukra is the perfect double agent—until his cover is blown and he is sent to Siberia (the mountains of Kurukṣetra), where his descendants bear (ironically?) the same name once given to the cows with which he was bribed.

Like Viśvarūpa, Śukra is a mediating, ambivalent figure; both of them perform a "good" sacrifice but then change it into a "bad" sacrifice—that is, they pervert its use and make it into a black mass. But, unlike Viśvarūpa, Śukra is regarded as a Brahmin first, a demon second. It is never entirely clear whether by nature Śukra is a priestly sage (i.e., a superhuman of some type) or a demon, any more than it is always clear whether Bṛhaspati is primarily sage or god; both names appear in the lineages of divine sages.[121] In the Ṛg Veda and afterwards, Bṛhaspati is often regarded as a god; Śukra is more difficult to understand. He is close to Tvaṣṭṛ and Bṛhaspati and even takes over some of their functions in the Ṛg Veda. He finds and releases cattle as Bṛhaspati usually does, and he fashions Indra's thunderbolt as Tvaṣṭṛ usually does; and he is sometimes said to be the father of Tvaṣṭṛ.[122] In the Ṛg Veda, Śukra is not yet the priest of the demons, though he assumes this role in the Brāhmaṇas, by which time he and Bṛhaspati are clearly functioning on opposed sides. Yet one always has the impression that the bond that unites Bṛhaspati and Śukra as priests, grandsons of Prajāpati, is far more important than the superficial factors that have caused them to align themselves with the gods or with the demons. Unlike the "true" demons—Viśvarūpa or Prahlāda, for example—Śukra never attempts to usurp Indra's position, though he often gives the demons themselves the power to do so.

Although the texts do not usually question or explain why a priest normally associated with demons should be accepted as priest of the gods, there is one interesting passage that does question why a priest might take the side of the demons in the first place. This text does not rely on the possibly demonic birth of Śukra (who is sometimes said to be the son of the priest Bhṛgu, begotten in Divyā, daughter of the demon king Hiraṇyakaśipu[123]), but refers only to matters of free choice. Asked (by Yudhiṣṭhira) how Śukra came to join the faction of the demons, Bhiṣma replied: "He became well disposed toward the demons because of his compassionate nature."[124] The meaning of this is not clear. Is it that Śukra pities the demons because they are always being beaten (usually in some underhanded way) by the gods? The commentator says that Śukra helped the demons and harmed the gods because the gods had beheaded Śukra's mother;[125] yet all known variants of the myth to which this refers are in complete and unmistakable agreement that the gods beheaded Śukra's mother because Śukra

[121] See Goldman, chap. 3, "Śukra, the Demons' Priest."

[122] *RV* 9.87.3; 1.83.5; 1.121.12; 5.34.2. [123] *Vāyu* 2.4.84; *Brahmāṇḍa* 2.3.1.78.

[124] *MBh.* 12.278.1–5. [125] Nīlakaṇṭha on *MBh.* 12.298.7 (Bombay).

was *already* the priest of the demons.[126] Evidently, although it is at least raised, the question is not satisfactorily answered, for Śukra is a most undemonic demon. Unlike the "true" demons, Śukra is immortal; when he becomes a serious nuisance to the gods, they see to it that he is swallowed;[127] but Śukra is always brought forth again. On one occasion when Śukra is swallowed, the text states explicitly that, since he was a Brahmin, he could not be killed.[128]

The knowledge that Śukra has is the same as (or better than) the knowledge and power of Bṛhaspati. Often the demons' victory is expressly attributed to the fact that Śukra's knowledge is superior to Bṛhaspati's; in particular, Śukra is often said to be the only one with the power to revive the dead.[129] Yet some texts say that the gods were able to revive those slain in battle,[130] and Bṛhaspati mutters the spell of magic revival over Indra and revives him.[131] These apparent contradictions may be resolved when one realizes that this power is one which the gods steal from the demons, as they steal the sacrifice, Soma, and the entire universe: "Gods and demons were fighting and only the demons could revive their dead. Then the gods practised asceticism and they became able to revive their dead, while the demons could not."[132] In order to preserve his advantage, Śukra often requests (and is granted) formulas that Bṛhaspati does not have.[133]

Śukra gives "good" counsel (Brahmin counsel, not demon counsel) to Vṛtra and Bali,[134] and he discourses at great length on the nature of the soul. But elsewhere he is said to use his Brahmin wisdom for demonic ends; in one Tamil text, he teaches the demons a most ingenious heresy, a travesty of certain orthodox concepts with immoral implications.[135] Śukra recognizes Viṣṇu in his dwarf disguise because Śukra alone among the demons has true spiritual insight, but he uses this insight to warn Bali not to promise Viṣṇu anything lest Viṣṇu take away his entire kingdom.[136] Śukra even curses Bali and the demons to lose their kingdom because they have disregarded his advice;[137] this curse is the same as the series of curses given by Bṛhaspati to Indra, and by Vasiṣṭha to Hiraṇyakaśipu, for the same sin—disregarding the guru.

Georges Dumézil has discussed the problem of Śukra, whom he describes as a sorcerer mediating between gods and demons:

> Each of the two factions has his *purohita*. . . . Despite the difference in their nature, the god Bṛhaspati and the superman Kāvya Uśanas are alike in their function, in their competition, and they both bear the title of Brahman. One might suggest that there is in this a warping of a tradition which, before the establishment of the strict system of *varṇas* [the four classes of society], would certainly have allowed for several types of sacred man:

126 *Vāyu* 2.35.95–302; 2.36.1–50; *Brahmāṇḍa* 3.72–73; *Matsya* 47.69–226; *Padma* 5.13.205–430.

127 *MBh.* 12.278.1–38. 128 *Padma* 6.18.82–90. 129 *MBh.* 1.71.7–8. 130 *Śata.* 2.6.1.1.

131 *Skanda* 3.1.11.35. 132 *Tāṇḍya* 12.5.23. 133 *Matsya* 47.81.

134 *MBh.* 12.270, and 13.100–101. 135 *Kantapurāṇam* 2.10.

136 *Bhāgavata* 7.15–9.20; *Skanda* 1.1.19. 137 *Bhāgavata* 8.20.14.

more of a magician, the *kavi* [the type of priest which Śukra represents] was not the equivalent of the sacrificial priests.[138]

It would appear from the Brāhmaṇa texts, however, that the difference between the two priests was not primarily a difference in the quality of their knowledge but rather a difference in the uses to which they put that knowledge–a purely partisan, functional difference, not a class difference. They are both wily and devious; hence the Machiavellian *Arthaśāstra* begins with an invocation to Śukra and Bṛhaspati, fitting patrons of politicians. Dumézil regards them as alike in function but different in nature; if by "nature" one denotes lineage (demon or divine) and by "function" one means religious activity (performing sacrifice), this is certainly true. But if one takes "nature" to denote class (*varṇa*, priest) and "function" to denote the result of religious activity (aiding the gods or demons), the statement must be reversed. "Nature" here corresponds roughly to svadharma, "function" to eternal dharma; Śukra's svadharma is, like Bṛhaspati's, that of a priest; yet Bṛhaspati's role in serving the gods, and Śukra's allegiance to the demons, reveal opposed functions, opposed choices–opposed absolute dharmas.

The "nature" of the demons may be no different from that of the gods, from whom only function distinguishes them; according to St. Augustine, there are good and evil angels, "dissimilar and contrary to one another, the one both by nature good and by will upright, the other also good by nature but by will depraved."[139] But the Hindu gods can rest only when both demonic nature and demonic will are overcome; thus Andhaka wisely pleads for mercy, saying, "Both my demon nature and my kingdom are gone."[140]

In Hinduism, knowledge–even religious knowledge–is morally neutral; the priests do not seem to care about the use to which their knowledge is put, as long as someone in power continues to foot the sacrificial bill; from their standpoint, svadharma easily supersedes eternal dharma. By the time of the Brāhmaṇas, sacrificial power automatically flowed toward the sacrificer without involving the deity; thus the demon priest could perform his functions on behalf of demons without becoming involved in any sacrilege. In later texts, though the demons are forbidden to drink the sacrificial Soma, they have the power of magic revival, their equivalent of the Soma, their power of life; thus both sides are able to remain alive and sacrificiant in order to continue the battle.

10. Indra Against Virocana

The same text that names Tvaṣṭṛ as a son of Śukra goes on to say that Tvaṣṭṛ's wife, mother of the three-headed Viśvarūpa, was the daughter of Virocana (while the mother of Vṛtra was the daughter of the demon Puloman).[141] Virocana, the

[138] Dumézil (1971), p. 160. [139] Hick, p. 68.

[140] *Skanda* 6.229.26. [141] *Brahmāṇḍa* 2.3.78.

son of Prahlāda (the archetypal Good Demon[142]), supplies the cows with which Indra bribes Śukra and appears in conflict with Indra in one of the earliest instances of sacrificial competition between gods and demons.[143] The archaism of this passage is evident from the fact that the two parties send not their two priests but the kings themselves, Virocana and Indra, to obtain religious truth; as usual, the demons fail because they do not understand truth as well as the gods do.

In a late Purāṇic text, Virocana is virtuous to the extreme, like his overgenerous son Bali. When Viṣṇu approaches Virocana in the form of an aged Brahmin, Virocana and his wife promise to fulfil all his desires, and even agree to give him their lives; then they attain final emancipation.[144] This would be an unequivocal bhakti myth were it not for one false note from the pre-bhakti period. Before this incident takes place, it is said that the gods went to Viṣṇu and requested him to kill Virocana (no reason is given, but none is needed: Virocana is a dangerously virtuous demon). Thus, though the original motive is petty jealousy, the myth is satisfied by the statement that Virocana died happily, knowing that he would obtain release.

11. Indra Against Bṛhaspati

Bṛhaspati is, like all the other characters in this incestuous cast, a complex figure, though not so ambivalent as most of the others. In one part of the Ṛg Veda he is said to be a demon begotten by Tvaṣṭṛ;[145] thus he is yet another brother of Viśvarūpa and Indra. In the earliest part of the Ṛg Veda, Bṛhaspati is an aspect of Indra, an epithet of Indra, "Lord of Sacred Speech"; he only becomes a figure in his own right later on,[146] whereupon he claims credit for many of the deeds formerly attributed to Indra.

Indra is said to have contended with or contradicted Bṛhaspati, a crime that is listed together with the slaughter of Tvaṣṭṛ's three-headed son and the giving of the heads of the sons of Varūtrin to the jackals. "From these sins against the gods, Indra walked away into the forest. The gods refused to sacrifice for him. Then Agni, Indra's best friend, performed a sacrifice for him, and he burnt away Indra's evil."[147] Here, as in several texts of the Viśvarūpa myth, an insult to Bṛhaspati forces Indra to find a new priest—now Agni rather than Viśvarūpa (perhaps because Indra has just killed Viśvarūpa as a direct result of the first of the series of crimes: insulting Bṛhaspati). Another text says that as a result of these crimes (killing Vṛtra and Viśvarūpa, contending with Bṛhaspati), the gods excluded Indra, leading him to seek help not from Agni but from the other ritual god, Soma.[148] To get the Soma, however, Indra had to steal it from Tvaṣṭṛ (since he

142 See below, sec. 14. 143 *Ch. Up.* 8.7–12; see above, chap. IV, sec. 4.

144 *Nārada Purāṇa* 2.32. 145 *RV* 2.23.2 and 2.23.17. 146 Schmidt, *passim*.

147 *Jai. Br.* 2.134; *Ait. Br.* 7.28; *Tāṇḍya* 14.6.8; *Kau. Br. Up.* 3.2. 148 *Ait. Br.* 7.28.

had been excluded from the drinking of Soma in punishment for this same group of sins[149]), and this theft is the very act usually cited as the first, not the last, in the series of conflicts between Indra and the descendants of Tvaṣṭṛ. Thus the cycle has revolved through a full three hundred and sixty degrees; the myth has bitten its own tale.

There is, from time to time in the Purāṇas, some loose talk about Indra and Bṛhaspati's wife: Indra is called "one who sleeps in his guru's bed" and even "one who kills his guru."[150] Bṛhaspati often curses Indra; on one of these occasions, Indrāṇī (Indra's wife) curses Bṛhaspati, who was in turn to be rejected and to have his wife, Tārā, carried off by Soma (in retaliation for Bṛhaspati's sin in procuring a husband—a *demon* husband, no less—for Indrāṇī while Indra was hiding from the fury of Brahminicide).[151] But Indra helps Bṛhaspati to get Tārā back (the occasion for yet another war between gods and demons, with Soma on the side of the demons), and Indrāṇī employs Bṛhaspati's help in winning Indra back when he has deserted her.[152] Bṛhaspati's conflict with Indra may in many cases derive from the large corpus of myths depicting conflict between priests and kings.[153]

12. Bṛhaspati Against Śukra

In spite of these conflicts, Bṛhaspati is usually said to be loyal to the gods. He is not above bribery, but usually manages to bribe only the right people; when the demons try to slay him, he offers a share of the sacrifice to the rulers of the worlds—sun, wind, and fire, rulers of heaven, the ether, and earth.[154] Bṛhaspati's treachery against the demons is made possible by the fact that he impersonates their own guru, Śukra, and causes Śukra to betray them. This impersonation is entirely comprehensible in the context of the well-trodden path between the sacrificial grounds of the gods and of the demons; indeed, one wonders how the two factions ever managed to tell their priests apart at all. According to some texts, Śukra is the priest of both the demons and the gods;[155] sometimes he defects to the gods, and sometimes the gods come to him for instruction.

The manner in which Bṛhaspati becomes priest of both sides is well known from the time of the Upaniṣads:

Bṛhaspati became Śukra, and for the sake of Indra's security he created a doctrine of ignorance for the destruction of the demons. By this doctrine, men say that the inauspicious is auspicious, and that the auspicious is inauspicious. They say, "Let there be a dharma which is destructive of the Veda and of other śāstras.*" This doctrine is false and barren; its fruit is mere pleasure.*[156]

[149] See below, chap. VI, sec. 3. [150] *Bhāgavata* 9.11.14; *Brahma* 96.10. [151] *Skanda* 1.1.16.6–7.
[152] *Brahmavaivarta* 4.47.50–161. [153] Muir, I, 296–400. [154] *Tāṇḍya* 6.7.1.
[155] *MBh.* 1.60.42; *Vāyu* 2.4.82; *Brahmāṇḍa* 2.3.78. [156] *Mait. Sam.* 7.9; *MBh.* 12.140.22.

The doctrine of ignorance taught by Bṛhaspati may be the Materialist doctrine called *Bārhaspatya* and traditionally attributed to him; as he invented it to teach to the demons, it is also called the demonic doctrine.[157] On other occasions, Bṛhaspati deludes the demon sons of Raji, making them devoid of dharma, in order to allow Indra to slay the demons.[158]

In an expansion of the impersonation myth, the demons initiate the false truce that Bṛhaspati suggests to Indra in the fight with Vṛtra, and Indra's daughter Jayantī assists Bṛhaspati. This episode, in which the daughter of Indra corrupts Śukra, may be a transformation of the Epic myth in which Kaca, the son of Bṛhaspati, corrupts Devayānī, the daughter of Śukra.[159] The gods treat Kaca as they often treat demon priests: they offer him a share of the sacrifice as a reward for his treachery against the demons. The parallels and inversions between the episode of Kaca, Śukra, and Devayānī and that of Indra, Śukra, and Jayantī are numerous and complex. In the first episode, the gods send a man to seduce the daughter of Śukra; in the second, they send a woman to seduce Śukra himself; instead of seducing the daughter, they kill the mother of Śukra; she is then revived as Kaca was in the first myth. Śukra eats and revives Kaca; Śiva eats and revives Śukra. In the first episode, the daughter must choose between father and lover, and she is responsible for the near death of her father, Śukra; in the second, Indra must kill Śukra's mother, but is saved from Śukra by his (Indra's) own daughter. The two episodes are directly related, for Devayānī is born as a result of the first encounter; she is the daughter of Śukra and Jayantī:

As the gods and demons were contending, Śukra left the demons and went to the gods. The demons asked him, "Why have you returned to the sacrifice, abandoning our kingdom?" But he calmed them and promised, "All of this is mine; only a portion belongs to the gods. I will give you all of this which I have kept for your sake." The gods, seeing the demons favored by the wise Śukra, decided to try to seize them before Śukra could instruct them. The demons sought refuge with Śukra, who said, "By various stratagems most of the chief demons have been destroyed, until only a few of you remain. I think there should be no more war; make peace until the situation changes, for I will obtain formulas from Śiva which will give us victory, and then we will fight with the gods and conquer them." The demons agreed to this and said to the gods, "We have laid down our weapons; clothed in garments of bark, we are going to the forest to practise asceticism." The gods thought that this speech of Prahlāda must be the truth, and they went away. But Indra, finding out the true reason for the truce, sent his daughter Jayantī to Śukra; at her request, Śukra cast a haze around them so that no one could witness their lovemaking. When the demons then sought their guru to obtain the incantations, they could not see him, and they went away in disappointment. Meanwhile, Bṛhaspati took the form of Śukra and went to the demons; they mistook him for their own guru and he instructed them. After some time, the real

[157] See above, chap. IV, sec. 4. [158] See below, chap. VII, sec. 2. [159] *MBh.* 1.76–77.

Śukra returned to the demons, but they failed to recognize him. Then he cursed them, saying, "Since you reject me, your wits will be destroyed and you will be defeated." Bṛhaspati vanished, and the demons realized that they had been deceived by him. They begged Śukra to forgive them, and he promised that they would regain their wits and conquer the gods. [He left Śaṇḍa and Marka in his place, but they defected to the gods, so that the demons were conquered.][160]

Bṛhaspati does not utilize his opportunity to corrupt the demons, who are overcome, not because they embrace a false doctrine, but simply because they infuriate their own preceptor and are cursed by him. Thus, although Bṛhaspati sets the stage for the demons' curse, their own guru destroys them, turning this myth into yet another episode in which the treacherous demon priest ruins his own people, first by deserting them (while dallying with Jayantī) and then by cursing them.

A later variant, however, shows that Bṛhaspati takes advantage of Śukra's absence to do some corrupting of his own:

Bṛhaspati, disguised as Śukra, said to Śukra, "You *are Bṛhaspati, author of the heresy of Materialism; you have taken my form to come here and delude the demons." Furious, Śukra departed; Bṛhaspati then taught the demons to despise the Vedas and the gods; he made them into Jains and Buddhists. Then Bṛhaspati departed, and Indra approached the demons, who told him that they had renounced the world in order to become monks, and that he could rule the universe. Indra agreed, and the demons, thus deluded, dwelled on the banks of the river Narmadā until Śukra awakened them from their vow and they again resolved to steal the triple world.*[161]

Several interesting developments have taken place. Bṛhaspati, with notable nerve and presence of mind, accuses Śukra of his own (Bṛhaspati's) treachery and his own heresy, Materialism. The double heresy of Buddhism and Jainism is used not merely as a technicality, by which the demons are disqualified from the power game, but as an actual philosophy, which causes them to renounce their kingdom; in earlier myths Vṛtra was tricked into renouncing heaven and accepting merely earth, but even this did not satisfy Indra, who killed him anyway; here the demons renounce all three worlds—until Śukra inspires them to fight again.

The demons are repeatedly duped and deserted in this myth. It begins with the Vedic episode in which Śukra (or, in some texts, the sacrifice itself, a particularly Vedic concept) leaves the demons and goes to the gods, but secretly aids the demons. Bṛhaspati tricks the demons, and Śukra curses the demons and abandons them. Finally, the first episode is recapitulated: the demon priests (now Śaṇḍa and Marka) abandon the demons to help the gods. Thus most of the previous threads

[160] *Vāyu* 2.35.95–302; 2.36.1–50; *Brahmāṇḍa* 3.72–73; *Matsya* 47.69–226; O'Flaherty (1975), pp. 290–300. [161] *Padma* 5.13.205–420.

are interwoven in this lengthy text, in which all the priests behave in much the same way and are equated. No one can tell the difference between Bṛhaspati and Śukra, and Śaṇḍa and Marka are explicitly said to be "the equals of Bṛhaspati."[162]

These chameleon-like Brahmins are set, nevertheless, in the cold black-and-white framework of the struggle between gods and demons, and the pattern remains set in spite of several different layers of religious values. At first, "the sacrifice" is what brings Śukra to the gods, but the second demon defectors (Śaṇḍa and Marka) are bribed with the much later concept of bhakti: the gods promise to be their devotees. In the first text, the demons merely pretend to be ascetics in order to cheat the gods in the typical Vedic manner; in the second text, they actually become ascetics, as the Purāṇic demon heroes do.

13. The Demon Devotee: The Bhakti Revolution

The many permutations of the myths of priestly demons in the early period demonstrate the impossibility of resolving the underlying conflict between traditional svadharma (according to which the duty of a demon is to interfere with the sacrifice and to kill the gods) and eternal dharma (according to which the duty of a demon is to sacrifice to the gods and to refrain from killing anyone). This paradox is heightened by two developments in the Upaniṣadic-Buddhist period: the demons have developed more specifically injurious characteristics (they rape and pillage and include in their ranks Rākṣasas and Piśācas, who drink blood), and eternal dharma, on the other hand, has developed more specifically noninjurious characteristics.

The solution offered by the *Bhagavad Gītā* has proven the basis for the spiritual perceptions of Hindus over many centuries and cannot be tossed off lightly; but one of the answers, and the one most pertinent to the subsequent mythology, is the bhakti answer: devotion to Kṛṣṇa makes it possible for Arjuna to fulfil both svadharma and eternal dharma. When applied to demons, this simple solution was not quite so simple. Two myths from the Indra cycle demonstrate some of the complications that arise even in the bhakti texts:

There was an evil man named Kitava ("rogue"), who reviled gods and Brahmins. One day he accidentally spilled on the ground some flowers he was going to give to a whore; they were offered to Śiva, and so when Yama came to take the evil one away, Kitava was released from Yama and even given the throne of Indra. He refused to have any contact with Indrāṇī, despite the panderings of Nārada, and he gave Airāvata and Uccaiḥśravas (Indra's elephant and horse) to the sages Agastya and Viśvāmitra, and he gave the wishing-cow to Vasiṣṭha. When Kitava's time was up, Indra regained the city of the gods (Āmarāvatī) and blamed Yama, saying, "You gave my throne to Kitava, who did this despicable thing, giving all my treasures away. Get them back for me." Yama said to

[162] *Matsya* 47.229–232, alt. reading.

Kitava, "You evil man, you should not have given away someone else's possessions; on earth, generosity is praised, but in heaven no one should give anything to anyone." Then Yama told Citragupta to throw Kitava down to hell, to punish him, but Citragupta refused, saying, "How can Kitava go to hell when he acted in such a praiseworthy way, giving those treasures to the sages? And his evil acts have been burnt to ashes by the grace of Śiva." Yama told Indra to ask Agastya and the others to give back the treasures, and he did. Then, through the ripening of his deeds, Kitava was reborn as the son of Virocana–as Bali.[163]

At first, this appears to be the story of a sinful mortal devotee who overcomes death and hell through the grace of Śiva.[164] But ultimately the devotee is reborn as a demon (and the name of Citragupta is reminiscent of Citraketu and Citraratha, the former incarnations of Vṛtra), the demon Bali, whose fatal flaw is his generosity. This, rather than his original depravity, would appear at first to be Kitava's flaw as well; though he resists the usual temptation (Nārada pandering for Indrāṇī), he betrays his ungodliness by acting like a mortal–far too generous for a god! And so, though Kitava's generosity saves him from hell, he is reborn as a demon, in punishment for an excess of this same virtue.

Another demon devotee of Śiva falls, like Viśvarūpa and Vṛtra, between the two stools of his own good nature and the evil women in his life, his wife and his mother:

Diti performed asceticism and gave birth to a son named Vajrāṅga, the equal of the gods. By his mother's command, he harassed the immortals in various ways, and when Diti saw the miserable state of Indra and the others she was very happy. Brahmā went with Kasyapa (Vajrāṅga's father) to Vajrāṅga, and persuaded him to release the gods. Vajrāṅga said, "Let the evil Indra enjoy his kingdom; I have no desire for the enjoyments of the world, and did this only because of my mother's command." Brahmā then created a lovely woman named Vajrāṅgī. Vajrāṅga took refuge in his good nature [sāttvika bhāva], *abandoned his demonic nature, and was happy. But there was no good nature in the heart of Vajrāṅgī; she asked him to give her a son to conquer the triple world and cause misery for Viṣṇu. When the wise and good Vajrāṅga heard his wife's words he was disturbed, but he thought, "If I fulfil my beloved's wish, the triple world and gods and sages will be greatly distressed; but if I do not, it will be hell for me. In both cases, dharma will be harmed." He granted his wife's request, and Tāraka was born.*[165]

The ambivalence is explicit, and devotion to Viṣṇu is not strong enough to overcome the female demonic allegiance. Blood again triumphs over moral choice.

Two other examples of conveniently explicit myths dealing with the conflict will point out other stumbling points:

[163] *Skanda* 1.1.18.53–120. [164] See below, chap. VIII, sec. 6. [165] *Śiva* 2.3.14.18–38.

There was a Yakṣa named Harikeśa, devoted to Brahmins and to dharma. From his very birth he was a devotee of Śiva. His father said, "I think you cannot be my son, or else you are indeed ill-begotten. For this is not the behavior for families of Yakṣas. You are by your nature cruel-minded, flesh-eating, destructive. Do not behave in this evil way (that is, worshipping Brahmins and Śiva); the behavior ordained by the Creator should not be abandoned; householders should not perform actions appropriate to the hermitage. Abandon this human nature with its complicated scale of rites; you must have been born from a mortal man, to be set on this wrong path. Among mortals, the appropriate ritual duty arises according to caste [jāti]*; and I too have ordained your duty in the proper way." But Harikeśa went to Benares and performed asceticism until Śiva accepted him as a great yogi, one of his own hosts.*[166]

The traditional doctrine of svadharma as explained by Harikeśa's father is rejected by the "good" demon, who prefers to worship Śiva and who is praised by the author of the text for doing so; bhakti has become the new eternal dharma, but this time one in which the particular is overruled by the general.

More elaborate, but similar in essence, is the tale of Sukeśin:

There was a great Rākṣasa named Sukeśin, who received from Śiva the boon that he could not be conquered or slain. He lived according to dharma, and one day he asked a hermitage full of sages to teach him about dharma. They began by describing the particular dharmas of gods (to perform sacrifice, know the Vedas, and so forth), Daityas (fighting, politics, aggression, devotion to Śiva), Yakṣas (study of the Vedas, worship of Śiva, egoism, aggression), Rākṣasas (raping other men's wives, coveting others' wealth, worshipping Śiva), and Piśācas (eating flesh, lack of discrimination, ignorance, impurity, falsehood). Then they went on to explain dharma in general, including the tenfold dharma for all classes, such as noninjury. They concluded: "No one should abandon the dharma ordained for his own class and stage of life; he would anger the sun god. Let no one abandon his svadharma, nor turn against his own family, for the sun would become angry with him."[167]

The sages' instruction is contradictory: they address Sukeśin as a Rākṣasa and warn him not to abandon his own dharma (raping, stealing), but then they tell him about eternal dharma, which involves self-restraint (not easily compatible with rape) and generosity (not easily compatible with stealing). The one ray of light in this dark conflict is the statement that it is part of the svadharma of Rākṣasas to worship Śiva. Sukeśin seizes upon this and begins to proselytize his people:

Sukeśin invited all the demons in his city to an assembly and taught them the primary and ancient dharma—noninjury, truth, and so forth (i.e., absolute dharma). All the demons

[166] *Matsya* 180.5ff.; cf. *Skanda* 4.32.1–175. [167] *Vāmana* 11–15.

began to practise this dharma, and their brilliant luster paralyzed the sun, moon, and stars; night was like day; the night-blooming lotuses did not bloom, thinking that it was still day; owls came out and crows killed them. People thought that the city of the demons was the moon, and that it had overcome the sun. Then the glorious sun thought that the entire universe had been swallowed up by the Rākṣasas, and he learned that they were all devoted to dharma, worshipping gods and Brahmins. Therefore the sun, who destroys Rākṣasas, began to think about their annihilation. Finally he realized the weak point of the Rākṣasas: they had fallen from their svadharma, a lapse which destroyed all their (absolute) dharma. Then, overpowered by anger, the sun cast upon the city of the Rākṣasas rays that destroy enemies. The city dropped from the sky like a planet that has exhausted its merit.

When Sukeśin saw the city falling he said, "Honor to Śiva!" and all the devotees of Śiva began to cry, and when Śiva learned that the sun had hurled down the city of the demons he cast his glance at the sun, and the sun fell from the sky like a stone. The gods propitiated Śiva and put the sun back in his chariot, and they took Sukeśin to dwell in heaven.[168]

The enmity of the sun—predicted by the wise sages—is based on a complex of factors, various reactions to the virtuous demon. As a god, the sun is naturally a destroyer of demons and automatically seeks to annihilate any who rise too high; this jealousy is enhanced by his offended amour propre when the demon outshines the sun.[169] But a more laudable motive may be seen in the fact that the demon, by being virtuous, is destroying not only his own dharma and the dharma of his own family (the factor which the sun uses as his excuse to destroy Sukeśin) but the dharma of the whole world—owls and stars and lotuses are disturbed by the sudden imbalance in the social order, for cosmic order is maintained by the proper performance of all svadharmas.

This is the traditional view: for a demon, evil is its own reward; a demon who tries to be "good" is violating his svadharma, paving the road for his own ruin as well as for the obstruction of cosmic order. Thus the virtuous Prahlāda is undone by his own generosity and the demons as a race are tricked into becoming so holy that they renounce the material world. Another example of this view may be seen in the myth of the churning of the ocean. When the gods and demons grasp the serpent who serves as the churning rope, the demons are given the tail; they complain that they should not have this "inauspicious" part of the animal, since they are given to reciting and hearing the Vedas and they are preeminent by birth and deeds. Viṣṇu smiles and accedes to their request, whereupon the demons grasp the serpent's head and are overcome by the smoke and flames that issue forth from his mouth.[170] Thus they are ill served by their Vedic virtue. Another explicit example of the svadharma view may be seen in the myth of Bali in the

[168] *Vāmana* 15–16. [169] See below, chap. IX, secs. 1–2. [170] *Bhāgavata* 8.7.1ff.

Kali Age;[171] even Bali's usual act of "giving" the universe to the dwarf Viṣṇu is regarded as an example of dangerous demon virtue; as a Sanskrit aphorism notes, "Because of his excess of generosity, Bali was captured. . . . Excess should always be avoided."[172]

But this svadharma doctrine is overthrown in the Sukeśin myth by the doctrine of bhakti. Śiva punishes the sun and reinstates the good demon by taking him out of the social fabric altogether, transposing him from a lower level to one where his virtue will no longer interfere with stars and owls—and gods. Thus bhakti does not so much contradict svadharma as move the problem into another realm, where the conflict no longer arises.

14. The Virtuous Demon King: The Perils of Prahlāda

Sukeśin and Harikeśa are not priests, nor are they rulers; they are simply rank-and-file demons of two cadet branches. Prahlāda, however, is a figure of considerable importance. Son of the evil Hiraṇyakaśipu, Prahlāda is a king of demons and father of royal demons. His story develops through ancient and medieval sources that demonstrate many of the historical permutations encountered in the myths of Indra and Tvaṣṭṛ's family.[173] Prahlāda is particularly interesting in the present context because his story is the mirror image of the tale of Indra and Vṛtra. Where Indra, the evil king of the gods, kills the demon Brahmin and wins (though he must undergo expiation for his sins), Prahlāda, the good king of the demons, respects Brahmins and loses.

In the Brāhmaṇas, Prahlāda is a typical, demonic demon—angry, lustful, opposing the gods. Prajāpati tries to keep his son Indra from being killed by the demons, while Prahlāda tries to keep his son Virocana from being killed by the gods.[174] The *Mahābhārata* knows Prahlāda as one of several demons who oppose dharma and fight against Indra.[175] It also describes Prahlāda as an enemy of Indra (by definition, since Prahlāda is king of the demons) but one whose virtue is his ruin:

Prahlāda took away the kingdom of the noble Indra; though he was a demon, he put the triple world in his power because of his virtuous nature and behavior. Then Indra bowed to Bṛhaspati and said, "I wish to know about religious merit and moral virtue." Bṛhaspati revealed knowledge to him but told him that he could learn more from Śukra. Śukra taught him but told him that Prahlāda had special knowledge of religious merit. Then Indra took the form of a Brahmin and went to Prahlāda and said, "I wish to know about religious merit." Prahlāda said that he was too busy, too involved in ruling the triple world, to spare him the time right then, but as "the Brahmin" waited patiently,

[171] *Vāmana* 49–51; see above, chap. II, sec. 9. [172] Böhtlingk, I, 26, no. 136, and 27, no. 137.

[173] Hacker, *passim.* [174] *Tait. Br.* 1.5.9.1. [175] *MBh.* 12.160.26–28.

Prahlāda was pleased and taught him about eternal dharma. Then Prahlāda asked the Brahmin to choose a boon, and the Brahmin said, "If you care for my welfare, O king, I wish to have your virtue." Prahlāda became afraid of him then, but he had to agree. Indra left, and Prahlāda's energy left him, saying, "I am your virtue, and I will leave you, to live in that fine Brahmin who was your pupil." Then dharma left Prahlāda, and truth departed, and good conduct, and finally prosperity.[176]

The transfer of the demon's power of truth to the god, and then the transfer of his prosperity (in the form of a woman)–worldly loss following spiritual–is an old motif.[177] The actual mechanism of the transfer (the god taking the form of a Brahmin and begging for virtue and prosperity) must surely be an ironic twist of the old myth in which Viṣṇu takes the form of a dwarf and begs the demon Bali for his kingdom.[178] The irony is increased when one recalls that in many versions of the Bali myth Prahlāda, the grandfather of Bali, warns Bali that the dwarf is Viṣṇu,[179] though he is unable to see through Indra's disguise when his own kingdom is at stake. In one version of the Bali myth, it is Indra himself who appears in disguise as a Brahmin beggar: In order to kill the king of the demons, Indra went to the palace of Bali and asked Virocana for a gift; the demon laughed and said, "If you wish, I will give you my own head, or this kingdom, or my very prosperity;" Indra said, "Give me your own head," and the demon son of Prahlāda cut off his own head and gave it to Indra.[180] As Indra replaced Viṣṇu so Virocana, Indra's old enemy, replaced Bali, but the motif remains unchanged. Also notable in the *Mahābhārata* text of the Prahlāda myth is the fact that Bṛhaspati sends Indra to learn from Śukra, whose knowledge of religious merit he acknowledges as superior to his own. The virtue of the demon king–his devotion to Brahmins, his eternal dharma–leads him to lose everything, even his svadharma as king of the demons.

The *Devībhāgavata* links Prahlāda with the story of Bṛhaspati and Śukra, and questions the morality of the gods' behavior in both myths. Referring to the Bṛhaspati story, the sage hearing the myth asks, "How could the guru of the gods trick the demons like that? If he, who taught the dharma of truth, lied to the demons, then who can be truthful?"[181] And this is the only text that raises ethical objections to the treatment of Prahlāda. At first there is a simple tale in which a wicked demon is made to see the light–by being killed by Viṣṇu:[182]

Hiraṇyakaśipu fought with the gods; when he was killed, his son Prahlāda became king. Prahlāda oppressed the gods, and there was a terrible battle between Indra and Prahlāda.

[176] *MBh.* 12.124.19–63. [177] See above, chap. IV, sec. 3.

[178] *Śata.* 1.2.5.1–9; *Tait. Br.* 3.2.9.7; *Vāyu* 2.36.74–86; *MBh.* 3.272; 3.215; 12.326; *Rām.* 1.29; *Vāmana* 47–51, 62–67; O'Flaherty (1975), 175–178.

[179] *Hari.* 71.48–72; *Matsya* 244–246; *Vāmana* 51. [180] *Skanda* 1.1.18.121–129.

[181] *Devībhāgavata* 4.13.1–35. [182] O'Flaherty (1975), pp. 171–173 and 241–250.

When Prahlāda was beaten, he achieved the highest knowledge and realized eternal dharma. Placing Bali on the throne, he went away to perform asceticism.[183]

The transfiguration of Prahlāda here takes place after his defeat and after the death of Hiraṇyakaśipu (in contrast with the later bhakti myths, where Hiraṇyakaśipu's death is a direct result of Prahlāda's virtue). But the Purāṇa then goes on to say that, while Prahlāda was practising asceticism, the gods began to win, Śukra went to obtain magic formulas from Śiva, Bṛhaspati impersonated Śukra, and Śukra cursed the demons.[184] In other texts, this curse is used to explain the subsequent episode of the treachery of Śaṇḍa and Marka (while Prahlāda alone of all the demons resists the heresies taught by Bṛhaspati[185]); but here, Śukra's curse leads to the episode of the "treachery" of Prahlāda (his devotion to the gods). Nevertheless, Prahlāda suddenly reverts to type; though called a devotee of Viṣṇu,[186] he returns to fight for the demons, and he argues convincingly that gods and demons are alike in both birth and behavior—as he, the godlike demon, can well understand:

When Śukra cursed the demons, the gods rejoiced, but the demons went to Śukra with Prahlāda. Pralāda begged Śukra to help them, and Śukra relented. The battle resumed, and the Goddess aided the gods. Then Prahlāda, the great devotee of Viṣṇu, praised the Goddess and said, "You are the mother of us all; how then can you discriminate between the gods and the demons who perform their own deeds? How could a mother discriminate between her good and bad sons [śubha *and* aśubha], *as you do between the gods and us? They and we both have our own interests at heart, and any distinction between gods and demons is a delusion. They are sons of Kasyapa, as we are, and both sides are always addicted to wealth and women. I think you have falsely instigated this strife because of your idle curiosity, your desire to see a fight. I know dharma, and so does Indra; yet we always fight for the sake of a share of the sacrifice. The gods and demons churned the ocean together, but the gods tricked the demons out of all the treasures that were churned forth. The gods did this wrongly, yet they became "good men"* [sādhus] *and the demons were overcome; what sort of dharma is that? Indra, who knows dharma, stole the wife of Gautama; Bṛhaspati raped his younger brother's wife when she was pregnant. My grandson Bali was truthful, without desire or anger, calm, generous, a sacrificer; but the deceitful Viṣṇu took the form of a dwarf and stole Bali's kingdom. Yet wise men say that the gods dwell in dharma. The gods speak with sweet tongues, and then when they are victorious they talk about dharma." But the Goddess said, "You all must go to hell and live there without fear or anger." The demons, protected by the Goddess, agreed and went to hell, and then the Goddess disappeared and the gods went to their world in heaven. Thus the gods and the demons lived without enmity.*[187]

[183] *Devībhāgavata* 4.10.33–40. [184] *Padma* 5.13.205–420.

[185] *Devībhāgavata* 4.11–14.

[186] *Ibid.*, 4.15.53. [187] *Ibid.*, 4.15.36–71.

In spite of the obvious truth in what Prahlāda says, the Goddess establishes peace and "protects" the demons out of their claims to heaven and earth, banishing them to hell. Prahlāda goes through two transformations: from demonic to godlike, and back to being a demon in hell once more; like Sukeśin in the first episode, Prahlāda is cast down—because of his virtue (in the *Mahābhārata*) or in spite of it (in the *Devībhāgavata*).

In bhakti texts, however, Prahlāda is born a devotee of Viṣṇu, remains devoted in spite of the threats and attacks by his own father (Hiraṇyakaśipu), and is ultimately rewarded with immortality in Viṣṇu's heaven; these myths follow the pattern of the second episode of the Sukeśin myth.[188] Prahlāda's father is furious, not because Prahāda is virtuous but merely because he has no respect for his father—in other words, because he is violating his svadharma, a matter of partisan loyalties rather than ethics. In these texts, Hiraṇyakaśipu tries in vain to have his prodigal son educated in demon etiquette by Śukra, Śaṇḍa, and Marka (who behave here like straight demons, opposed to the gods, in contrast with Prahlāda).

One text that combines the premises of the bhakti cycle with the double transition pattern of the *Devībhāgavata* is the *Kūrma Purāṇa*. Here Prahlāda begins as a demonic demon; Hiraṇyakaśipu sends Prahlāda to fight Viṣṇu (a task which Prahlāda obediently performs); but then, when Prahlāda is unable to vanquish Viṣṇu, he recognizes Viṣṇu as the supreme god and worships him; Viṣṇu then kills Hiraṇyakaśipu.[189] Prahlāda is "enlightened" by being conquered by Viṣṇu in battle (as in the *Devībhāgavata*) but as this enlightenment now takes place *before* the death of Hiraṇyakaśipu it allows the Purāṇa to depict the dialogue between the Vaiṣṇava son and the demonic father, the didactic core of the bhakti texts. Nevertheless, the demon Prahlāda still reverts to type after the death of his father, though the *Kūrma* attempts to rationalize this second shift of loyalties:

When Hiraṇyākṣa, the enemy of the gods, was slain, Prahlāda protected his kingdom; devoted to Viṣṇu, he abandoned his demon nature and sacrificed to the gods. But one day the demon failed to honor a Brahmin ascetic who came to his house; this was caused by the deluding magic of the gods [māyā]. *The Brahmin cursed Prahlāda: "Your heavenly devotion to Viṣṇu will be destroyed, since you use it to insult Brahmins." Then, by the power of the Brahmin's curse, Prahlāda was deluded and became attached to his kingdom; he oppressed Brahmins and was full of anger against Viṣṇu, for he recalled the slaughter of his father. Then Viṣṇu and Prahlāda fought in battle; Prahlāda lost again, sought refuge with Viṣṇu, meditated, and achieved final communion with Viṣṇu.*[190]

The motif used to explain Prahlāda's demonic backsliding is dreadfully trite; the "insult to a Brahmin" is a kind of *presbyter ex machina* used to explain Indra's

[188] *Viṣṇu* 1.15–20; *Bhāgavata* 7.1–10; *Śiva, Jñāna Saṃ.* 59–61.

[189] *Kūrma* 1.15.1–75. [190] *Ibid.*, 1.15.70–89.

frequent losses of power, Śiva's demotion to *liṅga* form, the onset of droughts, and what you will. What is more interesting is the fact that (as with the myths of Śukra and Viśvarūpa), the *Kūrma* finds it necessary to explain Prahlāda's demonic behavior (including his dutiful return to svadharma, to avenge his father) but not to explain why the demon should serve the gods in the first place, against all laws of demon nature. Prahlāda is reenlightened, as he is first enlightened, by being vanquished by Viṣṇu in battle; this seems to satisfy the Purāṇic bard, in spite of the fact that dozens and dozens of demons are vanquished by the gods on every page without seeing the light. In view of the *Mahābhārata* version of the Prahlāda myth, one is tempted to suggest that the "Brahmin" who curses Prahlāda may be Indra in disguise; the fact that Prahlāda becomes too attached to his kingdom is further reminiscent of the phrase with which he taunts Indra in the Epic—"I am too busy to teach you, too involved with my kingdom." Thus Prahlāda goes through one more stage here than in the *Devībhāgavata*: from demonic, to virtuous, to demonic, and finally to virtuous again.

The *Padma Purāṇa* returns yet again to the question that troubles the Hindu most—not the cause of Prahlāda's anomalous virtue, but the cause of his lapse from that virtue:

[*The sages asked,*] *A terrible doubt has come upon us; some wise men tell us, in the Purāṇas, how Prahlāda fought with Viṣṇu in the battle between gods and demons. How did he come to be killed by Viṣṇu and still enter into Viṣṇu's body?* [*The bard replied,*] *Listen to the story of the birth of Prahlāda as Brahmā himself told it. It is told differently in the Purāṇas.*[191]

The Brahmin Somaśarman wished to perform yoga and to die united with Viṣṇu. As the time of his death approached, demons came into Somaśarman's presence. Some of the sages there shouted, "Demons!" and as this great shout reached Somaśarman's ears he broke his meditation because of his fear of the demons, and he died immediately in this way, terrified of the demons. Therefore he was reborn in the house of a demon, as Prahlāda, the son of Hiraṇyakaśipu, and in the great battle between gods and demons he was killed by Viṣṇu. But as Prahlāda was fighting he saw the true form of Viṣṇu, and because he had practised yoga he remembered his previous life: "I was once named Somaśarman, and now I have entered the body of a demon. By my great merit and knowledge I will go from this body to the highest dwelling." When Prahlāda died, his mother Kamalā, the wife of Hiraṇyakaśipu, wept until the sage Nārada told her, "Do not grieve for your son. He was killed by Viṣṇu and will be reborn as your son, again called Prahlāda, but devoid of demon qualities of nature, endowed instead with godliness, and he will become Indra and will be honored by the gods." Then Nārada left, and Prahlāda was born again in the womb of Kamalā, and by the grace of Viṣṇu he became

[191] Cf. *Padma* 6.265, the conventional bhakti version.

king of the gods in heaven. Becoming a god and taking the place of Indra, he obtained release and the highest place of Viṣṇu.[192]

Until now, the question of the origin of Prahlāda's devotion to Viṣṇu was answered without reference to previous existences: he was conquered through a confrontation in battle, or was simply born virtuous. Now, perhaps through the influence of the *Kūrma Purāṇa*, the old myth of Prahlāda's fight against the gods reappears and the question arises: Why does the devotee fight against Viṣṇu?[193] This is not an entirely new question; the secondary episodes of the *Devībhāgavata* and *Kūrma* begin with the premise of Prahlāda's wickedness and then go on to explain why he became good and then evil again. But this is the first time that Prahlāda's *initial* antagonism against Viṣṇu is discussed, and a very inadequate discussion it is, at that. The *Padma* simply reverses the assumptions of all previous texts and asserts that by nature, by *birth*, originally, Prahlāda was good, and that only through a rather peculiar accident of *death* did he become bad. By postulating an earlier cycle of existence (like that of Vṛtra as the Gandharva Citraratha or Citraketu), the *Padma* bodly tacks on the premise of the straightforward bhakti texts (that Prahlāda was born virtuous) to the vacillating cycles of the *Devībhāgavata*, so that Prahlāda is now virtuous at first, then demonic, then virtuous, then demonic, then virtuous; this hardly clarifies the issue. In this way, however, the eternal dharma (devotion to Viṣṇu) is made primary, the svadharma (demon duty) secondary; the first need not be explained, and the second is easily explained by the equivalent of a curse—the curse that ruins Prahlāda in other variants.

Not content to let well enough alone, however, the *Padma* adds yet another rebirth for Prahlāda, this time as the nondemonic demon, devoid of precisely the quality of demon nature which he abandons by free will within one birth in the *Kūrma*; this is the ambivalent figure to which the myth inevitably returns. The final stage of the myth ends in the surprising statement that Prahlāda, now the godlike demon, actually became a god, that he became Indra, king of the gods, usurping Indra's place—the Vedic premise that began all the trouble in the very earliest texts, but here obviated by the fact that (since Prahlāda is now a god) the demons have not won after all. This is the final irony, one that is hardly vitiated by the usual tag line—that Prahlāda ultimately achieved release and reached Viṣṇu's heaven (vacating Indra's throne once again). In terms of ethics, role reversals, and the possibility of establishing priorities between relative and absolute dharma, we are more confused than ever. The frequent moral rapprochements, and even exchanges, between gods and demons have no effect, for power, not morality, is the motivating force of the myths, and only devotion can overcome the thirst for power.

[192] *Padma* 2.1.5.1–35. [193] Hacker, p. 200.

15. The Ambivalence of the Demon Priest

The good demon is an ambiguous being, whose ambiguity lies in his relation with the gods: he is a nongod and at the same time he shares attributes of the gods. He is by (ideal) definition inferior to the gods, just as the ascetic man is by (ideal) definition dependent on the gods; but in actuality he is equal or superior to the gods. These ambiguities could be removed either by denaturing the good demon or ascetic man (transforming him into a god) or by destroying his "godly" attributes (killing him, corrupting him, or removing his power). The first of these methods is rare in the case of demons (it does occur in the myth of Prahlāda) but common in the case of men; the second is, however, far more prevalent in both instances, particularly in pre-bhakti texts.

The particular virtue that characterizes most of the "good" demons, generosity, can perhaps best be understood in the human context of the Vedic sacrificial ritual. This has been brilliantly demonstrated by J. C. Heesterman; the sacrifice involves two competing parties, host and guest, giver and receiver:

> At the start the host is in possession of the goods of life; at the end the positions are reversed. But the guest and recipient has to pay the price of taking upon himself the onus of the death and destruction involved in the sacrificial largess. For, though it is the host who offers the "goods of life," it is the guest who is required to give the order for the killing and the preparing of the sacrificial food.[194]

(Similarly, the mistreated guest takes away his host's evil karma.[195]) Remarking on the parallels between the conflict of the two parties and that of gods and demons, he continues: "It does not seem fortuitous that still in Purāṇic mythology, the Asuras are often in the role of munificent sacrificial patrons," and he points out that the sacrificial fire is to be taken from the home of a rich man who is "like a demon."[196] The generous demon must "give" the sacrifice to the gods, only to have it taken back from him again; since the rich man is "like a demon," the sacrifice must be stolen from him as the Vedas are always "stolen back" from the demons (for if a demon "gives" a sacrifice, his virtue threatens the gods). The fact that the Soma or other parts of the sacrifice are supposed to be stolen can best be understood in the context of the battlefield nature of the ritual.[197] The second factor that is evident here is the transfer of guilt from the host to the guest, from the gods to the demons; this recurs in the mythology of the battle of Indra and Viśvarūpa, where the guilt of the sacrifice of Viśvarūpa (who is himself symbolic of the threefold sacrifice, the sacrificial beast) must be transferred from the gods; in ritual, the recipient of the sacrificer's sin is often the priest himself (who

[194] Heesterman (1978), pp. 87–88.

[195] O'Flaherty (1973), pp. 182–183; and see below, chap. X, sec. 4.

[196] *Kāṭh. Sam.* 8.12; 96.7; *Āpastamba Śrauta Sūtra* 5.14.1 Cf. *RV* 10.151.3.

[197] Heesterman (1962), pp. 22 and 24.

receives the sacrificial fee in payment for this), while in the myths the recipient of the sin is either the demonic priest or the patron who withholds payment from the priest,[198] a figure who is the inverse of the excessively munificent demon.

The ambivalence of the priest in the myths is twofold: the "bad" priest of the gods and the "good" priest of the demons. The first instance is relatively simple: where the victory of the gods is the absolute (to be achieved at any cost), the use of any means to defeat the demons appears to be justified. Moreover, the priest may change his patrons and his loyalties through motives neither of svadharma nor of eternal dharma, but rather through blatant self-interest–greed and opportunism. The demon priest is more complex and comes in a variety of types. The demon priest serving a demonic demon upholds the svadharma of demons and the svadharma of priests but comes into conflict with eternal dharma. The demon priest who serves a good demon creates no conflict unless he chooses to oppose the good demon, to exhort him in his demonic duties; then he upholds svadharma but violates eternal dharma, like the complying priest of the demonic demon.

The role of the demon priest in forming a transitional category between the opposed categories of svadharma and eternal dharma changes in each of the three periods. In the Vedic period, the priests mediate by shifting from one patron to the other without contradicting their own priestly nature. In the post-Vedic period, the priests mediate by providing the means to eliminate the ambiguous good demons–by corrupting them, making them consistently demonic. In the bhakti period, the priests as mediators sponsor consistency by bringing good demons under the hegemony of the gods. In all cases, the structure of relations between the gods and the demons is preserved; inconsistency (the self-contradictory category of the demon priest) makes possible consistency (the perpetual separation of the ideal categories). Mediation preserves distinction.

[198] See below, chap. VI, sec. 4.

Shall mortal man be more just than God?
Shall a man be more pure than his maker?
Job 4:17

VI

THE PARADOX OF THE EVIL GOD: The Transfer of Sin

1. Evil Arises on Earth from Parts of the Body of God

It is evident from the myths of the necessity of evil that, in Hinduism, evil (like good) is an integral part of God and stems from him. An important corpus of Vedic and Purāṇic myths views creation as the process of the dismemberment of the creator himself.[1] In the Vedas, this is an act of true and literal self-sacrifice on the part of the primeval creator, who destroys his body so that the four classes of mankind may be born from it: the Brahmin from his mouth, Kṣatriyas from his arms, Vaiśyas from his thighs, and Śūdras from his feet. But by the time of the Purāṇas, the dismembered god produces a more complex universe, with noxious elements arising from his own ignoble parts:

When Brahmā took on a body in which the quality of darkness [tamas] *was predominant, the demons were born from his thigh; he abandoned that body, which became night. He took another body in which the quality of passion* [rajas] *was predominant, and from him was born the race of men; he abandoned that body quickly, and it became the dawn.*[2]

[1] *RV* 10.90.1–16; 1.162; 1.163; *Bṛhadāraṇyaka Up.* 1.4; *Śata.* 2.1.4.11; 14.4.2.23; *Tait. Br.* 3.12.9.2; *Tait. Sam.* 4.3.10.1; 7.1.1.4; O'Flaherty (1975), pp. 27–35.

[2] *Viṣṇu* 1.5.28–67; O'Flaherty (1975), pp. 43–46. Cf. *Śata.* 11.1.6.1–11; *Ch. Up.* 8.7–11; *MBh.* 1.60; 12.160; *Bhāgavata* 2.5–6; 3.12.3; *Kūrma* 1.8; *Liṅga* 1.71; *Mārk.* 50–51; *Padma* 5.3; 5.6; 6.260; *Vāyu* 2.16; see above, chap. III, sec. 2.

In addition to those evil creatures expressly said to have been created by him on purpose, God creates a series of failures from his own flawed bodies.

The concept of "dismembered evil" recurs in Purāṇic texts: evil spirits (Guhyakas) arise from Kṛṣṇa's private part (*guhya*), his penis or anus, and injury, misfortune, death, and hell derive from the rectum of the creator.[3] Other forms of anal creation may be seen in the widespread Hindu belief that Brahmā eats rice and then emits us, as well as in the statement that Brahmā created the demons (Asuras) in the form of a breath (*asu*) from his rectum.[4] Thus man is a cosmic turd, and though the theological implications are not entirely clear, demons would appear to be of less consequence, or at least less substance–no more than a celestial fart.

Brahmā created from his behind defeat, ignorance, and adharma; the evil Adharma that arose from his back was a terrible, filthy creature made of his own sin [*pātaka*][5]–the flaw that would otherwise cause Brahmā himself to fall to hell. But Brahmā does not fall, for Adharma is created instead, and from Adharma are born deception, greed, wickedness, anger, and the Kali Age.

The Brāhmaṇas contain the seeds of the belief that evil originated in the body of the creator and was dispersed from him:

In the beginning, Prajāpati was alone and wanted to procreate; seeking in vain a second, a female, he saw the Brahmin and asked him to procreate with him, but the Brahmin refused, saying, "No, for you are in the grasp of evil; evil is upon your head." At Prajāpati's request, the Brahmin bound him at the nape of the neck, the waist, and the ankles, and with three strokes got rid of the evil for him. The evil was then divided into threefold prosperity (Śrī) and placed in the cow, in sleep, and in shadow. Then Prajāpati heated himself in order to create.[6]

Though the source of Prajāpati's evil is not discussed here, the pattern of the beginning of the myth is that of incest (the unsuccessful search for a woman other than his daughter) and the evil is on Prajāpati's head (the organ which is removed in punishment for incest in many other myths). Once Prajāpati has been purified he proceeds to create in the approved manner, by heating his body in asceticism. It is remarkable that the evil is changed into good before it is distributed; as Heesterman comments, "Here we see the reversal pāpman-śrī through the medium of the brahman power." Śrī often functions as the inverse of evil, but even without this explicit reversal the pattern of myths of dismemberment of the body of the creator god (or of the body of the slain demon) allows for either goodness or evil to be dispersed in this way.

[3] *Brahmavaivarta* 1.5.60–61; *Bhāgavata* 2.6.8. [4] *Liṅga* 1.70.199.

[5] *Bhāgavata* 2.6.9; *Kalki* 1.1.14–19. [6] *Jai. Br.* 2.369–70; Heesterman (1962), p. 26.

2. The Transfer of Evil

Thus the gods create forms of evil that trouble mankind forever after, sometimes in order to free the gods themselves from sin. Inherent in many creation myths is the belief that certain human troubles originate within the physical essence of the gods and might have remained outside the sphere of mankind had not the gods elected to inflict them on mortals, to transfer these troubles from themselves to mankind. This theme recurs in many myths in which evil (*moha, kalmāṣa, pāpa*, or a particular sin like Brahminicide), conceived of as a physical entity like karma, arises in a god who is then forced to rid himself of it by transferring it to men or women. This is the reverse of the motif (rare in Hinduism, but found in the later bhakti myths) in which God takes upon himself the sins of mankind, and it forms a bridge between two related but contrasting ideas of evil: that God creates evil against his will, and that he wishes to create it.[7] The myths of transfer form a mediating corpus, for although God does not wish to have evil arise in the first place, once it has been established he willingly "creates" it for mankind in order to free himself of it. Since, in the post-Vedic corpus, men do not necessarily fight on the side of the gods, men can at least serve as a convenient dump for celestial moral garbage.

The concept of the scapegoat appears in ancient Indian sources. In one ritual, the accumulated sins of the sacrificer are placed on the head of a man who is then chased away at the end of the ritual.[8] Another early text describes the transfer of sin from the sacrificer to his rival. This rite focuses on the sacrificer's wife, who is asked to name her paramours; in this manner, it is stated, the sin becomes less, untruth is turned into truth, and untruth is transferred to the rival, who is seized by Varuṇa.[9] The role of the woman is essential here as in all later myths of transferred sin; her guilt is assumed and is implicit in the rather leading question that is put to her, asking not if she has a paramour but who he is, or rather who *they* are (a "Have-you-stopped-beating-your-wife?" question if ever there was one). This guilt is then transferred to the sacrificer's rival (serving a double purpose, as in the agonistic sacrifices of gods and demons); "thus evil (*pāpman*) is taken away from the *aśvamedha* [horse-sacrifice] sacrificer by affinal relatives."[10] Marital union is said to be essential for release from Varuṇa's bonds;[11] the woman may be the cause of all evil, but it is she who takes the burden of it away from man. In other rites, the evil (*pāpman*) of the consecrated sacrificer is divided

[7] See below, chap. X, sec. 2, and above, chap. III, secs. 1 and 2.

[8] *Śata*. 13.3.6.5. Cf. *Tāṇḍya* 17.1.16 and *RV* 10.155.3.

[9] *Śata*. 2.5.2.20; *Tait. Br.* 1.6.5.3; Heesterman (1971), pp. 13–14.

[10] *Āpastamba Śrauta Sūtra* 8.6.20; *Tait. Br.* 3.8.4.1; cf. *Tāṇḍya* 5.6.10; Heesterman (1971), pp. 13–14.

[11] *Śata*. 2.5.2.17 and .36.

into three parts (like the evil of Prajāpati or Indra) and transferred to anyone who eats his food, to anyone who speaks of his evil (or says evil things about him), and to anyone who mentions his name (or to the ants who bite him).[12]

When evil is transferred not from a man to a man, or from a sacrificer to a priest, but from a god to a man, one of the basic Hindu responses to the problem of evil arises: evil afflicts mankind because it is *not* present in God; that is, we are now evil because God is (now) good. He must make us evil in order that he may remain good; thus our evil is proof that God is good, not a contradiction of this hypothesis. Since our own evil is not our fault, the sense of sin cannot be separated from a sense of having been sinned against–that is, of having evil thrust upon us. This appears to stand the whole Western approach to theodicy on its head. In village Buddhism, too, the relationship between god and man is based on this concept of evil flowing from heaven to earth–but here for the benefit of man:

> By transferring merit the devout worshipper is enhancing the salvation prospects of the gods. The gods in turn may reciprocate by assisting the worshipper to achieve his immediate mundane objectives. Merit transfer links man and deity in a complex ethic of mutual self-interest–man interested in the goods of the world and the deity interested in the rewards of salvation.[13]

The worshipper willingly "saves" his gods by giving them his own merit (and taking their sins), in part because he needs a pure god to accomplish his own ends. Similarly, people willingly accept Indra's sins in order to keep him alive and well for general purposes as well as to gain the particular benefits he offers them–worldly objectives of fertility and rebirth. This reciprocity is not unlike that of the Vedic sacrifice, in which gods wish *men* to remain pure in order that the gods may remain powerful and nourished by the sacrifice. The conventional idea of salvation is thus reversed: men try to save the gods. In many later bhakti myths, since the sacred shrines are all on earth, sinful gods must descend to earth in order to be purified; Indra must go on pilgrimage in South India (pretending to be on a royal hunt, to save face) in order to expiate his Brahminicide,[14] as Śiva must go to Benares to expiate this sin. Earth, not heaven, is the place to get ride of sin and evil.

For evil in India is not a moral problem but a problem of power, and power flows within the closed universe of the world-egg; there is a fixed quantity of everything, including evil, so that more *here* necessarily implies less *there*. God must be powerful in order for the universe (including mankind) to remain alive and to function properly; and he must rid himself of his sin in order to remain in power. The evil god must be kept powerful, no matter how evil he becomes; for

[12] *Kāṭh. Sam.* 23.6; *Mait. Sam.* 3.6.7; *Tāṇḍya* 5.6.10; Heesterman (1962), pp. 12–13.

[13] Obeyesekere, p. 26. [14] *Tiruviḷaiyāṭaṟpurāṇam* 1.

though sin does not negate divinity, the loss of power does. As power then becomes the summum bonum, certain rather cynical Hindu texts use the concept of power to determine what is and is not sinful: "No one in this world ever sees the fruits of dharma and adharma. Dharma is carried on power, like smoke on the wind; dharma belongs to the powerful. All is pure [*śuci*] for those who have power."[15]

Ronald Morton Smith has remarked that "if God is amoral, the essential sin must be the unsuccessful. . . . By removing ritual impurity, one is removing death, the acme of non-success."[16] Since death, rather than sin, is the quality that distinguishes god from man, Hindu mythology dwells at some length on the manner in which the gods removed the impurity of death from themselves —and gave it to men.[17] The transfer of other forms of ritual impurity that, like death, remove the power of the god is another recurrent motif of the myths.

The pattern of distribution and transfer appears in early Vedic texts associated at first, apparently, not with an impurity that must be disposed of, but on the contrary, with a desired object that must be sought and collected from various places:

Vāc [sacred speech] left the gods and hid in the waters. The gods claimed her from the waters, who gave her to the gods but asked for the boon that whatever unclean substance men might throw into them would not pollute them. Then Vāc entered the trees; the gods claimed her but the trees refused to give her up; the gods cursed the trees: "By means of your own handle [an axe with a wooden handle] as a thunderbolt they will cut you." Then the trees distributed Vāc in four things: drums, lute, axle, and reed-pipe [all of which "sing" and are made of wood].[18]

Waters and trees are the receptacles for the "good" thing, but the elements of pollution and curse are already present in seminal form. The waters are given the boon *not* to be polluted, but the men who throw unclean substances into them appear as objects of transferred sin in later variants;[19] and the axe that cuts the trees also recurs in those later texts. The one most frequent receptacle, along with waters and trees, is woman, who appears here as the central subject, the goddess Vāc. Thus, just as the pattern of creation from the dismembered body of God originally had benevolent motives and created good substances but later formed the basic pattern for the dismemberment of evil, so too the pattern of transferred sin arises first from the seeking and distribution of good. The role of water in the removal of pollution is obvious. The use of a tree or plant to receive evil is a very old Indian idea, perhaps derived from the miraculous properties of the Vedic Soma plant. The Atharva Veda addresses a "wiping-off" plant that removes all

[15] *MBh.* 12.132.1–7.

[16] Smith, p. 15.

[17] See below, chap. VIII, secs. 1–2.

[18] *Tāṇḍya* 6.5.10–13; cf. *Tait. Sam.* 6.1.4.1, *Mait. Sam.* 3.6.8, *Kāṭh. Sam.* 23.4.

[19] *MBh.* 12.273.

sins: "The sin, the pollution, whatever we have done with evil, by you we wipe that off."[20]

Another great remover of polluting evil is Agni, fire. Agni himself is delivered from his own sin so that the worshippers can then wipe off their sins on Agni;[21] again, the Lord is helped by those who would help themselves. Like Vāc, Agni flees from the gods and is collected from various hiding places in a manner that further expands the pattern of distribution.[22] At first, in the Ṛg Veda, Agni flees from the gods, hides in the waters and the plants, is discovered by Yama (god of the dead), and bribed with the promise of a full life-span and a share in the sacrifice.[23] Then Agni is said to hide in a bamboo stalk or a reed,[24] or, later, in the *śamī* tree from which the Vedic fire-sticks were made.[25] In the still later mythology of Śiva, Agni (the fiery seed of Śiva) hides in a clump of reeds from which Skanda is born.[26]

The next stage in the development of the Agni cycle appears in a text in which Agni is collected from his various hiding places and then redistributed, just as Vāc is redistributed when she is collected from trees:

Agni fled and entered the seasons, the waters, and the trees. Yama and Varuṇa found him, and the gods promised him a long life-span and a share in the sacrifice. He returned to the gods, and his bone became the pine tree of the gods (deodar); his fat and flesh became a fragrant resin; his sinew became sweet-smelling grass; his seed became silver and gold; the hair of his body and his head became two sorts of grasses; his nails became tortoises, his entrails, the Avakā plant, his marrow, sand and gravel, and his blood and bile became various minerals.[27]

Agni is distributed in a different, but still benevolent, manner in another text:

The sages sprinkled Agni with water; that water dripped off and became frogs, and the moisture burnt off by Agni became bamboo and lotuses.[28]

The life-span which Agni is granted in earlier texts when Yama finds him is then developed into an actual exchange between Agni and Yama, a motif that combines the idea of transfer (Agni exchanging his own mortality for food from the god of death[29]) with the idea of the god conquering death at the expense of men and animals (the fishes whom Agni makes mortal). This text also utilizes the theme of the curse:

Agni fled from the gods and entered the waters. A fish reported him and was cursed by

[20] *AV* 7.65.2. [21] *AV* 12.2.12–13. [22] See above, chap. V, sec. 6.

[23] *RV* 10.51.1–9; Sāyaṇa on *RV* 1.65.1. [24] *Śata.* 6.3.1.31. [25] *MBh.* 9.46.12–20.

[26] O'Flaherty (1975), pp. 105–115; (1973), 90–110; *MBh.* 3.213–216.

[27] *Bṛhaddevatā* 7.61–80; O'Flaherty (1975), pp. 99–100.

[28] *Śata.* 9.1.2.22. [29] See above, chap. V, sec. 6.

him: "They will slay you whenever they fancy." The gods found Agni, who asked to have a share of the offering. . . . Agni was in that world; Yama was in this. The gods said, "Let us exchange them." They offered Agni food and they offered Yama kingship over the departed ancestors. And so Agni is the food-eater of the gods, and Yama is the king of the dead ancestors. Thus Agni came to be in this world of the gods, and Yama in that world of the dead.[30]

In the *Mahābhārata,* the curse is extended to other substances in which Agni lodges; and the curse is now joined with its counterpart, the boon:

The gods searched for Agni, who was hidden in the waters. A frog told the gods where Agni was, and they found him; Agni cursed the treacherous frog to have no tongue, but the gods did a favor for the frogs, saying, "You will utter many kinds of speech, even though you will be tongueless, and you will live in holes and move about at night." Then Agni hid in an aśvattha *[sacred fig] tree, and an elephant told the gods where he was; Agni cursed the elephants to have their tongues bent backwards, but the gods did a favor for the elephants, saying, "Though your tongue will be bent backwards, you will eat all foods with it and utter loud sounds." Agni then entered bamboo, but when steam indicated where he was, he entered a* śamī *tree; a parrot told the gods where he was, and Agni cursed the parrot to be deprived of speech; but the gods, filled with compassion, told the parrot that he would be able to say "Ka" sweetly and indistinctly, like the speech of a child or an old man. And then the gods found Agni in the* śamī.[31]

In these two texts, Agni curses not the hiding place (the waters) but rather the aquatic animal who betrays him (the fish or the frog). His curse destroys their speech, the original desired thing (Vāc) that the gods sought in the waters. In another text, Agni curses the waters as Vāc did:

Agni fled and hid in the waters. The gods found him. Agni spat in the waters and cursed them to be spat upon and to be an unsafe refuge. From that (water and phlegm) arose the Āptya deities.[32]

In spite of the curse, the benevolent spirit in which Agni elsewhere creates (rather than curses) frogs reappears at the end, where Agni's phlegm in the water creates helpful deities. Moreover, the waters are the very deities who help Indra to rid himself of his sin. Thus the link between the two patterns—Agni hiding and Indra purifying himself—appears in this early text. This link is strengthened by two other texts in which, when Indra flees from the gods (after killing Vṛtra) and hides in a lotus stalk under water, Agni is persuaded by the gods to enter the water and find Indra.[33]

[30] *Tait. Sam.* 2.6.6.1–5; O'Flaherty (1975), p. 101.

[31] *MBh.* 13.84.20–47; O'Flaherty (1975), pp. 101–104.

[32] *Śata.* 1.2.3.1. [33] *Śata.* 1.6.4.1–2; *MBh.* 5.16.1–12.

3. The Expiation of Indra's Brahminicide

When Indra commits Brahminicide by destroying the Brahmin demon (Vṛtra or Viśvarūpa), he must face the consequences of that sin. In the Vedic context, the sin is merely the sin of the warrior, not the sin of the god;[34] his enemies are our enemies, the demons, the Others. As a warrior, he enters into a symbiotic relationship with the priest who restores him after battle. Thus when Indra has killed Vṛtra, he is grasped by an evil that causes him to grow old, an evil that is death, both Vṛtra's death (the evil of killing) and Indra's death (the evil of dying). He becomes free from evil by means of the sacrifice on the tenth day, the same sacrifice that purifies a mother and newborn child ten days after birth. When Indra has killed the demons he realizes that he has done a deed not heard of, and the gods perform a sacrifice that frees him from his evil.[35] By means of the sacrifice, the impurity of Indra is transferred from him to the priest who performs the sacrifice; as Heesterman has pointed out, Indra in the myth is burdened with evil by killing the demons just as the sacrificer is burdened with the impurity of killing the sacrificial victim. The threefold evil of the sacrificer or Indra is removed by the priest in the same way, for it stems from the same source: "Indra's killing Viśvarūpa and the dīkṣita's [sacrificer's] killing the sacrifice seems to carry the same meaning."[36]

The guilt of the warrior or the evil of the sacrificer was easily removed by the priest in Vedic times; but in post-Vedic mythology the demon killed by Indra ceased to be regarded merely as a sacrificial beast and was, on the contrary, generally said to be a demon priest (the very figure who, in Vedic ritual, removed the evil from the killer of the beast). Then the consequences of the slaughter become labyrinthine, for Indra destroys the very means of his own ritual expiation. In this view, Indra's sin is not merely that of manslaughter (a cheap crime to pay for in Vedic times) but that of Brahminicide, the most terrible of all sins (according to the Brahmin authors of the lawbooks). Indra is thus caught between two moral perspectives; as E. W. Hopkins drily remarks, "Curiously enough, though the act of slaying the demon is virtuous, evil always follows the slayer."[37]

By Epic and Purāṇic times, to add insult to injury, Indra is demoted and superseded by Viṣṇu and Śiva, so that he is no longer *the* god but merely *a* god; reduced to the role of a clown-king, a blustery figurehead mocked by the now dominant priests, he becomes no more than the hit man of the gods. His sin is somewhat diluted by this process; he is merely obeying orders. Thus it is said, "By Śiva's inviolable command, Indra protects the gods, kills the demons, and guards the worlds."[38] As he is a mere tool of Viṣṇu or Śiva, Indra's sufferings and

[34] Dumézil (1969 and 1970), *passim*. [35] *Jai. Br.* 2.324; *Tāṇḍya* 22.14.2.

[36] Heesterman (1962), pp. 22–24. [38] *Śiva* 7.2.2.27.

shortcomings are all the more acceptable to the worshippers of these gods, who would rather blame him for their troubles than blame Viṣṇu or Śiva. Yet, since Viṣṇu and Śiva advise and consent to the transfer of Indra's sin in later texts, they ultimately must be held responsible for the evil that appears among mankind in this way. Thus even in the later period, the myth of Indra's sin is the myth of *the* god's complicity in our evil.

In the earlier Agni myths, a "good" thing is collected; later, the corresponding "bad" thing is redistributed in the very sources from which the "good" had been collected; this pattern of development also applies to the Indra myths. When Indra killed Vṛtra, his power and strength went into the earth and appeared as plants and roots; cattle ate the plants and the gods milked the cattle; Indra drank the milk and regained his strength.[39] When Indra killed Vṛtra, grass grew over him; Agni burnt the grass, rain fell, plants grew, the plants were milked, and Indra was cured.[40] As the essence of Indra's strength is the Soma that nourishes him, other texts of this period place Soma in the very substances into which Indra's strength has flowed: Indra killed Vṛtra and hid; Agni found him; the gods collected Soma from cows, plants, and water, and Indra drank it.[41] Thus Vṛtra is identified with the Soma; but Soma, like Vṛtra, comprises all sorts of evil of nature and of moral life;[42] the treacherous Soma and Agni are identified with Vṛtra in very early myths.[43] Later, when Indra kills Vṛtra and is overwhelmed by Brahminicide, his strength leaves him and enters the wind;[44] this text does not tell how he recovers his strength, but in earlier texts the wind often acts, like Agni, to find Indra so that the gods may restore him, and the wind is the life's breath of the dismembered man;[45] so it may be implicit here that wind revives Indra.

Other texts of this period describe the distribution not of Indra's strength but of Vṛtra; and at first (as with Agni) this distribution is beneficial for mankind:

When Indra killed Vṛtra, the earth obtained various forms from Vṛtra, the sky obtained the stars, and in space (between heaven and earth) the white lotus of the ether appeared.[46]

This tripartite division recurs in the myths of the three-headed Viśvarūpa, whose three heads are said to become three kinds of birds; elsewhere, cocks are born from Vṛtra's blood, but it is explicitly stated that, because of this, cocks are unclean;[47] thus the distribution of the demon's body begins to take on unpleasant connotations. In a Tamil text, when three birds have appeared from Viśvarūpa's three heads (including the cock and the crow), Indra makes the female demons drink Viśvarūpa's blood.[48] This device foreshadows the roles of the female fury arising

[39] *Tait. Sam.* 2.5.3. [40] *Jai. Br.* 2.157.2. [41] *Śata.* 1.6.4.8. [42] Buschardt, *passim.*
[43] See above, chap. V, sec. 6. [44] *Mārk.* 5.8–11. [45] *RV* 10.90.
[46] *Tāṇḍya* 18.9.6; cf. *Mait. Sam.* 4.4.7. [47] *Bṛhaddevatā* 6.150, etc.; *MBh.* 12.273.58.
[48] *Tiruviḷaiyāṭaṟpurāṇam* 1.11.

from slaughter and the female whose impure menstrual blood will release Indra; it also draws upon the belief that demons (particularly demonesses) "eat" sins (punishing sinners and purifying them), thus further absolving Indra of the ill effects of his sin. Nevertheless Indra must atone for the murder in this text, and the slaughter of Vṛtra has even more dangerous consequences.

One Epic text still retains echoes of the Vedic myth in which the dismemberment of the conquered demon's body results in the distribution of good things. When Indra conquers the demon Bali, Śrī leaves Bali's body and Indra places her for safekeeping in four receptacles among men: earth, waters, the sacrificial fire, and truthful men.[49] The first three substances are traditional receptacles for Indra's sin, rather than his prosperity; the fourth, truthful men, replaces the traditional fourth, wicked women, providing an inversion appropriate to the distribution of desiderata. The demon's slaughter results in benefits not only because Indra takes Śrī from him (as he takes Soma from Vṛtra in the Vedic myth) but because Bali is here a good demon, who preaches to Indra for several chapters before departing from the scene. Śrī herself is often regarded as an ignoble deity because of her fickleness, and she is distributed in the urine and dung of cows rather than in the menstrual blood of women. There is a hint of this even in the myth under discussion, for Śrī remarks that no one knows if she is demonic or divine, and she is called Intolerable (Duḥsahā), the female aspect of a seminal demonic force.

The negative effect of the distribution of the dead demon is frequently encountered in these myths. Vṛtra's dead body gave off a foul smell, and the gods placed the smell in (dead) cattle[50]—the very cattle who, when alive, helped Indra to regain his strength. Similarly, while Indra hides in waters and is later purified by them, Vṛtra pollutes the waters:

Indra killed Vṛtra, who flowed stinking toward the waters. Some, disgusted at Vṛtra, rose higher and higher and so were not polluted; others were polluted by him and must be strained by a strainer made of the grasses which arose from the (unpolluted) waters.[51]

The role of grasses and waters is familiar from the Vāc and Agni cycles and is maintained in later mythology. The body of Vṛtra has a double issue: the polluted waters and the grasses that remove pollution.

This division of Vṛtra into "pure" and "impure" halves occurs in another important series of texts in which Indra manages to dispose of Vṛtra without actually committing Brahminicide. Vṛtra begged Indra not to kill him, saying, "You are now what I was" (ruler of the universe); Indra cut Vṛtra in half; the Soma half of Vṛtra survives in the moon, while the demon half survives in the stomachs of all creatures.[52] This dissection of the demon into eater and eaten is

[49] *MBh.* 12.218.1–30; for Bali, see above, chap. V, sec. 13; for Śrī, below, chap. XII, sec. 2; for Intolerable, above, chap. III, sec. 2. [50] *Śata.* 4.1.3.8. [51] *Śata.* 1.1.3.5. [52] *Śata.* 1.6.3.17.

reminiscent of the myths of the appeasement of the hungry Agni; it recurs in the myth of the demon Rāhu, whose head is cut off when he has stolen and eaten the Soma; Rāhu's severed head survives because it has eaten the Soma, and it continues to eat the moon each month, but his body falls to earth and is destroyed.[53] The Vṛtra text adds a postscript: "Therefore men say, 'Vṛtra is within us' "; that is, because of Indra's sin we are afflicted with hunger, the source of all our woes (a concept which Eliade has suggested may stem from "the serpentine appearance of the intestines."[54])

But Vṛtra's connection with hunger is developed in another text:

When Indra was about to kill Vṛtra, they made a compact that Vṛtra would enter into Indra, for Indra's enjoyment, and so Vṛtra entered into Indra. Vṛtra is the belly; hunger is man's enemy. Indra gave it [hunger?] to Viṣṇu.[55]

Much is unclear in this text, but it appears that Vṛtra bribes Indra not to kill him, by promising him "enjoyment"–and Indra is noted for his Gargantuan appetite, particularly for Soma (the divinity that is elsewhere said to be the essence of half of Vṛtra, and to make a similar compact with Indra). Once in Indra's belly, Vṛtra apparently enters all creatures as in the first text; although Viṣṇu accepts "it," hunger is explicitly said to be the enemy of *man*. Indra's enjoyment is our affliction.

The motif of Vṛtra entering Indra is developed in the Epic:

Vṛtra, smelling foul, entered the earth and stole its odor; Indra hurled his thunderbolt at Vṛtra, who left the earth and entered the waters, stealing their flavor; again the thunderbolt was hurled, and Vṛtra entered light (which lost its form or color), wind (which lost its touch), air (which lost the property of sound) and finally the body of Indra himself. Then Indra slew Vṛtra within his body by means of his invisible thunderbolt.[56]

Vṛtra now enters some of the places where Vāc, Agni, Indra's strength, and Indra's sin lodge: earth, water, and air. Vṛtra pollutes them and Indra frees them from pollution, restoring to them their natural properties. But then Vṛtra enters Indra himself and is destroyed (as the demonic Kāma within Śiva's body is destroyed[57]), and Indra is *not* polluted. In this way, many of the premises of the Vedic episode are reversed. Another reversal may be seen in those Epic and Purāṇic versions of the myth in which Vṛtra swallows Indra,[58] a typically demonic thing to do. Two patterns are in tandem here: the demon who devours and must be made to vomit back the god (Vṛtra, Śukra swallowing Kaca, Rāhu

[53] *MBh.* 1.15–17; O'Flaherty (1975), pp. 274–280. [54] Eliade (1965), p. 93.

[55] *Tait. Sam.* 2.4.12.5–7; cf. *Sata.* 1.6.4.15–18 and 6.6.3.26–32. [56] *MBh.* 14.11.6–20.

[57] O'Flaherty (1973), pp. 148–149; *Matsya* 154.235–248; *Skanda* 5.2.13.27–35.

[58] *MBh.* 5.9–13; *Skanda* 1.1.17.200–266.

swallowing Soma), and the god-fire who swallows up the demon-oblation (Indra swallowing Vṛtra, Śiva swallowing Śukra, Agni swallowing Soma[59]).

Often, Vṛtra is regarded as sin (just as he is hunger, the great evil), and in slaying Vṛtra, Indra is destroying sin, not committing a sin. This view appears throughout the Ṛg Veda and recurs in those many Purāṇic texts in which, as soon as Vṛtra is killed, all creatures rejoice, the skies are clear, plants bloom in season, and all is well. This version of the myth occurs in the Brāhmaṇas, too, though not often: "While Indra was killing Vṛtra, Vṛtra's coils encircled Indra. The evil had seized Indra; he repelled the evil with hymns."[60] Elsewhere in the Brāhmaṇas it is said, "Vṛtra is evil; Indra slew him and burnt him completely by means of Agni, and thereby burnt all his evil."[61] Apparently "his evil" in this context refers not to the sin of Indra in killing Vṛtra but to the evil of Vṛtra, that is, the evil that was the very essence of Vṛtra. It is also said that the gods warded off Vṛtra, evil, and were delivered from evil; Vṛtra is evil; with the help of Indra the slayer of Vṛtra, the sacrificer slays the evil Vṛtra, who keeps him from well-being, virtue, and good work; that is why he makes an offering to Indra the slayer of Vṛtra.[62] Here the slaying of the evil Vṛtra is clearly beneficial to mankind, keeping the evil represented by Vṛtra away from us; this is in striking contradiction of the later texts in which by killing Vṛtra Indra saves himself but brings evil to us. These two sets of texts disagree about the result of the destruction of Vṛtra but not about his evil nature. Another important text based on this concept of the evil Vṛtra combines the idea that the encircling coils are evil with the idea that Agni burnt away this evil:

Indra slew Vṛtra. When Vṛtra was dead, he bound Indra with sixteen coils. From the head of Vṛtra there came forth cows with a bull behind them. Indra thought, "He who offers him (the bull) shall be freed from this evil." He offered to Agni a cow with a black neck; to Indra, Indra offered a bull. When Agni was offered a share, he burnt into sixteen pieces the coils of Vṛtra, and by the offering to Indra, Indra bestowed power on himself.[63]

Even when Vṛtra is dead he threatens Indra's power, as he does in the later myths of expiation. But the good things that come forth from the body of the demon (good things that the gods want—sacrificial cattle) are used by Indra to bribe Agni to save him, just as Indra steals from the demons the cows with which he bribes *their* priest. Indra sacrifices to himself in order to restore his powers; and, in addition, he uses the booty stolen from the demon to free himself from the sin of killing the demon, a sin here symbolized by the encircling coils of the dead body.

In several of these texts, fire alone is sufficient to burn away the evil, as it is in other texts where the sin is Indra's, not Vṛtra's:

[59] O'Flaherty (1975), pp. 280–282; Dange, pp. 155–237. [60] *Tāṇḍya* 13.5.22–23.

[61] *Śata.* 11.1.5.7–8. [62] *Śata.* 9.5.2.4; 11.1.5.7. [63] *Tait. Sam.* 2.1.4.5–6.

Indra slew the three-headed son of Tvaṣṭṛ. An inauspicious voice addressed him. Agni sacrificed for Indra and drove away the voice, removing the evil.[64]

In other texts that acknowledge the sin of slaying Viśvarūpa, and even in those that list other, related sins (giving the ascetics to the jackals, killing Vṛtra, contending with Bṛhaspati), mere chiding or repentance seems to be sufficient for Indra: "all creatures were angry with him"; "all creatures condemned Indra";[65] "Indra was addressed by an evil voice, and when he recognized that he was unclean, he was purified by this."[66] The evil voice (Vāc), which had led him to seek the assistance of Agni, here leads him to confess his own sin and purify himself, just as he restores his own powers by sacrificing to himself. As a result of the group of crimes for which he is condemned, the gods exclude Indra from the sacrifice and deprive him of the Soma (which he later steals from Tvaṣṭṛ);[67] to restore himself, Indra must steal Soma back or seek purification in the contrasting power of Agni.

The need for purification by Agni is particularly intense in the Viśvarūpa cycle, where the "demon" is not evil; then Indra must expiate his own evil. The *Rāmāyaṇa* poet remarks, "If dharma were adharma, then Indra would not have performed a sacrifice when he had killed the sage."[68] But even the killing of the wicked Vṛtra must be atoned for, and Agni's role in the Vṛtra myth becomes more and more complex. At first, Agni himself hides and is distributed; then he finds Indra; then he burns away Vṛtra; then he burns away Indra's sin in killing Vṛtra; and finally he is one of the substances to receive a portion of the sin of killing Vṛtra. Fire as a primary purifying agent plays an essential role in the simplified variants of the myth and retains that role even in the more elaborate variants. Water, too, the complementary primary purifier, often suffices to relieve Indra:

Indra beheaded Viśvarūpa, the three-headed son of Tvaṣṭṛ. Divine speech (Vāc) said to Indra, "You are a Brahmin-slayer, lord of a hundred powers, since you slew Viśvarūpa who sought refuge." The sage Sindhudvīpa sprinkled Indra and said the hymn that begins, "O waters" for the removal of that inauspicious evil.[69]

The reappearance of Vāc in her positive aspect highlights, in retrospect, the role of her alter ego, the evil voice, in other myths of this cycle.

Most of the simple expiations by fire or water are expiations for the sin of killing Viśvarūpa, not Vṛtra. Several later texts distinguish between the two cases, remarking that the first is a more serious sin than the second but easier to expiate:

[64] *Tāṇḍya* 17.5.1.; cf. 13.11.28. [65] *Śāṅkhāyana Śrauta Sūtra* 14.50.1–2; *Jai Br.* 2.134; cf. *Ait. Br.* 6.33.4; *Tait. Sam.* 2.5.1; *MBh.* 5.13. [66] *Tāṇḍya* 13.11.28; cf. 19.18–19.

[67] *Ait. Br.* 7.28; see above, chap. V, sec. 11. [68] *Rām.* 6.83.29. [69] *Bṛhaddevatā* 6.150–153; cf. *RV* 10.9.

When Indra killed Vṛtra he said, "The sin of killing Viśvarūpa I placed in earth, water, and trees in return for favors which I gave to them. But how can I wipe off the slaughter of Vṛtra?" The sages told him to perform a horse sacrifice, and thus an evil even greater than the slaughter of Tvaṣṭṛ's son Viśvarūpa was brought to nought like snow melted by the sun.[70]

Here, and elsewhere in the Purāṇas, a horse sacrifice replaces the simple application of fire or water as the means of purifying Indra. In some Brāhmaṇas, Indra's slaughter of the demon is regarded as evil incarnate, and by becoming incarnate the evil becomes susceptible to Indra's main power, brute force:

Indra, using his foot, tore off the demon Namuci's head, from which was born a Rākṣasa who kept calling out "Where are you going? Where will you get rid of me?" Indra beat it off with lead.[71]

Though the sin starts a chain reaction—the demon Namuci producing a Rākṣasa, just as Viśvarūpa's death produces Vṛtra (sometimes from Viśvarūpa's dead body), and Vṛtra's death produces the demonic Fury of Brahminicide—the chain is cut as it is started, by violence. This text is exceptional, however; usually some element of expiation or sacrifice is required to atone for the violence.

In later bhakti texts, Indra is released from his sin by the direct grace of the god, Viṣṇu (who supplies Bṛhaspati with an amulet, which simply burns up the Fury of Brahminicide)[72] or Śiva (who purifies Indra after the slaughter of Vṛtra when Indra has performed asceticism for Śiva).[73] Both of these expiations involve forms of fire (a fiery amulet or the fire of ascetic power)—fire now efficacious not in itself but only as a tool of the purifying god. In a South Indian text, water, enhanced by the grace of Śiva, suffices to save Indra even when Vṛtra's murder is regarded as an exceptional crime and Indra as a great sinner.[74] Another Tamil text describes purification through water but requires a more complicated and protracted expiation:

A demon conquered the three worlds, and Indra fled from him and hid on the slopes of the Himālayas. There one day he saw the daughter of Bhṛgu and wished to possess her; he grabbed her by the hand. When Bhṛgu saw this he said to Indra, "Since you are acting like a Rākṣasa (by indulging in the Rākṣasa form of marriage), you will become one." Indra became a Rākṣasa, roaming the forests performing evil deeds.

In Indra's absence, the gods made a human king serve as king of the gods; he killed the demons and protected the world from Rākṣasas, but then, when one of the dancing-girls laughed at him, he returned to earth and performed asceticism at shrines sacred to Śiva; he lost interest in kingship and refused to return to the throne of heaven.

The gods were now again without a protector, so Nārada sought the Rākṣasa Indra in

[70] *Bhāgavata* 6.13.5–20. [71] *Śata.* 5.4.1.9–10. [72] *Brahmavaivarta* 4.47.50–78. [73] *Skanda* 3.2.19.5–35.
[74] *Tiruvārūrppurāṇam* 13.1–53; see above, chap. V, sec. 4, and below, chap. IX, sec. 2.

the forests. Indra tried to eat Nārada, but Nārada sprinkled water and recited a spell, and the Rākṣasa drew back his outstretched hand. Nārada led him to a sacred river and told him to jump in; when the Rākṣasa refused, Nārada shoved him in, and he emerged as Indra, in his old form and in a state of total amnesia. Nārada told him what had happened, and Indra returned to rule heaven.[75]

Although Indra fails to slay the demon and hides not from the sin of slaughter but from the demon himself, the myth follows the pattern of the Vṛtra-slaying myth: in Indra's absence a human king (Nahuṣa in the Sanskrit versions) rules heaven for him. The good human king and the evil demon here combine to play the role of the good demon who usurps Indra's throne in so many myths; together, they drive Indra away. The substitute Indra then assumes the Indra motif of encounter with the dancing girls, with the opposite emotion (he dislikes them while Indra likes them too much) but with the same result: loss of the throne. Indra, meanwhile, assumes the role of a Rākṣasa, from whom the substitute Indra protects his subjects. Indra here takes the actual form of his usual demonic deeds; the moralistic Tamil text treats Indra as he deserves, preserving the ideal moral opposition between gods and demons: the evil demon is Indra, the good god his substitute. The virtuous substitute Indra, like Bṛhaspati's victims, voluntarily relinquishes the throne, which Indra is able to resume when he has been purified (against his will, for as a straight demon, he does not *want* to become good again).

4. The Transfer of Indra's Brahminicide

In most texts, Indra's purification is no simple matter; his sin is a substance that cannot easily be annihilated by fire or water, but must be kept in circulation, distributed and transferred. At first Indra's own strength leaves him and is distributed; then negative aspects of Indra's divine substance flow from him and pollute the world:

Indra killed Vṛtra and stole the Soma. He drank it, and it flowed in all directions from him. From what flowed from his nose, a lion sprang; from his ears, a jackal; from the lower opening of his body, tigers and other wild beasts.[76]

The first substance to emerge is the mucous from his nose, which pollutes (just as Agni's phlegm pollutes the waters) and endangers in the form of a lion—a lion whose form is often taken by the ambivalent goddess Vāc.[77] The expelled mucous is the poisonous counterpart of the ingested Soma, and the particular danger involved in releasing mucous—sneezing—is given a new twist in another text:

[75] *Tirumūrttimalaippurāṇam*, paṭalam 9 and 10.

[76] *Śata.* 5.5.4.10. [77] *Śata.* 3.5.1.8–36; *Tait. Saṃ.* 6.2.7.

Indra was hurt. He spat, and from his saliva various jujube fruits arose. Then he sneezed, and they said, "Live!" and so he lived. Before this time, people used to die when they sneezed. From Indra's nose, two lionesses arose; from his ears, two tigers and other wild beasts.[78]

Though the noxious animals are still present, the danger is somewhat mitigated by the implication that (in return for saying "Live!" to Indra when he sneezed – the Indian equivalent of our "God bless you!") Indra made it possible for people to remain alive after sneezing. Thus the curse is coupled with a boon.

This device – the giving of a boon to compensate for the curse that the god inflicts upon nongods – may be traced back to the Agni cycle, but it would appear from that cycle, and from the Indra corpus, that the boon is an afterthought. In several texts, the sin of Brahminicide is distributed among various recipients who are *not* given any compensation:

Indra, fearing double Brahminicide from the slaughter of Viśvarūpa and Vṛtra, fled, and hid in the waters. The sages praised him and he became free of impurity; he divided Brahminicide among women, fire, trees, and cows.[79]

The first three substances are familiar from the Agni corpus; the fourth may be derived from the tradition that the evil smell of Vṛtra was placed in dead cattle, or that Indra's strength was re-collected from cattle. Elsewhere, where no boon is offered, the text nevertheless implies that Indra does some general good in return for ridding himself of sin:

When Indra had killed Vṛtra, he was overcome by falsehood and disorder [anṛta], *and by Brahminicide. He hid, and the world was destroyed, devoid of trees or rains. . . . The gods found Indra, performed a horse sacrifice, and distributed Brahminicide among trees, rivers, mountains, earth, and women. Indra was free of fever, purified of evil.*[80]

With Indra restored, trees and rains will return, since Indra is the god of rain and fertility. This may be the boon implicit in all texts in which Indra lodges his sin in trees and waters. Since they are forms of Indra himself, in purifying him they regenerate themselves, just as the worshipper strengthens himself by strengthening – or purifying – his god. The *Rāmāyaṇa* notes that, as long as Indra suffered from Brahminicide, he withheld himself (the rain) from the earth, causing a terrible drought, which desolated all creatures; when Indra was freed from Brahminicide, all creatures rejoiced.[81] Even when Indra's purification brings some form of evil upon us, it saves us from the greatest of all seeds of evil, drought and hunger (the latter incarnate in Vṛtra, the former implicit in the absence of Indra).

[78] *Jai. Br.* 2.156.1–9; 157.1. [79] *MBh.* 12.329.28–41.

[80] *MBh.* 5.10–13; *Devībhāgavata* 6.7–8. [81] *Rām.* 7.86.

Sometimes the boon offered by Indra is explicit, like the earlier curses:

When Indra killed Viśvarūpa, he was still scorched by the blazing corpse. Knowing that he would have to perform rigorous expiation afterwards, he persuaded a woodcutter to chop off the heads with an axe; in return, he promised the woodcutter a share.[82]

This is a reversal of the much earlier text in which Indra cursed the trees (which had betrayed him) to be cut by an axe; now the axe is given a reward for cutting apart Indra's enemy, just as a carpenter is often paid to initiate the ritual beheading of the human sacrificial victim.[83]

Even in the Vedic sacrifice of the Brāhmaṇas, someone other than the officiating priest kills the animal, outside the place of sacrifice.[84] Since the beheading of an animal is expressly said to be a demonic act,[85] Indra's quandary in beheading a demon who *is* the sacrifice (Viśvarūpa), like Śiva's in beheading the sacrificial goat (Dakṣa), is an inescapable logical development of the Vedic ritual itself, an impasse that can be resolved only through the assistance of an outsider—or, in later Hinduism, by the intervention of a non-Vedic bhakti god.

Sometimes a whole country receives the curse and boon:

When Indra killed Vṛtra, he was soiled by Brahminicide and he became hungry. The gods and sages purified him with sanctified water and placed the impurity [mala] *and hunger* [kārūṣa], *born of Indra's body, in the earth. Then, free of defilement and hunger, full of joy, Indra gave a boon to the place: "Let these two countries be famed as the Maladas and Karūṣas, bearing the defilement from my body, and may they prosper." And so for a long time these two places prospered and enjoyed good harvests.*[86]

Defiled by hunger (Vṛtra), Indra bestows good harvests (hence sufficient food) on the lands that remove his defilement. Another text places the sin directly from Vṛtra into the ground of a certain country, cleverly relieving Indra of any involvement at all:

When Vṛtra had been created by Tvaṣṭṛ, Brahmā told Indra to kill Vṛtra. Indra complained that he had already killed Viśvarūpa for the sake of the gods, and that he alone had become most evil; therefore he feared to kill Vṛtra. Brahmā, quoting the Arthaśāstra, *enlightened Indra: "There is no Brahminicide involved in killing a Brahmin who is trying to kill you." Then Indra killed Vṛtra, and from Vṛtra's body Brahminicide fell on the ground between the Ganges and the Yamunā, an auspicious place that purifies people. Because of the great defilement* [mala], *the country is famed as Mālva, where Vṛtra's great head lay. The gods cut up Vṛtra's body.*[87]

No boon need be given to make the place auspicious. The doab of Prayāga at

[82] *MBh.* 5.13.14. [83] Whitehead, p. 82.

[84] Heesterman (1975), *passim.* [85] Heesterman (1967), *passim.*

[86] *Rām.* 1.23.17–23. [87] *Skanda* 1.1.16.60–71; 1.1.17.270 ff. cf. *Brahma* 96.

Allahabad is the most sacred place in India, and the myth *assumes* its purifying power, like that of water or fire or the great shrines. The defilement falls there because the land is already blessed with the boon of the ability to purify. Only Vṛtra's head is defiling; the gods simply chop up the rest of the body, as the woodcutter chops up the heads of Viśvarūpa. The sin of Brahminicide itself (which ought not to have arisen at all, if one could trust the *Arthaśāstra*) vanishes in the holy confluence.

The myths of the Maladas and Prayāga may be regarded as elaborations on a traditional receptacle of Indra's sin, the earth, for the sin enters the ground in these places. Elsewhere, an entire country–and a race of human beings–is said to receive another of Indra's sins, again without any compensation. When Indra slaughtered the embryo within Diti, his fortunes waned; he bathed in a holy shrine and was delivered of his sin; men born of that evil were the Pulindas, who went to live in the mountains.[88] Savage mountain tribes are convenient outsiders (socially and geographically remote) on whom to thrust our sins; thus the descendants of Uśanas are sent to the mountains, the Kalindas are created when the Gandharvas are cheated out of a share in the three worlds, and the descendants of the wicked Vena are black mountaineers.[89]

Usually the recipient of the sin is not a man but a woman. One reason for this is that the sin itself is female, an avenging fury depicted as a hideous woman. Even in the Ṛg Veda, Indra is said to fear an "avenger" when he has slain Vṛtra,[90] and in later texts this avenger is the sin itself, a feminine noun and a wicked woman. Demonic women are often Indra's undoing; as early as the Atharva Veda, it is said that a demon woman put Indra down from among the gods.[91] (The commentator suggests that the female demon [*āsurī*] is merely the demon's power of illusion, which puts Indra in her power during the battle.) Another early text says that Indra fell in love with a demon woman and lived with the demons in order to be with her.[92] This action causes him to lose not only his stature as a god, but even his gender. He became a man among men and a woman among women, says the text, and hence he realized that he had been grasped by destruction (Nirṛti) and loss of manhood. The unfortunate tendency of gods to marry (or rape) demon women is well known and accounts for the mixture of paternal good and maternal evil in many lines of offspring. Indra is particularly susceptible to this weakness; even in the Buddhist Jātakas, where Indra (Sakka) is usually given an incongruously moral character, he takes the shape of a demon to win in marriage the daughter of a demon. After throwing the demons out of heaven, Indra fights them and is put to flight; he turns his chariot back, supposedly to go to his own certain death, for he wishes to avoid injuring the birds in his path; seeing him

[88] *Vāmana* 50.1–26; see above, chap. II, sec. 9.

[89] *Jai. Br.* 1.154–155; see above, chap. V, sec. 9, and below, chap. XI, sec. 1.

[90] *RV* 1.32.14. [91] *AV* 7.38.2. [92] *Kāṭh. Sam.* 13.5.

turn toward them, the demons retreat in confusion, and Indra later carries off the beautiful daughter of the demon king.[93] Even in this text, where Indra's usual violence and cowardice are reversed almost to the point of self-satire, his penchant for demon women is recalled.

Indra's most persistently troublesome demonic female is the Fury of Brahminicide. In one Tamil myth, she tries to stop the stallion that Indra is using in his expiatory sacrifice (an ironic reversal of the many myths in which Indra himself obstructs the sacrificial horse) until Indra promises her a refuge in earth, mountains, trees, sea, rivers, and women.[94] Indra usually transfers his Brahminicide to mortal women, to whom he grants in return the boon of having children.[95] This "boon" is usually regarded as a curse, the source of all evil, in the Purāṇic myths of the loss of the Golden Age, but in most of the Indra myths it is treated as a desideratum, a Vedic aspect of fertility and regeneration like the boons given to trees and waters:

When Indra had killed Viśvarūpa, he seized with his hand the guilt of slaying him and bore it for a year. Creatures called out, "You are a Brahmin-killer." He asked the earth to take a third of his guilt, and in return he promised her that, if she should be overcome by digging, within a year the dug-out portion would be filled again; and the third of his guilt that she took became a natural fissure. He asked the trees to accept a third of his guilt; they obtained the boon that when they were pruned, more shoots would spring up; the guilt which they took became sap. Women took a third of the guilt and obtained the boon of enjoying intercourse right up to the birth of their children; their guilt became the garments stained (with menstrual blood).[96]

Similarly, when Viṣṇu distributes Indra's Brahminicide in four parts, it appears as sap in trees, saline soil in earth, menstrual blood in women (who are given the same boons as above), and bubbles in waters (which receive the boon of having a plenitude of valuable substances in them).[97] When Brahminicide requests places in which to dwell if she leaves her present abode (Indra), Bṛhaspati and the gods distribute her in the same four places but specify the manner in which each of the four recipients is ultimately to be freed of the sin—that is, how the sin is to be transferred yet once more. Earth will be freed from evil when Kṛṣṇa is born; trees are to have their sin cut into many pieces (thus the usual curse, to be cut up, is made into a boon, a distribution of the distribution); waters are to purify all creatures (the quality that made them become involved with the sin of Indra in the first place), and the last portion of Brahminicide, appearing as lust in all women, will bear fruit for other men in the future.[98] In a Tamil text, the same four recipients have the sin of Viśvarūpa's murder released from them in the very

[93] *Kulāvaka Jātaka*, no. 31; cf. *Jātaka Mālā*, no. 11. [94] *Tirukkaṇṇapuram* 4.

[95] *Vaj. Sam.* 5.7. [96] *Tait. Sam.* 2.5.1. [97] *Bhāgavata* 6.9.6–10.

[98] I have mislaid this reference, but I believe the text is the *Skanda Purāṇa*.

form in which it is said to appear in them in several Sanskrit texts: it flows out of women in their monthly period, out of water in disgusting foam, out of trees in their sap, and out of the earth in salt soil—thus it will come out and vanish. In addition, the four receptacles are given boons, as in the Sanskrit texts, and the sin of the subsequent slaughter of Vṛtra is expiated when Indra comes to a shrine of Śiva.[99] The secondary transfer of the sin (from the substances that have taken it from Indra) appears to be a natural rather than a moral process, except in the case of women: the sin associated with the menstrual flow, and with the lustfulness of women, is sometimes transferred to lustful men. In this way, immoral men as well as immoral women begin to be involved. The *Mahābhārata* contains an example of this extension. When Brahminicide asked Brahmā to give her a dwelling place, he distributed her among Agni (to be transferred to any man who withholds oblations), trees (to be transferred to men who cut trees at full moon), waters (to men who put phlegm, urine, or excrement in water), or celestial nymphs (to men who sleep with menstruous women); then Indra performed a horse sacrifice and was freed of sin.[100] All four transfers have antecedents in the Brāhmaṇas. The first transfer may be traced back to a text in which Indra's sin is to devolve upon a man who withholds the priest's fee when he makes a sacrifice;[101] the second, to Agni's curse upon the trees; the third, to Agni's spitting into the waters; and the last, to the text that gives women the "boon" of bearing children.

The role of women in this secondary transfer remains constant even in texts that alter the functions of other recipients and place some of the blame on immoral men as well as women. In one text, Brahmā removes the sin (*enas*) of Brahminicide from the divinities and gives it (with appropriate boons) to the waters, the earth, women (who are therefore not to be approached during their menstrual periods), and to Brahmins who serve ploughmen, cowherds, merchants, and Śūdras.[102] The last category places directly upon the sinful Brahmin the portion which the *Mahābhārata* transferred from Agni to the man who sinned against Brahmins. A similar compression of the two-stage transfer into one appears in the *Rāmāyaṇa*. When Indra performed a horse sacrifice in order to be relieved of the sin of having killed Vṛtra, the gods gave a fourfold dwelling place to Brahminicide: one part to dwell in rivers in flood in the rainy season, one in saline soil, one to live for three nights each month with beautiful young women in order to humble their pride (an oblique reference to menstrual impurity), and one to dwell with those who slanderously destroy innocent Brahmins.[103] Thus the sin of Indra which, in early texts, causes impurity in various creatures is eventually said to be given to those who are already impure; the implications of this moral sleight-of-hand are complex.[104]

One of the earliest texts to suggest the secondary transfer is strikingly explicit

[99] *Tiruviḷaiyāṭaṟpurāṇam* 1.12–14. [100] *MBh.* 12.273; O'Flaherty (1975), pp. 86–90.

[101] *Śata.* 1.2.3.4. [102] *Skanda* 5.3.118.1–41. [103] *Rām.* 7.86. [104] Cf. *Tāṇḍya* 8.1.9–11.

in stating the necessity of this as well as of the primary transfer. It begins with the sequence in which Agni creates the Āptyas,[105] and then draws upon the Ṛg Vedic text in which Trita Āptya kills the three-headed Viśvarūpa (his first cousin):

Trita Āptya, sent by Indra, slew the three-headed one. Indra beheaded Viśvarūpa, cutting off his three heads.[106]

In this, the only Ṛg Vedic reference to the killing of Viśvarūpa, it appears that though Trita Āptya kills him Indra beheads him, just as, in the *Mahābhārata*, Indra kills him and the woodcutter beheads him. Noting this division of labor, the Brāhmaṇa text expands upon the theme:

When Indra slew the Brahmin Viśvarūpa, the Āptyas knew that he (Viśvarūpa) was going to be killed, and Trita killed him. Indra was free from that (sin) because he is a god. Then people said, "Let those be guilty of the sin who knew (Viśvarūpa) was going to be killed. Let the sacrifice wipe off the sin upon them." The Āptyas said, "Let us make this (sin) pass beyond us to him who makes offering without paying the priests." Thus the sacrifice wipes (the sin) off onto the Āptyas, and the Āptyas wipe it off on him who makes the offerings without offering a fee to the priest.[107]

The Āptyas (water deities) take the sin upon themselves by actually killing the Brahmin demon, though Indra is still given credit for the positive aspect of this deed; they must free Indra "because Indra is a god." The Āptyas are also divine, though not as divine as Indra, and though they are superhuman Brahmin-killers, they manager to pass on the sin to human Brahmin-cheaters, a less heinous but certainly more numerous class of sinners, the bêtes noires of the Brahmin compilers of these texts and hence the perfect scapegoats, on whom Indra's sin is often thrust. The role of the Āptyas as scapegoats is further expanded in other texts in which they choose as *their* scapegoats not tightfisted sacrificers but other despicable sinners, abortionists. When Grāhi, the demon of disease, has stricken someone, this prayer is said: "The gods wiped off their sin on Trita. Trita wiped it off on human beings. If Grāhi has reached you because of that, let the gods make it disappear. Wipe off evils on the embryo-slayer."[108] The gods' sin causes disease, and the gods will also remove it; the curse which threatens life is coupled with a boon, to be accomplished ultimately by the human sinner who takes life (as Indra takes the life of Diti's sons) by striking within the womb.

The Vedas refer elsewhere to sins committed "by the gods, by men, by the ancestors, and by myself," and to "god-committed sins" as well as "mortal-committed sins,"[109] a possible reference to the sin derived from the Āptyas. In discussing the possibility that this text might refer to sins committed *against*

[105] *Śata.* 1.2.3.1 [106] *RV* 10.8.8–9; O'Flaherty (1975), p. 71. [107] *Śata.* 1.2.3.2–4.

[108] *Tait. Br.* 3.2.8.9–12; *Mait. Sam.* 4.1.9; *AV* 6.113.

[109] *Vaj. Sam.* 8.13. Cf. *Vaj. Sam.* 8.27, *Śata.* 4.4.5.22, 12.9.2.4.

the gods, as well as devolving from them, Sten Rodhe remarks: "Sin, disease, evil and mishap appear together without any distinctions, and it is all believed to be derived from the gods through Trita. . . . The Vedic texts know of sins committed by gods, too, and relate how such sins may come to men and pollute them. . . . It is not improbable that the texts imply both possibilities of meaning."[110] Evils result from the gods' sins against us as well as from ours against them; there is a mutual interdependence of evil like the interdependence for the sake of mutual sustenance, completing the symbiosis of gods and men.

5. The Transfer of Śiva's Dangerous Energy

Through fair means or foul, Indra manages to get away with killing a Brahmin demon. Similarly, Śiva commits Brahminicide and performs expiation for it, a myth that involves more intricate rationalizations than simple transfer and distribution.[111] Even in the Indra myth there are hints that the two gods, alike in so many ways, rid themselves of evil not only in the same way but by actually sharing the physical means of purification.

When Śiva beheads Brahmā, he is forced to wander about holding the skull of Brahmā until he finds release in Benares. When Indra kills Vṛtra, he makes a cup from Vṛtra's skull,[112] and when Brahminicide grabs Indra after the slaughter of Viśvarūpa, the text says that the sin grabbed Indra "just like Śiva."[113] When Indra kills a Brahmin Rākṣasa named Skull-bearer (the name given to Śiva when he performs this expiation), Brahminicide oppresses him until he is purified at a Śaiva shrine.[114] An even more explicit connection appears in the *Skanda Purāṇa*: Bṛhaspati advised Indra to expiate the sin of Vṛtra's murder by going to Benares, where the skull had fallen from Śiva's hand; Indra bathed there and was purified.[115] The text further expands upon this overlap:

Vṛtra, born of Tvaṣṭṛ and the daughter of Puloman, was the soul of dharma; he abandoned his demon nature.[116]*. . . Indra killed him, but not knowing that Vṛtra was dead, he ran and hid. The gods brought him back, but he was oppressed by Brahminicide. Brahmā said to the gods, "He is full of evil Brahminicide for the sin* [enas] *of killing Vṛtra by a trick. We must therefore abandon him, or else we will incur evil ourselves. Even to look at him, let alone to touch him, brings sin." When Indra heard this and saw his own body devoid of energy and ill-smelling, he begged Brahmā to be gracious to him and to tell him how to expiate his sin. Brahmā told him that for killing Vṛtra, who was a pure creature* [*like the creatures before the Fall*[117]], *he must go on a pilgrimage to eighteen shrines and loudly confess himself a Brahmin-killer. Indra took the skull of*

[110] Rodhe, pp. 150 and 155. [111] See below, chap. X, sec. 2. [112] *Śata*. 4.4.3.2–12.

[113] *Bhāgavata* 6.9.6–10. [114] *Skanda* 3.1.11.7–70. [115] *Skanda* 4.81.1–25.

[116] See above, chap. V, sec. 4. [117] See above, chap. II, sec. 5.

Vṛtra and went to various shrines. At last the skull fell from his hand at the shrine of Śiva the Skull-bearer; the evil smell left Indra, and his energy returned.

At Brahmā's behest, Indra had made a golden image of himself, called the Evil Man, and given it to a Brahmin. But when this Brahmin was reviled by the citizens, who refused to touch him, he wished to return the gift and to destroy Indra with a curse. Indra assured him that there was no sin [pātaka] *in accepting the gift, and he promised that the Brahmin would become wealthy by performing all rites for the citizens who had despised him, and that the shrine there would be called the Releasing of the Skull. Then Indra vanished.*[118]

The evil smell once attributed to Vṛtra is now given to Indra himself, since Vṛtra has obtained the sweet odor of sanctity. Indra is now actually an Untouchable, as Śiva is in similar circumstances, and his expiation is said to follow Śiva's, since it takes place at the shrine already created by the skull-bearing Śiva (though here, anomalously, it receives its name not from the expiation of Śiva but from that of Indra). Untouchability then infects the Brahmin, who, by receiving the Evil Man (Indra's sin), functions like the indiscriminate Brahmin who receives a quarter of Indra's sin in an earlier text. This Brahmin is the mirror image of the usual scapegoat; instead of refusing to pay Brahmins, he is the unpaid Brahmin. The role of the tightfisted sacrificer is then assumed by the citizens of Benares, and the Brahmin is restored with the counterpromise that he will be a well-paid Brahmin with an assured ritual monopoly.

The premise that Śiva's sin precedes Indra's is not supported by textual analysis. Though Rudra may behead Brahmā–Prajāpati in the Ṛg Veda, the myth is fully developed only in the Brāhmaṇas, and even there the skull does not adhere to Śiva's hand but is transformed into a constellation. However, the seed of Brahmā, which is spilt in the course of this beheading, is distributed upon the earth, into the fire, and among various gods; later, the seed of Śiva is similarly distributed. Śiva promises Agni that he will be relieved of the torture caused by the seed if he releases it in the bodies of those women who warm themselves before him each month,[119] a possible reference to the sin associated with the menstrual flow. Śiva's seed is placed in fire, earth, and water, as well as in trees (reeds, bamboo), mountains, and women. The seed left over from the begetting of Skanda is distributed in bloody water (as the sin is placed in menstrual blood), in the rays of the sun, in earth, in trees, and on the mountain on which the sun sets in the West.[120] The pattern of the distribution of Indra's sin is also followed in the myth of the burning of Kāma (desire) by Śiva. After burning Kāma, the fire from Śiva's third eye, augmented by the fire of Kāma himself, threatens to burn all the universe until it is distributed among mango trees, Spring, bees, the moon, flowers, cuckoos, and the passion of lovers; among proud men and

[118] *Skanda* 6.269.16–152. [119] *Skanda* 1.1.27.69. [120] *MBh.* 3.220.10–11.

pleasure gardens.[121] The fever of Kāma tortures Śiva until Śiva transfers it to the son of Kubera, to whom he gives the ability to drive men mad,[122] a form of evil coming to mortals from the gods.

A final, direct link between the pattern of the distribution of Indra's sin and the distribution of Śiva's energy appears in the *Mahābhārata*, where the essence of Indra's Brahminicide is said to be derived from a force originally created by Śiva, partially distributed by him, and later transferred to Vṛtra, whence it entered Indra and was further transferred to other living creatures. The story is told in the context of the Vṛtra myth. When Indra was trying to kill Vṛtra, Agni and Soma helped him to create cold and fever heat.[123] When Vṛtra stupefied Indra by his power of illusion, Śiva made his own energy into a fever that entered Vṛtra and caused him to yawn, so that Indra could kill him.[124] In response to a question, the Epic then narrates the origin of that fever: it was born when Śiva beheaded Dakṣa:[125]

When Śiva destroyed Dakṣa's sacrifice, a drop of sweat fell from his forehead and became a great fire like the doomsday fire; then it became a man named Fever, short, red-eyed, red-bearded. Brahmā said to Śiva, "All the gods will give you too a share (in the sacrifice), for they and the sages find no peace because of your anger. If this man born of your fever wanders among men in one piece, the whole world will not be able to bear him. Restrain (him), and let him be divided into many." Śiva, thus implored and having been given a share, said, "So be it," and for the peace of all creatures he distributed fever among the hot exudations of mountains, moss in waters, barren saline patches on earth, slough of serpents, sore hooves of bulls, blindness of cattle, constipation of horses, moulting of peacocks, red eyes of cuckoos, disturbances in sheeps' livers, hiccups of parrots, fatigue of tigers, and fever among men.[126]

The destructive fever cannot be destroyed altogether,[127] so "for the peace of all creatures"—that is, to minimize its destructive effect—the god distributes it, first among many of the usual receptacles of Brahminicide (mountains, waters, earth), and then as various diseases of animals (including some animals associated with Vṛtra's evil: cattle, peacocks, and cuckoos). In a similar way, when Indra's substitute, Nahuṣa, kills a cow, the sin is divided into a hundred and one diseases which fall upon all creatures.[128] Śiva does not intend to do harm, and does less harm than would result if he left his energy in one piece or if he subsumed it into himself (for his weakness would have dire effects on the universe), but he is not

[121] *Matsya* 154.250–255; *Skanda* 1.2.24.42–43; *Haracarita* 9.59.

[122] *Vāmana* 6.45–55; cf. O'Flaherty (1973), pp. 283–286.

[123] *Tait. Sam.* 2.5.2.2–5. See above, chap. V, sec. 6.

[124] *MBh.* 12.272–273; O'Flaherty (1975), pp. 86–87. [125] See below, chap. X, sec. 1.

[126] *MBh.* 12.274.36–59; cf. *Brahma* 40.112–119; *Vāyu* 1.30.298–305; *Matsya* 72.11–16; *Padma* 5.24.26–32; O'Flaherty (1973), p. 284. [127] O'Flaherty (1973), pp. 282–292. [128] *MBh.* 12.254.46–47.

helping the farmers, who are now forced to deal with constipated horses and bilious sheep.

Motifs derived from both myths of fever (Indra against Vṛtra and Śiva against Dakṣa) are combined in another myth in which Śiva opposes Kṛṣṇa. Śiva sends fever to overcome Kṛṣṇa's army, and Kṛṣṇa then uses yawning to overcome Śiva[129] (just as the gods use yawning to overcome Vṛtra). This text is then modified and expanded; both Śiva and Kṛṣṇa create fevers, and Kṛṣṇa, not Śiva, is afflicted by yawning:

Śiva created a three-headed fever like the doomsday fire; it entered Kṛṣṇa and made him yawn and close his eyes, but then Kṛṣṇa created another fever to destroy the first one. A voice from the sky asked Kṛṣṇa to protect the (first) fever, and Kṛṣṇa granted it a boon that it should be the only fever in the world.[130]

The three-headed fever created by Śiva is reminiscent of the three-headed Viśvarūpa who is distributed by Indra. Here this fever is controlled rather than proliferated; and another variant of this text states that when the fever created by Kṛṣṇa had conquered the fever created by Śiva, Kṛṣṇa said, "Let the world be without fever."[131] But other variants, noting that Kṣṛṇa is asked to protect fever, not to abolish it, and perhaps recalling the story of Śiva's fever at Dakṣa's sacrifice, allow fever to expand:

Kṛṣṇa said to Fever: "You must wander and dwell among all classes of beings, divided into three parts: go among four-footed animals, stationary objects, and men. And let a fourth part take the form of a disease of the feet in birds. Among trees, you will live in the form of a worm, causing the withering of leaves; among fruits, as a disease called "pale-leaf"; and as moss in waters, moulting of peacocks, frost in lotus ponds, saline ground on earth, red chalk on mountains, epilepsy and sore hooves among cattle. Thus, Fever, you will be distributed on earth, and by the mere sight or touch of you living creatures will be slaughtered. No one but gods and men will be able to bear fever."[132]

There are several minor inconsistencies in this text. At first, fever is divided into three (as it is originally three-headed in this myth, and as Indra's sin is at first divided into three); but then, as in the Indra myth in many variants, a fourth part is added, among birds, where the three heads of Viśvarūpa originally lodged. Kṛṣṇa becomes suddenly merciful to men at the end, freeing them as well as the gods from the fatal effects of the dread disease, which pollutes everyone by sight as well as by touch, like the Untouchables infected by Brahminicide.

Yet another link between the sins of Indra and Śiva appears in one text in which Indra, in the form of a Skull-bearer, creates a number of heresies:

Pṛthu performed ninety-nine horse sacrifices, but Indra was jealous of him and stole the

[129] *Viṣṇu* 5.32–33. [130] *Hari.* 111.1–12.

[131] *Hari.*, 28 lines inserted after 111.5. [132] *Hari.*, 26 lines inserted after 111.9.

hundredth sacrificial horse. He fled like a heretic who mistakes adharma for dharma, wearing matted locks and carrying a skull and a club. Atri urged Pṛthu's son to kill Indra, saying, "Kill Indra, who has destroyed the sacrifice and is the lowest of the gods," but Indra vanished. Pṛthu himself took up an arrow to kill Indra, but the priests prevented him, saying that they would kill Indra by offering him as an oblation into the sacrificial fire, thus repaying Indra for his evil intentions. Brahmā, however, warned them, "Do not attempt to kill with a sacrifice Indra who is himself a form of the sacrifice. If you disregard Indra, you disregard all the gods. Desist from this sacrifice, for there is much evil obstinacy among the gods. Dharma has already been violated by the heretics made and released by Indra. Now you must protect dharma for your people, for Vena's evil actions almost destroyed dharma, and Indra's power of delusion has created a fierce path of heresy, mother of false dharmas, which you must destroy."[133]

When Indra fails to prevent Pṛthu from performing the sacrifice, he defiles it by creating heretics. Pṛthu agrees to stop sacrificing, Indra preserves his monopoly on a hundred horse sacrifices, and we are left with the burden of heresies, for the commentator remarks that the paths of heresy (Jains, Buddhists, Kāpālikas, etc.) existed from then on.[134] (Another of Indra's sins is said to have created a different heresy: Bṛhaspati is accused of having created the Materialist heresy to conceal the Brahminicide that arose when Indra killed Vṛtra.[135]) Thus the myth explains the origin of heresy among mankind through a weakness of Indra, the Brahmin-killer, who masquerades as Śiva the Skull-bearer Brahmin-killer. Moreover, as in the Dakṣa myth, Indra first destroys the sacrifice, then becomes the sacrifice (the oblation which the priests would offer to destroy him, just as Indra offered the ascetics as oblations to destroy them[136]), and is finally identified with all sacrifice. Thus the motif of the distribution of Indra's Brahminicide is elaborated in the myths of the distribution of Śiva's dangerous energy and reapplied to the Indra cycle once more.

6. The Transfer of the Evil of the Gods

Many of the Brahminicide distributions attempt to justify the transfer by placing the sin in people already sinful; this very measure, however, prevents the myth from being used in the larger context of the theodicy problem, for the transfer cannot explain why those people were evil in the first place. But the myth of Indra's stealing Pṛthu's horse does seem to describe the origin of heresy, and in other myths Indra's shortcomings account for the origin of certain forms of evil or impurity in men or women. When Indra refused to give the Soma to the Aśvins, the sage Cyavana conjured the demon of intoxication to devour Indra; Indra granted the Aśvins their portion of the Soma, and the demon of intoxica-

[133] *Bhāgavata* 4.19.1–38; see below, chap. XI, sec. 3. [134] Śrīdhara on *Bhāgavata* 4.19.1–38.

[135] *Padma* 5.13.296–297. [136] See above, chap. V, sec. 5.

tion was distributed among women, drinks, gambling, and hunting.[137] When Indra had seduced Ahalyā, her husband, Gautama, said to Indra, "This emotion which you have demonstrated here will also appear among men in the world, and the man who (commits adultery) will have half the sin, and you will have half." And Gautama cursed mortal women to have the beauty of Ahalyā, the cause of the trouble.[138] Such actions by the gods are usually accepted without comment, but this myth of Ahalyā is used to discredit the gods when Bṛhaspati corrupts the demons.[139] Indra is here responsible for the crime of adultery on earth—men being in this instance created in Indra's image—but in return Indra is made to take back upon himself half of the sin of the adultery of other men, a savior's role rather out of character for him.

There are a few other texts in which Indra and the gods do make an attempt to alleviate the force of evil that comes upon mankind from them:

These three worlds were united; the gods divided them into three. The worlds grieved that they had been divided in three, and the gods said, "Let us take the three sorrows from these three worlds." Indra removed their sorrow, and the sorrow which the god removed from this earth (f.) entered the whore; the grief which god removed from the atmosphere (n.) entered the eunuch; the grief from heaven (m.) entered the man who possesses sin [enas] *or the rogue* [kitava].[140]

The gods characteristically begin the trouble by dividing and separating the three worlds (even as they divide their own impurities), but this is the essential cosmic creative act, necessary for the survival of the universe.[141] The resulting sorrow is thrust upon the eternal scapegoat, Eve, and upon her symbolic complement (and constant companion in the harem), the eunuch—neutral, unnatural, inhuman, and the epitome of chastity. The rest devolves, as usual, upon the sinner. Since the gods themselves are not inconvenienced by the grief of the three worlds, it would appear that they (and Indra in particular) seem for once to have someone else's interests at heart. But sinners are still necessary; though the gods may not create sinners expressly to absorb the impurity of sorrow (the myth is unclear on this point), they certainly do not try to remove their sin. On the contrary, since the sorrow must remain within the bounds of the universe, we must be thankful that it is confined to unchaste women, impotent men, and rogues—so that we chaste, virile, virtuous creatures may live happily ever after.

7. Sin and Pollution

In commenting on the myths of plants and fire that "wipe away" sin, Sten Rodhe remarks, "We see that there is no distinction made between deliverance from

[137] *MBh.* 3.124–125; *Rām.* 7.86.1–17. [138] *Rām.* 7.30.20–45. [139] *Padma* 5.13.337–338.

[140] *Tāṇḍya* 8.1.9–11; *Jai. Br.* 3.72. [141] Ogibenin, *passim.*

sin, from uncleanness, and from curse. Sin is uncleanness, and uncleanness is something that man commits, Fire, water, plants deliver from every kind of evil."[142] Indologists have tended to maintain a distinction between the "moral" view of sin that is difficult to expiate and the "primitive" view (typical of the Indra myths) in which sin can be wiped away mechanically. Some have posited a degeneration from a moral conception of sin (such as the hymns to Varuṇa in the Ṛg Veda) to a physical one (Hindu ritual expiation); F. Max Müller was perhaps the most notorious champion of this theory. Others saw a gradual moral development from the idea of pollution in Vedic texts to the idea of the disobedience of the moral law of the gods;[143] the two trends in bhakti religion (sin as an error to be destroyed by knowledge, and sin as a personal offense to be forgiven by God) together have "displaced successfully the archaic conceptions of sin as a defiling stuff or as a ritual mistake, but they themselves have not yet been clearly reconciled."[144] It is, however, one of the most important functions of the "archaic" concept of sin as defilement to reconcile complex and conflicting moral ideas of evil, such as the two bhakti trends; hence the persistence of the "archaic" view even in bhakti texts. Thus the hypothesis of moral development is as unjustified as that of moral degeneration. As Rodhe rightly remarks, "It seems wise not to speak of any historical evolution on this point, but of various conceptions of sin, existing at the same time, sometimes involved in one another, sometimes isolated in various texts."[145] The two attitudes are often complementary rather than mutually exclusive: "Though sin is seen as a spiritual state, its consequences are believed to be physical; they usually take the form of sickness or other misfortune."[146]

The "primitive" view is typical of dualism: evil is not a true part of the good, which we wish to keep, but merely an accretion that can be chopped off. Max Weber has described the "primitive" implications of this type of Manicheanism:

> This view, then, connects easily with the doctrine of impurity found in tabooistic ethics. Evil appears as soiling, and sin—in a fashion quite like that of magical misdeeds—appears as a reprehensible and headlong fall to earth . . . leading to a state of contamination.[147]

Mary Douglas has discussed this problem at some length. She challenges the traditional view, derived from Sir James Frazer and Robertson Smith, which scorns "mechanical expiation" and regard for "unintentional sin," a view that leads to a "false assumption that ethics are strange to primitive religion. . . . It remains to show that pollution has indeed much to do with morals." She demonstrates the complex manner in which the view of sin as dirt (which typifies the Indra cycle) leads to an often profound moral view:

> Wherever ideas of dirt are highly structured, their analysis discloses a play upon such

[142] Rodhe, p. 150. [143] Keith (1926), p. 560. [144] de Smet, p. 172. [145] Rodhe, p. 161.
[146] von Fürer-Haimendorf (1974), p. 552. [147] Weber (1963), p. 145.

profound themes [as] the relation of order to disorder, being to non-being, form to formlessness, life to death. . . . The Pauline antithesis of blood and water, nature and grace, freedom and necessity, or the Old Testament idea of Godhead can be illuminated by Polynesian or Central African treatment of closely related themes.[148]

Mary Douglas goes on to describe several ways in which pollution may help to define and deal with moral evil:

Moral situations are not easy to define. . . . Pollution rules, by contrast with moral rules, are unequivocal. . . . When a situation is morally ill-defined [or] . . . when moral principles come into conflict, a pollution rule can reduce confusion by giving a simple focus for concern. . . . When moral rules are obscure or contradictory there is a tendency for pollution beliefs to simplify or clarify the point at issue.[149]

In the Indra myths, the complexity of roles and the conflicts between different value systems often lead to a logical impasse or a contradiction, where Indra must sin and yet must remain pure; the rite of expiation then defines his precise ritual status and resolves the conflict.

Writing from a very different vantage point, that of a Christian apologist, C. S. Lewis attributes to pain the function that Mary Douglas sees in dirt:

Now error and sin both have this property, that the deeper they are the less their victim suspects their existence; they are masked evil. Pain is unmasked, unmistakable evil; every man knows that something is wrong when he is being hurt.[150]

Dirt, pain, or evidence of ritual pollution (the Brahminicide that becomes embodied to haunt Indra) are physical entities which can point out obscure moral evil. More important, they show the way to the destruction of that evil:

There must be an advantage for society at large in attempting to reduce moral offenses to pollution offenses which can be instantly scrubbed out by ritual. . . . The social consequences of some offenses ripple out in all directions and can never be reversed.[151]

When the chain of karma seems inexorable, when sin begets sin and there is no way to reverse the hideous moral decline, ritual alone can step in from another plane and stop the chain reaction.[152] Again, C. S. Lewis sees this as an attribute of pain:

Of all evils, pain only is sterilised or disinfected evil. Intellectual evil, or error, may recur because the cause of the first error continues to operate. . . . Sin may recur because the original temptation continues. . . . But pain has no tendency, in its own right, to proliferate. . . . Pain requires no such undoing. . . . Thus that evil which God chiefly uses to produce the "complex good" is most markedly disinfected, or deprived of that proliferous tendency which is the worst characteristic of evil in general.[153]

The simplicity of pain contributes to the complex (moral) good; the "disin-

[148] Douglas, pp. 25–28, 129, and 5. [149] Douglas, pp. 130–131, 133, and 142. [150] Lewis, pp. 130–131.
[151] Douglas, p. 136. [152] See below, chap. XI, sec. 1. [153] Lewis, pp. 104–105.

fected" evil alone does not proliferate, as the "purified" sin alone ceases to reproduce itself in the chain of karma.

Paul Ricoeur sees two valuable and profound functions performed by the view of sin as defilement, impurity, and stain: the symbolic richness of the image of defilement and the usefulness of the theological implications of the view. For the first, he remarks that we cling to the image of defilement "in virtue of its unlimited potentiality for symbolization. . . . We shall have approached as close as possible to an experience which has not simply been left behind but has been retained, and which perhaps conceals something by which it survives through a thousand mutations." This is certainly true of Indian mythology, which retains the metaphor of impurity in diverse myths that invoke a more intricate concept of evil. The second function of the image of defilement in Ricoeur's view is closely linked to the fear of punishment for the sin indicated by the impurity: "Piety, and not only reason, will cling desperately to this explanation of suffering. If it is true that man suffers because he is impure, then God is innocent. Thus the world of ethical terror holds in reserve one of the most tenacious 'rationalizations' of the evil of suffering."[154] In India, however, impurity need not indicate sin at all, and God is clearly not innocent; yet the image of defilement serves this belief as well as, if not better than, it serves Ricoeur's corpus: because God is not innocent, he places his impurity upon us.

The mythology of the removal of pollution is able to symbolize, and often to introduce, a mythology of confrontation with moral evil. One example of this continuum is the oft-repeated list of the sins of Indra: the killing of Viśvarūpa, giving the ascetics to the jackals, quarreling with Bṛhaspati, and so forth. In many Brāhmaṇa texts, this cycle of sins is expiated by the removal of pollution, such as stealing Soma, employing the use of fire, or wiping the sin off on a plant, but even here Indra is sometimes made to confess his sin aloud and to recognize the evil in himself. When the Upaniṣads come to describe a new theory of good and evil to replace that of the Brāhmaṇas, they use this same list of sins on which to demonstrate their new morality; Indra brags that he has done all these things, "but not a hair of my head is harmed," for he has the knowledge of good and evil and is above all action.[155] Knowledge and repentance are ways of removing evil that are regarded as supplementary to, coterminal with, the ritual removal of pollution.

8. The Beast and the Snare

Sin and pollution in their most apparently contrastive forms intermingle in the Indian image of the beast and the snare. The "moral" side of the image is most highly developed in the theology of the Śaiva Siddhānta, a South Indian school

[154] Ricoeur, pp. 26 and 31. [155] *Kau. Up.* 3.1.

that produced texts in Tamil and Sanskrit dealing at great length with the problem of the origin of sin in man. The three elements on which the theology is based are the beast or soul (*paśu*), the snare or bond (*pāśa*), and the Lord (*pati*).[156] The soul is called *paśu* because it is bound by snares (*pāśas*), which bind it to sin (*āṇava,* "atomization," the separation of the soul from god), which is impurity (*mala*).[157] The snares are threefold, for the impurity is threefold: sin, karma, and illusion.[158] The original impurity grows into the creeper of desire, and then into the creeper of delusion; this leads man to commit faults or evil.[159] Sometimes the sin is said to be fivefold: unconscious impurity, ignorance, the root of evil, the original impurity, and the very condition of beasthood (*paśutva*).[160] As this sin is often identified with the snare, the snare is also divided fivefold: impurity, karma, illusion, the world that is a product of illusion, and the binding power.[161]

The role of God in binding and unbinding the soul is much debated in these texts. God has the power to remove the impurity, but some people may be "bound by God" to undergo a series of sinful experiences, at the end of which they may be emancipated by God.[162] Why then, the texts ask, does God allow impurity to affect souls and lead them away from God?[163] Some reply that it is not actually Śiva who does fetter the soul with snares, but the female power of Śiva, his *śakti*;[164] the dualistic (and misogynist) approach is clearly useful here. But other texts state outright that it is God himself who not only liberates the souls but binds them in the first place: "God [*pati*] binds his beasts with snares consisting of impurity, delusion, etc.; and he alone liberates them when he is well pleased with their bhakti. . . . By binding all beings, from the blade of grass up to the Brahmin, the lord makes them perform their duties."[165]

This admitted, the theologians are troubled by the close relationship between God and his snares; therefore it is said that God uses the impurities of karma and illusion in order to awaken the dormant soul,[166] and, moreover, that the triple impurity does not belong to the state of the soul (which is intimately connected to God) but merely sticks to it, and is, like dirt, easily washed off. The element of pollution in the "darkness of the soul" is clear: "What is *mala* [impurity]? It is supposed to be one non-spiritual stuff, which behaves with manifold functions. It is for this reason that when the *mala* is removed in one person it may function in other persons."[167] Impurity in this instance behaves precisely like good or evil

[156] *Mṛgendra Āgama* 2.2; Dhavamony, p. 347. [157] *Śivajñānacittiyār* 4.20; Dhavamony, p. 232.

[158] *Tirukkaḷi iṟṟuppatiyār* of Yuvanta, v. 4.3; (cited in Dhavamony, p. 187).

[159] *Ibid.*, 59.3–4; 93.1; 95.1; 42.3. [160] Dhavamony, p. 265.

[161] Śrīkumāra's commentary on Bhoja's *Tattvaprakāśa* 1.163; Dasgupta, V, 164.

[162] Dasgupta, V, 164. [163] *Irupāvirupatu* of Aruḷnanti, 4.27; Dhavamony, p. 246.

[164] Dhavamony, p. 119. [165] *Śiva* 7.2.2.12.

[166] *Irupāvirupatu* of Aruḷnanti; Dhavamony, p. 246. [167] Dasgupta, V, 164.

karma that sticks to a person until it is transferred to another. Impurity is regarded as sin, but it behaves like pollution.

In several texts, this impurity is equated with the very snare with which God binds the soul. Usually this snare is regarded as the source of evil, but one sect regards the snare as "the attachment or love of the two [*pati* and *paśu*, creator and creature]."[168] This is a surprising reversal of the generally negative function of the snare in Śaiva Siddhānta, though it is assumed in all of these texts that God does love the soul. Why, then, does he bind it? The Śaiva Siddhānta answer—for the good of the soul—is not supported by the pre-Śaiva Siddhānta use of the image of the beast and the snare.

There are strong Vedic resonances in the Śaiva Siddhānta use of the terms *lord*, *beast*, and *snare* (*pati*, *paśu*, and *pāśa*).[169] Varuṇa, the god credited with the highest moral tone in the Ṛg Veda, is personified as the god with the snares, and he is the god who binds the sinners. The tendency of the Vedic sages to attach great importance to similarities of words and sounds may have led them to express the evil from which they sought deliverance with a word similar to *pāpa* (evil): *pāśa*, snare.[170] Often the snare and a word for sin (*āgas* or *enas*) occur together;[171] thus even in the Vedas, the snare itself is a form of evil. The idea of Varuṇa as a god who binds with a snare because someone has committed a sin blends into the closely related, but contrasting, idea that the snare of Varuṇa is sin. Varuṇa brings all distress that one undergoes here on earth;[172] Varuṇa seizes with his noose him who is seized by evil.[173]

The other deities who bind us in their snares in later Vedic literature are unequivocally evil. Disease, destruction (*nirṛti*), the female demons, and Varuṇa;[174] Grāhi, the demon of disease,[175] destruction,[176] and death[177]—all ensnare us. That the gods' jealousy of man is the basis of this action is made explicit in one early text: "The gods were afraid of the warrior on his birth. While he was still within (the womb), they bound him with a snare. If he were not born caught in this snare, he would continually slay his foes."[178] The gods are responsible for the obstacle that prevents the warrior from excelling at his *svadharma*—and that prevents him from threatening the frightened gods. It is significant that this obstacle is placed upon us even in the womb; the gods prefer to cut down dangerous growths at the very root, as Indra chops up the potential Indra-killer in the womb of Diti.

The wicked Varuṇa with his snare bears a striking resemblance to Rudra, with whom he sometimes appears.[179] Varuṇa is bald, with protruding teeth and tawny eyes,[180] "an evil-minded, terrifying god, from whom man wants to

[168] Ramanujan (1973), p. 69; note on Basavaṇṇa 52. [169] Rodhe, p. 41. [170] *Ibid.*, p. 36.
[171] *RV* 1.24.15; 7.88.6–7. [172] *Śata.* 4.5.7.7. [173] *Śata.* 12.7.2.17. [174] *AV* 2.10.1. [175] *AV* 6.112.1.
[176] *AV* 1.31.2; 19.44.4; *Vaj. Sam.* 12.62; *Śata.* 7.2.1.1–17. [177] *Kaṭh. Up.* 4.2.
[178] *Tait. Sam.* 2.4.13. [179] *Śata.* 2.3.2.9. [180] *Śata.* 13.3.6.5.

be delivered. . . . In his terrifying aspects Varuṇa shows many resemblances to Rudra."[181] Vedic literature also speaks of the snares of Rudra Paśupati, Lord of Beasts: "May Aditi loosen this snare. I pay homage to the beasts and to the lord of beasts. I cast down the enemy and fasten the snare on him whom we hate."[182] In later literature, too, "Śiva carries a noose (*pāśa*) with which he binds refractory offenders."[183]

In the Vedas, Rudra earns the epithet of Paśupati after punishing Prajāpati for his sin; at this time, Prajāpati takes the form of a beast (*mṛga*), whom Rudra attacks.[184] Rudra is the lord of beasts wild and tame, domestic cattle (*paśus*) and the beasts of the forest (*mṛgas*).[185] This is a role that he may inherit from Indra, lord of creatures horned and tame,[186] but in his own right Rudra is a tamer of wild animals.[187]

A significant point in all of these Vedic texts is the undisguised antagonism between the lord and the beast. The word *paśu* may in some contexts refer to all animals, but it designates primarily the domestic animals or cattle (cows, horses, sheep, goats) used as sacrificial beasts and regarded as possessions (for *paśu* is cognate with the Latin *pecus*, from which we derive such terms as *impecunious*). The gods want beasts so that they can kill them and be wealthy through them. The gods divided the beasts among themselves, but they excluded Rudra; he looked on the beasts and the gods, wishing to kill them; when Rudra was about to kill Prajāpati, Prajāpati promised to make him Paśupati, and Rudra refrained from killing him.[188] The violence of the god's attitude to his beasts is even more obvious in a later variant of this myth, in which, when the gods perform a sacrifice without Rudra, he attacks them:

He knocked out the teeth of Pūṣan and the eyes of Bhaga and the two testicles of Kratu. All the gods, who were reduced to the condition of beasts, went to Rudra and bowed to him, but Rudra said in anger, "You have not given me a share of the sacrifice, though I was created before these gods, and because of this I have deprived them of their knowledge and deformed them." They praised and appeased him, and he said, "Let all of you be beasts and I will be your lord, and then you will obtain release." The gods agreed to this, and so he became lord of beasts, Paśupati. Rudra restored teeth to Pūṣan, eyes to Bhaga, seed to Kratu, and he gave full understanding to the immortals.[189]

Rudra wreaks simultaneous physical and intellecutal havoc upon the gods: he injures them and makes them into beasts by removing their knowedge. Thus our original state of ignorance, our beasthood, is due to the jealous wrath of the god. When he restores knowledge and promises release, he does so only on condition that the beasts will remain his share, his chattels, his beasts—here defined as

[181] Rodhe, pp. 64–65. [182] *Tait. Sam.* 3.1.4.4. [183] Daniélou, p. 218.
[184] *Śata.* 1.7.4.1–3; *Ait. Br.* 3.33–34; O'Flaherty (1975), pp. 29–30. [185] *AV* 11.2.24. [186] *RV* 1.32.15.
[187] *Tait. Br.* 1.115.8–9. [188] *Tāṇḍya* 7.9.16; *Mait. Sam.* 4.2.12. [189] *Varāha* 33.3–24.

creatures deprived of knowledge. Then he makes them physically and mentally whole again, a contradiction of this definition.

The gods divide up their precious cattle and cast the snares of delusion upon them, not (as the Śaiva Siddhānta would have it) for the good of the beast-soul, but out of sheer avarice:

Whoever among gods, sages or men became enlightened became the very self of the gods, and the gods had no power to prevent him. But whoever worships another divinity is like a sacrificial animal for the gods, and each person is of use to the gods just as many animals would be of use to a man. Therefore it is not pleasing to those (gods) that men should become enlightened.[190]

The Śaiva Siddhānta statement that god casts his illusion over men in order to make them perform their duties can be read in this context as a very selfish motive: he wants to make sure that they will serve him, belong to him, for Rudra Paśupati is rich in cattle,[191] a possessive god.

In the *Mahābhārata*, the gods promise that all beasts will belong to Rudra if he will destroy the Triple City, and he agrees to this.[192] This passage provides the basis of a more elaborate Purāṇic theology, when Śiva demands a sacrificial share from the gods before agreeing to kill the demons of the Triple City:

When the chariot was ready, Śiva demanded to be made lord of all beasts. The gods became suspicious and worried, but Śiva assured them that he would also give them a means of liberation from the state of being beasts, by practising the Pāśupata vow. The gods then agreed to this and bowed to Śiva. That is why gods, demons, and human beings are all called beasts. Rudra is the lord of beasts and the one who liberates beasts from their bondage.[193]

Later, when the Triple City had been destroyed, the gods came to Śiva and said, "The beast condition was established in the past in order to destroy the Triple City. Now we are worried about that beasthood." Śiva purified their beasthood by looking at them all, and ever since then, all the gods are called Pāśupatas; they performed asceticism for twelve years, were released from their bonds, and returned to heaven.[194] This text clearly considers the beast condition to be a bad thing, originally produced as a kind of blackmail by the power-mad god. At first it is said that all of us, gods, demons, and men, are beasts, but then the gods alone rise from that condition and are known as Pāśupatas (worshippers of Paśupati) instead, apparently leaving only men and demons ensnared in beasthood. But since mortals may also become Pāśupatas, it would seem that this text ultimately regards beasthood as a condition imposed by God in his malevolent aspect, and removed, in response to asceticism, by God in his more gracious form.

[190] *Bṛhadāraṇyaka Up.* 1.4.10; *Śata.* 14.4.2.21–22; see above, chap. IV, sec. 8. [191] *Ait. Br.* 3.33–34.
[192] *MBh.* 7.173.55. [193] *Liṅga* 1.72.34–45; see below, chap. VII, sec. 3. [194] *Liṅga* 1.80.1, 47–48, 54–58.

The image of the beast ranges from the wild sacrificial animal to the domestic sacrificial cattle and culminates in the most highly domesticated of all animals, the dog. To the Indian, the dog is the most unclean of all animals, a polluted scavenger, the very image of evil; domestication has not served to bathe away his sins in the eyes of the Hindus. The Tamil Śaiva Siddhāntins, when referring to their sinfulness before God, say, "I, a dog . . . ," and Śiva in his Untouchable aspect is often accompanied by a dog (as is the unclean Indra.)[195] For Buddhist villagers, too, the "animal world is moralized: dogs and beggars are all called *pau karayo* (sinners)."[196] Yet the dog is also the image of devotion in India. When Yudhiṣṭhira comes to heaven he wishes to take his dog with him; Indra and the gods are at first horrified but are forced to allow the devoted outcaste to enter heaven against their will (even as they must admit mortal devotees to heaven[197]); and then it is revealed that the dog is the god Dharma incarnate in disguise.[198] The *Bhagavad Gītā* notes that a wise man sees the same thing in a Brahmin or an outcaste, a cow or a dog—[199]the dog being to the cow in the world of beasts what the outcaste is to the Brahmin in the world of men. The long chain of sin in the myth of Vena is finally broken by a dog who is bathed in holy water at a shrine and brought to heaven.[200] Thus even the most impure beast may serve as a symbol of salvation.

In this context, the Śaiva Siddhānta theory of the origin of sin appears as another aspect of the late Vedic view of evil as an impurity placed upon man by God for the sake of God, not for the sake of man. In both the Vedic and the Śaiva Siddhānta view, God places his impurity on us by means of his power of delusion, and he may remove it if he wishes. But the two schools disagree about his purpose in so going. He does it to help us, say the Śaiva Siddhāntins; to defile us so that he may continue to be pure and powerful, say the ancient texts. The purpose of the gods, unfathomable in any case, is clearly secondary to our problem in facing the results of their actions, in accepting evil as the work of God. The Hindus of these widely divergent schools, the ancient "primitive" school and the later "moralistic" school, view God's purposes in very different lights, but they agree that evil *happens* that way, that God places his evil upon us and helps us to remove it, as we help him to remove it from himself.

[195] See below, chap. X, sec. 2; cf. *MBh.* 14.54.12-35. [196] Obeyesekere, p. 31.

[197] See below, chap. VIII, secs. 6-7; chap. IX, sec. 1. [198] *MBh.* 17.3

[199] *Gītā* 5.18. [200] See below, chap. XI, sec. 1.

And the Lord said unto Satan, Hast thou considered my servant Job, that there is none like him in the earth, a perfect and an upright man, one that feareth God, and escheweth evil? . . . And the Lord said unto Satan, Behold, he is in thine hand; but save his life.
Job 2:3 and 2:6

Let no man say when he is tempted, I am tempted of God: for God cannot be tempted with evil, neither tempteth he any man.
James 1:13

VII

THE CORRUPTION OF DEMONS AND MEN: The False Avatar

1. The Corruption of Demons by the Gods

The gods have at their disposal various methods for dealing with their arch enemies; the most basic procedure—to wage war—occurs from the earliest Vedic texts through the latest Purāṇas. The second method, which appears in the Brāhmaṇas and continues in Epic and Purāṇic literature, is to deny the demons access to the sacrifice by stealing it from them or by keeping them out of heaven. One Brāhmaṇa states that the gods repelled the demons by means of a Vedic chant and ascended the world of heaven; the commentator explains, "They prevented the demons from entering heaven."[1] Elsewhere this text says that the demons once had the whole sacrifice; by means of various formulae, the gods took from them all the sacrifices, one by one.[2] The gods corrupt the demons by denying them Vedic religion, but they do so by a physical or magical assault.

Other Brāhmaṇas state more explicitly the notion that the gods protect their own interests by corrupting their enemies:

The gods, speaking truth, were very contemptible and very poor, but the demons, speaking falsehood, were very prosperous. The gods then began to perform the sacrifice, and each time the demons came where they were preparing it, the gods snatched up the sacrifice and

[1] *Tāṇḍya* 8.9.15. [2] *Tāṇḍya* 8.6.5.

began doing something else. And the demons went away, thinking, "It is something else they are doing." Then the gods completed the sacrifice and they prevailed, and the demons came to nought.[3]

Although the gods seem to find virtue of little material assistance, while the wicked demons flourish like a green bay tree, the gods rely on the older aspect of virtue (the sacrifice) for their welfare, and they trick the demons into ignoring this source of strength. In other Brāhmaṇas, the gods hide the sacrifice from the demons and thus become supreme,[4] or they keep the demons out of heaven by mixing the Vedic verses with evil;[5] in the latter case the gods seem to destroy the purity of the sacrifice, but apparently this defiled sacred text is given only to the demons.

The gods make the demons evil, not to help mankind or to preserve the cosmic balance, but simply in order that the gods themselves may remain in power. In the Buddhist tradition, Indra is said to have brought about the fall of the demons from heaven because of his own jealousy and greed; thinking, "What good to us is a kingdom which others share?" he made the demons drunk and hurled them from heaven.[6] In this view, the fact that the demons are demons–that there was a fall from heaven, that the gods have enemies, that there is a force of evil to combat the force of good–is attributed to the decision of the gods, a decision based not on philosophical rationalization but on pure ritual competition.[7]

Lust is the gods' chief weapon against the virtuous demons, just as it is time's chief weapon against virtuous mortals. Indra uses his own wife, Śacī, to overpower a demon by playing upon the demon's desire for her,[8] just as Śiva destroys the demon Andhaka by playing upon Andhaka's desire for Pārvatī, the wife of Śiva.[9] Other demons are similarly overcome when weakened by their desire for the Goddess, but more frequent is the inverse: they are weakened when their own wives are seduced by the gods. The moral balance is a delicate one. Although by seducing a woman (the demon's wife) the "virtuous" god loses his own ascetic power of chastity, he thereby also destroys the power of chastity by which the demon's wife protected her husband; the enemy remains suppressed, while the god renews his powers.[10] When anyone attempts to seduce the wife of a god, on the other hand, the powers of the seducer are destroyed and the god remains intact; the god always emerges from the final conflict strengthened. Thus Śiva destroys Jalandhara by repaying him in kind. When Jalandhara disguises himself as Śiva and attempts to seduce Pārvatī, she immediately recognizes him and flees;

[3] *Śata.* 9.5.1.20–27. [4] *Gopatha* 2.2.2–11. [5] *Jai. Up. Br.* 1.16 and 1.18; see above, chap. IV, sec. 4.

[6] *Kulāvaka Jātaka*, no. 31; see above, chap. VI, sec. 4. [7] See above, chap. IV, sec. 3.

[8] *MBh.* 5.15.2–25. [9] *Vāmana* 9–10, 40–44; *Kūrma* 1.16.123–240; *Liṅga* 1.93.1–25; *Matsya* 179; *Varāha* 27.1–39; cf. O'Flaherty (1973), pp. 190–192; (1975), pp. 168–173.

[10] O'Flaherty (1973), pp. 178–180.

but when Śiva sends Viṣṇu, disguised as Jalandhara, to seduce Jalandhara's wife, Vṛndā, Viṣṇu succeeds and destroys the virtuous power of the demon, so that Śiva is able to kill him.[11]

These myths, in which lust is used as a crude weapon, shade off into the myths of heresy, in which a doctrine of lust is preached. Viṣṇu uses both levels of lust against the demon Ghora:

The demon Ghora attempted to throw the gods out of heaven and to occupy it himself. Brahmā instructed Indra to send Nārada to delude Ghora by causing him and his wife to become attached to adharma, and to make all of his people become evil, by any means possible. Nārada went there and said to Ghora, "The best way to propitiate the gods is by the enjoyment of sensual objects. Indra and the other gods all pursue pleasure; Śiva went to the Pine Forest to make love to the wives of the sages, and he knows the essence of the highest truth." Ghora forsook dharma under the influence of the false dharma taught by Nārada, and he ceased to honor Brahmins or the Vedas or Viṣṇu. He became fond of the wives of other men, and he regarded his own wife as poison. Nārada incited him to abduct Pārvatī; Ghora's wife tried to dissuade him, warning him of the dangers of naked Jain monks, but then Nārada deluded Ghora's queen so that she became devoted to Jains and heretics. Thus weakened, Ghora went to the mountains to carry off Pārvatī, and she killed him.[12]

The more traditional means of corruption—the use of a woman to seduce the enemy—is here combined with the details of heresy; together, they destroy the demon. Another woman, his wife, warns Ghora of the dangers of heresy; but, as she is poison to him, he ignores her, and when she too is corrupted by Nārada, the demon's last bastion of virtue falls.

By seducing the wives of demons or sages, the gods not only cause their enemies to lose their powers but they also transfer those powers to themselves. Just as sin may be transferred from one person to another, so the quantity of good karma amassed by a person may be transferred to another whom he has wronged in any way. After Jalandhara and his wife have been killed, having first been weakened by means of seduction, the energy of the wife emerges from her body and enters Pārvatī, and the energy of Jalandhara enters Śiva.[13] The law of karma thus provides an additional strong incentive for the gods to corrupt their enemies rather than merely destroy them, since by causing their opponents to sin the gods may hope to obtain their powers.[14] These general patterns of myths in which the gods corrupt their enemies, be they human or demon, appear in several important texts dealing with the origin of evil and heresy. For the heresies of Buddhism and Jainism (often combined or confused in Hindu texts) are grafted onto late

[11] O'Flaherty (1973), pp. 184–186. [12] *Devī Purāṇa*, chaps. 8, 9, and 13.

[13] *Śiva* 2.5.23–24; *Padma* 6.106.13–14; Dessigane, Pattabiramin, and Filliozat (1964), 42.23.

[14] *Pāśupatasūtra* 3.6–19; cf. O'Flaherty (1973), 182–184.

versions of two cycles of myths which stem from much earlier, more general tales of corruption: the myth of the sons of the human king Raji and the myth of the demons of the Triple City.

2. Indra Corrupts the Sons of Raji

In this myth, the king of the gods enlists the aid of his preceptor, Bṛhaspati, to overcome his human and demonic enemies. The presence of the Vedic priest-god, in place of the sectarian gods who usually appear in the Purāṇic myths dealing with the specific heresies of Buddhism and Jainism, suggests that this is an early myth. It is set in the context of the battle between gods and demons, though a mediating figure, a mortal man, proves the decisive pawn in the battle, just as Manu, the Gandharva, or Śukra may tip the scales in Brāhmaṇa texts.[15]

One basic variant of the story appears in the *Viṣṇu Purāṇa*:

During the battle between the gods and demons, it was learned that the faction which had king Raji fighting on their side would be victorious. Both gods and demons asked Raji to fight for them, and he said that he would fight for whichever side would make him their king. The demons said, "We cannot say one thing and mean another; we have our king, Prahlāda." But the gods agreed to make Raji their king; he fought on their side and the demon army was destroyed. Indra came to Raji and knelt at his feet and said, "I will be your son," and Raji smiled and said, "So be it." Then Raji returned to his own city (on earth), and Indra acted as king (of heaven).

When Raji died, his five hundred sons were urged by Nārada to demand the throne of heaven as their hereditary right. When Indra refused this to them, they overcame him by force and usurped his office. After some time Indra, who had been deprived of his share of the sacrificial offering, begged Bṛhaspati to secure for him a little sacrificial butter, even if no more than the size of a jujube. Bṛhaspati said, "If you had asked my help before, I could have done whatever you wished. Now I will try to restore your kingdom to you." He then undertook a magic rite to increase Indra's strength and to delude the wits of the sons of Raji. Deluded, the princes became Brahmin-haters, devoid of dharma and rejecting the Vedas. Then Indra killed them.[16]

The gods display none of the demons' scruples about being true to their word. Having lost his kingdom (by ignoring Bṛhaspati as usual), Indra tricks Raji out of the throne promised to him by flattering him and making Raji accept him as an adoptive son, a crown prince. In one text, Indra grasps Raji's feet, a maudlin gesture of inferiority and supplication, which makes Raji laugh but nevertheless enables Indra to take back his throne.[17] This stratagem is emphasized in other texts, which remark that the trusting Raji was fooled by Indra's deceptive words.[18]

[15] See above, chap. V, secs. 5 and 9. [16] *Viṣṇu* 4.9.1–22.

[17] *Bhāgavata* 9.17.1–16. [18] *Vāyu* 2.30.89; *Brahma* 11.3–25; *Hari.* 21–22.

Word-splitting proves ultimately ineffectual, however, and Raji's sons regain their throne by force; Indra is then weakened by his lack of sacrificial offerings, not because mortals are too wicked to offer sacrifice but merely because they are not offering sacrifice to *him*. This point of view cleverly resolves the conflict between the older premise that the gods are strengthened by virtuous mortals and the later one (which operates here and is even more obvious in later variants of the Raji myth) that they are threatened by virtuous mortals. The actual doctrine that corrupts Raji's sons is not described in any detail here, but it is significant that Nārada stirs them up (just as he incites Ghora), causing them to seek Indra's throne, an act which is their principle sin. A closely related text remarks that Bṛhaspati performed a ritual that deluded the wits of the sons of Raji and made them full of passion, desire, and anger.[19] Another variant says that Bṛhaspati offered an oblation so that Indra could break the strength of Raji's sons, and when they had fallen from the (true) path, Indra killed them all.[20]

Another group of texts omits the role of Bṛhaspati altogether and emphasizes instead the inborn, inevitable shortcomings of the demons and of Raji and his sons, which lead to their ultimate defeat and Indra's victory. Raji was such a great king that his royal power frightened Indra; when Raji asked the gods and demons to make him their king, he was motivated by self-interest and a desire for fame; the demons refused because they were full of pride and they realized his self-interest; when his sons took Indra's throne, they immediately became deluded, intoxicated by passion, devoid of dharma, and so they lost their strength and Indra regained his empire.[21] The *Harivaṃśa* follows this general pattern, and attributes these various threatening and weakening qualities to Raji and the demons; but it then reverts to the pattern of the first group of texts. When Raji reached heaven, like a god, his sons took away Indra's sacrificial shares; Indra asked Bṛhaspati for help, and Bṛhaspati devised an atheist doctrine inimical to dharma, pleasing to bad men; the sons of Raji were then overcome and Indra regained his place.[22] The first pattern—that Bṛhaspati must corrupt good mortals who have been promised a place in Indra's heaven—is combined with the second—that they erred all along the way and so were hoist by their own petard. In both of these texts, Raji himself is a threat to Indra from the very start, as a king and a would-be god; this ambition is evident even in the earliest texts, when Raji demands sovereignty over gods or demons as payment for assuring victory, but it is only regarded as the vital flaw in the otherwise virtuous king by this second group of texts. Raji's innate pride and ambition make the episode of his assistance in overcoming the demons superfluous; from the start, he is too powerful to be endured, and his sons prevent Indra from receiving the sacrifice, and so they must be destroyed. The passage in which Bṛhaspati devises the atheist

[19] *Vāyu* 2.30.92–100; *Hari*. 22.34–37. [20] *Bhāgavata* 9.17.12–16.

[21] *Brahma* 11.3–25. [22] *Hari*. 21.11; 22.34–37.

doctrine is rejected by the critical edition of the *Harivaṃśa*, and its redundant nature is obvious, for Raji and his sons already behave like atheists.

The idea of heresy is more appropriate, and more fully developed, in the *Matsya Purāṇa*, which may have influenced the spurious *Harivaṃśa* passage; here, as in the first series, Raji and his sons are virtuous:

Raji was a famous king, devoid of evil. He worshipped Viṣṇu and propitiated him with asceticism; Viṣṇu then granted Raji boons, so that he became a conqueror of gods, demons, and men. When the battle of gods and demons was at a deadlock, Brahmā told Indra and Prahlāda that the side with Raji fighting for them would win; the demons refused to make him their leader as he requested, and so he fought for the gods, destroyed the demons, and became Indra's "son". Raji gave the kingdom to Indra and went away to perform asceticism. But Indra's power became forcibly eclipsed by the sons of Raji, since they had such asceticism and power and virtue, and he lost his kingdom and his share of the sacrifice. Indra, who was proud of his strength, complained to Bṛhaspati, who produced a ritual to subdue evil planets and promote welfare; he deluded the sons of Raji and placed them beyond the pale of the Vedas and of dharma, making them Jains. Then Indra killed them.[23]

Two important developments may be seen here: Raji is not virtuous in the Vedic sense, but he is a devotee of Viṣṇu; he has nonsacrificial, ascetic powers. This asceticism now leads Raji not to challenge the gods (though he still makes his *pro forma* request to be king), but, on the contrary, to renounce his throne voluntarily, like the demons converted to Jainism by Bṛhaspati.[24] But Raji's sons are also great ascetics here, and they prove a threat to Indra. Bṛhaspati uses the usual Vedic and magic ritual, but now in addition he must use non-Vedic means to subdue the new threat; he not only deprives them of Vedic religion but makes them into Jains. The presence of Viṣṇu in this text is also significant, since it is he who appears as the Buddha in the later cycle of myths based on the Raji episode.

A final variant omits the technicality of Jainism and exaggerates the dangerous tendencies of Raji, which initiate the conflict:

Once there was a just king named Raji, who ruled his subjects with dharma as if they were his natural sons. No one died at the wrong time in his kingdom; rains came in season, and plants bore fruit. As he was ruling, the gods were fighting with the demons, who took away Indra's throne. Then Indra sought refuge with Raji, saying, "The demons have stolen the kingdom of the gods. Help me; destroy the demons." When Raji heard this he decided to fight the demons, for he coveted the position of Indra. Raji fought against the demons for five hundred years, destroying the demon leaders and sending the rest to hell. Then king Raji wanted the position of the lord of heaven; when Indra learned of this he folded his hands in supplication and begged Raji to consecrate him in the kingdom, saying,

[23] *Matsya* 24.35–49; *Padma* 5.12.77–91. [24] See above, chap. V, sec. 12.

"I am your son." Hearing this pitiful speech, Raji, who was full of pity, established that humble god as lord of the gods.

When Raji became old, he went to the Himālayas to perform asceticism, and his five hundred sons set their hearts on the kingdom of Indra, which their father had rightfully secured. But Indra, intoxicated with the idea of being king, decided to fight, and he lost his kingdom to the sons of Raji. He sought help from Viṣṇu, who told him to ask the Goddess; she said, "I will delude them and lead them upon an evil path, so that their power will quickly be destroyed. You will soon regain your own position." Then Indra killed the sons of Raji, who were deluded by the Goddess's power of illusion and set on a wrong path.[25]

The self-interest of Raji, mentioned in passing by some of the earlier texts, is now clearly stated: like the demons, he wants Indra's throne. Yet he is a good man; indeed, the episode in which he "adopts" Indra is here extended to the image of the paternalistic monarch who (like Aśoka) treats all of his subjects like sons. But if this virtue is in itself a threat to Indra, it is also dangerous for Raji himself, who simply gives the throne to Indra out of pity, like the typical overgenerous demon.[26] Viṣṇu appears but plays no part; the Goddess uses delusion to help Indra regain heaven.

3. Śiva Corrupts the Demons of the Triple City

Viṣṇu and the Goddess occasionally appear in later versions of another myth in this series, the myth of the Triple City of the demons, in which the elements of delusion (*māyā*) and corruption are again introduced into an ancient myth of simple conflict in which they originally played no part. This is one of the great myths of Śiva, an elaboration of his impersonal act of cosmic destruction. At the end of the Kali Age, Śiva will burn to ashes the triple world: heaven, the ether, and earth in the earlier Vedic cosmology; heaven, earth, and hell in the later Purāṇic cosmology. Much of the imagery of the myth as it appears in the *Mahābhārata* is Vedic. The three demons are the symbolic descendants of the triple-headed Viśvarūpa; the villain of the piece (the one who builds the triple cities for the demons) is Maya, the architect of the demons and the demonic counterpart of that old Vedic troublemaker, Tvaṣṭṛ, architect of the gods (like Tvaṣṭṛ, Maya remains aloof from the actual conflict; in some versions of the myth, he alone survives when the Triple City is burnt[27]); and the cosmology of the myth is Vedic rather than Purāṇic, the triple cities being located in heaven, the ether, and on earth:

The three sons of Tāraka practised such great asceticism that they obtained from Brahmā

[25] *Skanda, Kedara Khaṇḍa* 134.2–21; 135.1–33; 136.1–26.

[26] See above, chap. V, sec. 14. [27] *Śiva* 2.5.10.39.

several boons: they were permitted to establish three cities of gold, silver, and iron; they asked for immortality, which Brahmā refused, pointing out that no one lived forever; but Brahmā promised that after they had ruled for a thousand years, their three cities would become one and Śiva would destroy them with a single arrow. The inhabitants of the Triple City built a lake which revived any demon thrown into it; then the demons, who had achieved supernatural powers through their asceticism, oppressed all the worlds and frightened the gods, for the demons never suffered any loss in battle. They were overcome by greed and infatuation, and they lost their wits; shamelessly they plundered cities, routed the gods, destroyed virtuous sages, and wickedly violated all moral bounds. Indra attacked them but could not harm them, because they had been made invulnerable by the boon granted by Brahmā. Brahmā said to the gods, "These evil demons who hate the gods and offend dharma must be destroyed." Śiva mounted his chariot; the triple cities became one, and he destroyed them with a single arrow. All the demons were burnt by Śiva, for the welfare of the triple world.[28]

The demons here are not virtuous but merely powerful: they are ascetics. They do not become actively evil, however, until they violate the condition of their existence. Having been denied the boon of immortality, they create the demonic magic of revival, a magic lake, which places them on a level with (or even above) the gods and thus violates their pact. Then they become evil automatically, without the intervention of any corrupting god; the inevitable nature of this degeneration is emphasized by the very terms of the original boon: at the end of a thousand years the demons must be destroyed, just as all of us in the triple world must be destroyed at the end of the Kali Age. Therefore, at the end of this period they (and we) must be made evil by some means or other, to justify that destruction.

The lake of immortality is the central point of a Purāṇic variant of the myth in which Śiva is forced to trick the demons before his arrows can become effective against them:

This is how Rudra, the god of infinite deception, overcame Maya: Formerly, the demons were overcome in battle by the more numerous gods. They sought refuge with their guru, the deceptive Maya, and he fashioned three cities for them by his power of yoga. The demons, remembering their former enmity with all the gods, lived in those cities and destroyed the three worlds. Then the people and their lords begged Śiva to protect them from the inhabitants of the Triple City. Śiva took his bow and arrows and shot at the three cities, and when the demons were touched by the arrows, they fell down lifeless. But Maya the great yogi gathered them up and threw them into a magic well, and when they were touched by the water of immortality, they rose again as hard as thunderbolts. When Śiva saw this he became worried, but Viṣṇu devised a stratagem: Brahmā became a calf, and

[28] *MBh.* 8.24; cf. *AV* 5.28.9; *Ait. Br.* 1.23; 3.3.13; *Śata.* 3.4.4.3; 3.4.4.14; 6.3.3.25; *Tait. Saṃ.* 6.2.3; *Vāj. Saṃ.* 5.8; *Hari.* (app. 1, no. 43); O'Flaherty (1975), pp. 125–136.

Viṣṇu became a cow, and they entered the Triple City and drank up the well of the elixir of immortality. The demons stood by watching, bewitched, and when the great yogi Maya learned of this, he realized that it must be fate, against which neither gods nor demons, nor anyone else, could do anything. Then Śiva mounted his chariot and burnt the Triple City with his fiery arrows.[29]

This simple variant plays upon contrasting powers of illusion, those of the deceptive Maya and those of Śiva, for both Maya and Śiva are called great yogis. Nothing is said of the original virtue of the demons (they obtain their cities from a demon, Maya, not as a reward from a god, Brahmā), and hence they need not be made wicked; one may assume that they were always wicked, that their wickedness stems from their age-old enmity with all the gods. Other texts state that the demons became evil as soon as they received the boon from Brahmā; then the horrible demons of the Triple City oppressed the world too much, for they were proud of their boon.[30] This may also be the implication of the statement that the demons oppressed the sages and gods because they were proud of their strength.[31] Proud or not, the demons are indeed strong, and so their power must be stolen; the means used to do this–the creation of an illusory cow–is reminiscent of a trick played on a group of virtuous Brahmins,[32] a trick that results in the creation of a great heresy.

Śiva's use of deception is briefly foreshadowed in another text that describes the demons as originally powerful but not necessarily virtuous; indeed, they begin to commit outrages because they are proud of their powers, as usual, but then another cause of their wickedness is described. They were deluded by the great lord; therefore they shattered and trampled the paths of the gods and the fathers, making the gods miserable because the rituals that gave them their positions had been discontinued.[33] Here the myth reverts to the Vedic premise that it is the demons' *lack* of Vedic worship that troubles the gods, though that lapse is caused by Śiva, as it is in the texts which assume (in the Purāṇic manner) that it is the *presence* of the demons' worship (sacrificial or, later, devotional) that poses the threat. That threat applied only to Indra, in the myth of Raji; here all the gods are involved and so a more complete devastation is required.

Most Purāṇic texts preserve the simple premise that the demons were always evil and so Śiva had to destroy them. One such text reverses only the structual basis of the myth. There is only one demon, whose *name* is Triple City (Tripura), and instead of the three parts uniting in order to be destroyed, Śiva splits him into three when he kills him:

A demon named Tripura performed great asceticism, and Brahmā granted him the boon

[29] *Bhāgavata* 7.10.51–70. [30] 2 lines inserted after *MBh.* 7.173.55 ab.

[31] *Skanda* 5.3.26.1–169; *Hari.* (app. 1, no. 43, line 32).

[32] See below, chap. X, sec. 4. [33] *Hari.* (app. 1, no. 43, 1–172; esp. 32).

that he could not be killed by gods, demons, Gandharvas, Rākṣasas, Piśācas, or serpents. Then the demon recalled his former enmity (with the gods) and was furious; he set out to destroy the gods. The evil-minded demon caused all creatures who followed the dharma of their class and stage of life to dwell in three cities, and in that city [sic] *of the evil one, no one sacrificed or offered Soma or performed good deeds; there were no temples to the gods, nor any worship of the gods. Thus the might of the gods was cut off, and they wandered like mortals on earth, overcome by the demon. At last they went to Śiva in the city of Avantī, and he worshiped the Goddess, who gave him the marvellous Pāśupata weapon to conquer the evil demon. Then Śiva killed the great demon with a single arrow; with a weapon of delusion, Śiva split that deluding demon into three and killed him.*[34]

The evil of the demon is both Vedic (he prevents sacrificial offerings from reaching the gods and so weakens them that they are like mortals) and Purāṇic (he outlaws temples and worship); he is evil because he suddenly remembers that he is a demon, the natural enemy of the gods. Though Śiva kills him, he is actually destroyed by the power of the Goddess (thus, apparently, avoiding any violation of the promise that no *god* would kill him, the usual word-splitting evasion), and though no corruption or heresy is actually mentioned, there are hints of foul play. As in the episode of Maya and the cow, deception is used by both sides; the deluding demon is killed by a weapon of delusion (Pāśupata *śastra*), a possible play upon the term used elsewhere to describe the doctrine of the heretic god, his Pāśupata *śāstra*.

Other texts begin to insert explanations of the manner in which the demons become evil. The demons were ascetics who remained orthodox after obtaining their boon, chanting the Vedas, worshipping the gods, honoring Brahmins, and generally following dharma, until Alakṣmī, envy, thirst, hunger, Kali, and quarrels entered the city.[35] No further motivation is given for this sudden change of fortune, which may be assumed to have developed "in the course of time." Yet, after the evil has spread through the city, bringing sexual immorality, dishonor of the gods and Brahmins, and the destruction of temples and hermitages, the text remarks that the demons had been corrupted by Indra.[36] Indra's usual emissary in these affairs, Nārada, does appear, but only *after* the evil change has taken place; when evil omens and dreams appear in the city, Nārada comes and is received by Maya, who asks him about these omens and dreams; Nārada replies, "They mean that Śiva is coming in his great chariot to destroy the Triple City and you and the demons." The lord of demons was frightened by this, and he exhorted his soldiers to fight against the gods, conquer them, reign in heaven, and kill all the gods and Indra. "Then we demons will enjoy all the worlds," he concluded.[37] Apparently Maya himself is made to behave demonically only by the late warning of Nārada,

[34] *Skanda* 5.1.43.1–48. In *Padma* 1.76, Gaṇeśa kills Traipura, the son of the demon named Tripura. [35] *Matsya* 131.10–50. [36] *Matsya* 131.50. [37] *Matsya* 134.1–33.

who tells him nothing but the truth, reminding him that he is a demon (a recollection sufficient to stir the demon named Triple City, as well as other demons of the Triple City) and that he must kill the gods before they kill him.

Nārada plays a more important role in another set of texts, which pose a more serious theological problem. Here, the demons of the Triple City (now led by Bāṇa, a son of Bali) are said to be great devotees of Śiva, but they pose the usual Purāṇic threat:

Bāṇa ruled the Triple City. The gods and sages complained to Śiva that Bāṇa had performed great asceticism in order to obtain three cities, and that the great demons oppressed the triple world, stealing all of its gems—gold, jewels, and women. Moreover, Bāṇa's energy caused heaven to tremble and whirl about. Śiva conforted them and promised to devise a way to destroy the Triple City. He summoned Nārada and said, "The wives of the demons of the Triple City have such energy that they cause heaven to tremble and whirl about. Go and delude them." Nārada came to Bāṇa and said that he was full of curiosity to observe the famous chastity of the women of his city. Delighted, Bāṇa introduced Nārada to his queen, to whom Nārada taught a complicated erotic ritual. Then Nārada stole the minds of all the women, creating a chink in the virtue of the city, so that Śiva was able to destroy it.[38]

The precise nature of Nārada's doctrine is not clear, but it is evidently some variation on the loss of chastity, perhaps some form of Tantrism. Among the evil omens that appear in the city are dreams in which people wear red garments,[39] a possible reference to Buddhism. But some form of corruption is now necessary, since Bāṇa is a famous devotee of Śiva, one whom Śiva assists in many other myths; his participation in this cycle may be based on a linguistic attraction between his name and the word for the sacred arrow (*bāṇa*) which Śiva uses to destroy the Triple City; Śiva is the great archer, and Bāṇa is the instrument, the excuse, with which he destroys the universe. Bāṇa's energy, or that of his wives, threatens the gods, and the demons of his city behave demonically; this alone might well justify their destruction. But for Bāṇa himself, the steadfast devotee of Śiva, the more sophisticated episode of corruption is required, just as Somaka, a devotee of Śiva, must be converted to Buddhism by Bṛhaspati before he can be killed by Śiva.[40]

Another set of myths introduces a specific heresy, taught not by Nārada but by Viṣṇu (or by Viṣṇu aided by Nārada). Viṣṇu's role is foreshadowed in the *Harivaṃśa*, where he is said to help Śiva destroy the cities, at which time Viṣṇu is called the great yogi,[41] a term applied first to Maya and then to the deluding Śiva. From this brief allusion to Viṣṇu's assistance, the Purāṇas then develop the concept of Viṣṇu as the great deluder (Mahāmohin or Māyāmohin). In these

[38] *Matsya* 187.1–52; *Skanda* 5.3.26–27; *Padma* 1.14.1–36. [39] *Matsya* 188.12.

[40] See above, chap. V, sec. 2. [41] *Hari.* (app. 1, no. 43, lines 140 and 170).

myths, as in the *Mahābhārata*, the demons of the Triple City are the three sons of Tāraka, and Maya builds their three cities; but now they are said to be devotees of Śiva, as in the Bāṇa versions. They pose the threats caused not by Vedic demonic wickedness (stealing the sacrifice or stealing women, as the demons of Bāṇa's city do) but by Purāṇic demonic ascetic virtue (like that of Bāṇa himself): "Indra and the gods and Brahmins were burnt by the fire of the Triple City like trees burnt by a forest fire, and in fear of the demons they went to Viṣṇu."[42] This fire is the heat of asceticism, particularly asceticism devoted to Śiva: "All the demon women were true to their husbands, and the demons worshipped Śiva devotedly. By their asceticism they caused Indra and the other gods to wane away and to be burned by the demonic energy."[43] Elsewhere Viṣṇu states, "The demons are puffed up with pride, and evil, but they cannot be slain by the gods, because their worship of Śiva frees them from all sins."[44] In order to corrupt the demons, who are said to be full of dharma, Viṣṇu creates a man of delusion, Māyin, who may have been attracted to this myth by the presence of Maya or of mere abstract delusion (*māyā*), an accepted weapon in human battles from the earliest texts, where it is said to be particularly characteristic of "demonic" warfare and to be used against the wicked: the righteous warrior king invokes "Bali, son of Virocana, he who has *māyā*."[45] This delusion is Viṣṇu's weapon:

Viṣṇu taught Māyin a doctrine which deluded everyone; it was opposed to the Vedas and the dharma of class and stage of life. Viṣṇu sent Māyin to destroy the dharmas, Vedas, and lawbooks of the Triple City. Nārada assisted Māyin, and all the women of the city became unchaste and corrupt. Then by Śiva's command Alakṣmī entered the city, and by Brahmā's command Lakṣmī (who had been won by the demons' asceticism and worship of Śiva) departed from the city. Thus Viṣṇu established heresy and adharma, and Śiva abandoned the demons and was able to destroy them, for they were heretics, outside the path of the Vedas and the worship of Śiva.[46]

Now Alakṣmī's role is explained. She is sent by Brahmā's command, only after the women have been corrupted; she is the evil woman who replaces the good woman of the city (Lakṣmī). The fatal heresy is not only anti-Vedic and anti-bhakti, but Materialist (for Māyin teaches that heaven and hell are nowhere but right here) and lascivious, for good measure.

The heresy is more specific in another, greatly expanded text of this series; it is a combination of Jainism and Buddhism:

The demons of the Triple City had great virtue and practised Vedic rites; their energy scorched Indra and the gods, who went to Śiva in distress and said, "The demons have conquered the gods, shattered the sages, and ruined the universe. They themselves take all

[42] *Liṅga* 1.71.38. [43] *Saura* 34.23–24. [44] *Liṅga* 1.71.48, 66, 69; cf. *Śiva* 2.5.3.41–42.
[45] *Arthaśāstra* 14.1 and 14.3. [46] *Liṅga* 1.71.75–96; *Saura* 34.42–72.

the sacrificial shares, and they have set terrible adharma in motion, interfering with the sages." But Śiva said to the gods, "The ruler of the Triple City is virtuous and devoted to me. I cannot kill him." Viṣṇu said, "The demons of the Triple City are full of dharma and therefore invincible. Even when they commit great evil, they worship Śiva and are freed from all sins. Therefore I will create an obstacle to their dharma, and then I will destroy the Triple City for the sake of the gods." To destroy the enemies of the gods by destroying their Vedic dharma and Śiva worship, Viṣṇu created a man of delusion, who prepared a delusory doctrine in dialect. The man was bald, wore dirty clothes, carried a whisk broom, which he moved gently and constantly for fear of harming living creatures, and he wore a cloth over his mouth. At first, he had no success, but then Viṣṇu summoned Nārada, who became a formal convert, and the king of the demons said, "Since Nārada has become initiated, we will become initiated." He accepted the bald monk's teaching, which included nonviolence and other ideas taught in Buddhist texts. The monk satirized Vedic sacrifice and caste, preached against chastity, and completely deluded the demons' wits; and when the dharma of the women was destroyed, Viṣṇu was satisfied. The gods told Śiva that the demons had become Buddhists, and he burnt the Triple City of the demons, so that no one but Maya survived.[47]

There are a number of contradictions in this text. The gods say that the demons are evil, but the narrator says that the demons practised Vedic rites and Viṣṇu admits that they are full of dharma. Moreover, whatever the original nature of the demons, they remove their sins by worshipping Śiva, and their ruler is entirely virtuous. Nārada is therefore required to corrupt them and to make the women unchaste, yet he merely sets an example by becoming the first convert to a creed that has nothing unchaste about it. This creed seems far more like Jainism than like Buddhism (the man with the fan and the mask is clearly a Jain), and the commentator identifies it as Jainism,[48] yet there are frequent references to Buddhism, and the gods praise Śiva for making the demons take refuge in Buddhism.[49] This confusion persists in later myths.

More significant is the frequency of apologies in this text. There is, to begin with, disagreement about who is to take the credit (or the blame) for the corruption of the demons; Viṣṇu does the deed, but the text frequently remarks that it was by Śiva's command that Viṣṇu acted in this way. Since this is a Śaiva text, one can only assume that the author wishes to assimilate an already well-known achievement of Viṣṇu (the Buddha avatar) to the credit of Śiva. Yet if the author is proud of Śiva's action, he doth protest too much. Viṣṇu says to Māyin, "By my command, you will incur no fault";[50] the narrator remarks that, by Śiva's grace, Nārada and the bald monk did not become affected;[51] when Śiva hesitates to kill the demons because they are devoted to him and were merely

[47] *Śiva* 2.5.1–6; *Jñāna Sam.* 21.3–24. [48] Comm. on *Jñāna Sam.* 21.7–8.

[49] *Śiva* 2.5.6.28. [50] *Śiva* 2.5.4.17. [51] *Śiva* 2.5.5.62.

tricked into abandoning their dharma, Brahmā assures him, "There is no evil in this act, since you are the great lord and you yourself sent someone to delude them, and they abandoned their svadharma."[52] And finally it is said that those who were not opposed to the gods, and who worshipped Śiva, were saved, whether or not they were demons.[53]

These apologies seem to satisfy the author of this text, but the myth raised more serious problems in the minds of some Tamils who interpreted it:

The demons of the Triple City were invincible because they were great devotees of Śiva, but by their nature they caused the gods distress. Viṣṇu held a sacrifice and created spirits to destroy the demons, but they could not approach the demons whose powers were so great. Viṣṇu then created a man and sent him with Nārada to teach the demons a new doctrine: the Vedic path was false, there was no rebirth, and all matter perished each second. The man made the demons his disciples, while Nārada made the wives lose their chastity. Śiva was persuaded to go to war against them; he laughed and they were reduced to ashes.

But Nārada and the Buddha were stricken with remorse for what they had done, and they went to Kāñcī to expiate their sin. Śiva appeared to them and said, "The sin of teaching false doctrine can be expiated only after many millions of aeons. Even in order to help the gods it is a heinous sin to destroy someone's faith in Śiva. But because your sin can be expiated after many rebirths, the entrances to this shrine will be the doors to rebirth, and you will eventually attain release."[54]

The Vedic magic rite (which was sufficient to destroy the sons of Raji) is useless against these devotees, who require a subtler form of corruption; and this, in turn, requires modern methods of expiation. Another variant of this myth states that in expiation of the sin of causing apostasy, Viṣṇu was made to perform hard penance at Tirukal̲ukun̲ram.[55] Apparently the doctrine that the end justifies the means is not accepted by the Tamil texts; yet the sin is expiated, and all is well.

4. Viṣṇu as Buddha Corrupts the Demons

In early versions of the Triple City myth, Viṣṇu plays no part at all, or only a minor part; Śiva destroys the demons and arranges to have them corrupted by Nārada. But when the heresy becomes the specific doctrine of Buddhism, Viṣṇu teaches it; at this point there is some confusion between the roles of Viṣṇu and Śiva. In the *Vāyu Purāṇa*, Śiva is called the Buddha,[56] but the text does not expand upon or explain this identification. In general, the episodes in which Viṣṇu appears as the Buddha to help Śiva corrupt the demons of the Triple City are all later than the earliest in a series of texts in which Viṣṇu becomes the

[52] *Śiva* 2.5.6.36–46. [53] *Śiva* 2.5.10.40–44. [54] *Kāñcippurāṇam* 30.2–42.
[55] *Tirukal̲ukun̲ram, Pakshi Tīrtham*, pp. 5–6. [56] *Vāyu* 1.30.215 and 2.35.176.

Buddha to corrupt other demons, who have nothing to do with Śiva. Thus there are two separate and parallel lines of development (Śiva and Nārada in the Triple City, and Viṣṇu as the Buddha against other demons) and then a joining point: Śiva with Nārada and Viṣṇu as the Buddha in the Triple City. The second of these lines, the myth of Viṣṇu's Buddha avatar, has a complex history of its own.

Hindus came to regard the Buddha as an avatar of Viṣṇu between A.D. 450[57] and the sixth century,[58] for the Buddha avatar is not mentioned in the *Mahābhārata* (except in the Kumbhakona edition[59]) and appears first in the *Viṣṇu Purāṇa* (A.D. 400–500), where it is already established in full detail. The Buddha avatar is represented on the Gupta Daśāvatāra temple at Deogarh (c. A.D. 600) and mentioned in a seventh-century Pallava inscription[60] and on an eighth-century Tamil inscription.[61] The earliest texts that allude to the Buddha avatar[62] may antedate the *Mahābhārata*,[63] but this has yet to be proven.

The *Bhāgavata Purāṇa* refers to the Buddha incarnation in the form of several prophesies:

When the Kali Age has begun, in order to delude the enemies of the gods, Viṣṇu will be born as the Buddha, son of Ajana. . . . When the enemies of the gods come to know the Vedic rites and begin to oppress people, then he will assume an attractive and deluding form and teach adharma to the demons in the (three) invisible cities made by Maya, making them heretics. . . . With words he will delude those who are not deserving of the sacrifice. . . . Homage to Buddha, the pure, the deluder of the demons.[64]

The purpose of this incarnation is evident. Although the demons come to know the Vedic rites, they are not deserving of the sacrifice; their moral ambiguity makes it necessary for them to be corrupted as well as destroyed.

Sometimes Viṣṇu uses a combination of Buddhism and Jainism to corrupt the demons, as he does in the Triple City:

During the battle between gods and demons, the gods were defeated and sought refuge with the Lord; he became the son of Suddhodana, the very form of Māyāmoha, and deluded the demons, who became Buddhists and abandoned the Vedas. Then he became an Arhat (Jain) and made others into Arhats, and so the heretics came into being.[65]

A similar confusion of doctrines appears in the statement that, at the dawn of the Kali Age, in order to delude the enemies of the gods, Viṣṇu will be born as the Buddha, the son of Jina.[66] In one list of avatars, Viṣṇu is said to become incarnate as Ṛṣabha (the first Jain Tīrthaṃkara) and then as the Buddha.[67] This confusion

[57] Choudhury, p. 239. [58] Hazra (1948), pp. 103 and 41–42. [59] *Kumbhakona MBh.* 12.348.2; 12, app. 1, no. 32, lines 1–17. [60] Hazra (1948), p. 88; Banerjea, pp. 420–425. [61] Krishna Sastri, p. 5. [62] Banerjea, p. 392. [63] Schrader, pp. 43–47; Śāntātman, 39th avatar of the *Ahirbudhnya Saṃhitā*. [64] *Bhāgavata* 1.3.24; 2.7.37; 11.4.22; 10.40.22. [65] *Agni* 16.1–14. [66] *Garuḍa* 1.32; Śrīdhara on *Bhāgavata* 1.3.24, alt. reading. [67] *Bhāgavata* 2.7.10; cf. 1.3.6–22.

may derive from the fact that many Buddhist texts refer to the Buddha as Jina, or it may simply betray the Hindu tendency to lump together all non-Hindus.

The *Viṣṇu Purāṇa* adds further heresies to the doctrines of Buddhism and Jainism:

The demons, led by Prahlāda, had stolen the sacrificial portions of the gods, but they were so full of svadharma, Vedic worship, and asceticism that they could not be conquered. Viṣṇu created a man of delusion to lead the demons from the path of the Vedas; the man was naked, bald, carrying a peacock-feather fan; he went where the demons were practising asceticism on the banks of the Narmadā and made them all into Arhats, discouraging them from their asceticism and teaching them contradictory tenets about dharma. Then the man put on red garments and taught the rest of the demons that the sacrifice of animals was an evil act. He said, "If the animal slaughtered in the sacrifice is assured of arrival in heaven, why does the sacrificer not kill his own father?" Then the demons became Buddhists, and they caused others to become heretics, abandoning the Vedas and reviling the gods and Brahmins, discarding their armor of svadharma. The gods attacked them and killed them.[68]

Certain arguments, such as the satire on the Hindu rationalization of animal sacrifices and the appeal to "words of reason,"[69] may refer to the heresy of Materialism (a heresy also hinted at in some myths of the Triple City).[70] Viṣṇu's association with the Materialist heresy is further suggested by a text which states that the form which Viṣṇu assumes to corrupt the demons (Mahāmoha, great delusion) is responsible for other heresies: "The left side of Brahmā's body became known as Mahāmoha in order to found the Materialist and similar sects, for the seeking of liberation through eating flesh, drinking wine, and so forth."[71] Moreover, the phrase "words of reason" is also used in a pejorative sense in the myth in which Bṛhaspati, masquerading as Śukra, deludes the demons with his own Materialist heresy;[72] and at the end of that episode he leaves the demons practising asceticism on the banks of the Narmadā, precisely where Viṣṇu finds them here. Thus it would appear that the demons are made Materialists twice over, as well as Jains and Buddhists.

5. Śiva Corrupts Divodāsa

The threads of these three cycles—Raji, the Triple City, and Viṣṇu as the Buddha—are woven together in the last set of texts, which deals not with demons but with a mortal king like Raji—in fact, with a king who is an ancestor of Raji and whose story is linked with Raji's in some texts.[73] Like the myths of Raji and

[68] *Viṣṇu* 3.17.9–45; 3.18.1–34. [69] *Viṣṇu* 3.18.30; *yuktimadvacanam.*

[70] Cf. *Liṅga* 1.71.75–96; *Saura* 34.42–72; *Sarvadarśanasaṃgraha* 1, final verses "by Bṛhaspati."

[71] *Kālikā* 78.206. [72] *Padma* 5.13.370; see above, chap. V, sec. 12. [73] *Vāyu* 2.30; *Hari.* 21–22.

the Triple City, this story appears first without any reference to the heresy of Buddhism, and although the original version says nothing of the virtue of the king, the need to corrupt him (and, in particular, the need to corrupt his wife) is assumed:

Divodāsa was a famous king of Benares. At this time, a Rākṣasa named Kṣemaka entered the empty city, for it had formerly been cursed by Gaṇeśa to become empty for a thousand years, and for the duration of that curse Divodāsa lived in a charming city on the Gomatī, on the border of the kingdom. [The sages ask: How could Gaṇeśa, who is the very soul of dharma, curse a holy place? The bard continues:]

King Divodāsa lived in the city of Benares. Now, at this time Śiva married Satī and lived with his in-laws, but his mother-in-law, Menā, said to Satī, "Your husband does not behave properly in my presence. He is very poor and does nothing but sport with you." Satī begged Śiva to take her to his own home, and so Śiva looked over all the worlds and chose Benares as a pleasant place to live. But when he saw that Divodāsa was living there, Śiva summoned Gaṇeśa and said, "Go to the city of Benares and empty it. Use gentle wiles, for the king is very mighty." Gaṇeśa established a shrine in the city, and the chief queen of Divodāsa worshipped there and asked for a son, again and again. But Gaṇeśa did not give her sons, thinking, "If the king becomes angry at us, I will achieve my purposes." After a long time, the king did become angry at Gaṇeśa for failing to give him a son, and the evil-minded king foolishly destroyed the shrine of Gaṇeśa, whom he reviled as an "evil-minded, gluttonous maker of obstacles." Then Gaṇeśa said to the king, "Since you have destroyed my shrine when I had not offended you, your city will become empty." And so Benares became empty, and Śiva came and dwelt there with Satī.[74]

Śiva advises Gaṇeśa to use treachery because the king is very mighty, not very virtuous; Divodāsa is described as evil-minded and foolish, though this is said only after Gaṇeśa infuriates him. The city which Śiva destroys, however, is very virtuous, and this myth is introduced to explain why *it*, not the king, was cursed. The fact that a holy shrine is destroyed by the gods links this myth with the series of tales in which the gods destroy a shrine that has allowed too many people to enter heaven;[75] in these, as in the myth of Divodāsa, Gaṇeśa, "the maker of obstacles," is often the one who ruins the shrine. Thus Śiva corrupts an ordinary king and an extremely holy city simply because of a whim of his own, a whim that results from his own shortcomings (his failure to provide a satisfactory home for his wife).[76]

In spite of Divodāsa's innocence in this episode, there are several indications that he may have led a double life of questionable morality, though this takes place after Gaṇeśa produces the trouble. During the duration of the curse, Divodāsa lived in a charming city on the Gomatī. All variants of this text tell us

[74] *Hari.*, app. 1, no. 7, lines 57–140; *Brahmāṇḍa* 2.3.67.30–65; *Vāyu* 2.30.23–55.

[75] See below, chap. IX, sec. 2. [76] O'Flaherty (1973), pp. 213–221.

more about this "charming city": to get it, Divodāsa killed Bhadraśrena's one hundred sons and stole away his kingdom.[77] Indeed, this is the clue to the otherwise puzzling question of the connection between the Raji/Tripura story of the Buddhist heresy and the myth of Divodāsa. From the time of the Ṛg Veda, Divodāsa is famed as the destroyer of cities, sometimes aided by Indra.[78] Later, his favorite city is Benares; in the *Mahābhārata* he is famed as a king of Benares and as a king who took away the sacrificial fires from a conquered city when his son Pratardana destroyed it.[79] These Epic references to the sacrilegious king of Benares are then woven into a short tale:

Divodāsa became king of Benares after his father had ravaged the city by war. Then, by Indra's command, he rebuilt Benares and made it prosperous, crowded with members of all four classes; it was on the north bank of the Ganges and the south bank of the Gomatī, like another Amarāvatī of Indra, a city of the gods. The Haihayas came there and attacked Divodāsa, who fought a battle like the battle of gods and demons, but he suffered great losses and left the city in despair. He sought refuge in a hermitage, where a sage performed a sacrifice and gave him a son, Pratardana. This son returned to the city, killed the invaders and destroyed all their sons, leaving only one descendant, whom the demons mistook for Indra.[80]

This peculiar story contains *in nuce* a number of elements of the Buddha avatar as it is applied to Divodāsa. Divodāsa makes Benares prosperous and crowded, rivaling the city of the gods; he lives in Benares until he is driven out in a battle like that between gods and demons; he oversteps dharma in taking vengeance on his enemies; his enemy's son so rivals Indra that he deludes the demons into mistaking him for someone other than his true self. Thus the elements of the plot of the Triple City myth are all present in a crude, often metaphorical, form; the catalyst is the city of Benares, the city on the Ganges, the city of Divodāsa. Why should the Buddha avatar take place here? Perhaps because Benares is a city holy to worshippers of Śiva and in close proximity to the holy city of the Buddhists, Sarnath. A bard who wished to transpose the myth of gods and Buddhist demons to earth would find no better place to do it than here, and no better king to do it to than Divodāsa, already associated with violating dharma, stealing other peoples' cities, and enduring forced exile from Benares. (In a similar manner, Divodāsa's reputation for asceticism and virtue caused him to be identified by later Āyur-vedic tradition as an incarnation of Dhanvantari, physician of the gods, who brought forth the Soma at the churning of the ocean; Divodāsa taught the sages to heal illness and prolong life.[81] These associations with immortality and extended life-spans are clearly desirable in a physician but are liable to make the Hindu gods nervous.)

[77] *Hari.*, app. 1, no. 7, lines 65–67 and 139–143; *Brahmāṇḍa* 2.3.67.65–66; *Vāyu* 2.30.62–64. [78] *RV* 2.19.6. [79] *MBh.* 5.115.1; 12.97.20. [80] *MBh.* 13.31.15–55. [81] *Suśrutasaṃhitā* 1.1, 5.1, and 6.66.

The unrighteous side of Divodāsa's character is more fully developed in another series of texts, which tell of another city ruled by Divodāsa not only before the curse but, indeed, before his incarnation as Divodāsa at all:

In a former aeon, there was a six-year drought, which caused all creatures to tremble and to live like sages. [*Comm: eating fruits, roots, etc.*] *Some people ate flesh to keep alive. Anarchy arose, and all effort to create proved fruitless. Brahmā was worried that creatures would be destroyed, for as creatures decreased, sacrificial rituals decreased, and so those who eat sacrifices waned. As Brahmā worried, he saw a royal sage practising asceticism in Benares; this sage was Ripuñjaya, the very form of Kṣatriya dharma incarnate. Brahmā went to him and said, "Protect the earth, and I will give you a Nāga princess for your wife, and divine powers, and you will be called Divodāsa ('Servant of Heaven')." When Divodāsa asked why he had been chosen, Brahmā replied, "If you are king, the god (Indra) will send rain; for all the other kings are wicked, and the god will not send rain when an evil man is king." The king said, "I will accept your command, but let the gods stay in heaven, and not on earth, so that I may rule my subjects happily, without a rival." Brahmā agreed to this, and Divodāsa ordered a kettledrum to sound this proclamation: "Let all the gods go to heaven; let them not come back here, and let Nāgas and men stay in their own respective places, the underworld and the earth, while the gods remain in their own place." Then Śiva said to Brahmā, "I will go from here and practise asceticism on Mount Mandara for the duration of the time granted to him by your boon," and he went with Pārvatī to Mount Mandara. Then Viṣṇu left all the sacred Vaiṣṇava shrines here and went to Mandara, and Gaṇeśa left the Gaṇeśa shrines, and the sun and all the gods left the earth.*

Then Divodāsa reigned righteously. He shone like the sun; he punished like Yama the king of dharma; he burnt like Agni and was the very form of Rudra. By his ascetic powers he took the form of all the gods, and all the gods praised and worshipped him; his fort was like the twin brother of heaven, in which he desired to protect the Yakṣas and Rākṣasas, and the demons took the form of men and served him. When Divodāsa had been ruling for eight thousand years, the gods wished to produce an obstacle for him, and they took counsel with Bṛhaspati and said, "We gods will suffer great calamity if this king continues his acts of dharma and his sacrifices; though he injures the gods with his sacrifices that are hard to bear, they cannot avenge themselves. For though the king performs sacrifices, your friends do not enjoy those sacrifices very much. It is the nature of the gods who dwell in heaven not to be able to bear pressure from anyone else; Bali, Bāṇa, and others who opposed the gods were overcome, but Divodāsa rules with dharma; his women are chaste, and no one is childless or poor in his kingdom. There are no heretics, the gods are worshipped, and so there is no chink in his dharma." Then Bṛhaspati taught the gods who wished to harm that virtuous king various methods to do this, but they all failed. At last Divodāsa boasted, "By the power of my asceticism I will become Indra and give wheat to all my people, and I will become Agni, and by taking the form of water, the source of life for all creatures, I will bring creatures to life; what need is there for these fools? I will be the sun and moon for my subjects."

Meanwhile, on Mount Mandara, Śiva suffered restlessly in separation from his beloved Benares. Pārvatī urged him to go to Benares if he wished, but Śiva replied, "Brahmā granted Divodāsa a boon, and he rules the city with dharma. How can such a virtuous king be separated from Benares? What obstacles can I make to his dharma? Without some flaw in him, nothing can be done; old age, death, and disease cannot touch him." As he spoke to the Goddess, and looked at her, Śiva then sent his female ascetics to seduce the king from his dharma, but they failed. He sent the sun, but the sun split into twelve suns and established shrines there in twelve places. Gaṇeśa took the form of a Buddhist astrologer and deluded many of the people in the city, including the king's wife, but not the king. Then Viṣṇu took the form of a Buddhist, and his wife and Garuḍa became a Buddhist nun and a disciple, and they taught the Buddhist doctrine of non-injury; they said that caste distinctions were meaningless and that one should cultivate the pleasures of the body. Thus they corrupted the women of the city and the harem. Deeply upset, the king sent for a Brahmin to advise him.

Viṣṇu came to him in disguise, and Divodāsa said, "I am weary of ruling and wish to withdraw from the world. My one sin has been to regard the gods as mere blades of grass—but even that was for the good of my subjects, not for my own sake. Two sides are striving against one another in my mind. I have worshipped the gods and followed dharma, but I know how many have been destroyed because of the hostility of the gods. The demons of the Triple City, though true to their vows of dharma and devoted to Śiva, were destroyed by Śiva. I have no wish to oppose the gods, but I do not fear them, for they reached their places through sacrifice, and I have sacrificed; and my asceticism is greater than theirs." Viṣṇu said, "It is true that you have never been hostile to the gods, but the fault seems to me to lie in your heart, that you have kept Śiva, the Lord of Benares, far away. Now your life is fulfilled, and you may go to heaven to dwell eternally." Divodāsa established the liṅga *and worshipped it, and then he went to Kailāsa, Śiva's heaven, where he became a servant of Śiva, three-eyed and adorned with serpents like Śiva himself.*[82]

Divodāsa explicitly notes the parallel with the myth of the Triple City, but he fails to see how it applies to him; the fact that he cites in his own favor (that his asceticism is greater than that of the gods) is the very basis of the gods' resentment of him; he has banished them, surpassed them, and, the last straw, given refuge to demons in his fortress, a sin also committed by the demons of the Triple City. The gods admit that they cannot bear competition; Divodāsa established Vedic religion so firmly, and made the people so happy, "that the gods

[82] *Skanda* 4.1.39.26–70; 4.1.43.1–107; 44–58 *passim*. Cf. also *Gaṇeśa Upapurāṇa, Krīra Khaṇḍa,* chap. 39 (cited in Kennedy, p. 251).

became alarmed lest they should lose their supremacy."[83] Naively, Divodāsa says that he has no fear of the gods, since he has sacrificed to put them where they are; but the gods do not enjoy his sacrifices. He worships the gods, but somehow the Vedic underpinnings of that worship have been discarded; his sacrifices injure the gods, perhaps because they hate him and they know that he hates them. Divodāsa, for his part, cannot bear competition either; he refuses to rule unless the gods withdraw, for he demands the complete separation which the gods themselves usually insist on; he sends them back to heaven as they send presumptuous mortals back to earth. At first, Divodāsa competes with the gods only in metaphor, but then–when they attack him–he actually replaces them. Several attempts to corrupt him fail. First Brahmā tempts Ripuñjaya with a Nāga wife, but the king remains steadfast in his demand for the absence of the gods–and, significantly, the Nāgas–from his dominion. Then Pārvatī inspires Śiva to send female ascetics (a much reduced version of her role in other older tale of Divodāsa) in place of the celestial nymphs usually sent by Indra, but to no avail. The masquerade of Gaṇeśa also fails, for it is only a vestige from the earlier version (where it was successful), perhaps retained here because Gaṇeśa (like Viṣṇu and Śiva) is said to be forced to abandon his shrine in a country where no one is childless. Finally, the myth of the Buddhist heresy is introduced, though still without any effect on Divodāsa. At last, the gods grant him the reward of translation to heaven, using bhakti as a final resort to get the king out of Benares and to get Śiva (in the form of a *liṅga*) back in. As Divodāsa becomes a god, he is no longer a threatening, anomalous mortal, and everyone is happy.

The ostensible cause of all the trouble is a famine, which is used elsewhere to explain not only the general, original corruption of man in the Golden Age but the particular heresies taught as a result of the curse of the sage Gautama.[84] The true crux of the conflict between Divodāsa and the gods, however, is his demand that the gods leave earth. Divodāsa's inability to share Benares with the gods is noted by the *Brahmāṇḍa Purāṇa*: Śiva lives in Benares with Satī during the first three Yugas, but that city disappears in the Kali Yuga, whereupon the city (the Benares that we know) comes into existence again.[85] In this view, there are two Benareses–one the gods', the other Divodāsa's (or ours)–just as there is a divine city (Amarāvatī) and an earthly city (Avantī, Ujjain) in the Ripuñjaya myth, and two earthly cities (Benares and the other city on the Gomatī) in some of the Divodāsa stories. By living in Benares, therefore, Divodāsa automatically causes the gods to leave, even before he makes his explicit demand; this reveals the lack of peaceful coexistence between gods and men in Purāṇic mythology.

Since the gods normally dwell in heaven, Divodāsa's action can only be meant to indicate that he threw the gods out of their secondary dwellings on earth, out

[83] Kennedy, p. 251. [84] See below, chap. X, sec. 4. [85] *Brahmāṇḍa* 2.3.67.62–64.

of the temples where the gods dwell in the form of their images. Thus, when Divodāsa reestablishes the *liṅga* in Benares, Śiva returns to the city; the "house" that Satī seeks is the temple. This is the sacrilege for which Divodāsa must be punished: the destruction of the Purāṇic temple, an act entirely compatible with the statement that he continued to perform sacrifice and worship the Vedic gods. The full extent of the sin is revealed by another episode to which the myth refers, the tale of Ripuñjaya, who becomes Divodāsa in Benares but is best known as the last of the Bṛhadratha kings of Māgadha[86] and the king of Avantī. As one of the last kings in the Kali Age, he is also associated with Buddhism,[87] which may have led to the association with the "Buddhist" Divodāsa:

In a former aeon, anarchy arose, which worried Brahmā, for without men the gods are not able to sustain the world, since the gods live upon the nourishment from sacrificial gifts and prayers. Searching for a suitable king,[88] *Brahmā saw the royal sage Ripuñjaya performing asceticism, and Brahmā said to him, "Enough of this asceticism, my son. By your dharma you have conquered all worlds; now you should protect the world, for there is no other dharma like that." The royal sage bowed to Brahmā and said, "If I must protect the earth, then give me the charming city of Avantī [Ujjain]. The city of Amarāvatī [a mythical city said to be situated above Mount Meru] is renowned throughout the world of men as the place established as a dwelling place for the gods who have fallen from heaven. Let those who dwell in heaven remain outside my frontier; then I will rule the earth." Brahmā said, "What you wish will be granted. All the gods will obey your command always and be in your power, and you will be called 'Lord of the Gods.'" Then Brahmā vanished, and the king proclaimed to the gods, "Heaven is made for you, and earth for mankind," and the gods went to heaven. Then the king ruled his subjects in dharma, loving them like his own sons, and they were free of old age or death; the earth was like the world of the gods. As time passed, the gods were full of envy, and they tried hard to harm him, doing unpleasant things to his subjects again and again. Finally, Indra sent a great drought lasting a long time; but the king became a cloud, went up into the sky, and sent a good rain, which made his people happy. Indra then sent rain—he became the floods of doomsday; but the king became a wind and drove off the clouds. Fire disappeared from the earth, and so the king became fire to support his subjects and sacrifices and the gods. At this time, Śiva came with Pārvatī to the city; Ripuñjaya bowed to him in fear, and praised him. Śiva then granted the boon that was in Ripuñjaya's heart: that he would be invincible by all the gods always. And Ripuñjaya asked Śiva to make the city a place of pilgrimage, so that all the gods would dwell there always, so that Meru itself would be there. And Śiva, having granted this wish, made Ripuñjaya a lord of his hosts.*[89]

Many obscure points of the Divodāsa myth become clearer from this text, which

[86] *Viṣṇu* 4.23–24. [87] Wilson (1840), pp. 370–371.

[88] See above, chap. II, sec. 5. [89] *Skanda* 5.2.74.1–55.

was probably known to the author of the Divodāsa episode. The king is given a name more appropriate to his desires: he is a Lord of the Gods, not a mere Servant of Heaven. Yet Ripuñjaya at first shows none of the hostility to the gods that characterizes Divodāsa; he assumes not the forms but merely the powers of the gods, and then only in response to their own jealous attacks. Indeed, the very drought that initiates the Divodāsa episode is here depicted as an act of divine aggression, as it usually is in the mythology of Indra.[90] The bard even goes so far as to point out that by becoming fire Ripuñjaya is maintaining the life's blood not only of his own people but of the gods themselves. Yet even the unambitious virtue of Ripuñjaya is dangerous. His asceticism is a threat (Brahmā begs him to stop); he violates the natural order by banishing death and disease (as Divodāsa is said to be personally immune to death and disease) and by creating a heaven on earth (as Yayāti does[91]). Śiva knows that Ripuñjaya secretly desires to be invincible by the gods, though not necessarily to conquer them; he wishes to be left alone by the gods, the original motivation for his request to have them remain in heaven or in Amarāvatī, but not in Avantī. It is the gods who covet *his* heaven, not the reverse. Finally, since the city is Avantī and not Benares, the whole point of the conflict between the king and Śiva is removed, and Śiva comes to the king not to corrupt or test him but to reward him; yet, as in the Divodāsa myth, this reward accomplishes the gods' purposes more effectively than their antagonism does. Ripuñjaya chooses to have the gods come and live in his city forever, just as Divodāsa chooses to have Śiva come to Benares, and the dangerously virtuous king is translated to heaven where he is no longer an irritating anomaly. In view of the great consistency and simplicity of the Ripuñjaya text, as well as its relatively concise form, the absence of elaborate heresies, and its adherence to the older pattern of mythology (Indra versus the ascetic[92]), this tale may have contributed to the Divodāsa myth; but both episodes appear in the *Skanda Purāṇa,* and it is perhaps wiser to regard them as two regional Purāṇic variants on the older theme of the corruption of the cities of the demons.

Śiva and Divodāsa want to live in the same city, Benares, sacred city of Śaivas, just as Ripuñjaya and the gods compete for Avantī. It is ironic, but by no means uncharacteristic of the god, that, because Śiva wants to live in Benares forever (to make it sacred), he enters it by corrupting the virtuous people who live there—though their virtue may not originally have included devotion to Śiva. Śiva defends Benares (unsuccessfully) on behalf of another devotee in a Vaiṣṇava text:

When Kṛṣṇa was living in Dvārakā, Pauṇḍraka the king of Karūṣa sent a message to Kṛṣṇa, saying, "I *am Vāsudeva* [*Kṛṣṇa*]. *Come and fight with me, you pretender.*" *Now,*

[90] O'Flaherty (1973), pp. 40–54. [91] See below, chap. VIII, sec. 7. [92] O'Flaherty (1973), pp. 87–90.

the king of Benares was a friend of the king of Karūṣa, and fought on his side. Kṛṣṇa beheaded them both. Then Sudakṣiṇa, the son of the king of Benares, worshipped Śiva and asked him to help him slay his father's killer. Śiva told him how to perform a sacrifice to create a hideous, destructive fire, which appeared incarnate, naked, carrying a trident [like a Śaiva]. Sudakṣiṇa sent this fire to Dvārakā, but Kṛṣṇa commanded his discus to oppose it; the fire returned to Benares and burnt Sudakṣiṇa, and the discus destroyed all of the city of Benares.[93]

The wicked king of Benares is destroyed; his son attempts to avenge his death (as Divodāsa's son does); like Bṛhaspati in the city of Raji, Sudakṣiṇa uses a magic fire (in the shape of a heretical Śaiva) instead of a Buddhist. This ruse fails, and the city of Śiva is destroyed, not by him but rather in spite of his efforts to save it.

A Śaiva recasting of the myth retains this plot, but it gives Śiva a more prominent role, simplifying the myth and making it conform more closely to the Divodāsa pattern:

Pauṇḍraka, the king of Benares, worshipped Śiva by fasting for twelve years in the deserted city of Benares. Śiva granted him his request, to have the form of Vāsudeva, and the proud king boasted that he was Vāsudeva; he went to Dvārakā to conquer Kṛṣṇa, but Kṛṣṇa beheaded the king with his discus and caused the head to fall in the middle of the harem at Benares. Then Daṇḍapāṇi, the son of Pauṇḍraka, worshipped Śiva to avenge his father; Śiva gave him a witch with a trident, ashes, and a garland of human skulls. The king sent her to kill Kṛṣṇa, and she burnt all the earth like the fire of doomsday, but when she came to Dvārakā, Kṛṣṇa chased her back to Benares with his discus. Then the discus entered the city and burnt Daṇḍapāṇi and the whole city to ashes.[94]

The king of Benares who usurps the forms and the prerogatives of the gods is now assisted by a wicked female; he obtains his godly powers, as Divodāsa does, as the result of a twelve-year famine–here self-imposed, in an already empty city. These powers lead ultimately to the destruction of the holy city, now burnt to ashes like the Triple City.

The moral labyrinth of the Divodāsa myth, and the presence of Viṣṇu as the Buddha in it, led some English Indologists to assume that Divodāsa must have been a demon, to confuse him with the demons of the Triple City, though it is absolutely clear from all known Sanskrit variants of the myth (and from the entire literature of Indra, starting with the Ṛg Veda) that Divodāsa is a pious human king, a sage of royal blood (*rājarṣi*). Colonel Vans Kennedy inserted into one of the *Bhāgavata Purāṇa* passages about the Buddha[95] a parenthetical remark linking the myths of the Triple City and Divodāsa: Viṣṇu "preached heretical doctrines in the three cities founded by Maya (and in Kāsi [*sic*, Benares]), for the purpose of destroying, by deluding them, the enemies of the gods, steadfast in the

[93] *Bhāgavata* 10.66.1–42. [94] *Padma* 6.278.1–27. Cf. *Viṣṇu* 5.34. [95] *Bhāgavata* 2.7.37.

religion prescribed by the Vedas."[96] Kennedy justifies this insertion by stating that "part of the stanza refers to Viṣhnu's appearance in a former age in the city of the Tripura Asuras, and part to his incarnation as Buddha." He then proceeds to summarize the *Skanda Purāṇa* text of the Divodāsa story, omitting, however, the one line in the Sanskrit text that lends some weight to the concept of Divodāsa as a demon (or at least as a demonic mortal)–the statement that his city offered a refuge to Rākṣasas and demons.

Charles Coleman more thoroughly confused the two episodes:

> [Viṣṇu became the Buddha] (in some accounts it is said at the solicitation of Siva) to overturn the supremacy of the Asuras (or demons), the opponents of the gods, who, under Divodāsa, by their extraordinary virtue, piety, and practice of the holy doctrine of the Vedas, had become eminently powerful and happy. . . . Vishnu . . . by preaching doctrines of a more human character than those of the Vedas, caused Divodāsa and the Asuras to become apostates from that faith, and thus enabled the gods to overcome them, and establish their own supremacy on the subversion of their just and pious opponents. This legend, of which there are several versions, puerile, and we may add highly immoral as it may appear, is a correct specimen, in point of extravagance, of many others contained in the Puranas.[97]

In spite of his disdain for the Purāṇas, and his preference for Buddhism over Hinduism, Coleman was aware (unlike many Indologists to this day) that "there are several versions" of most Hindu myths, including this one; he has simply combined two versions from distinct, though related, myths.

6. Demons and Mortal Buddhists of the Kali Age

The confusion of human Buddhists and demons in Coleman's version is shared by the Hindus themselves. This confusion stems in part from a superimposition of the Buddha myth on two different patterns: stage one (gods versus demons in the Triple City, for the sake of mankind) and stage two (gods versus human challengers, Raji and Divodāsa). Kennedy noted the basic similarity between the myth of the Triple City and the myth of Divodāsa: "The appearance of Vishnu as Buddha is merely a repetition of a similar incident which occurred in the Kṛta Yuga [the destruction of the Triple City]";[98] in both episodes, he notes, "the king and his people had become the enemies of the gods, in consequence of their extreme piety and virtue, which threatened to deprive Indra and the immortals of heaven."[99] Precisely how the gods would lose heaven in the Divodāsa story is not evident from the texts; rather, they would lose heaven on earth, the holy city. But in both cases their exclusive right to divinity is threatened.

The oldest of these myths is the destruction of the Triple City, with its roots in

[96] Kennedy, p. 250. [97] Coleman, p. 185. [98] Kennedy, p. 261. [99] *Ibid.*, p. 251.

the Brāhmaṇas; but heresy does not enter the story until after the *Mahābhārata*. From the standpoint of pure common sense, the myths involving actual heresies of Buddhism and Jainism must originally have been composed with human beings in mind; that is, these episodes (inserted into older myths) must have arisen in order to justify the existence of heresy *on earth*. Kennedy, after telling the story of Viṣṇu's avatar as the Buddha to corrupt Divodāsa, remarks, "It is the common belief of the people in the west of India, that when Vishnu had been born in Kikata as Buddha, the son of Jina, and effected the apostasy of Divodāsa, having been prevailed upon by the Brahmans and holy men to terminate the propagation of his heretical doctrines, he immediately disappeared in a deep well at Gaya; and that he left behind him no writings or disciples."[100] This curious tradition, probably based on the *Bhāgavata Purāṇa* statement that the Buddha, son of Jina, was born among the Kīkaṭas,[101] removes from the myth the very premise that inspired it: the need to account for the actual existence of human Buddhists (who still existed in India, together with their Buddhist texts, in Kennedy's day).

The explanation of the origin of the existing sect of human Buddhists was best accomplished, however, with reference to the older pattern of the struggle between religion and antireligion—the battle between gods and demons, a struggle in which men often received physical or spiritual wounds as more or less innocent bystanders; these myths tended to describe evil—and heresy—as a kind of moral fallout from the nuclear wars of gods and demons. At this point, the Buddha myth was combined with the Raji myth (in which the war between gods and demons is a central element) or with the Triple City myth, and Divodāsa became the pivotal figure. Divodāsa is at first simply duped in the usual manner and only later made a Buddhist; there are veiled hints in the earliest variants of the Divodāsa myth that the king, far from being a demon, was destroyed by a demon. For although it is stated that, when Gaṇeśa's curse took effect, Śiva entered the city, it is also said that, as soon as the curse took effect and the city was emptied, a Rākṣasa named Kṣemaka entered the city.[102] Nothing further is said of this Rākṣasa, but he may have been sent by Śiva precisely in order to keep the city empty.

Thus a myth about mortals is framed in the pattern of a myth about demons. The cycle turns upon Raji (the mortal caught between gods and demons) and proceeds through at least seven distinct steps:

1. Bṛhaspati deludes the enemies of the gods (demons) by sacrifice.
2. Bṛhaspati deludes the enemies of the gods (mortals, Raji's sons) by sacrifice.
3. Bṛhaspati deludes the enemies of the gods (mortals, Raji's sons) by heresy.
4. Śiva deludes the demons of the Triple City by immoral teachings.

[100] *Ibid.*, p. 253. [101] *Bhāgavata* 1.3.24. [102] *Brahmāṇḍa* 2.3.67.26; *Vāyu* 2.30.23–27.

5. Viṣṇu deludes the demons of the Triple City by heresy.
6. Viṣṇu deludes mortals (Divodāsa) by heresy.
7. Viṣṇu's appearance as the Buddha becomes accepted as an avatar.[103]

The Buddha avatar may represent an attempt by orthodox Brahminism to slander the Buddhists by identifying them with the demons: "We may have in this conflict of the orthodox divinities and heretical Daityas some covert allusion to political troubles, growing out of religious difference, and the final predominance of Brahmanism."[104] This suggestion is supported by the fact that the Buddha incarnation, accomplishing the delusion of the demons, is said in many texts to be followed by the avatar of Kalkin, exterminating the heretics and barbarians of the Kali Age; these myths presuppose a political situation in the pre-Gupta period (precisely when the myth of the Buddha avatar first appears), when orthodox Brahmins were fighting a desperate battle on two fronts, against foreign invaders and a thriving Buddhist community at home.

The Buddha avatar may well have been inspired by the Kalkin avatar. The *Mahābhārata*[105] and the *Vāyu Purāṇa*,[106] which do not mention the Buddha avatar, say that Viṣṇu will be born as Kalkin in order to destroy barbarians and heretics. These passages may represent a reaction against the invastion of India by Greeks, Scythians, Pahlavas, and Kuṣāṇas during the centuries immediately preceding and following the turn of the Christian Era. The Kalkin avatar may be connected in some way with the idea of the Millennium, as it was current in Europe and elsewhere from the fourth to the seventh centuries A.D.;[107] but the main inspiration was probably the Buddhist doctrine of Maitreya, the future Buddha, which may have been derived from Zoroastrian doctrines,[108] perhaps brought into India by these same invaders. The fact that Kalkin appears as a warrior on horseback supports the possibility of some such political reference. Only later, in the Gupta period, when Jainism and Buddhism posed a serious threat to the fast-burgeoning Hindu revival, does the Buddha appear in the list of avatars, immediately preceding Kalkin.

When the Buddha avatar appears in these lists, it usually replaces the Kṛṣṇa avatar, occasionally producing strange juxtapositions. In the *Vāyu Purāṇa*, Kṛṣṇa is said to become incarnate to establish dharma and to destroy demons, including those dwelling in human bodies, deluding all creatures with his *yoga-māyā*;[109] he is then followed by Kalkin.[110] When this list appears in the later *Matsya Purāṇa*, Kṛṣṇa disappears and it is said that Viṣṇu became the Buddha to establish dharma and to destroy demons; he was an ascetic with the form of a god or a demon.[111] The deluding power attributed to Kṛṣṇa in the other lists—and more usually

[103] Gail, p. 921, for steps 2, 3, 5, and 7. [104] Wilson (1840), p. 272.

[105] *MBh*. 3.188.14–85. See above, chap. II, sec. 9. [106] *Vāyu* 2.37.390. [107] Thapar, p. 161.

[108] Basham, p. 309. See above, chap. IV, sec. 4. [109] *Vāyu* 2.36.96–103.

[110] *Vāyu* 2.36.103–155; *Brahmāṇḍa* 2.3.74.97–103. [111] *Matsya* 47.247; alt. reading.

applied to the Buddha—is *not* attributed to the Buddha in this text; he is said to establish dharma and destroy demons, a reference to the Tripura Buddha myth but not to the Divodāsa variant. The Kṛṣṇa and Buddha avatars are further telescoped by their coinciding at the beginning of the Kali Age. Traditionally, the Kali Age begins at the death of Kṛṣṇa; on the very day when Kṛṣṇa leaves the earth, Kali descends.[112] But, as Huntington remarks, "From the later vantage point of the Purāṇic authors engaged in combatting Buddhist teachings, the advent of the Buddha seemed to correspond more closely to the descriptions of what was to happen in the Kali Age."[113] And so the *Bhāgavata Purāṇa* and other texts simply assert that Viṣṇu will be born as Buddha at the beginning of the Kali Age; the mantle of incarnation passes directly from Kṛṣṇa to the Buddha.

The *Viṣṇu Purāṇa*, the first text to describe the Buddha avatar, also refers to Kalkin, who will come after invasions by Scythians, Greeks, Huns, and others have polluted India.[114] Viṣṇu as Buddha creates the barbarians and heretics whom he earlier (in terms of actual cult development) destroyed as Kalkin. Or, from the viewpoint of the texts, Viṣṇu first becomes the Buddha to destroy the demons and make them into heretics and then becomes Kalkin to destroy both heretics and barbarians These two avatars appear together in most Purāṇas, where their tasks are explicitly related and even confused. Viṣṇu became the Buddha and created Buddhists and other heretics; at the end of the Kali Age, Kalkin will suppress the barbarians and establish dharma; he will return to heaven, and the Golden Age will begin.[115] Viṣṇu as the Buddha is asked to protect the worshipper from heretics, and Viṣṇu as Kalkin is asked for protection from impurity.[116] The basic distinction—that the Buddha destroys the demons and Kalkin destroys heretic mankind—is blurred, since the demons are identified with heretic men. In commenting on this last text, Adalbert Gail remarks that "the basis of the Buddha avatar is here reduced to the absurd. The concept of the corruption of the demons by the Buddha is stood on its head. The billy-goat is made the gardener: Buddha is supposed to guard against the hordes of heretics"[117]—perhaps as a thief is set to catch a thief. Similarly, the Buddha is supposed to beome incarnate to protect us from nonawakening, fatal blunders, and heretic hordes, while Kalkin becomes incarnate to protect us against the black impurities of the Kali Age.[118] According to the myths, however, Buddha *produces* corruption by heretic hordes and Kalkin does destroy the black impurities of the Kali Age. This confusion may well arise, as Gail suggests, from an assimilation of the Buddha to the soteriological function of Kalkin, who follows immediately after.[119] The two avatars are almost never represented separately, but they appear together on reliefs of the ten avatars from the Gupta period onward.[120]

[112] *Viṣṇu* 5.38.8. [113] Huntington (1964). p. 29. [114] *Viṣṇu* 4.24.98.
[115] *Agni* 16.5–10. [116] *Garuḍa* 196.11. [117] Gail, p. 921.
[118] *Bhāgavata* 6.8.19. [119] Gail, p. 922. [120] Banerjea, p. 424.

As Buddha was considered to cause corruption in some texts, but to prevent it in others, so Kalkin's very name is ambiguous. Kalkin is one who possesses *kalka*, filthy residue, sediment, or impurity; he *has* the dregs of the Kali Age in some way—as the image of the barbarian who is impurity incarnate, or as the god who destroys that impurity. The frequent confusion of the Buddha and Kalkin avatars led to the invention of a version of the Buddha-Viṣṇu myth among the Buddhists themselves, in Ceylon, almost certainly because of their familiarity not only with the Hindu myth of the Buddha avatar but with that of Kalkin as well (to say nothing of the Maitreya myth from which Kalkin was probably derived):[121]

The gods . . . being aware of the increase of evil in the human world, go and beg Viṣṇu, one of the guardian deities of Ceylon, to do something about it. The dominance of heretical foreigners over Buddhist lands being the root of all evil, [Viṣṇu, after consulting Śiva, Indra, and Brahmā, decides to send a god to the human world,] to be born as a son of a pious king of Kāsi (Kashmir [sic]) in India. [He will be given the name of Vīrapōga, brought up by sages, and in the future he will come to Northeast Ceylon.][122]

Not surprisingly, the savior is not called Buddha in this Buddhist text, nor does he preach Buddhism; he is sent by Viṣṇu after consultation with Śiva and the other gods, and he becomes incarnate as the son of "a pious king of Kāsi" (which is the Sanskrit name for Benares, not Kashmir); this is all taken from the Divodāsa story. The rest of the myth, including the fact that this savior is to come in the future to destroy barbarian foreigners and to combat evil (rather than to create it), is derived from the Kalkin avatar.

The two avatars are both "historical" in that they occur at the beginning and end of the Kali Age, the age of reality. Since the Buddha is a truly historical figure, and the Kalkin to come is associated with other actual political groups of invaders, the texts often insert factual material into the descriptions of the avatars, as in the story of Vīrapōga in Ceylon. The *Mahābhārata* interpolates this passage:

At the beginning of the Kali Age, Viṣṇu will become the Buddha, son of Śuddhodana, and he will be a bald preacher who will speak in the Māgadha dialect and delude men. All men will become bald and take the ocre robe, and priests will cease to offer oblations or recite the Vedas. . . . Then, at the end of the Kali Age, a Brahmin named Kalkin, the son of Viṣṇuyaśas, will be born to uproot the barbarians and heretics, and the final dissolution will take place.[123]

The reference to the birth of Buddha as the son of Śuddhodana (as in the Pāli canon) is expanded in another text which preserves an even more historical tone;

[121] Malalgoda, p. 438n. [122] Malalgoda, p. 437; citing a MS called Dharmarājapota, Nevill MSS Vol. II, no. 350, British Museum. [123] *MBh.* 12, app. 1, no. 31, lines 1–22; *Kumbhakona* 12.348.

it lists the actual dynasties of the Śiśunāgas, Nandavardhana, and Mahānanda, and then remarks:

At this time, reminded of the Kali Age, the god Viṣṇu became born as Gautama, the Śākyamuni, and taught the Buddhist dharma for ten years. Then Śuddodana ruled for twenty years, and Śākyasiṃha for thirty. At the first stage of the Kali Age, the path of the Vedas was destroyed and all men became Buddhists. Those who sought refuge with Viṣṇu were deluded.[124]

After the lists of proper names have lulled us into a false sense of reality, the last line abruptly reminds us of the underlying myth.

The fact that Buddhism is regarded as having inititated the present Kali Age is cleverly used by the *Śiva Purāṇa* to explain why the corruption of demons should result in the existence of human heretics. The demons are corrupted in an earlier period (as Kennedy realized), but men become corrupt now, in the age of corruption:

Viṣṇu said to the man of delusion, "After spreading the dharma of darkness and destroying the Triple City, go to the wilderness and maintain your svadharma there until the beginning of the Kali Age. Then reveal your dharma and cause your disciples to spread it." . . . After the Triple City was burnt, the bald monks bowed to the gods and said, "Where shall we go? What shall we do? We have done a bad thing, to destroy the demons' devotion to Śiva, and now we will have to live in hell. But you wished us to do it, and you must tell us how to find peace." Viṣṇu, Brahmā, and the other gods said, "Do not fear. Since Śiva commanded this, nothing bad will happen to you. From today, this doctrine will be the ruin of men who adhere to it, in the Kali Age. You must hide in the desert until the Kali Age begins. Then you will establish your doctrine, and the fools of the Kali Age will be deluded and accept it." And so the bald monks returned to their hermitage.[125]

The forces of heresy lie in wait for the Kali Age, like other evil powers inadvertently created by Śiva;[126] spawned originally as part of a grand cosmic design, they linger on to accomplish a more banal corruption.

These temporal divisions are often blurred in the texts, however, where human Buddhists, demons, and the barbarians of the Kali Age all behave alike. As early as the *Śatapatha Brāhmaṇa*, barbarians are equated with demons,[127] and this confusion persists in later texts. When Brahmā tries to persuade Śiva to kill the inhabitants of the Triple City (demons who have now been converted to Jainism and Buddhism), he says, "You must slay the barbarian tribes in order to protect good men."[128] But another complication is added by several texts which suggest

[124] *Bhaviṣya* 3.1.6.35–42. [125] *Śiva* 2.5.4.19–21; 2.5.12.21–33.

[126] *Saura* 40.10–74; cf. above, chap. III, sec. 2. [127] *Śata.* 3.2.1.24. [128] *Śiva* 2.5.6.42.

that in destroying the Triple City, Śiva himself (or his deputy and alter ego, Agni) behaved like a barbarian. The destruction of the Triple City has been likened to the Hun invasion of India,[129] and in some descriptions of the burning cities, the women (who are being burnt alive) cry out to Agni, "You barbarian! Evil one! Even barbarians show mercy to women, but you are a barbarians' barbarian, mindless, impossible to fend off."[130] And like other barbarians, Agni responds lamely that he is only obeying orders.

Śiva the destroyer of barbarians is a barbarian; so too Viṣṇu is often said to have yet another avatar to complement that of Kalkin—he appears as a foreign barbarian among the Western barbarians,[131] possibly a reference to the Christ avatar.[132] Śiva destroys the triple cities and the barbarians in them in order to protect the good; in this way, Śiva takes upon himself the functions of Kalkin, an entirely appropriate assimilation, since it is Śiva who destroys the universe when barbarians and heretics are rife at the end of the Kali Age; the demons are barbarians as well as heretics. When the Triple City is corrupted, Kali enters the city, and then Śiva destroys it.[133]

7. The Positive Aspect of the Buddha Avatar

In spite of this association of Buddhists with demons and barbarians in the main corpus of myths, some non-Buddhists of the post-Purāṇic period came to accept the Buddha incarnation as a positive teaching by Viṣṇu. This attitude may be reflected in the text in which the Buddha is said to protect us from lack of enlightenment and from fatal blunders.[134] The *Varāha Purāṇa*, in listing the avatars, says that the worshipper should sacrifice to Bala and Kṛṣṇa when he wants sons, to Kalkin when he wants to destroy enemies, and to the Buddha when he wants beauty.[135] Similarly, the *Matsya Purāṇa* notes that the Buddha is lotus-eyed and beautiful as a god,[136] while offering homage to the peaceful Buddha.[137] Kṣemendra, a Jain writer of the eleventh century, described the Buddha avatar of Viṣṇu in a straight, heroic tale based on the standard episodes of Gautama's life as related in the Pāli canon.[138] Jayadeva, a twelfth-century Hindu, says that Viṣṇu became the Buddha out of compassion for animals, to end bloody sacrifices.[139] The *Devībhāgavata Purāṇa* offers homage to Viṣṇu, "who became incarnate as the Buddha in order to stop the slaughter of animals and to destroy the sacrifices of the wicked,"[140] adding a moral judgment to Jayadeva's more general statement; although the last phrase might be translated "to destroy wicked sacrifices" or taken to imply that all sacrificers are wicked, it is also possi-

[129] Shastri, J. L., II, 846. [130] *Matsya* 188.56; *Padma* 1.15.37–40; *Skanda* 3.28.68–69.

[131] Daniélou, p. 182n., citing "several astrological books." [132] *Ibid.*, p. 12. [133] *Matsya* 131.10–50.

[134] *Bhāgavata* 6.8.19. [135] *Varāha* 48.22. [136] *Matsya* 47.24. [137] *Matsya* 54.19.

[138] *Daśāvatāracarita* 9.1–74. [139] *Gītagovinda* 1.1.9. [140] *Devībhāgavata* 10.5.13, *duṣṭayajñavighātāya*.

ble that only wicked sacrificers (or demonic sacrificers) are condemned, not virtuous Hindu sacrificers.

One aspect of Hinduism that made possible such a positive identification of Viṣṇu and the Buddha was the tendency to regard "any genuine religious reformer . . . as an abode of divinity."[141] A text often cited in justification of this view is the *Bhagavad Gītā*, in which Kṛṣṇa says that he is reborn whenever dharma wanes and that those who worship other gods are actually worshipping him.[142] Elsewhere Kṛṣṇa declares, "Worshippers of the sun, Śiva, Gaṇeśa, Viṣṇu and the Goddess all reach me, just as all rains reach the sea."[143] The Muslim sect of the Imam Shahis believed that the Imam himself was the tenth avatar of Viṣṇu and that the Qur'ān was a part of the Atharva Veda.[144] Christ is sometimes included among the avatars of Viṣṇu, a practice that was once "a cause of great alarm among Christian missionaries."[145] Viṣṇu's protean nature even assimilates demons (as Śiva's ambivalent nature does): Hayagrīva and Viśvarūpa come to be regarded not as avatars but as important iconographic Vaiṣṇava forms.[146]

The moral ambiguity of the Buddha avatar has long posed an enigma to scholars. In 1790, Sir William Jones noted the contradiction posed by Jayadeva's praise of the Buddha avatar and the *Bhāgavata Purāṇa* references to demonic Buddhists; he suggested that there were two distinct historical Buddhas,[147] a bold but indefensible example of dualistic "splitting".

European scholars often emphasized the positive element of the Buddha avatar, rightly when applied to the secondary texts (Kṣemendra, Jayadeva, etc.) but wrongly with reference to the early corpus of Purāṇic myths. Charles Coleman, always eager to elevate Buddhists at the expense of the Hindus, falls into this second category, for he is referring to the myth of Divodāsa when he says:

> By some, the extensive sect of Buddha is supposed to have derived its origin from, and to have been identified with, the ninth avatar, or the last appearance of Vishnu on earth; when he is said to have appeared to reclaim the Hindus from numerous abominations into which they had fallen and to teach them more benevolent forms of worship than those which, through the means of human and animal sacrifices, they then practised.[148]

Coleman evidently confuses the Buddha avatar with that of Kalkin ("the last appearance of Vishnu on earth" and the one which is to reclaim the Hindus from the "abominations" of the Kali Age). But, unlike the Hindus, Coleman regards Vedic sacrifice itself as the primary abomination from which the Kalkin-Buddha "saved" them. Later scholars also applauded the concept of the Buddha avatar, probably with valid reference to the secondary, post-Purāṇic texts. Thus the

[141] Derrett, p. 50. [142] *Gītā* 4.7; 9.23. [143] *Padma* 5.90.63. [144] Ivanow, pp. 62–64.

[145] Daniélou, p. 12; Drekmeier, p. 146. [146] Van Gulik, *passim*; Maxwell, *passim*.

[147] Marshall, pp. 209 and 271. Cf. below, chap. XI. [148] Coleman, p. 184.

Buddha avatar has been called "a curious example of the desire to absorb whatever is good in another faith"[149] or a measure to combat Buddhism by making it appear that "there was little to distinguish the Buddhist laity from their Brāhmaṇical neighbours."[150] Drawing attention to Kṣemendra and Jayadeva, Helmuth von Glasenapp attributed these developments to a Hindu desire to absorb Buddhism in a peaceful manner, both to win Buddhists to Viṣṇuism and also to account for the fact that such a significant heresy could prosper in India.[151] He makes a clear distinction between the two groups of texts, noting that while Jayadeva emphasized the positive aspect of Buddha's teaching, polemicists (he does not specify, but clearly the Purāṇic mythologists must be included here) saw the purpose of this incarnation as the deluding of the wits and the establishing of a false system.

The first set of Purāṇic myths were composed at a time (the Gupta period) when Hinduism was still fighting a pitched battle against Buddhism, Jainism, and other heresies; it has been said that the Purāṇas "bear the scars of the battle to this day, in the form of numerous sharp and contemptuous denunciations of the Mohaśāstras ('scripture of delusion') and their non-Vedic adherents."[152] The texts of the second period were composed when Buddhism, though waning, was still a force to be reckoned with in India. A Kashmiri king of the tenth century had a magnificent frame made for "an image of the Buddha Avatara," and the image that he used was a Buddha figure that had probably been under worship by Buddhists; it has been suggested that this frame was made for the figure "in order to Hinduize it,"[153] just as the doctrine of the Buddha was placed in the "frame" of Purāṇic mythology to Hinduize it.

Jan Gonda's suggestion that the Buddha was identified with Viṣṇu in the early myths "because of Viṣṇu's general helpfulness to mankind in distress" seems unlikely, especially when Gonda goes on to explain that this characteristic of Viṣṇu made possible the identification with Rāma, Kṛṣṇa, and the Buddha, "noble and heroic men who are great benefactors of mankind,"[154] hardly the typical Purāṇic opinion of the Buddha. More apt are other scholars' references to the Buddha who approached the demons "not for their benefit but for their destruction," a negative avatar designed to render Buddhism "harmless to orthodoxy."[155] Hinduism has indeed tried to absorb whatever is good in non-Vedic Indian religions, notably in the doctrine of noninjury mentioned by Kṣemendra and the others, but this assimilation took place in the earlier, more tolerant period in which Buddhism and Hinduism grew up together and borrowed freely from one another, long before the texts in which Viṣṇu appears

[149] Keith (1917), p. 169. [150] Majumdar, Raychaudhuri, and Datta, p. 201.

[151] von Glasenapp (1962), p. 113. [152] Huntington (1960*a*), p. 33.

[153] Goetz, pp. 77–80; a frame in Srinagar Museum, of Śaṅkaravarman (r. 883–902).

[154] Gonda (1954), p. 159. [155] Choudhary, p. 241. Huntington (1964), p. 29.

as the Buddha, and again, centuries after these texts were composed. The idea of the future Hindu savior, Kalkin, may be one of these earlier Buddhist contributions—one that was ironically twisted when Kalkin was said to destroy the Buddhists.

An ingenious suggestion for the source of the Buddha avatar was made by Rao Bahadur H. Krishna Sastri, who asserted that this avatar "must have arisen out of the *pīpal* tree with which Buddha's 'enlightenment' is intimately connected, while the tree itself is worshipped by the Hindus as Vishṇu from even pre-Buddhist times down to the present day." The tree does unify several Buddhist and Hindu myths: Māra attacks Buddha under a tree, as Kāma attacks Śiva; the Buddha preaches under the tree, as Śiva does in the Pine Forest; and the sacred fig (the *pīpal* or *aśvattha*) was sacred in India long before the time of either Buddhism or Hinduism, for it appears on seals of the Indus Valley (c. 2000 B.C.) and on many early Indian stone carvings. But Sastri goes on to extrapolate even further, pointing out that the evil goddess Jyeṣṭhā is given the *pīpal* tree for her home in the *Liṅga* and *Padma Purāṇas* (which also state that she is to dwell in houses that contain images of Buddhist monks or the Buddha) and that the *pīpal* tree in the Purāṇas became, "evidently on account of its connection with Buddha, the home of 'goddess of ill-luck' (Jyeṣṭhā)."[156] The *pīpal* is, as Sastri states, as infamous in late Hinduism as it is sacred in early Hinduism, for it is the birthplace of the doomsday mare, though it is unlikely that this idea derives from the Buddhist association. But another valid symbolic link between Viṣṇu and the Buddha is chronologically inverted by Sastri: "This Paurāṇic theory of Buddha's intentional mislead in matters of Vedic ritual was perhaps an interpolation inserted after the crushing defeat which the Buddhist doctrine must have received at the hands of the Advaita teacher Śaṅkarāchārya." The myth of the Buddha avatar was incorporated into biographies of Śaṅkara, but this cannot explain the origin of the myth long before the time of Śaṅkara. (Sastri tacitly admits this anachronism when he comments that the *Daśāvatārastotra* attributed to Śaṅkara praises the Buddha avatar.) Sastri then suggests that the shared doctrine of noninjury may have led Vaiṣṇavas originally to accept the Buddha, as they accepted other human saints, "on account of his miraculous powers and his high position as a religious reformer," only later interpreting the non-Vedic aspects of the Buddha's teaching as a demonic ("āsura") form of religion; this is a reversal of the most likely trend of development. Finally, Sastri asserts that although the Buddha avatar was probably never worshipped, the Saṃhitās say that he could have been, "inasmuch as he was possessed of the quality of misleading the heretics to the advantage of the faithful"—a valid description of the hypocritical, anti-Buddhist bias of Viṣṇu in the early texts.

This persistent ambivalence in the Hindu attitude to Buddhists is evident

[156] Krishna Sastri, pp. 5–7; *Liṅga* 2.6.46–56; see above, chap. III, sec. 1, and below, chap. XI, sec. 4.

from V. S. Agrawala's statement that "good" demons like Bali and Prahlāda were often equated with Buddhists; "in spite of their Asura appellation, . . . no one could shut one's eyes that they were also good religious people believing in an ethical and moral religion."[157] The interplay of these conflicting attitudes is well illustrated by J. M. Macfie's analysis of the Buddha avatar:

> Modern writers dwell on the beauty of Buddha's character and the pity which he showed towards his fellow-men. But the compilers of the Purāṇas looked upon the teaching of both the Buddhists and the Jains with peculiar loathing, and found in it a manifestation of evil and not of good. . . . As a Hindu villager repeats for your information the list of Vishnu's descents, he includes that of the Buddha among the ten. Probably he knows nothing of the details of the story as it is told in the Purāṇas. On the other hand, the educated Indian . . . has little idea that the Buddha he is taught to admire was an illusion of Vishnu who came to deceive and destroy the demons by the inculcation of heresy and falsehood.[158]

Basham describes a similar inconsistency in the importance which modern Hindus place on the Buddha avatar: "Until quite recently the temple of the Buddha at Gayā [where the Buddha is said to have plunged into the ground[159]] was in the hands of Hindus, and the teacher there was worshipped as a Hindu god; but in general little attention was paid to the Buddha avatāra."[160] Even when Coleman visited India, he noted that "the Buddhas [*sic*] wholly, and the Brahmans partially, disavow this incarnation of Vishnu."[161] The ultimate reversal occurs within the Buddhist tradition. A legend apparently originating in medieval Ceylon refers to ten Bodhisattvas, one of whom is Viṣṇu,[162] who also appears as a Bodhisattva in a medieval text and is represented as one of the ten Bodhisattvas in Sinhalese temples, notably at Dambulla.[163]

It is ironic that the idea of Viṣṇu becoming incarnate as a "benefactor of mankind" may very well have been inspired by the popular and humanistic appeal of Buddhism, both in the human character of Gautama himself in early Buddhism and in the later ideal of the compassionate Bodhisattva who postpones his own release in order to remain among men. Nevertheless, the Buddha avatar, which appears in Purāṇic texts composed after the initial idea of human avatars (Kṛṣṇa and Rāma) has been accepted, is portrayed in order to discredit the Buddhist doctrines. In the myth of the conversion of the demons to Buddhism, the teaching is always clearly intended to be destructive, to be preached by God in bad faith.

The assumption of bad faith in the Buddha avatar is evident from the manner in which later sects used this device to discredit one another. The great Śaiva philosopher Śaṅkara (788–850), subject of several hagiographies, is said to have been an incarnation of Śiva, sent to earth to combat Viṣṇu's Buddha avatar:

[157] Agrawala (1964), p. xii. [158] Macfie, p. 8. [159] Kennedy, p. 253.

[160] Basham, p. 309. [161] Coleman, p. 184.

[162] *Anāgatavamsa*, pp. 33–54. [163] Personal communication from Dr. Richard F. Gombrich.

The gods complained to Śiva that Viṣṇu had entered the body of the Buddha on earth for their sake, but now the haters of religion, despising Brahmins and the dharma of class and stage of life, filled the earth. "Not a single man performs a ritual, for all have become heretics—Buddhists, Kāpālikas, and so forth—and so we eat no offerings." Śiva consented to become incarnate as Śaṅkara, to reestablish Vedic dharma which keeps the universe happy, and to destroy evil behavior.[164]

As usual, the heresy goes too far, destroying the allies as well as the enemies of the gods, and must be combatted by the intervention of God. As earth is filled, heaven is empty; to make heaven accessible and release attainable for creatures now impure by nature, Śiva becomes incarnate, a reversal of his usual motive in descending to earth in order to render heaven inaccessible.[165] The Buddha and Śaṅkara were both regarded by Aurobindo as inferior to Kṛṣṇa; though Aurobindo accepted Jayadeva's positive myth, he remarked that, in teaching that even bhakti must be sacrificed for release, "Buddha like Śaṅkara made a mistake."[166] As Huntington comments on this passage, "The essential negative character of the Buddha *avatāra* and the greatness of Kṛṣṇa are preserved, but at the expense of calling into question the divine wisdom behind the entire scheme of *avatāras*!"[167]

The chain of sectarian revisions does not end with Śaṅkara, however. Śaṅkara's followers opposed and persecuted the Vaiṣṇava philosopher Madhu or Madhva (1199–1278).[168] Madhva placed a new twist on the myth of the Buddha avatar: he said that the Śaiva scriptures were composed by Śiva at Viṣṇu's command, in order to delude men with false doctrines, to reveal Śiva and to conceal Viṣṇu.[169] This passage is based in part on the Purāṇic episode where Śiva agrees to teach false doctrines;[170] but the statement that this act destroys the true religion (Vaiṣṇavism) and replaces it with "false" Śaivism is an ingenious reversal of many of the assumptions behind the Buddha avatar. Śaṅkara was often accused of being a crypto-Buddhist because of his doctrine of illusion,[171] and this may be the basis of the myth taught by Madhva.

But the twists do not end even here. The hagiographical texts produced by Madhva's school created another myth based on a passage in the *Mahābhārata* in which Bhīma, a human hero regarded as an incarnation of Vāyu, the god of wind, attacks certain Rākṣasas and kills their leader, who is called Maṇimat.[172] According to the followers of Madhva, this passage of the Epic was rewritten and

164 *Śaṅkaradigvijaya* of Mādhava, 1.28–43. 165 *Ibid.*, 2.9.3; and see below, chap. IX, sec. 2.

166 Aurobindo, I, 406. 167 Huntington (1960*a*), p. 135 n.

168 See above, Chap. III, sec. 2; chap. IV, sec. 4; and below, chap. IX, sec. 1.

169 Madhva, *Brahmasūtrabhāṣya* 1.1.1, citing *Varāha Purāṇa*. I, 228.

170 *Varāha* 71.48–62; cf. *Padma* 6.263.24–36; see below, chap. IX, sec. 1, and chap. X, secs. 3 and 7.

171 *Tantrāvarttika* of Kumārila Bhaṭṭa; *Yājñavalkyasmṛti.*

172 *MBh.* 3.157.57–70; see above, chap. IV, sec. 4.

completed by Madhva himself;[173] and this is what the Mādhvas went on to say about it:

At the beginning of the Kali Age, knowledge of the Vedas, as taught by Kṛṣṇa and Bhīma, reigned supreme. . . . Then Maṇimat was born as a widow's bastard son, named Saṅkara [sic]. *The demons hailed him as their savior. On their advice he joined the Buddhists and taught Buddhism under cover of teaching the Vedānta, and he performed various wicked deeds. . . . Then Vāyu became incarnate as Madhva, to refute the teachings of Maṇimat-Saṅkara.*[174]

The idea of incarnation in order to corrupt begins with the Buddha myth and is countered by the Śaṅkara myth of the Śaṅkara-followers; now the Mādhvas assume the Buddha incarnation (for the earth is said to be "under the sway of Buddhism" before Maṇi was born, and Maṇi joins the Buddhists, instead of founding them), reverse the Śaṅkara incarnation (for he is now an incarnation not of the god Śiva but of a petty demon), and add a third incarnation, that of Madhva as Vāyu, the god who killed the demon Saṅkara in a previous incarnation, in the Epic. The idea that the gods are sent to corrupt the demons (as in the Buddha myth) combined with the implication that the resulting human heretics are demons (or are related to demons in some way) results in a major reversal, which smacks of Manicheanism; the demons are not the ones who are corrupted, but the ones who do the corrupting. (This may be an extension of the Purāṇic idea that the demons, once corrupted themselves, go on and corrupt others. The Mādhvas' identification of Śaṅkara as a demon is particularly harsh in light of the fact that the Mādhvas, alone among Hindu philosophers, believe that the demons and heretics are doomed to eternal damnation in hell.) Finally, this corruption takes place, as usual, in the Kali Age, and the Mādhvas take advantage of this fact to pun on the name of their enemy: Śaṅkara ("He who gives peace," an epithet of Śiva given to many Śaivas) becomes *Saṅkara*, a word that denotes indiscriminate mixture, particularly the breaking down of barriers between castes which is the principle sign of the advent of the Kali Age. In keeping with this name, Saṅkara is said to be the bastard son of a widow; similarly, the Mādhvas satirize Śaṅkara's famous monistic philosophy by stating that as a boy he was so stupid that he could only count to one.[175]

The hagiographies proliferated in this way. The *Basava Purāṇa* says that Nārada reported to Śiva that, while other religions were flourishing, the Śaiva faith was with few exceptions dying out among the Brahmins and so decaying among other castes also; Śiva then asked Nandin to become incarnate as the Vīraśaiva saint Basavaṇṇa to preach Vīraśaivism in keeping with orthodox dharma.[176] Another Vīraśaiva saint, Allama Prabhu, is said to have been an

[173] Grierson, p. 235. [174] *Maṇimañjarī* 5–8.

[175] Grierson, p. 235. [176] *Basava Purāṇa* II, 32; Dasgupta V, 43.

incarnation of Śiva who arrived in the world to combat the force of the incarnation of his consort, Pārvatī, who sent down her dark side, Illusion, to tempt him; Allama and the enchantress are elsewhere said to be mere minions of Śiva and Pārvatī, cursed to be born in the world.[177] In this way, sectarian Hindus regarded their own founders as incarnations of the true god, and the founders of rival sects as incarnations of the false god, or of the true god purposely setting out to delude his enemies. The emotional force of sectarian rivalry lends power to many revived dualistic myths—demons (the other sect) being held responsible for evil, often abetted by the eternal evil other, the woman.

The final blow to the "positive" interpretation of the Buddha avatar was dealt by another Mādhva philosopher, Vyāsatīrtha, who countered the argument that the Vedas must be accepted because God taught them, by stating that "Buddha himself is an incarnation of God, and yet he deceived the people by false teaching."[178] By this time, the bad faith of the gods was so widely accepted that to say that a scripture had been taught by a god was to discredit it. "The devil may quote scripture," we say; "Yes," say the Hindus, "but so may God."

[177] Ramanujan (1973), p. 143. [178] Dasgupta, IV, 203.

And the Lord God said, Behold, the man is become as one of us, to know good and evil: and now, lest he put forth his hand, and take also of the tree of life, and eat, and live for ever: Therefore the Lord God sent him forth from the garden of Eden . . .
Genesis 3:22–23

VIII
THE BIRTH OF DEATH

1. The Evil of Death

The Hindu mythologies of evil and of death are closely related; when sin and evil became increasingly important in Hinduism, particularly in the bhakti myths, the patterns established in the mythology of death were applied to the mythology of evil. Premature death is the very prototype of the condition that provokes theodicy: sudden accident and frustrations that beset human beings and require constant alleviation through symbolic techniques.[1] But even death at the proper time may be feared and challenged; though Hindu gods occasionally prove loath to share the good life, Hindus have always regarded death as the epitome of evil.

The myths of death and of evil share the same recurrent motifs, and often offer the same solutions to the different problems posed. Time is the corrupting factor in many of the myths of the origin of evil, and the word *kāla*, which means "time" in the Ṛg Veda and the Brāhmaṇas, later comes to mean "destructive time" or "death" in the *Mahābhārata.* In the absence of death, the earth becomes overburdened and men must be killed; the earth is similarly aflicted when it is overburdened either with men who are excessively good or with demons who are excessively evil. The origin of evil is inextricably associated with the appearance of sexual desire and hunger; death is also closely connected with these motifs, for sexual procreation produces the increase in population that death must counteract (and sexual sin provides the means by which death may be introduced or justified), and hunger is both an obvious natural cause of death and a condition that death (of part of the population) alleviates for mankind in general.

[1] Parsons (1954), pp. 197–211; Obeyesekere, p. 7.

In Buddhism, lust and death are combined in the devil. The Buddhist figure of Evil Māra (Māra Pāpimā) is derived from Pāpmā Mṛtyu of the Brāhmaṇas, Death who is Evil.[2] Buddha conquers death and lust, and so Māra is the incarnation of his opposition; Māra appears as a demon and is even given the name of a demon who opposes Indra as Māra opposes Buddha.[3] The battle between Buddha and Māra in later Buddhist texts is modeled closely on the classical struggle between gods and demons, but Māra symbolizes Indra himself as well as the enemies of Indra; he rides on an elephant (as Indra does),[4] and his daughters and assistants are celestial nymphs, like the agents of Indra. For Buddha as the quintessential ascetic incurs the enmity of the gods as well as the demons; as the good mortal, he is caught between the two.

Whereas in Buddhism the figure of lust-death is the devil, in Hinduism he is god, Śiva, who in his aspect of Kāla or Sthāṇu traces his descent back to the same Pāpmā Mṛtyu, evil death, from whom Māra is derived.[5] The resemblances between Māra and Śiva are striking: Māra, like Śiva, has snares;[6] he tempts the nuns by assuming the form of a handsome man, using his daughters to tempt the Buddha,[7] just as Śiva assumes the form of a handsome man to tempt the wives of the Pine Forest sages and is assisted by Pārvatī or Viṣṇu in the form of a beautiful woman who tempts the men.[8] Śiva the ascetic is death; Śiva the phallic god is lust; together they serve the function of Māra: "For just as he is death, so is he sex, that ungovernable urge that leads to yet more life and yet more death going on and on in a crazy whirlwind circle for ever and ever. Māra is Shiva."[9]

The corpus of death myths is further connected with evil by the moral element that recurs within it. The gods inflict death upon mortals either because they recognize its necessity or because they are jealous or inadequate. But death is regarded as an evil even in those myths which accept the premise of the need for the existence of the oppositional pair of life and death in an ambivalent cosmos. Although life and death may be regarded philosophically as the same god–and Prajāpati is sometimes called Death (Mṛtyu)–usually they are regarded psychologically as opposed gods, and Prajāpati fights against Death. Death occasionally results from man's evil (in those myths in which man is denied immortality as punishment for his sins) but more often prevents evil (in those myths in which the threat of death is regarded as the greatest inducement to morality on earth).

In the Vedas, death is evil; this is often stated as a simple equation. Like other forms of evil, Death has snares,[10] and the opposite of evil (*pāpa*) is long life (*āyus*).[11] In the Upaniṣads, too, death is sometimes called evil[12] and is listed together with forms of evil such as old age and sorrow, though this list also

[2] Windisch, pp. 185–195. Cf. Boyd, *passim*. [3] *Ibid.*, p. 185. [4] *Ibid.*, p. 197.

[5] O'Flaherty (1973), pp. 171–173. [6] Windisch, p. 196. [7] *Ibid.*, p. 202.

[8] See below, chap. X, sec. 5. [9] Zaehner (1974), p. 277. [10] *AV* 8.8.16; 8.1.4.

[11] *AV* 3.31. [12] *Bṛhadāraṇyaka Up.* 1.3.10; 1.5.23.

includes day and night, and good works as well as evil among the "evils."[13] For the more typical Upaniṣadic view is that life—the cycle of rebirth—is evil, and the highest goal is release from life—*mokṣa*, the complete cessation of earthly life, which a Ṛg Vedic hero would have shunned as a form of eternal death. But Purāṇic Hinduism derives its attitude in this matter (as in most) from the Ṛg Veda, largely disregarding the Upaniṣads: Death is evil, and the sure sign of the gradual waning of dharma in each of the four Ages is the steady decrease of the human life-span.

The Ṛg Veda poet prays, "Deliver me from death, not from immortality."[14] By immortality, however, the ancient sages meant not a literal eternity of life, but rather a full life-span (*sarvam āyus*), reckoned as a hundred years. The Brāhmaṇas declare, "He who performs the consecration ceremony is delivered from all death, all murderous blows; old age becomes his death."[15] The only death that is feared is premature death; thus one offers this prayer for a little child: "Let father heaven and mother earth give you death in old age [*jarāmṛtyu*], that you may live for a hundred years."[16] (The use of "death in old age" in this context may indicate a double meaning in the frequent Purāṇic statements that people are "free from old age and death" [*jarāmṛtyuvivarjita*]; it may mean, more precisely, that they are freed even from natural death in old age).

2. The Conquest of Death

In the later Brāhmaṇa period, people did aspire to be free even from the "unevil," natural death; they wanted literal immortality. This double level of expectation persisted throughout the Purāṇas; sometimes people sought eternal immortality, sometimes merely a full life. Much—some might even say all—of Indian religion is dedicated to the attempt to achieve immortality in one form or another. In the Ṛg Veda, the magic Soma plant conveys immortality; later, mystical methods replaced the (perhaps lost) Soma plant, but the goal remained the same. In many of the Brāhmaṇas, Death is conquered and no problems seem to arise from this; the gods become immortal, and their immortality is renewed by the sacrificer who performs the ritual correctly, thereby also ensuring his own immortality. In these early texts, while god and man are still interdependent, the gods seem willing to share their immortality with the men who provide for the continuing immortality of the gods.

At first, gods alone can aspire to true immortality, often obtained effortlessly, as part of their very nature: "The serpents set aside their old skins, conquered death, and became the Ādityas" (solar gods, sons of Aditi).[17] This simple, natural image is then superseded by a more elaborate ritual of immortality, still expressly

[13] *Ch. Up.* 8.4.1. [14] *RV* 7.59.12; *Śata.* 2.6.1.12; *AV* 18.3.

[15] *Śata.* 5.4.1.1 Cf. Edgerton, *passim.* [16] *AV* 2.28.4. [17] *Tāṇḍya* 25.15.4.

limited to the gods: "The gods have dispelled evil from them and are free from death; though the sacrificer cannot obtain immortality, he attains the full measure of life."[18] But when this text later repeats almost the same sentiment,[19] it suddenly adds that the sacrificer "becomes immortal." Sten Rodhe has discussed this transition:

The gods, whom the priests want to subordinate under the sacrifice and themselves, have not yet lost their characteristic of being free from death in contrast to men. But the priests want to deprive them of this significance, and so they very carefully end their passage by saying that man can become *amṛta* [immortal], just as the gods.[20]

The two levels of immortality for man are linked in some texts, which make one form of immortality dependent on the other. One must live for a full hundred years in order to obtain heaven (as Prajāpati performed a rite for a thousand years to become immortal[21]): "Whoever lives for a hundred years becomes immortal, for the life of a hundred years procures heaven";[22] "Whoever knows this conquers recurring death and attains a full life-span; this is freedom from death in the other world and life here."[23]

A full life-span for the gods is a thousand years, but they too may strive for complete immortality, with more frequent success than that granted to men. In addition to these parallel dualities, the immortality sought by both gods and men is divided in another way: immortality of the soul or breath, and that of the body. In one text, the body of Prajāpati actually becomes immortal: "In the beginning, Prajāpati was both mortal and immortal; his breaths were immortal, his body mortal. By the sacrifice he made his body immortal; by the sacrifice, the sacrificer makes his body immortal."[24] Here mortals as well as gods achieve double immortality; there are no differentiations left at all. But several texts state that Death is always given the body as a share.[25] Sometimes this statement is applied to gods as well as to men (and one may again see the hand of the priests who wish to lower the gods). But often it is applied neither to gods nor to men; death is given no share at all, and again gods and men are equal.

The early level assumes that death is an enemy who can be conquered by gods and men; in this way, death is treated like a demon. In one Brāhmaṇa, the struggle between Prajāpati and Death is actually said to replace the struggle between gods and demons:

They say the gods and demons fought against one another. Truly, the gods and the demons did not then fight against one another. Prajāpati and Death fought against one another. Now the gods were close to Prajāpati, for they were his dear sons. They struck and thrust off death, evil, and went to the heavenly world.[26]

[18] *Śata.* 2.1.3.4. [19] *Śata.* 2.2.2.14. [20] Rodhe, p. 92. [21] See below, *Śata.* 10.4.4.1–3.
[22] *Śata.* 10.2.6.7. [23] *Śata.* 10.2.6.190; cf. *Kau. Up.* 3.2. [24] *Śata.* 10.1.4.1.
[25] See above, chap. VI, sec. 2. [26] *Jai. Up. Br.* 2.10.1–22. Cf. above, chap. III, sec. 2.

Other myths follow the Vedic pattern of the struggle between Indra and Vṛtra:

The gods and Yama were fighting against one another for this world. Yama took to himself the power and strength of the gods, who realized that Yama had become what they were. They sought help from Prajāpati, who made a cow and a bull from his body and offered them to Viṣṇu and Varuṇa; these two seized Yama and drove him away, taking his power for Indra.[27]

The gods are in direct opposition against Yama, not for their own lives but for the sovereignty of the universe, a power which Yama steals from them as Vṛtra usually steals it from Indra. The gods voice the very complaint that Vṛtra brings against Indra ("You have become what I was"), an accusation that is often applied to presumptuous mortals. Cattle are used (as usual) to bribe two gods to conquer the demonic Yama and drive him away, and Indra is supreme again. There is nothing in this myth to indicate that Yama is the god of the dead rather than a demon.

Death is the enemy, however, in certain texts that utilize other patterns of the Vṛtra myth:

Prajāpati created living beings. He created the gods, and mortal beings, and above the mortal beings he created Death as their devourer. Half of Prajāpati was mortal, and the other half immortal; with the part of him that was mortal he was afraid of Death, and so he split into two, clay and water, and entered this earth. Death said to the gods, "What has become of him who created us?" "In fear of you," they said, "he has entered the earth." "Let us search for him," said Death, "for I will not injure him." The gods gathered him out of this earth and said, "Let us make him immortal." They made him immortal by encompassing his mortal forms with his immortal forms (building the altar of clay bricks and layers of earth).[28]

The god Prajāpati is split in two, mortal and immortal, just as the demon Vṛtra is half mortal and half immortal. Prajāpati hides in the earth, where Indra hides from Vṛtra or places the sin of killing Vṛtra; when he is found and strengthened, again like Indra, Prajāpati still remains half mortal, but his form is arranged in such a way that he achieves immortality. Death too is ambivalent. At first he is said to be the devourer of mortal beings, but then he promises not to harm Prajāpati; he remains "above the mortal beings" here, and only the one god is freed from death.

Sometimes, however, the gods help men to conquer death:

Prajāpati became pregnant with all beings; while they were in his womb, evil Death seized them. Prajāpati said to the gods, "With you I will free all these beings from evil Death."

[27] *Tait. Sam.* 2.1.4.3–4.

[28] *Śata.* 10.1.3.1–7; cf. *Mait. Sam.* 1.6.12; *Tāṇḍya* 9.67; *Tait. Br.* 1.1.10.1.

When they asked what benefit they would have from this, he granted them a share and lordship, and he freed all beings from evil Death.[29]

The gods are bribed with lordship and a sacrificial share; in return, all creatures are made immortal, a condition that does not seem to trouble the gods or the author of this text. Other texts usually qualify either the degree of this immortality (limiting it in time) or the people to whom it is given. An instance of the latter stratagem assumes the former as well:

When Prajāpati was creating living beings, evil Death overpowered him. He performed asceticism for a thousand years, striving to leave that evil behind him, and in the thousandth year he purified himself entirely; the evil that he washed clean is his body. But what man could obtain a life of a thousand years? The man who knows this truth can obtain a thousand years.[30]

The text begins with the earlier premise that only Prajāpati can be immortal (for the rest of us would die before we could complete the ritual to conquer death, a Vedic "catch-22"). Implicit in this premise is the distinction between man's life-span and that of Prajāpati; for elsewhere it is said that Prajāpati "was born with a life of a thousand years; even as one might see in the distance the opposite shore, so did he behold the opposite shore of his own life."[31] This glimpse inspires Prajāpati to seek complete immortality, which he achieves, as he does in the above text that describes his purification and extends this achievement to a limited group of enlightened mortals in addition to Prajāpati.

A later text reverses some of the Vedic assumptions. Where the Brāhmaṇas often state that Prajāpati alone was immortal, or that he taught the gods how to achieve immortality, the Upaniṣads describe the manner in which Prajāpati creates the gods (through incestuous, androgynous intercourse, and through the production of Soma and Agni) but then remark, "This was the surpassing creation of Brahmā, for he created the gods, who were better than him, when he, being mortal, created immortals."[32] Here immortality is limited by being denied to Prajāpati.

Another way of limiting the range of immortality is to deny it to the sinner:

Brahmā delivered all creatures over to Death; only the Brahmacārin [the chaste student of the Vedas] was not delivered to Death. Death said, "Let me have a share in this one, too," but Brahmā said, "Only when he neglects to bring the firewood (will he be subject to death)."[33]

This text assumes that all creatures are mortal, by the wish of the gods, and merely qualifies this with a single exception, an exception which is then requalified to

[29] *Śata.* 8.4.2.1–2. [30] *Śata.* 10.4.4.1–3. [31] *Śata.* 11.1.6.6.

[32] *Bṛhadāraṇyaka Up.* 1.4.6. [33] *Śata.* 11.3.3.1.

make him, too, mortal if he sins, like the demons who are granted immortality—"but." This indicates the reversal of the assumption that the gods try to win immortality for men; for the jealousy of the gods becomes manifest even in these early texts.

A Kharia myth about death demonstrates how this jealousy may conflict with the Vedic premise of the symbiosis of gods and men:

[After Ponomosor had destroyed mankind by fire, he could find no survivor, and therefore no one could give him sacrificial food. He was forced to make an agreement with Dakai Rani in order to find survivors. It is because of this agreement that Dakai Rani has seven eighths of men's bodies (the portion that is subject to death) and Ponomosor has only one eighth (the soul that survives death).][34]

Ponomosor's quandary is the familiar one. Though he is at first forced to corrupt or destroy men (because of their evil behavior or because of the threat posed by their virtue—the usual hypothesis of post-Vedic mythology), he needs the sacrificial offerings which they can supply only when uncorrupted or undestroyed (the Vedic premise). The bargain with death, the awarding of a share, is a typical solution for the Brāhmaṇas, though the proportion allotted to each side in this tribal myth betrays the cynicism with which the Kharias regarded the gods' compromise with the power of evil.

In the Brāhmaṇas, jealousy sometimes so overbalances the need for sacrifice that the gods become almost totally destructive of mankind:

Prajāpati created all existing things, those with breath and without, gods and men. Then he felt as if he were emptied out, and he was afraid of death. He wondered, "How can I get these beings back into my body? All existing things are in the threefold Vedas; therefore I will make for myself a body that contains the whole threefold Vedas." He put the Vedas into his own self and made it his own, and he became the body of all existing things, and he ascended upwards.[35]

It is not clear whether "all existing things" suffer by being reabsorbed into Prajāpati's body, but his intentions toward them are irresponsible, if not actually hostile, and he rises in the end, evidence of his wish to surpass his creatures. Destruction may be implicit in Prajāpati's wish to reverse the creative process, to reabsorb what he has spewed forth, for he swallows up the three Vedas as the three-headed demon Viśvarūpa swallows the triple world, and as Vṛtra swallows Indra, his enemy.

In swallowing the universe in this way, reversing creation, Prajāpati behaves not only like a demon but like Death himself; and in several texts this identification is explicit:

The year is death, for he destroys the life of mortal beings by means of night and day, and

[34] Roy, p. 417. [35] *Śata.* 10.4.2.2–3, .22, and .27.

then they die. The gods were afraid of this Prajāpati, the year, death, the ender, for they feared that he would put an end to their lives. They performed sacrifices but they did not attain immortality. They continued to exert themselves, and Prajāpati taught them the proper ritual to perform, so that they became immortal.

Then Death said to the gods, "Surely in this way all men will become immortal, and then what will be my share?" The gods said that the body would not be immortal but would be the share of death, while the rest of the man who had achieved immortality through knowledge or ritual acts would become immortal.[36]

In this myth, differentiation into dualities takes place on several levels. The year is at first both creator (Prajāpati) and destroyer (Death); when these functions become separate, Prajāpati teaches the gods how to overcome Death, just as he has taught them how to make him immortal. Yet a portion must be given to Death. Everyone must have a share, and mortal man is the bone thrown to Death to pacify him when the gods have become immortal; the gods win their immortality by denying man his. Creatures are divided into immortal (gods) and mortal (men), the latter further divided into mortal bodies and immortal spirits, a division achieved by yet another contrasting pair, knowledge and ritual.

In another text where Prajāpati assumes the role of death, the identification persists even when Prajāpati becomes benevolent; death simply becomes benevolent (a role that reemerges in Epic mythology):

Prajāpati created beings who went away, fearing that he would devour them. He said, "Return, and I will devour you in such a way that you will be procreated more numerously." Through the hymn, Death here devours creatures and makes them procreate.[37]

At first, creatures flee from Prajāpati as he himself flees from Death; then he shows the creative aspect of death, an aspect that may be implicit in the text in which he reabsorbs his own creation. Death makes procreation possible, and thus ultimately augments creation.

The two strands—Prajāpati as the enemy of death, and Prajāpati as death himself—are brilliantly interwoven in a myth that describes how the opposition of Prajāpati and Death (Mṛtyu) leads to their ultimate union:

Prajāpati and Death were competing in sacrifice. Prajāpati's weapons were praise, recitation, and ritual; Death's weapons were song accompanied by the lute, dance, and what is done for no point [i.e., no ritual point, or art for art's sake]. They were equally great, and after many years there was no victory. Then Prajāpati wished to conquer Death, and he saw numerical equivalence and computation in the sacrifice [i.e., the precise formula of the ritual]. With that he conquered Death, who retreated for refuge.

[36] *Śata.* 10.4.3.1–9. [37] *Tāṇḍya* 21.21; cf. *Jai. Br.* 2.254.

The parts of the sacrificial ritual—praise, ritual, the instruments of sacrifice—became the music of the lute, and dance, and what is done for no point, and the various parts of the lute [i.e., musical instruments became ritual instruments; Prajāpati absorbed Death]. Then they said, "Here there is no Soma sacrifice performed by two competing sacrificers; there is no second sacrifice but only one; Prajāpati is the sacrifice."[38]

Ritual absorbs art; the priest absorbs the creative spirit; Apollo absorbs Dionysos. Whatever the process, the end result is clear: by becoming death, Prajāpati conquers death; he eliminates the competition by means of a ritual merger. Ritual rules supplant the rules of true competition as the competition is absorbed; death is no longer the enemy; death is supplanted by ritual error, the only danger to the Brahmin.

But the image of death as the devourer remains untempered in another myth, which identifies Death with the creator, father of the year:

In the beginning there was nothing here. Death, who is hunger, covered this universe. He worshipped and produced for himself thought, the waters, the earth, and fire. . . . Death united with hunger and produced the year; for a year, Death carried him and then produced him. He opened his mouth to devour the newborn one, and the child cried. Death thought, "If I kill him now, I will have less food than if I kill him later." At the end of a year, Death slaughtered him and ate all that he had created. Whoever knows this conquers recurrent death, and death has no hold on him; he attains a full life-span and becomes one of the deities.[39]

Death refrains from devouring his own creature, not out of any pity for him but out of selfish hunger; he makes him not more numerous but simply a bigger meal, beef instead of veal. This postponement lasts only for the natural life-span of the creature—the year lives for a year—as does the "immortality" granted to the sacrificer: he attains a full life-span. But then it is said that the limited group of enlightened mortals will not only conquer recurrent death (that is, obtain release from the cycle of rebirth) but become gods themselves.

Where Prajāpati and the gods, or the gods and men, obtain the same type of immortality through the sacrifice, the myth rests satisfied; the gods wish men to have what they themselves have. The Ṛg Veda allows the worshipper to imagine that he has changed place with the god—making a better job of it than the real god does: "Agni, if you were mortal and I were immortal, I would not give you up to calumny or evil. My worshipper would not be living in want, distress, or evil."[40] The worshipper hints that, given a longer life-span, he would be more moral than he is now (he would not live with his "evil," which Sāyaṇa glosses as "a vicious mind") and more moral than the god (who gives his worshipper up to

[38] *Jai. Br.* 2.69–70; cf. Heesterman (1962), p. 20.

[39] *Śata.* 10.6.5.1–7. [40] *RV* 8.19.25.

evil). Similar prayers are addressed to Indra ("If I were you . . ."[41]), apparently without fear of offending the god, who is then asked for favors. The tolerance of the Vedic gods, particularly Indra, wears thin after the Vedic period, and any mortal who wishes to become immortal like the gods—let alone in place of a god—is quickly put down.

In the Upaniṣads, in spite of the general striving toward complete release (release from life as well as from death), a few Brāhmaṇa myths are preserved and expanded. The story of Naciketas[42] is retold in the Upaniṣads.[43] Naciketas is sent by his father to Death, where he obtains three boons and returns to his father. In this version (though not in the earlier Brāhmaṇa), the second boon is to reach the world of heaven, where there is no fear, death, old age, or sorrow. The third boon is knowledge about death; this is obtained against the will of Death, who says, "Do not question me about dying," and tempts Naciketas with earthly pleasures (lovely maidens, song and dance). But Naciketas, like Yayāti,[44] rejects these blandishments and wishes to come into the presence of the undecaying immortals. In the Brāhmaṇas, death may sometimes be conquered by ritual; in the Upaniṣads, it may be conquered by knowledge.

3. The Victory of Death

This optimism vanishes in the post-Vedic period, where death (Mṛtyu or Yama) requires not merely a sacrificial share but the right to perform his own job, his svadharma—killing. The possibility of the absence of death is considered in the *Mahābhārata* but ultimately rejected:

Once, the gods were preparing a sacrifice, and they made Yama their slaughterer of sacrificial animals. Then Yama did not kill any creatures, and so they became numerous. Therefore the gods went to Prajāpati and said, "We are frightened by this increase in men, and we have come to you for refuge." Prajāpati said, "What fear have you from men, since you are immortals? A mortal can be no danger to you." The gods said, "Mortals have become immortals, and there is no distinction, because of the lapse of death. Therefore, wishing for such a distinction, we have come here." Prajāpati said, "Since Yama is engaged in the sacrifice, men are not dying. When he has completed his ritual, there will be death in the end [antakāla] *for them." Then the gods went back to the sacrifice.*[45]

By performing a ritual, Yama in effect grants universal immortality, just as mortals achieved immortality through ritual in Vedic times. But since this text regards the ritual as merely a temporary episode, the problem of the absence of death does not really arise; the overcrowding, which characterizes the universe

[41] *RV* 7.32.18; 8.14.1 [42] *Tait. Br.* 3.11.8.
[43] *Kāṭha. Up.* 1.4–6. [44] See below, sec. 7. [45] *MBh.* 1.189.1–9.

before Death is created as well as when he withdraws temporarily, ceases when the ritual ceases. The explicit need for a distinction between gods and mortals is a manifestation not only of the jealousy of the gods but of the philosophy of caste: there must be a hierarchy, a separation of roles; and Yama must perform his own.

A later version of this myth offers more complex problems and solutions:

Once the sages made Yama their slaughterer of sacrificial animals. No one died then except those animals slaughtered for the sacrifice; mortality became immortality. Heaven became empty and the mortal world, ignored by death, became overcrowded. The gods said to the demons, "Destroy the sacrifice of the sages." The demons attacked the sacrifice, but the sages begged Śiva to help them, and he himself completed their sacrifice. The sages then said to the gods, in anger, "Since you sent the demons to destroy our sacrifice, let the evil demons be your enemies." And thenceforth the demons became the enemies of the gods.[46]

In this myth, evil for the gods originates in the absence of death; supposedly there were no bellicose demons until the gods sent them to interfere with the sages. The opposition between gods and mortals in the *Mahābhārata* is here replaced by the opposition between sages and demons. Nothing is said of the return of Yama to the world, and the solution for the problem of overcrowding is not the primary, simple one of the *Mahābhārata* (to destroy everyone) but the later one typical of the Purāṇas (to destroy virtue–that is, by distracting Yama, to destroy the sacrifice that makes men immortal). Even this temporary solution is rejected, however, for Śiva completes the sacrifice (as he completes Dakṣa's sacrifice when Śiva's own demonic hosts have destroyed it); thus the original problem of overcrowding is forgotten, and the machinations of the gods backfire, apparently leaving them with still increasing mankind, as well as demons who harass not mankind but the gods themselves. This confusion arises in part from the author's ambivalent attitude toward the role of sacrifice; on the one hand, the gods need the sacrifice (which they themselves perform in the earlier version and which the demons, their enemies, obstruct), but on the other hand, the virtue of the sacrificer threatens the gods. This ambivalence is enhanced by the ambiguous position of the sacrificers, sages who are semidivine, mediators between gods and men.

Another myth that begins with the absence of death among mankind is resolved by the intervention of Viṣṇu rather than Śiva:

Formerly, in the Golden Age, when there was no fear or danger, the eternal, primeval god (Ādideva) acted as Yama, and while he did so no one died, but people continued to be born. All creatures increased, birds and cows and horses and wild animals, and men

[46] *Brahma* 116.1–21.

increased by the millions. This dangerous crowd overburdened the Earth, who sought refuge with Viṣṇu. He said, "Do not worry. I will see to it that you are lightened." He became a boar who grasped the Earth with his tusks and raised her up. A great trembling arose, frightening the gods, who sought refuge with Brahmā; he assured them that there was no danger from the demons, and they went home.[47]

The original assumption that Death is put hors de combat by officiating at the sacrifice is here slightly modified; another, more merciful god takes the place of Death. A further assumption, that the overcrowding is caused by an excess of people in general, is here replaced by the secondary motif, that virtuous people cause this excess; this is implicit both in the statement that the myth takes place in the Golden Age, when men are all still virtuous, and in the assertion that Yama found no one to kill. The other possible modification, that an excess of wicked people is causing the trouble, is suggested by the gods' fear that demons are responsible for the disturbance of the Earth; this fear arises because the demons are usually to blame for the earth's distress when Viṣṇu assumes the form of a boar to rescue her. But Brahmā assures the gods that the demons are not to blame, and all is well; again, this text ultimately takes the form of a mere episode resolved, apparently, by a return to the previous state (Yama resumes his official duties) rather than by a reconsideration of the nature of death.

The confusion between the problems of an excess of people in general and an excess of extremely virtuous or evil people allows the pattern of this myth to be applied to a related cycle that expresses the necessity of punishment rather than of death. This correlation is apparent from the earliest myths of the origin of evil, in which the rod of punishment wielded by a king becomes necessary when the evil nature of man first develops. Another link is furnished by the myths in which the punishment of the evil demons is offered as a solution for the problem of overcrowding on earth. One myth of punishment begins, like several myths of death, with Brahmā's involvement in a sacrifice:

This is how punishment arose in order to protect the moral law, for punishment is the eternal soul of dharma. Brahmā performed a sacrifice in order to create, and as happiness prevailed, punishment vanished. A confusion arose among men: there was nothing that was to be done or not to be done, nothing to be eaten or not to be eaten. Creatures harmed one another and grabbed from one another like dogs snatching at meat; the strong killed the weak, and there were no moral bounds. Then Brahmā said to Śiva, "You should have pity on the good people and abolish this confusion." Then Śiva created punishment, which was his own self, and he created Yama and Mṛtyu.[48]

This myth seems to imply that the world cannot function when there is nothing

[47] *MBh.* 3, app. 1, no. 16, lines 70–126. [48] *MBh.* 12.122.14–29.

but happiness, that even in the Golden Age the law of dog eat dog—or fish eat fish—will prevail; men will harm one another unless punishment is introduced to protect the good from the wicked. But it also implies that unqualified happiness is undesirable in itself, that there must be a distinction between oppositions, for the universe cannot function when there is nothing to be done or not to be done. The word used for this indiscriminate mixture of moral elements (*saṃkara*) is the term often used to denote intermixture of castes, and clearly concepts of hierarchy are in play here: there must be punishment not only to prevent evil, but to separate good men from evil men. That Śiva creates Yama and Mṛtyu immediately after punishment has been established follows both from the interaction of the two mythologies and from the fact that Yama is the overseer of the dharma and adharma of the universe, in fear of whose rod of punishment all creatures follow dharma.[49] (Similarly, the Buddha remarked that when men live for more than a hundred thousand years they forget about birth, old age, and death, and would therefore not be interested in salvation, though he also remarked that when men live less than a hundred years they become exceedingly corrupt.[50]) Death and punishment are necessary to preserve virtue among mankind. Yama, for all his evil, is on the side of law and order; though Vedic texts treated him like a demon, later myths describe the banishment of Yama as one of the worst consequences of the conquest of the universe by demons.[51]

4. The Office of Death: Śiva (Sthāṇu) Opposes Brahmā

Although normally Brahmā is the creator and Śiva the destroyer, there is a series of myths in which these roles are superficially reversed, and Brahmā prevents Śiva from creating immortals.[52] In several myths of this series, it is at once evident that Śiva must cease creating immortals in order to avoid the familiar problem of overcrowding:

Brahmā began to create by meditation, but darkness and delusion overcame him. When his mind-born sons, all passionless yogis devoted to Śiva, refused to create, Brahmā performed asceticism, but still he was unable to create. He begged Śiva to help him, and Śiva agreed, but the creatures that Śiva made were immortals like himself, and they filled the universe. Brahmā said, "Do not create this sort of creatures, but make them subject to death." Śiva said, "I will not do that. Create such mortals yourself, if you wish." Then Śiva turned away from creation and remained with his seed drawn up in chastity from that day forth.[53]

The traditional roles of Śiva and Brahmā are retained in this myth. Śiva refuses to

[49] *Matsya* 11.18–22; *MBh*. 3, app. 1, no. 8, 1.5. [50] *Jātaka* 1.48; cf. Shaw's "Back to Methuselah."
[51] *Kāñcippurāṇam* 2.17.6. [52] O'Flaherty (1973), pp. 111–140.
[53] *Śiva* 7.12–17; cf. *Vāyu* 1.10.42–59; *Liṅga* 1.6.11–22.

create, in part because Brahmā asks him to refrain, and in part because Śiva is by nature an ascetic; this is evident from the references to the passionless sons of Brahmā, who, in their devotion to Śiva, imitate him by disobeying Brahmā's command to create mortals.

The ascetic nature of Śiva's withdrawal from creation is stressed in another version of this myth, in which Śiva also rejects the anthropomorphic aspect of creation, his wife:

Brahmā performed asceticism and created Rudra, the androgyne, who divided himself as Brahmā commanded him to do. Dakṣa then took the female half of the androgyne to be his daughter, and he gave her to Rudra. Brahmā said to Rudra, "Śiva, lord of Satī, perform creation," but Rudra said, "I will not. Do it yourself, and let me destroy. I will become Sthāṇu ["*the pillar," an ascetic*]." *And having commanded Brahmā to create, Śiva went to Mount Kailāsa with Satī.*[54]

The implications of Śiva's epithet, Sthāṇu, may be traced back to the Brāhmaṇas, where the worshipper seeks to be freed from the snares (*pāśas*) and pillars (*sthāṇus*) of death; when he overcomes these, he obtains a full life-span.[55] Thus the basic meaning of the Sthāṇu form of Śiva is death; as Sthāṇu, he withdraws from creation. Śiva has his own role, his svadharma, which is to destroy, and he commands Brahmā to follow Brahmā's svadharma, to create.

This simple division of labor is reversed in a series of myths that recognize the necessity of an ambiguous, mortal creation:

Brahmā asked Rudra to create, and the three-eyed Rudra created perfect hosts just like himself, free from old age and death, three-eyed, immortal. Brahmā then stopped him, saying, "Let not creation be thus. Only that creation which is composed of good and evil [śubhāśubha] *is prescribed." And so Rudra ceased creating and became Sthāṇu.*[56]

The realization that Rudra's creatures are too numerous or too powerful (immortals, like Rudra) frightens Brahmā, who introduces death. (Elsewhere, these dangerous creatures are made in Brahmā's own image but, fortunately, they corrupt themselves.[57]). Śiva's refusal to create may also be interpreted as superficially destructive, but this is not its ultimate effect; for, by refusing to create mortals instead of immortals, Śiva indulges in a kind of preventive euthanasia, a reversal of the reversal, so that he ends up creative after all. That he has the welfare of mankind at heart in refusing to create mortal creatures is apparent; yet, one version of this myth returns to the premise of Śiva's destructive role and justifies this as a favor to mankind: "Out of compassion, Rudra gives final peace to all creatures, effortlessly, for he gives passionlessness and release."[58]

Usually, however, Śiva does not wish to inflict the sorrows of mortality upon

[54] *Skanda* 7.2.9.5–17. [55] *Ait. Br.* 3.14. [56] *Matsya* 4.30–32.

[57] See above, chap. II, sec. 5. [58] *Brahmāṇḍa* 2.9.68–92; *Liṅga* 1.6.10–22.

his creatures. When Śiva creates beings free of death and passion, Brahmā tries in vain to make them subject to birth and death, and Śiva withdraws from creation; when Brahmā asks Śiva to create beings subject to birth, death, and fear, Śiva smiles in pity and says, "I will not create beings subject to death and fear, devoid of energy, in the power of karma, sunk in an ocean of misery. Create such miserable creatures yourself."[59] In all of these myths, however, Śiva's withdrawal from mortal creation is made possible only because it is understood that Brahmā will perform this role; each, by following his own svadharma, ensures that the universe is supplied with both mortality and immortality; each of the oppositions must be preserved. This is evident from those version of the Sthāṇu myth in which, when for some reason Brahmā's creatures fail to increase (a common inverse of the overcrowding motif), Śiva immediately comes to his assistance and participates in creation.[60]

The premise of overcrowding as a justification for the existence of death is also reversed in a South Indian text:

The primeval serpent [Ādiśeṣa] was weary of supporting the earth, and asked Śiva for help. Śiva ordered an Untouchable to beat his drum and cry, "Let the ripe decay"; in exchange, the Untouchable was granted sustenance (from funeral offerings), but he found this sustenance too small, so he cried, "Let the ripe and the unripe decay," in order to increase the death rate. People in mid life and children began to die. Śiva remonstrated with the Untouchable and gave him further privileges.[61]

The excessive zeal of death—here in the form of ar. Untouchable, symbolizing the undesirable aspect of death—must be curbed, just as his occasional lack of zeal must be overcome. Śiva as death commands the Untouchable to beat the drum; but Śiva as antideath keeps him from beating a tattoo of premature death—the death of young children and people in their prime, the aspect of death that the goddess of death herself finds hard to accept.[62] Death must have his share, but no more than his share.

An interesting variant of the Sthāṇu myths appears in a text that introduces a moral consideration of the nature of the creatures to be killed. Their fault is not merely that they are immortal or too numerous, but that they pose a violent threat to Brahmā. This version incorporates the concept of the Rudras as dangerous or evil creatures, as they are in other myths of death:

Brahmā created the mind-born sages, who remained celibate and refused to create. Then he created Rudra from his anger, and gave him various wives, and told him to create. Rudra created beings like himself, who swallowed up the universe on all sides, burning up the skies with their blazing eyes. Prajāpati was frightened, and he said, "No more of these

[59] *Kūrma* 1.10.17–40; *Śiva* 2.1.15.49–64. [60] *Saura* 23.16–52; 25.5–20; *Kūrma* 1.10.17–40.

[61] Thurston, VI, p. 116. [62] See below, sec. 5.

creatures! Perform asceticism for the sake of all creatures and create the universe as it was before." Śiva agreed, and he went to the forest to perform asceticism.[63]

Brahmā objects not to immortality in general in this text, but merely to the creation of immortals who threaten to upset the balance of the universe, to swallow everything up like demons.

These two objections are combined in yet another variant:

Brahmā began the process of creation, but he succeeded only in producing adharma, delusion, suffering, death, disease, old age, sorrow, and anger. These offspring were miserable, and they had no wives or children. Then Brahmā said to Rudra, "Create creatures," and Rudra mentally created creatures like himself, carrying skulls and drinking Soma, their seed drawn up in chastity. They had thousands of eyes and were of such terrible aspect that one could not look upon them, for they were great ascetics with great energy, the Rudras who devour oblations. When Brahmā saw them he asked Śiva to create instead beings who would be subject to death, for, said Brahmā, "Creatures free from death will not undertake actions or holy rituals." Śiva refused and remained thenceforth as Sthāṇu, his seed drawn up in chastity.[64]

The myth begins with the familiar episode of Brahmā's accidental creation of adharma and all the subsequent evils, including death. Although he is not satisfied with this creation, Brahmā nevertheless objects even more strenuously to Rudra's immortals (who are destructive heretics as well–skull-bearing Kāpālikas). Yet Brahmā reiterates the need for an ambiguous creation: "Creatures free from death will not undertake actions or rituals." Only the threat of evil death compels creatures to remain virtuous and to offer the sacrificial food that the gods need to remain free of death; therefore the gods include death within creation for much the same reason that they tolerate other demons. But a more general good is served as well, for just as mortality and immortality are interdependent, so too are the moral oppositions: "Only that creation which is composed of good and evil is prescribed."

In this way, Brahmā and Śiva combine forces to produce the necessary balance of the universe. Mortality is necessary on one level, but it can be transcended on another (just as the doctrine of svadharma itself can be transcended by bhakti); Brahmā's creatures must die, but those who are devoted to Śiva are freed from the wheel of rebirth.[65] The motif of overcrowding can best be understood in the context of the Hindu universe, the closed world-egg whose total contents can never increase but can only be redistributed. No one is ever destroyed, for the belief in reincarnation allows only a kind of recycling; but when temporary bottlenecks arise in certain places (on earth, or in heaven), death or corruption must be introduced in those places.

[63] *Bhāgavata* 3.12.1–26. [64] *Liṅga* 1.70.300–342. [65] See below, sec. 6.

In keeping with these views of the relativity of death, certain texts emphasize the cyclic nature of the universe, the manner in which periodic creation and dissolution (*pravṛtti* and *nivṛtti*) alternate, just as Brahmā and Śiva alternate in their tasks. An extended version of the Sthāṇu myth, which appears in two closely related texts of the *Mahābhārata*, begins with the assumption of an amoral necessity for death (a dangerous overcrowding brought about by an excess of people whose only flaw is that they do not die) but soon introduces moral judgments regarding not mortals but Death itself, in the form of a Goddess, Mṛtyu:

Long ago, Brahmā produced creatures who increased greatly but did not die. There was no space anywhere for people to breathe in the triple world. When Brahmā saw that the universe was unrestrained, he began to worry about destroying or restraining it; a fire arose from his anger and began to burn the universe on all sides, enveloping heaven and earth in a halo of flames that killed everything. Then Śiva, in the form of Sthāṇu, lord of those who wander at night, came to Brahmā and said, "You have created these creatures, but now your angry energy is burning them. When I see this, I am filled with pity; have mercy; do not be angry." Brahmā said, "I am not angry, nor do I desire that there should be no creatures. But the goddess Earth, oppressed by her burden, is sinking into the water, and she begged me to bring about a universal destruction for her sake. Since I do not know how to destroy all these increased beings, anger entered me." Sthāṇu said, "Those whom you have burnt to ashes will never again return. Restrain your energy and devise some other means for the welfare of all creatures, so that they may return." Then Brahmā restrained his energy within himself and created periodic creation and dissolution. And from him as he restrained the fire of his anger there appeared a black woman with red garments and red eyes, and Brahmā called her Death and told her to destroy everyone.[66]

The first half of this myth combines (or confuses) two related motifs: God kills men either because they have increased in numbers (as is usually the case) or because they have increased in years (aged, ready to die); the latter meaning (aged in years) appears in the tribal mythology of death, but the former is more likely and fits the context better. At several points, the myth implies that death comes about because of some shortcoming or mistake of God. Brahmā does not know how to destroy things properly, and though he at first denies that anger has entered him, he later admits that it has. Moreover, he expressly states that he does not wish to do what he is doing, and finally, when he does restrain his destructive energy, it is not wholly destroyed but is merely transferred to someone else—a woman, as usual.

[66] *MBh*. 12.248.13–21; .249.1–16; also 7, app. 1, no. 8, 35–120.

5. The Svadharma of Death

The myth then continues, developing the problems of this goddess:

Death wept and said, "How could you create a woman such as I am? How could I perform such a cruel task? I fear adharma, and I will not kill sinless children or old people, dear ones and sons and brothers and mothers and fathers. Evil-doers go to the house of Yama when they die; let me not go to the house of Yama; have mercy on me and let me perform asceticism." Brahmā said, "Death, I created you to destroy creatures. Do it, and do not worry, for you cannot do otherwise, and you will not be blamed in the world." Death did not agree, but stood there in silence, determined not to destroy any creatures, for she wished for their welfare. Brahmā smiled and restrained his anger, and Death performed asceticism until Brahmā said, "There will be no adharma in you. Creatures oppressed with diseases will not blame you. The tears that you shed will be diseases which will oppress men when their time has come. At the time of death, you will cause creatures to be attached to anger and desire, and so you will escape adharma. Yama, who is eternal dharma, will assist you, and so will diseases." She said, "If it must be so, then grant me this: let greed, anger, envy, wrath, malice, delusion, shamelessness, and cruelty split the body into separate parts." Brahmā said, "It will be so. Your dharma will be to kill creatures. Adharma will kill those of vicious conduct. Purify yourself, and abandon desire and anger, and kill living creatures." Fearing a curse, Death agreed, and so at the time of death she deludes creatures with desire and anger and kills them, having abandoned her own desire and anger. At the proper time, just as the Destroyer herself takes away the breath of creatures, creatures all kill themselves, and it is not Death who kills them. Because of this, even the gods are known as mortals.[67]

Death is a woman here, which is unusual in Sanskrit mythology, but she behaves like Alakṣmī, Jyeṣṭhā, and other female personifications of evil. Her concern for the wickedness of her assigned task is not dismissed, as it is in other myths of this nature, with a simple reference to the doctrine of svadharma, though Brahmā does use this as one of his arguments when he says, "Your dharma will be to kill creatures." Like Śiva, Death wishes to perform asceticism instead of obeying Brahmā; but, unlike him, she is not allowed to do this, for there is no one else to assume the role she wishes to reject (destruction), as Brahmā assumes Śiva's role (creation). The relationship between Death and Yama is a confused one. Sometimes Death seems to fear that Yama will punish her for her own sins; sometimes she seems to feel that there is no need for her, as Yama already carries off evil-doers; and sometimes Yama appears as her assistant. A similar confusion is apparent in her relationship with disease. Sometimes it is said that she creates

[67] *MBh.* 12.249.17–22; .250.1–41; also 7, app. 1, no. 8, 121–249.

diseases, but elsewhere their role seems to be to separate her from the blame of death; just as Brahmā has transferred to her his own guilt of destruction, so she transfers it to the diseases, who kill people either by her command or in her stead. The metaphor of transference leads to a series of measures by which Death is absolved of the guilt of killing, measures that turn upon her relationship with desire and anger. Death fills creatures with desire and anger at the time of death so that she herself is free of adharma; by corrupting them before she kills them, making them deserving of death, she avoids the sin of killing virtuous people—a stratagem familiar from the myths of the pattern of the Buddha avatar. Moreover, if she frees herself from her own desire and anger, and kills people emotionlessly, unattached, she will commit no sin; this more sophisticated concept of the role of desire and anger also appears in the *Bhagavad Gītā*, where Kṛṣṇa justifies killing as long as one does not kill while under the influence of desire and anger.[68] So Death purifies herself of these emotional flaws, transferring them to her victims; as usual, mortal men are made evil so that the gods may remain free of evil.

In a sensitive retelling of the tale of Death, William Buck places this incident directly after the myth of the Fall: the fallen creatures remain immortal, and the earth cannot bear their weight. Śiva appeals to Brahmā's mercy, but Brahmā replies, "I have no kindness. . . . I have no grace." Brahmā then consents, against his better judgment, to restrain his fire; Death is created and flees until Brahmā promises,

I will make them equal. You will not have to take them, either men or gods or devils. I will make greed and anger and malice and shame and jealousy and passion. I will make them this way and that way. I will make disease and war from your tears. Those two only I will make that way. Do nothing—they will all come to you, soon or late. There is nothing to do, nothing to stop doing, for you or for them. But only greet them well in their hour. You have nothing else to say, they will kill themselves. And only the foolish will weep over what none can avoid." Then Shiva began his dance, for till then, though he raised his foot, he could not put it down."[69]

Śiva's raised foot indicates the suspension of the Sthāṇu episode—the suspension of death itself—until Death is acquitted of complicity in evil. Then Death begins her work, Śiva his dance.

The disinclination of Death to perform her own svadharma appears in another text in which Death is, as is more usual, a god rather than a goddess:

When Brahmā had created the Rudras and they asked him for a livelihood, he gave them lust and adharma as their assistants. The son of Adharma was Death, whom Adharma instructed to kill people, but Death replied, "How can you tell me to hurt people, to perform such an evil action?" Adharma said, "There will be no sin in you if you hurt people. You will direct old age, disease, fever, and the other ills which I have created, and

[68] *Gītā* 2.38. [69] Buck, pp. 318–320.

by those means people will die. Wherever I dwell, there you will dwell. Destruction is your nature, and you will put auspicious diseases into all bodies." Then Adharma created various diseases, of whom the eldest was Fever, with three heads and nine eyes; and Death took his army of Injury, Quarrels, and the others, and wandered among men.[70]

Here again Death is freed of the responsibility for death by transferring it to the actual diseases that are the technical cause of death, including the demonic three-headed Fever, which afflicts the sinful Indra and Śiva in other contexts; the particularly Śaiva aspect of the Fever is evident from the fact that each head has three eyes, as Śiva has. Yet the element of evil still clings to Death, for he is told that destruction is his nature, and now Adharma incarnate (whom the female Death so fears in the *Mahābhārata*) assigns the task in place of Brahmā.

The Sthāṇu myths thus demonstrate a continuous interplay between an absolute and a relative morality in the attitude toward death. The more basic Hindu view is the relative view that just as each person has his own svadharma, so there must be a god whose svadharma is destruction. But this view is constantly challenged by a more absolute morality, which questions the necessity of death and clearly associates it with evil. This conflict is similar to that raised by the destructive svadharma of demons; in early texts, Death is sometimes regarded as demon, the natural enemy of the immortal gods. The myths in which Śiva refuses to create mortal beings deny his own svadharma to kill and justify this refusal by invoking the doctrine of bhakti–Śiva's devotion to living creatures–as the virtuous demons do. These texts seem to try to solve the problem of evil death by thrusting responsibility onto someone other than God himself. Even though it is often said that Śiva's svadharma is destructive, the psychological impetus of the Sthāṇu myths makes it easier for the devotee to accept this aspect of his god, just as the creation of diseases (or, more pertinent, of desire and anger) makes it easier for Death to accept her own evil role. At a later, more fully rationalized stage of bhakti religion (and at a stage when Vedāntic philosophy is more fully integrated in the myths), the bhakti idea is pushed still farther and the god becomes responsible for everything that happens in the world, including destruction. But the present body of myths takes the narrower view that the loving god is not personally responsible for death.

6. The Death of Death: Śiva Opposes Yama

The bhakti corpus then progresses one step farther by asserting that Śiva prevents Death from afflicting any of his devotees. This idea may be traced back to the many Brāhmaṇa texts which state that certain enlightened men are not subject to death. The Upaniṣadic force that challenges death–the force of knowledge–is

[70] *Bṛhaddharma* 3.12.48–60; see above, chap. III, sec. 2.

then replaced by the force of bhakti, and it is said that Yama may not touch any of the worshippers of Viṣṇu.[71] Yama himself allows his own "devotee," his wife, to stay him from his appointed rounds in one myth:

Yama married Vijayā, the daughter of a Brahmin. Though he forbade her to enter his southern domains, she disobeyed him and discovered the wicked in torment. When she saw her own mother there, she asked Yama to release her. Yama said that someone living on earth must sacrifice and transfer the merit of that act to Vijayā's mother; this was done, and she was released.[72]

The "merit transfer," known from village Buddhism as well as Hinduism,[73] is here coupled with the power of a woman, and Yama is seduced. Even in the Epic, the devotion of a woman prevents Yama from taking her husband's life;[74] but these isolated incidents do not pose the more serious problems that arise when Yama declares a general strike or when he grants exemption to a significant number of devotees.

The pattern of the myth of the immortal devotee derives from the pattern of earlier Yama myths. First Yama fights against the gods; then he fights in order to be given a mortal body as his share; then he neglects his job or (like the goddess of Death) does not wish to do it; and finally, in the myths of overcrowding in heaven,[75] he demands to be allowed to do his job, to apply his vocation to everyone, including devotees on their way to heaven. Yama loses every one of these battles but the second (where he succeeds in obtaining a share, the bodies of mortals). Another pattern that contributes to this cycle is that of the Sthāṇu myth. At first Śiva is death; then he refuses to be death; and now he refuses to allow death to touch his devotees.

The epithet Yamāntaka or Kālāntaka ("Death, the Ender") was originally applied to Yama himself; later it was transferred to Śiva, reinterpreted as "The Ender of Death", and explained by a myth:

Mārkaṇḍeya, a devotee of the gods, was fated to die at the age of sixteen. He was meditating and worshipping the Śiva-liṅga when this moment arrived, and Yama's messengers came to bind his soul and take it to Yama. At that moment, Śiva burst out of the liṅga in great anger and kicked Yama in the chest, almost killing him. Yama realized that he must not treat a devotee of Śiva like an ordinary mortal, and he went away. Śiva said that Mārkaṇḍeya would remain sixteen years old forever.[76]

This story is then applied to other devotees, to the wicked as well as to the virtuous:

A very wicked Brahmin named Devarājā ("king of the gods") committed many sins: he

[71] *Viṣṇu* 3.7. [72] *Bhaviṣya*, cited in Wilkins, pp. 82–83.

[73] See above, chap. VI, sec. 2. [74] *MBh.* 3.281–283 (Sāvitrī).

[75] See below, chap. IX, sec. 1. [76] *Bhāgavata* 12.8–10; cf. Rao, II, 1, 156–164.

left his wife for a harlot, killed his mother and father and his wife, ate forbidden foods, drank wine, and so forth. One day he accidentally overheard a discourse on Śiva at a temple. Later, the Brahmin died of a fever, and Yama's attendants bound him with snares to take him to Yama; but Śiva's attendants thrashed Yama's servants, released Devarājā and took him to Kailāsa, while Yama, the king of dharma, was afraid to interfere.[77]

The Brahmin (whose name may intend a pun on the title of the most wicked of the gods, Indra) is the epitome of unrepentant wrongdoing, but his sins are erased by his *accidental* particpation in the worship of Śiva. Usually, however, the devotee is virtuous, at least at the start; this is certainly true of Śveta, probably the first Śaiva devotee to whom this pattern was applied. Śveta appears in the *Mahābhārata* as a royal sage who is able to revive his dead son (apparently without the help of any god)[78] and for whose sake Śiva kills the demon Andhaka.[79] According to the Śaiva Siddhānta school, Śveta was an incarnation of Śiva, a sage who composed the Śaiva Āgamas.[80] The *Śiva Purāṇa* says that when Brahmā performed asceticism, Śiva rewarded him by becoming the young sage Śveta, who taught Brahmā the secret of perfect knowledge.[81] Elsewhere in Śaiva scriptures, Śveta is regarded not as an actual incarnation of Śiva but merely as a particularly devout worshipper:

When the sage Śveta had reached the end of his life-span, Death (Kāla) came to take him. Śveta challenged Kāla, saying that he was a devotee of Śiva the Death of Death (Mṛtyor Mṛtyu). When Kāla persisted, Śiva appeared, and Yama took one look at Śiva and fell down dead. The gods rejoiced to see Death (Antaka) dead.[82]

This story mixes together indiscriminately the various aspects of Death: Kāla, Yama, Mṛtyu, and Antaka; it ends without seriously addressing the problems caused by the death of death in any or all of these aspects. For the myth is intended merely to demonstrate the complete power of devotion to Śiva, and is told (to the sages in the Pine Forest) with other stories about devotees who conquer Death.[83] But other Purāṇas, dissatisfied with this simple ending, further developed the myth:

A royal sage named Śveta worshipped Śiva. When Death (Kāla) came to take Śveta away, Rudra asked Death to give the devotee to him. Thinking of his own nature, Death attacked Rudra, who struck him with his left foot, and Death (Mṛtyu) died. But Brahmā then begged Rudra to let Death live, since he had committed no fault and was obeying Rudra's orders. Rudra agreed to this, and Death lived.[84]

[77] *Śiva, Śivapurāṇa Māhātmya*, 2.1–40. [78] *MBh*. 12.149.63. [79] *MBh*. 13, app. 1, no. 18, 107–108.
[80] Dasgupta, V, 66–69. [81] *Śiva* 7.1.5.5. [82] *Liṅga* 1.30.1–25.
[83] *Liṅga* 1.29.63. [84] *Kūrma* 2.35.12–38.

In this text, Śiva revives not only his mortal devotee but the dead god of death himself; he kills Death and revives him.

The motif of the revival of Death introduces a new thread to be woven into the present fabric of myth, a thread based on the well-known myth of Śiva and Kāma, the god of lust. When Kāma attempted to arouse the ascetic Śiva, Śiva burnt Kāma to ashes, only to revive him at the entreaty of the gods; ever since then, Kāma has been bodiless and invisible, since Śiva destroyed his physical form.[85] Like Death—for he is Death—Śiva destroys the body but not the immortal essence of his creatures. Śiva derives the epithet Kāmāntaka, "Destroyer of Kāma," from this myth; as he is also known as Kālāntaka, "Destroyer of Death," the Kāma myth is easily applied to the Kāla cycle: Śiva burnt Kāla, who praised him: then Śiva revived Kāla but told him that he would remain invisible.[86] Here, as in the Kāma myth,[87] Śiva does not actually diminish the power of the creature who is burnt; on the contrary, he releases that power, frees it from the narrow confines of a physical body, for the power is his own—lust or death.

The motif of Kāma's bodiless revival from ashes is combined with the imagery of the Mārkaṇḍeya story and introduced into the Śveta myth:

Kāla came to take Śveta away when he was worshipping Śiva. Śiva emerged from the liṅga and burnt Kāla to ashes; he made Śveta into one of his own hosts and disappeared. From that time forth, Kāla has never been seen by anyone, for he has no body.[88]

The myth is then further expanded along the lines of the Mṛtyu cycle:

Śveta was a virtuous king, a devotee of Śiva; everyone in his kingdom was happy. Yama and Kāla came to take him one day when he was worshipping Śiva. Then Śiva, the Destroyer of Kāla, looked at Kāla with his third eye and burnt him to ashes in order to protect the devotee. Śiva said to Śveta, "Kāla eats all creatures, and he came here to eat you in my presence and so I burnt him. You and I will kill evil men who violate dharma, heretics who wish to destroy people." But Śveta said, "This world behaves properly because of Kāla, who protects and creates by destroying creatures. If you are devoted to creation, you should revive Kāla, for without him there will be nothing." Śiva did as his devotee suggested; he laughed and revived Kāla with the form he had had. Then Kāla praised Śiva the Destroyer of Kāla, and Kāla went home and told his wife Māyā and all his messengers never to bring any devotees of Śiva to the world of death, but to bring all other sinners.[89]

Although Kāla is revived in his previous form, and does not remain invisible, as Kāma usually does, the argument about the necessity of his job (familiar from the Mṛtyu corpus) is here utilized in a pattern suggested by the Kāma myth, for the gods persuade Śiva to revive Kāma by convincing him that Kāma, the source

[85] O'Flaherty (1973), pp. 141–150. [86] *Śiva* 5.26.9–10. [87] O'Flaherty (1973), pp. 155–163.

[88] *Viṣṇudharmottara* 1.236.1–21. [89] *Skanda* 1.1.32.4–92. Cf. *Tirukkaṭavūr* 18.

of creation, must be revived "or else there will be nothing." Śiva himself is here quite willing to usurp the position of Kāla (since it is a svadharma that he shares anyway), though he would limit its function to evil men; but Śveta is wiser than his god and points out the need for Death as a separate force, though still limited only to sinners. As happens so often, the evil of mortality is countered by the argument of the evil of mortals; this argument is useless, however, to justify the death of the virtuous mortal, who must therefore be made immortal.

Two other myths in this cycle illuminate the moral aspects of the problem of death. In these myths, Yama himself is moved by the virtue of the dead mortal and resigns of his own accord (like Mṛtyu in the *Mahābhārata*) rather than at the insistence of Śiva.

A five-year-old boy died, and his Brahmin parents, who had had him late in life, mourned bitterly. The Brahmin cursed Yama to be sonless as he himself was now, and Yama, who had only performed his svadharma, was saddened when he heard the curse. He went to Brahmā and bowed and said, "I will stop doing my appointed job, for if I have no son there will be no one to offer ancestral oblations to me." Indra told Brahmā that it was Yama's job to take people at any time, even in youth; though Brahmā agreed, he could not change a Brahmin's curse, but he created a hundred and eight diseases and told them to assist Yama on earth, so that no one could curse Yama. Yama took the diseases back to his world and told his messengers not to touch the devotees of Śiva at the Hāṭakeśvara shrine.

Then Yama took the Brahmin's son back to him, for he was moved by compassion. The Brahmin rejoiced and embraced his son and said, "Since I have a son, let Yama have a son. And let no one who makes an offering to Yama at this shrine grieve for his son." Yama agreed to this and returned to his world.[90]

Although Śiva does not actually intervene (for the Brahmin curses Yama directly, and Yama himself relents), it is Śiva's shrine which provides the exception to the universal sovereignty of death, not only for this devotee but for all who grieve for their sons. The Mṛtyu cycle supplies not only the argument about the svadharma of Yama but the superficial solution provided by the creation of diseases, which replace sins as the link between death and mortals. Mortals who are either sinful or diseased are subject to death; the myth does not distinguish between physiological and ethical flaws.

Yama's attitude in this myth is unclear. Though the Brahmin's curse is what causes him to resign his post, he is said to be motivated by compassion as well. The curse disappears (or is replaced by a suicide threat) in another, greatly expanded variant of this myth, which emphasizes the compassion of Yama:

A merchant whose eldest son died in the prime of life was so grieved that he and his wife resolved to die with their son. Hearing them weep, Yama was full of pity; he left his own

[90] *Skanda* 6.139.1–64.

city and began to meditate upon Kṛṣṇa on the banks of the Godāvarī river. Therefore, after just a short time, people increased everywhere and filled the earth, for no one died. Earth said to Indra, "Without slaughter, I am oppressed by a heavy burden. Tell Yama to destroy creatures." Indra could not find Yama, but the sun, Yama's father, said, "He is performing asceticism on the Godāvarī; I don't know why." Then Indra shouted, "That wretched Yama has ruined my position as sovereign of the gods; he must wish to usurp my place." Indra commanded his celestial nymphs to interfere with Yama's asceticism, but no one dared to try. Then Indra became angry and said that he himself would take the armies of the gods and kill the enemy who was trying to obtain heaven by means of asceticism. But Viṣṇu learned of this and protected Yama.

Finally, Indra sent the nymph Gaṇikā ("whore"), who sang so that Yama's mind wavered; she plunged into the Godāvarī and went straight to heaven, because of the power of the shrine there. The sun said to Yama, "My son, fulfil your own karma; destroy creatures." Yama replied, "I will not do this despicable work," but the sun said, "What, precisely, is despicable about it? You can do it. Didn't you see the Whore, who sang and went to heaven after bathing in the shrine? Go back to your own city." Yama returned to his own city and stopped worrying about killing creatures.[91]

There are a number of significant reversals in this myth. Viṣṇu, not Śiva, is the devotee's god, but this is of secondary importance since in both this and the preceding myth it is the *place* which poses the obstacle to death; this development is far more prominent in the related cycle of myths about the conquest of heaven,[92] to which this episode is linked by Indra's fear that Yama wishes to obtain heaven by means of asceticism. The mourning of the parents of the dead boy rouses the pity of Yama, just as the story of Mṛtyu's compassion is told to assuage the grief of mourning parents.[93] This grief is the result of the reversal of the natural order in which parents die before their children, a modest form of immortality, which is all that is asked for in the Ṛg Veda: "Let not the sons die before the fathers." Yama is moved to resign, with the usual results: no one dies and the Earth complains. This simple fact is not sufficient to persuade him to return to his work, however; Indra, pigheaded as ever, is sure that someone is after his throne, and so he treats Yama like a dangerous mortal or demon. He seduces him, first (unsuccessfully) with a miscellaneous group of nymphs and then by combining the attention-getting powers of a nymph with the special powers of the shrine; having stirred Yama's mind (demonstrating to him the inadequacy of his asceticism), she then goes to heaven (demonstrating the superfluity of his asceticism). The shrine in this myth first provides a loophole in the universality of Yama, a compromise between immortality and mortality, by limiting immortality to a select few; then it establishes a philosophical point:

[91] *Brahma* 86.8–50. [92] See below, chap. IX, secs. 1–3. [93] *MBh.* 12.249–250.

since bhakti assures entrance into heaven, svadharma is irrelevant. Here, however, the argument is taken one step farther: Yama evidently reasons that, since svadharma is irrelevant, it cannot be evil. He therefore obeys his father, the sun, who is an eloquent advocate of the doctrine of svadharma in confrontations with virtuous demons;[94] Yama himself here plays the role of such a demon, for he succumbs to parental persuasion just as the wicked demons become demonic at their parents' request, and he goes back to killing, no longer bothering his head about morality.

A similar expiation by Yama, one which again enables him to continue doing his work, appears in a Tamil text:

Once Yama thought to himself, "For a long time I have been devouring living creatures, even though I know that the Vedas and Purāṇas all say that noninjury is the highest dharma. I must rid myself of this sin." He went to Tiruvāñciyam and worshipped Śiva, who appeared and forgave him. Yama returned to his city, but after a while he again became deluded and sinned against Śiva because of the power of time (or death [kāla]*). By Śiva's grace, his delusion departed, and he returned to the shrine and said, "Forgive me for my sins against Mārkaṇḍeya, Śveta, and the others." Śiva forgave him and commanded him to stay at the shrine in order to chase away sinners who came there to die.*[95]

Although Yama is right in thinking that his job is a violation of eternal dharma, and although he is said to become deluded again when he resumes his work (deluded by time, just like ordinary mortals in the Golden Age, even though Yama himself *is* time–Kāla), Śiva continually forgives him, just as any good royal chaplain continually absolves his monarch; someone must fill the evil office of King of the Dead. Śiva does not allow Yama to go on carrying off Śaiva devotees like Mārkaṇḍeya and Śveta, yet he allows him to go on carrying off everyone else. In addition, Śiva gives Yama a special task: he must keep sinners from dying at the shrine (which would give them access to the world of Śiva), in order to prevent precisely the type of unrepentent, accidental salvation which the wicked Devarājā achieved; as usual, the Tamil text adds a moral element foreign to the Sanskrit corpus. Śiva gives these sinners to Yama as a sign that Yama's job has become ethical; he is to avoid the devotees and make a special effort to kill sinners.

7. The Devotee's Conquest of Death: Yayāti Opposes Indra

The reversal of the normal order of death (parents dying before children) lies at the heart of another series of myths in this cycle, the myths of Yayāti, which begin in the *Mahābhārata*:

[94] See above, chap. V, sec. 13.

[95] *Tiruvāñciyakṣettirapurāṇam*, no. 38.

King Yayāti was the son of Nahuṣa, who usurped Indra's throne; Yayāti married Devayānī, the daughter of Śukra, but when he then dishonestly married a second wife, Śukra cursed Yayāti to fall victim to old age, though he tempered this curse so that Yayāti could pass on his old age to someone else for a thousand years without incurring evil. In order to continue to enjoy Devayānī, Yayāti persuaded his fourth and youngest son, Puru, to exchange his own youth for Yayāti's old age. After a thousand years of pleasure, in which he ruled virtuously, Yayāti was sated with lust; he gave Puru back his youth and made him king.

When Yayāti went to heaven, he was honored by the gods, but he boasted to Indra that no one among the gods, men, Gandharvas, or sages equalled him in ascetic power. Then Indra said, "Since you look down upon your equals and betters, your merit is gone, and you will fall from heaven." Yayāti was granted his request to fall among good men; as he fell he said, "I conquered Indra's world, and Prajāpati's, the worlds of each god, and I lived in their place as I pleased. The gods honored me, and I rivalled their power and majesty. But then I fell from heaven, having spent the merit I had amassed, and I heard the gods saying, sorrowful and compassionate, 'Poor Yayāti has used up his merit and fallen from heaven.' " For a while, Yayāti was suspended between heaven and earth, but then he fell among his daughter's four sons, who placed him back in heaven by giving him a portion of their own merit.[96]

Yayāti wins youth, only to lose it, and wins heaven, only to lose it, but in the end he triumphs. His ambivalence and mediation are graphically expressed by the image of suspension between heaven and earth. (Similarly, when Triśaṅku insists upon bodily entering heaven, despite the opposition of Indra, a compromise is reached whereby he remains suspended in heaven as a constellation, head downwards.[97]) At first he violates the natural order, exchanging his youth with his son, but this leads to the more galling offense of conquering Indra's world. Yayāti boasts, as Divodāsa does, that his ascetic power is greater than that of the gods, and Indra jealously casts him out of heaven, though Yayāti's own pride is blamed for this; one suspects a note of hypocrisy when the "compassionate gods" talk of "poor Yayāti"—they are relieved to see him leave heaven. Yayāti's offspring then make an exchange that is considered natural (though Yayāti at first protests against it, not wishing to demean himself by accepting charity)—they give him some of their own merit, a transfer of karma common in Indian mythology.[98]

The thinly submerged hostility of Indra in this episode, and the importance of lust in inspiring Yayāti to seek eternal youth, are further developed in Purāṇic versions of the myth. The *Mahābhārata* simply states that, after a thousand years of pleasure, Yayāti lived in the forest with Brahmins for another thousand years, fasting on water alone, torturing himself between the five fires, standing on one

[96] *MBh.* 1.76–80, 83–84, 88, 91; 5.118–120; cf. *Matsya* 32–42 and Dumézil (1973), *passim*.

[97] *Viṣṇu* 4.3.14–15; *Hari.* 9.89–100, 10.1–21; *Rām.* 1.56.10–1.59.33.

[98] See above, chap. VI, sec. 2, and below, chap. XI, sec. 1.

foot, eating only air; then he went to heaven (until, after a short period of bliss, Indra cast him out).[99] The Purāṇas add a significant modification: when Yayāti gave the kingdom to Puru and took back his old age after a thousand years, he went to the forest *with his wife*; then he went to heaven;[100] Yayāti fasted to death and went to heaven with his wife.[101]

The translation to heaven with a woman plays an important part in later variants of the myth. In the Epic, Yayāti's troubles begin when he desires a forbidden woman (his second wife); the forbidden woman in the Purāṇas is often a celestial nymph:

When Yayāti obtained Puru's youth, he ruled justly and virtuously, until he became attached to the celestial nymph Viśvācī; then his lust was insatiable, even after a thousand years. Seeing how desire could never be satisfied, Yayāti renounced sensual pleasure; he took back his old age from Puru and practised asceticism in the forest.[102]

The episode in which Yayāti becomes disgusted with sensual pleasures—a set piece from the *Mahābhārata*—here results not from satiation with the normal enjoyment of virtuous marital pleasures (or even bigamous pleasures) but rather from lack of satiation with a celestial nymph; it is not explained how she comes to Yayāti, but one suspects the hand of Indra; and it is significant that in this text Yayāti does not ever go to heaven.

Another part of the Purāṇic myth is supplied by the *Bhāgavata Purāṇa*. When Yayāti became disgusted with sensual pleasures (no nymph appears here), he went to the forest, after giving Puru back his youth; then in a moment he was released like a bird from a nest, and he found his refuge in Viṣṇu.[103] This final element, the bhakti element, is used to release Yayāti from the complicated tangle of all the other strands (ursurpation, lust, violation of the natural order) in the extended version that appears in the *Padma Purāṇa*. This text begins with the reversal of two assumptions of all other variants: Indra tries to get Yayāti to heaven, not to keep him out, and Yayāti first seeks heaven and only then seeks youth. Moreover, Yayāti himself creates a second heaven—on earth:

The sage Nārada told Indra about the virtue of King Yayāti on earth, and Indra said, "Nahuṣa usurped my place before, and this king is just like his father. He will certainly take my place unless you bring him to heaven somehow." Indra sent his charioteer to Yayāti, who engaged him in a long discussion about good and evil, karma, and old age; finally, Yayāti resolved not to go to heaven but to make heaven on earth himself, by means of his asceticism, svadharma, and good nature. He announced this to Indra, who worried all the more and continued to try to contrive a way to bring Yayāti to heaven. Then Yayāti made all his subjects devotees of Viṣṇu, virtuous, happy, without passion or

[99] *MBh.* 1.81.6–16. [100] *Vāyu* 93 (2.31).13–69.

[101] *Brahma* 12.1–48; *Liṅga* 1.67.1–25.

[102] *Viṣṇu* 4.10.1–18; *Brahmāṇḍa* 2.3.68.29–94. [103] *Bhāgavata* 9.19.1–25.

hatred. Free of the flaws of death, all people lived for a long time, together with their sons and grandsons; all men on earth appeared to be twenty-five years old forever. No one was mortal; there was no death, nor sorrow, and the earth was the very form of heaven.

Then the servants of Yama fell and were abused by the servants of Viṣṇu; weeping, they told Yama how the king of earth had made the earth free of death. Then Yama, Lord of Dharma, thought about what was best for everyone, and he went to Indra and said, "Men have become immortal, free of old age or disease, greed or delusion, and they do no evil; they perform their svadharma and worship Viṣṇu. One generation meets another—sons, grandsons, great-grandsons. My work is destruction, and my job has been destroyed; I have fallen from my place, deprived of business. If you wish to please me, bring the king to heaven somehow." Indra summoned Kāma and the Gandharvas and celestial nymphs and told them to bring Yayāti to heaven; they took the form of mimes and acted the story of Viṣṇu's dwarf avatar and the demon Bali. Old age took the form of a beautiful woman and sang so sweetly that Yayāti was deluded by her song and by the bewitching magic of Kāma. In this deluded state, the king forgot to wash his feet when he had urinated and defecated; at that moment, old age seized him, in order to secure the welfare of Indra. And when the dance was over, and the dancers had gone away, the king had become an old man.

The naïve king, still bemused by lust, went hunting one day and found a beautiful lake; there he saw a lovely woman singing. He was overcome by passion for her and begged her to unite with him, offering her his kingdom and his own life if she would gratify his desires. Her companion told the king who the woman was:

"When Kāma had been burnt by Śiva, Rati, the wife of Kāma, wept at this lake; her tears fell into the water, and from those tears were born sorrow, old age, separation, misery, and grief. Then from the left eye of Rati the tears of bliss gave birth to this woman. Enjoy her forever, for she performed asceticism in order to obtain a husband; but her husband must be a young man, and your body is riddled with old age. Get one of your sons to give you his youth, if you want to enjoy her." The foolish king, deluded by Kāma, persuaded his son Puru to exchange his own youth for Yayāti's old age. When the girl still hesitated to marry him because he already had two wives, Yayāti promised to obey her every command, and she married him. Yayāti enjoyed her for a long time, and all his subjects remained undecaying, unageing, full of asceticism and truth, all meditating upon Viṣṇu. Then Indra feared the noble Yayāti all the more, and he told the daughter of Rati to bring him to heaven somehow. The girl said to Yayāti, "Great king, you are so mighty that you interfere with Yama and Indra, for you have made the world of mortals free of disease or evil. If your truth and dharma are so great, why can't you go to the world of the gods in the sky?" "You are right," the king replied, "I can do anything; but I do not go to heaven, for if I do, then death and the gods will give me a share, and so all my subjects will be deprived of me and become subject to death." But she pleaded with him, and he began to reason, "Each man's fate is determined by his own good or evil karma,

and various diseases are the causes of death for creatures who have breath. The ripening of my own inescapable karma has come to me in the form of this woman; those actors who came to my home caused old age to enter my body, and the king of gods sent his charioteer to bring me to heaven before, and now that karma has ripened." Then he said to her, "My mind is divided. If I go to heaven, my subjects will suffer, for the wicked Yama will torment them with diseases. But I will go to heaven with you." As he prepared to leave, he summoned Puru and said, "Give me back my old age, take back your youth, and rule the kingdom; do anything to make your subjects happy." When Yayāti set out for heaven, his subjects wanted to go wherever he went, even to hell, and so the king took all his subjects with him to heaven; he went to Indra's world and sent all his subjects to the world of Viṣṇu. Then the gods honored him, and Indra welcomed him, saying, "Enter my house and enjoy all the heavenly pleasures." But Yayāti went to Viṣṇu's world and was allowed to be Viṣṇu's slave forever.[104]

This complicated myth contains several episodes of the reversal and restoration of the natural order. At first, Yayāti seeks heaven, but he seeks it not in heaven but on earth. This preference of mortals for earthly heavens is not uncommon in folk Hinduism; even in village Buddhism, where the doctrinally sanctioned goal is *nirvāṇa*, "for most Sinhalese Buddhists the most desired reward for meritorious living is that which takes the form of a satisfactory future life on earth. This is more desirable than the prospect of any future existence in heaven."[105] In Purāṇic Hinduism, too, rebirth in heaven supersedes release from rebirth and is in turn superseded by "heaven on earth." This goal is, however, not tolerated by the gods, who regard it as a kind of usurpation (fearing that Yayāti will follow in his father's footsteps, as demons often do). Yayāti's virtue is explicitly described as an obstacle to Yama and Indra, for Yayāti is a kind of shrine on earth, creating heaven not for himself but for everyone else. With Yayāti's heaven on earth, there is no death nor any evil; the order of generations is violated (sons living with great-grandsons), everyone remaining twenty-five years old forever, like the Hindu gods,[106] a world of Peter Pans, which is idyllic but unacceptable, for not only will it deprive Yama of his job, and the gods of breathing room, but it destroys variety, an essential quality of life.

To restore order, the gods resort to three episodes of seduction based on the catalytic figure of the forbidden woman (the second wife, the nymph, or even the first wife). First, Yayāti is seduced by Kāma himself and the nymphs who try to catch the conscience of the king by enacting what is actually happening to him; like Bali, Yayāti has usurped heaven, and the gods have appeared in disguise, dwarf-like, to steal it back from him. Yayāti falls for the ruse; the technicality on which he is disqualified is the one ritual chink in his virtue (failing to wash his

[104] *Padma* 2.64–71; 72–77; 79–83. [105] Obeyesekere, p. 29. [106] *Rām.* 3.4.13–14.

feet after urinating[107]), but the true flaw is lust, which leads to old age, just as the spirit of old age is born from Rati. The second episode of seduction is the meeting with the daughter of Rati (the sister and alter ego of old age), which merely undoes the effect of the first seduction, forcing Yayāti to regain his lost youth and thus to violate the natural order once more; again the generations are wrongly mixed, the father being younger than the son.

This leads to the third seduction, the one at which the previous two have aimed: the nymph leads Yayāti to heaven. This episode contains a number of apparent reversals of earlier premises of this and other myths in the cycle. Unlike the typical shrine myth or the Epic myth of Yayāti, this text states that Indra *wants* Yayāti to come to heaven, for a number of complex reasons. Since Yayāti has the effect of a shrine, only by removing him from earth can Indra stop the general spread of virtue and immortality which pose a far greater problem than that of Yayāti alone. In this, Indra is effecting a kind of exchange. Yayāti must sacrifice the happiness of all his subjects in order that he may remain with his wife, just as he sacrifices the happiness and youth of his son for this same selfish reason. If the gods and death give Yayāti a share (i.e., make him immortal), his subjects will die; this is the decision that the "virtuous" Yayāti makes. Hypocritically, he makes Puru promise to make all his subjects happy, though he knows full well that he has made a bargain designed to ruin their happiness. Like the virtuous demon Vajrāṅga, Yayāti allows his wicked wife to stir him up against the gods in heaven in order that he may avoid the living hell of a marital squabble. This bargain with the gods is greatly limited by two further reversals. Yayāti's decision is rationalized by arguments of karma (and by the familiar justification that various diseases—not death itself, nor Yayāti's selfish choice—will destroy his subjects), but then bhakti intervenes and they all go to heaven after all—to Viṣṇu's heaven, not Indra's or Yayāti's. The bhakti heaven mediates between the opposed heavens of gods and mortals; though Yayāti "falls" as he does in the Epic (he succumbs to Indra's ruse and loses his heaven on earth), he is able to win a far more valuable prize.

The other reversal implicit in Indra's desire to bring Yayāti to heaven is the manner in which this episode follows the general pattern of myths in which Indra tries to bring *Yama* back to work; when Yayāti comes to heaven, Yama will start to function again. Indra seduces Yayāti with the same ruse that he used to seduce Yama on the banks of the Godāvarī: a nymph comes to him and then returns to heaven (just as the nymphs sent to Vṛtra return to Indra's heaven and lure Vṛtra to his doom).[108] Yama in that myth is a devotee of Viṣṇu, as Yayāti is here, and the fight between the servants of Viṣṇu and Indra/Yama takes place here as there. At first this fight is awkwardly placed in the Yayāti myth; the servants of Viṣṇu

[107] See above, chap. III, sec. 2, and cf. the sin of Nala, *MBh.* 3.56.3–5.

[108] See above, chap. V, sec. 4.

abuse the servants of Yama and antagonize him, just as they do in the myths of death and the devotee, but nothing comes of this encounter, for Yama is already angry at the loss of his job. The second encounter is the decisive one. Yayāti's subjects are willing to go to hell (the house of Yama), but through the power of devotion they are all transported to Viṣṇu's heaven instead. Once more, apparently, death is conquered; no one seems to worry that Yama has no job or that Puru has no subjects to rule; the myth has moved into a different dimension, where these questions do not occur.

8. The Tribal Mythology of the Origin of Death

It is not surprising that many of the classical themes of the Sanskrit texts occur in the myths recorded by anthropologists in India, since these tribes have a strong Hindu heritage and have in turn influenced the development of Hindu ideas. The Kharia myth of the bargain with death[109] could almost have come from a Brāhmaṇa text, and other close correspondences have been cited from time to time in this work. The differences, however, are equally significant, and many of the myths seem to be more similar to those of tribes in other countries than they are to the Purāṇic corpus. In the final balance, the Hindu (or at least the Indian) element seems to prevail, and it is therefore useful to consider these myths alongside those of the Sanskrit texts.

The motif of overcrowding is basic here, as it is to the Sanskrit corpus. As Verrier Elwin remarks, "The notion that if nobody died the world would become overcrowded and unable to support the population is widely distributed."[110] A typical example of such a myth appears among the Rengma Nagas:

> [At first there was no day and night, and the dead lived in the same world as the living. God had to divide day and night, so that the dead would work at night, and he moved the dead] to another world, too, for when the dead and the living lived in the same world they were so numerous that there was danger of there not being enough land.[111]

The Hindu belief in the need for differentiation of all kinds, between day and night as well as mortal and immortal, the need for a separate place for each of the two groups, combines here with the motif of overcrowding.

As in the classical corpus, this motif is often embroidered with the secondary theme of corruption: when death becomes necessary, sin enters the world. Among the Bondo this corruption is spontaneous, but it involves food and women, as usual, and a snake, as in Eden: At first there was no death, and not enough room; the gods sent a snake to bite a child, who died; the mother roasted the snake and ate it, and henceforth there was witchcraft.[112] In another Bondo

109 Roy, p. 417. 110 Elwin (1949), pp. 411 and 416; (1943), p. 182.

111 Mills, p. 27; Elwin (1949), p. 411. 112 Elwin (1949), p. 416.

myth the woman is omitted but God personally ensures the destruction of man: At first there was no death, and the earth was overcrowded; Mahaprabhu sent mangoes; men ate them and died.[113] From this text it is not clear whether the eating of the mango is considered a sin (as in Eden) or merely a poisonous weapon, like the snake in the other Bondo myth. The element of corruption is unmistakable, however, in a similar Juang myth in which the gods take an even more active part and provoke a classical Indo-European sin: When the initial absence of death led to overcrowding, Mahapurub tricked a couple into eating their own children, and after that there was death.[114] Yet another variant of this motif seems explicitly to deny the Hindu doctrine of reincarnation: The dead used to be cremated and then to return to earth; there were too many people, and at last Mahapurub cursed mankind so that no one should ever return from the dead.[115]

In the majority of these myths, the gods introduce death upon earth for a good reason, almost always for the benefit of mankind. A few myths of this type, however, offer no clear reason for the gods' decision to make men mortal:

In Koeli-Kacchar lived a Baiga and a Baigin. When Bihi Mata saw that nobody was dying she was troubled; she made from the dirt of her body a Sahis and his wife and sent them to the Baiga, saying, "Make a drum of earth and go and dance in front of these Baiga." The Baiga could not help it, he fell in love with the Sahis woman. Now, before that time, man and woman had never been to one another and that was why there was no death in the world. But when the Baiga met the Sahis woman alone in the forest there was an earthquake. Mother Earth trembled and the Baiga died immediately. From that time there has been death in the world.[116]

The connection between death and sex, the woman sent by the gods to corrupt an unoffending mortal, and the trembling of Earth under the burden of procreation—these motifs link the myth closely with the classical Hindu corpus. Other tribal myths seem also to imply that "death comes into the world by the treachery of the gods"[117]:

[In olden times, milk shrubs used to grow out of a rock.] Out of the rock came a boy and girl. They drank the milk of the shrubs and kept themselves alive. At first this milk was sweet but when Burha Pinnu saw that men would drink the milk and live for ever he made it bitter. . . . They married and from them all human beings have come.[118]

Here the usual premise—that when sexual procreation arises, death becomes necessary—is reversed; only after death is introduced does sexual procreation become possible.

The belief that death arises because of some ill will among the gods toward men is implicit in a Baiga myth:

[113] Elwin (1953), p. 508. [114] Elwin (1949), p. 421. [115] Elwin (1949), p. 416.
[116] Elwin (1949), p. 414; cf. p. 415. [117] Elwin (1943), p. 182. [118] Elwin (1949), p. 288.

Bhagavan grew tired of the Baiga. He wanted other *jīv* [living creatures] in the world. But he could not kill Nanga Baiga. So he made the sensation of itching. . . . One day, when Nanga Baiga picked up a stick to scratch himself, Bhagavan turned it into a cobra. It bit him and he died. We would never have been subjects of death if Bhagavan had not tricked us. . . . [As Nanga Baiga died, he told his sons to boil and eat his flesh.] But Bhagavan, seeing what would happen if they ate their father's flesh, was frightened and came to them disguised as a sadhu. [He told them not to eat the flesh, for he said that that was a great sin.] They were afraid of the sadhu, so they did as he told them [and threw the flesh into the river]. . . . All the rest of Nanga Baiga's magic was lost to us through this Hindu god's deceit. Down the river, three women ate Nanga Baiga's flesh and became witches.[119]

The Hindu elements are acknowledged by the storyteller, who blames it all on "this Hindu god's deceit." The motif of eating the father's flesh to become immortal is the inverse of the Juang myth in which people become mortal by eating the flesh of their children. The connection between sin and death is also reversed. Bhagavan tricks the Baiga into dying by telling them that it would be a sin for them to do that which he knows would give them immortality; in this he behaves precisely like God in the Garden of Eden, a myth that supplies all the essentials of the Baiga myth: food tabu, wicked women, and snakes.

The Hindu belief that death and evil result from the gods' mistakes or weaknesses combines with the motifs of hunger, women, and death in a Gadaba myth that attributes death to the hunger of the gods:

[At first there was no death. The gods could only eat human corpses, and so they were always hungry. God killed a child and made him into bread; he took the form of an old woman and gave the bread to men. They ate it and died.][120]

The gods here behave like Rākṣasas (who eat corpses and are always hungry) and also like the gods of Vedic mythology, who depend on men for their food (the sacrificial offering in those texts being replaced here by the actual physical bodies of the mortal worshippers). The hunger of the gods leads to the hunger (the violating of a food tabu) of the worshippers, who are tricked into committing a grave sin unconsciously; and this sin, as in other tribal myths of death, involves the death of a child, the event that provides the starting point for most Sanskrit myths questioning the justice of death.

The pollution of death is literally transferred in a Gond myth:

[The sixty-four Yoginis who lived in the underworld bathed in the sea once when they were menstruating. The shadow of a hawk fell on their blood and a girl was born. The Yoginis gave her men as her food. But men at this time kept the Water of Immortality in a hollow bamboo and were able to return to life after the girl ate them. When she became hungry again she sent the sixty-four Yoginis to Mahadeo. He stole the Water of Immortality and there was death in the world.][121]

[119] Elwin (1939), pp. 328–329 and 414; cf. Elwin (1949), p. 451; see above, chap. IV, sec. 4.

[120] Elwin (1953, p. 509. [121] Elwin (1949), p. 420.

The sin usually committed by mortals–the sexual procreation symbolized by menstruation–appears here among the demonic Yoginis but ultimately results in the mortality of mankind. The episode of the stealing of the elixir, which is widespread in Indo-European mythology, is here reversed: the elixir is stolen not by men from the gods, as it is usually, but by the gods from men. A closer parallel might perhaps be seen in the myths in which the gods steal the secret of revival from demons, who are here (as so often in Sanskrit mythology) replaced by men, whereas the Yoginis (who are given the traditional dwelling place and diet of demons) are abetted by the gods in their destruction of mankind.

The belief that there must be death in order for Yama to keep his job appears in tribal myths;[122] sometimes this motif is transferred to the god himself, Mahapurub:

In the Middle World no man died, and Mahapurub wondered how he was to get souls for his kingdom. . . . He had a son. He killed him and prepared to carry him out for burial. But when his wife heard of it, she ran weeping to the place and, taking her son from him, sat with the corpse in her lap. [He tricked her into imagining that she had become a witch and was eating the corpse.] She wept bitterly but gave the body to Mahapurub. He buried it, and from that day, death has been in the world.[123]

God needs "souls for his kingdom" so badly that he sacrifices his own son for this purpose, in contrast with Yama of the Sanskrit myth who gives up his kingdom in order to have a son. The elaborate mirage created to make his wife think that she had become a witch is typical of Sanskrit myths of corruption by the gods.

Another classical strain in the tribal mythology of death may be seen in a series of myths that recognize the positive aspects of mortality. At first there was no death, but there was old age; the old men asked Mahapurub for death, and then everyone–even some young people–died.[124] The implication here is that death is a mixed blessing: it is better than old age, but it is not welcome to the young. This concept, supported by hierarchical Hindu social values, also occurs among the Toda:

At first no Toda died. After a time a Piedr man died. [At the funeral, some people wept, but others danced and sang. The goddess Teikirzi, seeing the people weeping] took pity and came to bring the dead man back to life. [But then she saw that some people seemed quite happy, and she decided not to raise the dead man. Then she decreed that at funerals some would weep, while others would be happy.][125]

This ambivalent attitude toward death merges with the more sophisticated belief that death signifies union with God, in a Juang myth:

[At first there was no death. Mahapurub thought, "None died, what shall I do?" There was a little boy whom all loved. Mahapurub had him killed and brought to him, but when

[122] *Ibid.*, p. 509. [123] Elwin (1943), p. 182; cf. (1949), p. 426.

[124] Elwin (1949), p. 426. [125] Rivers, p. 400.

his messenger saw how much everyone mourned for the little boy, he returned the child to earth.] But the boy had been very happy with Mahapurub. He had as much food as he could eat and there were always games to play. He had no desire to stay on earth. [He fasted until he died, and henceforth there was death in the world.][126]

Hunger is, as usual, the weapon that destroys mankind; it appears first in the boy's wish to taste again the food of heaven and then in his fatal fast on earth. Although no reason is given for Mahapurub's initial desire to kill men, he behaves as he does in those tribal myths in which he inflicts death upon men for his own benefit: he murders a beloved child. Yet, perhaps under the influence of the Hindu doctrine of blissful release, God's act is interpreted as one of favor to mankind, since death is viewed as a pleasant life in God's company.

A final "classical" variation in tribal mythology may be seen in those myths in which a general increase in mankind leads to an increase in wicked men, who must be destroyed not only to relieve the earth of an intolerable burden but also to satisfy outraged morality:

Originally all men were immortal, but they increased too much and fought among themselves and were wicked, till one day Khazangpa got angry and said, "Let all the men in the world die." [Two survived and created the human race again.][127]

The precise nature of this wickedness is suggested by a similar Kharia myth:

[Ponomosor, the Supreme Being, created the world and people.] They multiplied and soon there was a scarcity of food. [He gave them more food, but] men annoyed Ponomosor by cutting down fruit-bearing trees and he sent a flood to destroy them. [Again they displeased him and he sent a rain of fire, which only a few survived.][128]

Hunger leads to the violation of a food tabu (the destruction of the magic trees); the flood and the fire of universal destruction are sent in punishment. It is evident even from this selected corpus of texts that the origin of death and the origin of evil are as closely intertwined in Indian tribal mythology as they are in the Sanskrit texts.

126 Elwin (1949), p. 422. 127 Parry, pp. 488ff.; cf. Elwin (1949), pp. 25–26.

128 Roy, pp. 414ff.; cf. Elwin (1949), pp. 24–25, and see above, chap. II, sec. 9.

And the Lord God commanded the man, saying, Of every tree of the garden thou mayest freely eat: But of the tree of the knowledge of good and evil thou shalt not eat of it: for in the day that thou eatest thereof thou shalt surely die. . . . And the serpent said unto the woman, Ye shall not surely die: For God doth know that in the day ye eat thereof, then your eyes shall be opened, and ye shall be as gods, knowing good and evil.
Genesis 2:16–17 and 3:4–5

IX
CROWDS IN HEAVEN

1. The Danger of Crowds in Heaven

Throughout the Vedas, the creation of space and the expansion of form are synonymous with the creation and sustenance of life; an important word for sin, *aṃhas*, has the primary meaning of restriction or compression.[1] General overpopulation is the primary justification for the creation of death (the primary evil) and for the Fall of man, but the crisis caused by an excess of virtuous people—a recurrence of the problem posed by the original Golden Age—may be resolved by the use of corruption rather than death. The gods object to any excess which threatens the balance of the universe. When there is an excess of evil, the more conventional mythology prevails and the gods fight the demons;[2] when there is an excess of virtuous people, however, the gods corrupt the offending demons or mortals.

The image of disproportion when too many people go to heaven is brilliantly expressed in a Tamil verse in which a prince boasts that he will kill so many heroes (who, having died in battle, will go to heaven) that "the back of the sky will be dislocated, and the back of the earth relieved."[3] Many early Sanskrit texts deal with the basic disinclination of the gods to allow crowds in heaven, a manifestation of their jealousy of mortals.[4] In the Upaniṣads, rebirth is offered as a solution to overcrowding: "Do you know how the world beyond is not filled up?" asks the sage,[5] and the cycle of karma is then described. But the doctrine of karma is not accepted as a working assumption by the authors of the Purāṇas—nor, apparently, by the gods. The Brāhmaṇas state that the gods, having conquered heaven, tried

[1] Ogibenin, pp. 137–142. [2] See above, chap. IV, sec. 6. [3] *Kamparāmāyaṇam* 2497.
[4] See above, chap. IV, sec. 8. [5] *Ch. Up.* 5.3.3.

to make it unattainable by men; they drained the sacrificial sap or hid the sacrifice and concealed themselves.[6] In spite of the detrimental effect this must have had on the gods—depriving them as well as us of the elixir—the gods would happily ruin it all rather than share it. Although this is a Vedic text, the gods' opposition to human virtue (their wish that men should not perform the sacrifice) results from the confusion of the gods' need for Soma with their fear that men will use it to become immortal. Numerous texts echo this idea: the gods obtained heaven by sacrifice and then blocked the way so that men would not follow them there.[7] A vivid description of the disdain of the gods appears in another text: "The Ṛbhus won the privilege of drinking Soma among the gods by means of their asceticism. But the gods loathed them because of their human smell."[8] The human smell is as offensive to the gods as is the notorious odor of demons such as Vṛtra and Pūtanā ("the putrid").

Another Brāhmaṇa elaborates on this uneasy symbiosis:

The gods and demons were fighting. The gods created the thunderbolt, which was a man, and they sent it against the demons; it destroyed the demons and came back to the gods. But the gods feared it, and broke it into three pieces, and they saw that the hymns that are divinities were inside this man. They said, "After he has lived virtuously on this earth, he will follow us by means of sacrifice and well-performed asceticism. Therefore, let us act so that he does not follow us: let us put evil in him." They put evil in him—sleep, exhaustion, anger, hunger, love of dice, desire for women. Then the gods said, "These hymns, divinities, that are in the man—with them we will conquer the demons." They did so, and so they drove the demons out of this world and heaven, and took their cattle. Then the gods were supreme.[9]

Men here are pawns necessary to the gods, not only to give them sacrifice, but to be used as weapons in the battle against the demons; and they must be destroyed to serve this latter purpose, to be the thunderbolt, just as the noble sage Dadhīca had to be murdered so that his bones could make the thunderbolt for Indra to kill Vṛtra.[10] The image of the pawn might suggest the Manichean battlefield, but the myth does not justify this inference, for it is the gods, not the demons, who make men evil in order to win the battle, to keep men as well as demons out of power. Indeed, Fr. Heras, S.J., discusses this myth in a chapter entitled "The intervention of the demons in the original fall of man" and remarks, "These *devas* [gods who placed evil in man] had evidently been expelled from heaven, for they realized that man living well on earth would succeed to them in heaven. They were

[6] *Śata.* 1.6.2.1–4; cf. 3.1.4.3, 3.2.2.2, 11.28.

[7] *Tait. Saṃ.* 6.5.3; cf. *Śata.* 4.3.1.4–20; *Tait. Saṃ.* 6.3.4.7; *Ait. Br.* 2.1.

[8] *Ait. Br.* 3.30. See above, chap. V, sec. 3. [9] *Jai. Br.* 1.98–99.

[10] *RV* 1.84.13–15; *Bṛhaddevatā* 3.22–24; *MBh.* 3.100–101; 12.329; *Bhāgavata* 6.10; *Liṅga* 1.35–36; cf. O'Flaherty (1975), pp. 58–59.

therefore *asuras*."[11] They certainly behave like demons, but that is not uncommon; yet they do not fear, as Fr. Heras suggests, that men will replace them in heaven; the gods are still in heaven, always in heaven, but they do not want to share it. Therefore they corrupt mankind, destroying their human weapon after it has served its purpose, just as they drain the sacrificial sap after it has brought them to heaven.

Even in the Upaniṣads there is evidence that the gods wish to keep heaven an exclusive club; just as they wish to keep men as "beasts" and thus conceal true knowledge from them, so too it is said that "god causes those whom he wishes to lead downwards from these worlds to perform bad actions; those whom he wishes to lead upwards he causes to perform good actions."[12] This accounts for virtue as well as sin, but the later texts emphasize the sin and fear the virtue:

Formerly, all creatures were virtuous, and by themselves they obtained divinity. Therefore the gods became worried, and so Brahmā created women in order to delude men. Then women, who had been virtuous, became wicked witches, and Brahmā filled them with wanton desires, which they in turn inspired in men. He created anger, and henceforth all creatures were born in the power of desire and anger.[13]

Here the usual weapon, Eve, suffices to keep man in his place; elsewhere, Viṣṇu uses heresy to thin out the ranks of heaven:

Formerly, the inhabitants of the earth all worshipped Viṣṇu and reached heaven, filling the place of Release. The gods said, "How will creation take place, and who will live in hell?" Viṣṇu assured them that in the Kali Age he would create a great delusion, causing Śiva to teach the Naya Siddhānta and Pāśupata doctrines in order to delude men and place them outside the path of the Vedas.[14]

Just as the Kali Age itself and the subsequent universal destruction are necessary to bring death to the entire world so that "creation will take place," so the heresies taught by Viṣṇu or Śiva at this time are necessary to prevent the dead from swamping heaven.

The heresies of the Kali Age appear in another myth, which begins with a variant of the usual problem of crowds in heaven:

King Pratardana, an ardent worshipper of Śiva, obtained a boon from Brahmā enabling him to rule a kingdom in which there was not a single heretic or sceptic or Buddhist. Everyone worshipped Viṣṇu and Śiva and all the gods, following the way of dharma, and the gods always received the supreme oblation. After a long time, all the most evil demons and barbarians, having worn out their bad karma, went to heaven, for those whose descendants followed the true path of the Vedas were released from hell and went to

[11] Heras, p. 237. [12] *Kau. Up.* 3.9; cf. above, chap. VI, sec. 8.

[13] *MBh.* 13.40.5–12. [14] *Varāha* 70.29–42.

Amarāvatī, city of the gods. How could the ancestors of those who worshipped Viṣṇu and Śiva dwell in hell, and what could the servants of Yama do in that kingdom? What a miracle this was: everyone went to heaven, Yama had no business, and all the gods were worshipped everywhere. Yama became worried and said, "The evil in hell are released by the religious acts and offerings of their sons," and Indra said, "What is there to distinguish us from lowly creatures? Bṛhaspati, formerly you taught the Materialist and Buddhist doctrines, by which the demons were made to stray from the Vedic path. Do this now." But Bṛhaspati replied, "There is not a single Materialist, Buddhist, Jain, Greek, nor even a Kāpālika in his kingdom. How then can I do this?" Finally, Bṛhaspati suggested that one of the gods appear as a Vaiṣṇava and destroy Śiva worship in the kingdom, so that all the ancestors of Pratardana's subjects would return to a cruel hell. The gods said to one another, "This is not a pretty task," and no one agreed to do it. Indra then commanded a centaur [kinnara, *a horse-headed man or human-headed horse*] *to go in disguise as a Vaiṣṇava to destroy the worship of Śiva. He told the people in the kingdom that Śiva lived in a burning ground, naked, adorned with snakes, carrying the head of Brahmā. Though the king defended Śiva, many people were persuaded by the centaur; the spirit of Kali entered the Brahmins, and they began to argue. Atheism grew strong. Pratardana worried, "The evil one is injuring the lord Śiva, and according to the lawbooks I should kill him. But then people will wrongly call me a Brahmin-killer." At this time, the ancestors of those who reviled Śiva all fell from heaven, their good karma burnt to ashes and dissipated like Ganges water in wine. The hells became full again. Then Viṣṇu, who was asleep, was inundated by a wave of blood and awakened by the screams of Lakṣmī when she saw this horrifying sight. She said to him, "Mountains are falling, the seas are lifted by winds, the sun no longer shines, and the earth is about to be destroyed. You must do something." They went to Mount Kailāsa with the gods, who apologized to Śiva for their act of deception, saying that they had done it in order to protect creation. At that moment, Pratardana decapitated the centaur, his followers, and all their cattle and horses. Śiva then assuaged Pratardana's anger and joined the horses' heads to the men's bodies and the reverse, giving horses' heads to those who had spoken against Śiva and horses' bodies to those who had acted against him.*

Then Brahmā said, "In the Kali Age, when the earth is full of barbarians and men have falled from good conduct, a very evil Brahmin living in the South will beget in a widow a son named Madhu. As the Kali Age progresses, Madhu will hate Śiva more and more, and he will preach a false doctrine of delusion. His followers will be even worse than Buddhists, Jains, or Kāpālikas, and even the sight of them will be polluting." The gods departed, and Pratardana, having made his kingdom free of heretics, died and found release. But in the Kali Age there will be many pupils of Madhu, and Madhu will be a Materialist in disguise.[15]

The initial problem of a crowd of *evil* people in heaven is easily solved, only to

[15] *Saura* 38.20–96; 39.1–80; 40.61.

give rise to another extreme, the overcrowding of hell, which brings about natural catastrophes portending the end of the universe. The true danger of Pratardana's virtue is not the one first stated by the gods but one which they do mention in passing: without the evil-doers in hell, there is nothing to distinguish the gods from the nongods. Virtue on earth leads to salvation for the evil in hell, since the virtuous sons redeem their (evil) fathers by means of a form of merit transfer. (Pratardana is noted for precisely this kind of redemption, for he is one of the four grandsons whose good karma transferred to Yayāti, the enemy of Indra, sends him back up to heaven. The enmity between Indra and Pratardana may be traced back to the Upaniṣads, where Pratardana, son of Divodāsa, has such martial virtue that he is able to go to Indra's heaven, where he haughtily refuses a boon from Indra and hears Indra boast of all his unpunished sins.[16]) The gods openly admit the selfishness of their intention and hesitate to carry it out, but they later justify themselves to Śiva by saying that they produced their deception "in order to protect creation." Yet another justification for the gods' behavior is implicit in their assertion that they must destroy their traditional enemies, the demons, by corrupting their descendants in Pratardana's kingdom; and they ask Bṛhaspati to delude the demons as he did before. In fact, however, it is men who are deluded, not demons, and it is for this that the gods apologize to Śiva. As in the myth of the Buddha avatar, heresy comes to men in the Kali Age as an accidental by-product of the gods' plot to subvert the demons; the heresy is even taken as an opportunity for a thinly veiled attack on the philosopher Madhva (or Madhu), and Pratardana (as well as being the grandson of Yayāti) is the son of the archetypal human-demon pawn, Divodāsa.[17]

Thus the Pratardana myth explains the otherwise embarrassing fact that people in the Kali Age hate Śiva; their hatred, like Dakṣa's,[18] is sought in earlier obscure causes and curses. The Kali Age almost begins during Pratardana's reign ("Kali" enters the Brahmins, as he does when his time has come, though here the term may only indicate the spirit of quarrel) but is then postponed, as often happens; and the true heretic of the Kali Age is an intellectual heir, if not necessarily a direct descendant, of the reviling centaur. The physical duality of this creature is utilized to resolve a moral ambivalence. Pratardana is caught between two dharmas, the wish to combat heresy and the fear of Brahminicide; finally, he kills the Brahmin heretic, but is saved by Śiva, who restores the animal heads of the heretics, as he restores other decapitated enemies (Brahmā, Dakṣa, Gaṇeśa). Indra gives a horse-head to Dadhyañc (Dadhīca) in similar circumstances. Dadhyañc gives the Soma to the Aśvins (horse-headed figures like the heretic centaur), who lend him a horse-head for Indra to decapitate and who

[16] See above, chap. VIII, sec. 7, and *Kau. Up.* 3.1.

[17] See above, chap. VII, sec. 7 and sec. 5.

[18] See below, chap. X, sec. 1.

finally restore his own head;[19] Dadhyañc, like Pratardana, threatens Indra and is attacked but ultimately saved. The image of the centaur is then used to express another duality, sacrilegious words (the horse-heads) and sacrilegious acts (the horse-bodies); together, they assure a balance between the populations of earth and heaven.

2. The Destruction of Shrines on Earth

The problems caused by the absence of death or the unemployment of Yama are even more acute when shrines become the gates to heaven. When pilgrimage to shrines (*tīrthas*) came to replace asceticism as a means of achieving religious power, the gods who had previously destroyed asceticism or corrupted virtuous Vedic kings began to destroy the shrines: first Benares and Avantī, and then Dvārakā and Somanātha.[20] But the gods themselves made use of certain shrines. Indra, who at first performed horse sacrifices and Soma sacrifices to expiate his sins, then performed asceticism and finally went on pilgrimages on earth. This led to a rephrasing of the old quandary: the gods now need shrines for their own purposes (as they needed Soma), but they fear that mortals may use them to challenge the gods.

At this stage, the Purāṇas begin to narrate myths about the overcrowding of heaven in order to demonstrate the miraculous efficacy of some local shrine:

The mere sight of Skanda at the shrine of Kumāra was sufficient for anyone to reach the world of heaven, no matter how sinful he might be; women, Śūdras, dog-cookers, all went to heaven. Learning of this, Yama went to Śiva and complained, "Each of the gods has his own job to do; but now that even the most evil are transported to heaven by a sight of your son, leaving my kingdom of hell, what am I to do?" Śiva replied, "The evil within these people is dispelled by the sight of the shrine. Those women and Śūdras and dog-cookers whose acts are due to the force of karma from their previous lives have become purified even in evil actions." Śiva then taught the doctrine of the unity of all the gods, and Yama departed.[21]

This text stretches the doctrines of pantheism and bhakti to overrule svadharma. To the complaint that heaven is full of evil people, Śiva simply replies that they are no longer evil, ignoring the other half of the complaint, that heaven is full.

In other texts, the problem posed by Skanda's grace is overcome by the creation of Gaṇeśa, the second son of Śiva, who is usually worshipped as the remover rather than the inciter of obstacles: "Heaven became overcrowded by

[19] *RV* 1.117.22; *Śata.* 14.1.1.18–24; *Jai. Br.* 3.64; *Bhāgavata* 6.9–11; *Bṛhaddevatā* 3.15–25; O'Flaherty (1975), pp. 56–57. [20] See above, chap. VII, sec. 5.

[21] *Skanda* 1.1.31.1–78.

pilgrims. So Parvati made Ganesha, who created obstacles to men going to heaven by diverting their longing for pilgrimage to desire for the acquisition of wealth."[22] An expanded version of this myth attributes the original problem to the kindness of Śiva:

During the period right before the Kali Age, women, barbarians, Śūdras, and other sinners entered heaven by visiting the shrine of Somanātha [Śiva lord of Soma]. Sacrifices, asceticism, donations to Brahmins, and all the other prescribed rites ceased, and heaven became crowded with men, old and young, those skilled in the Vedas and those ignorant of them. Sacrifice was destroyed, earth became empty, and heaven was so overfull that people had to stand holding their arms up. Then Indra and the gods, distressed at being overcome by men, sought refuge with Śiva, saying, "Because of your favor, heaven is pervaded by men. Give us a place to live. Yama, King of Dharma, is struck dumb when he contemplates the record of their evil deeds and the seven hells, which are empty." Śiva could do nothing, as it was he who had granted entrance into heaven, but Pārvatī created Gaṇeśa from the dirt on her own body and said to the gods, "For your sake I have created this being to make obstacles to men so that they will be filled with great delusion, their wits struck down by desire, and they will not visit Somanātha but will go to hell." The gods were delighted at this, relieved of their fear of mankind.[23]

To justify the behavior of the gods, this text, like the story of the shrine of Kumāra, argues that the worshippers were not excessively virtuous but excessively sinful, undeserving people who took advantage of the automatic release granted by the shrine and neglected Vedic rites. In challenging the power of God's grace to save unrepentant sinners like Devarājā, the myth assumes a moral veneer similar to that of the Tamil texts.[24] But the jealousy and ill will of the old, pre-bhakti gods reemerges in the statement that the gods were relieved from all fear of mankind.

The role of Gaṇeśa in this myth is a reversal of his normal role as the remover of obstacles. Another Purāṇa comments on his ambivalence in this respect:

Bṛhaspati said to Śiva, "Those who wish to harm the gods propitiate you for the accomplishment of their desires, in order to remove obstacles. Create some good obstacles for those who wish to harm the gods; this is our wish." Then Śiva created Gaṇeśa and said to him, "You have become incarnate in order to destroy demons and to help the gods and Brahmins; create obstacles against dharma in the path to heaven for those who offer sacrifice without giving a payment to the priest." And so Gaṇeśa created obstacles to the dharma of demons.[25]

Śiva's notorious affection for demons is here openly held against him; to make up

[22] Thomas (1958), p. 25. [23] *Skanda* 7.1.38.1–34.

[24] See above, chap. VIII, sec. 6. [25] *Liṅga* 1.105.5–29.

for this—for his own "removal of obstacles" from the path of sinners—he creates Gaṇeśa to produce obstacles for the usual enemies of the gods and Brahmins, virtuous demons and tightfisted sacrificers. In this way, Gaṇeśa opposes dharma and keeps people out of heaven; originally he was meant to act only against demons, but, as usual, his hegemony is quickly extended to mortal enemies of the priests.

Gaṇeśa appears as the obstacle of obstacles in a Tamil myth:

A king was performing a sacrifice to deprive Indra of his throne. Indra sent Vighna ("obstacle") to put obstacles in the path of the king, but when Vighna ruined all *sacrifices, the sages sought the help of Śiva, who sent Gaṇeśa to earth to help them. Gaṇeśa fought against Vighna, who worshipped Gaṇeśa and was made one of his attendants, with orders to trouble all those who failed to worship Gaṇeśa Lord of Obstacles.*[26]

The myth turns on the pun implicit in Gaṇeśa's title, Lord of Obstacles, which can indicate either that Gaṇeśa creates obstacles or that he overcomes them. Obstacle becomes incarnate in Vighna, the servant of Indra, and so the enemy of Vighna must be the enemy of Indra; thus Gaṇeśa might appear at first to be in favor of the worshipper who challenges the gods as the king does here. But when Vighna destroys not only the threatening individual mortal but sacrifice in general, the post-Vedic assumptions with which the myth begins (gods against a mortal) are replaced by Vedic assumptions (gods, deprived of sacrifice by a demon, wish to help virtuous mortals), and Gaṇeśa is seen to be on the side of the gods after all—as well as on the side of mortals, as is possible in the bhakti alignment. Vighna is identified with Śiva as Kāla in a Sanskrit variant of this myth,[27] but even in the Tamil text Gaṇeśa and Vighna-Kāla are basically reconciled; they help those who worship the gods and only oppose sinners, a moral distinction which resolves so many of these conflicts.

The holiness of Assam is extolled in a variant of the myth of overcrowding which accounts for the gods' inadvertent creation of a heresy:

The people who worshipped in Assam [Kāmarūpa] obtained Release or became servants of Śiva, and Yama could not impede them or lead them to his dwelling place. The messengers of Yama became frightened, and Yama said to Brahmā, "I have no function in Assam. Restore the usual rules." Viṣṇu said, "Men in Assam are becoming gods or immortals, since Yama has no power, and when Yama is cast off, there are no moral bounds." Śiva took his troops to Assam and began to drive everyone away, but the sage Vasiṣṭha became angry when he was harassed, and he cursed the Goddess to be worshipped in the left-hand manner. Then he said, "Since these stupid troops wander like barbarians, let them be barbarians dwelling in Assam, and since Śiva tried to expel me, an ascetic Brahmin, as if

[26] *Vināyakapurāṇam* 71.18–118. [27] *Skanda*, cited in Daniélou, p. 294.

I were a barbarian beyond the pale of the Vedas, let Śiva be dear to barbarians, and let him wear bones and ashes." And so it happened, and in a moment Assam was under the sway of Yama. Later, when Viṣṇu came there, the shrine was freed from the curse, but then, so that men and gods would not be able to worship there, Brahmā devised a means to hide the shrine. He flooded all the shrines in Assam, and by hiding them in this way he fulfilled the curse of Vasiṣṭha.[28]

The gods' desire for the old-fashioned, orthodox religion is manifest in their statement that in the absence of Yama the usual rules and moral bounds do not function. Śiva does not intend to corrupt the worshippers—he intends merely to keep them from the shrine and from heaven—but his action ultimately has this effect and is performed in response to the threat that usually causes the gods to corrupt mankind (the insufficiency of sinners for Yama to rule over). Later, when Brahmā destroys the shrines, this too is hastily attributed to Vasiṣṭha's curse rather than to the malice of the gods. The pattern of the myth thus contradicts the professed blameless intentions of the gods and reveals their baser motives. Just as the gods are often inadvertently weakened by the corruption of their sacrificers in the older texts, so Śiva is tarred by the brush of heresy when he destroys the sanctity of the shrine. Thus the gods' inept reaction to the sudden increase in virtuous mortals results in the creation of evil on earth, evil that rebounds against the gods as well as against mortals.

In another variant of this theme, the gods take similar measures to destroy a holy place, but this time in vain:

*When Śiva had established the Sthāṇu-*liṅga *beside a lake, heaven was soon filled with men, because one gains heaven merely by looking at that liṅga. Then all the gods sought refuge with Brahmā, saying, "Protect us, for we are in danger from men." Brahmā said, "Let the lake be filled with dust immediately," and Indra caused dust to rain for seven days, filling the lake. But when Śiva saw this rain of dust, he held the liṅga and the sacred fig tree on the bank in his hand, and this liṅga and fig tree grant the wishes of anyone who performs the ritual here. When the sages saw the lake full of dust, they smeared their bodies with the dust and their sins were shaken off with the dust, and they were honored with the gods and reached the abode of Brahmā.*[29]

The preliminary conflict between too virtuous mortals and gods in an overcrowded heaven is soon superseded by a conflict between the gods of the old religion (led by Indra) and the devotional Śiva, who proves ultimately victorious, as he is victorious over Yama in similar circumstances. The original problem is simply exacerbated by the gods' attack, for now, in addition to the shrine, the fig tree and the dust meant to destroy the shrine send people to heaven.

[28] Hazra (1963), p. 232; *Kālikā* 84.1–36. [29] *Vāmana, S.* 24.6–17.

In a South Indian variant of this myth, Indra covers a shrine with dust in order to prevent people from reaching heaven while endowed with bodies; because of this, Vṛtra takes Indra's throne from him, Indra kills Vṛtra, and Indra is forced to remove the dust from the shrine so that he can expiate his own sin in it—incidentally restoring it to mankind as well.[30] The demonic behavior of the gods in these myths is emphasized by a tradition that categorizes shrines and calls certain ones demonic (*āsura*) because they were once covered up by demons such as Vṛtra, Yama, Namuci, Andhaka, and Maya.[31] Not only does this description fit the behavior of the gods, but the one god most frequently associated with this crime, Yama, is actually listed among the demons.

In keeping with the usual sectarian biases of this motif, the Vaiṣṇava Pāñcarātras have their own version:

> The Pāñcarātra was first in the Kṛta age proclaimed by god Brahmán [Brahmā] to the sages of sharpened vows, who taught it to their disciples. All people followed the Pāñcarātra and were liberated or went to heaven; hell became naught and a great decrease of creation took place. [Brahmā complained to Viṣṇu,] "All men, being full of faith and masters of their senses, sacrifice as prescribed in the Great Secret; and so they go to the place of Viṣṇu from which there is no return. There is (now) no heaven and no hell, neither birth nor death." This, however, was against the plan of the Lord, and so He started, with the help of Brahmán, Kapila, and Śiva, five more systems (Yoga, Sāṅkhya, Bauddha, Jaina and Śaiva), conflicting with each other and the Pāñcarātra, for the bewilderment of men.[32]

This text is unique in attributing the teaching of the Buddhist and Jain heresies to the threat of a general excess of virtuous mortals (rather than particular mortals or demons). The original problem of the loss of the Golden (Kṛta) Age is here combined with the multiform (an overcrowded heaven) by the simple expedient of setting the origin of the Pāñcarātra school in the Golden Age.

In spite of their obvious axes to grind, these myths demonstrate an underlying assumption that it is not good for everyone to go to heaven. A peculiar example of this line of thought may be seen in the episode in which the mountain Himālaya, personified as a king, becomes so devoted to Śiva that he is about to leave earth and go to heaven. This would deprive the earth of all the valuable gems, minerals, and magic herbs of which Himālaya is the prime source, and to prevent this Śiva himself comes to Himālaya disguised as a Vaiṣṇava Brahmin and reviles himself just enough to make Himālaya lose his pure devotion and remain on earth,[33] where he belongs.

[30] *Tiruvārūrppurāṇam* 13.1–53; see above chap. VI, sec. 3.

[31] *Brahma* 70.25 and 70.35–36.

[32] Schrader, p. 83, citing the *Padma Tantra*, part I, chap. 85, and *Viṣṇutilaka*, 11.146ff.

[33] *Śiva* 2.3.31.1–52; 2.3.32.1–65.

3. The Earth Overburdened by Sinners

The gods are also endangered by any excess of wickedness among mortals. Here the motif of overcrowding combines with the rarer motif of the scourge sent to punish or destroy the wicked on earth in a series of myths in which the Earth, overburdened by wicked demons, begins to sink into the cosmic floods, from which Viṣṇu rescues her:

Formerly, the demons were full of anger and greed, intoxicated with their strength, and they increased so that the gods could not bear them and could find no refuge. The gods saw that the Earth was oppressed and overcrowded by the terrible demons, and that she was sinking. In fear they said to Brahmā, "How can we bear this oppression from the demons? Hiraṇyākṣa has seized the earth and we cannot enter his water fortress [beneath the ocean, where he hid the earth]." Brahmā said, "The sage Agastya will drink the water." The gods begged Agastya to protect them, and Agastya drank the ocean in an instant. Then Viṣṇu became incarnate as the boar, and he entered the earth and the demon abode below, and he conquered all the demons there.[34]

In the earlier layers of the mythology as it appears in the Brāhmaṇas, the earth simply sinks into the cosmic waters in the course of time, and it (or she) is rescued by a fish, a tortoise, or a boar. Later, these three animals become the first three avatars of Viṣṇu, and the boar is made to battle demons as well as to rescue the earth. The amoral motif of the earth sinking into the waters is then combined with the idea that a demon has carried her away to the demonic subterranean (or subaquatic) hell, and from here it is merely one additional step to say that she sinks into the waters because of the weight of the demons upon her.

Viṣṇu rescues the overburdened earth in another avatar as well, that of Kṛṣṇa. This story first appears in the *Mahābhārata*:

In the Golden Age, the entire earth was filled with many creatures. In this flourishing world of men, the demons were born. For the demons had often been defeated in battle by the gods, and having fallen from their superior position, they took birth here on earth. Wanting to be gods on earth, the proud demons were born from men and from all creatures that live on the earth. And when they were born and went on being born, the wide earth could no longer support them. When Earth was thus oppressed by the great demons, she came to Brahmā for help. Brahmā dismissed her and told the gods to be born on earth, to purify the earth and throw off her burden. And so the gods descended from heaven to earth to destroy the enemies of the gods and for the welfare of all the worlds. They killed demons and Rākṣasas in great numbers.[35]

As usual, it all begins as the gods' fault: they rid themselves of demons, as they rid themselves of sin, by throwing their garbage down to earth. Demons are often

[34] *MBh*. 12.202.7–33. [35] *MBh*. 1.58.1–52; 1.59.1–9.

said to live on earth because the gods stole heaven from them; and when the demons strike back, the gods in their turn are thrown out of heaven and made to wander on the surface of the earth like men.[36] Thus earth, rather than heaven or hell, becomes the cosmic battlefield from time to time. This action makes it possible for the gods to equate their two groups of enemies with each other, for demons are born as men; if men are evil, it is because they are demons driven out of heaven. The sign that distinguishes these "demon men" from mere men is that the former wish to be gods on earth—the intolerable sin of ambition, the fatal flaw of many mortals.

In one variant of this myth, when the demons fall to earth they wish not to become gods on earth but simply to reach heaven again; to prevent this, Kṛṣṇa becomes incarnate:

The gods sent Nārada to Viṣṇu to say, "The demons that you killed in battle have gone to earth in Mathurā. Taking human form, they oppress men on earth. A demon fallen from heaven goes to earth; but one who has a man's body and is killed on earth has a hard time reaching heaven under your careful scrutiny."[37]

By driving the demons from heaven, the gods have brought injury upon mankind; nevertheless, by sending Kṛṣṇa to earth they intend to undo this harm, to kill demons who are not merely the enemies of the gods but, as in Vedic times, the oppressors of men as well.

The battle between demon-men and god-men which results from this double descent is the *Mahābhārata* war, in which Kṛṣṇa is said to have become incarnate "to establish dharma and to destroy demons."[38] In particular, Kṛṣṇa subdues "demons dwelling in human bodies,"[39] a statement which is used to justify the genocide that Kṛṣṇa perpetrates. Sometimes it is not the careless wrath of the gods in general that leads to this slaughter of men, but the sin of one god—Indra, as usual:

When Indra violated Ahalyā, he lost his beauty and power. The powerful demons saw that Indra had lost his power and tried to conquer him, and they were born as kings on earth. The Earth, afflicted by their weight, complained to the gods: "Demons that you have killed have been born in the world of men, and so I am sinking downwards." The gods descended from heaven to earth, to help creatures and to alleviate the burden of Earth.[40]

Indra's loss of power prompts the demons to attack the gods, apparently unsuccessfully; but the demons then try to conquer the gods by becoming men, for the Earth says that the demons were killed by the gods and then were reborn as

[36] *Skanda* 3.1.6.8–42. [37] *Hari.* 44.10 and 44.75–79. [38] See above, chap. VII, sec. 6.
[39] *Vāyu* 2.36.96–103; *Hari.* 31.143–148; *Brahmāṇḍa* 2.3.74.97–103. [40] *Mārk.* 5.14–26.

men. Any or all of the flaws of the gods—weakness, success, or indiscriminate killing—may here be held accountable for the birth of the human demons.

Some Purāṇas distinguish between demonic and human enemies: "The earth was oppressed by millions of armies of demons and proud and deceitful kings"; the overburdened earth seeks refuge with Viṣṇu, who agrees to become incarnate as Kṛṣṇa "to lift up the burden of the earth,"[41] killing both demons and wicked mortals. Other Purāṇas describe the wickedness of Kaṃsa, Kṛṣṇa's archenemy, who is elsewhere said to be a reincarnated demon[42] and is identified with demons.

When Kaṃsa was flourishing in his wickedness, the earth was oppressed by her excessive burden, and she went to heaven and said to the gods, "Numerous armies of proud demons are upon me, and I am tortured by the weight of them and cannot support myself. Help me so that I do not fall down into hell." Brahmā asked Kṛṣṇa's help in removing the oppression caused by the numerous demons. Viṣṇu raised up the Earth, established dharma, and banished evil.[43]

The gods have a ready answer for all eventualities: When the earth is overburdened by human virtue, the gods introduce corruption; when it is overburdened by demonic evil, they remove corruption. Unfortunately, it is not always easy to distinguish mortals from demons, or virtue from evil.

4. The Destruction of the Human Race and the Shrine of Dvārakā

In the *Mahābhārata* and many Purāṇas, the demonic nature of Kṛṣṇa's enemies is quickly forgotten, and what is described is a massacre of human beings. The first hint of this shift of target comes in texts which say that the intention is, as usual, to destroy demons—but that to do this Kṛṣṇa became incarnate in a particular human family, that of the Yadus, a family descended from Yayāti and hence already sullied by an ancestor noted for his attempt to usurp the prerogatives of the gods. What Kṛṣṇa then accomplishes is the extermination of not only the demonic enemies of the Yadus (the wicked Kaṃsa and his ilk) but the Yadus themselves—Kṛṣṇa's own family, the good guys—and the destruction of their holy city, Dvārakā (also known as Dvāravatī). The war has been described as a great potlatch,[44] in which both sides destroy themselves, good and evil alike. By provoking the final drunken debacle, Kṛṣṇa decimates the population and thus reduces the burden of the earth, as god does at doomsday. Zaehner remarks on this holocaust: "There must be war if 'justice' is to be preserved. Strife and war are quite as much part of the true earthly equilibrium and 'justice' as are tranquility and peace. The divine 'justice' in this case reached what must have

[41] *Bhāgavata* 10.1.17–22 and 11.4.22.

[42] *Bhāgavata* 10.1–4; *Hari.* 47–48; O'Flaherty (1975), pp. 206–213.

[43] *Viṣṇu* 5.1.12–60; *Devībhāgavata* 10.5.11–12; *Padma* 6.272.12–25.

[44] Mauss, p. 52.

been an all-time record in terms of 'kill-count'–1,660,020,000 dead, as against 24,165 survivors."[45] The great Armageddon of the *Mahābhārata* begins on the battlefield of Kurukṣetra, one of the holiest places in India, and ends in the dangerously holy shrine of Dvārakā. That Kurukṣetra itself is a battlefield on which men die as part of a sacrifice performed by the gods–a truly human sacrifice–is a concept that may be traced back to the Brāhmaṇas, where the gods perform their sacrifice on Kurukṣetra (a sacrifice that excludes the Aśvins, divine benefactors of mankind).[46] The *Mahābhārata* itself tells a story of the sanctity of Kurukṣetra, which places the Epic battle firmly in the context of the battle between gods and men:

Kuru, a great sage, ploughed the fields of Kuru until Indra came from heaven and asked what he wanted; Kuru replied that he wanted all men who died there to go to heaven. The gods feared that if men dying there gained heaven without sacrifice, the gods would have no share; Indra then offered a more limited boon to Kuru: men who fasted to death there, or who died in battle there, would go to heaven, and Kuru agreed to this.[47]

The shrine is limited in such a way that only a bloody battle will allow the widespread migration so feared by the gods; and when the gods themselves become incarnate as the heroes doomed to die on Kurukṣetra, they preempt many of the free tickets to heaven, simultaneously assuring their own return aloft and the reduction of the number of true mortals who will be able to ascend in this way.

But Dvārakā is the place of the final holocaust and the place where the gods most clearly destroy only the virtuous among mankind, not their theoretically demonic enemies. At first it is simply stated that Kṛṣṇa will cause Dvārakā to fall into the ocean,[48] a classical doomsday image. The one text which does *not* describe the destruction of Dvārakā by the ocean provides instead a reversal, an account of Dvārakā's creation that could have justified its destruction by water. Kṛṣṇa, choosing the site for the city of Dvārakā to be built, asked the ocean to withdraw from the shore for twelve leagues to give space for the city; the ocean complied, and Viśvakarman built the city there, making it like Indra's city.[49] If the sea has yielded the land, against nature, it would be fair for it to reclaim it in the end; and the city "like Indra's city" is reminiscent of the competitive threat of cities like Avantī (which is flooded, like Dvārakā[50]). This aspect of the city's link with the ocean is not further developed here, but the *Mahābhārata* offers another reason for the destruction of the city:

A group of Yadu boys, driven by fate, had once mocked three sages: the boys dressed Sāmba, the son of Kṛṣṇa, as a pregnant woman and asked the sages to bless her child;

[45] Zaehner (1974), p. 90; (1970), p. 183. [46] *Śata*. 4.1.5.13, 14.1.1.2. [47] *MBh*. 9.52.4–21.
[48] *MBh*. 3.12.31. [49] *Hari*. 86.35–53. [50] See above, chap. VII, sec. 5.

seeing the trick, the sages cursed Sāmba to give birth to an iron bolt that would someday exterminate the entire race of Yadus. Sāmba brought forth an iron bolt, which was pulverized and thrown into the sea. . . . Years later, when evil dreams and portents were seen in the city, and people began to show disregard for Brahmins, Kṛṣṇa realized that the time had come for the fulfilment of the curse which Gāndhārī (mother of the Kurus slain by Kṛṣṇa) had spoken in grief. He told the inhabitants of Dvārakā to go on a pilgrimage to the sea, to Prabhāsa. The Yadus and their families set out, but at Prabhāsa they got drunk and began to fight, for they were perverted by time (or doomsday, kāla). *Kṛṣṇa himself, seeing his son Pradyumma killed, took up a handful of grass, transformed it into a bolt of iron like a thunderbolt, and killed all before him. Son killed father and father killed son; madly they fell like moths flying into a flame. Seeing that Sāmba was among the fallen, Kṛṣṇa became angry and killed the rest.*

When Kṛṣṇa himself was dying, wounded by a hunter named Jarā (old age), he said to Dāruka, his charioteer, "You must protect the women, so that the barbarians do not harm them." Dāruka went to Dvārakā and spoke to Arjuna and to Kṛṣṇa's father, warning them of the imminent destruction of the city. Arjuna took the women and children out of Dvārakā, to Indraprastha. Then Dvārakā was flooded, but when the evil barbarians saw the women being led away by Arjuna, their wits were overcome by greed and lust, and they attacked them and carried off the women. But Arjuna took the remainder of the family, the old men, children, and women who had survived the general slaughter, to live in Indraprastha, in Kurukṣetra, and there he installed as king the Yadu Vajra, grandson of Kṛṣṇa.

Arjuna was deeply upset when he learned that the city had been destroyed, but the sage Vyāsa reminded him that the race of Yadus had been cursed by Brahmins, and that he should not sorrow, since it was fated to happen. "Even though Kṛṣṇa could have averted the disaster," he said, "he overlooked it because it was fated to be. Since Kṛṣṇa can master the entire triple world, surely he can overcome the curse of mortals. The women of the city had been cursed by an angry sage, and so the power of the city was destroyed. Having removed the burden of the earth, releasing the world, Kṛṣṇa went to his own highest place."[51]

The portents that appear in the city and the Brahmins' curse of "women" are strongly reminiscent of the destruction of other cities—the Triple City and Divodāsa's Benares. (In one text, this episode follows the myth in which Benares is destroyed by the king of Dvārakā.[52]) Kṛṣṇa is responsible for the Yadus' demise in numerous ways. He massacres the Kurus, sons of Gāndhārī, who then curses Kṛṣṇa to see his own sons slain and his women carried off;[53] he begets the boys who enrage the sages and incur their curse; and seeing these boys at last fallen

[51] *MBh.* 16.2–9. [52] *Padma* 6.278; see above, chap. VII, sec. 5. [53] *MBh.* 11.25.39–42.

under the double curse, he himself picks up the iron bolt and physically cuts down the remaining drunken warriors. The multiplicity of explanations—the curse of the Brahmins and of Gāndhārī, the repeated and desperate recourse to fate, and the final release that he grants them all as a favor—shows that the author felt the need to apologize for Kṛṣṇa's behavior, and to find someone else to blame. First the mother of the Kurus and then the previous members of the Yadu race, naughty boys, are blamed—transposing the origin of evil to the past, as usual, but even here involving Kṛṣṇa, who kills the Kurus and whose son does the mischief. Then the actual race is deluded by wine or "perverted by time," as in the original Fall, to make them fit for slaughter. And finally the women are carried off by outsiders, barbarians (though it is Kṛṣṇa who originally inspires the curse that dooms them to this fate and who then actually sets up the rape, by telling Arjuna to lead the women out of the fortified city of Dvārakā to the lands of the barbarians). The evil woman as source of the curse appears in the form of Gāndhārī, who is superseded in later texts by the women of the Yadu race itself (here foreshadowed by the boy who impersonates a woman).

Kṛṣṇa's determination to destroy the virtuous race of Yadus is evident even when he specifically warns them that a flood is coming—a flood that he has created to kill them *all*; yet the *Mahābhārata* tries in vain to temper the genocide by having Kṛṣṇa send Dāruka to rescue "the inhabitants of Dvārakā," of whom there should be none left, since Kṛṣṇa has sent them all, with their families, on a pilgrimage. Even when these survivors (women, children, and old men unfit for pilgrimage, one must suppose) are massacred by barbarians, the *Mahābhārata* says that a few remaining members of the family, women included, survived this third extermination and lived after all at Kurukṣetra—a direct contradiction of the frequent assertion that Kṛṣṇa destroyed the entire race of Yadus. One man, at least, survives—Vajra, who is taken to Indraprastha (Delhi; the *Viṣṇu Purāṇa* says that he was taken to Mathurā[54]) and consecrated as king. As Wilson remarks drily on this survival, "Vajra . . . was established as chief of the Yādavas at Indraprastha, and . . . therefore escaped the destruction which overwhelmed their kinsmen . . . of Dvārakā. This was a fortunate reservation for the tribes which in various parts of Hindustan . . . profess to derive their origin from the Yādavas."[55] From the standpoint of the author of the text, faced with an existing race of Yādavas, a loophole must be found for someone to survive, just as a "seed" of the human race survives the final doomsday; yet clearly the original intention of Kṛṣṇa was to destroy both the people and their city.

Vyāsa's explanation of Kṛṣṇa's behavior seems to satisfy Arjuna, but, as S. K. Belvalkar remarks, "The explanation would not probably fully satisfy the layman,

[54] *Viṣṇu* 5.38.34. [55] Wilson, (1840), p. 480.

who expects the divine Avatara to always do the right thing and save the sufferers."[56] The Purāṇas, unable to accept Vyāsa's rationalization, dwell at greater length on the destruction of Dvārakā:

Kṛṣṇa killed the demons and the wicked kings for the sake of the universe; he removed the burden of the earth by destroying numerous armies. Then, on the pretext of a curse by Brahmins, he destroyed his own family. For Nārada and other sages, angered by the mischief of some boys of the Yadu tribe who dressed as women, had cursed the Yadus to be destroyed, and the wise Kṛṣṇa did not wish to oppose what had been ordained by fate.

One day the gods sent Vāyu to Kṛṣṇa to say, "More than a hundred years have passed since you descended to earth in order to do a favor for the gods and to remove the burden of the earth. The wicked demons have been killed, the burden removed; now you should return to heaven." Kṛṣṇa said, "I know all that you say, but the earth is still burdened with the excessively numerous Yadus, and I will remove this burden immediately by killing them. When I have placed Dvārakā in the ocean and destroyed the Yadus, I will go to heaven. Jarāsandha and the others who caused the burden have been killed, but even a youth of the Yadu race is no less a burden for the earth than they. When I have taken this great burden from the earth, I will return to protect the world of the immortals." And so, when dreadful portents occurred in Dvārakā, Kṛṣṇa said to the Yadus, "Let us go to Prabhāsa," and when he had killed the race of Yadus and abandoned Dvārakā, he went to heaven, and the ocean flooded Dvārakā.[57]

A number of the thornier points of the *Mahābhārata* text are clarified or changed here. It is now actually said that the Brahmins' curse is just an excuse for Kṛṣṇa to do what he wishes to do,[58] but still he claims only to be obeying the dictates of fate. The gods beg him to stop killing everyone (as they beg another avatar, the boar, to stop destroying things once he has fulfilled the purpose of the incarnation[59]), but Kṛṣṇa has a ready answer: The virtuous Yadus are even more of a threat than the wicked demons, for the burden that they cause is greater than that of the demons. In this way, the demons incarnate as kings are split apart again; the demons are one problem, the kings another, greater problem. Another text of this myth differs slightly on this point. Kṛṣṇa says, "Jarāsandha and the others who were causing the burden of the earth were slain, and the burden was taken up by the Yadus."[60] Here the mortal enemies are not greater than the demons but simply complementary, a second string of battle reinforcements; in any case, they must be wiped out.

In the *Viṣṇu Purāṇa*, as in the *Mahābhārata*, the slaughter at Prabhāsa takes place, Dvārakā is flooded, and Arjuna leads away the women, who are carried off

[56] *MBh.*, *Mausala Parvan*, introduction, p. xxxiv.

[57] *Viṣṇu* 5.37.1–36. [58] *Liṅga* 1.69.83; *Bhāgavata* 11.1.5.

[59] *Kālikā* 30–31; cf. *Bhāgavata* 10.59; *Hari.* 55; *Liṅga* 1.95–96; *Śiva* 3.11; 3.22–23; *Skanda* 5.1.66; *Viṣṇu* 5.29; O'Flaherty (1975), pp. 187–197. [60] *Brahma* 210.1–27.

by barbarians. This time there is no remnant of surviving women and children; only Vajra lives to be king. The total annihilation of the women prompts the author of this text to adduce yet another "previous curse" in justification:

The gods had overthrown the demons and were celebrating on the summit of Mount Meru. Thousands of beautiful celestial nymphs on their way to the celebration passed the deformed sage Aṣṭavakra, engrossed in asceticism; they praised him and he granted them the boon of being reborn as the wives of Kṛṣṇa, but when they mocked his deformity he cursed them to be carried off by barbarians. They appeased him again and he promised that they would afterwards return to the world of the gods. These women were the wives of Kṛṣṇa carried off by the barbarians.[61]

The destruction of the women is now their own fault; they, not boys dressed to impersonate them, provoke the curse (which may be alluded to in the *Mahābhārata*'s statement that the women of the Yadu race were cursed by sages); this is a more satisfying sop to Purāṇic misogyny, but even here the curse takes place (like the entire incarnation of demons in most texts) as a result of the gods' successful slaughter of the demons. Moreover, Kṛṣṇa's advice to Arjuna to lead the women away is the immediate cause of the rape; the *Liṅga Purāṇa* may have this in mind when it remarks that the wives of Kṛṣṇa were carried off by barbarians because of the curse of Aṣṭavakra and also because of the power of Kṛṣṇa's own delusion (*Māyā*).[62] Once again, the success of the gods is paid for by the destruction of men.

But after describing the massacre of the entire race of Yadus, the *Viṣṇu Purāṇa* tempers this by mentioning the survival of the one thing that was doomed from the start: the holy city of Dvārakā, whose very name indicates that it "has the doorway"—to heaven:

The ocean rose and submerged the whole of the empty city of Dvārakā, all except the dwelling of the deity of the race of Yadu. The sea has not yet been able to wash that temple away, and there Kṛṣṇa constantly abides, even in the present day. Whoever visits that holy shrine is liberated from all his sins.[63]

In direct contradiction of the Epic statement that the entire city was destroyed, this text says that the temple of Viṣṇu survived to give salvation to all who visit it, the classical Purāṇic shrine that angers the Vedic gods. Yet, even in the Epic, the shrine must somehow be regarded as surviving, because—like human Yadus and Buddhists—the shrine of Dvārakā was there, existing on earth "even today," at the time of the composition of the texts, standing "at the extremity of the peninsula of Gujerat."[64] It has been suggested that the physical location of the shrine, at the very westernmost part of India, on the shore of the ocean, may have

[61] *Viṣṇu* 5.37.36–57; 5.38.70–85. [62] *Liṅga* 1.69.87.

[63] *Viṣṇu* 5.38.9–11, 13–28. [64] Wilson (1840), p. 482 n.

caused the town to be "originally considered the sacred gate to Varuṇa's world (which is also situated in the West in the classificatory system)."[65] Dvārakā is the pied-à-terre of the god of the underworld, and hence the city of death, the city where the human race must die at Kṛṣṇa's hands.

This sanctity of the (surviving) shrine of Dvārakā was, according to the commentator, the very reason that Kṛṣṇa tricked the inhabitants into a useless pilgrimage to their appointment in Samarra: "In dying in Dvārakā," he says, "there would be Release for the Yadus, who are incarnations of the gods. Thinking that this must not be, Kṛṣṇa told them to go to Prabhāsa, which is the place to obtain the world of heaven; and so he said, 'Let us go to Prabhāsa to allay these portents.' "[66] In this way, Kṛṣṇa prevented them from achieving total Release, but not from reaching heaven—their true home, as gods incarnate, and the home to which the raped women are also to return. This return to the original Epic premise (the battle between heroes and villains seen as a battle between gods and demons on earth) makes it appear that Kṛṣṇa is doing the Yadus a favor by taking them away from the holy city and killing them and their wives. In the Epic, Kṛṣṇa's murderous activity is said to "release" the whole world, but now he apparently wishes to avoid this. The argument given by the commentator implies a return to the Vedic premise that heaven is preferable to Release, combined with the Purāṇic premise that God does a favor to those whom he kills.[67]

Kṛṣṇa becomes incarnate to remove a double threat: the demons who overburden the earth must be killed, and the city of Dvārakā must be destroyed. The link between these two destructive acts is created by the Yadus who live in Dvārakā; in the early Purāṇas, they, like the wicked demons, pose an excessive burden; hence they and their city must be destroyed. But now they must be destroyed in a particular way because they are gods, not demons—a fact stated in all texts but ignored by the pattern of the myth, which treats them as demons or virtuous mortals, antigods of some sort. Since Dvārakā is too holy for gods, they must be kept from the shrine if it is not destroyed; this is the case in the *Viṣṇu Purāṇa* text that prompted the commentator's rationalization. The Purāṇa feels that the sanctity of Dvārakā is far superior to that of Prabhāsa, that Release is superior to heaven—for all of us, but not for the human gods whom Kṛṣṇa destroys, gods with Vedic values. The survival of the shrine in the *Viṣṇu Purāṇa* is a bhakti interpolation, a superimposition of the "survival of the shrine forever and ever" motif on the older plot of total destruction. The two themes are not entirely incongruous, for even in the myth of total cosmic dissolution there is often said to be a particular area of sanctity that survives the deluge: the sage Manu, or the seven sages, or the Vedas, or even a purified seed of men to begin the new Golden Age.

[65] Kuiper, p. 113. [66] Śrīdhara on *Viṣṇu* 5.37.29–34. [67] See below, chap. X, sec. 6.

The *Bhāgavata Purāṇa* also states that the shrine at Dvārakā survived the flood, and the memory of Kṛṣṇa there is said to remove all evils (*aśubha*).[68] Here, as in the Epic but unlike the *Viṣṇu Purāṇa*, some of the women survive with Vajra; there is no rape by barbarians, but the poet still finds it necessary to offer a reason for the destruction of the men:

Kṛṣṇa became a householder in Dvārakā and married many wives, and had many sons and grandsons. In the race of the Yadus, no one was poor; everyone had many children, lived a long life, and respected Brahmins. But they were so numerous that one could not count them even in a hundred years. The terrible demons who had been slain in the battle of the gods and demons were born among men, and so at the command of Viṣṇu the gods became incarnate in the race of Yadus to repress the demons. . . . When Kṛṣṇa had killed the demons, and thus relieved the burden of the earth, he thought, "The earth is still overburdened by the unbearably burdensome race of the Yadus. No one else can overcome them, since they are under my protection." . . . Deluded by Kṛṣṇa's power of delusion, and cursed by the Brahmins, they were all destroyed, and when his entire family had been destroyed, Kṛṣṇa said, "The burden has been removed."[69]

Kṛṣṇa alone can destroy the Yadus, since they take refuge in him, just as Śiva alone can destroy the demons of the Triple City, who are his devotees. But the overnumerous Yadus, who cover the entire surface of the earth,[70] are in large part the result of his own zealous pursuit of the householder's life, born of his own seed and begotten in the women previously cursed by Aṣṭavakra. When his anxiety about this burden leads Kṛṣṇa to destroy his own family on the pretext of the Brahmins' curse, the commentator remarks drily, "This is said to indicate why he destroys his own family, an unseemly act."[71] Even in the *Mahābhārata*, it is the sight of his fallen sons that drives Kṛṣṇa to participate in a battle in which "son killed father and father killed son," a telling description of his own role in the battle. Kṛṣṇa must destroy his own destructive offspring after he has raised up the earth, just as the boar avatar is forced to kill himself and his sons, who are wreaking similar havoc (weighing down the earth), after he had raised up the Earth and married her; and Rāma is prevented from killing his own wife when the gods remind him that he has completed the demon-killing for which he became incarnate.[72] In all of these episodes, the avatar seems to forget his cosmic purpose when he becomes deluded by earthly involvement, primarily the involvement with children.

The need to exterminate the Yadus precisely because they are born of Kṛṣṇa's own seed is made explicit in the *Liṅga Purāṇa*:

68 *Bhāgavata* 11.31.1–28. 69 *Bhāgavata* 10.90.27–44; 11.1.1–4; 11.30.1–25.

70 *Padma* 6.279.59; *Bhāgavata* 11.1.1–4. 71 Śrīdhara on *Bhāgavata* 11.1.1–4.

72 *Rām.* 6.106.28–29; O'Flaherty (1975), pp. 197–204; (1973), pp. 282–283.

One of Kṛṣṇa's wives asked Kṛṣṇa to give her a son equal to the lord of the gods. Kṛṣṇa performed asceticism for Śiva, who granted him a son, Sāmba. Kṛṣṇa took sixteen thousand maidens for his pleasure, and then, under the pretext of the Brahmins' curse, he destroyed his own family and lived in Prabhāsa. After living for a hundred and one years in Dvārakā, where he had removed the sorrow of old age, he made the curse of the sages come true.[73]

The threat to the gods is here created by Kṛṣṇa himself, who succumbs to his wife's entreaties as Vajrāṅga and Yayāti do, knowing that no good will come of it; Kṛṣṇa produces a son equal to Indra, a son who is directly responsible for the curse of the Yadus (since it is he who masquerades as the pregnant woman and prompts the sages' curse). Moreover, Kṛṣṇa creates other god-men, for it is said that he removed old age (and hence mortality) from the inhabitants of Dvārakā as many dangerously virtuous kings do, notably Divodāsa and Yayāti. Kṛṣṇa must therefore destroy Dvārakā and move to Prabhāsa, on the pretext of the curse brought about by his own son.

The role of Sāmba is greatly expanded in another text, which further emphasizes the antagonism between Kṛṣṇa and his offspring and revives the theme of the unchaste women:

One day Nārada came to Dvārakā to see Kṛṣṇa. All the Yadu boys received him with respect, but Sāmba, proud of his young beauty and deluded by the fated, inevitable force of the curse, disregarded Nārada. To teach Sāmba a lesson, Nārada told Kṛṣṇa that all of Kṛṣṇa's sixteen thousand wives were in love with Sāmba. Sāmba was summoned, and the women, whose minds were blurred by wine, showed unmistakable signs of passion when Sāmba appeared. Furious, Kṛṣṇa cursed them to be carried off by barbarians after his death, and he cursed Sāmba to be afflicted by leprosy. Therefore the women were carried away under the very eyes of Arjuna. Later, Sāmba remembered what had happened before, and as he was impelled by inevitable fate, he enraged the sage Durvāsas and prompted the curse that destroyed his whole family.[74]

The handsome son deformed by a jealous father, an important theme in Hindu mythology,[75] here accounts for Sāmba's sin in insulting two sages, first Nārada, then Durvāsas; these episodes are in turn explained by the statement that Sāmba misbehaved because of the force of fate or because of the curse he was about to receive—a fatalistic cycle if ever there was one. Sāmba's mischief and that of the women combine here in one neat episode: he misbehaves with them. Thus the destruction of the race of the Yadus is blamed on Kṛṣṇa's wives, on Kṛṣṇa's son, and on the jealous rage of Kṛṣṇa himself.

In spite of this, the *Bhāgavata Purāṇa* states that the entire family is not

[73] *Liṅga* 1.69.71, 82–84. [74] *Sāmba* 3.6–55; *Bhaviṣya* 1.72–73. [75] O'Flaherty (1973), pp. 150–151; (1975), pp. 262–269; *Bṛhaddharma* 2.60. See below, chap. XI, sec. 9.

destroyed; the women and Vajra reach Indraprastha safely, and there is no barbarian attack. Thus, in spite of Kṛṣṇa's intention to wipe them all out, in this text both the Yadus and their shrine survive. In another text, however, the destruction of the race is painstakingly complete. The slaughter takes place at Prabhāsa; Dvārakā is totally flooded; all the women are carried off on the way to Indraprastha; and not even Vajra survives to continue the line.[76] The total loss of the women is explained again by the curse of Aṣṭavakra (who actually calls them whores[77]), and it is all in a good cause: "For the sake of all the gods, and to destroy the burden of the earth, and to kill all the Rākṣasas, and to release all the inhabitants of Nandavraja [Kṛṣṇa's home], Dvārakā, and Mathurā, Kṛṣṇa became incarnate."[78] The author doth protest too much; the multiple excuses betray a guilty conscience, particularly since the final argument—that he wishes to give them all Release (as in the Epic)—has been unmasked by the commentator, who pointed out that Kṛṣṇa sent them to Prabhāsa to prevent them from obtaining Release.

The genocide of the Yadus takes place at the start of the Kali Age. "Kṛṣṇa decided to destroy his own race and to perform actions to remove the impurities of the Kali Age. . . . Though the Lord was omniscient and omnipotent, he did not want to alter the Brahmins' curse; and since he was the very form of doomsday [*kāla*], he rejoiced in it."[79] Even in the *Mahābhārata*, the warriors are "deluded by doomsday,"[80] and the description of what transpires at Prabhāsa—the warriors fighting to the death for no apparent cause—is an exact description of what will happen in the Kali Age, when Viṣṇu as Kalkin will incite the slaughter: "When Kalkin comes in the Kali Age, he will kill all but a remnant seed of the human race; then people will be overcome by karma, deluded, and angry with one another for no cause."[81] Moreover, the rape of the women by barbarians is the telltale sign of the Kali Age. The behavior of Kṛṣṇa in some ways prepares mankind for the Kali Age, destroying the last of the virtuous races so that the barbarians may take over; the Kali Age is the time when the gods are no longer present on earth, for Kṛṣṇa has killed them all. After Viṣṇu becomes incarnate as Kṛṣṇa, to kill his own race of god-men, he becomes incarnate as the Buddha to corrupt other mortal men; then, at the end of the Kali Age, he becomes incarnate as Kalkin to kill all these evil mortals.[82] The similar function of these last three avatars (in spite of the supposedly benevolent intentions of Kṛṣṇa) caused the Purāṇas to confuse Kṛṣṇa with both the Buddha and Kalkin,[83] for Viṣṇu's last three appearances on earth represent three different stages in the systematic destruction of the human race by the jealous gods.

This jealousy is often veiled in the Kṛṣṇa story, masked by the increasingly

[76] *Padma* 6.279.56–97. [77] *Padma* 6.279.94. [78] *Padma* 6.279.97.

[79] *Bhāgavata* 11.1.10–11; 11.1.24. [80] *MBh.* 16.4.12. [81] *Brahmāṇḍa* 2.3.73.114–116.

[82] *Padma* 6.279.110–111. [83] See above, chap. VII, sec. 6.

dominant attitude of devotion, which turns a deaf ear to the malevolent overtones of the ancient myth. But jealousy is blatantly apparent in other myths of this pattern–myths of the destruction of holy cities such as Benares –particularly when the destroyer is not God but merely a god, a petty tyrant inordinately fond of his own pied-à-terre. Kṛṣṇa's destruction of Dvārakā is linked to the more traditional pattern of Indra's destruction of holy cities in a cycle of myths centering upon Mahābalipuram (Mamallapuram) near Madras. The pattern may be traced back to the myths in which Kṛṣṇa leaves Dvārakā to fight against a Śaiva king of Benares;[84] the best-known variant of this myth (and one which is juxtaposed with the tale of Kṛṣṇa and King Pauṇḍraka[85]) is the story in which Kṛṣṇa conquers the demon Bāṇa, a devotee of Śiva said to reside in various cities other than Benares or Mahābalipuram.[86] This cluster of myths is then utilized by the local Brahmins in glorifying Mahābalipuram: The demon Bali was the founder of Mahābalipuram. When his son, the demon Bāṇa, was taken prisoner and brought to Mahābalipuram, Kṛṣṇa came from Dvārakā and laid siege to the city, conquering Bāṇa in spite of Śiva's assistance to the demon. Years later, a prince named Malleśvara fell in love with an Apsaras who had come down to bathe in a fountain near the city; the prince begged to be brought in disguise to see Indra's court,

> a favour never before granted to any mortal. The Rājā returned from thence with new ideas of splendour and magnificence, which he immediately adopted in regulating his court. . . . and an account of its magnificence having been brought to the gods assembled at the court of Indra, their jealousy was so much excited at it, that they sent orders to the God of the Sea to let loose his billows, and overflow a place which impiously pretended to vie in splendour with their celestial mansions. This command he obeyed, and the city was at once overflowed by that furious element, nor has it ever since been able to rear its head.[87]

The link between the shrine on earth and the city of the gods in heaven persists in a Tamil variant of the myth of the flood, in which, when the ocean begins to flood the shrine, the gods fear that their city, too, will be flooded.

The basic pattern of malevolence is embroidered with motifs retained from the earlier myths of Yayāti and Divodāsa–the nymph by the fountain who leads the king to his doom in heaven, the plot that shifts smoothly from demonic enemies to human victims of the gods. The legend of Malleśvara is further expanded in the local Purāṇa, which clearly draws upon the legend of the founding of Dvārakā[88]: When King Malleśvara was ruling over Mahābalipuram, the sage Puṇḍarīka came there and wished to cross the sea; Viṣṇu came in disguise and caused the sea to recede; on the place where Viṣṇu appeared, a temple of seven

[84] See above, *Bhāgavata* 10.66.1–42. [85] See above, *Padma* 6.278; *Viṣṇa* 5.34.

[86] *Viṣṇu* 5.34; *Hari*. 112–113. [87] Chambers, pp. 156–157. Cf. *Tiruviḷaiyāṭaṟpurāṇam* 18–19.

[88] *Hari*. 86.35–53.

pinnacles arose.[89] Here, as in the *Mahābhārata* story of the receding of the sea at Dvārakā, nothing is said of the ultimate submersion of the shrine; but the seven pinnacles are part of the legendary submerged structure, not the existing shrine. Mahābalipuram is an appropriately ambiguous site for the myth of the shrine that is both destroyed and saved; for though several temples do survive, and the shrine therefore exists, it is, like Dvārakā, on the very brink of the sea, and legend has long maintained that there are other "pagodas" hidden underwater.

The Hindu texts often preach that Viṣṇu became incarnate to help mankind, to destroy evil, and to preserve dharma, and this statement is often parroted by scholars. When Kṛṣṇa is confronted by the sage Uttaṅka and accused of failing to prevent the genocide of the Yadus, he cites this argument among others. Like Vyāsa, he says that it was fated to happen, and then he reminds the sage of the traditional purpose of the avatar: he becomes incarnate to protect dharma, to kill those who behave in adharma; and then he undercuts this justification by saying that those whom he killed (as well as the righteous who died in spite of his efforts to save them) are all now happy in heaven.[90] This last fact is established elsewhere in the Epic, where a vision appears of Kurus and Pāṇḍus joyously reunited, father with son, brother with brother, and all blissfully translated to heaven.[91] This happy ending is, however, in striking contrast to the scene in which Kṛṣṇa actually participates, the wholesale slaughter of father by son, son by father, brother by brother. It appears that, in this view, the gods may allow men to be happy in heaven (where they are tantamount to gods and thus cease to be competitive or anomalous) but never on earth. When they become too overpopulous, the gods kill them on the pretext of killing wicked demons; when men become too virtuous, the gods send a flood to destroy their shrine, an inversion of the motif of the flood sent to punish or destroy sinners. A correlated inversion is implicit in the slaughter of the overpopulous mortals, for in killing these sinners (and demons), Viṣṇu causes the cosmic floods to recede from the earth which he raises up.

An examination of the texts in which the last three incarnations occur shows that neither the intention nor the achievement of Viṣṇu is beneficial to mankind; he becomes incarnate as the result of a curse[92] just as often as he acts through a sense of self-sacrifice, and what good he achieves in destroying demons is easily overbalanced by the destruction of his own race. Viṣṇu does indeed desire to save mankind when dharma wanes; but he also destroys mankind when adharma wanes, sometimes out of inadequacy or malevolence, and sometimes through a frank recognition of the role of evil in his own creation.

[89] Carr, pp. 173–175, citing the *Mamallāpurī-māhātmya*, professing to be chapters 93–100 of the *Kṣetrakhaṇḍa* of the *Brahmāṇḍa Purāṇa*. [90] *MBh*. 14.53.11–22. [91] *MBh*. 15.41.

[92] *Padma* 1.13.244–247; *Brahmāṇḍa* 3.3.85–106; 72.3–17; *Matsya* 47.99–103.

Yea, surely God will not do wickedly, neither will the Almighty pervert judgment.
Job 34:12

X
GOD IS A HERETIC

The concept of the creation of evil for the benefit of mankind, in the spirit of bhakti, is the culmination of Hindu mythological theodicy. Whereas Viṣṇu taught heresy to the demons as a curse upon them, Śiva teaches heresy as a release from a previous curse; and whereas Viṣṇu's teaching is destructive in effect as well as in intent—for he teaches the damning doctrine of Buddhism—Śiva brings about a Hindu heresy that serves a useful, religious purpose. Even in Viṣṇu's act there is an element of ambiguity. Some Hindus (such as Jayadeva) looked on the work of the Buddha as intrinsically valid, others (the major Purāṇic texts) regarded it as the epitome of evil. This ambiguity is heightened a thousandfold in the myths of the Śaiva heresies, which are regarded by some Śaivas as the very essence of Hindu scripture but by many Vaiṣṇava texts as a blasphemy no better than Buddhism. The myths in this complex cycle are the episodes of Dakṣa's sacrifice, Śiva as the Kāpālika (or Kapālin), Gautama and the Seven Sages, and Śiva and the Pine Forest sages.

1. Dakṣa and the Curse of Heresy

The myth of Dakṣa, which is told in many texts,[1] states that Dakṣa gave a sacrifice and did not invite Śiva, who was traditionally excluded from the sacrifice; Śiva destroyed the sacrifice and beheaded Dakṣa, who then recognized Śiva's divinity

[1] *Liṅga* 1.35–36; *Kūrma* 1.14; *Vāyu* 1.30; *MBh.* 12, app. 1, no. 28; 12.274.2–58; *Brahma* 34, 39–40, 109; *Matsya* 72; *Varāha* 33.4–34; *Rām.* 1.66; *MBh.* 7.202; 10.18; 12.343; 13.76; *Bhāgavata* 4.2–7; 10.88; *Śiva* 2.2.26–43; 5.16–20; *Vāmana* 2.4–6; etc. Cf. O'Flaherty (1975), pp. 123–125.

and praised him. Śiva restored the sacrifice and replaced Dakṣa's head (which had been thrown into the fire) with that of a goat.

In many versions of this myth, which forms the first stage of the series, a heresy is established. Dakṣa curses Śiva to be denied a share in the sacrifice, to be impure and banished from heaven, to be king of ghosts and Piśācas.[2] Then a chain of curses occurs:

Dakṣa called Śiva a heretic and cursed him to be outside the Vedas; Nandin, the servant of Śiva, said that Dakṣa's curse was false; Dakṣa then cursed Nandin and all the servants of Śiva to be beyond the Vedas, heretics, outcastes. Nandin cursed Dakṣa to be a hypocrite, full of lust and greed, a false Brahmin.[3]

In other versions of this myth, Dadhīca (who assumes the role of Nandin) curses the Brahmins who hate Śiva, so that they will be beyond the pale of the Vedas, forbidden to sacrifice, taking pleasure in the behavior of heretics; they are to be reborn in the Kali Age as Śūdras, to say prayers for Śūdras, to go to hell, to be outside the Vedas, their minds struck down by evil.[4] Śiva sometimes mercifully forgives Dakṣa and allows him to find Release or even to become a leader of Śiva's hosts.[5] Śiva released Dakṣa from the evil of dishonoring Śiva, and Dakṣa entered the liṅga that he had worshipped, called the Lord of Dakṣa.[6] When Nandin curses Dakṣa's priests to be poor and greedy, Brahmin Rākṣasas, Śiva chastises him for losing his temper with Brahmins.[7] But Dakṣa's curse takes effect, as the sects which he curses (Kālāmukhas and Kāpālikas) were actual heretical Śaiva sects, and Dakṣa's own adherents are condemned to something worse (from the partisan Śaiva standpoint): they are doomed to hypocritical Vaiṣṇava orthodoxy:

Nandin said, "May those who hate Śiva be deluded by the flowery speech of the Vedas; let them be magicians and ascetics, omnivorous, delighting in wealth and sensuality, wandering beggars."[8]

A similar exchange of heresies results from an encounter between Śaṅkara and his enemies, who are often prone to this sort of accusation:

Śaṅkara's kinsmen refused to give him sacred fire for his mother's funeral rites, for they called him "Rogue, ascetic," and said that (as an ascetic) he had no authority over Vedic rites. Śaṅkara then cursed them to be forever prohibited from the study of the Vedas, to live near the cremation grounds, and to be unacceptable as donors of alms to ascetics, and so they have been ever since.[9]

Like Śiva, of whom he is an incarnation, Śaṅkara is justly excluded from the

[2] *Bhāgavata* 10.88.32. [3] *Śiva* 2.2.26.14–40; *Skanda* 1.1.2.23–26; 1.1.2.26–37.

[4] *Saura* 7.38–39; *Tantrādhikāranirṇaya*, p. 35; *Mārk.* 49.13; *Skanda* 7.29.90ff; *Kūrma* 1.15.28–33; *Kanta Purāṇam* 6.10.24. [5] *Kūrma* 1.15.76–77. [6] *Saura* 7.1–4, 53–59.

[7] *Skanda* 1.1.38. [8] *Bhāgavata* 4.2.21–26. [9] *Śaṅkaradigvijaya* 14.46–53. See above, chap. VII, sec. 7.

sacrifice; nevertheless he curses those who exclude him to be themselves excluded.

The myth is not content with this exchange of imprecations, however, but seeks to trace a more basic cause in the source of Dakṣa's hatred of Śiva. Here, as throughout the cycle, there is no clear Śaiva/Vaiṣṇava demarcation, though sectarian biases are often at play; for both Śaiva and Vaiṣṇava texts seek to explain Dakṣa's rejection of Śiva (whom all texts regard as a great god, if not always the great god) and Śiva's creation of the heretic Kāpālikas and Pāśupatas (whom most texts regard as sub-Vedic, if not necessarily anti-Vedic).[10] The myth of Śiva's destruction of Dakṣa's sacrifice is an ancient one involving many Vedic threads, not all of which are pertinent to the present discussion.[11] Although the Purāṇic myth is used to justify and assimilate the heterodox Śiva, many of the Vedic antecedents of the myth indicate that Rudra beheaded the Dakṣa figure (Prajāpati) in order to protect the orthodox moral order, to punish the incestuous creator, or to "stretch his bow against the hater of religion."[12] Thus, at first this myth represents a conflict between a moral Śiva (Rudra) and an immoral Dakṣa (Prajāpati), roles that are apparently reversed in the Purāṇic versions.

Some of the ambiguities in the Purāṇic myth result from the combination of two separate, though complementary, Vedic myths, elements of each of which appear in scattered passages throughout Vedic literature. The first group is united by the basic premise of Prajāpati's incest as the precipitating factor of the myth: Prajāpati was about to commit incest with his daughter; she took the form of an animal to elude him and he took the form of an animal to pursue her; the gods created Rudra to avenge this outrage; Rudra shot an arrow at the Prajāpati beast.[13] The second group is smaller and more consistent, based on the premise of Rudra's exclusion from the sacrifice: Prajāpati (and the gods) excluded Rudra from the sacrifice and divided the beasts among themselves; Rudra beheaded the sacrificial beast; the gods gave Rudra a portion of the sacrifice, for he is a slayer of cattle.[14] This Vedic antagonism between the gods and Śiva is implicit in the Sanskrit texts, in which all the gods but Śiva attend Dakṣa's sacrifice and are punished by Śiva. The gods are linked with demons in opposition to Śiva in two devotional Tamil reworkings of the myth. In the first, Dakṣa (like Divodāsa) obtains ascetic powers and build a proud city in which the king of demons takes refuge; later, however, the gods (in addition to the Brahmins) side with Dakṣa and are cursed to be overcome by the demons[15]—their equivalent of the mortal

[10] O'Flaherty (1971), pp. 272–287. [11] Meinhard, pp. 35–91; O'Flaherty (1973), pp. 128–130; 210–218. [12] *RV* 10.61.5–7; *AV* 10.10.16; *Bṛhaddevatā* 4.110–111; *Tai. Sam.* 3.4; 10.3; *Tāṇḍya* 8.2.10; *Bhāgavata* 3.13; *Mārk.* 50; O'Flaherty (1973), pp. 25–31. [13] *RV* 1.71.5–7; *Ait. Br.* 13.9–10; *Śata.* 1.7.4.1–8; O'Flaherty (1975), pp. 116–188; (1973), pp. 111–141.

[14] *Gopatha* 2.1.2; *Tāṇḍya* 7.9.16; *Śata.* 1.7.3.1–4; see above, chap. VI, sec. 8.

[15] *Kanta Purāṇam* 6.2.26–28; 6.10; 6.15; *Takkayākaparaṇi* 437 ff.

heresy that results, in Sanskrit texts, from the conflict between the god Śiva and a mortal enemy (Dakṣa). In a second Tamil text, the gods at Dakṣa's heretical sacrifice are joined by demons and are reborn as demons—an even stronger indictment of the gods and a more consistent and devout reversal of the Sanskrit tradition, in which Śiva is a heretic whose demonic hosts destroy the sacrifice.

Some texts begin to combine elements of the two Vedic myths, starting with Prajāpati's incest but including references to Rudra's being given a portion of the sacrifice.[16] Finally, in the Purāṇas, the Dakṣa myth combines these motifs in a single myth: Dakṣa does not want Śiva to marry his daughter (and Dakṣa has incestuous tendencies); he excludes Śiva from his sacrifice; Śiva destroys the sacrifice and beheads Dakṣa, replacing Dakṣa's head with that of the sacrificial beast; Śiva is given homage. Thus Śiva is simultaneously the defender of orthodox morality (the incest tabu) and the unorthodox interloper (the violator of the sacrifice).

This ambiguity is essential to the ritual myth in which Śiva plays the mediator who resolves the ambivalence of both of the Vedic myths. In many cosmogonies, it is necessary for primeval creation to be incestuous (as the original One creates the female with whom he then procreates), but incest is forbidden by the social law. Therefore Prajāpati must commit incest, but he must be punished for it; and the act of his punisher is ambiguous—necessary, but sinful, like the original creation itself. Similarly, the sacrificial beast must be killed, but killers are usually unclean in the view of later Hinduism; so the sacrificer is made exempt from the stigma of killing, as the sacrificial beast is said to go to heaven. Only Rudra, who is the killer par excellence, can simultaneously destroy the sacrifice and perform it (by throwing the beast's head into the fire as an oblation). Śiva thus mediates between Vedic and non-Vedic views of ritual; he resolves incest and the tabu against incest, sacrifice and the tabu against killing. Though he is at first said to have no share in the sacrifice, he is then given a share in the sacrifice; though at first excluded, he is then included, bridging the gap between two conflicting ritual needs and traditions.

Śiva uses the evil Dakṣa himself as a sacrificial offering, and in so doing purifies Dakṣa. That Dakṣa's sacrifice is originally an evil one, like the sacrifice performed by Viśvarūpa or that of the ascetics whom Indra threatens to use as sacrificial offerings,[17] is implicit in the myth and clearly elaborated in a late variant:

The gods were becoming victorious in battle with the demons, and so Śukra sacrificed a goat; a drop of blood fell into the fire and became a goat-headed demon who put the gods to flight. Śiva then made the fire of his third eye into a ghost to subdue Śukra and the goat-headed demon. Śukra fled and took refuge in Śiva's stomach, emerging through

[16] *Śata.* 1.7.4.1–4; *Mait. Sam.* 4.2.12.

[17] See above, chap. V, sec. 5.

Śiva's penis after praising him. The goat demon also asked Śiva to pardon him and let him be the dwelling place of the gods, which Śiva granted, making him into Vāstupa.[18]

Vāstupa is the deity of the temple, originally a Vedic form of Rudra-Śiva himself; Vāstoṣpati is the deity who punishes the incestuous Prajāpati. Like Dakṣa, this goat-headed creature begins as a demonic force but is transmuted into a literal site of divinity (a form of Śiva originally created in order to kill Dakṣa-Prajāpati), just as Dakṣa is taught to worship Śiva when previously he had hated him for this same act of aggression.

The fact of Dakṣa's hatred of Śiva was well established by the time of the *Mahābhārata*, and several different reasons for this hatred are stated in different versions of the myth. Rudra himself gives Dakṣa his evil disposition, according to one early text,[19] and another text falls back upon fate to explain it: "There arose an enmity in Dakṣa toward Śiva for no reason, by chance."[20] Hardly more explicit, but more reminiscent of the classical Hindu myths of evil, is the statement that Dakṣa reviled Śiva "because of the curse of Nārada," perhaps as a result of the conflict between Nārada and the sons of Dakṣa.[21] This text also invokes the curse of Dadhīca, which explains the conflict between Dakṣa and Śiva by having recourse to a previous conflict between their representatives, Kṣuva (a king) and Dadhīca (a Brahmin), who are assisted by Viṣṇu and Śiva, respectively, during an argument about the relative importance of kings and priests.[22] As a result of this conflict, Dadhīca curses Viṣṇu and the gods to be burned by the fire of Śiva's anger (i.e., in the course of Dakṣa's sacrifice),[23] a sequence that seems to explain the myth as one of sectarian and class conflict. Sectarian conflict crops up in many myths of this cycle; the clash between kings and priests is well known from the Indra-Bṛhaspati myths and recurs here in the encounter between the Seven Sages and the king.[24]

Many myths attribute Dakṣa's hatred of Śiva to the fact that Śiva married Satī, the daughter of Dakṣa. These conflicts may be traced to the Vedic episode in which Śiva punishes Prajāpati (the ancestor of Dakṣa) for committing incest with his daughter, a connection that persists in those passages in which Śiva curses Dakṣa to become incestuous.[25] In other texts, Dakṣa objects to Śiva's marriage to his daughter because Śiva is an ascetic and therefore an unsuitable son-in-law.[26] But most texts attribute Dakṣa's antipathy toward Śiva to a former slight or

[18] *Īśānaśivagurudevapaddati* III, 25, 93ff; von Stietencron (1972), pp. 82–83.

[19] See above, chap. III, sec. 2. [20] *Brahmavaivarta* 4.38.5.

[21] *Liṅga* 1.99.14–15; cf. *Vāyu* 65; *MBh.* 1.70; *Bhāgavata* 6.5; *Brahma* 3; *Viṣṇu* 1.15; 5.1; 5.15; *Śiva* 2.2.13; O'Flaherty (1973), pp. 74–76; (1975), pp. 46–53. [22] *Śiva* 2.2.38.1–63; 2.2.39.1–48.

[23] *Liṅga* 1.36.72–74. [24] See above, chap. V, secs. 4 and 11.

[25] *Bhāgavata* 4.2.22–23; *Kūrma* 1.14.61; *Vāyu* 1.30.61; *Skanda* 7.2.9.42.

[26] *Bṛhaddharma* 2.34–37; *Śiva* 2.2.26.16; *Kūrma* 1.14.63; *Vāyu* 30.61; *Devībhāgavata* 7.30.27–37.

imagined slight. Once Śiva honored Dakṣa as was customary, but Dakṣa wished for more honor than he deserved, and he reviled Satī, saying, "All my other sons-in-law are better than your husband, Śiva."[27] Other texts state that Rudra actually did slight Dakṣa by failing to bow to him; Dakṣa complained to Satī, "My other sons-in-law honor me more than your husband does; Śiva vies with me and dishonors me always, going against my grain."[28] In one Hindi version of the myth, the fault is entirely Dakṣa's:

> Brahmā . . . made Dakṣa chief of the Lords of creation. When Dakṣa was invested with such high office, he became exceeding arrogant; never was a man born into the world whom dominion did not intoxicate. [He gave a sacrifice but did not invite Śiva, who said to Satī,] "Dakṣa has summoned all his daughters, but because of his quarrel with me he has left you out. Once he was displeased with me in Brahmā's court, and that is why he slights me to this day."[29]

The deep devotional spirit of this author makes it impossible for him to entertain the notion that Śiva might have been responsible for Dakṣa's hatred of him. Dakṣa himself, in a Sanskrit text, is aware of Śiva's divinity, but he admits to irrational feelings: "Although I know that Śiva is the Ancient Man, I have always been unable to brook him"; but Dakṣa then goes on to justify himself by explaining "the root of it: I command the eleven Rudras, who are a part of Rudra; yet Brahmā made me give my daughter to him. Therefore I hate him."[30]

2. Śiva as Outcaste and Heretic; The Kāpālika

The apparent nonsequitur in Dakṣa's statement arises from the fact that the text cited above is a misquotation of an earlier text in which Dakṣa explains to Dadhīci (*sic*) that he does not honor Śiva, because although he knows eleven Rudras, he does not know Maheśvara (Śiva).[31] This is the actual historical basis of the mythological conflict: Although the eleven Rudras (or Maruts) are Vedic storm gods who serve Indra, the individual Rudra who eventually subsumes and commands them all is non-Vedic in almost all essentials, a combination of the Indus Valley Paśupati, a tribal god of destruction, a Vrātya ascetic, the Agni of the Brāhmaṇas, and various other local strains all grafted onto the shadowy Rudra of the Ṛg Veda (himself a strange god hated and feared, worshipped with offerings at crossroads but never with a share in the Vedic sacrifice).[32] Several Brāhmaṇa texts state that Rudra-Śiva was excluded by the other gods from the sacrifice, or that, when the gods reached heaven, Rudra was left behind.[33] This

[27] *Kūrma* 1.14.53–65. [28] *Śiva* 2.26.11–12; *Vāyu* 1.30.42–49; *Brahmāṇḍa* 2.13.44.

[29] *Rāmacaritamānasa*, pp. 34–35. [30] *Bṛhaddharma* 2.35.24–33; 2.33.34–50.

[31] *MBh.* 12, app. 1, no. 28, 40–45; *Brahma* 39.30–33; *Vāyu* 1.30; cf. *Bṛhaddharma* 2.37.50–66.

[32] O'Flaherty (1973), pp. 8–11, 83–90.

[33] *Tāṇḍya* 7.9.16; *Mait. Sam.* 4.2.12; *Gopatha* 2.1.2; *Tait. Sam.* 2.6.8.5; *Śata.* 1.7.3.1.

exclusion and enforced mortality, albeit temporary, results in a kind of avatar on a grand scale, which in the later bhakti cult is developed into the myth of Śiva's voluntary wanderings on earth, an intentional gesture of love on the part of the god, who willingly becomes involved in his own deluding magic.[34]

The apparent result of Dakṣa's curse is actually its cause; because Śiva was always a heretic, denied a share in the sacrifice, Dakṣa curses him to be such. This circular reasoning (which accounts for many other heresies and evils) is apparent from many versions of Dakṣa's curse:

"The Brahmins will not sacrifice to you along with the other gods, for Śiva has defiled the path followed by good men; he is impure, an abolisher of rites and demolisher of barriers, [who gives] the word of the Vedas to a Śūdra. He wanders like a madman, naked, laughing, the lord of ghosts, evil-hearted. Let Śiva, the lowest of the gods, obtain no share with Indra and Viṣṇu at the sacrifice; let all the followers of Śiva be heretics, opponents of the true scriptures, following the heresy whose god is the king of ghosts."[35]

Since Śiva has no share of the sacrifice, he is cursed to be a heretic; since he is a heretic, he is denied a share in the sacrifice.

The temporal ambiguity of Dakṣa's curse is evident from other versions of the myth in which Dakṣa explicitly curses Śiva to be a heretic because he is already a heretic:

"You are excluded from the rituals and are surrounded by ghosts in the burning ground; yet you fail to honor me, while all the gods give me great honor. Good men must scorn all heretics; therefore I curse you to be outside the sacrifice, outside caste; all the Rudras will be beyond the Vedas, avowing heretic doctrines, Kāpālikas and Kālamukhas."[36]

In particular, Dakṣa says he hates Śiva because Śiva is a Kāpālika,[37] a skull-bearer, and when he refuses to invite Śiva to his sacrifice he uses this as his excuse: "In all sacrifices, there is no share ordained for Śiva, the naked Kāpālika."[38] Although Śiva is said to be "the eldest, most noble, most eminent, and first of the gods," Dakṣa excludes him, saying, "He is a Kapālin."[39] Here the listeners ask the bard, "How did Śiva become a Kapālin?"

The answer to this question is a story well known throughout India, a multiform of the myth of Śiva's fight with (and beheading of) Dakṣa. In the course of an argument, Śiva beheaded Brahmā, whose skull stuck to Śiva's hand; Śiva wandered for years performing the Kāpālika vow, naked, until at last he reached the shrine of Kapālamocana ("Skull-releasing") in Benares, where he was

[34] Deussen (1917), *passim*. [35] *Brahma* 2.13.70–73; *Garuḍa* 6.19; *Bhāgavata* 4.2.10–32.

[36] *Skanda* 1.1.1.20–40; *Śiva* 2.2.26.14–27; 2.2.27.42–54. [37] *Padma* 5.5.42–50; *Kālikā* 16.19ff., 17.1–16.

[38] *Kūrma* 1.15.8–11; *Vāmana* 2.27, 4.1. [39] *Vāmana* 2.17–18; *Kālikā* 63.4–5.

purified.[40] In some Vaiṣṇava variants of this myth Śiva is released by Viṣṇu, who creates a lake of tears for Śiva to bathe in at Benares[41] or produces streams of purifying blood from his own body.[42] In view of the sectarian conflict between the Vaiṣṇava Dakṣa and the Śaiva group (Nandin, Dadhīca, Satī, and Śiva himself), Viṣṇu's intervention in these variants is significant.

The myth of the skull-bearer may be traced back to the Vedic conflict between Rudra and Prajāpati and to the myth of Indra's pursuit by Brahminicide, but the Śaiva corpus adds many more complex reasons for the beheading of Brahmā. One myth of this group explains the beheading with the circular reasoning typical of myths of heresy:

Once when Śiva mounted Brahmā's shoulder, Brahmā's fifth head said to him, "Be a Kapālin," thus addressing Śiva by his future name. Śiva became angry at the word kapāla (*skull*) *and cut off the head, which stuck to his hand.*[43]

The myth seems aware of the confusion of time cycles, for it notes the incongruity of Brahmā's use of Śiva's "future name"; Śiva becomes a Kapālin because he is called Kapālin, apparently deciding to have the game as well as the name. Since the name *is* the person in Hindu thought, by naming Śiva, Brahmā makes him what he calls him, a Kapālin.

From these and other texts, it would appear that the story of the beheading of Brahmā by Śiva, and the existence of a Kāpālika sect of which Śiva is a member, are mutually dependent on each other, like the chicken and the egg. David Lorenzen has discussed this paradox:

The relative priority of the Śaivite myth and the Kāpālika ascetics themselves is also uncertain. Did the Kāpālikas invent the myth in order to provide a divine model for their ascetic observance, or did they model the observance on the myth? The evidence is inconclusive.The sources in which the myth first appears, the Purāṇas, also mention human Kāpālikas, and there are no references to the ascetics significantly earlier than these works. In some respects this question is a needless one. Since both the penance for killing a Brāhmaṇa and the association of Śiva, the god of death and destruction, with skulls undoubtedly antedated the Śiva-Kapālin myth, Śaivite ascetics who observed the Mahāvrata might also have antedated it. Whether or not such ascetics existed and whether or not they themselves invented this myth, it is certain that the later Kāpālikas adopted it as their divine archetype.[44]

Although, as Lorenzen points out, the myth of Śiva as the Kapālin first appears in the Purāṇas, this myth has precedents in the Vedic corpus of Rudra and

[40] *Varāha* 97.1–27; *Śiva* 3.8.36–66; 3.9.1–57; *Jñāna Saṃ.* 49.65–80; *Bhaviṣya* 3.4.13.1–19; *Kūrma* 2.30–31; Rao, II, 1, 295–300; *Kathāsaritsāgara* 2.13; Lorenzen, p. 78; O'Flaherty (1973), pp. 111–141. [41] *Nārada Purāṇa* 2.29. [42] *Padma* 1.14; *Matsya* 183.83–108.

[43] *Varāha* 97.2–8. [44] Lorenzen, pp. 79–80.

Prajāpati, as well as in the tale of Indra and Vṛtra. These texts are far earlier than the earliest reference to the Kāpālikas, but they do not include the vital motif of the skull sticking to the hand; hence the debate remains open.

Viṣṇu, who often helps Śiva to expiate his sin (particularly in texts with a strong Vaiṣṇava bias), sometimes causes that sin, as in one pro-Śaiva text: Once the avatars of Viṣṇu became intoxicated with pride, splitting the earth, oppressing towns, and frightening wild animals; Kṛṣṇa became adulterous, while Paraśurāma destroyed many Kṣatriyas in vengeance against one of them; Śiva was angered by these wicked acts and assumed the form of the Kāpālika, who beheaded the avatars and carried their skulls, causing them to lose their pride and granting them boons in return; then Śiva replaced the skulls and returned them to life, and that is how the school of Kāpālikas arose.[45] In this myth, Śiva restores the Vaiṣṇava figures even as he restores the (Vaiṣṇava) Dakṣa, blessing them as he often blesses enemies whom he has chastised. The motif of the wicked avatar that must be suppressed is taken from earlier myths of the chastisement of the crashing boar and the genocidal Kṛṣṇa (here adulterous rather than murderous).

In spite of the sins of Brahmā that justify the beheading, Śiva is frequently criticized for the act, as Indra is for killing Brahmins even when they are actually demons. In an allegorical play, Anger cites this as an instance in which he overpowered Śiva, and another play treats with sarcasm the Kapālin who ostensibly praises Śiva for establishing his vow. The Kapālin assures his girl-friend that the skull he carries can be purified, for, he says, "Our lord was released from the sin arising out of the beheading of the Grandfather."[46] The skull-bearer is the epitome of Śiva's demonic side: Rākṣasas drink out of skulls and carry tridents.[47] The beheading is sometimes regarded as bringing evil upon mankind, as Indra's Brahminicide does; the head of Brahmā that Śiva cut off united with the Nāga gods to torment mankind and extort offerings.[48]

Later, more devotional Śaiva texts insist that Śiva established the vow "for the sake of his devotees," that he could have made the head fall from his hand had he not wished to suffer for the sake of his worshippers. This is a rare example of a Hindu savior myth, the inverse of the far more typical myth on which it is based, the myth in which the god inflicts his own sin upon mankind, as Indra distributes his Brahminicide. One myth of the inverted corpus explicitly states that Śiva could have avoided the punishment had he wished to do so:

Brahmā desired Sarasvatī and asked her to stay with him. She said that he would always speak coarsely. One day when Brahmā met Śiva, his fifth head made an evil sound and Śiva cut it off. The skull remained stuck fast, and though Śiva was capable of burning it up, he wandered the earth with it for the sake of all people, until he came to Benares.[49]

[45] *Gorakṣa Siddhānta Saṃgraha*, p. 20. [46] *Prabodhacandrodaya* 2.31; *Mattavilāsaprahasana* 17.
[47] *Hiraṇyakeśin Gṛhya Sūtra* 2.3.7. [48] Oppert, p. 301. [49] *Śiva, Jñāna Sam.* 49.65–80.

Other myths are not satisfied with this rationalization and find it necessary to remove Śiva himself from the scene of the crime and the punishment, substituting for him a man whom he creates, a factotum like Viṣṇu's Buddhist man of deluding magic:

Once when Brahmā and Viṣṇu were arguing about which of them was supreme, a flame liṅga appeared between them, and from it there emerged a three-eyed man adorned with snakes. Brahmā's fifth head called the man his son; thereupon the man, who was Rudra, became angry; he created Bhairava and commanded him to punish Brahmā. Bhairava beheaded Brahmā, for whatever limb offends must be punished. Brahmā and Viṣṇu were terrified; they praised Śiva, who said to Bhairava, "You must honor Viṣṇu and Brahmā, and carry Brahmā's skull." Then Śiva created a maiden named Brahminicide, and he said to her, "Follow Bhairava until he arrives at the holy city of Benares, after wandering about, begging for alms with this skull and teaching the world the vow that removes the sin of Brahminicide. You cannot enter Benares, so leave him there." Bhairava wandered, pursued by Brahminicide, until he came to Viṣṇu, who gave him alms and said to Brahminicide, "Release Bhairava." But she said, "By serving him constantly under this pretext (of haunting him for his sin), I will purify myself so that I will not be reborn." Then Bhairava entered Benares with her still at his left side, and she cried out and went to hell, and the skull of Brahmā fell from Bhairava's hand and became the shrine of Kapālamocana.[50]

Bhairava is first created as a *Stellvertreter* in the Dakṣa myth, where several texts state that Śiva created him and sent him to do the dirty work. Here he is assimilated to the related myth of Śiva and Brahmā, so that Śiva is not only freed from the stigma of having committed the sin but is even said to create the punishment (which is inflicted on him against his will in less devout versions). Moreover, rather than being defiled by his sin, he purifies the very sin itself (herself); this cumbersome justification accounts for the otherwise embarrassing fact that the god was associated with the most serious of crimes: he did it for the good of the sin, as well as for mankind in general (to whom he "taught the vow that removes the sin of Brahminicide").

This late justification of the Kapālin myth represents an important development in Hindu theology. The motif of the head sticking to the hand may be traced back to the Vedic mythology of Indra, who in one episode is pursued by a Rākṣasa born of the head of Namuci torn off by Indra.[51] Another important precedent occurs in the *Mahābhārata*:

Rāma beheaded a Rākṣasa, whose head accidentally became attached to the thigh of the sage Mahodara who happened to be wandering in that forest. The sage went on pilgrimages to shrine after shrine, and finally was released from the skull at the Shrine of

[50] *Śiva* 3.8.36–66; 3.9.1–57. [51] *Śata.* 5.4.1.9–10; see above, chap. VI, secs. 3–4.

Uśanas on the Sarasvatī; this shrine, where Uśanas had performed asceticism for the demons in battle, became known as Kapālamocana thenceforth, for it was there that the sage was purified and freed from sin (kalmaṣa).[52]

Although nothing is said here about Brahminicide, and the sage receives the skull accidentally rather than by explicit agreement, it is evident that he receives the sin of murder along with the skull, for he must be purified and made free of sin as well as physically released from the skull. The fact that this release takes place at the shrine of Uśanas provides a further link with the Indra-Vṛtra cycle in which Uśanas (Śukra) is prominent.

Although Śiva sometimes distributes his destructive energies as Indra does,[53] this pattern is rarely applied to the story of Śiva's Brahminicide. When Śiva absorbs the Indra myth and Indra is replaced by more "moral" gods, certain reversals must soon take place; thus Śiva is said to free the mortal Vālmīki from Brahminicide,[54] where Indra gives his Brahminicide to other mortals. Śiva's role as savior may have been influenced by the Mahāyāna Buddhist ideal of the Bodhisattva who willingly suffers in order to teach others how to find Release, saying, "I take upon myself the deeds of all beings. . . . I take their suffering upon me. . . . I must bear the burden of all living beings, for I have vowed to save all things living. . . . It is better that I alone suffer than the multitude of living beings."[55] The transition from the pattern of the Indra myth to that of the Śiva myth may also be associated with the bhakti belief that God (Śiva) loves mankind, whereas Indra in the post-Vedic corpus feared or even hated mankind.

The Kāpālika may be regarded as an avatar of Śiva (though Śiva's human incarnations are usually called *svarūpas*, his "own forms" rather than avatars). The myth in which the Kāpālikas are created to counteract the wicked avatars of Viṣṇu may indicate a Śaiva tendency to make this aspect of Śiva serve as a counterpart to the avatar; in this context, it may be significant that the *Mahābhārata* story of Kapālamocana (the oldest text to describe the origin of the shrine) associates it with a Vaiṣṇava avatar, Rāma, rather than with Śiva. Official lists of Śiva's avatars created in imitation of those of Viṣṇu do not mention the Kāpālika, but they do say that Śiva will become incarnate as Daruka in the Pine Forest,[56] and Śiva usually enters the Pine Forest as a Kāpālika.[57] Moreover, there is an ambivalence in the attitude toward the cause of the avatars of both Viṣṇu and Śiva. Just as Śiva is sometimes cursed to become a Kāpālika and sometimes assumes this role of his own will for the sake of mankind, so Viṣṇu is often said to have been cursed to be born seven times among mankind as punishment for his sin of killing a woman, although the text quickly adds that he became incarnate

[52] *MBh.* 9.38.1–20. [53] See above, chap. VI, sec. 5. [54] *MBh.* 13.18.7–8; Drekmeier, p. 43.
[55] *Vajradhvaja Sūtra*, cited in Basham, p. 278. [56] *Liṅga* 1.24.100; *Vāyu* 1.23.184.
[57] *Āpastamba Dharmasūtra* 1.9.24.15 and Kullūka on *Manu* 11.72.

"for the sake of the world"[58] or to establish dharma.[59] Śiva's appearance on earth as the Kāpālika more closely approaches the idea of the savior than do Viṣṇu's incarnations, for Kṛṣṇa ultimately destroys men and their greatest Vaiṣṇava shrine (Dvārakā), whereas Śiva as the Kāpālika (and at Dakṣa's sacrifice) restores all that he destroys and establishes the great Śaiva shrine at Benares. Viṣṇu's appearance as Rāma is selfish in motivation as well, for when the gods and Indra are terrorized and humiliated by the Rākṣasa Rāvaṇa, Viṣṇu is forced to become incarnate as a man to kill him; Brahmā tells the gods, "Rāvaṇa asked to be invincible by Gandharvas, Yakṣas, gods, demons, and Rākṣasas, but since he despised men he did not enumerate them in his list; therefore he may only be killed by a man."[60] Here, as elsewhere, only by becoming a mortal man can a god kill his own enemies, the demons; and only by becoming a man can a god seek his own expiation by worshipping at shrines such as Kapālamocana.

Although both Śiva and Viṣṇu are sometimes said to act in the spirit of play, *līlā*, an attitude sometimes said to absolve them of responsibility for their actions,[61] Viṣṇu merely assumes his roles superficially, resuming full divinity whenever he pleases, while Śiva truly suffers as the Kāpālika. Śiva also acts as a savior when he drinks the poison that emerges from the ocean to threaten the universe.[62] The concept of the sinful avatar may be directly related to the more general doctrine of sinful rebirth: "This implies that the God who incarnates is not perfect because he still possesses a trace of desire which must be worked out in an earthly locus and in a human form. . . . One ends by supplicating oneself to an imperfect God."[63] "Imperfect" is a generous adjective for most Hindu gods; as Brahmin-killers, Indra and Śiva are regarded as the very scum of heaven, and yet they do suffer for their sins. As they must rid themselves of their guilt, they place it where it was known to exist: among mankind. But Śiva, who invented Brahminicide, invented also the vow to expiate Brahminicide, just as Śiva Lord of Beasts invented the Pāśupata rite to free the beast from the snare.

Many Śaiva versions of the Kāpālika myth, which have been revised to reflect credit upon Śiva, claim that he acted as he did in order to benefit various people. According to one such text, Śiva beheaded Brahmā for Brahmā's own good, though it is still felt necessary to have Śiva create a factotum to teach the expiation (albeit not to do the deed itself):

Once when Brahmā was trying to create, he produced a beautiful woman and grabbed her by force. When he asked her to make love with him, she became angry and said, "This fifth head is inauspicious on your neck. Four faces would be more suitable for you." She then

[58] *Padma* 1.13.244–247; *Brahmāṇḍa* 3.3.85–106; 72.3–17; *Matsya* 47.99–103.

[59] *Matsya* 47.235; cf. *Gītā* 4.7. [60] *Rām.* 1.14.13–14. [61] See above, chap. I, sec. 1.

[62] *MBh.* 1.15.1–4; 1.16.1ff; *Matsya* 249.1–3, 250.1ff.; *Vāyu* 1.54.47–82; *Brahmāṇḍa* 4.6.31–47.

[63] Herman, pp. 377–378.

vanished, and the fire of Brahmā's anger burnt up all the water on earth. Rudra appeared and severed the fifth head with his nails; he then took up the severed head and became the Kāpālika. When he reached Kapālamocana, the skull fell from him, the gods praised him, and he was purified. Śiva then created an ascetic who wandered and taught the Kāpālika vow.[64]

In addition to benefiting mankind in general—both by destroying the head that blazes so destructively and by creating an ascetic to teach the vow—Śiva's action helps Brahmā in creation, by removing the "inauspicious" fifth head. This head is sometimes considered inauspicious for demonophile rather than incestuous tendencies:

Brahmā's fifth head was helping the demons to devour the gods. When the gods asked Viṣṇu to cut it off, he said, "If the head is cut off it will destroy the universe." They praised Śiva, who agreed to cut off the head and hold it, since the earth could not bear it and the ocean would have been dried up in a minute. Then, out of pity for the world, Śiva held the head until he placed it in Benares.[65]

Here, as in other versions, the head is particularly dangerous because of its fiery quality. This quality is offensive to the gods even when it is not destructive, for it is competitive:

Brahmā's fifth head had such excessive energy and shone so brilliantly that all the gods and demons were unable to see or move, for it was far brighter than the sun, and it swallowed up the glory and power of the gods.[66]

The demonic affiliation of the head cited in justification of Śiva's action in the earlier text is not valid here, where the head is said to be as dangerous to demons as it is to the gods. The threat it poses is the recurrent one of an excess of energy (*tejas*), the quantity which must be limited in anyone bad or good, the virtuous demon or the immortal Rudras. This same energy threatens Brahmā's sons in yet another version of the myth:

Śiva created Brahmā, who had five heads. When Brahmā failed to create, he asked Śiva to be his son, whereupon Śiva said that he would cut off Brahmā's head. Brahmā then created a five-headed son, Rudra, and sent him to Himālaya, but Brahmā became foolish and proud, thinking that he had created everything. His fifth head produced an energy so great that it destroyed the wits of his sons, just as lamps fail to glow when the sun has risen. His sons took refuge with Śiva, telling him how Brahmā's fifth head had destroyed their energy and asking him to restore things as before. Śiva overwhelmed Brahmā with his energy, and he cut off Brahmā's head.[67]

The justification for Śiva's action in destroying the glowing head is somewhat

[64] *Bhaviṣya* 3.4.13.1–19. [65] *Brahma* 113.1–22.
[66] *Padma* 5.14.92–115. [67] *Skanda* 5.1.2.1–65.

weakened by the statement that Śiva's energy was even greater than Brahmā's, and would supposedly produce an even greater danger. A further confusion is evident in the implication that Śiva is his own grandfather (for he is the son of his son Brahmā, a situation that occurs in other Purāṇas and in the Ṛg Veda,[68] but is usually less blatantly apparent). Once again, stumbling-blocks in the logic reveal a moral dilemma; the author finds it difficult to justify the actions of the Kāpālika, and most Śaiva theologians consider the episode to reflect discredit on Śiva.

Dakṣa has a particular reason to object to the Kāpālika Śiva, for the Dakṣa myth is a multiform of the Vedic myth of the beheading of Prajāpati by Rudra. We have, therefore, yet another logical circle: Śiva beheads Dakṣa because Dakṣa has insulted Śiva because Śiva beheaded Dakṣa (Prajāpati). Thus Śiva is a heretic long before Dakṣa curses him to be so. Śiva appears in the *Mahābhārata* as a naked Kirāṭa, an outcaste hunter.[69] He is said to be an outcaste, lower than a Śūdra,[70] and he is involved sexually with outcaste women.[71] The image of Śiva as the beggar (Bhikṣāṭanamūrti)–the form in which he appears in the Pine Forest–has a bell tied to his leg; as bells were worn by outcastes in order to warn the upper castes of their approach, the iconography "emphasizes in a way the belief that the god was outside the pale of orthodox Vedism."[72] In this form, Śiva is often accompanied by a dog, the scavenger outcaste of the animal world.

The belief that God himself is a heretic results in a number of theological labyrinths. For whereas Viṣṇu taught the heresy of Buddhism falsely and maliciously to non-Hindus, so that Hindus may simply dismiss this episode as a divine trick which need not concern them, Śiva teaches Hindus doctrines which he intends for their good (and, in some texts, declares to be valid doctrine), though they are regarded as heresies by many Hindus, even by some members of the sects which profess them. In the context of the historical background of Śiva as an outcaste and heretic, the Dakṣa myth, which seems at first to exclude Śiva, actually represents his assimilation into the orthodox pantheon. After the curses have been exchanged, Śiva comes to the sacrifice and destroys it, and he forces Dakṣa and his faction to acknowledge him and to give him a share in the sacrifice. The first part of the myth, containing the tirades against Śiva, represents an earlier stage at which the more obviously non-Vedic characteristics of Śiva had not yet been rationalized. Thus, from the initial premise of Rudra's heresy, the myth comes full circle to the episode in which Dakṣa curses Śiva to be an outcaste and his followers to be heretics, while Dadhīca/Nandin (the representative of Śiva himself) produces yet another group of heretics, the followers of Dakṣa. Because of the different historical levels preserved within a single myth, the

[68] von Stietencron (1969), *passim*, and *RV* 10.90.5. [69] *MBh*. 3.40.1–5. [70] *Skanda* 4.2.87–89.

[71] *Manasābijay* of Bipradās, pp. 1–235; cited in Maity, p. 79. [72] Banerjea, p. 483.

relationship between the heretical god and his more orthodox followers, on the one hand, and the relationship between the "reformed" god and his still unregenerate followers, on the other, led to various paradoxes. Chief among these was the problem of imitation, which applies not only to Śiva but to other gods of the Hindu pantheon as well (primarily Indra and Kṛṣṇa), whose immoral behavior was a source of embarrassment to the more pious members of their sects.

3. The Problem of Imitation

When Śiva was transformed from an outcaste to the supreme god, many of his worshippers remained outcaste, forcing their god to justify his actions in having created sects of which he now was said to disapprove, sects that were an awkward reminder of his former, disreputable status. Śiva became dissociated from some of the more extreme members of his own sects, who still nevertheless maintained that it was he who taught them to behave as he had done. Śiva is said to have remarked, "The left-hand [*vāma*, i.e., Tantric] ritual, though declared by me, was intended for Śūdras only. A Brahmin who drinks liquor is no longer a Brahmin; let it not be done."[73] The implication here is that Śiva himself no longer indulges in alcohol, though the Śūdra members of his sects do so by his instruction. Similarly, Pārvatī remarks to Śiva, "I fear that those rites which were enunciated by you for the welfare of men have been perverted in the Kali Age,"[74] implying that Śiva himself had never behaved as his worshippers did now, in the Kali Age.

The difficulties that arise from the attempt to dissociate the god from the heresies that he creates are evident in a statement made by Śiva after he has taught heretical doctrines at the request of Viṣṇu:[75] "In order to delude those outside the Vedas, I propounded these doctrines. But I am the very form of the Vedas, and my true form is not known to those who speak the doctrine of other texts. I am to be known by the Vedas."[76] A more lengthy discussion of this point of view appears in the *Padma Purāṇa*:

Pārvatī said to Śiva, "You have said that one should avoid conversation with heretics. What sort of people are they?" Śiva replied, "Those who carry skulls and bones and wear ashes, those who use non-Vedic rites and do not follow the lawbooks, they are all heretics." Pārvatī was amazed and said, "But you yourself carry skulls and bones and ashes; why is this reviled?" Śiva then told the great secret about his own behavior:

"Formerly, the demons delighted in Viṣṇu and were pure, devoid of all evils. Indra and the gods were disturbed and full of fear of the demons, who shook off their sins by means of asceticism and were invincible. Viṣṇu then told me, 'Create a heretical dharma in order to delude the enemies of the gods. Narrate Purāṇas of darkness to Gautama, Bṛhaspati,

[73] Wilson (1861), I, 252n., citing Kāśīnātha's *Dakṣiṇācara Tantra Raja*.

[74] *Mahānirvāṇa Tantra* 1.64–65. [75] See above, chap. IX, sec. 1. [76] *Varāha* 70.41–43.

and the other sages; teach them the Pāśupata doctrine. Bear the skull, ashes, and bones yourself, to cause the people in the triple world to worship you in this form, and I will worship you in this form in order to delude the creatures of darkness.' I was very upset about this, fearing that it would destroy me, but Viṣṇu said, 'Do as I say, for the sake of the gods, and you will restore yourself by reciting my thousand names.' Then for the sake of the gods I created the way of heretics, entering Gautama and the other Brahmins. The Rākṣasas obtained boons from me and they all became attached to sense objects, devoid of truth and strength, and they were conquered by the gods, falling from all dharma to the lowest place. Thus I created the reviled sects of outcastes proclaiming the Śaiva, Pāśupata, Nyāya, Sāṅkhya, Materialist, and Buddhist heresies. The doctrine that Viṣṇu had taught in the form of the Buddha, to destroy the demons, that very doctrine of Buddhism I taught in the Kali Age, to delude the universe."[77]

The myth begins as usual with the need to corrupt virtuous demons but results in the corruption of mortal Brahmins. The text retains several nonsectarian motifs (such as the role of Bṛhaspati and the use of Buddhist as well as Materialist heresies) and adds others associated with the Śaiva cycle, such as the reference to Gautama and the Pāśupata heresy. Like Death, Śiva at first objects to his appointed wicked svadharma, but is finally persuaded to perform an evil act for a good end; his action is to the disadvantage of mankind, though it is to the advantage of the gods. Śiva manages to clear himself by publicly denouncing the heresies he teaches, taking refuge in the worship of Viṣṇu, and falling back on the final argument that he was only obeying orders. (This rationalization is further extended by the *Varāha Purāṇa*,[78] which, like the *Padma*, has a Vaiṣṇava bias, which leads it to attribute *all* the deeds of Śiva, good or evil, to Viṣṇu's command.)

These texts deal with the first of the pair of conflicts, that between the purified god and his still impure worshippers. More troublesome, however, is the complementary conflict between the impure god and his purified worshippers. When Śiva was eventually accepted into the orthodox pantheon, his previously documented antisocial behavior raised serious problems when regarded as a possible model for the worshipper. The evil actions of the god were used to explain the vice that is in the world, justified, as Vyāsa justified Bṛhaspati's dishonesty and heresy, by the accepted analogy between human and divine emotions:

Śiva's cobra, hungry, wishes to eat the rat of Gaṇeśa;
And the peacock of Skanda wishes to eat the cobra.
The lion of Pārvatī is greedy for the snake-eating bird.

[77] *Padma* 6.263.1–91. [78] *Varāha* 70.41–43.

Since there is such strife even in the house of Śiva,
How could it be otherwise in the universe, which is
The very form of that household?[79]

The belief that the behavior of the gods has not only an analogous but a causal effect on human behavior appears in an inverted use of the same animal metaphor. When Śiva performs asceticism and becomes completely calm, the natural enmities of the animal kingdom are overcome, and cows play with tigers, deer with lions, snakes with rats, dogs with cats.[80] If the gods, then, behave badly, how can man aspire to virtue? "If Brahmā is unceasingly employed in the creation of worlds; if the eye of the god who destroyed the sacrifice of Dakṣa burns with desire when he embraces Gaurī, how can tranquility be obtained by man?"[81]

The next logical step, from the model of explanation to the model for imitation, recurs throughout Hindu writings but is ultimately rejected. Nārada attempts to convert Ghora to hedonism by citing the fact that Śiva, who knows the highest truth, seduced the wives of the Pine Forest sages.[82] Kṛṣṇa assumes that men imitate the gods when he says that he keeps working because men would follow his example if he did not; the example that Kṛṣṇa sets by committing adultery must then be justified by elaborate arguments,[83] and in certain sects such as the Sahajiyās of Bengal, Kṛṣṇa's example does lead to behavior contrary to the Hindu norm. As Eliade writes,

> One becomes truly a man only by conforming to the teaching of the myths, that is, by imitating the gods. . . . Even the most barbarous act and the most aberrant behavior have divine, transhuman models. . . . Religious man sought to imitate, and believed that he was imitating, his gods even when he allowed himself to be led into acts that verged on madness, depravity, and crime.[84]

The gods, like men, often justify their wickedness by citing each other's sins. When Indra kills a woman he excuses himself on the grounds that Viṣṇu killed Śukra's mother (which he did at Indra's behest);[85] Indra is said to have brought adultery into the world by his bad example,[86] and when Nahuṣa attempts to seduce Indra's wife, he replies to the gods' objections by stating that they never objected when Indra raped Ahalyā and committed other deeds contrary to dharma.[87] Rāma is urged to slay a female demon by the reminder that Indra once slew Virocana's daughter when she intended to destroy the earth.[88] The *Bhāgavata Purāṇa* even goes so far as to justify Kṛṣṇa's adultery with reference to human behavior, saying that since even the sages are uncontrolled and act as they

[79] *Pañcatantra* 1.159; cf. *Subhāṣitaratnakoṣa*, verses 70 and 97. [80] *Manmathonmathana* 2.21.
[81] *Prabodhacandrodaya* 2.28. [82] *Devī Purāṇa*, chaps. 8, 9, and 13; see above, chap. VII, sec. 1.
[83] *Gītā* 3.23; *Padma* 6.272.176; *Bhāgavata* 10.33.34–36. Cf. Bhagavan Das, p. 98; Pal, p. 68; Muir, IV, 48–54. [84] Eliade (1959), p. 100 and p. 104. [85] *Rām.* 1.24.17–19.
[86] *Rām.* 7.30.20–45. [87] *MBh.* 5.12.6–7. [88] *Rām.* 1.25.15–22.

please, how could one possibly restrain Viṣṇu when he becomes voluntarily incarnate?[89]

As early as the Upaniṣads, Indra boasts of his unpunished sins and offers to share his immunity with his worshippers:

"I killed the three-headed son of Tvaṣṭṛ and delivered the ascetics to the jackals; I broke a treaty and overcame the demon Prahlāda and the descendants of Puloman. Yet not a hair of my head was harmed. So he who understands me is not injured by any deed, not even by stealing, killing an embryo, matricide or parricide. If he has committed any evil, he does not become pale."[90]

Paul Deussen suggests that the worshipper is thus immune from the consequences of his deeds because they are no longer his deeds.[91] One might say that the manner in which Indra seems to be able to perform, unscathed, acts forbidden to Hindus bound by strict caste law functions as a kind of vicarious release, a safety valve for his worshippers; the myth functions as the negative example of a difficult reality. The moral dilemma arises only when the ordinary worshipper is allowed to share the god's immunity; then the model leaves the realm of the ideal, becomes an actuality, and must be justified by the doctrine of imitation.

Certain theologians were able to justify the heretical behavior of their sects by referring to the heretical behavior of their gods: "What the gods do and what the worshippers do in their service cannot according to Hindu opinion be judged by ordinary laws of right and wrong. The god is supra-moral; the worshipper when he enters the temple leaves conventionality outside."[92] The more orthodox view holds that the gods alone are supra-moral, but the "left-hand" sects maintain the validity of imitation and hold the "released" worshipper equally unbound by the morality of *svadharma*. This view, though of special benefit to the esoteric sects, is obviously supported by the social atmosphere of orthodox Hinduism, which is so thoroughly conditioned to the idea that there are natural divisions between men, that what is appropriate for the elect (the Brahmin) is not appropriate to the Śūdra, that "quod licet Jovi non licet bovi." The hierarchy of morality thus serves both to support and to challenge the doctrine of imitation, depending on the status of the mortals involved in the action. The gods rank above mankind, and are therefore not to be imitated, but the "enlightened man" (and sometimes the Brahmin) also ranks above mankind and may behave immorally without suffering the consequences of his action.

The doctrine of imitation was more often rejected and criticized for the abuses it encouraged than accepted as dogma. In the Vedic period, when gods were primarily good and benevolent, men were encouraged to imitate them; this is the

89 *Bhāgavata* 10.33.35. 90 *Kau. Up.* 3.1; see above, chap. V, secs. 5 and 11; chap. VI, sec. 3.

91 Deussen (1897), p. 41n; cf. Zaehner (1974), *passim*. 92 Eliot, II, 168.

basis of the sacrifice. But when the conflict between gods and men became more important than their mutual dependence, it was regarded as a sin to imitate even the good behavior of the gods, let alone their evil behavior.[93] Whatever the laws of the actions of the gods, they do not apply to man; Brahmā's incest is justified by the statement that the ways of divine beings can be known only by the gods, not by men, who should not talk about them.[94] Thus, for one reason or another, men were not supposed to imitate the evil behavior of the gods. The Śaivas who tried to justify their excesses by saying that they were merely copying their god became the object of satire and disapproval.[95] The wicked Kali complains about this double standard when he says to the gods, "Let Brahmā sport with any girl, and you amuse yourselves with celestial nymphs, but Kali must live in celibacy. You preach dharma and yet you do things that one can hardly bear to hear about,"[96] and Prahlāda makes a similar accusation of hypocrisy against the Hindu gods.[97]

The gods are said to commit serious sins in order "to awaken people to a sense of the dangers of *adharma*"[98]—that is, as a negative moral example. The divine extremes of Tantrism are considered suitable only for people at the extremes of the moral scale—the gods and truly enlightened sages, on the one hand, and the degraded mortals of the Kali Age, on the other. The usual justification for Tantric practice—that the enlightened man may achieve salvation by the very acts that cause common men to burn in hell[99]—was often explicitly cited and rejected. Thus, when Śiva is criticized, Nārada remarks,

> "If [Pārvatī] be married to Śaṅkara, everyone will regard even those faults as virtues. . . . The sun and fire devour all sorts of food, but no one blames them for it. Though both pure and impure water flow in the Gaṅgā, no one calls the river foul. The powerful, sire, can do no wrong, like the sun and the fire and the Gaṅgā. But if any stupid man, wise in his own conceits, would do as they do, he falls into hell and stays there for an aeon. Can the creature be compared to God?"[100]

Similarly, it is said (in explaining why Kṛṣṇa's adultery cannot be taken as license for men to do the same) that Rudra alone may drink poison unharmed, just as no blame is imputed to fire, which consumes all fuel.[101] Another reason for men to refrain from imitating Kṛṣṇa's adultery is simply a rephrasing of Kali's complaint about the gods' moral hypocrisy: "We should act as the gods say, not as they do; let no one other than a superior being even think of acting thus."[102] Śrīdhara comments on this:

[93] Indrabhūti's *Jñānasiddhi*, chap. 15; Eliade (1958), p. 263; Zaehner (1974). [94] *Matsya* 4.3–5.

[95] *Mattavilāsaprahasana* and *Karpūramañjarī*. [96] *Naiṣadhacarita* 7.122–123.

[97] See above, chap. V, sec. 14. [98] Rajagopalachari, p. 40. [99] Eliade (1958), p. 263.

[100] *Rāmacaritamānasa*, pp. 37–38. [101] *Bhāgavata* 10.33.30–31; see above, chap. VI, sec. 2.

[102] *Bhāgavata* 10.33.31–32.

In order to refute the charge (of immorality) against the supreme deity, the author speaks of the behavior of the great, the transgression of dharma. He mentions the outrageous behavior seen in Prajāpati, Indra, Soma, Viśvāmitra, and the others, and says that no fault is attached to them because of their energy. But if anyone else should act in this way, not being divine (there would be a fault attached to them).[103]

The idea that we must heed the teachings of the gods but not imitate their actions also appears in Mahāyāna Buddhism, though it arises from a very different philosophy; the Buddha says, "Knowing (men) to be perverted, infatuated, and ignorant, I teach final rest, myself not being at rest."[104] The belief that man should behave better than God appears in the teachings of the Buddha, who is said to have remarked that human beings are ideally situated to seek moral perfection or release, because they are more highly endowed than animals (who lack the intellect to strive for salvation) but less privileged than the gods (who enjoy such happiness in heaven that they are not motivated to strive for salvation).[105]

These conflicting philosophical attitudes are all pertinent to the problem of Śiva as a heretic and as the author of heresies. Ultimately, the majority opinion, and certainly the orthodox opinion, compromised by maintaining that the god was not to be imitated by his worshippers in all his immoral actions, but that the heresies that he introduced specifically for the sake of immoral men were to be followed, at least by those men. The major Śaiva heresies are said to have been propounded by Śiva for certain special groups of men, not those set above the normal moral law (such as the "enlightened" men and Brahmins exempted by the Upaniṣads and other esoteric texts) but those specifically set below the normal moral law: the heretic groups created by the curses of Dakṣa, Dadhīca, the Seven Sages, Gautama, and Bhṛgu. We have already seen how the first two groups arose; now let us consider the final groups, all of whom are associated with the Pine Forest in some way.

4. Gautama and the Seven Sages in the Great Drought

Gautama is listed among the greatest heretics in the *Padma Purāṇa* conversation between Śiva and Pārvatī cited above, and his curse is an accepted source of heresy: "Either because of the curse of Gautama and the others, or because of the great evil, men outside the Vedas and those who are born of mixed castes, as well as women and Śūdras, take the Tantras as their text."[106] "The curse of Gautama" may be interpreted objectively or subjectively—that is, a curse given by Gautama

[103] Śrīdhara on *Bhāgavata* 10.33.30–32; Muir, IV, 48–54. [104] *Saddharmapuṇḍarīka* 15.21.

[105] Vasubandhu's *Abhidharmakośa*, cited by von Glasenapp (1970), p. 29.

[106] *Tantrādhikāranirṇaya*, p. 25.

or to him—for there are two myths of heresy in which he plays an important role, first as author of the curse and then as its recipient.

In the first myth, Gautama is a virtuous sage, who retains his virtue even under the great pressure of hunger, the force that produces the inevitable corruption of normal men. The story of Gautama and the great drought may be traced back to the Ṛg Veda, where Gotama is said to have produced a magic spring or to have received water from the Maruts when he was thirsty.[107] In the Purāṇas, Gautama's hermitage situated on the banks of the Godāvarī is a place of special sanctity and safety in time of drought, like Divodāsa's city:

During a terrible drought which lasted for twelve years, people began to starve. They went to Gautama and requested food. By the power of his asceticism, Gautama caused the Ganges to flow there and produced food, with which he fed them. When the drought ended, people returned to their homes and Gautama resumed his asceticism.[108]

This tradition—that Gautama has the power to create a miraculous river in time of drought, or that his hermitage always has this property and is resorted to in time of drought—underlies the entire corpus of this series.

Another strand interwoven with it is originally connected not with Gautama alone but with the Seven Sages as a group (of which Gautama is a member), the very group that later comes to oppose the Gautama of the miraculous hermitage and to represent vice in contrast with his virtue. This myth also begins with drought:

Once when there was a terrible drought and widespread starvation, the Seven Sages and Arundhatī wandered the earth in search of food. They saw a dead boy, and, as they were starving, began to cook him. While they were cooking him, King Vṛṣādarbhi came to them and implored them to refrain from eating what should not be eaten, and he offered them food and riches. They refused to accept a gift from a king, but they left the boy uncooked and went to find food in the forest. The king sent his ministers to spread gold before them, but they refused this too. Then the king became furious, and he performed a sacrifice which produced a hideous witch, whom he sent to destroy the Seven Sages and Arundhatī. Meanwhile, the sages were joined by a wandering mendicant named Śunaḥsakha ("friend of a dog"), with whom they shared their fruits and roots. One day they saw a beautiful lotus pond guarded by the hideous witch created by Vṛṣādarbhi. The sages approached the pond to gather and eat the lotus filaments, and as the witch was about to devour them, Śunaḥsakha struck her on the head and reduced her to ashes. The sages then gathered the filaments with great effort and put them on the bank while they performed their ablutions in the pond, but when they emerged the lotuses had disappeared. They all cursed the unknown thief: Atri said, "Let whoever stole them touch a cow with his foot," and the others cursed the thief to commit similar evil acts. But then Śunaḥsakha confessed

[107] *RV* 1.88.4, 1.116.9, 4.4.11. [108] *Nārada Purāṇa* 2.72.

to having taken the filaments in order to test them, and he told them that he was Indra and that he had killed the witch in order to protect them. "Your lack of greed," he said, "has procured for you unperishing worlds. Arise and go there." And they went to heaven with Indra, for even when they were hungry they had had no greed.[109]

The sages' lack of greed even under pressure of hunger is proven by their refusal to accept the gifts of a king; apparently their intention to eat a human child is permissible in time of emergency (*āpad*); Viśvāmitra, another of the Seven Sages, is chastised by an Untouchable for violating a food tabu in time of famine,[110] just as the group is here chastised by a king, but in both myths the sages are vindicated. It is not clear how Indra tests their virtue; Vṛṣādarbhi has already established their high-mindedness, and when Indra takes their food they react with hysterical vengeance. But the wording of the first curse—that someone will strike a cow—and the subsequent curses that are to turn the thief into a person guilty of various evil and heretical acts (curses with no effect in this variant) are motifs that persist, with a very different twist, in later variants of the myth.

Another text states that the Seven Sages lived in a hermitage where there were no atheists or sinners, no diseases or death, no hunger, until they cooked a dead child; then they were forced to wander about in search of food. (Apparently their hermitage loses its magic properties because of their transgression, just as Gautama's obtains its powers because of his virtues). The king (who is nameless) appears only after the child-cooking episode and cannot therefore chastise them for it, but he offers them food, gold, and *a cow*; they refuse his offer and no more is heard of the king (he does not create a witch to trouble them), but they meet Indra, enter the lotus pond, and enter heaven.[111]

The last variant of this episode begins not with the virtue of the sages' hermitage but with the evil that arises in it in time of drought:

Once there was a twelve-year drought in the hermitage of the Seven Sages. People abandoned all dharma and rituals and ate improper things; mothers abandoned their sons, men their wives, and everyone stole, oppressed by hunger. The Seven Sages wandered until they found a dead boy, and were cooking him when Vṛṣādarbhi came upon them and said, "What is this disgusting act, to eat human flesh as if you were Rākṣasas? I will give you food; leave the dead boy." But they replied, "There is expiation for eating human flesh, but one must never accept a gift from a king." Furious, the king decided to test them: he left gold for them on the ground, but they rejected this too. They wandered on and met Śunomukha ("face of a dog"), entered the pond, and cursed the unknown thief of the lotus filaments to be omnivorous, hypocritical, a drinker of wine and eater of meat, a whoremaster and a horse-dealer. Indra revealed himself and told them that he had only

109 *MBh.* 13.94.3–44; 13.95.1–86.

110 See above, chap. II, sec. 7.

111 *Padma* 5.19.210–391.

tested their dharma; they remained there performing asceticism until they obtained immortality.[112]

This text actually states that the king is testing the sages, though Indra is still said to test them as well. The cooking of the child is discussed at greater length and ultimately dismissed as a necessary evil in time of misfortune; but the fanatical antimonarchical bias of the Brahmin redactor does not yield an inch. The unknown thief is now cursed to eat many forbidden things; this is used to provide a bridge between the eating of the dead child and the kicking of the cow in later variants that describe the eating of a cow.

The sin of the Seven Sages in the famine, the sin of eating a cow, is an important element in the myth of Satyavrata (Triśaṅku):

Satyavrata attempted to commit adultery, and for this he was driven out by his father, the king, and Indra sent no rain for twelve years. Satyavrata became a Caṇḍāla and fed the wife and sons of Viśvāmitra on the meat of wild animals, in return for which favor Viśvāmitra helped Satyavrata ascend bodily to heaven.

Other texts elaborate upon this with significant variations:

Satyavrata was cursed by the sons of Vasiṣṭha to be an outcaste; in return, Viśvāmitra cursed the sons of Vasiṣṭha to be outcastes. During the drought, Satyavrata fed Viśvāmitra's sons and himself by killing the magic wishing-cow of Vasiṣṭha, for which he was cursed to be called a Triple Sinner (Triśaṅku), having displeased his father, killed a cow, and eaten its flesh. Nevertheless, and in spite of the opposition of Indra, Viśvāmitra enabled Satyavrata to ascend to heaven, where he became a constellation, suspended head downwards forever.[113]

Through this widespread myth, the Seven Sages are clearly associated with a twelve year drought, the eating of a cow, the curse of being outcaste, and the opposition of a group of sages to a single sage who provides food. The original myth, set in the Vedic context of ritual competition between kings and priests (or between two different kinds of priest) presents a simple Vedic solution: the priest wins, and the sinner goes to heaven. (No expiation or release is stipulated for the sons of Vasiṣṭha, who are cursed to be outcastes). But the Purāṇic myths of the sinful sages reject the Vedic solution and enter into a more complex series of purifications.

The first of these variants states the opposition between the wicked Seven Sages and the virtuous individual sage, who is here called Garga rather than Gautama:

[112] *Skanda* 6.32.1–100.

[113] *Viṣṇu* 4.3; *Hari.* 9–10; *Rām.* 1.56.10–1.59.33.

The sage Viśvāmitra had seven sons who became the pupils of Garga. When there was a terrible drought, they left Garga's hermitage to live in the woods, and they decided to eat his cow. Having resolved upon this evil, they minimized the sin by offering the cow as food for their ancestors. When they had eaten the cow, they told their guru that it had been stolen by a tiger. Then they became hunters, and later they were reborn as deer, birds, and finally as ascetics.[114]

Hunger, which led to the attempted eating of a child by all the sages and the kicking of a cow by their unknown enemy, which caused the sages to refuse the gift of a cow from the king and to curse their enemy to be omnivorous, now causes them themselves to eat a cow belonging to the virtuous Garga/Gautama, and to be doomed (by their own evil action) to a life of wickedness and polluting slaughter, as hunters; yet even here their sin is limited, and their ultimate salvation (as yogis) is promised as usual.

The final group of texts in this cycle transfers the apparent sin of cow-killing from the Seven Sages to Gautama, but now the cow is merely a delusory cow, like the cow used to corrupt the demons of the Triple City:[115]

Formerly, in the Pine Forest, there were householder sages who performed asceticism for Śiva. One day a terrible drought destroyed all living creatures, and the sage Gautama fed the Pine Forest sages, at their request, for twelve years. Then the drought ended and the sages wished to leave Gautama, but he wanted them to stay. They created the illusion of a cow, who died at Gautama's touch, and they used this as an excuse to refuse his food and to return to the Pine Forest to practise asceticism. When Gautama discovered that the cow-slaughter was an illusion, he cursed them to be beyond the pale of the Vedas.[116]

As usual, the curse is attributed ultimately to a drought and hunger, the source of the first sin (and the inverse of the flood that avenges that sin) in the myth of the Fall. Several versions of this episode emphasize the force of famine and the causal force of time and karma:

Once, Indra sent no rain for fifteen years. Because of the drought, food was scarce; it was not possible to count the corpses in every house. Some people ate horses and others ate human corpses; a mother would even eat her child, and a husband his wife, all were so tortured by hunger and famine. . . . Formerly, in the ripening of time, and by the force of the karma of living creatures, there was a twelve-year drought. Men behaved in evil ways because of their desire for food; some were so deluded that they killed and ate others; some ate elephants and horses.[117]

The original image of the cooking of the dead boy is now heightened by the image of the mother eating her own child, and of people killing their human

[114] *Matsya* 20.1–25. [115] See above, chap. VII, sec. 3. [116] *Kūrma* 1.15.95–108.

[117] *Devībhāgavata* 12.9.1–10; *Tantrādhikāranirṇaya*, p. 29; from the *Skanda Purāṇa*, *Yajñavaibhava Khaṇḍa*, p. 32. See above, chap. VIII, sec. 8.

food. These texts revive the tradition that the one exception to the universal evil arising from famine is the hermitage of Gautama or the Seven Sages; now it is said that in Gautama's hermitage, even in these desperate times, there was no fear of famine, demons, or anything else, and it is for this reason that all creatures, including the Seven Sages, take refuge with him.

The Ṛg Vedic motif of Gautama's particular ability to produce water in time of drought is then appropriately reintroduced: just as he was able to bring the Ganges to his hermitage, so he can control other rivers. In several texts, Gautama obtains the boon of unlimited water from Varuṇa (god of water as well as of morality);[118] in one, the boon of the magic river is given after the drought has ended and the illusory cow has been killed; Brahmā grants the original boon that makes Gautama's heritage a haven, promising that there will always be food there, but nothing is said about water; after the cow has been killed, however, the hypocritical sages assure Gautama that the cow is not actually dead, but merely unconscious, and that she will revive when immersed in the water of the Ganges; then the myth cotinues:

Gautama propitiated Śiva by performing asceticism for a hundred and one years, begging Śiva to give him the Ganges that was in Śiva's matted locks. Śiva gave him a lock of hair, with which Gautama revived the dead cow, and at that spot a great river arose, auspicious and purifying. When the Seven Sages saw that marvel they returned and said, "Bravo! Bravo, Gautama, for causing the Ganges to descend to the Daṇḍaka forest." Then Gautama realized that the whole cow-slaughter had been an illusion, and he cursed the sages to take the vow of matted locks and ashes falsely, to be outside the three Vedas and Vedic rites. When the Seven Sages heard this, they said, "Let this not be for all time," and he replied, "My curse is never in vain; it will take place now, but then in the Kali Age men will have bhakti. Brahmins in the Kali Age will practise no rituals, for they will be burnt by the fire of your words, but if they bathe in this bovine river, the Godāvarī, and give as many cows as they can, they will go to heaven, and they will save their ancestors who have fallen to hell, and these ancestors will go to heaven and find eternal Release."[119]

The myth has been expanded here by the insertion of a multiform of the famous episode in which the sage Bhagīratha persuades Śiva to use his matted locks to help bring the Ganges to earth, in order to revive Bhagīratha's ancestors, who have been burnt to ashes,[120] like the sages "burnt" to hell by Gautama's curse. The river in this text offers redemption to the sinners who have killed the cow; like the sages in the Vṛṣādarbhi myths, they will ultimately find heaven despite the temporary curse that Gautama inflicts on them. In spite of the variations in the name of the forest (Pine Forest or Daṇḍaka) and the river (Ganges or

[118] See below, n. 123. Śiva 4.27.23–46. [119] *Varāha* 71.10–46.

[120] *MBh.* 3.104–108; *Brahmāṇḍa* 3.46–53; *Bhāgavata* 9.8.1–31; 9.9.1–15; *Rām.* 1.37–43; *Liṅga* 1.66.15–20; *Vāyu* 88.143–169; *Viṣṇu* 4.4.1–33.

Godāvarī), it is evident that the forest and the river are to provide release in the Kali Age for the sinners created in the myth, freeing their parents and ancestors from hell, as often happens in bhakti texts.[121]

Another variant supplies yet another member of the Ganges-Godāvarī group: Gāyatrī, the wife of Brahmā (often associated with Sarasvatī, another river-speech goddess). This text dwells at length on the nature of the heresy that Gautama brings upon the other sages:

When Gautama learned that the sages had created the illusion that he had killed a cow, he was furious, and he cursed them to hate Śiva and to be outside all sacrifices, Vedas, and lawbooks, to be evil men, adulterers, initiated in the Buddhist, Jain, Pāśupata, Kāpālika, Śākta [Tantric] sects and other heresies. When the sages begged for mercy, Gautama said, "You will be reborn in the Kali Age, and if you honor the feet of Gāyatrī you will be released from the curse." Therefore the sages were born as heretics in the Kali Age, doomed to return to hell because of their karma.[122]

Although there is an apparent moment of mercy, when the sages are promised salvation if they worship Gāyatrī (i.e., return to the Vedic rituals, for Gāyatrī is a Vedic hymn), the curse of heresy would seem to make such worship impossible, and they are finally doomed to hell.

The question of Gautama's mercy toward the sages is central to the *Śiva Purāṇa* version of this myth, which consists of two different variants explicitly compared precisely from the standpoint of mercy. The first of these versions is largely the same as the text that mentions Gāyatrī, with certain significant changes, notably the attempt to explain the quarrel in terms of a different basic human flaw—sexual desire instead of hunger:

When Gautama saw the sages suffering from famine, he performed asceticism for Varuṇa and obtained the boon of unlimited water. His hermitage became fruitful and he fed everyone. But one day the evil wives of the sages, who felt dishonored because of the water, became angry and spoke to their husbands spitefully about Gautama. The sages stupidly created the illusion of a cow, who died at Gautama's touch, but when Gautama found out about the cow he became angry and he cursed the sages, saying, "You evil ones who have caused me misery will be outside the Vedas, devoid of faith in the Śaiva path which gives release. You will fall to hell, and my curse will affect all your descendants, who will not be Śaivas, and you will dwell in hell with your sons." And so all the sages and their sons lived together, beyond the pale of Śaivism, and at the beginning of the Kali Age there will be many wicked men.[123]

This text implies that the sages are reborn first in hell and then on earth in the Kali Age, though no ultimate Release is given for them here, for their descen-

[121] See above, chap. IX, sec. 1, and below, chap. XI, sec. 1.

[122] *Tantrādhikāranirṇaya*, p. 31; *Devībhāgavata* 12.9.1–97.

[123] *Śiva* 4.27.23–46.

dants are specifically denied any power to help them. Although the motif of famine remains, it is subservient to the wickedness of the sages' wives, which is an essential point of many of the Pine Forest myths. The role of the wives is here obscure (they seem to feel it demeaning to accept Gautama's charity, which may also be the source of the malice of the sages themselves); their role is more fully developed in the other version of the myth, which the bard refers to as having occurred "in a different era":

Formerly, the sage Gautama lived with his virtuous wife Ahalyā, performing asceticism. One day a drought arose for a hundred years, and Gautama performed asceticism for Varuṇa, who granted him a fabulous well, which irrigated his hermitage and made it continuously fruitful, a place of refuge for everyone. Sages came there by the thousands and lived there with their wives and children. One day Gautama's disciples went to the well and were abused by the wives of the sages, who insisted upon drawing their water first; then Ahalyā went there and was abused by them. The evil-minded women lied to their husbands about what had happened, and when the sages heard of this, they were overpowered by the force of their future karma, and they became angry with Gautama and propitiated Gaṇeśa to make an obstacle against Gautama, to throw Gautama out of the hermitage. Gaṇeśa at first objected, saying, "It is not right to become angry with someone who has not offended you. You will be destroyed, for you are deluded by your wives." Yet, when they insisted, he agreed to do as they asked, and the illusion of the cow was created; it was Gaṇeśa who became the cow. The sages and their wives abused Gautama and Ahalyā and threw stones at them and drove them out of the hermitage.

Gautama begged the sages to tell him how to expiate his sin, and they prescribed a lengthy series of expiations, which Gautama faithfully performed. At length Śiva appeared, and when Gautama asked to be made free of sin, Śiva said, "You always were free of sin, but these evil sages deceived you. By the mere sight of them, let others become most evil, for they have become murderers and there is no expiation for them anywhere." But Gautama said, "The sages did me a favor, since if they had not acted as they did I would not have seen you. I am grateful to them for this favor, for their evil action has brought good fortune to me." Gautama then asked Śiva to let the Ganges flow through his hermitage and to remain there himself in the form of a liṅga.

When people heard of the miraculous powers of the river and the liṅga in Gautama's hermitage, they came from far and wide to worship there, and the sages who were Gautama's enemies also came there to bathe, but when the Ganges saw them she vanished, saying, "These are the most evil murderers, heretics who must not even be looked upon." But Gautama said to her, "These men were blinded by their passion for women, and he who does a favor to those who have offended against him will be purified." The Ganges appeared again and said that the sages must beg Gautama's forgiveness before she would reveal herself to them. Then the former murderers became ashamed and begged forgiveness.[124]

[124] *Śiva* 4.25.1–58; 4.26.1–57; 4.27.1–22.

Gautama is the husband of Ahalyā, with whom Indra commits adultery; this may serve to link this version with the episode in which Indra "tests" the famished sages, as well as with the group in which Indra's failure to send rain provides the initial impetus. Ahalyā is here not the epitome of female evil but rather the foil against which the wickedness of the other Pine Forest wives is displayed (a role played elsewhere by Arundhatī[125]). The phrase here used to justify the sages' subservience to their wives ("because of their future karma") is used in the first *Śiva Purāṇa* version to explain why the cow falls dead;[126] the two incidents are directly related, and both are unavoidable. In the vain attempt to find a first cause for the seed of evil, the myth falls back on the image of the fabulous, fruitful garden of virtue which is ruined by hunger and sinful women.

More significant changes may be seen in the manner in which the myth attempts to trace the further consequences of evil, to see how the chain, whatever its origin, may ultimately be broken. The question of expiation is first applied to Gautama rather than to the sages, for in this text they throw him out of the hermitage instead of fabricating an excuse to leave it themselves. In order to do this, they enlist the aid of Gaṇeśa, just as Śiva uses Gaṇeśa to throw Divodāsa out of Benares, and Gaṇeśa at first refuses to bring about this evil, though it is his svadharma to cause such obstacles. Gaṇeśa's objections are expressed not in moral terms, however, but rather in terms of the logic of transferred karma. He worries that by offending against an innocent man he and the sages will be destroyed, for he will obtain Gautama's bad karma and Gautama will obtain Gaṇeśa's good karma as a result of the unjust accusation.[127] This logic pervades the myth, for Gautama at the end says that he is grateful to the sages for having inadvertently done him a favor by attempting to do him a disservice; moreover, he advises the Ganges to reveal herself to them even though they do not deserve it, since in that way she will be doing a favor to those who have committed an offense, and thus she too will gain merit. In this way, by suffering a curse that he does not deserve, and by performing an expiation for a sin that he has not committed, Gautama gains great merit; realizing this, he does not curse the sages– Śiva himself makes them into heretics denied the right to expiation.

The expiation of the sages is a more difficult problem, for Śiva has made them so evil that the purifying water of the Ganges is too pure for them to use, and it is only by interceding in the name of mercy that Gautama is able to break the otherwise infinite chain of punishments. But the mercy is ultimately Śiva's, for he alone can free the sages from the heresy that he has inflicted on them, by bringing the Ganges down to earth for them and all other sinners.

[125] *MBh.* 3.213–216; *Skanda* 1.1.27.44–102; *Śiva, Dharma Saṃ.* 10.96–214; *Kūrma* 2.38.33–39; O'Flaherty (1973), pp. 98–103; (1975), pp. 108–110.

[126] *Śiva* 4.27.31; 4.25.8; *bhāvikarmavaśāt.*

[127] *Pāśupatasūtra* 3.6–19; Ingalls, pp. 287–291; O'Flaherty (1973), pp. 182–184; Lorenzen, pp. 187–188.

The roles of Śiva, the Ganges, and Gaṇeśa in this myth are further illuminated by another text, in which these three figures are bound together by a more coherent logic, and which exposes them in a rather malevolent conspiracy. This myth is evidently a development of the episode in which a lock of Śiva's hair produces the Ganges to revive the cow. The Ganges in this new version is the starting point of the entire myth:

Pārvatī, the wife of Śiva, was jealous of Śiva's second wife, the Ganges, who lived in his hair. Pārvatī asked Gaṇeśa to find a way to remove the Ganges from Śiva's hair. Now, at this time there was a great twelve-year drought everywhere but in Gautama's hermitage, because Brahmā had granted that no hunger or disease should exist there. Knowing of this, all the sages came as pupils to Gautama's hermitage. Then Gaṇeśa said to his mother, "Gautama could shake the Ganges from the matted locks of the three-eyed Śiva," and he went in the form of a Brahmin to Gautama's hermitage, accompanied by his brother and Jayā. There he said to the sages, "Let us ask Gautama's permission to return to our own hermitage," and when Gautama prevented them, because of his affection for each of them, Gaṇeśa said to the sages, "What, have we been bought with food? Let us go home." And then Gaṇeśa said to Jayā, "Without letting anyone else know of it, take the form of a cow and go where Gautama is, and eat the wheat, and when he strikes you, make a pitiful noise and fall down dead." She did so, and the sages cried out and went away. But then Gaṇeśa advised Gautama to bring the Ganges down from Śiva's hair and to sprinkle the cow with that water. "Then," he said, "we will all live here with you in your house as before." When Gaṇeśa and Jayā had returned to heaven, having accomplished their purposes, and when all the Brahmins had gone, Gautama wiped out his sins with asceticism. By meditation, he learned that his own sinful state was for the sake of the gods, so that he could help the world and Śiva and Pārvatī by bringing down the Ganges for everyone's welfare. "But there is no sin in me," he realized, and he propitiated Śiva, thinking, "I will bring down the Ganges and Pārvatī will be pleased with me, for her co-wife is in Śiva's hair." Gautama went to Kailāsa, praised Śiva, and was offered a boon. "Give me the Ganges" he said, and this was granted, and so the hermitage of Gautama became a holy place.[128]

This episode is now made to serve an entirely different purpose—to satisfy the whim of a deity—but Gautama still does not resent being made a fool of; he is only too happy to oblige his god when the latter is embroiled in marital difficulties, and it never occurs to him to curse the sages who have put him to such trouble. Pārvatī's well-known jealousy of the Ganges[129] is here used to motivate the gods to create the heretical deception that is usually the result of their jealousy of mortals; Gautama is Pārvatī's innocent dupe just as Divodāsa is when Pārvatī wants to move house. But in this bhakti text, Gautama is

[128] *Brahma* 74.8–88; 75.1–50.

[129] O'Flaherty (1973), pp. 226–232.

ultimately strengthened rather than weakened by the actions of the gods; his hermitage is twice blessed, by Brahmā and by Śiva, as the myth combines those episodes which place the boon at the beginning with those in which Śiva grants it at the end.

For this is a synthetic text, combining the episode in which Gaṇeśa (unprompted by Pārvatī) becomes the cow with the episode in which Śiva gives Gautama a river from his hair. This latter text describes the curse of the heretical sages in great detail and also provides most explicitly for their release; when Gautama has promised to have the Godāvarī purify the descendants of the sages, the sages visit Śiva on Kailāsa (as Gautama does to ask for the Ganges):

The sages said, "In the Kali Age, sages will have your form, with matted locks; give them some sacred texts." Śiva gave them the Pāśupata text and said, "Long ago, when I took the form of Bhairava to help the gods destroy the demons, tear-drops fell from me and became the Raudras, lovers of wine, women and evil. The Brahmins will be born in the line of the Raudras because of Gautama's curse; but those of them who delight in my command will obtain heaven, while those who revile the Śaivas will go to hell by my command, for these Brahmins burnt by Gautama's fire are heretics."[130]

The evil sons of Rudra who elsewhere act against Śiva's will to bring evil to mankind here free mankind from other evils wrought by Śiva. The sages are to be reborn in the Kali Age, as usual, at which time Śiva provides for their release from the curse of Gautama by giving them heretical texts that are suitable for them. This text, like that of the *Padma Purāṇa*, is narrated by Śiva himself to explain why he created delusory texts; but unlike that Vaiṣṇava text, this variant raises one heretical doctrine, the Pāśupata, to the level of the god himself, instead of stating that all the Śaiva heresies were taught by him in bad faith. The myth introduces the element of free will into the fate of the sages, assigning some of them to hell and some to heaven, while allowing some to worship Śiva correctly in spite of their heresy (just as they are elsewhere said to worship the Gāyatrī in spite of their heretical status).

Thus the myth of Gautama and the Seven Sages explains the Fall of a group of Brahmins and provides for their ultimate release in the Kali Age. Similarly, the pollution arising from a sin against a cow is the basis of a myth told by many Untouchables to explain their "Fall" from caste: There were four Brahmin brothers; one, to be helpful, removed a dead cow from their common kitchen; the others considered him polluted and banished him; his descendants were the Untouchables. The anthropologist who recorded this myth remarks, "The injustice of their position is tied in, then, with the injustice of pollution."[131] The arbitrary and accidental manner of the brother's pollution, like that of Gautama

[130] *Varāha* 71.48–62.

[131] Kolenda, p. 75.

falsely accused and tricked, removes any onus of guilt from the Untouchables or from Gautama, though in the Sanskrit myth it is the conniving "brothers" (the sages who do *not* touch the cow) who fall from caste. To this extent, the Gautama myth, unlike the Untouchable myth, regards pollution as just rather than unjust punishment, inflicted for the conscious sin of falsely accusing a pure man of being polluted.

5. Śiva Cursed in the Pine Forest: The "heresy" of Liṅga-worship

The sin of false accusation underlies the myths of Śiva in the Pine Forest, in which the sages abuse him as they have abused Gautama. The sectarian bias of each version of the myth of Gautama obviously affects the Purāṇa's attitude to the content of the heresy that Śiva eventually teaches; and this ambiguity is compounded in the Pine Forest myths. But the question is further complicated by the basic Hindu attitude toward the purpose of heresy, which is used sometimes to destroy an enemy (as in the case of the demons) but sometimes to release a friend (as in the case of the mortals of the Kali Age).

These ambiguities are further complicated by the contrasting attitudes toward the liṅga-worship that is the basis of the Pine Forest myth. After beheading Brahmā, Śiva entered the Pine Forest disguised as a naked beggar; the sages' wives fell in love with him and the jealous sages cursed him to be castrated; his phallus wrought havoc among them until they placated him and he taught them to worship the liṅga.[132] In some of these myths, Śiva is cursed to be worshipped in the form of a liṅga (i.e., the liṅga cult is regarded as a kind of inferior religion, if not necessarily as a heresy), while in others he curses the hostile sages to worship him in this form (a double-edged incident, depending on whether Śiva regards liṅga worship as a true doctrine to save them or a false doctrine to corrupt them). Yet, in the final encounter with the sages, it is evident that the cult which he establishes in the Pine Forest is a great boon for them, and one which he establishes because of his mercy toward them; there is no question of any curse.

It should be noted at the outset that almost all the myths which treat liṅga worship as the result of a curse upon Śiva are late texts. One anomalous Sanskrit text of this group is not part of the Pine Forest corpus:

One day when the sage Atri was performing asceticism with his wife Anasūyā, Brahmā, Viṣṇu and Śiva came to him and offered him a boon. When Atri continued to meditate, the three gods went to Anasūyā; Śiva had his liṅga in his hand, Viṣṇu was full of erotic feeling, and Brahmā, beside himself with desire, said, "Make love to me or I will die." When she heard this coarse speech, Anasūyā made no reply, for, although she feared the anger of the gods, she was true to her husband. But the three gods were overcome by

[132] O'Flaherty (1975), pp. 141–149; (1973), pp. 172–209.

delusion, and they raped her by force. Then she became angry, and she cursed Śiva to be worshipped as a liṅga, Brahmā to be worshipped as a head, and Viṣṇu to be worshipped as feet, in order to ridicule them all, and she cursed them all to be reborn as her sons. Because of this, Śiva was born as Durvāsas.[133]

The relationship between Brahmā and Anasūyā, and the way she criticizes him for his "coarse speech," are reminiscent of the incestuous relationship that leads to the beheading of Brahmā by Śiva in an adjacent chapter of this Purāṇa;[134] this is reinforced by the fact that Anasūyā curses Brahmā to be worshipped as a head, the form in which he participates in the Kāpālika myth. That Anasūyā regards liṅga-worship as an insult to Śiva is evident from her statement that she cursed them all in order to ridicule them.

In the majority of the Sanskrit myths of the Pine Forest, however, it is by no means clear that liṅga-worship is regarded as a curse. Usually Śiva is cursed by the sages, but he is merely cursed to be castrated; it is as a result of the difficulties that arise from this castration that the sages are cursed in return (or at least forced) to worship the liṅga. Thus even in the Sanskrit texts the element of antipathy is present, as in the Dakṣa myth. Śiva is spurned by the sages until he forces them to acknowledge his greatness and to worship him as the liṅga; once they have been forced to recognize him, however, Śiva is gratified by their worship of him in this new form, a form which he has established for their own benefit.[135] The clear division between these two aspects of the myth–the curse of castration and the beneficial establishment of liṅga-worship–is apparent from a text in which Sāvitrī, whom Śiva has wronged, curses him to be castrated in the Pine Forest, whereupon Gāyatrī, whom Śiva has assisted at Sāvitrī's expense, turns the curse into a boon, saying, "When your liṅga has fallen, men will honor you and will thereby win heaven. You will exist forever by the banks of the Ganges in the form of a liṅga."[136]

Within the Pine Forest myths, several layers of development may be seen. First, Śiva is in the power of desire, seduces the women, and is castrated; then an apologetic layer is composed: the women seduce him, or he wishes to test the sages;[137] and, finally, he comes to teach the sages a lesson, and to establish the cult of the liṅga.[138] The "test" introduced in the apologetic layer, perhaps inspired by Indra's "test" of the Seven Sages in the drought, is an ambiguous, mediating phase. Śiva acts didactically, not, supposedly, under the influence of lust (as he

[133] *Bhaviṣya* 3.4.17.67–78; O'Flaherty (1975), pp. 53–55.

[134] *Bhaviṣya* 3.4.13.1–19; cf. *Śiva, Jñāna Saṃ.* 49.65–80.

[135] *Brahmāṇḍa* 2.27.1–127; *Śiva, Dharma Saṃ.* 10.79–215; *Jñāna Saṃ.* 42.1–51; 4.12.1–54; *Skanda* 6.1.5–64; 7.1.187ff.; 7.3.39.5–38; 5.3.38.6–68.

[136] *Padma* 5.17.269–271.

[137] First: Nīlakaṇṭha, *Padma*; second: *Vāmana, Liṅga, Kūrma, Saura.*

[138] Deussen (1917), *passim.* Cf. O'Flaherty (1973), pp. 172–184, 192–204.

was in the first layer), but his wife prompts him to attack the sages, while their wives prompt them to curse Śiva. Thus even in the apologetic texts, Śiva's motives are somewhat suspect. There is no such ambiguity, however, in the submotif of the Pine Forest myths in which Bhṛgu curses Śiva to be worshipped as a liṅga.

6. The Curse of Bhṛgu

Like the episode of Śiva in the Pine Forest, the myth of Bhṛgu's curse was originally applied to Agni and then later transferred to Śiva.[139] The conflict between Bhṛgu and Agni first occurs in the *Mahābhārata*:

When Pulomā, the wife of Bhṛgu, was pregnant, a Rākṣasa fell in love with her and wanted to carry her off, but first he had to know the name of her husband. He asked Agni, who was forced to reveal the truth, and then the demon carried off the woman, whose child slipped from her womb and was born as Cyavana. When the Rākṣasa saw the child fall, he dropped Pulomā, but Bhṛgu cursed Agni to be omnivorous, a curse which the gods later modified by stating that only the flames of Agni, but not his entire body, would devour anything, and thus render it pure.[140]

This episode is a reversal of the Vedic cycle in which Agni himself curses those who have spoken to betray him.[141] It is elaborated in Purāṇic texts in which the demon, now called Tālajaṅgha, disguises himself as Bhṛgu and asks the three Agnis to tell him who the woman is[142]—a further echo of the Vedic tale of the hiding of the three Agnis.

This myth is then transferred to Śiva by means of a number of Epic and Purāṇic links: Bhṛgu curses Agni to be omnivourous—Śiva gives Agni the same curse in many texts;[143] Bhṛgu curses Agni for the crime of rape, as Anasūyā curses Śiva; Bhṛgu and Śiva compete for another woman, Pārvatī;[144] and Bhṛgu curses Viṣṇu to become incarnate.[145] These elements are then combined and rearranged in the myth in which Bhṛgu objects to Śiva's union with Pārvatī and therefore curses him to be worshipped in the form of the liṅga.

A final link is provided by another Purāṇic text:

Bhṛgu was performing asceticism for Śiva in an anthill, and Pārvatī asked Śiva why he failed to reward Bhṛgu. Śiva replied, "He is still full of anger; I will show you." Then Śiva told his bull to dig up the anthill and throw Bhṛgu down on the ground. The bull did so, and Bhṛgu cursed the bull to be destroyed. When the bull vanished and Bhṛgu saw

[139] O'Flaherty (1973), pp. 90–110. [140] *MBh.* 1.5–7. Cf. Goldman, *passim.*

[141] See above, chap. VI, sec. 2. [142] *Skanda, Sahyādri Khaṇḍa* 2.5; *Skanda* 5.3.82.

[143] *Skanda* 1.1.27.42; *Padma* 5.17.165; *Kumārasambhava* 9.16; O'Flaherty (1973), pp. 273–277.

[144] *MBh.* 12.329.49.1–5. [145] *Vāyu* 97.137–142; *Matsya* 47.39.

the three-eyed Śiva laughing, he prostrated himself in shame and praised Śiva. Śiva was pleased; he established a shrine of Śiva and Pārvatī there and promised that anger would never enter Bhṛgu again.[146]

The original premise of this myth is identical with that of many Pine Forest texts: Pārvatī makes Śiva demonstrate by a test (inevitably failed) that a sage is unworthy. Bhṛgu curses not Śiva but Śiva's bull (a symbol of his virility, like the liṅga, and the male counterpart of the cow that Gautama's enemies curse), and Śiva establishes a shrine—androgynous, and therefore probably the liṅga in the yoni, as in the Pine Forest.[147]

This bare framework of the Pine Forest conflict is then joined with the myth of Bhṛgu's curse of Agni to produce the myth of Bhṛgu's curse of Śiva:

The gods asked Bhṛgu to decide for them who was the greatest among the three gods. Bhṛgu went to see Śiva on Mount Kailāsa, but Nandin prevented him from entering Śiva's house, saying, "Śiva is making love to Pārvatī. Turn back if you wish to stay alive." After many days of waiting at the door, Bhṛgu said, "Since he dishonors me while he is making love to a woman, let his form be that of the liṅga in the yoni. And since he does not recognize me, a Brahmin, let him be no Brahmin, and let his worshippers be heretics, outside the Vedas, smeared with ashes."[148]

This myth may be identified as a variant of the Pine Forest myth in two ways: both myths account for the origin of liṅga-worship, and Bhṛgu is active in both (for he is one of the Seven Sages). Moreover, in the *Bhāgavata* variant of this myth, Bhṛgu is said to have been sent by a group of sages, rather than gods, to test the three gods; when Śiva saw Bhṛgu, he arose and tried to embrace him like a brother, but Bhṛgu objected to this, saying, "You are a heretic"; then the god became angry and raised his trident to kill Bhṛgu, but the Goddess placated him.[149] Like Dakṣa, Bhṛgu curses Śiva because Śiva is already a heretic, and Nandin defends Śiva against both opponents; indeed, Bhṛgu is responsible for cursing the worshippers of Śiva to be heretics in the *Bhāgavata* version of the Dakṣa myth. Thus Bhṛgu's curse makes Śiva or his followers into heretics. An interesting Tamil variant substitutes Nārada for Bhṛgu and inverts the role of the heresy: Nārada is sent to test the three gods in an episode precipitated when Brahmā fears that men on earth will become sinful in Viṣṇu's absence,[150] a fear directly at variance with the intentions of the gods and the sage in the Sanskrit texts.

Bhṛgu is the antagonist in another version of the liṅga-worship myth that was cited by Abraham Roger in the seventeenth century. In this version, Bhṛgu is a "Lord of Sages" who comes to see Śiva when he is with Pārvatī ("Therefore the

146 *Matsya* 193.23–49. 147 O'Flaherty (1973), pp. 201–204, 256–257.

148 *Padma* 6.282.20–36; 6.255.6–43. 149 *Bhāgavata* 10.89.1–7. Cf. 4.2.27–32.

150 *Veṅkaṭācalamāhātmiyam*, pp. 10–20; cf. *Skanda* 2.1.3–8.

sage came at an inopportune moment"), is made to wait, and curses Śiva to become that with which he is at the moment involved; later, however, the sage ordains that anyone who worships the liṅga in the yoni will be blessed.[151] Both the curse and the blessing appear in the version of the myth recorded by the Abbé Dubois in the late eighteenth century, by which time the one sage had become a group again:

[Brahmā, Viṣṇu and Vasiṣṭha, with many sages, came to visit Śiva] and surprised him in the act of intercourse with his wife. He was not in the least disconcerted by the presence of the illustrious visitors, and so far from showing any shame at being discovered in such a position, continued to indulge in the gratification of his sensual desires. . . . At sight of him some of the gods,and especially Vishnu, began to laugh; while the rest displayed great indignation and [cursed him to be banished from honest society. Śiva and his wife] died of grief in the same position in which the gods and the penitents had surprised them. [Śiva said,] "My shame has killed me; but it has also given me new life, and a new shape, which is that of the lingam." [And he wished that men would offer him worship in that form.][152]

Nothing is said here of any benefits that might be given to worshippers of the liṅga; Śiva seems to attempt to make the best of an unfortunate situation, and it is he who ordains that liṅga-worship should take place, though he is embarrassed by the entire episode. It is significant that the gods and sages banish Śiva from honest society, making him an outcaste.

A rather loose variation of the Dubois version of the myth was narrated recently by a Brahmin in Benares:

Śiva had been discovered in bed with his wife Durga by Brahma, Vishnu and other gods. He had been so drunk that he had not thought it necessary to stop. The majority, all except Vishnu and a few of the broader-minded, thought them nasty and brutish and said so. Śiva and Durga died of shame in the position in which they were discovered; but before they expired Śiva expressed the wish that mankind should worship the act manifest in the form which he now took to himself, the lingam.[153]

Here Śiva is merely said to be "nasty and brutish," and this is given as a descriptive statement rather than a curse. Another contemporary version of the myth eliminates even this vague pejorative statement but restores a vital element from the older Pine Forest stories; here it is Śiva who comes into the forest where the sages are practising asceticism, rather than they who come to his house as in the Bhṛgu series:

Shiva one day roamed into a forest with his wife where some Rishis were practising austerities and, forgetting that the spot was sacred to the sages, suddenly became amorous. In the heat of the moment he lost all sense of decorum and embraced his spouse in an open place. As ill-luck would have it some of the sages who inhabited the woods came that way, and saw Shiva and his wife in each other's arms. The outraged saints converted Shiva into a Lingam by a curse.[154]

[151] Roger, pp. 247–248. [152] Dubois, pp. 629–630.

[153] Newby, p. 39. [154] Thomas (1959), p. 114.

Although Śiva is not cursed to be a heretic in this text, it is clearly stated that he was cursed to become a liṅga, not merely castrated, in contrast with other late texts in which he himself (freely or under compulsion) creates the practice of liṅga-worship.

A final contemporary version returns to the primary Pine Forest pattern but again omits the reference to heresy:

> [After the death of Satī, Śiva wandered like a demented creature through the forest. The young wives of the sages asked him the cause of his distress, and Śiva told them that his beautiful wife had killed herself because he had been insulted by her father, Dakṣa. One of the women laughed and said that] he looked indeed a man for whom a beautiful young woman would commit suicide! This taunt so infuriated the god of virility that he violated her. Her husband came on the scene and cursed the god to be worshipped as the Lingam.[155]

Śiva's direct sexual encounter is with the wife of a sage, rather than with his own wife (as in most episodes of Bhṛgu's curse), but Satī is still the root of the trouble, since her death causes both his entrance into the forest in a "demented" state and the insult that leads him to violate the sage's wife. Here the Pine Forest encounter takes place immediately after the clash with Dakṣa, rather than after the clash with Brahmā, which is more usual; the two episodes are interchangeable. Satī, who often urges Śiva to test the Pine Forest sages, here indirectly drives him to do this by committing suicide after Dakṣa curses Śiva; and this action eventually leads to another curse, the sage's curse of liṅga-worship. Śiva, who is often said to be mad with lust, or with wine, is now simply said to be mad (apparently as a result of his grief), the final excuse for the irrational or evil behavior of a god.

Thus the myth develops from the Sanskrit texts, in which Śiva, though in many ways antagonistic toward the sages and cursed to be castrated, establishes liṅga-worship for their benefit, through the episode where Bhṛgu curses him to be a heretic and to be worshipped as the liṅga, into the texts in which (probably under the influence of European abhorrence of phallic cults) the form of worship itself is taken to be heretical and unclean, inflicted on Śiva against his will. The tension between the apparent antagonism between Śiva and the sages in terms of the plot, and the recurrent insistence that Śiva came to the forest in order to help the sages, is evident even in the Sanskrit texts, where the ambivalent attitude of the god toward his heretical worshippers results in various contradictions and confusions. The antagonism is evident not only from the exchange of curses but also from the historical context, for Śiva is traditionally opposed to sages whose excessive asceticism threatens the universe, a fault sometimes attributed to the Pine Forest sages.[156] The Brahmin redactors of the Purāṇas were thus able to use

[155] *Ibid.*

[156] O'Flaherty (1973), pp. 199–201.

the myth as a vehicle to cast abuse on any number of enemies, depending on the author's own particular bête noire. As Vaiṣṇavas, the authors could discredit Śaivas; as priests, ascetics; as high caste Śaivas, low caste Pāśupatas; and finally, worshippers of the liṅga could use the myth to excoriate and satirize opponents of liṅga-worship.

This last, perhaps most numerous group, maintained that Śiva acted only out of the highest motives:

When Śiva entered the Pine Forest, he intended to do a favor for the forest-dwellers there. . . . Śiva entered the Pine Forest in disguise and enlightened the sages dwelling there. . . . When Śiva was cursed by the sages, he himself let his liṅga fall, in order to instruct them.[157]

At the end of the myth, however aggressively Śiva may have acted toward the sages, he always shows them his favor: "The Goddess pitied the sages and begged Śiva to give them peace from passion and hatred; thus implored, Śiva looked upon them with favor and removed their delusion, giving them peace."[158] A commentator explains both the aggression and the favor implicit in two epithets of Śiva: "He is called 'Greatly Reviled' because he was reviled by the sages, who said, 'He came into the Pine Forest in order to bewitch the minds of our wives, for he is an evil wretch.' . . . He is called 'Giver of Peace' because after the sages of the Pine Forest had reviled him he gave them peace by destroying their doubts and giving them knowledge of the true nature of things."[159] The initial aggression is necessary, for only by spending their wrath on him can the sages be enlightened. "The sages of the Pine Forest became angry at Śiva. . . . They did not recognize him. . . . As soon as they had cursed him, they knew him to be the lord, and they sought refuge with him."[160] The sages hurl things at Śiva (a tiger, fire, snakes, or their curses[161]) in order to kill him; but these things then become the attributes of Śiva (his bracelets, his loincloth), and thus inadvertently the sages are doing him a favor.

This twisting of the worshipper's aggression into devotion, almost against his will, is known in Sanskrit theology as *dveṣa-bhakti*, "Hate-devotion," a kind of ritual *Hasslieb*. This concept derives from the Hindu belief that *any* contact with a god, even a negative contact, is beneficial; thus when the heretic reviles the god he is regarded as actually worshipping him. After Kṛṣṇa had killed the ogress Pūtanā, her body gave off a sweet smell when it burned, for she had been purified by her death at his hands; in fact, she won salvation by suckling Kṛṣṇa, even though she did it with the intention to poison him. Similarly, when Kaṃsa, having slaughtered Kṛṣṇa's relatives, was afraid that Kṛṣṇa would try to kill him,

[157] *Śiva* 4.12.11; *Brahmāṇḍa* 2.27.2; *Yāgīśvaramāhātmya* 26b.3. [158] *Darpadalana* 7.70–71.

[159] Nīlakaṇṭha on *Mahābhārata* 13.17.202 (13.17.99 in Poona ed.). [160] *Kathāsaritsāgara* 3.6.131–133.

[161] *Kōyil Purāṇa*, cited by Rao, II, 1, 235–236. *Kantapurāṇam* 6.15.32.

he saw Kṛṣṇa everywhere he looked, on all sides of him, pervading his world;[162] this is precisely the same attitude as that of the enlightened man, who realizes that God actually does pervade his world, and thus Kaṃsa's hatred of the deity drew him into the proper philosophical outlook that he would have reached through bhakti. Even Pauṇḍraka's offense of falsely declaring himself to be Kṛṣṇa is rewarded when Pauṇḍraka is actually given the form of Kṛṣṇa,[163] as his *imitatio dei* is translated from a challenge offered in hatred into an act of loving worship.

A variation of this motif appears often in Śaiva mythology, in which the most abandoned sinner inadvertently commits, by his very sin, an act of salvation. Thus Guṇanidhi abandoned his wife for a prostitute and robbed the temple of its offerings, but he was saved from the tortures of hell because he had made a new wick for the temple lamp (though he made it in order to see what there was worth stealing).[164] This doctrine, though sometimes challenged in bhakti texts which demanded a conscious turning toward God, was often upheld in texts justifying heresies: "Those who become non-Vedic Pāśupatas and decry Nārāyaṇa [Viṣṇu] really worship the latter through the spirit of hostility (*dveṣa-buddhi*)."[165] The *Bhāgavata Purāṇa* makes explicit the effect of this belief: "Desire, hatred, fear, or love toward the lord, filling the heart with bhakti, destroy all sins and bind one to the lord: the cow-herd girls [*gopīs*] by desire, Kaṃsa by fear, the wicked kings by hatred, and his kinsmen the Vṛṣṇis by affection were bound to him as we are by bhakti."[166]

Dakṣa is bound to Śiva by a kind of hate-love, and Dakṣa acts, like the Pine Forest sages, to create an attribute of Śiva intended to harm him: Dakṣa was angry with Śiva, for the destruction of his sacrifice, and so he performed asceticism and created an eye in Śiva's forehead.[167] In the Pine Forest as well,[168] and in many other Purāṇic texts, Śiva's opposition to evil sages or demons leads them to recognize and praise him; even the virtuous Arjuna comes to recognize and bow to Śiva only after waging a long battle against him when Śiva is disguised as an outcaste, heretic hunter,[169] the form he takes in the Pine Forest. (The hate-love works in reverse, as well; often the god, intending to harm a mortal or demon, helps him, as when the god frees the demon's soul by killing him.[170]) Thus Śiva is "cursed" by the sages to be worshipped as the liṅga, but this makes him great; and he "curses" them to worship him, but this gives them salvation. Śiva's most famous act of salvation—the swallowing of the poison that makes his neck blue—inspired an inverted myth of aggression against him: Śukra fought against

[162] *Bhāgavata* 10.6.24, .34–36; 10.2.24. Cf. *MBh.* 2.42.1–3; *Viṣṇu* 4.14–15.

[163] *Bhāgavata* 10.66.24. See above, chap. VII, sec. 5.

[164] *Śiva* 2.1.17.48–2.1.18.38. See above, chap. VIII, sec. 6.

[165] Hazra (1948), p. 99n.

[166] *Bhāgavata* 7.1.29–30; 10.44.39.

[167] *MBh.* 12.330.41–71; 12.329.14.4.

[168] Kulke, p. 88.

[169] *MBh.* 3.39–42.

[170] Andhaka in O'Flaherty (1973), 190–192; (1975), pp. 168–172; Mahiṣa in O'Flaherty (1975), pp. 238–249.

Śiva, and his snakes bit Śiva's throat, making it blue.[171] In this way, even the myths of the post-Vedic corpus in which the god clearly intends to harm the worshipper may be utilized and transformed in the bhakti texts so that the god ultimately helps the worshipper; his cruelty is now regarded as a kindness that hurts him more than it hurts the devotee, whom he attacks for his own good. In this theological context, it is entirely appropriate for the sages to worship Śiva after they have cursed him and felt his wrath.

7. Śiva Enlightens the Pine Forest Sages

Often, particularly in later texts, Śiva comes to the Pine Forest in order to teach the sages a lesson. In sculpture, Śiva preaching to the Seven Sages is represented as Dakṣiṇāmūrti, a benign aspect sometimes identified as Tantric; sculptures depicting him in this form, teaching Bhṛgu, Gautama, and the other sages, appear in South Indian temples from the eighth century.[172] In the simpler versions of the Pine Forest myth, Śiva enlightens the sages by teaching them the nonheretical, though non-Vedic, cult of liṅga-worship. In later versions, however, Śiva comes to the Pine Forest to teach the sages other, heretical doctrines, and yet even here is is said to act for their benefit. These heresies are said to be taught by Śiva to release the sages from the previous curses of heresy given them by Dakṣa and Gautama. The Pine Forest encounter is foreshadowed at the end of the *Kūrma Purāṇa* version of the Gautama myth, which seeks, like other variants, to temper the curse with a hope of release:

When Viṣṇu learned that Gautama had cursed the sages to be outside the pale of the Vedas, he went to Śiva and said, "There is not even a drop of merit in a man who is beyond the Vedas. But nevertheless, because of our devotion to them, we must protect them even though they will go to hell. Let us make texts of delusion to protect and delude the evil ones beyond the Vedas." Śiva agreed, and they made the Kāpāla, Pāśupata, Vāma [*i.e., Tantric*] *and other texts. For the sake of the sages, Śiva descended to earth when the force of the curse had come to an end, and he begged alms from those who were outcaste, deluding them as he came there adorned with skulls, ashes, and matted locks, saying, "You will go to hell, but then you will be reborn and gradually work your way to the place of merit."*[173]

The ambivalent moral status of the sages in this version of the myth is evident from Viṣṇu's statement: the men are evil, and doomed to hell, but the gods must protect and delude them so that they will ultimately find merit. Even though the doctrines that Śiva teaches are mediating ones—below the Vedas but above damnation—he cannot teach them while the sages are still cursed to be heretics;

[171] *MBh.* 12.329.15. [172] Kulke, p. 64; Rao, II, 1, 276–278; Long (1972), *passim.*

[173] *Kūrma* 1.16.109–120; *Tantrādhikāranirṇaya*, p. 27.

he must come "when the force of the curse had come to an end" to teach them new heresies, just as he comes when the force of the Kali Age is spent to destroy mankind and initiate the Golden Age. The prediction that he pronounces at the end of the myth is similar to that which is described at the end of the myth of Dakṣa and Dadhīca:

Śiva promised that those sages who read the Vedas would go to heaven; that those who did not would become householders, and he would release them from their sins by coming to them at noon, smeared with ashes, begging alms from them. Whoever gave alms to him would go to heaven.[174]

This prediction is realized in the Pine Forest, where Śiva releases the sages by begging from them.

An even more explicit link between the myth of Dakṣa and the myth of the Pine Forest appears in a South Indian Sanskrit text: when Dakṣa sneers at Śiva, Dadhīca rebukes him and tells him the story of the Pine Forest.[175] In other texts, the episode of Dakṣa's sacrifice takes place before the Pine Forest episode, for Śiva comes to the Pine Forest precisely in order to release the Brahmins who had been cursed by Dakṣa. One text explains how it is that Śiva hopes to free the Pine Forest sages from heresy by teaching another heresy:

There are various non-Vedic texts in the world, such as the Vāma, Kāpālika, and Bhairavāgama. They were expounded by Śiva for the sake of delusion and have no other cause; they were taught because of the curse of Dakṣa, Bhṛgu, and Dadhīca. In order to raise up, in the manner of stairs, step by step, those Brahmins who were burned by the curse and forced outside the path of the Vedas, Śiva expounded the Śaiva, Vaiṣṇava, Saura [sun-worship], Śākta [Tantric], and Gāṇapātya [Gaṇeśa-worship] scriptures; even though there is here and there a bit which is opposed to the Vedas, there is no sin in their being taken up by Vedic worshippers.[176]

Another text explicitly connects the curses of Dadhīca and Gautama in a chain, one leading to the other:

Formerly, in the sacrifice of Dakṣa, Brahmins were burned by the curse of Dadhīca, who said, "These Brahmins and others who were burned by the curse of the noble Gautama will be born in the Kali Age and will follow vows outside the Vedas, evil ways. Then in the Kali Age, Rudra will bring salvation to men and gods. He will become incarnate to establish the Vedas and lawbooks for the sake of his devotees."[177]

Gautama's curse precedes Dadhīca's, and Śiva releases the sages from both, in the Pine Forest. Elsewhere, the sages responsible for the curses of heresy are merely

[174] *Skanda* 7.2.94–96, 136–142.

[175] *Dakṣa Kaṇḍa* 13.1–16; cited in Kulke, p. 85. *Kantapurāṇam* 6.13.30–127.

[176] *Devībhāgavata* 7.39.26–32. [177] *Kūrma* 1.29.27–34.

listed in a group, which sometimes includes Bhṛgu; all three of these sages are included in the group of Seven Sages, or Pine Forest sages, so that the perpetrators of the curse as well as the recipients benefit from Śiva's grace at the end. Gautama, who appears most often as both subject and object of the curse, is implicated in two further offshoots of heresy: he is the author of several heresies, and he is one of the Seven Sages who are guilty of cooking the dead boy. Śiva releases all of these sages from the curse of heresy by begging from them in the Pine Forest.

The Pine Forest sages are often said to be heretics. In the *Mahābhārata* they are simply atheists:

Certain Brahmins abandoned their houses and went to the forest, thinking, "This is dharma," and they engaged in chastity. Indra had pity on them and told them to give up their asceticism and to devote themselves to their own svadharma as householders, to practise Vedic rituals. Then they abandoned the way of atheists and took to the householder dharma.[178]

This accusation of "atheism" is apparently based on the antiascetic tradition that regarded any asceticism, particularly when practised by householders, as a threat. Another form of atheism is described in a text that identifies the sages specifically as those of the Pine Forest:

Formerly in the Pine Forest there were Brahmins performing asceticism, vying against each other in various ways, but they did not achieve fulfilment. Then they thought, "The sages did not speak the truth when they said that success in everything is obtained by asceticism." Overcome by impatience, they put aside their dharma of asceticism and became atheists. But at this time a voice said to them, "Do not despise the scriptures. Do not blame asceticism or dharma, but blame yourselves. You strive against each other, desiring success, and because of that your asceticism is fruitless, destroyed by desire, egotism, anger, and greed. Go to the Mahākāla woods and propitiate the liṅga of Śiva and you will obtain success." The Brahmins were amazed, and they obeyed the voice and worshipped the liṅga of Śiva and obtained fulfilment.[179]

The philosophical commitment of this text is directly opposed to that of the *Mahābhārata*: where the Epic considered the householder's asceticism to be atheism, this text regards the discontinuation of asceticism (or the false performance of asceticism) to be atheism. Indra converts the ascetics from the first excess; Śiva converts them from the other extreme by teaching them liṅga-worship. Here, as throughout the cycle, the actual *content* of the heresy is of little importance; the worshippers are "heretics" if their doctrine is at variance with that of the author of the text. In some texts, the flaw in the ascetics is not their overzealous ritualism alone, but the fact that they lack bhakti for Śiva; when

[178] *MBh.* 12.11.1–28.

[179] *Skanda* 5.2.11.1–26.

he terrorizes them, they prostrate themselves before him, and Śiva, full of pity, gives them knowledge of his greatness, the other quality they had lacked.[180] In later texts, the heresy is usually less subtle; a South Indian variant states that the sages of the Pine Forest had left the path of the Vedas, each sage believing that he was Brahmā.[181] This may be a satire on the Upaniṣadic concept of the identification of the individual soul with the world-soul (*brahman*), but it also suggests the pattern of the proud sage who wishes to become a god (Brahmā).

A contemporary Indian text states that "several heretic sages refused to believe in the gods and in the Triad. Shiva decided to visit them in their forest home and teach them the truth."[182] These sages are atheists of the most simple and obvious kind. Other late versions of the Pine Forest myth identify other heresies:

> It came to the knowledge of Shiva that there resided in the Tāragam forest ten thousand heretical rishis, who taught that the universe is eternal, that souls have no lord, and that the performance of works alone suffices for the attainment of salvation. Shiva determined to teach them the truth. [He seduced the sages and their wives.][183]

This heresy is difficult to identify; it has elements of pure atheism, Buddhism, and the ritualism that Śiva challenges in other versions of the Pine Forest myth.[184] It is also suggestive of the Mīmāṃsā philosophy, which is cited in another variant set in the same forest (Tāragam = Taraka): "In the forest of Taraka dwelt multitudes of Heretical Rishis, followers of the Mimansa. Thither proceeded Śiva to confute them."[185] The Mīmāṃsā is one of the six classical Hindu schools, hardly a heresy, as it is based on exposition of and absolute obedience to the Vedas (though a Vedāntin would regard the Mīmāṃsā as incomplete).

A few late versions of the myth regard the sages as Buddhists:

> The Buddhist Bhikshus . . . did not understand the true significance of Linga and fell a prey to moral lapses, even taking recourse to sex-perversions. Notwithstanding the fact that they apparently derided Linga worship, the women folk in their camp were seen overpowered by erotic impulse. It is this hypocrisy found amongst their order that is brought to light in this satirical incident. . . . The trend of the story is a subtle reflection on the morals of the Buddhist monks in the monasteries who were ultimately converted to the way of the Pāśupatas in putting their faith in the efficacy of the Linga.[186]

The view that the sages were Buddhists is supported explicitly by no Sanskrit text, although one does state that Śiva himself took the form of a Buddhist monk (*kṣapaṇaka*) to enter the Pine Forest in order to show Pārvatī that even sages are not calm.[187] The Pine Forest heresy was identified as Buddhism by several nineteenth-century Europeans, who based their belief on the mistaken assumption that the Gautama of the Pine Forest was the same as Gautama the Buddha. One American Indologist tells the tale of Gautama much as it appears in the

[180] *Dakṣa Kaṇḍa* 13.29 and 14.1–47; Kulke, p. 85. [181] *Paḻanittalapurāṇam* 8.37–67.
[182] Ghosh, p. 108. [183] Nivedita and Coomaraswamy, pp. 310–311. [184] *Kūrma* 2.37.60–62, 129–131.
[185] Rao, II, 1, 235. [186] Agrawala (1964), p. 86 and p. xiv. [187] *Kathāsaritsāgara* 3.6.131–133.

Sanskrit texts (the drought occurs, the illusion of the cow is created, Gautama finds out about the trick and curses the sages), but the author then remarks: "Gautama is the principle divinity of the Burmese. According to tradition, he was so offended with the Brahmins that he determined to separate himself from them and establish a new religion."[188] He accompanies this statement with a drawing of a Buddha, entitled, "Gautama, or Budh." Colonel Kennedy came to a similar conclusion about the story of Gautama and the illusory cow: "Gautama, according to tradition, was so offended with the conduct of the Brahmans on this occasion that he determined to separate from their communion and to establish a new religion."[189] Wilkins adds that this religion "for a time eclipsed Brahmanism."[190]

As heresy in general, and Buddhism in particular, is so often associated with demons, it is not surprising that at least one text identifies the Pine Forest sages as demonic. At first it is said that the sages cursed Śiva because of fate; but then (as it so often is) this impersonal force is superseded by a more immediate power, and the sages are said to have cursed Śiva not through their own fault but because they were overcome by the doctrine of the demons, and for this reason it was necessary to destroy the demons.[191] Apparently the sages themselves are not demons, nor is it necessarily implicit that demons actually corrupted them. The doctrine of the demons, according to this text, is full of darkness (*tamas*), while that of the gods is made of goodness (*sattva*); this could merely indicate the demon heresy of Materialism taught and accepted by any mortal, but as it is then stated that the demons themselves had therefore to be destroyed, it is probable that they have actively participated in the Pine Forest heresy.

This text is South Indian, as are the only other sources of the myth that involve demons. The South Indian poetess Kāraikkal Ammaiyār described the dance of Śiva surrounded by the demons in the forest of Tiruvālaṅgād, and is even said to have changed herself into a demon to dance with him.[192] In contemporary worship at the Chidambaram temple, Śiva is invoked as the god who is worshipped in the forest by gods and demons,[193] and the form that he assumes in several late South Indian variants of the Pine Forest myth—the form of Hari-Hara, Viṣṇu-Śiva—is said to have been taken to confute heretics and demons.[194] In one variant of the Pine Forest myth, Śiva himself is cursed by the sages to become a Rākṣasa, since he has behaved like a Rākṣasa (stealing their wives).[195] Śiva is

[188] *Śiva* 4.2.25; Wright, pp. 14–17. [189] Kennedy, p. 253. [190] Wilkins, p. 231.

[191] *Yāgīśvaramāhātmya*, cited in Jahn (1916), pp. 310–315.

[192] *Pĕriya Purāṇam* 5.4.1–66, *Kāraikkalammaiyārpurāṇam.*

[193] Personal communication from Anne-Marie Gaston (Añjali).

[194] *Skanda* 6.247.1–44; cf. Oppert, p. 508; Dessigane, Pattabiramin, and Filliozat (1967), pp. 84–85; *Bhāgavata* 10.88.14–36. [195] *Brahmāṇḍa* 1.2.27.1–123; O'Flaherty (1975), pp. 141–149.

often worshipped by demons, particularly in the form of the liṅga that is established in the Pine Forest: gods and demons worship his liṅga;[196] Rāvaṇa worships the liṅga to obtain a boon, and Śukra, the guru of the demons, often wins Śiva's favor in this way. Śiva's behavior in destroying Dakṣa's sacrifice is the epitome of demonic activity, and he is said to reside in the subterranean hell,[197] with the demons. All of the gods behave like demons on many occasions,[198] but Rudra is the demonic god par excellence. These general links between heretics and demons, and between Śiva and demons, may have led to the association of the demons with the Pine Forest heresy.

In the context of the original myth, the heresy is of secondary importance. Once in the forest, Śiva seduces the wives of the sages, and the heresy is merely a later rationalization of the adulterous behavior that Śiva inherited from the Epic myth of Agni and the sages' wives.[199] René Grousset places the heresy in its proper historical perspective—as an afterthought to justify Śiva's less rational intentions in the earlier versions of the myth:

> In a fit of virtuous indignation at an act of incest contemplated by Brahmā, Śiva cut off one of the culprit's five heads, after which he was . . . overcome by madness. This madness went so far as to make him commit various strange actions, such as the seduction of the wives of the anchorites in the forest of Taragam—though, to be sure, the anchorites were heretics![200]

The madness, sometimes said to be induced by lust, wine, or grief, is here vaguely connected with an act of violence. This madness serves better than the sages' "heresy" to explain Śiva's "strange actions," such as the seduction of the sages' wives, an act of scant doctrinal meaning.

A similarly illogical juxtaposition of the seduction and the vague heresy appears in another contemporary account:

> The God Shiva as Bhikshatana (the beggar) had to atone for his crime of cutting off Brahma's head, by begging for his food from door to door. In the course of his wanderings he used to infuriate the Brahmins, who did not believe in him, by amours with their wives.[201]

Seducing the sages' wives is bound to make them acknowledge Śiva's existence, though not, perhaps, his divine nature; clearly the fact that the Brahmins "did not believe in him" is as superfluous to this myth as it was to the earliest Sanskrit versions. Yet, if one goes back still further, to the Vedic Prajāpati myth underlying the Pine Forest episode (and still associated with it in these late versions), the heresy proves to be an ancient element of the myth; the gods/Prajāpati/Dakṣa are punished because they refuse to give Rudra a share—that is, they do not believe in him.

[196] *Matsya* 154.350. [197] *Śiva, Dharma Saṃ.* 49.23–86; O'Flaherty (1975), pp. 138–141.
[198] See above, chap. IV, sec. 5. [199] O'Flaherty (1973), pp. 90–97; (1975), pp. 105–115.
[200] Grousset, pp. 191–192. [201] Khandalavala, p. 52.

Whether or not the sages of the Pine Forest were heretics, Śiva himself enters the forest in the role of a heretic. He is depicted as a heretic in sculptures of the myth (as Bhikṣāṭana), and he is treated as a heretic by the sages themselves. An amusing development of this aspect of the myth appears in the legend of a Vīraśaiva saint who converted people to faith in Śiva

by any means whatever: bribes, favours, love, and if needed, physical force, coercing or persuading them to wear the Śaiva emblem of holy ash on the forehead. One day, Śiva himself came down in disguise to see him. But he did not recognize Śiva and proceeded to convert him, offering him holy ash, trying to force it on him when he seemed reluctant. When his zeal became too oppressive, Śiva tried in vain to tell him who he was, but was forced down on his knees for the baptism of ash—even Śiva had to become a Śaiva![202]

As in the Pine Forest, Śiva comes in disguise to test the devotee, whose failure to recognize the god results here not in a curse and the ultimate conversion of the devotee but rather in the conversion of the god himself from his apparent heresy.

The "heresy" from which Śiva usually appears to suffer in the Pine Forest is not, as here, lack of devotion to himself but rather the same heresy that is at the heart of the conflict with Dakṣa: the Kāpālika cult representative of the sin of Brahminicide. Though Śiva as the Kāpālika is older than Śiva in the Pine Forest, the Kapalika motif is introduced into the Pine Forest story only in relatively late versions. The Pine Forest myth often directly follows the episode of the beheading of Brahmā,[203] and texts of the Pine Forest myth contain explicit references to the Pāśupata and Kāpālika cults.[204] The Kāpālika aspect of the Pine Forest myth appears in two versions which are also reminiscent of the related myth of Dakṣa:

Formerly, there was a great sacrifice in the Mahākāla forest, and all the Brahmins went there. Śiva appeared as a Kāpālika, with a skull in his hand and skulls for ornaments, bald, smeared with funeral ashes. When the sages reviled him and started to throw him out, he promised to go away when he had been fed, but when he threw the skull upon the altar the sages, failing to recognize him, killed him and threw the skull out. But another skull immediately took its place, and when millions of skulls appeared in this manner the Brahmins realized that the man was Śiva. They praised him, and Śiva said, "In the midst of all the skulls, there is a liṅga which will dispel the sin of Brahminicide, in expiation for which I was wandering as a Kāpālika myself. Worship it and you will be absolved of your sins." They praised him and worshipped the liṅga.[205]

As usual in the Sanskrit texts, the original antagonism between the sages and Śiva

202 Ramanujan (1973), p. 29.

203 Meinhard, pp. 41–42; von Stietencron (1972), *passim*. Sāmba 16–17; *Skanda* 5.2.8.1–14; 5.3.38.6–68; *Varāha* 97.1–18; *Skanda* 1.1.6.2–68; *Padma* 5.17.35–55; Baldaeus, pp. 17–18; Dessigane, Pattabiramin, and Filliozat (1967), pp. 84–85.

204 *Kūrma* 2.37.131–142; 1.16.117; *Brahmāṇḍa* 2.27.116ff.; *Vāmana* 6.87.

205 *Skanda* 5.2.8.1–45.

(based here, as in the Dakṣa myth, on the Kāpālika's exclusion from the sacrifice) results in his favor to the sages and the granting of the boon of liṅga-worship. The motif of expiation supplies an important link: the liṅga absolves the sages of their (unspecified) sins, presumably including the sin of having offended their god, just as it apparently releases the god himself from the sin (Brahminicide) that caused them to offend him in the first place.

Another Pine Forest myth that stresses the skulls goes into more detail about the sins from which the Brahmins are to be released:

Śiva entered the sacrificial grounds carrying a great skull and adorned with skulls. He begged for alms, but the priests reviled him and threw out the skull; more and more skulls appeared to replace it. The priests accused him of coming there for their women, and they beat him until he cursed them, saying, "You will be beyond the Vedas, devoid of the Vedas, wearing matted locks, adulterers without progeny, begging for alms and living on the scraps of others, taking pleasure in prostitutes and dice. But those who live without egoism or wealth will be born again in good families. And those who are peaceful and constrained and devoted to me will not lose their knowledge, wealth, or descendants." Thus he gave them a curse and a boon, and he vanished.[206]

This is the most emphatic of all the texts in its description of Śiva's curse upon the sages, but their heresy is still indefinite. The sages are to be outcastes (beyond the pale of the Vedas) but their lust is emphasized, as in the early myths of corruption, and only the statement that they are to have matted locks implies a particularly Śaiva heresy. Thus Śiva curses them to be heretics in his own image, but even here (as in the myths of Gautama and the drought) the curse is tempered with mercy, allowing the heretics the free will to rise from their doom in subsequent rebirths.

How can Śiva give the sages salvation by teaching them a new heresy? The myth offers several answers based on the concept of moral relativity. Though the sages are doomed to hell, Viṣṇu and Śiva decide to help them by giving them *some* religion, albeit a heresy, since they are denied the Vedas; the heresy serves as a staircase between non-Vedic and Vedic religion.[207] Because of the curse upon them, the sages need something to bridge the gap between true religion and complete darkness, to purify them enough so that they can enter the waters of purification: they need an orthodox heresy to break the ritual chain of impurity, just as other sinners need a sacrifice prompted by the emotion of bhakti to break the logical chain of sin.

The concept of "weaning" is expounded by apologists for the Tantras:

Śiva knowing the animal propensity of their common life must lead them to take flesh and wine, prescribed these [Tantric] rites with a view to lessen the evil and to gradually wean

[206] *Padma* 5.17.75–84. [207] *Devībhāgavata* 7.39.26–32.

them from enjoyment by promulgating conditions under which alone such enjoyment could be had, and in associating it with religion. "It is better to bow to Nārāyaṇa with one's shoes on than never to bow at all."[208]

Śūdras and the victims of curses are forbidden to study the Vedas; certain others are incapable. Out of pity for all of them, Śiva teaches heresy, raising them up "step by step," a doctrine that may have been influenced by the Buddhist idea of "skill in means"–suiting the teaching to the level of the person to be enlightened.

In addition to Buddhism and Tantrism other doctrines have been regarded as serving this intermediary role in the Pine Forest:

Mention is made of certain Brahmanas who had lost the privilege of studying the Vedas through the curse of the sage Gautama, and who were directed by [Śiva and Viṣṇu] to write on and teach other sciences of a perverted character, showing their utility for the confounding of the wicked, and thereby find a way to the expiation of their sins. It is not easy to describe what these sciences were, but one thing is clear, that all this means a covert attack aimed at the schisms consequent on that nascent spirit of innovation exhibited in the various forms of Śākta, Vaiṣṇava, and Śaiva worship which sprung up in medieval India after Buddhism had been stamped out.[209]

Whatever the content of the heresy, it is non-Vedic and thus saves the sages who have "lost the privilege of studying the Vedas"; their own use of this heresy is more likely to prove useful to them than their application of heresy to "confound the wicked," a motif more appropriate to the cycle of Divodāsa and the demons.

For the basic principle in these chains of heresy is that of homeopathic curses: One can teach heresy only to a heretic; "You can't cheat an honest man." The curse merely emphasizes the fault that inspires it; thus, the Goddess says that she created the Kāpāla, Bhairava, Vāma, Jain, and other doctrines opposed to the Vedas and lawbooks, in order to delude in the next life those who here delude men with evil doctrines.[210] Only the corrupt are susceptible to divine corruption (though the "good" demons are a notable exception to this rule), and only they can profit by it, as it is better than the corruption in which they already dwell. Viṣṇu is said to have become the Buddha because of the lack of enlightenment, the force of heresy, and the madness prevalent at the time[211]–that is, to root out evil with evil, just as Prajāpati curses those demons who are already evil. In one text, Śiva says that he reveals himself primarily for the sake of atheists, to keep them from being evil-doers;[212] elsewhere, he is said to become incarnate for the sake of all creatures, and as an instruction to atheists.[213] He destroys the Triple City in order to convince the wicked that he is the supreme god,[214] and when he appears as Hari-Hara, devotees of Śiva and Viṣṇu cease arguing and merge;

[208] Woodroffe, p. 570. [209] Mukhopadhyāya, p. xxv. [210] *Kūrma* 1.12.256–259.
[211] *Bhāgavata* 6.8.19. [212] *Padma* 4.110.244. [213] *Kūrma* 2.36.2 and 2.37.37. [214] *Śiva* 2.5.9.44.

heretics and logicians leave their false paths and seek Release.[215] Were there only believers, God would not need to participate in religious life or to prove his existence; God needs heretics just as he needs demons. A similar sentiment, though given a Vaiṣṇava bias, appears in Madhva's statement that the Śaiva scriptures were composed by Śiva at Viṣṇu's command, in order to delude men with false doctrines, to reveal Śiva and to conceal Viṣṇu;[216] Viṣṇu needs Śaivas, just as Śiva needs (and creates, at Dakṣa's sacrifice) Vaiṣṇava heretics. The distinction which the post-Vedic gods are always so concerned to maintain between themselves and mortals is here extended to a sectarian conflict more characteristic of later bhakti mythology.

In this view, Śiva makes men heretics in the first place so that he can ultimately enlighten them; similarly, he destroys Himālaya's love for him to give himself an opportunity to reinspire that love.[217] It is Śiva who makes us into beasts, and Śiva who releases us from the condition of beasts. When Śiva has destroyed Dakṣa's sacrifice, Viṣṇu asks him why he has deluded them all with his magic illusion (*māyā*)—that is, why he has made Dakṣa hate him. Śiva replies, "I punish those who are overcome by my delusion"[218]—admitting to having caused as well as cured the sin of Dakṣa—but then he immediately adds: "It was not I who destroyed Dakṣa's sacrifice; I never hurt anyone; if one hates another, that recoils upon him."[219] Once again, karma is used to absolve the god, but in the context of the animosity between Dakṣa and Śiva, this abstract force is of secondary importance. Śiva deludes men in order to reveal their weaknesses, their beast nature—lust and hatred; he punishes them but ultimately enlightens them, releasing them from that nature.

For the heretics, this enlightenment at first appears as a heresy, which they reject; and indeed it is a heresy, in comparison with the ideal, Vedic worship. But the heresy is their only salvation, a heresy taught as a favor to the prodigal sages.[220] The Śaiva Purāṇas revel in the story of Viṣṇu as the Buddha, and the Vaiṣṇavas relate the story of the Śaiva heresies with evident gusto; it is easy for these texts to admit, grudgingly, the value of heresies for *other* people, taught by gods other than their own. More unusual from the western point of view, but quite common for Hindus, is the statement made by sectarian authors that their own god had created heresies for a good reason; thus the *Viṣṇu Purāṇa* tells of the Buddha avatar, and the *Śiva Purāṇa* describes the various heresies taught to the Pine Forest sages. The heresies taught to heretics serve either to make them slightly

[215] *Skanda* 6.247.1–44.

[216] Madhva, *Brahmasūtrabhāṣya* 1.1.1, citing *Varāha Purāṇa*; see above, chap. IX, sec. 1.

[217] *Śiva* 2.3.31–32; *Manmathonmathana* II, 1–19; O'Flaherty (1973), pp. 213–217.

[218] *Śiva* 2.2.41.2. [219] *Śiva* 2.2.42.4–6.

[220] Nīlakaṇṭha on *MBh.* 13.17.202; *Yāgīśvaramāhātmya* 26b.3; *Śiva* 4.12.11; *Brahmāṇḍa* 2.27.2; *Darpadalana* 7.70–71.

better, so that they may start on the path back to the Vedas, or to make them so evil that they must reach the farthest point of the cycle and then rebound from the extreme, to become good again, like all the creatures of the Kali Age—all of us.

And Abel was a keeper of sheep, but Cain was a tiller of the ground. . . . And the Lord had respect unto Abel and to his offering: But unto Cain and to his offering he had not respect. . . . And the Lord said unto Cain. . . . "If thou doest well, shalt thou not be accepted? And if thou doest not well, sin lieth at the door." . . . And it came to pass, when they were in the field, that Cain rose up against Abel his brother, and slew him.
Genesis 4:2–8

XI

THE SPLIT CHILD: Good and Evil Within Men

1. The Myth of Vena and Pṛthu

The story of the birth of king Pṛthu is often told to explain the origin of kingship on earth, but the symbolism of the myth reveals wider and deeper concerns, for the story is developed into an attempt to solve the problem of evil in the relationship between parents and children. The symbolism emerges even from a bare outline of the myth:

Once there was a king named Vena, who was so wicked that the sages killed him; since he had left no offspring to succeed him on the throne, the Seven Sages churned his body, and from it there emerged a son, Pṛthu. Pṛthu was as good as his father had been wicked; the two bards who recite the genealogies of kings were born to praise him. In order to restore prosperity to his subjects, who were suffering from famine as a result of Vena's evil rule, Pṛthu took up his bow and arrow and pursued the earth to force her to yield nourishment for his people. The earth assumed the form of a cow and begged him to spare her life; she then allowed him to milk her of all that the people needed. Thus did righteous kingship arise on earth, among kings of the lunar dynasty, who are the descendants of Pṛthu.

Almost all of these elements occur in all variants of the Pṛthu myth. In addition, the churning of Vena is usually said to take place twice: from his right arm, Pṛthu is born; from his left leg, a wicked son is born. Sometimes the opposition is between right and left, sometimes between hand and leg, sometimes both, but the opposition is always between upper/dextrous/good and lower/sinister/evil.

This is the tale as it appears in the Epics and Purāṇas, but, as Georges Dumézil has pointed out in his brilliant analysis of the story,[1] it must be much earlier in origin; other Indo-European sister versions indicate that it was well known at an early period, and these versions also give an idea of some of the ancient forms of the myth.[2] The tale of Tarquin in Rome shows particularly striking similarities. Tarquin had dared to cause the three tribes to be mixed; he was punished violently for this; Servius was then legitimized by the corpse of Tarquin, according to Tarquin's widow (who, in some versions, is said to have poisoned Tarquin herself).[3] The basic parallels between Tarquin/Servius and Vena/Pṛthu are fairly obvious; the secondary motifs of mixed tribes, lying widows, and poison are also relevant, as we shall see.

The earliest existing stratum of Indian literature, the Ṛg Veda, does not tell the Vena tale in full, but it does mention Pṛthu and almost always refers to him as the son of Vena;[4] thus even at this time they were known as a pair. Moreover, one Ṛg Vedic hymn refers to a Vena who has "impelled" the calves of the speckled cow who is the earth, whose white udder yields Soma as milk for the gods.[5] The earliest full recitals of the myth appear several centuries later, in the Brāhmaṇas; these narrate the episode of Pṛthu, while Vena appears only as a patronymic epithet:

Pṛthin, son of Vena, was consecrated first of men. He desired that he might appropriate to himself all good, and he did this.[6] *Abundance in the form of a cow ascended and came to men; men called to her, "O rich in cheer, come!" Manu son of Vivasvat [the sun] was the calf; earth was the vessel; Pṛthin son of Vena milked her; from her he milked cultivation and grain. She was then similarly milked by demons, who milked illusion out of her; by the dead ancestors, who milked death out of her; by the Seven Sages, who milked ascetic power out of her; by the gods, who milked strength out of her; by the Gandharvas, who milked sweet odor out of her; and by the serpents, who milked poison out of her.*[7]

Thus at the earliest level, Vena and Pṛthu are linked as father and son; first Vena appears in the Vedas as the one who forcibly milks the earth-cow with her calf; then Pṛthu appears in this same role. The Seven Sages who here aggressively milk the earth appear in the later variants to "milk" Vena to produce his sons. The

[1] Dumézil (1943), p. 99. See esp. chap. 3, part 5, "La vache d'abondance et la vache d'empire."

[2] *Ibid.*, p. 101. [3] *Ibid.*, pp. 215–217.

[4] *RV* 10.148.5; 10.94.14; 8.9.10, cf. *RV* 1.112.15; *Jai. Up. Br.* 1.10, 1.34, and 1.45; cf. Wallis, pp. 34–36; Charpentier, pp. 299–306. [5] *RV* 10.123.1–5; 5.52.16; 1.84.10–11; 8.6.19; 2.34.2; 5.60.5; 8.101.5; *Śata.* 1.8.3.15; *Kau. Br.* 8.5. [6] *Śata.* 5.3.5.4–7. [7] *AV* 8.10.22–29.

myth at this early stage appears to be about food—all kinds, demonic and divine, milk and poison.[8]

The Pṛthu story, omitting the episode of Vena, appears in the *Mahābhārata*, which refers to Pṛthu as the son of Vena and tells how he milked the earth.[9] Several Purāṇas similarly refer briefly to Vena and then describe the birth of his single son, Pṛthu, and the milking of the earth; here Vena is usually given a father, named Aṅga ("portion" or "body"), and sometimes a mother, Sunīthā.[10] A closely related text states that Aṅga was born of Ūru ("thigh");[11] this is particularly significant as a source of the idea that Vena's sons were "thigh-born" in fact as Aṅga was in name. In this text, Vena's left hand produces a Niṣāda (a dark-skinned, tribal non-Hindu), his right hand Pṛthu, who is said to have had two sons himself;[12] nothing further is heard of this pair, who form a superfluous complement to the other dualities of the myth.

Elsewhere, the Epic introduces an important episode that elaborates on the nature of the two sons of Vena, one good and one evil, one a civilized cultivator and one a barbarian hunter:

Vena destroyed dharma among his people. The sages killed him and churned his right thigh, from which was born a deformed little man, dark as a burnt pillar, with red eyes and black hair; he was the ancestor of the Niṣādas, the barbarians who live in the mountains. Then they churned Vena's right hand, and from him was born Pṛthu, who milked the earth-cow.[13]

In addition to the black son, the *Mahābhārata* adds details about Vena's "black" parentage, for here it is said that Vena's mother, Sunīthā, was the daughter of death, and Vena's father is the son of Anaṅga. Anaṅga, "the bodiless one," is an epithet of Kāma, Desire, whose body was destroyed by Śiva.[14] Thus Vena's paternal ancestors include either the body (with all its connotations of fleshly corruption) or desire (the source of that corruption and its spiritual counterpart, bodiless emotion). One text calls Vena's father Atibala, "excessive might," himself the son of Anaṅga; Atibala falls prey to his passions.[15] Sāyaṇa says that Vena is Kāma in the Ṛg Veda, and several texts comment on the lust of Vena.[16] Despite his name, Vena's father is regarded as a virtuous man, born in an illustrious family descended from Manu the Self-created. But Vena's mother has now become the villain of the piece, associated with that part of his body (not specified, but contrasted with the right hand, and hence either the left hand or either thigh) which gave birth to his evil descendants.[17] Vena is thus constituted

[8] *Jai. Up. Br.* 2.13.1–5. [9] *MBh.* 7, app. 1, no. 8, 763–827.

[10] *Kūrma* 1.13.9–11, 15–20; *Agni* 18.11–18; *Skanda Kedāra*, 6.7–16; *Vāyu* 2.1.91–98; *Brahma* 2.20–28. [11] *Vāyu* 2.1.91. [12] *Vāyu* 2.2.22. [13] *MBh.* 12.59.99–103.

[14] See above, chap. VIII, sec. 6. [15] *MBh.* 12.59.99–103; Sāyaṇa on *RV* 10.123.

[16] *Matsya* 10.3–10; *Padma* 5.8.1–10; *Manu* 9.67. [17] *Padma* 5.8; *Matsya* 10.8.

of contradictory principles, which result in contrasting progeny; he mediates between ambivalent parents and ambivalent children, transmitting the qualities of good and evil from one to the other. His own wickedness may be traced back to his two grandfathers, desire and death.

The *Bhāgavata Purāṇa* emphasizes the inherited, inevitable nature of Vena's sin and introduces the idea that the creation of the black Niṣāda not only produces a new king but frees Vena of his guilt:

Vena took after his maternal grandfather, Death, who was born of a portion of adharma, and so Vena was devoid of dharma. He went hunting and killed all the poor wild animals; he would violently strangle children of his own age at play as if they were beasts. He told the sages to sacrifice to him instead of to the gods, and he became more and more evil. The sages killed him, remarking, "One can feed a serpent on milk, but he remains evil by nature." But Sunīthā, his mother, took up the corpse of her son and preserved it magically. Then, realizing that they needed a king descended from Vena, the sages churned the thigh of the fallen king, and the black Niṣāda was born; when he was born he took away Vena's impurity. Then the sages churned Vena's two arms, and a pair of twins was born: from his right hand Pṛthu appeared, born of a portion of Viṣṇu, and from his left hand Pṛthu's wife appeared, born of a portion of Lakṣmī.[18]

The churning of Vena's body now has two distinct purposes: first he is churned to remove his impurity, which is transferred to the Niṣāda, the bad king; only then can Vena be churned to produce a good king. The text further distinguishes between the evil maternal heritage of Vena producing black descendants and the virtuous paternal heritage producing the shining Pṛthu (and his equally shining wife), incarnations of deity; good and evil are separated physically, if not physiologically. Vena's father is no longer called the son of Desire, and it is the maternal grandfather whom the evil Vena resembles; the male/female dichotomy is now clearly added to the other symbolic oppositions, Lakṣmī appearing from the *left* hand.

This distinction between the good father and the bad mother is maintained throughout the later mythology; the next set of texts then begins to elaborate on the role of Vena's good and evil progeny:

The sages churned Vena's left thigh and the black Niṣāda was born of Vena's impurity; then the angry sages churned Vena's right hand as if it were a fire-stick, and Pṛthu was born from that hand, shining forth like fire. When Pṛthu was born, all creatures rejoiced everywhere, and Vena went to the triple heaven, for by the birth of a good son he was protected from hell.[19]

In earlier texts, the Niṣāda is born directly out of the impurity of Vena, a black

[18] *Bhāgavata* 4.13.25–47; 4.14.1–46; 4.15.1ff.

[19] *Brahmāṇḍa* 2.36.127–227; *Skanda* 7.1.337.72–175; *Hari.* 5.1–21; 6.1–49; *Brahma* 4.28–122.

exudation in a material form; the bad son removes the king's bad qualities and thus frees the good qualities so that the good son can be born. This is a primitive view of sin as pollution; it reemerges in certain Tantric texts that speak of "burning the black man of sin out of the body." But in the version just cited, the Niṣāda, though born of Vena's impurity, does not remove it; now it is the good son, Pṛthu, who sends his father to heaven and who is henceforth responsible for removing the sin of Vena, a substance complementary to but separate from the impurity transferred to the Niṣāda. The son is said to save (*tra*) his father from the hell called Put (by offering the oblation to the ancestors), and hence a son is called *putra.* A similar folk etymology appears in another version of the Vena myth which states: A son is one who saves his ancestor (*pitṝṃs trāyate*).[20] On the psychological level, this episode of Pṛthu demonstrates the child's concern for the object, Vena, which does not enter into earlier texts.

Another text states that the birth of both sons is necessary for the purification of Vena: "When the Niṣāda was born, the evil went out of king Vena and his sin was destroyed; and when Pṛthu was born, Vena went to heaven, for he was protected from hell by this noble son."[21] Thus the idea that a good son protects his father combines with the older concept of transferred sin, and Vena is doubly saved. The manner in which the good son saves his evil father is further expanded in several texts:

After Vena had been killed, Pṛthu asked the sage Nārada whether Vena had gone to heaven or to hell. Nārada told Pṛthu that Vena had been reborn among the barbarians, afflicted with consumption and leprosy. Pṛthu went to the country of the barbarians and took his father upon a palanquin to the shrine of Śiva as Sthāṇu, but when they approached to bathe there at mid-day the wind in the sky said to Pṛthu, "Do not do this rash deed; protect the shrine. This man is enveloped in a terrible evil which would destroy the shrine, and this would be a great sin." Pṛthu then resolved to perform expiation for the sake of his father, and the birds in the sky said to him, "There is a holy place where your father's great evil may be destroyed; it is Goṣpada ["cow's footprint"]. When the gods and demons churned the ocean of milk, the Mothers of the World came with the gods to this shrine, and there they saw, imprinted upon the mountain stone, the footprint of Nandinī (the daughter of the magic wishing-cow). Henceforth this place was known as Goṣpada, and it is the only shrine that can release your father." King Pṛthu went there and performed the rite, and Vena went to the triple heaven.[22]

This text considers the problem that arises from heteropathic purification from sin; that is, in those texts in which the *evil* son releases his father, homeopathically taking the evil from him, there is no problem of pollution of the son; but when the *good* son is given this task, he is faced with a logical dilemma: since Vena is

[20] *Vāmana S.* 26.31. [21] *Viṣṇu* 1.13.7–41.

[22] *Skanda* 7.1.336.95–253; cf. *Garuḍa* 6.4–8; *Viṣṇudharmottara* 1.106.5–66.

wicked, he is barred from participation in the ceremonies that might purify him. Only the devotional sacrifice of one who is pure (the son) can break the chain of evil karma. That he is able to do this only at a shrine made sacred by the child of the magic wishing-cow is an important point to which we will return later. The transfer of evil karma from a parent to a son (or the giving of the son's merit to the father) occurs in village Buddhism as an antidote to karma: "The living can transfer their merit to the dead and thus enhance the salvation prospects of the latter. . . . Many people seek to transfer merit (*pin*) to their dead kinsmen."[23] In a popular Buddhist myth, the son of a thief enlightens his father. "This," explains the priest, "illustrates how the good *karma* of the son affected that of the father, for the virtue and wisdom of the son (expressions of his arrival at a superior stage of karmic evolution) counteracted the sin of the father, enabling the latter to reform before he was inextricably ensnared in the effects of his own bad *karma*."[24]

A close variant of this episode omits the shrine of the Cow-footprint but allows Vena to become purified at the Sthāṇu shrine to which he first is taken; however, in place of Nandinī, Śiva himself intervenes to help Vena:

Once when Manu sneezed, from his mouth there came forth a king who was the defender of dharma. This king married Bhayā [fear], the daughter of death [Mṛtyu Kāla], and from him was born the wicked Vena. When the king saw the face of his son, he went to the forest, performed asceticism, and attained the heaven of Brahmā. Vena behaved evilly because of the fault of his maternal grandfather, and he was killed by the sages, who churned the Niṣāda and Pṛthu out of him. . . .

At the Sthāṇu shrine there was a dog who had been a man in a previous life but was sinful and hence reborn as a dog. The dog came to the Sarasvatī river and swam there, and his impurities were shaken off and his thirst slaked. Then he became hungry and entered Vena's hut; when Vena saw the dog he was afraid, and, having gently touched the dog, he bathed in the Sthāṇu shrine. The dog showered him with water from the shrine, and by the power of the shrine, Vena was saved by his son. Śiva offered Vena a boon, and Vena said, "I plunged into the lake out of fear of this dog, for I have been forbidden by the gods to bathe in this shrine. The dog did me a favor, and so I ask you to favor him." Śiva was pleased and promised that the dog would be freed from sin and would proceed to the heaven of Śiva. Then Śiva said to Vena, "I am pleased with you. You will dwell in my presence for a long time, and then, born from my body, you will be reborn as the demon Andhaka, and, because of your former adharma—reviling the Vedas—you will become full of passion for the Mother. Then I will destroy you and purify your body with my trident, freeing you from all impurity, and you will become Bhṛngin, leader of my hosts."[25]

This text begins with an episode that foreshadows, in reverse, the main theme of

[23] Obeyesekere, p. 26; see above, chap. VI, sec. 2.

[24] Sharma, p. 352. [25] *Vāmana S.* 26.4–62; 27.1–23.

the purification of a wicked father by a good son; for the virtuous father of Vena leaves his evil son but manages to attain heaven by his own efforts. In Vena's case, the virtuous son must accumulate good karma and transfer that back to his father, even as he transfers the water from the shrines to his father, who is forbidden to touch them directly. In addition to this, another submotif of transfer is introduced. The unclean dog transfers the holy water from his body to that of Vena, and Vena in turn intercedes for the dog with Śiva (who is himself often accompanied by a dog when he comes to release heretics from their evil, as in the Pine Forest). The dog acts like Pṛthu (or the cow) in helping the father to obtain purifying water, but he also acts like the Niṣāda because he is impure. Thus the dog mediates between the impure Vena and the pure shrine, and for this he is rewarded. Finally, it appears that even these episodes are insufficient to free Vena from the entire burden of his guilt, and the chain continues into two more rebirths: first as the evil demon who will sin because of Vena's sin, and then, after the intercession of Śiva again, as the virtuous leader of Śiva's hosts, born of "a portion" of Śiva's body even as Pṛthu is born of Viṣṇu. In this way, Vena is purified, first by his two sons (one evil and one virtuous) and then by becoming two "sons" of Śiva (first evil and then virtuous).

In a later text, the precise nature of Vena's wickedness has a definite effect on the role of Pṛthu:

When Vena left the path of dharma, all classes and castes became mixed, for when the sages told him that mixing castes led to hell, he announced his intention to cause them to intermarry thoroughly. The atheist Vena caused Brahmins to beget sons in Kṣatriyas, Kṣatriyas in Vaiśyas, and so forth, producing the mixed castes of the Māgadhas and others. Then from the body of Vena himself was born a son named Barbarian, from whom were descended various foreign tribes. Seeing these creatures who were born of the transgression of dharma, the sages killed the evil Vena and churned both of his hands. Pṛthu and his wife were born of the body of Vena, and dharma was once again established, for Pṛthu reinstated all the castes, and by Pṛthu's decree all the castes became devoid of evil.[26]

The barbarian races, which in all versions of this myth are created from the body of Vena, appear here, but this motif is then repeated in another form as well, and Vena creates other impure castes by explicit decree. (A similar duplication may be seen in the texts in which Vena not only produces barbarians but is born as an unclean leper among them.) Both evil groups appear *before* Vena is killed in this version, and the dualistic birth from his dead body is maintained by the statement that it produced a male/female pair (as in the *Bhāgavata Purāṇa*) in place of the usual good/evil pair. (Since the female is associated with evil throughout this

[26] *Bṛhaddharma* 3.13.1–60; 3.14.1–45.

corpus, and placed on the left, the moral dichotomy is preserved.) Nothing is said of the purification of Vena himself, but Pṛthu is born in order to "purify" one set of Vena's offspring, that is, to make the mixed castes devoid of evil.

A final, greatly expanded version of the myth returns to the question of Vena's personal salvation, which is achieved by the direct intervention of a god (Viṣṇu), who takes upon himself at least part of the responsibility for Vena's corruption as well as his salvation; for the myth still seeks the ultimate cause in the past:

When the Niṣādas and other evil barbarians were born from Vena's body, the sages knew that the king's sins were gone. When Pṛthu was born from Vena's body, the king became spotless and righteous again and his sin was obliterated, the sin derived from his grandfather, Death.[27]

At this point the myth is interrupted, and the statement that is accepted in almost every version of the myth (that Vena was wicked because Death was his grandfather) is now challenged by the listeners, who first of all question the evil nature of death (a question that haunts the Hindu mythology of the origin of death). The bard at first answers this with a simple statement: "Death is the commander of evils and of evil thoughts; an evil-doer by his evil deeds reaches hell, where Yama heats him, while a good man obtains heaven."[28] This straightforward answer is then expanded in an episode that demonstrates not the evil but the virtue of Death—and the wickedness of his daughter:

Though Sunīthā was virtuous, because of the ripening of her father's karma she struck the ascetic Suśaṅkha and said to him, "My father punishes the evil and not the good, and there is no fault in that, but merely merit." But she continued to strike the sage, who cursed her, saying, "Since you struck me, you will have an evil son." Sunīthā practised asceticism in order to obtain a virtuous husband.

The sage Aṅga, son of Atri, obtained from Viṣṇu the promise that he would have a virtuous son. When Sunīthā learned of this she decided to marry him, for she thought that, because of his boon from Viṣṇu, Aṅga would beget a virtuous son in her, and Suśaṅkha's curse would be in vain. They married and had a son, Vena, who ruled virtuously, though Sunīthā worried about his origin and about the sage's curse, especially when people began to diminish.[29]

Although the ostensible purpose of this episode is to justify the evil of Vena as an inescapable result of his ancestry, it has the opposite effect. Sunīthā repeats the bard's statement that Death harms only the evil, but she is nevertheless driven by the force of Death's karma to commit a sin—teasing a sage and receiving the curse of evil offspring, like the female ancestors of the doomed Yadus.[30] The myth gives Death the role of the virtuous father of an evil child, a multiform of Aṅga and

[27] *Padma* 2.27.19–46 (Calcutta 2.28). [28] *Padma* 2.29.1–46. See above, chap. VIII, sec. 5.

[29] *Padma* 2.29.47–82; 2.30.1–73; 2.32.1–25; 2.33–35. [30] See above, chap. IX, sec. 4.

inverse of Pṛthu. Since the evil of Sunīthā is cancelled out by the virtue of Aṅga (and by the explicit boon of Viṣṇu), Viṣṇu must intervene again to undo the good he has done, to make the sage's curse come true, and to account for the corruption of Vena after all. To do this, Viṣṇu assumes the familiar form of a crafty Jain monk to corrupt the virtuous Vena, in spite of the warnings of Aṅga.[31] The sages churn Vena, and the Niṣāda and Pṛthu are born, neither of whom is said to purify Vena. Thus it is necessary for Viṣṇu to return yet again in the final episode, this time in his natural form, to teach Vena how to find salvation through asceticism and a horse sacrifice.[32] In this text, Vena is said to be corrupted in a number of ways (by being descended from Death, by the sin of his mother, and by falling prey to Viṣṇu's heresy); and his salvation is even more complex. He is said to be purified first by his contact with the sages who kill him, then by the birth of Pṛthu, then by his own asceticism and horse sacrifice, and finally by the teachings of Viṣṇu. The birth of the Niṣāda also contributes to Vena's purification by signalling the departure of his sins, and Pṛthu at the end practises asceticism to purify the land of Vena even as, in other variants, he purifies Vena himself or his people. The Seven Sages, who churn Vena and milk the earth in almost all variants of the myth, here lend several motifs to the character of Vena himself. He is taught a heresy as a part of the release from the curse of his mother, just as the sages are taught a heresy to release them from Gautama's curse, and he breaks the chain of evil by bathing in a river as they do.[33] The Seven Sages are associated, like Vena, with sin in time of famine (in particular, with aggression against a cow, the pivotal motif of the Vena/Pṛthu myth); they are the perfect foil for his wickedness, for where he clashes with sages as a result of refusing to pay them, they clash with a king as a result of refusing to accept food from him.

The multiplicity of explanations and the persistent interruptions and questions that characterize this last text demonstrate the degree to which the Vena myth remained troublesome to the Hindu mind and raised more questions about the nature and origin of evil than it could resolve. Always the myth reverts to the past for reasons; even at the end of the long text, Vena asks Viṣṇu to let him bring his parents with him to heaven; ultimately, the conflict between kings and priests, gods and mortals, is reduced to the conflict between parents and children.

This complicated story, which spans the entire range of Hindu mythology from the Vedas through post-Vedic Hinduism to both Vaiṣṇava and Śaiva bhakti movements, is susceptible of analysis on many levels. It may be seen as a historical justification of the social order, and on the symbolic level as a myth about the social meanings and referents of certain symbols. It is certainly, first and foremost on the explicit level, a myth of the nature of kingship and the social order; the bad king mixes the classes (as Tarquin mixes the tribes, and is punished), usurping for himself the sacrificial privileges of the Brahmins and incurring their wrath,

[31] *Padma* 2.36–37. [32] *Padma* 2.38.1–45; 2.124.1–17. [33] See above, chap. X, sec. 4.

while the good king establishes the proper hierarchy.[34] Vena is famous in India as a king who mixed the classes and castes;[35] the name Veṇa (often wrongly used for Vena himself) properly denotes a caste arising from the "mingling" of an Ugra man and a Kṣatriya woman (the Ugra himself being a savage hunter born of a Kṣatriya father and a Śūdra mother); that the words are so frequently confused may well indicate a general feeling that Vena is associated with mixed tribes. Vena's misrule results in drought and famine, the archetypal cause and result of sin; Pṛthu restores food and establishes civilization, order, and morality. Under Pṛthu's direction, the earth yields to each class of beings the specific, distinct thing that it needs; this is the function of dharma. The bad king is a cruel hunter, and his black descendants are hunters; the good king lays aside the bow and arrow with which he is born, and he establishes pastoral herds and cultivated crops. In the *Mahābhārata*, Pṛthu's very raison d'être is to restore the social order, which has disintegrated as the Kali Age progresses; when the integrated classes of the Golden Age fall into chaos, the gods create kingship–and Pṛthu–to restore order.[36] To do this, classes must be separated and kept distinct, an act originally symbolized by the separation of Vena himself into the two basic classes, evil and good.

But the myth does not end here. The proliferation of oppositional pairs suggests other, deeper meanings, as well. The primary contrast is indeed between Vena and Pṛthu, the evil king and the good king, but there are many other oppositions. Vena is given a good father and a bad mother; he himself produces an evil son and a good son; the two courtly bards produced at Pṛthu's consecration are an oppositional pair, for the Sūta is said to be the son of a Kṣatriya father and a Brahmin mother, the Māgadha the son of a Brahmin father and a Kṣatriya mother.[37] (Sometimes it is Vena's sin, not Pṛthu's virtue, that leads to the birth of these bards, for the Māgadhas are listed among the mixed tribes that arise from the mixture of classes instigated by Vena.[38]) Thus even the apparently social materials play a symbolic role, as do the kinship relationships. Sometimes Vena gives birth to Pṛthu and his wife; almost always, Pṛthu himself has two sons. The oppositions between white and black, right and left, male and female, hand and leg, good and evil, culture and nature, order and disorder, are mutually reinforcing. Too much has been written about the coincidence of opposites in India, and I doubt that any lengthy reference to this large body of scholarship would greatly illuminate the present myth, though it is certainly relevant to it.[39]

The problem of good and evil–the second level of the myth, after the level of historical justification–may be viewed in the context of the patterns established in the previous chapters of the present work. By usurping the privileges of the

[34] Dumézil (1943), pp. 59–60. Cf. Greimas, pp. 162–170; Muir, I, 297–306. [35] *Manu* 9.66–67.
[36] See above, chap. II, sec. 8. [37] *MBh.* 12.59.118. [38] *Bṛhaddharma* 3.13–14.
[39] Eliade (1958), pp. 244–273; (1959), p. 156; see also Hertz, and Needham (1973).

gods–demanding that sacrifice be offered to him in their stead, as he does in all texts of the myth–Vena joins the ranks of the many kings (Divodāsa, Yayāti, et al.) whose *virtue* threatens the gods, though Vena remains evil until the very end and merely becomes "godlike" by official decree. The clash and reconciliation of Vena and the gods serves here, however, as merely one aspect of a more basic conflict, the conflict between parents and children. For Vena is the epitome of parenthood, of both father and mother; as early as the Atharva Veda, he is the nonsexual parent of Brahmā and all the gods, himself being born of the abstractions of water and fire (the symbiotic elements of the golden seed).[40] To understand this level of the myth, one must view the story from Pṛthu's standpoint; though it is the episode of Vena which provides the complexities of detail (in contrast with the generally uniform narrations of the episode of Pṛthu milking the earth-cow), the Indian tradition calls this the myth of Pṛthu and generally devotes more space to him as the greatest Indian culture hero. On an explicit level, the myth is about the relationship of a son to his father; covertly, however, it may be seen as a myth of the relationship of a child to his mother, and in order to support this view it is necessary to reconsider the symbolism of cows and milk.

2. The Symbolism of Cows and Milk

The earliest Indian variant of the myth is the story of Pṛthu milking the earth-cow; though she grants him all that he desires, he must first attack her aggressively; she flees from him and begs him not to kill her. Thus his relationship with this cow is ambivalent: at first she is his enemy, then his nourisher. Moreover, her milk itself is ambivalent: she yields nourishment for men and gods, but illusion for demons and poison for serpents. The opposition between death and nourishment continues in the contrast between Death as the grandfather of Vena, and the nourishing earth, who is the granddaughter of Vena, for Pṛthu makes the earth his daughter in many texts. This opposition continues in the contrast between Vena as a king who causes famine and death and Pṛthu as the king who makes the earth yield all food. The opposition between poison and milk recurs in the Vena myth when the sages, referring to Vena, remark that you can feed a serpent milk, but he remains evil.[41] (Poison also occurs in the Roman and African variants of the myth, in which the queen poisons the wicked king,and in the Irish variant.) The marvellous cow that Pṛthu milks also reappears as Nandinī, whose footprint marks the sacred place where Vena is purified and who is the actual calf of the magic cow, even as Pṛthu becomes the symbolic calf.

[40] *AV* 4.1.

[41] *Bhāgavata* 4.13–15.

Nandinī and Pṛthu appear together in an Epic myth:

Nandinī was the magic wish-granting cow born of Surabhi (the daughter of Dakṣa) and Kasyapa; she was given to the sage Vasiṣṭha, and her milk had the property that any mortal who drank it would live for ten thousand years without losing his youth. One day Pṛthu and the other Vasus came to the wood where Vasiṣṭha lived. The wife of one of the Vasus wanted to give the cow to a mortal princess who was her friend, Jinavatī, a woman famed for her beauty, to make her the only one among mortals to be free from age and disease. To please her, Dyaus, Pṛthu, and the other Vasus stole the cow, for which crime Vasiṣṭha cursed them all to be born as mortals on earth.[42]

Pṛthu (here identified as one of the Vasus) may have been attracted to this myth because of his well-known aggression toward magic cows; he helps to steal this cow (as Prometheus steals the fire from Zeus) in order to help a mortal defy the challenge of the gods, to become free from age and disease—the definitive crime which the jealous Hindu gods cannot tolerate. (It is ironic that the Indian counterpart of Zeus—Dyaus, now demoted in status—is the would-be thief of immortality.) Surabhi is here said to be born of Dakṣa (father of many other troublesome women) and to be married to Kasyapa (father of many troublesome demons as well as gods); the mortal for whose sake the primeval theft of immortality is committed, and the demigod who urges the theft, are both female. Thus Surabhi, Nandinī, the Vasu's wife, and the mortal princess form two opposed female groups: two good, chaste cows and two wicked, lustful women, one who uses her beauty to corrupt her husband and the other whose beauty tempts her to challenge the gods. In this myth, Pṛthu takes the side of the erotic women against the maternal cows, a role somewhat inconsistent with his character in the myth of Vena.

Nandinī appears in the Vena myth in association with the place where the Mothers went when they came forth from the churned ocean. The Epic myth of the churning of the ocean of milk—whence comes forth every desired thing, including ambrosia and poison[43]—is a clear multiform of the pre-Epic myth of the milking of the magic cow. In many passages of the Ṛg Veda, the Soma juices are said to be churned or milked from the ocean—that is, from the Soma vats metaphorically regarded as an ocean—and this may well have been the source of the Epic myth of the churning. A close link between the two episodes (the churning of the ocean and the milking of the cow) may be seen in the statement that the magic cow, Surabhi, is produced when the ocean of milk is churned; and in return the ocean of milk is said to flow forth from the udder of Surabhi.[44] Thus the cow and the ocean are each other's mothers. This logical circle is stated explicitly: Surabhi, the mother of cows, was born of the ambrosia when Brahmā,

[42] *MBh.* 1.93.5–35. [43] *MBh.* 1.15–17; *Rām.* 1.45; *Bhāgavata* 8.6–12; *Matsya* 249–251; *Padma* 3.8–10; 5.4; 5.14; *Viṣṇu* 1.9. See O'Flaherty (1975), pp. 273–279. [44] *MBh.* 1.23.50; *Rām.* 7.23.21.

sated with it, spat it forth from his mouth; from the milk of Surabhi, the ocean of milk arose on earth, and four cows were born from her; when the gods and demons churned the ocean that was mixed with the milk of these cows, they obtained the horse Uccaiḥśravas, and Lakṣmī, and the ambrosia; Surabhi's milk is ambrosia to those who drink ambrosia, wine to those who drink wine, elixir (*svadhā*) to those who drink elixir.[45]

The verb for "churning" is *manth*, which indicates vigorous backwards and forwards motion of any sort; in the Vedas, it refers primarily to the twirling of the two fire-sticks to produce the sacred flame, an act often given sexual connotations in the Ṛg Veda[46] and in later bhakti poetry, where fire is regarded as androgynous, like Vena:

Suppose you cut a tall bamboo
in two;
make the bottom piece a woman,
the headpiece a man;
rub them together till they kindle:
tell me now,
the fire that's born,
is it male or female,
O Rāmanātha?[47]

Manth also applies to the churning of milk into butter and, in addition, often describes violent attack. Adalbert Kuhn has demonstrated the close interrelationship between the myths of churning fire and producing Soma;[48] he sees links between the verbal root *manth* and the base forms of Pro-metheus and Mandara (the mountain used as the axis in the churning of the ocean), as well as with the modern Irish *maedar* (a vessel or churn) and the grotesque Pramathas, servants of the fire-god Śiva. The basic meaning of the verb may be to snatch away or to steal, particularly to steal Soma;[49] thus *manth* applies to the kindling of fire or the churning of butter, since both are metaphors or multiforms of Soma through the myth of the stealing of the Soma-fire from heaven. *Manth* applies to the churning of butter,[50] and to the stealing of Soma by the eagle.[51] Indra is usually the eagle in this myth; Vena is identified with Indra and with the bird that flies to heaven to get the Soma;[52] thus Vena is both the subject and the object of the churning-kindling-stealing of the Soma.

This same verb, *manth*, is used to describe what the sages do to Vena; the vague and contradictory statements of what they did to him before this "churning"

[45] *MBh.* 5.100.1–13. [46] *RV* 3.29.1–3. [47] Ramanujan (1973), p. 110. *Dēvara Dāsimayya* 144.

[48] Kuhn, pp. 15–17, 218–223. [49] *RV* 5.30.8; 6.20.6. Cf. Narten, pp. 121–135.

[50] *Kāṭh. Sam.* 11.5; *AV* 7.70.2. [51] *RV* 1.93.6; 9.77.2; *Mait. Sam.* 4.8.1; *Kāṭh. Sam.* 37.14; O'Flaherty (1975), pp. 280–282; (1973), p. 277. [52] *Kau. Br.* 8.5; *RV* 10.123.6.

began (they grabbed him, or killed him with sharp blades of grass, or cursed him to die) indicate that they did not originally kill him *before* churning him but rather *by* churning him, violently attacking him (*manth*). In several texts, the sages churn Vena's arm or leg "as if it were a fire-stick," and Pṛthu emerges "shining like a fire," while the Niṣāda is black as a burnt stick;[53] Dumézil takes the verb in the Vedic sacrificial sense and says that the sages produce Pṛthu as they generate the sacred fire.[54] But the episode of the "churning" of Vena is not Vedic but Epic; it is the Epic analogue to the Vedic episode of the milking of the cow, and so it may well indicate that the sages churn or milk Pṛthu out of the Vena-cow in addition to "sparking" him out of the Vena fire-stick.

In other words, Vena acts symbolically as the mother of Pṛthu, and Pṛthu is born out of the female Vena's "milk" in place of the male Vena's fiery seed. There are many other examples of a man creating male offspring from his thigh in Indian mythology, and the Ṛg Veda calls the phallus a "boneless thigh."[55] Demons and Vaiśyas are created from Prajāpati's thigh; Tvaṣṭṛ churns the body of the dead Viśvarūpa and Vṛtra is born[56] (the part of the body that is churned is not specified, but the same verb is used as in the Vena myth, *manth*). The head of the demon killed by Rāma adheres to a sage's thigh,[57] an apparently demonic part of the body; another demonic thigh-born child is Aurva (whose name is said to be derived from *ūru*, "thigh," the name of Vena's grandfather), the sage who is transformed into the submarine mare. Kuhn suggests that Vena himself was originally thigh-born, like Zeus, Aurva, and Soma;[58] the episode of the demonic, thigh-born Niṣāda was then added, and only later was Pṛthu said to be born from the right hand of Vena. A line of males is thus thigh-born from males (though it must be noted that Aurva is born of his mother's thigh and indeed turns into a female himself; in this he is perhaps closer to the pattern of the Vena myth than Kuhn suspected). Elsewhere it is said that in the ritual the wives must pour water along their right thighs, for the semen of the man is emitted from the right thigh.[59] As seed is equated with milk, to "milk" the man's thigh of seed is equivalent to milking the woman's breast of milk, and the Kāmasūtras liken the action of the yoni on the liṅga to that of the milkmaid's hand on the cow's udder.

The thigh-born nature of Vena himself, as well as of Pṛthu, is supported by an ancient myth:

Kutsa was created from the thigh of Indra; he was identical to Indra and slept with Indra's wife, the daughter of Puloman; when she was questioned by Indra she told him, "I could not tell you two apart." Indra said, "I will make him bald, and then you will be

[53] *Vāyu* 2.1.125. [54] Dumézil (1943), p. 216. [55] *RV* 8.4.1.

[56] See above, chap. VI, sec. 1; and cf. *MBh.* 12.329.27.4. [57] See above, chap. X, sec. 2.

[58] Kuhn, pp. 148–151; O'Flaherty (1971*b*); (1973), pp. 289–292; (1975), pp. 159–161; cf. *Tait. Sam.* 6.1.11.1; *RV* 10.123.6. [59] *Tāṇḍya* 8.7.10.

able to distinguish between us." Indra made Kutsa bald, but Kutsa disguised himself and slept with Indra's wife again. Then Indra sprayed dust on Kutsa's chest and said, "Be a Malla!" [*a mixed tribe born of an outcaste Kṣatriya man and a Kṣatriya woman*]. *Kutsa begged Indra to spare him, his own son, and to give him a livelihood. Indra said, "Shake the dust off your chest." Kutsa did this, and the dust* [rajas] *became the kingdoms known as Rajas and Rajīyas, and Kutsa was their king. Kutsa forbade his priests to sacrifice, saying, "Whoever sacrifices will be beheaded. The gods do not eat when there is no sacrifice." Indra persuaded Kutsa's priest, Upagu, to sacrifice; Kutsa cut Upagu into pieces, but Upagu's father prayed to Indra, and Upagu was revived.*[60]

The incestuous conflict between father and son (like that between Tvaṣṭṛ and Indra); the dismemberment and resurrection (like that of Kaca and Jarāsandha[61]); the thinly masked beheading-castration motif (here Indra merely removes the hair from his son's head, but Upagu is threatened with actual beheading, and in other variants of this motif Rudra beheads his father Brahmā so that Rudra's wife will be able to distinguish between them in bed;[62] Kutsa is said to grab Indra by the testicles, and Gautama—whose form Indra takes, as he "has" Kutsa's form—castrates Indra for adultery with his wife[63]); the creation of two sets of barbarian tribes, one with a false etymology like that of Pṛthu, who is said to be a king (*rājan*) because his people rejoice (*rañj*) when he is born (and like that of the Niṣāda, said to receive his name when he is told to sit down [*niṣīda*], and the Maladas born of Indra's filth [*mala*][64]); the conflict between kings and priests; the impious king who forbids sacrifice in order to starve the gods—these elements foreshadow the myth of Pṛthu, who hates Indra because Indra is his father.[65]

From these myths of unilateral creation of sons by fathers—and from the simple fact that Vena has no wife—it becomes apparent that Vena acts as the evil cow-mother out of whom Pṛthu is milked, in contrast with the good cow-mother whom Pṛthu milks and makes his daughter. Cows and milk enter the Vena myth even before the myth enters India, for there is a Celtic multiform in a collection of Middle Irish stories probably redacted in the eleventh or the twelfth century:

King Bres . . . demanded from every rooftree in Ireland a hundred men's drink of the milk of a . . . cow. They formed three hundred cows of wood with dark brown pails in their forks in lieu of the udder. These pails were dipped in black bog-stuff. . . . All the bog stuff they had was squeezed out as if it was milk of which they were milked. . . . Bres was under a tabu to drink what should be milked there. . . . He drinks it all! Some say that he was seven days and seven months and seven years wasting away because of it, and he traversed Erin seeking a cure till he reached the same cairn, and there he died.[66]

Dumézil sees this as the counterpart of the cow of abundance which the generous

[60] *Jai. Br.* 3.199–202; cf. *Tāṇḍya* 14.6.8. [61] See above, chap. V, sec. 7. [62] O'Flaherty (1973), p. 127.
[63] *Tāṇḍya* 9.2.22; O'Flaherty (1973), pp. 85–87. [64] See above, chap. VI, sec. 4.
[65] See above, chap. VI, sec. 5. [66] Stokes, p. 439ff, no. 46, "Carn Húi Néit."

and nourishing king Pṛthu forced to satiate men with its inexhaustible and providential pseudo-milk; for the cow of Bres acts as a scourge, punishing the greedy and destructive king with abundant but fatal pseudo-milk.[67] But this "Celtic negative" is present in the Indian myth as well. Vena, like Bres, is plagued by disease and wanders in search of remedy; he produces poisonous "black milk" like the black bog-stuff in the form of the black Niṣāda who is churned out of him; and by ordering people to sacrifice to him alone, Vena in fact takes the Brahmins' traditional fee, the sacrificial cow, thus usurping all the cows in the country just as Bres does; Pṛthu then restores the cows that Vena has stolen.

Vena is thus in many ways the symbolic "evil mother" of Pṛthu, just as Vena's own evil is blamed on *his* mother. The misogynist bias of the Hindu myth is reversed in the Roman text, where the woman plays a more positive role; the widow (not the mother) of Tarquin makes it possible for the good king to assume the throne, albeit illegitimately, preserving the corpse just as Vena's mother magically preserves his corpse.[68] In this context, it is interesting to note that Vena is said to have been responsible not only for the confusion of classes but also for the practice of the remarriage of widows.[69] Vena himself leaves no widow, for he has no wife (himself assuming the role of the mother).

Seen from Pṛthu's standpoint, the grandmother (the daughter of Death) is the source of evil; in writing of the archetype of the mother, Jung remarks that

> the transition from mother to grandmother means that the archetype is elevated to a higher rank . . . and it frequently happens that the opposities contained in this image split apart. We then get . . . a benevolent goddess and one who is malevolent and dangerous. . . . As the distance between conscious and unconscious increases, the grandmother's more exalted rank transforms her into a "great mother."[70]

This splitting is central to an understanding of the Pṛthu/Vena myth.

The symbolism of cows and milk has deep roots in Indian religion. The good cow, the nourishing earth, is a central Vedic image; the swollen plant from which the Soma juice is pressed is likened to an udder milked of juices like cows, yet Soma is a bull.[71] Later, the milk from the breasts of Pārvatī confers immortality or eternal youth.[72] This magic milk, equated with the elixir of immortality, is primarily good, as one would expect; it is nourishing and gives life. Indra is said to drink Soma from his mother's breast, regarding Soma as an udder.[73] The mother's love for her child makes her milk flow spontaneously; indeed, even when Pārvatī is merely a "proxy" mother with no biological function, her breasts fill with milk the moment that, unknown to her, her "son" Skanda is born far away.[74] But just as milk flows because of love, so it can also be withheld because of

[67] Dumézil (1943), p. 240. [68] *Bhāgavata* 4.13–15. [69] *Manu* 9.66–67. [70] Jung (1972), p. 36.

[71] *RV* 3.48.3; 4.23.1; 7.101.1; 8.9.19; 9.68.1; 9.69.1; 9.107.5; 9.97.9; Wasson, pp. 43–45.

[72] *Kālikā* 80; *Saundarya Laharī* 73; *Śata*. 2.5.1.3–6. [73] *RV* 3.48.2–3.

[74] *Matsya* 154.554–60; *Skanda* 2.7.9.94; 1.1.27.81–83; Dessigane, Pattabiramin, and Filliozat (1967), p. 19; O'Flaherty (1973), pp. 252 and 274.

hate, and the milk that gives knowledge can also give ignorance.[75] In Śaiva Siddhānta theology it is said that because of the threefold bonds or snares, the self is a barren cow who drinks the toddy of illusion instead of nectar.[76] In the Vedas, the demons possess milk that destroys knowledge; the same "milk of illusion" that the demons milk from the earth-cow under Pṛthu's command is used to befuddle the mind of the bitch Saramā when Indra sends her to bring back the cows stolen by the demons.[77] When the ocean of milk is churned, it yields not only Soma but poison, and in Indian tribal mythology God transforms the sweet milk of immortality into the bitter milk of mortality.[78] Thus milk in India may be said to be morally ambivalent, moderating between the good Soma and the evil poison; there is good milk and bad milk.

Often the opposition is stated not in terms of good and bad milk but in terms of good and bad breasts, for in India (particularly in South India) the sacred power of a woman was thought to reside in her breasts.[79] In the Ṛg Veda, Aditi–generally a good, nourishing mother–pushes away (from the breast) her eighth son, Mārtāṇḍa, the sun, so that he dies; she bore him to be born and to die again.[80] Agni in the Ṛg Veda is said to be a calf born of an udderless cow (the female fire-stick), who cannot suckle him.[81] In later Hinduism, Pārvatī is sometimes an unsatisfying mother; once, when Skanda wished to suckle at her breast, she left him in order to practise asceticism; he called her "the woman whose breasts are not sucked" (Apītakucā), an epithet which she retained; Pārvatī allows dolls to suck at her breasts, which were never sucked by Skanda.[82] Certain yogis were cursed because they made slighting remarks about Pārvatī's breasts.[83] Pārvatī's inability to bear children in the normal manner, let alone to nurse them normally, is often remarked upon to her discredit; her adopted son, Aiyanar, is worshipped at crossroads in order that he may learn from wayfarers "about the peculiar position in which he stands in regard to his mother," and another son took to eating corpses because he was unsatisfied by his mother's milk.[84] Skanda is often given wet nurses because Pārvatī cannot nurse him herself; the Pleiades, or Kṛttikās, usually suckle him, but he is also nursed by the gruesome Kālī. The aggression implicit in this relationship is made explicit in the Epic:

[75] *Periya Purāṇa* 6.1 (*Tiruñāṉacampantamūrttināyārpurāṇam*) 66–76. See above, chap. II, sec. 7.

[76] Dhavamony, p. 178 (citing *Tiruvuntiyār*); see above, chap. VI, sec. 8.

[77] *RV* 10.108.1-11; *Bṛhaddevatā* 8.24–36a; O'Flaherty (1975), pp. 71–74.

[78] See above, chap. VIII, sec. 8. [79] Hart, pp. 98–99. [80] *RV* 10.72.8–9. [81] *RV* 10.115.1

[82] *Skanda* 1.3.2.21; *Tiruvilaiyāṭaṟpurāṇam* 4.32. [83] Briggs, p. 57.

[84] *Brahmāṇḍa* 4.10.41–77; *Brahmavaivarta* 3.2.19–24; *Mahābhāgavata* 12.18–21; *Bṛhaddharma* 2.41.106–108; *Rām.* 1.34.12–20; 1.36.7–9; *Vāmana* 25.1–20; 31.5–18; *MBh.* 3.104–108; *Brahma* 74–75; O'Flaherty (1973), pp. 267–271; Dessigane, Pattabiramin, and Filliozat (1964), pp. 76–77; Oppert, p. 509; *Cutalaimātācuvāmivipattu*, 1–6.

When Skanda was born, Indra asked the Mothers of the World to kill him. They agreed and approached him, but when they saw him and realized that he was invincible, they sought refuge with him and said, "You are our son. Let us all rejoice in you as in a son, for our breasts are flowing with milk and we are full of love." Skanda granted their desires, for he wished to drink from their breasts.[85]

The milk of their breasts flows here not because of love but rather because of fear; he conquers them and forces them to give him their milk almost as a peace offering. (The Mothers of the World indirectly offer their milk to Vena by establishing the shrine of the cow that releases him).

In another myth of this corpus, the aggression again begins with a wet nurse, Pūtanā, a hideous ogress. In one text, Pūtanā nurses Skanda,[86] but she is more famous for having "nursed" Kṛṣṇa:

The ogress Pūtanā, a devourer of children, was sent to kill the infant Kṛṣṇa; she assumed a charming form and let him suck her breast, which she had smeared with a virulent poison. But Kṛṣṇa, pressing her breast hard with his hands, angrily drank out her life's breaths with the milk and killed her, having cut off her breasts.[87]

According to a psychoanalytic analysis of this myth, "Pūtanā is obviously a representation of the child's conception of the bad mother, the mother with poisoned milk. To create such a demoness externally is to protect one's inner feelings about one's own mother by denying any ambivalent feelings."[88] Psychoanalysis has more to say about this myth, but for the moment the central image may be supported by several similar episodes revealing some sort of aggressive attitude toward a breast often regarded as inadequate or aggressive itself. The first element, aggression toward the breast, is particularly focused on the cow-mother in Tamil poetry, where wicked men are said to cut the udders of cows.[89] Another example of aggression toward the breast appears in the mythology of the Gonds:

[Pārvatī suckled the Gond gods, but they sucked her right breast until blood came, and they continued to suck blood until the breast shrivelled up. Having sucked her blood, they could not be controlled by anyone on earth.][90]

Blood replaces milk here, as in one variant of the Pṛthu myth in which the Rākṣasas milk the earth to obtain blood, their food.

A Sanskrit myth first describes the aggressive breast and then reverses this

[85] *MBh.* 3.216–217; O'Flaherty (1975), pp. 113–115. [86] *MBh.* 9.45.16; 3.219.26–27.

[87] *Bhāgavata* 10.6.1–44; *Agni* 12; *Brahma* 184; *Hari.* 50.22; *Padma* 6.245; *Viṣṇu* 5.5.

[88] Masson (1974*a*), p. 459. [89] *Puṟanāṉūṟu* 34.

4.10; O'Flaherty (1975), pp. 213–218.

[90] von Fürer-Haimendorf (1948), pp. 102, 129–137; Robinson and Joiner, pp. 1–37; cf. *Hari.* 6.30–31, *Bhāgavata* 4.18.21.

image, as the child uses the breast to transform the mother back into her loving aspect:

The demon Dāruka could only be killed by a woman. The Goddess Kālī made a body out of the poison in Śiva's neck (which he had placed there when it had come forth during the churning of the milky ocean). She killed Dāruka, but then she went mad. Śiva became a little boy in order to drink away her anger with her milk; she suckled him and thus was made calm. Then he danced to please her, and she danced with him.[91]

Another variant of this text retains the three episodes (the killing, the nursing, and the dance) but reverses the sexes:

Formerly a female Asura named Daruka had through devotion obtained such power, that she consumed like fire the gods and Brahmans. . . . Parvati created from her own substance a maiden of black colour [who] destroyed Daruka. . . . Shiva also appeared as an infant in a cemetery surrounded by ghosts, and on beholding him Kali took him up, and caressing him gave him her breast. He sucked the nectareous fluid; but becoming angry, in order to divert and pacify him, Kali, clasping him to her bosom, danced . . . until he was pleased and delighted.[92]

Kālī's dark side appears twice here, in the female Dārukā and in the dark female whom Pārvatī creates from her own body, rather than from Śiva's. In keeping with the inversion of the demon's gender, the episodes of suckling and dancing are reworked. The milk makes Śiva angry instead of calming her, and so she dances for him where he had danced for her; the events are the same, but the genders, and hence the emotional currents, are reversed. Yet the underlying significance of the two final episodes remains intact: a mammary contact is followed by an erotic contact; the mother becomes the wife, and only then is there peace.

The poisonous breast appears in another significant context: in weaning Indian children, a violent and abrupt process, "the mother may cover her nipples with a bitter paste."[93] A plant called Hālāhala (the same name given to the poison that emerges from the churned ocean) has a fruit said to resemble the teat of a cow;[94] this image links the Soma-poison opposition of the milk-churning myth with the milk-poison opposition of the breast image. Weaning is also a recurrent image in the mythology of heresy. We must be "weaned" gradually from our evil doctrines (poison) to the religion of the Veda (Soma); metaphysical growth recapitulates infantile growth.

In early Indian mythology, milk is often contrasted with blood rather than with poison, as in one myth remarkably similar in symbolic structure to the myth of Pṛthu:

[91] *Liṅga* 1.106; cf. *MBh.* 7.173, 16 lines inserted after 60.

[92] Kennedy, pp. 337–338, from *Liṅga* 2.100.

[93] Carstairs, pp. 63–64. [94] *Bhāvaprakāśa* (see *Hālāhala*), cited in *Śabdakalpadruma* V, 532.

Bhṛgu, the son of Varuṇa, thought himself above his father and above the gods. He went to the other world, where he saw two women, one beautiful and one hideous; he saw a river of blood guarded by a black, naked man with yellow eyes, a club in his hand; and a river of butter guarded by golden men who drew all desires from it into golden bowls. He returned and asked his father the meaning of what he had seen; his father told him that the two women were faith and lack of faith, and the black man was anger.[95]

The strife between father and son is expressed in terms of the familiar opposition between good and evil women, black and golden men, black "clubs" (often symbolic of the phallus in Śiva mythology) and golden bowls (often symbolic of the womb), blood that pollutes and butter that yields all desires.

Soma, poison, and blood are thus symbolically linked with milk throughout Indian mythology.[96] Yet another liquid pertinent to the Pṛthu myth is seed, or semen, which functions in true dialectial fashion sometimes as milk, sometimes as the opposite of milk. "Seed is milk; milk is female and seed is male, and so together they give life; the god of fire desired the sacrificial cow; his seed became that milk of hers."[97] In Ceylon, too, eight drops of blood are said to constitute a drop of semen; blood gets heated in a woman and turns into milk; thus blood forms the link between the male essence (semen) and the female essence (milk); blood pollutes, while milk purifies.[98] The woman's "seed" is often equated with her menstrual blood (*rajas,* a word also used to denote passion and symbolic of the source of all sexual procreation), with which the man's semen unites to produce a child.[99] Blood is the basis of the woman's productive liquids; a demonic daughter of the evil Duḥsaha[100] is the "thief of menses" (Ṛtuhariṇī); her three daughters steal the breasts of maidens, their genitals, and newborn children when the proper rituals are neglected.[101]

Hindus believe that "in the male the principle of life is in the semen (*retas*); in the female it is in the milk, known as *payas*, which latter word is also frequently used to mean semen."[102] The drinking of semen, likened to Soma or milk, occurs widely in the mythology; the mare Saṃjñā drinks the seed of the sun stallion, and the barren Pārvatī drinks Śiva's seed.[103] The drinking of semen is recommended in medical textbooks as a cure for impotence, though this is generally regarded as a

[95] *Jai. Br.* 1.44.12–13; *Śata.* 11.6.1–7. Cf. the story of Maṅkaṇaka, *Vāmana S.* 17.2–23; *MBh.* 3.81; 9.37; *Kūrma* 1.5; 2.34; *Padma* 1.27; O'Flaherty (1973), pp. 245–247; (1971*c*), pp. 26–35; (1975), pp. 173–174.

[96] O'Flaherty (1973), pp. 277–279. [97] *Śata.* 9.5.1.55–56; 2.5.1.16; 2.3.1.14–15. [98] Yalman, p. 30.

[99] Eliade (1958), pp. 239–254; Meyer (1930), II, pp. 359–362; see above, chap. II, sec. 4.

[100] See above, chap. III, sec. 2. [101] *Mārk.* 48.103–104. [102] Brown (1942), p. 87.

[103] *Śiva* 2.4.2.46; *Manu* 4.222; *Kāma Sūtra* 2.9; *Matsya* 158.33–50; *Padma* 5.17.165; *Skanda* 1.1.27.42; *Vāmana* 28.50; *Brahmavaivarta* 3.8–9. For Pārvatī, see *Matsya* 158.33–50, *Haracarita* 9.217; for Saṃjñā, see O'Flaherty (1973), pp. 261–277, 280–282.

sin or a perversion in mythological texts.[104] Urine, like semen, is drunk as a substitute for Soma/milk. The Avesta gives evidence that the urine of the cow or bull was used in purificatory rituals, and it has been suggested that the drug properties of the Soma remained potent in the urine of anyone who had drunk the Soma, so that it became the practice to drink such urine.[105] In the *Mahābhārata*, Indra (who often represents the stallion or bull) is said to urinate Soma as an elixir for the sage Uttaṅka, the same hapless Brahmin who, elsewhere in the Epic, is forced to swallow the urine and dung of an enormous bull.[106] In later Hinduism, it became the practice to drink the "five productions of the cow" (milk, curds, ghee, dung, and urine; note the conspicuous absence of another liquid cow-product, blood), in order to purify and absolve the sinner; thus the drinking of the stallion's Soma/urine was replaced by the drinking of the cow's milk. A myth explaining this practice is placed in the context of the struggle between gods and demons:

The goddess of fortune (Śrī) left the demons and went to the gods. After many years she went to the cows and asked to dwell within them; at first they refused, since she was so inconstant and fickle; at last she said, "No part of your bodies is disgusting; let me live somewhere in you." The cows agreed to let her dwell in their urine and dung.[107]

Just as the universe is sometimes visualized as the excrement of God, or Soma as the urine of Indra, so the cows as creators par excellence place within their apparently least venerable parts that aspect of womanhood which is both sought after by gods and demons and most dangerous to them: fickle fortune.

The dialectical opposition between milk and semen has another manifestation in the Indian variation on the concept of "the breast that feeds itself"–Melanie Klein's formulation of the infant's belief that when he is denied milk it is because the "bad breast" keeps it for itself. The implications of this hypothesis will be discussed below in another context; here the relevant development is the close parallel between this idea and the Indian concept of the phallus that holds back its seed, the yogi who seals his powers within himself,[108] a widespread idea that is manifest in the mythology of the drinking of the seed. The parallels between milk-mythology and seed-mythology in India are numerous and striking. On the one hand, women are thought to have seed, as men have;[109] there is an associative link between milk, seed, and urine in cows, with the cow acting as a symbol of a woman with a phallus.[110] One South Indian myth tells that the goddess Mīnākṣī was born to a king who had wanted a son and treated her like a son; she had three breasts, one of which disappeared when she met her husband,

[104] *Suśrutasaṃhitā, Śārīrasthānam* 2.41. [105] Alsdorf, p. 64; Wasson and O'Flaherty, *passim*.

[106] *MBh.* 14.54.12–35; 1.3.100–105. [107] *MBh.* 13.81.1–86; see above, chap. IV, sec. 3.

[108] Hayley, *passim*; cf. O'Flaherty (1973), pp. 261–276. [109] *Suśrutasaṃhitā, Śārīrasthānam* 2.35–45.

[110] Melanie Klein in *Imago*, vol. 11, cited in Daly, pp. 34–35.

Śiva.[111] A psychologist has commented on this myth: "The third breast stands for the male sex organ. Its withering stands for castration . . . as the way to the transformation of a man into a woman, i.e. identification with the mother."[112] The woman whose father "transformed" her into a man is retransformed when the phallic breast disappears.

Another South Indian tale of a breast that leaves a body and symbolizes aggression appears in the great Tamil epic, where the chaste heroine twists off her left breast and throws it down; Agni appears before her in the form of a black Brahmin with "milk-white teeth"; she tells him to destroy all evil-doers in the city of Madurai, but to spare Brahmins, good men, chaste woman, old people, children, and cows; the city goes up in flames after the immortals have abandoned it.[113] (In a related text, cows, Brahmins, women, the sick, and the childless are warned to leave before a city is besieged.[114]) Upon the well-known theme of the doomed city (for Agni declares that he was commanded "long ago" to destroy Madurai), the city abandoned by the gods, the evil city from which only a handful of "the good" survive at doomsday, the South Indian text superimposes the symbolism of the destructive left breast that contains chaste fire—while Fire himself, in complementary inversion, contains "milk" in the form of teeth. In a modern retelling of the epic, this symbolism is made explicit, for the heroine curses the city "for depriving me of the joy of having a child to be fed at my breast."[115]

The two normal breasts, like the abnormal third breast, may be replaced by a phallus. In a Buddhist tale, a woman cuts off her breasts in order to nourish a starving woman about to devour her own child; after this act, she returns home to her husband, whose oath restores her breasts. But Indra fears that she will cause him to fall from his throne of power; he takes the form of a Brahmin, begs from her, and asks her if the story of her act is true. She replied that she did it, and not for the sake of heaven, or Indra, or anybody else, but in order to tame the untamed; by that truth, she asks to become a man, and at that very moment she is transformed into a man, and Indra rejoices.[116] Again the classical pattern of the gods' antipathy to human virtue is embroidered with the motif of the woman who nourishes everyone with her breasts (here blood-yielding rather than milk-yielding) and contrasts with the woman who not only does not feed her child but is about to devour him—the extreme instance of the breast that feeds itself, and the classical sin arising from famine. The heroine becomes a non-woman twice; at first she is restored by her husband, but when the archetypal male (Indra) appears, she changes the breast for the phallus forever.

The fierce goddess Bhagavati has been described as a hostile virgin, whose

[111] Whitehead, p. 54; *Tiruvilaiyāṭarpurāṇam* 1.5.42–43. [112] Spratt, p. 268.

[113] *Cilappatikāram* 21.43–57; cf. above, chap. VII, sec. 3, and chap. IX, sec. 4.

[114] *Puṟanāṉūṟu* 9; cited in Hart, p. 80. [115] Ayyar, p. 132. [116] *Dīvyāvadāna* 32, pp. 307–309.

"snake ornaments, weapons, projecting tongue . . . indicate that she is a phallic mother, the 'mother with a penis' who is a common phantasy for European children, too"; for this reason, menstruous women are feared in India and a menstruating virgin is too terrifying to deflower.[117] Here again, blood mediates between the milk of the breast and the seed of the phallus.

On the other hand, just as the udder or breast of the cow or Goddess can function as a phallus, with seed, so Vena's limbs or body or thigh can be churned or milked. This anomalous sexuality is not uncommon in Indian mythology. In the Ṛg Veda, the god of rain is personified as a cloud (Parjanya) who is said to be "sometimes a sterile cow, sometimes one who gives birth; he makes his body whatever he wishes; the mother takes the father's milk."[118] The androgynous nature of the cloud is preserved in later Hinduism, where the same word (*payodhara*, literally "liquid-bearing," a masculine noun) denotes a breast or a cloud. In the Atharva Veda, Tvaṣṭṛ is a pregnant male, a bull filled with milk; his seed is milk, butter, and his calf.[119] Here the Vena parallel is particularly strong, for the father's milk becomes the calf; the father is milked of his son. Prajāpati is said to rub up milk and butter from himself, and thus to propagate;[120] here the verb simultaneously indicates the rubbing out of semen, the milking of milk, the churning of butter and the bringing forth of a male child. Prajāpati, the male creator, is also said to have the breasts and womb of a woman; the two breasts of Prajāpati are milked by the priest to obtain whatever he desires (i.e., Prajāpati is the wishing-cow), and after creation takes place Prajāpati is milked out and empty; Prajāpati becomes pregnant, with creatures in his womb.[121]

In the Epic, too, semen is produced like butter: "As butter is churned out from milk by the churning-sticks, so seed is churned out (of a man) by the churning-sticks born of bodily desires."[122] But the absence of sexuality also transmutes seed into Soma or butter; the man of continence, who restrains his seed, is said to have seed as rich as butter (like the rich milk of the breast that feeds itself). Thus either sexual "churning" or its inverse can turn seed to butter. The Epic also relates a story of the simultaneous transfer of both milk and pregnancy from woman to man:

King Yuvanāśva ["possessing young horses"] performed thousands of horse sacrifices and other sacrifices, but he had no son. The sage Bhṛgu and other sages consecrated a pot of water and filled it with their own ascetic power so that when Yuvanāśva's queen, Saudhyumnī, drank it she would bring forth a godlike son. One day, when Yuvanāśva had been fasting, he became parched with thirst; he found the pot of consecrated water and, not knowing its special properties, drank it all. When Bhṛgu discovered this accident he was angry at the improper deed that, he said, the king had committed; the king would

[117] Gough, pp. 74–75. [118] *RV* 7.101.3. [119] *AV* 9.4.1 and 9.4.3–6; see above, chap. V, sec. 3.
[120] *Śata.* 2.2.4.1–8. [121] *Tāṇḍya* 13.11.18; 9.6.7; *Śata.* 8.4.2.2. [122] *MBh.* 12.207.21.

have to bring forth a son, as the sages had decreed, but they performed a sacrifice so that he would give birth to a son the equal of Indra, without having labor pains. After a hundred years, a boy came out of his left side, and Yuvanāśva did not die—this was a marvel. The gods asked Indra, "Whom will he suck?" and Indra answered, "He will suck me [mām . . . dhāsyati]*," and put his thumb in the boy's mouth; and so the child was called Māndhātṛ.*[123]

The pregnant male, the seed in the pot, the birth from the left side (the thigh or the right or left "womb," according to variant readings), the suckling as well as the child-bearing by a man (the thumb replacing the breast as the thigh replaces the womb)—all is relevant to the Vena myth. The description of thirst leading to an improper deed and the curse of Bhṛgu are also familiar from the mythology of heresy, as is the involvement of Indra (here as surrogate wet nurse) with a king whose name indicates association with young horses but who has no young sons, a king who performs horse sacrifices and wants a son equal to Indra; all of this is particularly reminiscent of the episode of Indra and the stallion of the son of Pṛthu.[124] Another Epic male pregnancy is that of Śukra: When Śukra swallows Kaca, Kaca is born from Śukra's stomach and tells Śukra's natural daughter, Devayānī, that he "dwelled where she had dwelled."[125] Similarly, when Agni drinks the seed of Śiva, he and all the gods not only find themselves pregnant but begin to lactate, a condition which they themselves find both uncomfortable and embarrassing.[126] This self-conscious literal-mindedness in the myth—interpreting in commonsense terms an episode originally designed to convey only a symbolic meaning—is even more extreme in a Tamil tale:

A Vidyādhara's wife who was pregnant persuaded her husband to carry her embryo while she went to a temple festival. She neglected to return, however, and when the fully developed embryo could not come out, the Vidyādhara died.[127]

The mythical image of the pregnant male is retained as a possibility at first, only to be challenged as unsatisfactory in the cold light of reason.

The association of milk and cows with phalluses in India supports Melanie Klein's hypothesis, as two myths will demonstrate:

[A cow would give no milk and so was driven out. She went to the forest. One day the owner followed her and saw her spilling her milk on a stone image, the Śiva-liṅga. He tried to dig it up, but could not reach the bottom, and blood poured forth. Then he worshipped it as the great liṅga.]

[A pious boy saw a cowherd brutally assaulting a cow. He took over the job of cowherd and the cows yielded more milk than they could hold, so he used the extra milk that they spilled to water liṅgas. Then the jealous ex-cowherd accused him of stealing and wasting

123 *MBh.* 3.126.1–26; Meyer (1930), II, 372–374; cf. *Viṣṇu* 4.2.12–17. 124 *Bhāgavata* 4.19–20.

125 See above, chap. V, sec. 7. Cf. also Sāmba, above, chap. IX, sec. 4. 126 *Saura* 62.5–12.

127 Venkatasubbiah, pp. 113–114.

milk; the boy's father kicked a "mound of sand," not knowing that it was a sacred liṅga, and the boy cut off his father's leg. Śiva appeared and made the boy one of his immortal servants.][128]

The Oedipal aggression in both episodes is patent. The cow is a loving and generous mother with superabundant milk; the father opposes first the cow/mother, then the phallus (which bleeds instead of yielding either milk or seed), and finally the child, who cuts off the father's "leg" as the father had attempted to cut off the (boy's) phallus. In the classical Tamil myth on which the two above modern retellings are based, the father kicks not the liṅga but the pails of milk (an example of the interchangeability of the liṅga/seed and the udder/milk), the son cuts off both of his father's legs, and Śiva revives the father and takes both father and son to heaven.[129] The offending "leg," familiar from the Vena myth and the myth of Yama and the Shadow,[130] is thus restored and purified, a significant development in the light of the conflict and reconciliation between Vena and Pṛthu.

Another Śaiva myth of this type incorporates other motifs familiar from the Vena corpus:

A Brahmin lady on her deathbed asked her two sons to throw her bones into the water of the Ganges. The elder son agreed, and when she died he set out with her corpse. On the way, he observed this scene:

A Brahmin had gone away for the day, and when he returned he found that his wife had not milked the cow, who was distressed. He tied up the calf in order to milk the cow, but the calf kicked him, and the angry Brahmin beat the calf and left him tied up away from the still unmilked cow. The cow cried out and told the calf that she was determined to make the Brahmin suffer as she had suffered for her calf; only then would her sorrow be assuaged. Her son tried to enlighten her philosophically, but she added, "My son, I know that you are right, that we are all the slaves of our own karma; nevertheless, we are swallowed by illusion and we experience misery. In the morning, I will kill him by striking him with my horns, and then I will go to a special shrine to expiate the sin of Brahminicide." But in the morning the Brahmin said to his son, "I must go out on business; you milk the cow." The Brahmin left, the son went to get the calf, the cow became angry and struck him with his horns, and he died. The boy's mother wept in misery and beat the cow and untied her. The cow, who had been white, then appeared to be black, and people marvelled at this; but she raised her tail and went quickly to the banks of the Narmadā and plunged in and became white.

The Brahmin carrying his mother's corpse was amazed that Brahminicide could be so easily dispelled; he himself plunged into the river and then he met a beautiful woman, the goddess of the Ganges; she told him to throw his mother's ashes into the river, and he did.

128 Whitehead, p. 126; Rao, II, 1, 205–209.

129 *Periya Purāṇam* 4.6.1–60, "Caṇṭecuranāyaṇār."

130 See below, n. 142.

His mother obtained a celestial form, praised her son, and went to heaven, by the grace of Śiva.[131]

The dualistic oppositions in this compact myth are rife. There are three sets of mothers and sons: the Brahmin lady and her two sons in the frame story; the mother who fails to milk the cow, and her son; and the cow and her calf. There are two river goddesses (Ganges and Narmadā); and there are two cows, the white cow and the black cow, united to form the image of the ambivalent mother to mediate between the other two mothers, one good (the Brahmin lady) and one wicked (the woman who neglects the cow and so is indirectly responsible for the death of her son). The good mother dies and her son survives; the bad mother outlives her son. The relationship of sons to parents is that of virtue to vice. The innocent son of the cow owners is killed because his parents mistreat the cow; indeed, he is killed in place of his father, for had his father milked the cow as usual the son would not have died. The calf tries in vain to enlighten his murderous mother, and the son in the frame story purifies his mother's (unspecified) sins by taking her to a shrine, as Pṛthu takes Vena. In both stories, only the shrine can break the chain of karma, a chain whose power the cow explicitly acknowledges but nevertheless defies; she prefers to take direct action and knowingly commits a sin in the anticipation of salvation through Śiva's grace. One could hardly imagine a more complete exposition of the moral ambivalence of the cow-mother and the necessity of a son to forgive and purify her.

3. The Stallion and the Mare

The concept of a cow whose udders are symbolically linked with phalluses is further strengthened by the manner in which cows come to replace stallions in Indian mythology. The cow is benign and procreative, nourishing and sacred, essential to Hindu ritual; the bull, however, is dangerous and (though sacred to Śiva) is not used in rituals; the bull is erotic but not procreative in post-Vedic Hinduism, a distinction of importance throughout Hindu myth. The stallion, on the other hand, like the cow, is benign and procreative, as well as sacred, and is used in the Vedic horse sacrifice, a fertility ritual; the mare, like the bull, is dangerous and erotic, and is not used in ritual; the mare is the form taken by the fire beneath the sea, which emerges at doomsday to destroy the universe; the doomsday mare is created by the thigh-born Aurva.[132]

The ancient Indo-European fertility ritual involved the king and a mare (a

[131] *Śiva* 4.6.1–32, 40–65.

[132] O'Flaherty (1971*b*), pp. 10–23; *RV* 1.163.1–2; *Tait. Sam.* 5.5.10.6; 7.5.42.2; *MBh.* 1.181–182; 9.51; *Brahma* 110, 113, 116; *Brahmāṇḍa* 3.50–56; *Hari.* 1.45–46; *Matsya* 175–176; *Padma* 5.18; *Varāha* 147; *Skanda* 1.1.9.90; 1.1.17; 7.1.29–33; O'Flaherty (1973), pp. 286–292; (1975), pp. 159–161; (1975*a*), pp. 1–7.

ritual still echoed in the Vedic myth of the sun god and the mare). In the Near East, however, the mating took place between the queen and a bull. The Vedic Indian horse sacrifice supplies the uneasy (and soon discarded) mediating point: the Indo-European mare (already regarded as dangerous) is replaced by the queen, who mates with a stallion instead of a bull.[133]

In the Vedic period, before the rise of the misogynist tradition, which split the erotic, genital woman from the fertile, breast woman, the mare-woman played an important ritual role, even as the sacrificer's wife served a ritual function, for in the course of the horse sacrifice, the queen enacted ritual intercourse with the consecrated stallion. In the post-Vedic period, this ritual became unacceptable, incompatible with the new concept of woman; the "unchaste" queen is mocked in the ritual texts of the Brāhmaṇas or said to be seduced by Indra, who takes the form of a stallion to accomplish his end.[134] The fact that only the male horse is ritually acceptable in post-Vedic Hinduism is evident from a tradition which states that horses used to have breasts until Śiva cut them off (simultaneously cleaving the hooves of bulls, but not castrating them); another version of this myth states that Śiva did not actually cut off the breasts of the horses but merely made them vanish, simultaneously destroying not the hooves of the bulls but their teeth;[135] the anomalous breast of the horse, the enduring element of the episode, is the symbolic inverse of the anomalous phallus of the cow.

Much of this oppositional symbolism may be explained in historical terms. In Vedic times, the stallion was bred for attack and revered for martial qualities of virility; in later, Hindu times, in a pastoral society, cows were more useful and the female of the species more revered. Ritually and symbolically, therefore, the cow's milk came to replace the stallion's seed. In the Ṛg Veda, Soma is the stallion's seed; it is the male substance mixed with (female) milk to make it productive.[136] The stallion and the cow form a productive pair; the mare and the bull are their dark complement.

The symbiotic relationship between the stallion and the cow is evident from one version of the Pṛthu myth which adds another episode after the milking of the earth-cow:

Pṛthu performed ninety-nine horse sacrifices and prepared to perform the hundredth, inspiring the jealousy of Indra, who stole the sacrificial stallion. Pṛthu's son chased Indra with a bow and arrow, but Indra vanished, having released the horse, and then Pṛthu's son became known as Vijitāśva, "the conqueror (or controller) of the horse." But when Pṛthu himself took up an arrow to strike at Indra, the priests sacrificed against Indra, and Brahmā said to Pṛthu, "You should not be angry with Indra, for he is your very

[133] Puhvel, pp. 159–172.

[134] *Vaj. Sam.* 20–32; *AV* 20.136.1–16; *Ait. Br.* 6.36; *Sarvadarśanasaṃgraha*, pp. 6–7; cf. *Hari.* 118.11–17.

[135] *MBh.* 8.24, app. 1, no. 4, lines 15–21; *Matsya* 138.40–42.

[136] *RV* 1.164.34–35.

self." Pṛthu agreed and bestowed his filial affection (literally, "calf-love," vātsalya) *on Indra; Indra began to touch Pṛthu's feet in a gesture of love, for he was ashamed of his own behavior, but Pṛthu embraced Indra and gave up his hatred.*[137]

This is the other side of the coin, the problem of the son's conflict with his father. Just as Vena created heresies that Pṛthu must rectify, so too does Indra create evil that Pṛthu must undo; but this time the horse sacrifice, which Pṛthu uses elsewhere to undo the evil of Vena, is itself the source of new evil–competition between the son and the stallion father. Pṛthu must deal with an evil god-father as well as an evil human father; the priests side with Pṛthu against evil, in contrast with the priests who opposed the evil Vena, but Brahmā himself intervenes and reconciles them all. Pṛthu's son simply steals back the stallion and becomes the horse tamer, an image that recurs in this corpus; Pṛthu's own involvement is more complex, however. Indra himself is the stallion, the symbol of aggressive masculinity, and he often impersonates or steals sacrificial horses, usually to hide them in the ocean, the womb of horses and source of the sun-stallion;[138] thus Indra here reverses the process of ocean-churning. In coming to terms with Indra, Pṛthu again comes to accept his evil parent; he bestows his "calf-love" on Indra (the term usually used to describe a mother's love), and Indra's power is described as the "mother of adharma"–the female source of evil. Yet Pṛthu relents when he realizes that Indra is not only a god but his other self, that in rejecting his father, he rejects his own heritage and nature. Indra, in his turn, repents and embraces his son (who, by ending the sacrifice, ceases to compete with him); the dissension and disintegration in this part of Pṛthu's nature is mended by the son's voluntary withdrawal from conflict with a malevolent, or at least jealous, father. This text demonstrates how the conflict between man and god so central to the Hindu mythology of theodicy–here manifest in Vena's refusal to sacrifice as well as in Pṛthu's excessive sacrifice–functions as a variant of the more basic conflict between a son and his father.

4. The Good and Evil Mother

As the stallion is an emotionally and morally ambivalent symbol of the father, so too is the cow a dualist figure of the mother. The good cow is symbolic of the good mother, producing good milk, and bad cows are sacred to the bad mother, Nirṛti, the goddess of disease and bad luck; a barren, black cow is offered to Nirṛti in the house of a woman who has no son.[139] The speckled earth-cow milked by Vena in the Vedic myth is milked only once and then is barren; (here, as in the Vena myth, milking and bringing forth young are equated). Agni

[137] *Bhāgavata* 4.19.1–38; 4.20.18ff.; cf. *Padma* 2.134; see above, chap. VI, sec. 5.

[138] *RV* 1.163.1–2; *Tait. Saṃ.* 7.5.25.2; *Śata.* 10.6.4.1; O'Flaherty (1971*b*). [139] *Śata.* 5.3.1.13; 5.3.2.13.

(engendered, like Vena, by "churning") is said to be a calf nursed by two mothers, a black cow and a white cow, who are night and day.[140] The cow milked in the original Pṛthu myth is an integrated image of the two mothers: she yields death to the ancestors and life strength to the gods. Nandinī, the magic wishing-cow, yields milk and elixir like Soma itself to the good sage Vasiṣṭha, who owns her, but when the wicked king Viśvāmitra steals her and beats her, she brings forth ferocious barbarian races from her ass, urine, excrement, and froth,[141] just as the Vena-cow (opposed by sages) is milked of barbarian Niṣādas while Pṛthu's cow is milked of nourishing substances.

An important Vedic myth of two mothers is the story of Saṃjñā, the wife of the sun (Vivasvat):

Saṃjñā gave birth to twins, Yama and Yamī, and then left her husband, creating as a substitute in her place an identical goddess called Chāyā ("dark shadow"). Her husband discovered the deception only when Chāyā mistreated her stepson, Yama; Yama tried to kick Chāyā and was cursed by her to lose his leg, a curse which his father later modified so that Yama fell to the underworld, the first mortal to die and king of all subsequent dead people. Vivasvat pursued Saṃjñā, who had taken the form of a mare, and in the form of a stallion (whose seed she drank) he begat the twin Aśvins upon her.[142]

The oppositional pairs of the good and bad mother, the bright image (*saṃjñā*) and dark shadow, are linked with the motif of the fertile solar stallion pursuing the erotic, destructive mare. The sun himself is said to have been rejected and pushed from the breast by his mother, Aditi, or to have been threatened by her asceticism while still in her womb, becoming mortal because of this;[143] and Chāyā's hatred of her stepson results in a curse that makes Yama into the king of the dead. Thus the wicked, false mother is the source of the greatest of all evils, the kingdom of the dead.

Aditi is the good mother, the good nourisher, chaste and fertile; Nirṛti, her "elder sister" (even as the Niṣāda is Pṛthu's elder brother) is the bad mother, barren and lascivious. In post-Vedic mythology, Nirṛti/Alakṣmī/Jyeṣṭhā appears with poison, just as her contrasting sister, Śrī or Lakṣmī, appears with Soma when the ocean of milk is churned.[144] Diti and Aditi are the two wives of Kasyapa. From Diti all the evil demons are born, and from Aditi all the gods; thus the war between the gods and demons, the basis of Hindu mythological theodicy, is a fraternal conflict. The relationship between Indra and his stepmother, Diti, is one of conflict with sexual overtones; Indra keeps killing Diti's sons, and she keeps

[140] *RV* 6.48.22; 1.95.1; 1.96.5. [141] *MBh.* 1.165.1–45.

[142] *RV* 10.17.1–2; *Nirukta* 12.10; *Śata.* 1.1.4.14; *Tait. Br.* 1.1.4.4; 1.1.9.10; 3.2.5.9; *Tai. Sam.* 2.6.7.1; 6.5.6.1; 6.6.6.1; *Mārk.* 103–105; *MBh.* 1.66; *Brahmāṇḍa* 3.59–60; *Matsya* 11; *Padma* 5.8; *Vāyu* 2.3; *Viṣṇu* 3.2; cf. O'Flaherty (1975), pp. 60–70; cf. also *Gopatha* 1.1.3.

[143] *RV* 10.72.8–9. [144] *MBh.* 1.15–17; *Liṅga* 2.6.

trying to have a son to kill Indra. When she is pregnant with such a potential son on one occasion, Indra enters her womb and cuts to pieces his unborn brothers; a similar tale is told of Aditi's elder and younger sons.[145] Thus by a sexual assault upon the black mother Indra simultaneously overcomes his "black" brothers, the demons.

Another myth from this corpus includes elements from the cycle of the cow and the stone liṅga:

A woman named Sudevā had no son. She brought her younger sister Ghuśmā to her husband and begged him to marry her. He did, and Ghuśmā gave birth to a fine son. Though the husband loved Sudevā best, she was jealous, and one night she took a knife and cut off all the limbs of the son and threw them into a lake. Ghuśmā threw a liṅga made of earth into the lake, as she did each day, and she saw her son standing on the bank of the lake. Sudevā begged to be forgiven, and she was.[146]

Again the wicked stepmother threatens the son, but now it is she who dismembers him, not the reverse as in the myth of Indra and Diti. Whereas Indra had to justify his sin by pointing out a ritual error committed by Diti, or by suffering the loss of his throne, Sudevā, like the murderous cow, is forgiven by the grace of Śiva.

The most explicit Hindu myth of "split" mothers is the story of the Goddess who, upon being teased by Śiva about her dark skin (he being noted for his white color), practised asceticism until she sloughed her black skin and became known as Gaurī, "the golden one", while the skin became the goddess Kālī, "the black one" (or the female form of time and death, Kāla), also known as Kauśikī ("born of the sheath").[147] (The Niṣādas are, like Kālī Vindhyavāsinī, "dwelling in the Vindhyas," black people who inhabit the Vindhya mountains, the geographical boundary between North India—the land of the Aryans, in Purāṇic tradition—and the land of the Dravidians.) The image of the split woman may be traced back to a Vedic myth of a girl who sloughs her diseased skin (which becomes a porcupine, alligator, and chameleon) and obtains a golden skin, by the favor of Indra.[148] The mother who is simultaneously terrifying and enchantingly beautiful appears throughout Hindu mythology in the motif of the *Liebestod* of

[145] *Rām.* 1.45–46; *Bṛhaddevatā* 4.47–56; *Bhāgavata* 3.14–17; 6.18; *Brahmāṇḍa* 2.3.5; *Matsya* 7; *Hari.* 1.3; *Padma* 2.25; 5.7; *Vāmana* 45–56; *Viṣṇu* 1.22; *Tait. Sam.* 6.1.3.4–8; *Śata.* 3.2.1.27–28; von Stietencron (1966), p. 149n.; O'Flaherty (1975), pp. 91–94; see above, chap. II, sec. 9, and chap. VI, sec. 3. [146] *Śiva* 4.32.1–52; 4.33.1–56.

[147] *Skanda* 1.2.27–29; *Devībhāgavata* 5.23; *Kālikā* 47; *Matsya* 139, 154–157; *Padma* 5.41; *Śiva* 7.1.25–27; *Vāmana* 28; *Skanda* 5.2.18; O'Flaherty (1975), pp. 251–262; *Mārk.* 85.37–41.

[148] *RV* 8.80; *Bṛhaddevatā* 6.99–107; Coomaraswamy (1935*b*), pp. 8–9.

the demon who desires the Goddess, fights against her in battle, and is killed by her.[149]

Another tale of split mothers appears in South Indian tradition:

[Reṇukā (whose name may mean "mote of light") was the mother of Paraśurāma; one day she became unchaste and, at the behest of his father, Paraśurāma beheaded Reṇukā; at the same time, he beheaded a dark-skinned, low-caste woman. Paraśurāma pleaded with his father to revive Reṇukā; given permission at last, the boy went in the dark and revived both bodies, but accidentally he placed the wrong head on each body. The woman with Reṇukā's head was accepted as Reṇukā; the other became a Mātaṅgī, a low-caste woman.][150]

This myth adds a new element to the corpus. The split women, dark and light, low and high caste, are reunited in a totally integrated form, each with half of the other, even as the Niṣāda and Pṛthu form the dark and light halves of the dead Vena. This reuniting motif appears in one Epic myth that makes strikingly clear certain themes that are deeply submerged in the Vena myth:

King Bṛhadratha had two wives, twins, but neither of them bore him a son. A sage gave the king a mango, which he gave to his two wives; they split it in half, and each ate a half, conceived, and brought forth half a body. Each half had one eye, one arm, one leg, one buttock, half a stomach, and half a face. The queens, frightened, had their nurses discard these pieces of flesh, but then there appeared a female named Jarā ("old age"); she was a female Rākṣasa but not (like) a female Rākṣasa; she lived upon flesh and blood but had celestial golden beauty; she had been created by Brahmā to destroy demons. She took up the two halves and joined them, and they united into a sturdy child, Jarāsandha ("joined by Jarā"). Then the two queens, whose breasts were full of milk, came forth to receive their child, drenching him with their streams of milk.[151]

The king who is born in pieces is not as anomalous in Indian myth as he is in the West;[152] his ambivalence remains, for he is one of the "human demon" kings whom Kṛṣṇa destroys. The mother who joins him is the ambivalent female, demonic and divine, a demoness by birth and diet but not in all her acts or in her appearance; created to destroy demons, she is also the archenemy of a presumptuous mortal king, Yayāti, and she alone can integrate the split king, who is rejected by his dual mothers only to be taken back by them and drenched by their milk.

[149] O'Flaherty (1973), pp. 184–191; 236–239; and cf. the myths of Andhaka and Mahiṣa, see above, chap. X, sec. 6. [150] Elmore, p. 95; cf. Clough, pp. 85ff; Thurston, IV, 306ff. See, too, Thomas Mann, *The Transposed Heads*. For the classical myth of Reṇukā, see *MBh.* 3.116.1–18.

[151] *MBh.* 2.16.12–51; 2.17.1–5. [152] See the Maruts (*Vāmana* 46; *MBh.* 9.37.28–31); Kṛṣṇa (*Hari.* 47–48, O'Flaherty [1975], pp. 206–213; *Bhāgavata* 10.1–4; *Liṅga* 1.69; *Viṣṇu* 5.1–3); and Skanda (O'Flaherty [1973], pp. 267–271 and 321).

5. The Androgynous Parent

Perhaps the most famous split figure in Indian mythology is the primeval, incestuous androgyne born of the Creator, who separates to unite again sexually. Vena himself functions as an androgyne: he is both the father and the mother of Pṛthu; he has no wife, but creates Pṛthu incestuously or unilaterally. Similarly, some versions of the Vena myth state that Pṛthu and his wife were born of Vena and thus form an incestuous pair; Pṛthu treats his wife like a half of himself.[153] In many Purāṇas, the god divides himself into male and female; the female half then further separates into the white goddess (Gaurī and her descendants) and the black goddess (Kālī and her troop of Mothers);[154] thus the male/female contrast is made parallel to the white/black, good/evil opposition at an early stage. In the many textual and graphic representations of the androgynous form of Śiva and Pārvatī, the woman is always on the left side. Ila, another king born, like Pṛthu, in the lunar dynasty, is noted for having changed from a man into a woman, and back again, on several occasions (or, sometimes, to alternate as a woman for a month and a man for a month; or to become an androgyne or a centaur [Kinnara], half man, half horse).[155] The transformation of Ila into a woman (and of his stallion into a mare) takes place when he inadvertently witnesses—and thus separates—the sexual union of Śiva and Pārvatī, the original androgyne. The female Ilā gives birth to children who oppose the children begotten by the male Ila; indeed, the *Mahābhārata* states that Ila, a descendant of Vena, was both the mother and the father of Purūravas, who was born "in her."[156] The text goes on to describe the behavior of this child of the androgyne: Purūravas, a human, was surrounded by nonhumans (Gandharvas and a celestial nymph whom he married); he came into conflict with the Brahmins and stole their gems; the sages tried to reason with him, but he took no notice, and so they cursed him and he perished at once, overpowered by greed and arrogance. In other words, he repeated the doomed actions of Vena, his androgynous ancestor. In this context, Vena's status as both the literal father and the symbolic mother of Pṛthu is neither bizarre nor irrelevant, and it is further supported by the antiquity of the Indian concept of the pregnant male.

The sexual ambivalence of Vena has counterparts not only in Indian and

[153] *Bṛhaddharma* 3.13–14; *Bhāgavata* 4.16.17.

[154] *Vāyu* 9.75; *Liṅga* 1.70.324–327; *Viṣṇu* 1.7.12–13;

Śata. 14.4.2; *Manu* 1.32; *Viṣṇu* 1.7.14; *Saura* 24.55–67; 25.5–29; *Matsya* 3.30–44, 4.11–21; O'Flaherty (1973), pp. 111–113, 256–258. Cf. Eliade (1965), pp. 103–114.

[155] *Matsya* 11.44; *RV* 10.95.18; *MBh.* 1.75.18–19; *Liṅga* 1.65.19–25; *Viṣṇu* 4.1.8ff.; *Padma* 5.8.75; *Brahma* 7.3ff.; *Hari.* 1.10.3ff; *Mārk.* 111.6–18; *Bhāgavata* 9.1.3ff.; *Rām.* 7.87; *Brahmāṇḍa* 3.60; *Devībhāgavata* 6.27–29; 8.8; von Stietencron (1972), chap. 11; O'Flaherty (1973), pp. 304–306.

[156] *MBh.* 1.70.13–20. Cf. Meyer (1930), pp. 374–376.

Indo-European mythology[157] but in Africa. The Nyoro myth of the origin of the first king is strikingly similar to the myth of Pṛthu and contains all of the Vena/Pṛthu oppositions, including the sexual ambivalence, the symbolism of black and white cows, left and right cows, hunter and savage, half bodies, evil mothers and good fathers.[158] Several points of particular interest relate to the symbolism of cows in Nyoro mythology. Among the Nyoro, cows are normally milked from the right side, but when the king dies a special cow is milked from the left side, and some of the milk is poured into the mouth of the corpse; the king, at a ceremony performed every morning, passes the evil of the past night into a black cow–significantly, through a white spot on its forehead against which he places his head. The cow in this corpus would seem to play the role assumed by the dog in the myth of Vena: the morally ambivalent animal whom the king's sin is transferred, a role also fulfilled by the Niṣāda. Rodney Needham has pointed out the implications of some of this symbolism:

> In that Mpuga [the first king] is both colours, he symbolizes in his person both the principle of opposition itself and the alien, uncategorized, and essentially disorderly nature of his own condition and intent. . . . The narrative describes a transition from nature to culture; it states the perennial and complementary opposition between order and disorder.[159]

All of these principles are essential to the myth of Vena and Pṛthu.

The African myth offers a further clue to the interpretation of the Hindu parallel by its very existence. If the Vena story appears in a non-European culture (to which it is unlikely that it could have been transported by Europeans), then we must not look for "Indian" or "European" or "African" meanings in it at all; we must look for universal, human meanings, the kind of archetypal meanings for which Jung and lesser students of comparative mythology have been so often mocked, meanings that apply not merely to kings but to us all, to all mortals who are nourished at the breast–indeed, to all mammals, if we ever decipher the mythology of dolphins and tigers.

6. The Split Child

The best known European image of the man who splits into two separate people is that of Dr. Jekyll and Mr. Hyde.[160] This splitting, which is rare or pathological in adults, is universal and normal in children. We are all familiar with it:

> At first children are very confused about what is inside themselves and what is outside themselves. Thus they can project one of their repressed wishes into the environment and mistake it for something quite outside themselves. In fact this distinction between inner

[157] Plato tells the story of the primeval androgyne in the *Symposium*.

[158] Needham (1967), pp. 425–452. [159] *Ibid.*, pp. 445–446.

[160] Joan Rivière, in Klein et al. (1955), p. 362.

and outer life is a tradition, like logical thinking, which even adults have only built up after thousands of years of civilized society; and each new generation has to learn it afresh. In a twinkling a small child will say that his teddy bear was naughty and made a wet patch on the floor.[161]

This psychologist extends the pattern to adult behavior:

Parts of the mind are liable to be in opposition to other parts of the mind, and the child is prevented from becoming a mature adult with an integrated personality. An extreme case of this is imagined by Robert Louis Stevenson in *The Strange Case of Dr Jekyll and Mr Hyde*.[162]

This theory, most originally and fully developed by Jean Piaget, brings to light a close structural resemblance between a young child's symbolic processes and the archetypes postulated by Jung:

One category of general symbols contains those which are common to the thought of the child, to dreams, and to the various symbolic forms of adult thought.[163]

Piaget speculated on the possible reasons for this resemblance:

Either there is an innate, unconscious tendency common to all men, which actuates the child of today as it determined the representations of our ancestors, or else it is a question of mere imaged representations . . . which can be general in so far as the products of infantile thought influence "primitive" forms of thought. . . . However far back we go into history, or pre-history, the child has always preceded the adult, and it can be assumed that the more primitive a society, the more lasting the influence of the child's thought on the individual's development. . . . Symbolism can, thanks to the truly primitive character of the mechanisms of the child's thought, acquire the same degree of generality that Jung found in his hypothesis of a "collective unconscious."[164]

Piaget's theory has been attacked by many anthropologists[165] who seem to feel that he is saying that primitives are childlike, or that they think like children whereas we of the nonprimitive world of science think like grown-ups. But Piaget is merely saying that the cultures of primitive, prescientific people preserve many of the symbols that all children (primitive and civilized) use but that are often discarded or superseded in nonprimitive cultures. In Piaget's view, myths reveal a level of symbolism that is shared by children everywhere, preserved by many prescientific cultures, and indeed preserved in many "scientific" cultures as well, cultures which (like that of India) continue to derive their spiritual values from the traditions of their more primitive ancestors.

Thus Mr. Hyde, the naughty teddy, and the black Niṣāda may be regarded as expressions of equivalent symbolic function. What this level of explanation gains in simplicity and generality it unfortunately also gains in banality. Is this all that the Vena myth is about? If so, why the recurrent cow imagery, which, though of

[161] Pickard, p. 78. [162] *Ibid.*, p. 24. [163] Piaget, p. 198.

[164] *Ibid.*, pp. 196–198. [165] Douglas, pp. 88 and 115–116.

obvious ritual significance in Hindu and Nyoro culture, can have little meaning for the Western child with his naughty teddy? To answer this, we must go yet farther back into childhood, and here we enter the realm of psychoanalysis. Dumézil has indeed established beyond any doubt that the myth of Vena is about society, but this does not mean that it is *only* about society. On another level, the myth is about what much of psychoanalysis is about: the child's earliest perception of his parents.

7. The Breast that Feeds Itself

Freud's theory of ambivalence suggests that there is a dissociation in some men between heavenly love and earthly desire, that the child hates the "genital" mother and loves the "breast" mother.[166] This appears in post-Vedic Indian mythology as the conflict between the chaste but fertile cow-mother associated with the breast, and the erotic but barren genital mother associated with the mare. The Freudian view could be supported by a large number of Hindu myths of the *vagina dentata* type, myths in which the yoni, or female organ of generation, is explicitly said to castrate or to kill.[167] (In later Tantric painting, this symbolism is often reversed, together with so many other traditional Hindu values, and the genital mother becomes the beautiful white mother who embraces her supine husband, while the breast mother becomes the dangerous black mother with blood flowing in place of milk from her headless torso.[168]) Melanie Klein's major innovation is in applying the theory of ambivalence specifically to the breast of the mother; the child projects hatred and love onto concrete objects–bad and good breasts and milk–rather than onto a vague maternal persona:[169]

> In the earliest phase the persecuting and the good objects (breasts) are kept wide apart in the child's mind. When . . . they come closer together, the ego has over and over again recourse to . . . a splitting of its imagos into loved and hated, that is to say, into good and dangerous ones. . . . The mother, first of all her breast, is the primal object for both the infant's introjective and projective processes. . . . It is not only what are felt to be destructive and "bad" parts of the self which are split off and projected into another person, but also parts which are felt to be good and valuable. . . . The child [attempts] to get hold of "good" substances and objects (ultimately, "good" milk . . .) and with their help to paralyze the action of the "bad" objects and substances within its body.[170]

The concept of the breast that feeds itself stems from this hypothesis:

> Whenever he is hungry or neglected, the child's frustration leads to the phantasy that the

[166] Klein (1948), p. 365.

[167] Elwin (1949), pp. 360–361; O'Flaherty (1973), pp. 186–192; *Śiva* 2.5.59.1–32; 7.1.24.26–47; 4.10.18–24; *MBh.* 1.173.1–24; *Bhāgavata* 9.9.24–39; *Matsya* 155–158; *Padma* 5.41; *Skanda* 1.2.27–29; *Padma* 6.18.82–90. [168] Rawson, plate 86. [169] Klein (1948), p. 357.

[170] Klein et al. (1955), pp. 308 and 310; cf. (1948), p. 265.

milk and love are deliberately withheld from him, or kept by the mother for her own benefit.[171]

In India, this view of the mother has a male counterpart: the man is said to withhold his seed within himself, preventing not the feeding of the child but the very creation of the child. This parallelism makes possible the symbolic equivalence of the production of milk from the breast and the production of seed from the thigh; thus Vena is "milked" of Pṛthu.

In analyzing the Bhagavadi myths, Kathleen Gough refers to Melanie Klein and interprets the image as one of repressed hostility to and fear of the mother: "That Bhagavadi dismembers and eats the demons reflects the infant's projection upon the mother of his own oral frustrations in the period of suckling (commonly prolonged to the age of three or four, but abruptly terminated if a sibling is born)."[172] The genital mother not only holds back her milk but "sucks" the milk (seed) of the male instead, the inverse of nursing: "In India, the woman –outside her role as mother–is the temptress who saps the male's strength, reflected in the image of the blood-thirsty goddesses."[173] The nonmother goddess who drinks the man's seed appears also as the antimother who devours her sons. The breast that feeds itself appears in the Pṛthu myth when the earth is said to withhold her herbs and seeds and keep them herself; the earth-cow admits that she swallowed the herbs herself in order to keep them from being eaten by evil men[174]–the men who overran the world in the reign of Vena. Thus the evil mother keeps the food away from the evil, hateful son (Vena, himself a mother who yields evil milk) and is forced to give food to the good son (Pṛthu).

How does this view of infant perception relate to the older boy with his naughty teddy and the still older Jekyll-Hyde or Pṛthu-Niṣāda? Basically, the normal human being outgrows both the infant's "breast" split and the child's "naughty teddy" split:

In normal development, with growing integration of the ego, splitting processes diminish and the increased capacity to understand external reality, and to some extent to bring together the infant's contradictory impulses, leads also to a great synthesis of the good and bad aspects of the object. This means that people can be loved in spite of their faults and that the world is not seen only in terms of black and white.[175]

This ability to resolve contradictions is one of the central concerns of myth;[176] thus whatever its relevance to the study of actual personality development, Melanie Klein's hypothesis, with its images of black and white cows and breasts, is certainly closely tied to mythological thinking about normal personality development.[177] Pathology is also relevant, for the attitudes of psychosis preserve (as do mythological images) the universal experiences of infancy:

[171] Klein (1960), p. 8. [172] Gough, p. 74. [173] Koestler, p. 230. [174] *Bhāgavata* 4.17.24; 4.18.7. [175] Klein (1960), p. 9. [176] O'Flaherty (1973), pp. 33–38; Lévi-Strauss (1958), p. 64; (1967), pp. 29–30; (1963), p. 229. [177] Klein (1948), p. 305.

In the first few months of life the child goes through paranoid anxieties related to the "bad" denying breasts, which are felt as external and internalized persecutors. . . . The tendency of the infantile ego to split impulses and objects . . . results in part from the fact that the early ego lacks coherence. But . . . persecutory anxiety reinforces the need to keep separate the loved object from the dangerous one. . . . This combination of mechanisms and anxieties . . . in extreme cases becomes the basis of paranoia and schizophrenic illness.[178]

Yet the "greater synthesis of the good and bad aspects of the object," which is characteristic of maturity, is also characteristic of "anti-Manichean" cultures, which know no devil or personification of evil:[179]

One gains the impression . . . that the opposite of "right cultures" . . . is not "left cultures" but *intermediate or balanced cultures*, which are less concerned with the triumph of a principle than with the harmonious balance between a number of principles which are complementary to each other. . . . Even night, even death find their place here instead of being eliminated–in the Manichean manner–by the eschatological process. In the cyclic conception of the *Indians* the dancing Shiva holds in his four hands the symbols not only of life but also of death, the necessary condition of life.[180]

The integration of good and evil, which underlies the Hindu view of the necessity of evil, is thus regarded as a social expression of the integration of the mature personality; but, as we have seen,[181] this is not the only Indian view of evil. In the great corpus of myths involving cows and mothers, some seem to emphasize the first stage, the splitting apart characteristic of the earlier perception of evil (the myth of Gaurī/Kālī is typical of this group). Other myths, however, such as the tale of Jarāsandha (and the bhakti variants of the Pṛthu myth) tend to emphasize the more mature view of differentiation, the reintegration.

8. The Splitting of Gandhi

An interesting example of the application of psychoanalytic insights to the life of an Indian is offered by Erik Erikson's analysis of Gandhi; its relevance to the present study lies in the fact that Erikson found in Gandhi's attitudes many of the symbolic values typical of Hindu mythology, particularly of the myth of Vena and Pṛthu.

Erikson begins with an analysis of Indian family life, pointing out many of the tensions that we have already noted, particularly with reference to the mother, whose diffusion in the joint family means that she "can belong to the individual child only in fleeting moments":

The child feels guilty in a way largely unknown in the West (except to those on the border of schizophrenia). For the child wants his mother to himself, while she must

[178] Klein (1960), pp. 7–8. [179] Fritsch, p. 19.

[180] *Ibid.*, p. 41. [181] See above, chap. III, secs. 1–2.

spread her love. He cannot blame her for a single and consistent betrayal as the Oedipal boy in the West can, who therefore also has a clear rival enemy and hero, his father.[182]

The Oedipal conflict does occur in Indian myth, but it is greatly undercut by the factors indicated by Erikson, and is hence often reversed.[183]

Gandhi's attitude to evil was one of unequivocal denial, which places him firmly within the "splitting" category. He was fond of the story of Prahlāda, the virtuous son of an evil demon father;[184] but, as Erikson points out, Gandhi's lifelong emphasis on the innocence (i.e., sexlessness) of children–indeed, his almost pathological insistence on chastity–indicates an inability to recognize the demon king in himself: "And this *must* be pointed out because the demons triumph in all hidden and disguised ambivalences: however and whenever we let our children down, we become their demons."[185] By refusing to acknowledge his own demon, Gandhi made his father into a demon–like Prahlāda's father, or Pṛthu's father. This ambivalence then led to a split within Gandhi himself, and a projection of evil not only onto his father but onto his childhood alter ego, Mehtab:

Mohandas, one must conclude, was somehow addicted to Mehtab. For Mehtab played perfectly the personage on whom to project one's personal devil and thus became the personification of Mohandas' *negative identity*, that is, of everything in himself which he tried to isolate and subdue and which yet was part of him.[186]

This is the view of pollution as a detachable, transferable substance, which characterizes Indian mythology of the Indra pattern and the early myths of Vena and the Niṣāda. In Gandhi, this attitude established "the main contestants for Gandhi's lasting identifications: Mother, Father, and Evil Other."[187]

Even closer to the Pṛthu imagery is Gandhi's obsession with milk and cows, particularly in its close association with his attitude toward women and chastity. Erikson has described this preoccupation: "Much of his deep ambivalence toward the 'good' and the 'bad' mother survived in his dietary scruples.[188] . . . In the end he abjured even milk in order not to feel unduly eroticized. . . . [Gandhi feared] woman as a source of evil. . . . and . . . milk as a 'dangerous substance.' "[189] He regarded milk as a temptation inextricably linked with sexual temptation, an attitude revealed by his own statement that, when he had determined to fast and vowed to take no milk or milk products, his wife tempted him with a sweet (milkless) porridge; unable to resist the temptation, he ate, and "the angel of death" appeared to him in the form of acute dysentery.[190] Gandhi's assertion that he would not drink milk because of the cruelties inflicted on cows during milking is reminiscent of the mythology of tortured cows; and he drew

[182] Erikson, p. 42. Cf. Masson (1974*b*). [183] See below, sec. 9.

[184] Erikson, p. 243. See above, chap. V, sec. 14. [185] Erikson, p. 244. [186] *Ibid.*, p. 135.

[187] *Ibid.*, p. 145. [188] *Ibid.*, pp. 154–155. [189] *Ibid.*, p. 234. [190] *Ibid.*, p. 332.

upon the symbolism of this cycle when he told of having been offered milk to break his fast and remarked, "How could I, who would not take even *amrit* [Soma] except at the proper hour, swallow such a thing?"[191] But the cow was to Gandhi a symbol of his ambivalent attitude to his mother, and Erikson remarks on Gandhi's desire to unite "the mother who gives and the mother who denies," a desire leading to "sinister rages and . . . confused imagery" which can only be understood through "the study of universal mythology and of the deepest mental pathology."[192]

Gandhi's "sinister rages" and fanatic ideas about chastity led him into conflict not only with his father but also with his sons, whom he expected to be chaste and whom he bitterly and destructively humiliated when they married.[193] In this way, as in the Vena myth, the conflict is carried on from father to son to grandson. One result of these conflicts was the production of a kind of spiritual androgyne within Gandhi: "Gandhi, one may conclude from all the parental themes we have recounted, had wanted to purify his relationship to his father by nursing and mothering him; and he had wanted to be an immaculate mother."[194] We have seen this reconciliation with the "demon" father in Pṛthu's nursing of the leprous Vena; but the desire to be a mother as well as a father is a characteristic of Vena himself. Gandhi "almost prided himself on being half man and half woman. . . . He undoubtedly saw a kind of sublimated maternalism as part of the positive identity of a whole man, and certainly of a homo religiosus."[195] This sexual fusion is a symptom of a moral fusion in Gandhi, a progression from the projected devil of his childhood to a mature acceptance of his own moral as well as sexual dualism; Gandhi's nonviolence enabled him to see "how much of what we used to ascribe to the Devil's wiles or to the id's inexorable demands can be tolerated, if absorbed by love rather than negated by violent moralism."[196]

This final acceptance is the great achievement of Gandhi, an achievement of personal as well as political significance, of both psychological and sociological import; the hateful person contains his hate and learns to "love the opponent as human. . . . In all these and other varieties of confrontation, the emphasis is not so much (or not entirely) on the power to be gained as on the cure of an unbearable inner condition."[197] Power is very relevant to the opposition of good and evil in Indian mythology, particularly to the Indra corpus; but the conversion of hate to love (as in the doctrine of *dveṣa-bhakti*, which is the culmination of the myths of Dakṣa and the Pine Forest sages) is certainly also important. Together, these two trends form the basis of the Hindu myths of theodicy, among which one could certainly list Erikson's reconstruction of the myth of

[191] *Ibid.*, pp. 381–382; Gandhi (1958–), XIV, 266. [192] Erikson, pp. 155–156.

[193] Koestler, pp. 143ff. [194] *Ibid.*, p. 405. [195] *Ibid.*, pp. 402–403.

[196] *Ibid.*, p. 248. [197] *Ibid.*, p. 437.

Gandhi or Gandhi's own mise-en-scène—in his own life—of the mythical figures in the Hindu drama.

9. Splitting and Integration

The myths of Vena and Pṛthu span a period of more than three thousand years, and it is not surprising that there are various attempted solutions, some more fully integrated than others. In the more primitive view, evil is in some ways "other" than oneself, thrust onto a black scape-cow, heteropathically removed; but in other texts, evil is also a part of oneself, homeopathically assimilated. The expulsion of evil is viewed in terms of the killing and revival of good and evil progeny; evil progeny separate the good from the evil, while good progeny ensure the fructification of good. The two separate factions are constantly under tension, balancing, gravitating toward an integration. The early myths seek to delve into the wicked ancestry of Vena to find someone (his parents, of course, particularly his mother) to blame for his sin; later, the emphasis shifts to the relationship between Vena and his son Pṛthu, who accepts the evil of his parent (of whatever sex, literally male or figuratively female) and comes to terms with it within himself; by assuming responsibility for Vena's sin, Pṛthu reintegrates that sin within his own personality and accepts it. One way in which the texts express this maturity of Pṛthu, his protection of his parents, is in the image of reversed parenthood. When Pṛthu becomes reconciled with the denying mother, the wicked earth-cow, the earth then begs him to think of her as his daughter, and he agrees;[198] in another text, Pṛthu asks the earth to become his daughter, and she agrees.[199]

The original antagonism between father and son (a line that is developed in tandem with the ambivalent relationship between mother and son) is a well-known characteristic of an early stage of personality development in the Freudian view. In India, the Oedipal conflict is generally weighted in such a way that the father, rather than the son, plays the aggressive role. This is true of the myth of Paraśurāma, whose father urges him to decapitate his mother,[200] and it is true of the myths in which Śiva jealously mutilates his handsome son, Gaṇeśa,[201] and Brahmā destroys all of his sons. But the early Pṛthu myths are closer to the Greek/Freudian model, and Pṛthu is (indirectly) responsible for the death of his father. This pattern also occurs in ancient Tamil texts: the newborn son is a threat to the father, who first visits him in war dress; the milk of the nursing

[198] *MBh.* 7, app. 1, no. 8, line 791. [199] *Hari.* 6.6 and 6.40. [200] *MBh.* 3.116–117.

[201] Leach (1962, pp. 82–90; *Bhaviṣya* 3.4.14.45; *Varāha* 23.16–19; *Śiva* 2.4.16–19; O'Flaherty (1973), p. 150; (1975), pp. 261–269. And cf. Kṛṣṇa and Sāmba, above, chap. IX, sec. 4.

mother is also dangerous to the father[202] (as is menstrual blood in North India). In another sense, all Hindu sons are responsible for the deaths of their fathers, for the son must give the offering that sustains his father after death, releasing him from the bad karma that would otherwise keep him an uneasy ghost, just as Pṛthu releases Vena. This offering makes the father dependent on the son in a way that reverses the flow of power in the Oedipal conflict.

In Vedic mythology, the god Tvaṣṭṛ ("old father, old artificer") is the pivotal figure of two Vedic myths of father-son conflict. Tvaṣṭṛ's son, Indra, kills him, but Tvaṣṭṛ also trims the excessive energy of his own son-in-law, Vivasvat, the sun, when Tvaṣṭṛ's daughter Saṃjñā flees from him. In this way Tvaṣṭṛ, who provides the ambivalent key to the fraternal conflict of gods and demons, also provides the archetypal image of both aspects of the conflict between father and son in India. The mythology of Indra supplies several other motifs relevant to the psychology of the Vena corpus. Jyeṣṭhā is sometimes called the mother of Indra, and Indra is famed for releasing the stolen cows of the Paṇis; he kills his father in order to obtain the Soma (milk) which Tvaṣṭṛ has withheld from him.[203] As Tvaṣṭṛ is the pregnant male, the "bull filled with milk," he here clearly plays the role of the breast that feeds itself, and meets with the violent aggression of his son, Indra, who actually boasts that he does not hesitate to kill his father or his mother.

The aggression of son toward father is evident in the Tamil reworking of another classical "two-mother" myth, the story of Rāma whose evil stepmother, Kaikeyī, causes him to be banished. In the Sanskrit version, Rāma's brother Bharata excoriates Kaikeyī (Bharata's own mother) and explicitly contrasts her with Surabhi, the cow that shed tears of compassion for her two sons. But in the Tamil version, Bharata blames himself and laments that he has killed his father, injured his brother, stayed in the hell of his mother's womb and sucked her breasts—for he regards her as a demonness.[204] Still more explicit is a Tamil myth in which a Brahmin boy commits incest with his mother, and, when caught *in flagrante* by his father, kills his father by striking him with a spade; the father's ghost, in the form of Great Sin, pursues the boy for many years (as Brahminicide pursues Indra), until Śiva grants him release from the crime (a crime which, as Devī points out, would otherwise have doomed the boy to an eternal hell).[205]

Other examples of the Oedipal aggression of the son toward the father may be seen in the myths of the cows and the liṅga, as well as in the myth in which Śiva beheads his father, Brahmā. One Hindu myth that retains details strikingly similar to that of the Greek Oedipus myth is the tale of the demon Andhaka, son

[202] Hart, pp. 94–96. [203] See above, chap. V, sec. 3; O'Flaherty (1975), pp. 56–60.

[204] *Rām.* 2.68.15–24; *Kamparāmāyaṇam* 2264–2280.

[205] *Tiruviḷaiyāṭarpurāṇam* 26.1–41.

of Śiva and Pārvatī, who becomes blind and lusts for his mother.[206] It is surely significant in this context that in one text of the Vena myth Śiva says to Vena, "You will be born from my body again as the demon Andhaka, and because of your former, terrible adharma you will become full of passion for the Mother."[207] Andhaka is then killed by his father, Śiva, in a way that splits him appropriately in two: the lower half of his body is dried up by the hot rays of the sun, and the upper half is drenched by water from the clouds;[208] thus he is split and purified by the two complementary ritual elements, fire and water.

In the later myths, Pṛthu overcomes the Oedipal conflict and revives the father that he had earlier (inadvertently) killed. Pṛthu also opposes and becomes reconciled with his "father" in the episode of the stallion and Indra. For as the earth-cow is his symbolic mother, the Indra-stallion is his symbolic father, the epitome of "extraverted masculinity . . . all those qualities which are traditionally most prized in men."[209] Hindu mythology provides numerous examples of sons who save, and become reconciled with, evil fathers; thus the son of Yayāti takes his father's old age, and Yayāti's grandsons give him their merit so that he can reach heaven.[210] Other virtuous sons of evil fathers "help" them by destroying them totally; thus Prahlāda encourages Viṣṇu to disembowel his demonic father, Hiraṇyakaśipu.[211] When the father is regarded as totally demonic, he is destroyed, like Hiraṇyakaśipu (and Vena in the early myths), but when the human element is emphasized, he may be forgiven by his son.

One set of "disintegrated" tentative solutions may be seen in those texts which describe a proliferation of splittings, a lack of resolution which, at the psychological level, usually indicates pathology. At first it is a relatively simple matter, the one wicked father of one good son; but soon there are two sons, one good and one evil, and two parents of Vena similarly contrasted (the good father and the bad mother); by the juxtaposition of these two ambivalent generations on either side of Vena, his own nature is no longer wholly black but becomes, by association, itself ambivalent. The two halves of Vena may be viewed in social terms (such as our civilization—Pṛthu, the culture hero—opposed to theirs—Niṣāda, the impure outcaste); in religious terms (Vedic religion opposed to heresy); or simply in terms of good and evil, with all of their psychological, theological, and symbolic implications.

Many of the apparent inconsistencies in these myths arise from the combination of two very different underlying assumptions about the role of the

[206] *Vāmana* 9–10, 33, 40–44; *Kūrma* 1.16; *Liṅga* 1.93.1–25; *Matsya* 179.1–86; *Padma* 5.43.1–95; *Saura* 29.11–50; *Śiva, Dharma Saṃ.* 4.4–208; *Śiva* 2.5.42.1–2, 2.5.49.40; *Skanda* 7.2.9.151–163; *Varāha* 27.1–39; *Viṣṇudharmottara* 1.226.1–82; O'Flaherty (1973), pp. 190–192; (1975), pp. 168–173. See Ramanujan (1972) and Halder.

[207] *Vāmana S.* 26.4–62.

[208] *Śiva* 2.5.46.38.

[209] Huntington (1960*a*), pp. 84 and 74.

[210] See above, chap. VIII, secs. 6 and 7.

[211] See above, chap. V, sec. 14.

individual. The first assumption is that the individual is merely a particle of cosmic power, a manifestation of an entity (neither good nor bad) that behaves in accordance with the consequences of other cosmic entities; in this view, when the "entity" becomes dirtied or weakened it must be purified and strengthened. The second view sees the individual playing some spontaneous role in the development of events; in this view, when a sin is committed it must be expiated. To remove evil, in the first view, is to objectivate it; in the second view, evil is subjectivated.

The first view prevails in early myths, epitomized by the cycle in which Indra transfers his sin to other elements.[212] In early variants of the Vena myth, even when Vena is dead, the cosmic "something" is alive (as the dead body of Viśvarūpa or Vṛtra continues to threaten Indra), a neutral microcosmic power. The Indo-European response to this power is to color it with good and evil, and to divide it; this dualistic mode of thought is so basic to Indo-European linguistic and (hence) perceptual processes that one need not look into an actual tradition to explain it; tradition conveys thought patterns but does not make them. The isolated African example may be seen as yet another instance of this type of thought process, a process that underlies both sane and insane concepts of the individual in the Indo-European mental frame (and in other cultures marked by this pattern of intellectual structuralism). The cosmic power must be divided because of some event; the event itself presupposes evil, without which nothing would happen.

This obsessive need to find the event emerges from the Vena myth when we consider the simple question: What did Vena do? The sins attributed to him are traditional (he mixed the castes, he cheated the priests) but not personal. The flaw is sought first in genetic inadequacies (his mother was the child of death) and then in the first event, the first mistake. This obsession emerges also from the myths of the loss of the Golden Age, where, again, there *is* no "first mistake"; man is doomed *before* he commits his sin of lust or hunger. Yet in spite of fate, in spite of doom, there is a moment when the individual might have been able to change his fate. The idea of free will is alien to the concept of the individual as a manifestation of cosmic power; yet Hindu myth superimposes the idea of free will upon later myths and introduces the (contradictory) view of the spontaneous role of the individual. Thus Vena's mistake was in not acting to change his fate. The Vena myth presents an extremely detailed description of the effect of his sin, but (with one notable exception) a very vague idea of the cause; for the myth functions on two levels, one of which assumes the cause (cosmic predetermination), the other of which tentatively introduces a totally different cause (Vena's own inability to oppose fate). The myth is about what happened to Vena (his evil), not about what he did (his sin); for in India the significant evil is what

[212] See above, chap. VI, sec. 4.

happens to one, not what one does. The myth seeks to explain inexplicable causes by describing visible effects.

Both points of view exist simultaneously in the myths; there is a constant shift from one field of reference to another, specific instances of nondynamic unity superimposed on an assumption of dynamic cosmic power. As the myth flows back and forth from one plane to another, inconsistencies proliferate. Many Hindus assume that man is doomed to unhappiness; when we view the individual's sin as a manifestation of power, it is impossible to negate the doom, which can merely be traced backwards or projected (transferred) forward. But Hindus also believe that there is no beginning to the stream of consciousness, and hence there can be no beginning of doom—in fact, there can be no doom. The stream begins each time a life begins; in spite of karma, the individual can choose to accept his fate or to challenge it. This view emerges clearly from the bhakti myths in which Vena's inherited sin (whatever its cause) breaks the chain, through the help of God but also through the spontaneous choice of Pṛthu, who learns how to move from the premise of evil to the choice of good. In early myths, Vena is washed away in the tide of karma, leaving Pṛthu clean; later, Vena swims against the current, with Pṛthu's help. The myth attempts various explanations of Vena's dilemma—to split him, to blame Sunīthā, to absolve Sunīthā, to blame or absolve Death, and finally (the old reliable standby) to blame the curse of a sage—but it reaches a solution only in the bhakti period, when the good son and the (good) god help to redeem Vena and pull him out of the flow of the cycle of rebirth. The problem endures for centuries until the religious context of the myth changes in such a way as to allow a solution.

The opposition of good and evil takes place on two planes of kinship, with Pṛthu as its pivot: the fraternal plane (Pṛthu vs. the Niṣāda, Abel vs. Cain) and the parental plane (Vena and Pṛthu, Satan and Job). The fraternal struggle is more prominent in most of Indian mythology as it forms the basis of the cosmic struggle between gods and demons. The battle between gods and men, however, is a paternal one. The *Mahābhārata* massacre takes place on both levels, for gods fight demons and "demonic men" simultaneously; and so it is said that son kills father, father kills son, and brother kills brother. The story of Pṛthu emphasizes the parental struggle; Vena, not the Niṣāda, is the significant evil other of the myth, and it is in the relationship of father and son that the clue to the riddle of evil must be sought, for evil is transmitted lineally through time.

The myths of struggle between gods and demons often correspond more closely to the model of a game than to that of the structural definition of a myth; that is, they proceed from a state of uneasy and ultimately unreal symmetry and cohesion (a truce or state of equality between gods and demons) to a state of real separation and balance (gods supreme, demons banished[213])—though the myth

[213] Long (1975), *passim*; see above, chap. IV, sec. 1.

recognizes that this state of separation cannot endure and must proceed again through integration and refragmentation ad infinitum. Creation, too, is a process of separation: heaven splits away from earth, light from darkness, the male half of the androgyne from the female half. But there is another aspect of Hindu mythology which better fits the Lévi-Straussian definition of a myth as proceeding from asymmetry to symmetry[214]; this is the level of mythology that deals with conflicts within the individual, conflicts that may be (and in Hinduism sometimes are) viewed in terms of the Manichean struggle of divine forces within the body, but are more often seen as problems in which the solution to be sought is not separation but integration. The conflict of the erotic and ascetic impulses within Śiva may be analyzed by this model, as may the myths of Kṛṣṇa and Rādhā, the myths of the devotee (even of the demonic devotee, which we have analyzed from a different perspective–viewing the cosmic balance as a whole–rather than from the point of view of the demon himself[215]) and the myth of Vena and Pṛthu.

In the Hindu view of personality, qualities are transmitted to the individual not only from his own soul in a previous birth (his own personal karma) but from his parents. It is said that sons resemble the father, daughters the mother; that all human beings take after the mother, not the father; or that the child inherits the karma of both parents.[216] Another theory is more appropriate to the causation underlying Vena's ancestry (as well as to Freudian concepts of personality development):

> Generally, a daughter inherits the qualities of her father, and a son gets the qualities of his mother. Thus Mṛtyu's daughter, Sunīthā, got all the qualities of her father, and Vena inherited the qualities of his mother. . . . The child born of King Anga became the follower of his maternal grandfather. According to *smṛti-śāstra*, a child generally follows the principles of his maternal uncle's house, . . . the qualities of his maternal family. If the maternal family is very corrupt or sinful, the child, even though born of a good father, becomes a victim of the maternal family.[217]

Although even here the tendency is to blame the mother for the evil of a child of either sex, it is the son, in particular, who suffers from her wickedness (which she, in turn, acquires from her father).

The parents split the responsibility for one's physical makeup: the mother gives flesh and blood, the father bone, sinew, and marrow.[218] The moral component given by parents is equivalent to one's svadharma, also given by one's parents. The son of a potter is a potter (though his chance to play this role is in part determined by his behavior in his previous life); and, the Vena myth seems to

[214] O'Flaherty (1973), pp. 35–38. [215] *Ibid.*, *passim*, esp. chaps. V–IX; see above, chap. V, secs. 13–14.

[216] *Rām.*, app. 1, no. 14, lines 55–56; 3.13.32; *Agni* 151.18.

[217] Bhaktivedanta, IV, 2, 574 (on *Bhāgavata* 4.13.39) and IV, 3, 849 (on *Bhāgavata* 4.21.30).

[218] *MBh.* 12.293.16–17. Cf. *Agni* 369.31–32; 370.19–20.

say, the son of an evil potter is an evil potter–unless he chooses not to be, to deny the evil aspect of his svadharma as the good demons may deny theirs with the help of bhakti. The two forces interact; both are inherited from the past, and together they entirely determine the starting point of the individual's life. What he does with that life is further influenced by chance factors, the grace of God, and his own free will.

The child, Vena, inherits certain bad qualities from his mother; by splitting the personality he gets rid of the bad qualities and breaks the chain of karma: Pṛthu is good, and so are Pṛthu's offspring. This ritual splitting can interrupt the logical trend of karma by removing the myth to another plane, where logic and time are irrelevant. Mary Douglas has described a similar process among the Dinka: "When an act of incest has been committed, a sacrifice can alter the common descent of the pair and so expunge the guilt. The victim is cut in half alive, longitudinally through the sexual organs. So the common origin of the incestuous pair is symbolically negated."[219] A combination of projection (onto the sacrificial victim, the scapegoat) and splitting reverses the flow of time. In Vedic times, this interruption of karma could be achieved through sacrifice; in bhakti myths, it is achieved through the grace of God. Both methods are used in the Pṛthu myth.

The belief that the sins of the fathers are visited upon the children appears even in the Ṛg Veda, before the idea of karma was fully developed: "Set us free from the misdeeds of our fathers, and from those that we ourselves have perpetrated; let Vasiṣṭha loose like a cattle thief (set free), like a calf (set free) from the rope that binds him."[220] Vena is the cattle thief; Pṛthu is the calf who milks the earth-cow; and the rope that binds the calf is the noose of sin that God uses to bind his beasts.[221] The Atharva Veda asks forgiveness for the sins of the brother and the mother as well as for those of the father: "What sin [*enas*] my mother, my father, and what my own brothers, what we have done, let this divine tree protect us from them."[222] In present-day village Hinduism and Buddhism, it is still believed that children suffer from their parents' karma, that the sins of the fathers are visited upon the heads of the children. A young boy was crippled, and his father said that this was "due to the bad *karma* of both father and son in past lives."[223] A similar theory was expounded by a nineteenth-century psychologist, who maintained that heterogenous personality resulted when the traits of character of incompatible and antagonistic ancestors were preserved alongside of each other.[224] As to the literal validity of this theory, William James remarked airily, "This explanation may pass for what it is worth–it certainly needs corroboration."[225]

[219] Douglas, p. 67. [220] *RV* 7.89.5. [221] See above, chap. VI, sec. 8. [222] *AV* 10.3.8.
[223] Sharma, p. 351. [224] Smith Baker, in *Journal of Nervous and Mental Diseases*, September, 1893, cited in James, p. 175. [225] James, p. 175.

The "incompatible and antagonistic" characteristics usually derive, in Hindu myths, from a wicked mother and a good father; when there is only one parent (as often occurs in supernatural births), that parent must contain both sets of characteristics; thus Vena is both male and female, both good and bad. Since Vena serves as mother as well as father, the other female (the earth-cow) is a mother-surrogate, a wicked stepmother, and so Pṛthu's relationship to his surrogate is one of cruelty, appropriate to the nonbreast mother or the genital mother.

In early texts of the myth, there is blatant conflict between father and son; in later texts, there is harmony. At first, the son disowns the father and splits himself away from his past in order to go on being untainted himself. In India, the split between the two halves of the self was often viewed as the split between the erotic and the ascetic tendencies.[226] In the Vedas it is often said that a man learned in the Vedas has two kinds of seed: from the seed above the navel (i.e., mental seed, by which Prajāpati and the sages create their mind-born, sinless, nonprocreating offspring) he produces offspring when he initiates pupils and teaches the Vedas; from the seed below the navel he procreates the offspring of his body.[227] One can thus "father" children in good or bad ways: good children from above the navel (Pṛthu generated from the hand of Vena), bad children from below the navel (the Niṣāda from the leg of Vena). But these two ways are connected by the spine, which transmutes the "bad" type of seed (semen) into the other type of seed (Soma, in the head). The art of yoga is devoted to this difficult psychospiritual alchemy, which may be viewed as the microcosmic parallel to the shaman's attempt to rise from earth to heaven through the pillar separating them (the pillar which is the macrocosmic form of the human spinal column).[228] Blood mediates between semen and Soma–blood, the essence of human life and mortality–and is thus the key to the transmutation of the evil procreation resulting from the chain of karma (transmitted through semen) into the good procreation resulting from individual effort (transforming semen into Soma). Base animal instinct is thus transformed into religious insight.

This process requires that the evil seed be retained, not split away, for it is the raw material required for the transmutation into good seed.[229] The pathological part of the personality is retained in the process of healing,[230] and one may see this process at work in the Pṛthu myth: "The very fact that the Niṣāda is not immediately destroyed, but is retained in the conscious sphere in an inactive role, is to be taken as testimony that the forces of healing have gained the ascendancy."[231] A recent interpretation of this myth seeks to reintegrate even the Niṣāda:

[226] O'Flaherty (1973), pp. 40–54, 76–82. [227] *Tait. Sam.* 3.25.1.

[228] Eliade (1958), and cf. Butterworth. [229] O'Flaherty (1973), pp. 255–292.

[230] Jung (1954), p. 71. [231] Huntington (1960*a*), p. 73.

> The Naiṣādas are not allowed to live in cities and towns because they are sinful by nature. As such, their bodies are very ugly, and their occupations are also sinful. We should, however, know that even these sinful men . . . can be delivered from their sinful condition to the topmost Vaiṣṇava platform by the mercy of a pure devotee.[232]

When Pṛthu becomes fully integrated, at the end of the myth, he is praised by both gods and demons;[233] he has come to terms with evil as well as good.

The Vena-Pṛthu myth has been seen as a myth about civilization, about the development from hunter to civilization, from the savage who must kill the animal who supplies his food, to the pastoral king who merely milks it. In this context milk is symbolic of the preservation of animal life, and this life is both poisonous and ambrosial. Just as Pṛthu tames the cows so that they may be milked rather than slaughtered, so too must the savage parts of the individual's personality be retained, though tamed or "paralyzed" (as Melanie Klein suggests) in order to be brought into harmony with the valued parts. Vena and the Niṣāda are only hunters; Pṛthu begins as a hunter and develops into a pastoral king. An early Indian myth states that the creator had to master both the tame world of men and the wild world of the gods;[234] he completes the sacrifice with tame beasts, and "father and son part company"; in another text, father and son part company when the sacrifice is completed with wild beasts.[235] Pṛthin the son of Vena is described as a hunter who became overlord of both kinds of cattle,[236] that is, over both wild and tame. The taming of the beast is an image familiar from Śaiva theology, where our own souls are the beasts bound, tamed, and released by God; in the Pṛthu myth, it is the individual himself who must tame the beast within him (often with the help of God). Jung remarked that wild horses in dreams often symbolize powerful instinctive drives emerging from the unconscious, and the taming of horses is an Indian image used to denote the control of the senses;[237] in this we are reminded of Pṛthu and Indra fighting for the stallion, and of the conflict between the good stallion and the dangerous mare.[238] In Sanskrit literature, the dangerous, demonic doomsday mare is wild, while the consecrated stallion is, by virtue of that consecration, tame. In Tamil literature, this distinction is made between tame men and wild women: woman is identified with culture and domesticity, man with nature; therefore "woman is dangerous unless she is carefully controlled; left in her natural state, she is a threat."[239] Woman is likened to a fire that is "destructive in its natural state, but is a source of light when constrained by the wick of the lamp."[240] The fiery horse is the Indian symbol of raw human energy, potentially evil in a state of nature, potentially good when curbed and harnessed.

[232] Bhaktivedanta, IV, 2, 618–619 (on *Bhāgavata* 4.14.46). [233] *Bhāgavata* 4.16.27.

[234] *Śata.* 13.2.3.1–4. [235] *Tait. Br.* 3.9.1.2. [236] *Tāṇḍya* 13.5.20.

[237] *Kaṭha Up.* 3.4–6; *Buddhacarita* XV.1–13. [238] O'Flaherty (1976).

[239] Hart, p. 111. [240] *Ibid.*, p. 112.

The gods are able to live with all their contradictory forces unreined, untamed; but men must be civilized. This is perhaps the ultimate "splitting," the separation of the wild parent (the god) from the tame child (the mortal man). Indra (or Śiva) often functions like a trickster god: a raw, uncontrolled, amoral embodiment of the infantile unconscious, deceiver and deceived, androgynous, ambivalent, the phallus a detached and self-animated entity, the right side warring against the left.[241] Vena, too, is part trickster, a split male who becomes pregnant and bears sons. The trickster god's ambivalence is sometimes unacceptable in its primitive state: his later worshippers split him into god and buffoon, and some regard him as a god, some as a devil. He has been compared to the figure of God in the Book of Job, the trickster being an integrated concrete image of the moral ambivalence which is denied (split dualisically) in the Hebrew myth. He is uncivilized and anti-social; but the men who delight in trickster myths cannot indulge in trickster capers. The process of maturity applies not only to human civilization but to the human individual, who overcomes his savage instincts—his tendency to view the evil parts of himself and his parents as pollution and to split them away from him—in order to tame and integrate the good and the evil within himself.

[241] Paul Radin, *The Trickster, A Study in American Indian Mythology*, with commentaries by C. G. Jung and Karl Kerényi, and a new introduction by Stanley Diamond (New York, 1972).

Out of the mouth of the most High
proceedeth not evil and good?
Lamentations 3:38

XII

CONCLUSION: The Many Paths of Theodicy

1. The One and the Many

The constrasting attitudes to the presence of good and evil within the individual may be subsumed under the general rubrics of dualistic and monistic: one regards evil and good as essentially different and divisible; the other regards them as essentially harmonious and inseparable. The ability to regard a problem from two (or more) separate viewpoints simultaneously is one of the many great strengths of Hindusim, one which is particularly useful in approaching the problem of evil. The Hindus were aware of the many alternative methods of tackling theological problems, though often one was considered better, or at least higher, than another: "There are two knowledges to be known . . . a higher and also a lower. Of these, the four Vedas are the lower; the higher is that whereby the Unperishing is understood."[1] The higher truth is this context is monism, the lower pantheism;[2] though God seems divided, he is undivided.[3] Similarly, the Buddhists distinguished between worldly empirical truth and the absolute truth.[4] This conflict between multiplicity and unity was seen by Teilhard de Chardin as a kind of Manichean battle between gods and demons: "It was then that Unity, overflowing with life, joined battle through [the process] of creation with the multiple, which, though non-existent in itself, opposed it as a contrast and a challenge."[5]

[1] *Muṇḍaka Up.* 1.1.4–5. [2] Zaehner (1974), pp. 120–121. [3] *Gītā* 13.16.

[4] *Mūlamādhyamakakārikā* of Nāgārjuna, 24.8–9.

[5] Teilhard de Chardin (1965), p. 114; trans. Zaehner (1974), p. 167.

However reconciled the Indians may have been to the multiplicity of possible solutions (or rather nonsolutions), or the unity of truths, or the hopelessness of reaching a balance between the two views, the student of myths of theodicy may be tempted to steer a Middle Path of his own. Here the resources of comparative religion, which we have single-mindedly (perhaps pigheadedly) ignored until now, can no longer be spurned, for in formulating a schematic approach to Indian theodicy, it is useful to draw upon studies of theodicy in other religions. It will surely have become evident to the reader at numerous points in the present study, particularly in the preceding chapter, that many if not all of the "solutions" offered by Hinduism occur elsewhere, often in different contexts and with different relative valences. The Indian motifs must first be seen in their own historical context, but their value as reactions to universal human problems can only be fully assessed in comparison with other cultural approaches to these problems.

Paul Ricoeur's essay on the symbolism of evil is particularly illuminating in this regard, for he attempts to create a "typology" based on a study of *all* the myths of the origin of evil in the Western tradition:

Can we live in all those mythical universes at the same time? . . . And if we had some reason for preferring one of them, why did we have to lend so much attention and understanding to myths that we were going to declare abolished and dead? . . . They all speak to us in some fashion. . . . It is only by discovering in each of these myths an affinity for the other that we shall be able to account for the possibility of their confusion; and in thus making the contamination intelligible through a play of underground affinities, we shall have stretched to the limit our endeavor to comprehend all the myths, including the most contrary ones, in the light of the dominant myth.[6]

Setting aside for the moment the concept of the "dominant myth," let us turn to the question of methodology; how are all of these "mythical universes" to be inhabited at the same time? Ricoeur states the problem and a possible solution:

If the mythical consciousness in primitive civilizations remains very much *like itself*, and if, on the other hand, mythologies are *unlimited in number*, how shall we make our way between the One and the Many? . . . We shall try to follow the counsels of Plato in the *Philebus*, when he tell us . . . always to seek an intermediate number that "multiplicity realizes in the interval between the Infinite and the One." . . . I should like to think, as Cl. Lévi-Strauss does in *Tristes tropiques*, that the images which the myth-making imagination and the institutional activity of man can produce are not infinite in number, and that it is possible to work out, at least as a working hypothesis, a sort of morphology of the principal images.[7]

This task may be undertaken inductively, working from the material to the possible classes in a kind of empirical taxonomy of mythological symbolism.[8] Professor Ricoeur, however, begins from the hypothesis of the primacy of the

[6] Ricoeur, pp. 306 and 330. [7] *Ibid.*, pp. 171–172. [8] O'Flaherty (1973), pp. 11–33.

experience of sin, guilt, and confession in generating the images of theodicy; hence his "dominant myth," in terms of which all other myths of evil must be understood, is the Adamic myth of Eden. Yet he grants that this myth, in turn, cannot be understood without the others in the "system":

> Thus the Adamic myth raises up one or more counterpoles to the central figure of the primordial Man, and from those counterpoles it gets an enigmatic depth by which it communicates subterraneously with the other myths of evil and makes possible what we shall call further on a system of the myths of evil.[9]

Ricoeur's system has four main components, all of which find parallels in the corpus of Indian materials:

1. "The drama of creation and the 'ritual' vision of the world," typical of Babylonian mythology.[10] This group includes myths of various types, which seem clearly separate in India: the original creation, which contains an inevitable germ of evil (our chapter III, the necessity of evil); myths in which "the principle of evil is polarly opposed to the divine as its original Enemy"[11] (Manichean myths, chapter IV, section 3); myths in which the younger gods kill the older gods through self-perpetuating violence[12] (the myths of consanguinity of gods and demons, chapter IV, section 1); myths which imply that these younger gods, our gods, are murderers, that "the intentions and actions which the mythographers ascribe to the gods are the same as those which man recognizes as evil for himself"[13] (the myths of the evil gods who murder demons, chapter VI). This category also includes myths in which gods use death as a weapon against man[14] (chapter VIII), and, finally, a subtype of the "Hellenic titan"[15] (the good demon, chapter V). It is perhaps questionable whether a category so diversified is a true category at all.

2. The dominant myth: "The 'Adamic' myth and the 'eschatological' vision," the Judeo-Christian myth.[16] The Fall and the vision of the last things occur in Hinduism too (chapter II), but are not as fruitful as they are in the West. The myths of karma do blame man for evil, but they neutralize any implication of personal, individual guilt by shifting the blame to a previous existence, of which one cannot be conscious (and for which one cannot truly experience guilt), though one can still make personal efforts to dispel that evil in the future. Moreover, the myths of karma were widely rejected in India and hence cannot be regarded as "dominant," in spite of the efforts of western scholars to force them to play this role.

3. "The wicked god and the 'tragic' vision of existence," the Greek myth[17] (chapters VI, VII, IX, and X).

[9] Ricoeur, pp. 234–235. [10] *Ibid.*, pp. 175–210. [11] *Ibid.*, p. 213. [12] *Ibid.*, pp. 178–179.
[13] *Ibid.*, p. 182. [14] *Ibid.*, pp. 187–190. [15] *Ibid.*, pp. 206–210.
[16] *Ibid.*, pp. 213–278. [17] *Ibid.*, pp. 211–241, and see above, chap. IV, secs. 8–9.

4. The Orphic myth of the exiled soul[18] (some Manichean myths–chapter IV, section 4–and myths of the dichotomy within man–chapter XII).

These myths are all seen by Ricoeur as responses to the experience of sin; yet in Hinduism all these forms arise in the conspicuous absence of any recognition of personal sin; hence Hinduism emphasizes myths of type three (which blame God), while Ricoeur's corpus centers upon type two (which blame man). Type one, which blames an Evil Other, plays only a small role in Hinduism in comparison with its Western occurrence, still less than type two but subservient to that type:

> More refined onto-theologies have not ceased to appear, according to which evil is an original element of being. . . . The fact that theogony revives under ever new forms gives cause for reflection. . . . The recognition of a non-human source of evil, included even in the confession of the human origin of evil, revives tragedy; and, *since tragedy is unthinkable* [italics mine], theogony offers itself as the ultimate means of saving tragedy by converting it into logic.[19]

Even in the "confession of the human origin" there is a resistance against blaming man; the Western theologian cannot bear to blame God and therefore persists in blaming the devil. In India, however, tragedy is very thinkable indeed, and yet the Indian system of myths of evil develops in a manner quite similar to that suggested by Ricoeur. The myths of chaos and the drama of creation (Vedic myths persisting in the Purāṇas) lead to myths of the "Adamic" type, but–and herein lies the crucial difference–both of these myths are quickly superseded by the tragic myth, which remains the dominant Indian myth, in restless coexistence with its many enduring predecessors.

Ricoeur's system differs from the Indian model in some points of emphasis, but it is nevertheless a useful *point d'appui* in constructing a comparative mythology of evil. Another useful model was suggested by Max Weber, who regarded dualism as one of three possible approaches to theodicy, the other two being the doctrine of predestination and the doctrine of karma.[20] Dualism is logically consistent, but not so much a solution of the problem as a declaration of its philosophical insolubility;[21] predestination requires the renunciation of the hypothesis of benevolence and implies that all creatures are wicked per se, while God's motives are inaccessible to finite human understanding,[22] again a tacit admission of philosophical and logical failure. In preference to these two theodicies, Weber praised the theory of karma, which "stands out by virtue of its consistency as well as by its extraordinary metaphysical achievement: it unites virtuoso-like self-redemption by man's own efforts with universal accessibility of salvation, the strictest rejection of the world with organic social ethics, and

[18] *Ibid.*, pp. 209–210 and 279–305. [19] *Ibid.*, p. 327 and p. 329.

[20] Weber (1946), p. 358.

[21] Parsons, in Weber (1963), xlviii. [22] *Ibid.*

contemplation as the paramount path to salvation with an inner-worldly vocational ethic."[23] The ability of karma to sustain apparently contradictory goals may be seen as another manifestation of dualism, or at least of dialectic, and indeed Weber regarded all three of his categories of theodicy as expressions of dualism in a broader sense: the ethical dualism of religions of providence (in which a sacred majestic god, the *deus absconditus*, confronts the ethical inadequacy of all his creatures); spiritual dualism (the bisection of all creation into light and pure vs. dark and sullied matter, the classical form of Zoroastrianism); and ontological dualism (the theory of karma, providing a contrast between the world and the eternal order). Of this last he remarks, "This is the most radical solution to the problem of theodicy, and for that reason it provides as little satisfaction for ethical claims upon god as does the belief in predestination."[24] He goes on to remark upon the unsatisfactory nature of all "pure" theodicies and concludes that only a combination of various theories can even begin to solve the problem of theodicy, "as a result of mutual interaction with each other and above all in attempts to satisfy the diverse ethical and intellectual needs of their adherents."[25]

A similar combination of methods was recommended by William James, who distinguished between "healthy-minded" religion (a dualism characteristic of the "splitting" approach, regarding evil as a "waste element, to be sloughed off and negated") and monism, in which evil must be "kept and consecrated and have a function awarded to it in the final system of truth."[26] James regarded healthy-mindedness as the less satisfactory of these two possibilities: "Healthy-mindedness is inadequate as a philosophical doctrine, because the evil facts which it refuses positively to account for are a genuine portion of reality; and they may after all be the best key to life's significance, and possibly the only openers of our eyes to the deepest levels of truth."[27] As an alternative, he regarded the most complete religions as "those in which the pessimistic elements are best developed,"[28] a type of religion which he characterized as "sick-soul" philosophies in their extreme form, and which included Buddhism and Christianity, religions which maximized rather than minimized evil.[29] The greatest religious insights have arisen neither in the healthy-minded nor in the totally pessimistic but from those who, like Bunyan and Tolstoy, have experienced the depths of the sick-soul and then returned to a new, more balanced form of dualism:

> When disillusionment has gone as far as this, there is seldom a *restitutio ad integrum*. One has tasted of the fruit of the tree, and the happiness of Eden never comes again. ... Neither Bunyan nor Tolstoy could become what we have called healthy-minded. They had drunk too deeply of the cup of bitterness ever to forget its taste, and their redemption is into a universe two storeys deep. Each of them realized a good which broke

[23] Weber (1946), p. 359. See above, chap. I, sec. 2. [24] Weber (1963), pp. 146–147.

[25] *Ibid.* [26] James, p. 142. [27] *Ibid.*, p. 169.

[28] *Ibid.*, p. 171. [29] *Ibid.*, p. 140.

the effective edge of his sadness; yet the sadness was preserved as a minor ingredient in the heart of the faith by which it was overcome.[30]

This is the evolution of qualified monism (what Rāmānuja might have called *viśiṣṭa advaita*), which James endorses with the symbolism of mythological theodicy—the loss of Eden, the drinking of the bitter-sweet Soma-poison: to begin with healthy-mindedness (to discard the evil "dirt," as Vena discards the Niṣāda); then to experience the insights of the involuted monism of the sick soul (Vena doomed to evil); and finally to arrive at a synthesis which grants evil a function in the final system of truth, revering both the purity of healthy-mindedness and the dirt of the sick soul.

Vedic religion is largely healthy-minded, ignoring (rather than denying) the more tragic aspects of life, aspiring to heaven, and invoking benevolent gods. The Upaniṣads introduce the insights of the sick soul and pave the way for a vision of the essentially evil nature of life, a vision which largely colors the image of the Hindu gods themselves in the early period: malevolence or inadequacy motivating the divinities who determine our fates. The rest of Hinduism, Epic and Purāṇic, might well be subsumed under James's period of resolution and mending; evil is recognized as horrible, death terrifying, heresy wicked, but these are accepted and integrated with the healthy goals of the Vedic life-view.

The existence of diametrically opposed but equally valid approaches to theodicy is affirmed within the Hindu myths themselves. The ritual and philosophical contrast may be reconciled when mythology strikes a balance between a philosophically profound *crie de coeur* and an emotionally satisfying argument;[31] here, if anywhere, *le coeur a ses raisons que la raison ne connait point*. The Buddha recognized this quandary when he at first hesitated to teach, fearing that no one would understand him; he then realized that men have various capacities to receive the truth, just as in a lotus pond there are some lotuses thriving far below the water surface, some already rising out of the water, no longer adhered to by the water, and others just at the surface; he agreed to teach[32]—perhaps for the sake of this last, intermediary group. Later, Mahāyāna Buddhism expanded this simple metaphor into the doctrine of skill in means, suiting dogma to pupil. The myths of the Kali Age heresies recognize the need for different spiritual paths for different individuals, ranging from the Vedic to the Tantric;[33] the Purāṇas mediate between these two extremes of spiritual competence. Mythology, too, serves a purpose for those wavering between the deeply submerged theodicy of village devil cults, which never really come to terms with the problem of evil at all, and the full-blooming karmic philosophy, out of reach for all but the relatively few enlightened Vedāntists. Purāṇic mythology brings some measure

[30] *Ibid.*, pp. 163 and 192. [31] See above, chap. I, sec. 4.

[32] *Vinaya Piṭaka, Mahāvagga*, 1.5.11–13. [33] See above, chap. X, sec. 7.

of light to those in the intermediary gloom between the *tamas* of Tantric cult and the *sattva* of Vedāntic philosophy.

2. The Varieties of Hindu Experience

This book almost certainly tells more about Hindu theodicy than most people will want to know, but the sheer volume of the material is in itself a significant fact; as in Marx's and Engel's development of the Hegelian dialectic, when quantitative factors attain substantial enough proportions, they undergo a transition into qualitative factors. The number of myths that the Hindus told about this subject says, as no brief summary could say, how deeply troubled they were by the problem and how difficult it was for them to solve it. Give someone a round peg to put in a round hole, and ask him to write an explanation of how he did it, and you will probably get a short paragraph. Take a round peg and a square hole–the problem of theodicy, to be squeezed into a pseudo-logical framework––and give it to ten thousand people, and ask them to tell you how they could *not* do it, and you will get a very long book. Insoluable contradictions generate infinite numbers of incomplete solutions.[34]

One must therefore speak of the Hindu approaches and solutions–in the plural, and not of *the* Hindu approach or solutions–to theodicy. This is the fascination of Hinduism–*all* the possible solutions are there, somewhere, so that Hinduism in itself offers the full spectrum of varieties of religious experience, the diversity essential to a complete theodicy. But unlike the synethetic works of James, or Frazer, or Stith Thompson, the strength of this total view is not invalidated by a dispersal among noncommunicating cultures or individuals; many Hindus at many times knew all, or at least most, of the ways that the peg would not go into the hole. Like a kaleidoscope, the myths contain and constantly rearrange vivid episodes like bits of colored glass through which one sees one's own personal reality; never is the pattern quite the same twice over, never is it at rest.

The awareness of multiplicity is a characteristic of Hindu mythology[35] and of Hindu art; at least one of the purposes of the many heads and arms depicted on Hindu iconographic figures is to signify the multiplicity of powers and possibilities of divine action. Multiplicity equally characterizes the possibilities of human action in the Hindu view of society, though the individual was often forced to one of the two poles of human potential: complete variety of an arbitrarily assigned range of roles, denying choice; or choice of an equally arbitrary nature, on the presupposition of only one valid possibility to choose, like the candidate in a Soviet election.

[34] O'Flaherty (1973), pp. 36–38. [35] *Ibid.*, pp. 16–21.

The first of these views is characteristic of the doctrine of svadharma, which assumes that, just as all roles, good and evil, are necessary for the infinite variety which constitutes society as a whole, so too the full variety of all moral possibilities in human life, including all evils (death, injustice, suffering), and the full variety of religious views (including all heresies) are necessary to the fulfilment of human life. Although the individual has no choice of roles, society is disposed in such a way that each individual contributes in some manner to the totality of human possibility, all roles being equally valid, equally necessary (though not equally good). Action and variety are the values of this system. The individual creates his life not out of the full range of material but, as it were, out of *objets trouvés*, and each individual is expected to create a different part of the mosaic, some of these parts necessarily involving suffering, heresy, or other evils provided by the gods, who are caught up in karma as we are.

This view, which persists throughout orthodox Hindu texts, was then directly challenged by the group of doctrines which substitute the individual, a universally applicable morality, and a single goal (release from involvement in the cycle of rebirth) for the svadharma, relativism, and variety of the orthodox view. Under the influence of Buddhism, the Upaniṣads, and the bhakti cults, the individual is given a choice of action, freedom from the strictures of caste; instead of creating his life from *objets trouvés*, he may choose his medium and free himself from karma. (In terms of doctrine, the choice is not entirely free. In Buddhism, the choice is conditioned by past karma; in bhakti theory, God chooses the worshipper. But viewed in terms of action, as it is in mythology, the individual consciously changes his life.)

The freedom implicit in the bhakti view is counterbalanced by a corresponding restriction of goals; everyone must, theortically, seek to create the same type of life, the life which achieves release. The variety and action celebrated by the orthodox view are replaced by uniformity in doctrine; peace or quiescence (*nirvāṇa, mokṣa, śānti*) is the single goal. In this view, certain aspects of existence are rejected–immoral behavior in the individual, certain inherently "evil" possibilities of action, certain roles that are provided for under the doctrine of svadharma–and, as the ultimate abstraction, existence itself is considered either evil or nonexistent. God here is on the side of good, working to help man free himself from evil behavior and, ultimately, from the world of variety, action, and life.

The moral relativism of the svadharma view is based on the contrast between purity and impurity, rather than good and evil; in this context, evil is defined as the threat of impurity, defilement, wrong intermingling of classes; impurity can never be dispensed with, however, nor can it become an autonomous principle (as in classical dualism), for it is always regarded as functioning in the service of purity. The bhakti texts, on the other hand, regard good and evil as antagonistic and no longer interdependent; thus one may hope to cleave to the one and avoid the other entirely. The svadharma view of orthodox Hindusim is an ethical system based on the pluralism inherent in the social system of caste (whose goal is the preservation of social and moral balance); the bhakti philosophies deny the validity of the caste system in favor of a more universalistic and apparently more individualistic ethical system, whose goal is salvation.

The first of these two views is in some ways less challenging but more realistic than the second; each individual knows what is expected of him, and need make no choice, yet all possibilities are accounted for. The second view requires a moral decision on the part of the individual, but its assumption of a single universal goal simplifies this decision. Both views assume that the gods wish man to have that for which he strives—either the necessary evil of the svadharma view or the universally applicable good of the bhakti view (i.e., release, which is beyond dharma and adharma). It is only in the transitional stages (when asceticism is a human goal that is not acceptable to certain of the older gods) that a conflict arises between man and god, and this conflict spills over into some svadharma- or bhakti-oriented texts as well, for asceticism may be used to obtain powers or salvation.

These intricate intertwinings and discrepancies reveal the complexity of the Hindu mythology of evil, particularly when one bears in mind the fact that two viewpoints which seem to agree in one particular will not only disagree in others but even in the reasons for which they apparently agree in that one. Thus apparent unanimity may conceal true discrepancy; and, on the other hand, apparent multiplicity may be seen as unanimity. One text explicitly remarks upon the multiplicity of paths leading to a single goal:

There are many religions—that of the Vedas, Sāṅkhya, Yoga, the Pāśupatas, Vaiṣṇavas—and one person chooses this path, another person another path; because of the variety of preferences, favoring a straight path or a winding, you are the one goal for men, as the ocean is the one goal for all rivers.[36]

The gods generally act on behalf of men in all views except that of the asceticism-oriented mythology, but they do so for very different reasons and in very different ways: sometimes in order that they themselves may survive on sacrificial offerings, sometimes out of love for mankind. The gods are responsible for the creation of evil for various reasons: in orthodox Hinduism, because dharma is only possible, and valuable, when adharma also exists to balance and to contrast with it; in asceticism mythology because the gods fear that men will become too powerful and overcome the gods; and in devotional mythology because God wishes to descend to the level of evil, and to participate in it, to help or free mankind.

[36] *Mahimnastotra* 7. See above, chap. VII, sec. 7.

Thus, the conflict between "good" and "evil" tends to disappear, or is disregarded, in various ways: the early texts (the Brāhmaṇas) brush the problem aside in favor of ritual solutions; the orthodox texts attempt to reconcile good and evil and thus to avoid the conflict. The Buddhists, and certain Hindus, sidestep the problem by positing karma as the only cause of good and evil; this results in an infinite chain of earlier and earlier causes which, like Achilles and the tortoise,[37] approach but never reach a final solution. But later texts, under the influence of Buddhism, the Upaniṣads, and bhakti, reveal an insight into the problem on a cosmic as well as an individual level. This is made possible by the manner in which Hindu mythology superimposes on older views certain conflicting later views and balances the two. Thus it is possible for a Hindu myth to imply that the evil in human life is necessary, desirable, and intended by God, that everything in life is relative, and yet to assume at the same time a universally valid "good" toward which all mankind should strive. "Evil" must be accepted, but "good" must be sought; these views together provide a working solution to the problem of evil, a framework in which mankind as a whole, and each individual, may function in the face of an ultimately insoluble problem. Although some Hindu texts seem to welcome the presence of evil, and others envision an escape from karma and from the evil inherent in it, the total corpus affirms a universe of possibilities.

[37] Toporov, pp. 59 and 67.

Bibliography

Abbreviations

AARP	Art and Archaeology Research Papers. London
ABORI	*Annals of the Bhandarkar Oriental Research Institute*
AGSWK, AWL	*Abhandlungen der Geistes- und Sozialwissenschaftlichen Klasse, Akademie der Wissenschaften und der Literatur*
AKT	All-India Kashiraj Trust
ALB	*Adyar Library Bulletin*
ASA	Association of Social Anthropologists
ASB	Asiatic Society of Bengal
ASS	Ānandāśrama Sanskrit Series
Bib Ind.	Bibliotheca Indica
BSS	Bombay Sanskrit Series
BST	Buddhist Sanskrit Texts
ERE	*Encyclopedia of Religion and Ethics*. Ed. James Hastings. 13 vols. Edinburgh, 1908–26
GOLSBS	Government Oriental Library Series, Bibliotheca Sanskrita
HOS	Harvard Oriental Series
HR	*History of Religions*
IIJ	*Indo-Iranian Journal*
JAOS	*Journal of the American Oriental Society*
JAS	*Journal of Asian Studies*
JBBRAS	*Journal of the Bombay Branch of the Royal Asiatic Society*
JRAI	*Journal of the Royal Anthropological Institute of Great Britain and Ireland*
JRAS	*Journal of the Royal Asiatic Society*
KSS	Kāshī Sanskrit Series
POS	Poona Oriental Series
PTS	Pāli Text Society
SBE	Sacred Books of the East
SDSIUH	Schriftenreihe des Südasien-Instituts der Universität Heidelberg
TCAAS	*Transactions of the Connecticut Academy of Arts and Sciences*
TSS	Trivandrum Sanskrit Series
WZKSO	*Wiener Zeitschrift zur Kunde des Sud- und Ostasiens*
ZDMG	*Zeitschrift der Deutschen Morgenländischen Gesellschaft*

Sanskrit and Pāli texts, by title

* denotes primary version used, cited in bibliographic notes unless otherwise indicated. Frequently cited works are referred to in footnotes by the abbreviations that follow the full bibliographic citation here.

Abhidhānacintāmaṇi of Hemacandra. Ed. Pandit Śivadatta and Kāśīnātha Pandurang Parab. Abhidhānasaṃgraha, nos. 6–11. Bombay, 1896.

Agni Purāṇa. ASS no. 41. Poona, 1957. (*Agni*)

Ahirbudhnyasaṃhitā. Ed. F. O. Schrader. Adyar Library, no. 4–5. 2nd ed. Madras, 1966.

Aitareya Āraṇyaka. Ed. and trans. A. B. Keith. Anecdota Oxoniensia: Aryan Series 9. Oxford, 1909. (*Ait. Ar.*)

Aitareya Brāhmaṇa With the comm. of Sāyaṇa. Bib. Ind. Calcutta, 1896. (*Ait. Br.*)

Amarakośa of Amarasiṃha. With the comm. of Maheśvara. Bombay, 1896.

Anāgatavaṃsa of Kassapa. Ed. J. Minayeff. *Journal of the Pali Text Society*. London, 1886. Pp. 33–54.

Āpastamba Dharmasūtra. Ed. G Bühler. BSS, nos. 44 and 50. 2nd ed. Bombay, 1892–94.

Āpastamba Śrautasūtra. Gaekwad Oriental Series, nos. 121 and 142. Oriental Institute, Baroda, 1955 and 1963.

Arthaśāstra of Kauṭilya. Ed. R. S. Shastry. GOLSBS, no. 54. Mysore, 1919.

Atharva Veda. With comm. of Sāyaṇa. Bombay, 1895. (*AV*)

Baudhāyana Dharmasūtra. With the comm. of Govinda Svāmī. Ed. C. Śastri. KSS, no. 104. Benares, 1934.

Baudhāyana Śrauta Sūtra. Ed. W. Caland. Bib. Ind. New Series. 3 vols. Calcutta, 1904–24.

Bhagavad Gītā. With the comm. of Śaṅkara. Ed. Dinkar Vishnu Gokhala. POS, no. 1. Poona, 1950 (*Gītā*)

Bhāgavata Purāṇa. With the comm. of Śrīdhara. Bombay, 1832. (*Bhāgavata*)

Bhaviṣya Purāṇa. Bombay, 1959. (*Bhaviṣya*)

Brahmāṇḍa Purāṇa. Ed. J. L. Shastri. Delhi, 1973. (*Brahmāṇḍa*)

Brahma Purāṇa. Gurumandal Series, no. 11. Calcutta, 1954. (*Brahma*)

Brahmavaivarta Purāṇa. ASS, no. 102. Poona, 1935. (*Brahmavaivarta*)

Brahmasūtrabhāṣya of Madhva (Ānandatīrtha). Calcutta, 1911.

Bṛhaddevatā of Śauanaka. Ed. A. A. Macdonell. HOS, no. 5. Cambridge, 1904.

Bṛhaddharma Purāṇa. Ed. H. Śastri. Bib. Ind. Calcutta, 1888. (*Bṛhaddharma*)

Bṛhannāradīya Purāṇa. Ed. Pandit Hrishikesha Shastri. ASB. Calcutta, 1891. (*Bṛhannāradīya*)

Buddhacarita of Aśvaghoṣa. Ed. E. H. Johnston. Panjab University Oriental Publications, no. 31–32. 2 parts. Calcutta, 1935–36.

Dakṣa Kāṇḍa of the *Skanda Purāṇa*, *Śankara Saṃhitā*, *Śiva Rahasya Khaṇḍa*. Ms. copied by T. Ramalinga Dikshitar, Cidambaram, cited by Kulke, q.v.

Darpadalana of Kṣemendra. Kāvyamālā Series, no. 6. Bombay, 1890.

Daśakumāracarita of Daṇḍin. Ed. N. B. Godbole. 11th ed. Bombay, 1928.
Daśāvatāracarita of Kṣemendra. Ed. Pandit Durgāprasād and Kāśīnātha Pāndurang Parab. Kāvyamālā Series, no. 26. Bombay, 1891.
Devībhāgavata Purāṇa. With comm. Benares, 1960. (*Devībhāgavata*)
Dhammapada. Ed. Sūriyagoda Sumangala Thera. London, 1914.
Dīgha Nikāya. Ed. T. W. Rhys Davids and J. E. Carpenter. PTS. London, 1890–1911.
Dīvyāvadāna. Ed. P. L. Vaidya. BST, no. 20, Darbhangar, 1959.
Garuḍa Purāṇa. Benares, 1963. (*Garuḍa*)
Gītagovinda of Jayadeva. With 3 comms. Ed. A. Sharma, K. Deshpande, and V. S. Sharma. Sans. Acad. Series 19 A 16. Hyderabad, 1969.
Gopatha Brāhmaṇa. Ed. D. Gaastra. Leiden, 1919. (*Gopatha*)
Gorakṣa Siddhānta Saṃgraha. Ed. Gopi Nath Kaviraj. Princess of Wales Saraswati Bhavana Texts, no. 18. Benares, 1925.
Haracaritacintāmaṇi of Jayadratha. Ed. Pandit Śivadatta and K. P. Parab. Kāvyamālā Series, no. 61. Bombay, 1897 (*Haracarita*)
Harivaṃśa. Ed. V. S. Sukthankar, S. K. Velvalkar, and P. L. Vaidya. Poona, 1969–71. (*Hari.*)
Hiraṇyakeśin Gṛhya Sūtra. Ed. J. Kirste. Vienna, 1889.
Jaiminīya (Talavakāra) Brāhmaṇa. Ed. R. Vira. Sarasvati Vihāra Series, no. 31. Nagpur, 1954. (*Jai. Br.*)
Jaiminīya Upaniṣad Brāhmaṇa. Ed. by Hanns Oertel in *JAOS* 16, no. 1 (1894): 79–259. (*Jai. Up. Br.*)
Jātakas. With comm. Ed. V. Fausboll. 6 vols. London, 1877–96.
Kālikā Purāṇa. Bombay, 1891. (*Kālikā*)
Kalki Purāṇa. Ed. Kālīprasanna Vidyāratna. Calcutta, no date. (*Kalki*)
Kāma Sūtra of Vatsyāyana. 2 vols. Bombay, 1856.
Kārikā of Gauḍapada. Ed. and trans. R. R. Karmarkar. Poona, 1953.
Karpūramañjarī of Rājaśekhara. Ed. Sten Konow. Trans. Charles Lanman. HOS, no. 4. Cambridge, 1901.
Kāṭhaka Āraṇyaka. Ed. L. von Schroeder. Berl. Sitz. Ber., no. 137. (*Kāṭh. Ār.*)
Kāṭhaka Saṃhitā. Ed. L. von Schroeder. 4 vols. Leipzig, 1900–1910. (*Kāṭh. Sam.*)
Kathāsaritsāgara of Somadeva. Ed. P. Durgaprasād and K. P. Parab. Bombay, 1930.
Kauśītaki Brāhmaṇa. Wiesbaden, 1968. (*Kau. Br.*)
Kumārasambhava of Kālidāsa, with the commentary of Mallinātha. Bombay, 1955.
* *Kūrma Purāṇa*. Ed. A. S. Gupta. AKT. Benares, 1967. (*Kūrma*)
Kūrma Purāṇa. Ed. Nīlmaṇi Mukhopadhyāya. Bib. Ind. Calcutta, 1890.
Liṅga Purāṇa. Ed. Pañcānanatarkaratna. Calcutta, 1890. (*Liṅga*)
Mahābhāgavata Purāṇa. Bombay, 1913. (*Mahābhāgavata*)
* *Mahābhārata*. Ed. V. S. Sukthankar et al. Poona, 1933–1960. (*MBh.*)
Mahābhārata. With the comm. of Nīlakaṇṭha. Bombay, 1862.
Mahābhāṣya of Patañjali. Ed. Vedavrata. 6 vols. Jhajjar, 1963.
Mahānirvāṇa Tantra. Ed. with comm. of Hariharananda Bharati, by Arthur Avalon. Tantrik Texts, no. 13. Madras, 1929.

Mahāvagga of the *Vinaya Piṭaka*. Ed. H. Oldenberg. London, 1879.
Mahimnastotra (*Haramahimnastotra*) of Puṣpandanta. With comm. of Madhusūdana. KSS, no. 21. Benares, 1924.
Maitrāyaṇī Saṃhitā of the Yajur Veda. Ed. L. von Schroeder. Leipzig, 1881. (*Mait. Sam.*)
Mānavadharmaśāstra. With the comm. of Medhātithi. Bib. Ind. Calcutta, 1932. (*Manu*)
Mānavadharmaśāstra. [*The Laws of Manu*]. Trans. Georg Bühler. SBE, no. 25. Oxford, 1886.
Maṇimañjarī of Nārāyaṇa Paṇḍita. Bombay, 1934.
Manmathonmathana of Rāma. Ed. R. Schmidt. *ZDMG* 69 (1909): 409–37 and 629–54.
Mārkaṇḍeya Purāṇa. With comm. Bombay, 1890. (*Mārk.*)
Matsya Purāṇa. ASS, no. 54. Poona, 1909. (*Matsya*)
Mattavilāsaprahasana of Mahendravarman. TSS, no. 50. Trivandrum, 1917.
Mitākṣarā of Vijñāneśvara. Comm. on *Yājñavalkyasmṛti*. Ed. W. L. S. Pansīkār. Bombay, 1909.
Mūlamādhyamakakārikā of Nāgārjuna. With comm. of Candrakirti. Ed. and trans. H. Chatterjee, Calcutta, 1957 and 1962.
Naiṣadhacarita of Śrīharṣa. Ed. Jīvānanda Vidyāsāgara. Calcutta, 1875–76.
Nārada Purāṇa. Summarized by K. Damodaran Nambiar, in supplement to *Purāṇa* 15, no. 2 (July 1973): 1–56. (*Nārada*)
Nārada Smṛti. Ed. Julius Jolly. Bib. Ind. Calcutta, 1885–86.
Nirukta [*The Nighaṇṭu and the Nirukta*] of Yāska. Ed. Lakshman Sarup. Oxford, 1921.
* *Padma Purāṇa*. ASS, no. 131. Poona, 1894. (*Padma*)
Padma Purāṇa. Calcutta, 1958.
Pañcatantra of Pūrṇabhadra. Ed. Johannes Hertel. HOS, no. 11. Cambridge, 1908.
Pañcatantra. Trans. Arthur Ryder. Chicago, 1956.
Pāśupatasūtra. With the comm. of Kauṇḍinya. Ed. Anantakrishna Sastri. TSS, no. 143. Trivandrum, 1940.
Prabandhakośa of Rājaśekhara. Ed. Jina Vijaya. Singhi Jaina Series, no. 6. Shantiniketan, 1935.
Prabodhacandrodaya of Kṛṣṇamiśra. With comms. Ed. Vāsudeva Śarman. Bombay, 1898.
Rāmacaritamānasa. See Dās, Tulsī.
* *Rāmāyaṇa* of Valmīki. Ed. G. H. Bhatt. Baroda, 1958–. (*Rām.*)
Rāmāyaṇa of Valmīki. 2nd ed., published by N. Ramaratnam. Madras, 1958.
Ṛg Veda. With the comm. of Sāyaṇa. Ed. F. Max Müller. 2nd ed. London, 1890–1892. (*RV*)
Śabdakalpadruma of Raja Sir Radhakant Deb Bahadur. Calcutta, 1886.
Saddharmapuṇḍarīka. Bibliotheca Buddhica, no. 10. St. Petersburg, 1908.
Śaṅkaradigvijaya of Mādhava (Vidyāraṇya). Ed. with comm. Poona, 1915.
Śaṅkaravijaya of Ānandagiri. Ed. J. Tarkapañcānana. Bib. Ind. Calcutta, 1868.

Śaṅkhāyana Śrauta Sūtra. Ed. A. Hillebrandt. Bib Ind. Calcutta, 1888–99.
Sarvadarśanasaṃgraha of Mādhava, son of Sāyaṇa. Ed. Pandita Ishvarachandra Vidyāsāgar. Bib. Ind. Calcutta, 1858.
Śatapatha Brāhamaṇa. Ed. Albrecht Weber. Bib. Ind. Calcutta, 1903. (*Śata.*)
Saura Purāṇa. ASS, no. 18. Poona, 1923. (*Saura*)
* *Śiva Purāṇa*. Benares, 1964. (*Śiva*)
Śiva Purāṇa. *Jñānasaṃhitā* (*Jñāna Sam.*) and *Dharmasaṃhitā* (*Dharma Sam.*) With comm. Bombay, 1884.
* *Skanda Purāṇa*. Bombay, 1867. (*Skanda*)
Skanda Purāṇa. Kedāra Khaṇḍa. Bombay, 1910.
Skanda Purāṇa. Sahyādri Khaṇḍa. Ed. J. Gerson da Cunha. Bombay, 1877.
Subhāṣitaratnakoṣa of Vidyākara. Ed. D. D. Kosambi and V. V. Gokhale. HOS, no. 42. Cambridge, 1957. (Trans. D. H. H. Ingalls. HOS, no. 44. Cambridge, 1965.)
Subhāṣitāvali of Vallabhadeva. Ed. Peter Peterson. BSS, no. 31. Bombay, 1886.
Śukranītisāra. With comm. Ed. Jivānanda Vidyāsāragara. Calcutta, 1882.
Sumaṅgalavilāsinī of Buddhaghosa. PTS. London, 1886.
Suśrutasaṃhitā. Ed. Kaviraj Ambikadatta. KSS, no. 156. Benares, 1954. 2 vols.
Sutta Nipāta. PTS. London, 1900.
Taittirīya Āraṇyaka. With comm. of Sayaṇa. Bib. Ind. Calcutta, 1872. (*Tait. Ār.*)
Taittirīya Brāhmaṇa. With comm. of Sāyaṇa. Ed. Rajendralala Mitra. Bib. Ind. Calcutta, 1859. (*Tait. Br.*)
Taittirīya Saṃhitā. With comm. of Mādhava. Bib. Ind. Calcutta, 1860. (*Tait. Sam.*)
Tāṇḍya Mahābrāhmana. With the comm. of Sāyaṇa. Ed. Anandacandra Vedantavāgīśa. Bib. Ind. Calcutta, 1869–74. (*Tāṇḍya*)
Tantrādhikāranirṇaya of Bhaṭṭojī Dīkṣita. Benares, 1888.
Tantrāvarttika of Kumārila Bhaṭṭa. Comm. on Śabarasvāmin's *Jaiminīya Mīmāṃsā Sūtra* commentary. Ed. Gangadhara Śastrī. KSS, nos. 5–72. Benares, 1903.
Triṣaṣṭiśalākāpuruṣacaritra of Hemacandra. Bombay, 1904–9.
Upaniṣads. With the commentary of Śaṅkara. Ed. Hari Raghunath Bhagavan. Poona, 1927. (*Chāndogya: Ch. Up.; Kauśītaki: Kau. Up.; Maitrāyaṇi: Mait. Up.*)
Upaniṣads. One Hundred and Eight Upanishads. 4th ed. Bombay, 1913.
Vaikhānasasmārtasūtra. Bib. Ind. Calcutta, 1927.
Vājasaneyi Saṃhitā. Ed. Albrecht Weber. Berlin, 1851–59. (*Vaj. Sam.*)
Vāmana Purāṇa. Ed. A. S. Gupta. AKT. Benares, 1968. (*Vāmana. S: Saromāhātmyam*)
Varāha Purāṇa. Ed. Hrishikeśa Śastri. Bib. Ind. Calcutta, 1893. (*Varāha*)
* *Vāyu Purāṇa*. Bombay, 1867. (*Vāyu*)
Vāyu Purāṇa. ASS, no. 49. Poona, 1860.
Vedapuristhalapurāṇa. Summarized by T. Mahalingam, Mackenzie mss. Madras, 1972. Pp. 255–256.
Viṣṇu Purāṇa. With the comm. of Śrīdhara. Ed. Sītārāmadāsonkāranātha. Calcutta, 1972. (*Viṣṇu*)
Viṣṇudharmottara Purāṇa. Benares, no date.

Visuddhimagga of Buddhaghosa. Ed. Henry Clark Warren. HOS, no. 41. Cambridge, 1950.

Yāgīvaramāhātmya. India Office ms. 3719. Reproduced by Wilhelm Jahn, *ZDMG* 70 (1916): 310–320.

Yājñavalkyasmṛti. With comm. of Viśvarūpāchārya. TSS, nos. 74, 81. Trivandrum, 1922–1924.

Tamil texts, by title

Cilappatikāram of Iḷaṅkovaṭikal. Madras, 1968.

Cutalaimātācuvāmivipattu of M. Muttucāmipillai. Maturai, n. d.

Kamparāmāyaṇam. Madras, 1957.

Kāñcippurāṇam of Civañāṉayoki. Kancipuram, 1933.

Kantapurāṇam of Kacciyappacivācāriyar. Madras, 1907.

Katirkāmapurāṇavacanam of C. Tāmotaram Piḷḷai. Cuṉṉākam, 1937.

Paḻanittalapurāṇam of Pāla Cuppiramaṇiya KKavirāyar. Madras, 1903.

Pĕriyapurāṇam eṉṟu vaḻaṅkukiṟa Tiruttoṇṭarpurāṇam of Cekkiḻār. Ed. Āṟumukanāvalar. Madras, 1916.

Takkayākaparaṇi of Oṭṭakkūttar. Ed. U. V. Svāminātha Ayyar. 2nd ed. Madras, 1945.

Tirukaḻukuṉṟam of M. M. Kumarasami Mudaliyar. Madras, 1923. (In English)

Tirukkaṇṇapurasthalapurāṇam. In Sanskrit and Tamil. Madras, 1912.

Tirukkaṭavūrpurāṇam, trans. [from Sanskrit?] by Pālakiruṣṇa Tīkṣitar. Madras, 1905.

Tirumūrttimalaippurāṇavacanam of Aruṇācala Kavuṇṭar. Madraṣ, 1936.

Tiruvāṉaikkāvalmāhātmiyam of Pa. Pancāpakeca Cāstiri. Srirangam, 1932.

Tiruvāñciyakṣettirapurāṇam of S. Pālacupramaṇiya Cĕṭṭiyār (Tamil prose retelling). Kumpakoṇam, 1939.

Tiruvārūrppurāṇam of Campantamuṉivar. Madras, 1894.

Tiruviḷaiyāṭaṟpurāṇam of Parañcotimuṉivar. Madras, 1965.

Tiruvŏṟṟiyūrpurāṇam of Ñāṉapirakācar. Madras, 1869.

Venkaṭācalamāhātmiyam of I. Muṉucāmināyaṭu. Cittur, 1928. *Tiruppati Tirumalai Yāttirai Venkaṭācala Māhātmiyam eṉṉum sthalapurāṇam.*

Vināyakapurāṇam (*Pārkkavapurāṇam eṉṉum vināyakapurāṇam*) of Kacciyappamuṉivar. Madras, 1910.

Viruttācalapurāṇam of Ñāṉakkūttar. Madras (?), 1876.

Works in European languages, by author

Agrawala, V. S. *Vāmana Purāṇa, A Study*. Benares, 1964.

———. *Śiva Mahādeva, The Great God*. Benares, 1966.

Aiyangar, K. V. Rangaswami. *Rājadharma*. Adyar, 1941.

Alsdorf, Ludwig. *Beiträge zur Geschichte von Vegetarismus und Rinderverehrung in Indien*. *AGSWK*, no. 61 (1961). Wiesbaden, 1962.

Altekar, A. S. *State and Government in Ancient India.* 3rd ed. Delhi, 1958.
Ambedkar, Bhimrao Ramji. *The Untouchables.* New Delhi, 1948.
Archer, W. G. *The Hill of Flutes: Life, Love and Poetry in Tribal India.* London, 1974.
Auboyer, Jeannine. *Everyday Life in Ancient India.* London, 1965.
Aurobindo, Sri. *On Yoga, Book Two.* International University Centre Collection, vol. 6. Pondicherry, 1958.
Ayyar, A. S. P. *Kovalan and Kannaki.* Madras, 1947.
Baldaeus, Philippus. *Naauwkeurige beschryvinge van Malabar en Choromandel. . . .* Amsterdam, 1672.
Banerjea, Jitendra Nath. *The Development of Hindu Iconography.* 2nd ed. Calcutta, 1956.
Basham, A. L. *The Wonder That Was India.* London, 1954.
Beals, Alan R. *Gopalur, a South Indian Village.* New York, 1962.
Bhaktivedanta, A. C. Swami Prabhupāda. *Śrīmad Bhāgavatam.* New York, 1975.
Bhandarkar, D. R. *Some Aspects of Ancient Hindu Polity.* Benares, 1929.
Böhtlingk, Otto. *Indische Sprüche.* 3 vols. Kaiserliche Akademie der Wissenschaften. St. Petersburg, 1872.
Bosch, F. D. K. "Het Lingga-Heiligdom van Dinaja." *Tijdscrift voor Indische Taal-, Land-, en Volkenkunde,* Batavian Society of Arts and Sciences 64 (1924): 227–291.
Boss, Medard. *A Psychiatrist Discovers India* (trans. Henry A. Frey). London, 1965.
Bowker, John. *Problems of Suffering in Religions of the World.* Cambridge (England), 1970.
Boyd, James W. *Satan and Māra: Christian and Buddhist Symbols of Evil.* Studies in the History of Religions (supplements to *Numen*) 27. Leiden, 1975.
Briggs, George Weston. *Gorakhnath and the Kanphata Yogis.* Calcutta, 1938.
Brown, W. Norman. "Proselyting the Asuras." *JAOS* 39 (1919): 100–103.
_______. "The Ṛgvedic Equivalent for Hell." *JAOS* 61 (1941): 76–80.
_______. "The Creation Myth of the Ṛg Veda." *JAOS* 62 (1942): 85–98.
_______. "Indra's Infancy according to Ṛg Veda IV.18." In Dr. Siddheshwar Varma presentation volume, Hoshiapur, 1950.
_______. "Duty as Truth in the Veda." In *India Maior,* congratulatory volume presented to Jan Gonda, Leiden, 1972. Pp. 57–67.
Buch, Maganlal A. *The Principles of Hindu Ethics.* Baroda, 1921.
Buck, William. *Mahabharata.* Berkeley, 1973.
Bühler, Georg. See *Mānavadharmaśāstra.*
Burrow, Thomas. *The Sanskrit Language.* London, 1955.
Burton, Sir Richard F. *Vikram and the Vampire.* London, 1893.
Buschardt, L. *Det rituelle Daemonrab i den Vediske Somakult.* Copenhagen, 1945.
Butterworth, E. A. S. *The Tree at the Navel of the Earth.* Berlin, 1970.
Carr, M. W. (ed.). *Descriptive and Historical Papers Relating to the Seven Pagodas on the Coromandel Coast.* Madras, 1869.
Carstairs, G. Morris. *The Twice-Born.* London, 1957.
Chambers, William. "An Account of the Sculptures and Ruins at Mavalipuram." In *Asiatick Researches* I, pp. 145–170. Calcutta, 1788.
Charpentier, Jarl. "Rig Veda VIII.100." *Vienna Oriental Journal* 25 (1911).

Chattopadhyaya, Debi Prasad. *Lokāyata: A Study in Ancient Indian Materialsm.* New Delhi, 1959.

Choudhary, Radhakrishna. "Heretical Sects in the Purāṇas." ABORI 37 (1957): 234–257.

Church, Cornelia Dimmitt. *The Yuga Story.* Unpublished Ph. D. dissertation, Syracuse, 1970.

———. "The Purāṇic Myth of the Four Yugas." *Purāṇa* 13, no. 2 (July 1971): 151–159.

———. "Eschatology as the Denial of Death in Indian and Iranian Myth." Paper presented at the annual meeting of the American Academy of Religion, Chicago, November 8–11, 1973. (1973*a*)

———. "The Indian Yugas and the Magnus Annus in Iran and Greece." Paper presented at the 29th International Congress of Orientalists, Paris, July 16–22, 1973 (1973*b*)

———. "The Myth of the Four Yugas in the Sanskrit Purāṇas—a Dimensional Study." *Purāṇa* 16, no. 1 (January 1974): 5–25.

Clough, E. R. *While Sewing Sandals.* New York, 1899.

Coleman, Charles. *The Mythology of the Hindus.* London, 1832.

Coomaraswamy, A. K. "Angels and Titans, an Essay on Vedic Ontology." *JAOS* 55, no. 5 (1935): 373–419. (1935*a*)

———. "The Darker Side of Dawn." Smithsonian Miscellaneous Publications, vol. 94 (Washington: Smithsonian Institution), 1935, no. 1. (1935*b*)

Daly, C. D. *Hindu-Mythologie und Kastrationaskomplex, eine psychoanalytische Studie.* Vienna, 1927. Reprinted from *Imago* 13 (1927).

Dange, Sadashiv A. *Legends in the Mahābhārata.* New Delhi, 1969.

Daniélou, Alain. *Hindu Polytheism.* London, 1964.

Das, Bhagavan. *Krishna.* Madras, 1929.

Dās, Tulsī. *The Holy Lake of the Acts of Rāma* [*Rāmacaritamānasa*]. Trans. W. D. P. Hill. London, 1952.

Dasgupta, Surendranath. *History of Indian Philosophy.* 5 vols. Cambridge, 1922–55.

Derrett, J. D. M. *Religion, Law and the State in India.* London, 1968.

Dessigane, R.; Pattabiramin, P. Z.; and Filliozat, Jean. *Les legendes Çivaites de Kāñcipuram.* Institut Français d'Indologie, no. 27. Pondicherry, 1964.

———. *La legende de Skanda selon le Kandapurāṇam tamoul et l'iconographie.* Institut Français d'Indologie, no. 31. Pondicherry, 1967.

Deussen, Paul. *Sechzig Upaniṣads des Vedas.* Leipzig, 1897.

———. "Ueber das Devadāruvanamāhātmya", *ZDMG* 71 (1917): 119–120.

Dhavamony, Mariasusai. *Love of God in Śaiva Siddhānta.* Oxford, 1971.

Douglas, Mary. *Purity and Danger: An Analysis of Concepts of Pollution and Taboo.* London, 1966.

Dracott, Alice E. *Simla Village Tales.* London, 1906.

Drekmeier, Charles. *Kingship and Community in Early India.* Stanford, 1962.

Dubois, Abbé Jean Antoine. *Hindu Manners, Customs and Ceremonies.* (Paris, 1825.) 3rd ed., trans. Henry Beauchamp. Oxford, 1959.

Dumézil, Georges. *Servius et la Fortune*. Paris, 1943.
_______. *Heur et malheur du guerrier*. Paris, 1969.
_______. *The Destiny of the Warrior*. Trans. Alf Hiltebeitel. Chicago, 1970.
_______. *The Destiny of the King*. Trans. Alf Hiltebeitel. Chicago, 1973.
_______. *Mythe et épopée*. Vol. II. Paris, 1971.
Edgerton, Franklin. "The Fountain of Youth." *JAOS* 26, no. 1 (1905): 1–67.
Eliade, Mircea. "Notes de Démonologie." *Zalmoxis* 1 (1938): 197–203.
_______. *Yoga: Immortality and Freedom*. Trans. Willard R. Trask. Bollingen Series, vol. 56. New York, 1958 (Paris, 1954).
_______. *The Sacred and the Profane*. New York, 1959.
_______. *Mephistopheles and the Androgyne*. Trans. J. M. Cohen. New York, 1965.
Eliot, Sir Charles. *Hinduism and Buddhism*. 3 vols. London, 1921.
Elmore, Wilbur Theodore. *Dravidian Gods in Modern Hinduism*. Nebraska, 1915.
Elwin, Verrier. *The Baiga*. London, 1939.
_______ *The Agaria*. Bombay, 1942.
_______. *Maria Murder and Suicide*. Oxford, 1943.
_______. *Myths of Middle India*. Oxford, 1949.
_______. *Tribal Myths of Orissa*. Bombay, 1953.
Emeneau, Murray B. *Kota Texts*. Berkeley, 1944–46.
Erikson, Erik H. *Gandhi's Truth. On the Origins of Militant Nonviolence*. London, 1970 (New York, 1969).
Forster, E. M. *The Hill of Devi*. London, 1965.
Frazer, Sir James George. *The Golden Bough*. 13 vols. London, 1915.
Fritsch, Vilma. *Left and Right in Science and Life*. London, 1968 (Stuttgart, 1964).
von Fürer-Haimendorf, Christoph. *The Aboriginal Tribes of Hyderabad. Vol. 3: The Raj Gonds of Adilabad. I: Myth and Ritual*. London, 1948.
_______. "The Sense of Sin in Cross-cultural Perspective." *Man*, n.s. 9 (1974): 539–556.
Gail, Adalbert J. "Buddha als Avatar Viṣṇus im Spiegel der Purāṇas." *ZDMG*, 1969, supplementa 1, Vorträge, Teil 3, pp. 917–923.
Gandhi, M. K. *An Autobiography, or The Story of My Experiments with Truth*. Trans. from the Gujurati by Mahadev Desai. Ahmedabad, 1927.
_______. *Collected Works*. Delhi, 1958–.
Geldner, Karl Friedrich. *Der Rig Veda*. 3 vols. *HOS* nos. 33–35. Cambridge, Mass., 1951.
Ghosh, Oroon. *The Dance of Shiva*. New York, 1965.
Ghoshal, U. N. *A History of Indian Political Ideas*. Oxford, 1959.
von Glasenapp, Helmuth. *Von Buddha zu Gandi*. Wiesbaden, 1962.
_______. *Buddhism: A Non-theistic Religion*. Trans. Irmgard Schloegl. London, 1970 (Munich, 1966).
Goetz, Hermann. *Studies in the History and Art of Kashmir and the Indian Himalaya*. Wiesbaden, 1969.
Goldman, Robert P. *Myth and Metamyth: The Bhārgava Cycle of the Mahābhārata*. New York, 1976.

Gombrich, Richard F. *Precept and Practice: Traditional Buddhism in the Rural Highlands of Ceylon*. Oxford, 1971.

———. "Ancient Indian Cosmology." In *Ancient Cosmologies*, ed. Carmen Blacker and Michael Loewe, pp. 110–142. London, 1975.

Gonda, Jan. *Aspects of Early Viṣṇuism*. Utrecht, 1954.

———. *Der Jüngere Hinduismus*. Stuttgart, 1963.

Gough, Kathleen E. "Female Initiation Rites on the Malabar Coast." *JRAI* 85 (1955): 45–80.

Greimas, A. J. "Comparative Mythology" (an anlysis of Dumézil's analysis of the Pṛthu myth). In Pierre Maranda (ed.), *Mythology: Selected Readings*, pp. 162–170. Harmondsworth, 1972. Abridged and trans. from *Du sens: essais sémiotiques*, pp. 117–134. Seuil, 1970.

Grierson, G. A. "Mādhvas." *ERE* 8: 232–235.

Grousset, René. *The Civilization of India*. Trans. Catherine Alison Phillips. New York, 1931 (Paris, 1930).

van Gulik, R. H. *Hayagrīva*. Utrecht, 1935.

Hacker, Paul. *Prahlāda: Werden und Wandlungen einer Idealgestalt*. Wiesbaden, 1960. *ABGSWK*, no. 6, 1959.

Halder, R. "The Oedipus Wish in Iconography." *Indian Journal of Psychology*, 1938.

Hart, George L., III. *The Poems of Ancient Tamil, Their Milieu and Their Sanskrit Counterparts*. Berkeley, 1975.

Hayley, Audrey. "Aspects of Hindu Asceticism." In *Symbols and Sentiments*, ed. Ian Lewis, ASA Monographs. Tavistock, 1976.

Hazra, Rajendra Chandra. *Studies in the Purāṇic Records on Hindu Rites and Customs*. Bulletin no. 20. Dacca, 1948.

———. *Studies in the Upapurāṇas. I: Saura and Vaiṣṇava Upapurāṇas. II: Śākta and Non-sectarian Upapurāṇas.* Calcutta Sanskrit College Research Series 11 and 22. Calcutta, 1958 and 1963.

Heesterman, J. C. "Vrātya and Sacrifice." *IIJ* 6, no. 1 (1962):1–37.

———. "Brahmin, Ritual, and Renouncer." *WZKSO* 8 (1964): 1–31.

———. Review of Alsdorf, *IIJ* 9 (1966): 148.

———. "The Case of the Severed Head." *WZKSO* 11 (1967): 22–43.

———. "On the Origin of the Nāstika." Festschrift Erich Frauwallner, *WZKSO* 12–13 (1968–69): 171–185.

———. "Kauṭalya and the Ancient Indian State." *WZKSO* 15 (1971): 5–22.

———. "Veda and dharma." In *The Concept of Duty in South Asia*, ed. Wendy Doniger O'Flaherty, pp. 80–94. (London, 1975).

Heras, H. S. T."The Devil in Indian Scripture."*JBBRAS* 27, part 2 (June 1952):214–241.

Herman, Arthur Ludwig. *The Problem of Evil and Indian Thought*. Ph.D. dissertation, University of Minnesota. Published by Motilal Barnarsidass (New Delhi, 1976).

Hertz, Robert. *Death and the Right Hand*. Trans. Rodney and Claudia Needham. London, 1960.

Hick, John. *Evil and the God of Love*. London, 1968.

Hill, W. D. P. See Dās, Tulsī.

Holwell, J. Z. *Interesting Historical Events relative to the Provinces of Bengal.* London, 1766, 1767, 1771. Reprinted in Marshall, pp. 45–106.

Hopkins, Edward Washburn. "Gods and Saints of the Great Brāhmaṇa." TCAAS 15 (July 1909): 19–70.

———. "The Divinity of Kings." *JAOS* 51 (1913): 300–316.

———. *Epic Mythology.* Strassburg, 1915. (Encyclopedia of Indo-Aryan Research, III, 1, B.)

Huntington, Ronald. *A Study of Purāṇic Myth from the Viewpoint of Depth Psychology.* Unpublished PhD. dissertation. University of Southern California, 1960. (1960*a*)

———. "The Legend of Pṛthu, a Study in the Process of Individuation." *Purāṇa* 2 (July 1960): 188–210. (1960*b*)

———. "Avatāras and Yugas: Purāṇic Cosmology." *Purāṇa* 6 (1964): 7–39.

Ingalls, D. H. H. "Cynics and Pāśupatas, The Seeking of Dishonor." *Harvard Theological Review* 55 (1962): 281–298.

Ivanow, W. "The Sect of Imam Shah in Gujurat." *JBBRAS* 12 (1937): 19–70.

James, William. *The Varieties of Religious Experience.* (The 1901–2 Gifford Lectures). London, 1960.

Jung, C. G. *Answer to Job.* Trans. R. F. C. Hull. London, 1954 (Zurich, 1952).

———. *Four Archetypes. Mother. Rebirth. Spirit. Trickster.* Trans. R. F. C. Hull. London, 1972. "I: Psychological Aspects of the Mother Archetype," from "Die psychologischen Aspekte des Mutter-Archetypus," *Von den Wurzeln des Bewusstseins* (Zurich, 1954).

Kane, P. V. *History of Dharmaśāstra.* 9 vols. 2nd ed. Poona, 1968.

Keith, Arthur Berriedale. *Indian Mythology.* Vol. 6, part 1, of *The Mythology of All Races,* ed. L. H. Grey. Boston, 1917.

———. *The Religion and Philosophy of the Vedas and Upanishads. HOS* no. 31–32. Cambridge, 1925.

———. "Sin, Hindu." *ERE* 11 (1926): 560.

Kennedy, Colonel Vans. *Researches into the Nature and Affinity of Ancient and Hindu Mythology.* London, 1831.

Khandalavala, Karl. "Some Paintings from the Collection of the late Burjor N. Treasurywala." *Marg* 1, no. 1 (October 1946).

Klein, Melanie. *Contributions to Psychoanalysis 1921–45.* London, 1948.

———. *Our Adult World and its Roots in Infancy.* London, 1960.

Klein, Melanie, et al. *New Directions in Psychoanalysis.* London, 1955.

Koestler, Arthur. *The Lotus and the Robot.* New York, 1961.

Kolenda, Pauline Mahar. "Religious Anxiety and Hindu Fate." *JAS* 23, no. 2 (1964. Supplement, "Aspects of Religion in South Asia."): 71–81.

Kuhn, Adalbert. *Mythologische Studien. I. Die Herabkunft des Feuers und des Göttertranks.* Gütersloh, 1886.

Kuiper, F. B. J. "The Bliss of Aša." *IIJ* 8, no. 2 (1964): 96–129.

Kulke, Herman. *Cidambaramāhātmya.* Wiesbaden, 1970.

Lamotte, Étienne. *Histoire du bouddhisme Indien.* Louvain, 1958.

Leach, Edmund R. "Pulleyar and the Lord Buddha: An Example of Syncretism." *Psychoanalysis and the Psychoanalytic Review* (Summer 1962): 81–102.

———. "Genesis as Myth." In *Genesis as Myth and Other Essays*. London, 1969.

———. *Lévi-Strauss*. London, 1970.

Lévi, Sylvain. *La doctrine du sacrifice dans les Brāhmaṇas*. Bibliothèque de l'école des hautes études. Sciences religieuses, vol. 73. Paris, 1966.

Lévi-Strauss, Claude. "The Structural Study of Myth." In Thomas A. Sebeok (ed.), *Myth: A Symposium*. Bloomington, Indiana, 1958.

———. *Structural Anthropology*. Trans. Claire Jacobson. New York, 1963 (Paris, 1958).

———. "The Story of Asdiwal," Trans. Nicholas Mann. In Edmund R. Leach (ed.), *The Structural Study of Myth and Totemism*, ASA Monograph no. 45. London, 1967.

———. *The Raw and the Cooked.* (*Mythologiques: Introduction to a Science of Mythology. I.*). London, 1970. (Paris, 1964).

Lewin, Thomas Herbert. *The Wild Races of Southeast India*. London, 1870.

Lewis, C. S. *The Problem of Pain*. London, 1957.

Ling, T. O. *Buddhism and the Mythology of Evil*. London, 1962.

Lingat, Robert. "Time and the Dharma, on Manu 1.85–6." In *Contributions to Indian Sociology*, no. 6 (1962): 7–16.

———. *The Classical Law of India*. Trans. J. D. M. Derrett. Berkeley, 1973.

Long, J. Bruce. "Śiva as Promulgator of Traditional Learning and Patron Deity of the Fine Arts." *ABORI* 52 (1972): 67–80.

———. "Life out of Death: A Structural Analysis of the Myth of the Churning of the Ocean of Milk." In Bardwell Smith (ed.), *Hinduism: New Essays in the History of Religion*. Leiden, 1975.

Lorenzen, David N. *The Kāpālikas and Kālāmukhas: Two Lost Śaivite Sects*. Berkeley, 1972. Australian National University, Centre of Oriental Studies, Oriental Monograph Series, vol. 12.

Lovejoy, Arthur O. *The Great Chain of Being. A Study of the History of an Idea*. (William James Lectures, Harvard, 1933.) New York, 1960.

Macfie, J. M. *The Vishnu Purana. A Summary with Introduction and Notes*. Madras, 1926.

Maity, Pradyot Kumar. *Historical Studies in the Cult of the Goddess Manasa*. Calcutta, 1966.

Majumdar, R. C.; Raychaudhuri, H. C.; and Datta, Kalinkinkar. *An Advanced History of India*. London, 1958.

Malalgoda, Kitisiri. "Millennialism in Relation to Buddhism." *Comparative Studies in Sociology and History*, Cambridge University, vol. 12 (1970), pp. 424–441.

Mann, Thomas. *The Transposed Heads. A Legend of India*. Trans. H. T. Loew-Porter. New York, 1941.

Marshall, Peter J., ed. *The British Discovery of Hinduism in the Eighteenth Century*. Cambridge, 1970.

Masson, J. L. "The Childhood of Kṛṣṇa: Some Psychoanalytic Observations." *JAOS* 94, no. 4 (October–December 1974): 454–459. (1974*a*)

———. "India and the Unconscious: Erik Erikson on Gandhi." In *International Journal of Psychoanalysis* 55, part 4, 1974, pp. 519–526. (1974*b*)

Mauss, Marcel. *The Gift: Forms and Function of Exchange in Archaic Societies.* Trans. Ian Cunnison. London, 1970 (Paris, 1925).
Maxwell, Thomas S. "Transformational Aspects of Hindu Myth and Iconology: Viśvarūpa." AARP 4 (December 1973): 59–79.
Meinhard, Heinrich. *Beiträge zur Kenntnis des Śivaismus nach den Purāṇa's.* Bessler Archiv. Berlin, 1928. Pp. 1–45.
Meyer, Johann Jakob. *Sexual Life in Ancient India.* 2 vols. New York, 1930.
_______. *Trilogie der Altindischer Mächte und Feste der Vegetation.* Zurich, 1937.
Mayrhofer, Manfred. *Concise Etymological Sanskrit Dictionary.* Heidelberg, 1963.
Middleton, John (ed.). *Myth and Cosmos.* New York, 1967.
Mills, J. P. *The Rengma Nagas.* London, 1937.
Moulton, James Hope. *Early Zoroastrianism.* (Hibbert Lectures, 2nd series, 1912.) London, 1913.
Muir, John. *Original Sanskrit Texts.* 5 vols. 2nd ed. London, 1872.
Mukkopadhyāya, Nīlmaṇi. See *Kūrma Purāṇa,* Calcutta, 1890.
Narayan, J. K. "Khasi Folk-lore." *New Review* 16, (1942): 454–462.
Narten, Johanna. "Das Vedische Verbum *Math.*" *IIJ* 4, no. 4 (1960): 121–135.
Needham, Rodney. "Right and Left in Nyoro Symbolic Classification." *Africa* 37, no. 4 (October 1967): 425–452.
_______ (ed.). *Right and Left, Essays on Dual Symbolic Classification.* Chicago, 1973.
Newby, Eric. *Slowly Down the Ganges.* New York, 1966.
Nivedita, Sister, and Coomaraswamy, Ananda K. *Myths of the Hindus and Buddhists.* London, 1913.
Obeyesekere, Gananath. "Theodicy, Sin and Salvation in a Sociology of Buddhism." In Leach, Edmund R. (ed.), *Dialectic in Practical Religion.* Cambridge Papers in Social Anthropology, no. 5, pp. 7–40. Cambridge, 1968.
O'Flaherty, Wendy Doniger. "The Origin of Heresy in Hindu Mythology." *HR* 10, no. 4 (May 1971): 271–333. (1971*a*)
_______. "The Submarine Mare in the Mythology of Śiva." *JRAS* 1971 (1), pp. 9–27. (1971*b*)
_______. "The Symbolism of Ashes in the Mythology of Śiva." *Purāṇa* 13, no. 1 (January 1971): 26–35. (1971*c*)
_______. *Asceticism and Eroticism in the Mythology of Śiva.* Oxford, 1973.
_______. *Hindu Myths. A Sourcebook Translated from the Sanskrit.* Harmondsworth, 1975.
_______. "The Hindu Symbolism of Cows, Bulls, Stallions, and Mares." AARP 8 (December, 1975), pp. 1–7. (1975*a*)
Ogibenin, Boris L. *Structure d'un Mythe Védique: Le Mythe Cosmogonique dans le Ṛgveda.* The Hague, 1973.
Oppert, Gustav. *On the Original Inhabitants of Bharatavarsha or India.* London, 1893.
Orme, Robert. India Office, Orme Manuscript 1.179. I am indebted to Dr. Peter J. Marshall for the transcript of this manuscript.
Pal, Dhirendra Natha. *Śrīkṛṣṇa.* Calcutta, 1923.
Pantulu, N. K. Venkatesam. "The Legend of Vena and the Atharva Veda." *Quarterly*

Journal of the Mythic Society of Bangalore 29 (April 1939): 289–303.

Pargiter, Frederick Eden. See *Mārkaṇḍeya Purāṇa*.

Parry, N. E. *The Lakhers*. London, 1932.

Parsons, Talcott. *Essays in Sociological Theory Pure and Applied*. Glencoe, Illinois, 1949. 2nd ed. 1954. See also Weber, Max (1963).

Piaget, Jean. *Play, Dreams and Imitation in Childhood*. Trans. C. Gattegno and F. M. Hodgson. London, 1962 (*La Formation du Symbole*, Geneva, 1951).

Pickard, P. M. *The Activity of Children*. London, 1965.

Pocock, David. "The Movement of Castes." *Man*, 1955.

———. "The Anthropology of Time-Reckoning." In *Contributions to Indian Sociology*, no. 7 (1964), pp. 18–29. Reprinted in Middleton, pp. 303–314 (1967).

Potter, Stephen. *Some Notes on Lifesmanship*. London, 1950.

Prasad, Beni. *Theories of Government in Ancient India*. Allahabad, 1927.

Puhvel, Jaan. "Aspects of Equine Functionality." In Puhvel, Jaan (ed.), *Myth and Law Among the Indo-Europeans*. Berkeley, 1970. pp. 159–172.

Raghavan, V. "The Manu Saṃhitā." In *Cultural Heritage of India*, vol. II, pp. 335–363. Calcutta, 1962.

Rajagopalachari, C. *Rāmāyaṇa*. 5th ed. Bombay, 1965.

Ramanujan, A. K. "The Indian Oedipus." In Arabinda Podder (ed.), *Indian Literature, Proceedings of a Seminar*. Indian Institute of Advanced Study, pp. 127–137. Simla, 1972.

———. *Speaking of Śiva*. Harmondsworth, 1973.

Rao, T. Gopinatha. *Elements of Hindu Iconography*. 4 vols. Madras, 1916.

Rawson, Philip. *The Art of Tantra*. London, 1973.

Ricoeur, Paul. *The Symbolism of Evil*. Trans. Emerson Buchanan. Boston, 1969.

Rivers, W. H. *The Todas*. London, 1906.

Robinson, Marguerite S., and Joiner, L. E. "An Experiment in the Structural Study of Myth." *Contributions to Indian Sociology*, n.s. 2 (1968): 1–37.

Rodhe, Sten. *Deliver Us From Evil: Studies on the Vedic Ideas of Salvation*. Swedish Society for Missionary Research. Lund, Copenhagen, 1946.

Roger, Abraham. *Offne Thür zu den Verborgenen Heydenthum*. Nürnberg, 1663.

Roth, Rudolph. "On the Morality of the Veda." *JAOS* 3 (1853): 329–349.

Roy, S. C. and R. C. *The Kharias*. Ranchi, 1937.

Ryder, Arthur W. (trans.). *The Panchatantra*. Chicago, 1956.

Sastri, D. R. *Short History of Indian Materialism, Sensationalism and Hedonism*. Calcutta, no date.

Sastri, Rao Bahadur H. Krishna. "Two Statues of Pallava Kings and Five Pallava Inscriptions in a Rock Temple at Mahabalipuram." *Memoirs of the Archaeological Survey of India*, no. 26. Calcutta, 1926.

Schmidt, Hanns-Peter. *Bṛhaspati und Indra. Untersuchungen zur Vedischen Mythologie und Kulturgeschichte*. Wiesbaden, 1968.

Schrader, F. Otto. *Introduction to the Pāñcarātra*. Adyar Library no. 3. Madras, 1916.

Sharma, Ursula. "Theodicy and the Doctrine of *karma*." *Man*, n.s. 8 (1973): 348–364.

Shastri, J. L. (trans.). *Śiva Purāṇa. Ancient Indian Tradition and Mythology*, vols. 1–4. New Delhi, 1970.

Shastri, Suryakanta. *The Flood Legend in Sanskrit Literature.* Delhi, 1950.

Shivapadasundaram, P. *The Śaiva School of Hinduism.* London, 1934.

Sinha, Hara Narayana. *The Development of Indian Polity.* New York, 1963.

Sircar, Dines Chandra. *Studies in the Society and administration of Ancient and Medieval India.* Calcutta, 1967.

de Smet, R. V. "Sin and Its Removal in India." *Indian Antiquary* 1, no. 3 (July 1964): 163–173.

Smith, Ronald Morton. "Sin in India." Unpublished paper presented at a conference on Tradition in South Asia, School of Oriental and African Studies, University of London, 15 May 1970.

Spratt, Philip. *Hindu Culture and Personality: A Psychoanalytic Study.* Bombay, 1966.

Staal, Frits. *Advaita and Neoplatonism, a Critical Study in Comparative Philosophy.* Madras, 1961.

———. "Über die Idee der Toleranz im Hinduismus." *Kairos. Zeitschrift für Religionswissenschaft und Theologie,* pp. 215–218. 1959.

———. *Exploring Mysticism: A Methodological Essay.* Berkeley, 1975.

von Stietencron, Heinrich. "Bhairava." *ZDMG* 1969, Supplement I, Vorträge, Teil 3, pp. 863–871.

———. *Indische Sonnenpriester: Sāmba und die Śākadvīpīya-Brāhmaṇa.* SDSIUH, 3. Wiesbaden, 1966.

———. *Gaṅgā und Yamunā. Zur symbolischen Bedeutung der Flussgöttinnen an Indischen Tempeln.* Wiesbaden, 1972.

Stokes, Whitley. "The Prose Tales in the 'Rennes Dinsenchas.' " *Revue Celtique* 15 (1894): 272–335 and 418–484.

Strabo. *Geography.*

Strauss, Otto. *Ethische Probleme aus dem Mahābhārata.* Florence, 1912.

Tagore, Debendranath. *Autobiography.* London, 1914.

Tambiah, S. J. *Buddhism and the Spirit Cults in Northeast Thailand.* Cambridge (England), 1970.

Teilhard de Chardin, Pierre. *Écrits du temps de la guerre.* Paris, 1965.

———. *Christianity and Evolution.* London, 1971.

Temple, R. C. *Legends of the Punjab.* 3 vols. Bombay, 1884, 1885, 1900.

Thapar, Romila. *A History of India. Volume I.* Harmondsworth, 1966.

Thomas, P. *Epics, Myths and Legends of India.* Bombay, 1958.

———. *Kāma Kalpa.* Bombay, 1959.

Thurston, E. *Castes and Tribes of Southern India.* 7 vols. Madras, 1909.

Toporov, V. N. "Madkh'iamiki i Eliaty: Neskol'ko parallelei." In *Indiiskaia Kul'tura i Buddizm.* Moscow, 1972. Pp. 51–68.

Venkatasubbiah, A. "A Tamil Version of the *Pañcatantra.*" *ALB* 29 (1965): 113–114.

Venkateswaran, C. S. "The Ethics of the Purāṇas." In *The Cultural Heritage of India,* vol. II, pp. 287–300. Calcutta, 1962.

Wallis, H. W. *The Cosmology of the Rig Veda.* Edinburgh, 1887.

Wasson, R. Gordon, and O'Flaherty, W. D. *Soma: Divine Mushroom of Immortality.* New York, 1968.

Watts, Alan. *The Way of Zen*. New York, 1957.
———. *Beyond Theology*. New York, 1964.
Weber, Max. *Essays in Sociology*. Trans. and ed. H. H. Gerth and C. Wright Mills. New York, 1946.
———. *The Religion of India. The Sociology of Hinduism and Buddhism*. Trans. and ed. Hans H. Gerth and Don Martindale. New York, 1958.
———. *The Sociology of Religion*. Trans. by Ephraim Fischoff, intro. by Talcott Parsons. 4th ed. London, 1963.
West, Martin Litchfield. *Early Greek Philosophy and the Orient*. Oxford, 1971.
Whitehead, Henry. *Village Gods of South India*. Oxford, 1921.
Wilford, Francis. "On Egypt and Other Countries . . . from the Ancient Books of the Hindus." *Asiatick Researches* 3, pp. 295–468. Calcutta, 1792.
Wilkins W. J. *Hindu Mythology, Vedic and Purāṇic*. 2nd ed. Calcutta, 1900.
Wilson, Horace Hayman. *Sketches of the Religious Sects of the Hindus. Vol. I*. London, 1861–62.
———. *The Vishnu Purāṇa*. 3rd ed. (London, 1840). Calcutta, 1961.
Windisch, Wilhelm Oscar E. *Māra und Buddha*. Leipzig, 1895.
Woodroffe, Sir John George. *Shakti and Shakta*. Madras, 1959.
Wright, Caleb. *Lectures on India*. New York, 1848.
Yalman, Nur. "On the Purity of Women in the Castes of Ceylon and Malabar." *JRAI* 93, part 1 (January-June 1963): 25–58.
Zaehner, R. C. *Dawn and Twilight of Zoroastrianism*. London, 1961.
———. *Concordant Discord*. Oxford, 1970.
———. *Our Savage God*. London, 1974.
Zimmer, Heinrich. *Myths and Symbols in Indian Art and Civilization*. New York, 1946.

Index